Lecture Notes in Computer Science 8233

Commenced Publication in 1973
Founding and Former Series Editors:
Gerhard Goos, Juris Hartmanis, and Jan van Leeuwe

Sihan Qing   Jianying Zhou
Dongmei Liu (Eds.)

Information and Communications Security

15th International Conference, ICICS 2013
Beijing, China, November 20-22, 2013
Proceedings

 Springer

Volume Editors

Sihan Qing
Dongmei Liu
Chinese Academy of Sciences, Institute of Software, Beijing 100190, China
E-mail: qsihan@mail.ss.pku.edu.cn; dongmeiliu77@gmail.com

Jianying Zhou
Institute for Infocomm Research, Infocomm Security Department
1 Fusionopolis Way, #21-01 Connexis, South Tower, Singapore 138632, Singapore
E-mail: jyzhou@i2r.a-star.edu.sg

ISSN 0302-9743   e-ISSN 1611-3349
ISBN 978-3-319-02725-8   e-ISBN 978-3-319-02726-5
DOI 10.1007/978-3-319-02726-5
Springer Cham Heidelberg New York Dordrecht London

Library of Congress Control Number: 2013950171

CR Subject Classification (1998): E.3, D.4.6, K.6.5, K.4.4, F.2, C.2

LNCS Sublibrary: SL 4 – Security and Cryptology

© Springer International Publishing Switzerland 2013

Typesetting: Camera-ready by author, data conversion by Scientific Publishing Services, Chennai, India

Printed on acid-free paper

Springer is part of Springer Science+Business Media (www.springer.com)

Preface

The 15th International Conference on Information and Communications Security (ICICS 2013) was held in Beijing, China, during November 20–22, 2013. The ICICS conference series is an established forum that brings together people from universities, research institutes, industry, and government institutions, who work in a range of fields within information and communications security. The ICICS conferences give attendees the opportunity to exchange new ideas and investigate developments in the state of the art. In previous years, ICICS has taken place in Australia (1999), China (2011, 2009, 2007, 2005, 2003, 2001 and 1997), Hong Kong (2012), Singapore (2002), Spain (2010, 2004), the UK (2008), and USA (2006). On each occasion, as on this one, the proceedings have been published in the Springer's LNCS series.

In total, 113 manuscripts from 19 countries were submitted to ICICS 2013, among which 23 regular and six short papers from 12 countries were accepted. The accepted papers cover a wide range of disciplines within information security and applied cryptography. Each submission to ICICS 2013 was anonymously reviewed by three reviewers. We are very grateful to members of the Program Committee, which was composed of 66 members from 16 countries; we would like to thank them, as well as all the external reviewers, for their valuable contributions to the tough and time-consuming reviewing process.

ICICS 2013 was organized and hosted by the Institute of Software, Chinese Academy of Sciences (CAS), the Institute of Software and Microelectronics, Peking University and the State Key Laboratory of Information Security of the Institute of Information Engineering, Chinese Academy of Sciences (CAS). The conference was sponsored by the National Natural Science Foundation of China under Grant No. 60970135 and No. 61170282.

We would like to thank the authors who submitted their papers to ICICS 2013, and the attendees from all around the world. Finally, we would also like to thank Ying Qiu for managing the conference website and the EasyChair system, Publicity Chair Xinyi Huang for making the wide distribution of the call for papers, and other local Organizing Committee members for providing logistical support.

August 2013

Sihan Qing
Jianying Zhou

ICICS 2013

15th International Conference on Information and Communications Security

Beijing, China
November 20–22, 2013

Organized by

Institute of Software, Chinese Academy of Sciences (CAS)
Institute of Software and Microelectronics, Peking University, China
SKLOIS, Institute of Information Engineering, CAS

Sponsored by

National Natural Science Foundation of China (NNSFC)

General Chair

Dongdai Lin — Institute of Information Engineering, CAS, China

Program Chairs

Sihan Qing — Chinese Academy of Sciences and Peking University, China
Jianying Zhou — Institute for Infocomm Research, Singapore

Program Committee

Michel Abdalla — ENS and CNRS, France
Endre Bangerter — Bern University of Applied Sciences, Germany
Zinaida Benenson — University of Erlangen-Nuremberg, Germany
Marina Blanton — University of Notre Dame, USA
Ioana Boureanu — EPFL, Switzerland
Bogdan Carbunar — Florida International University, USA
Aldar Chan — Institute for Infocomm Research, Singapore
Ee-Chien Chang — National University of Singapore, Singapore
Liqun Chen — Hewlett-Packard Laboratories, UK
Songqing Chen — George Mason University, USA

Weiping Wen   Peking University, China
Duncan Wong   City University of Hong Kong, China
Wenling Wu   Institute of Software, China
Yongdong Wu   Institute for Infocomm Research, Singapore
Li Xu   Fujian Normal University, China
Shouhuai Xu   University of Texas at San Antonio, USA
Fangguo Zhang   Sun Yat-sen University, China
Futai Zhang   Nanjing Normal University, China
Jie Zhang   Nanyang Technological University, Singapore
Wentao Zhang   Institute of Information Engineering, CAS,
                          China
Yuliang Zheng   UNCC, USA
Yongbin Zhou   Institute of Information Engineering, China

Publicity Chair

Xinyi Huang   Fujian Normal University, China

Publication Chair

Dongmei Liu   Chinese Academy of Sciences, China

External Reviewers

Zeeshan Bilal	Takuya Hayashi	Patrick Schweitzer
Shaoying Cai	Stephan Heuser	Jie Shi
Hua Chen	Shuhui Hou	Masaaki Shirase
Jiageng Chen	Georgios Kambourakis	Ben Stock
Xihui Chen	Divyan Konidala	Benjamin Stritter
Chen-Mou Cheng	Barbara Kordy	Wenhai Sun
Cheng-Kang Chu	Nan Li	Ying-Kai Tang
Su Chunhua	Wei Li	Haibo Tian
Xingmin Cui	Zhengqi Li	Aggeliki Tsohou
Sabrina De Capitani Di	Junrong Liu	Christian Wachsmann
Vimercati	Yang Liu	Bing Wang
Prokopios Drogkaris	Yang Lu	Jianfeng Wang
Changlai Du	Weiliang Luo	Wei Wu
Junbin Fang	Takashi Nishide	Hong Xu
Carol Fung	Kazumasa Omote	Jia Xu
Yuichi Futa	Jun Pang	Zhiqian Xu
Wei Gao	Panagiotis Rizomiliotis	Weijia Xue
Jinguang Han	Rodrigo Roman	Qiben Yan

Table of Contents

Trusted and Trustworthy Computing

Authentication and Security Protocols

Intrusion Detection and Recovery

Side Channel Attacks and Defense

Engineering Issues of Crypto

Cryptanalysis

Attribute-Based Encryption

Cryptographic Primitives and Applications

Defending against Heap Overflow by Using Randomization in Nested Virtual Clusters

Chee Meng Tey and Debin Gao

Singapore Management University, Singapore
{cmtey.2008,dbgao}@smu.edu.sg

Heap based buffer overflows are a dangerous class of vulnerability. One counter-measure is randomizing the location of heap memory blocks. Existing techniques segregate the address space into clusters, each of which is used exclusively for one block size. This approach requires a large amount of address space reservation, and results in lower location randomization for larger blocks.

In this paper, we explore the possibility of using a cluster for 2 or more block sizes. We show that a naive implementation fails because attackers can easily predict the relative location of 2 blocks with 50% probability. To overcome this problem, we design a novel allocator algorithm based on virtual clusters. When the cluster size is large, the randomization of larger blocks improves by 25% compared to existing techniques while the size of the reserved area required decreases by 37.5%.

1 Introduction

Randomization of heap memory location belongs to a larger class of anti-malware techniques collectively known as address space layout randomization (ASLR). These techniques attempt to defeat attackers by limiting their knowledge of the absolute or relative location of particular memory objects, and have gained widespread acceptance among mainstream OS [1–4]. There are also standalone allocator projects [5–7] that provide ASLR for various OS.

One of the ways in which heap memory is randomized involves the location of memory blocks returned by the C library function malloc. Existing techniques segregate the address space into clusters, each of which is divided into equally sized slots. Both the alignment and size of slots are power of 2 multiples of the minimum (typically 16 bytes). To handle a memory allocation, the allocator rounds up the requested block size to the next power of 2 multiple of the minimum, determines the cluster to use, randomly chooses an unused slot in that cluster and returns its location.

An example of the memory layout of such an allocator is shown in Figure 1. There are 2 salient features of such a method of allocation. Firstly, due to alignment restrictions, the larger the block size, the fewer the number of choices to place the block. The relative and absolute location of large blocks are therefore easier to guess. Secondly, a large area of the address space needs to be reserved.

In this paper, we study an alternative allocation algorithm where blocks of different sizes can be allocated from the same cluster by first structuring such a

S. Qing et al. (Eds.): ICICS 2013, LNCS 8233, pp. 1–16, 2013.

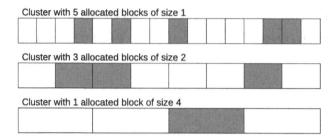

Fig. 1. A heap memory snapshot for an application using a randomizing heap allocator. Shaded blocks are allocated. In this snapshot, the application has allocated 5 blocks of size 1, 3 blocks of size 2 and 1 block of size 4. In practice, allocators do not allocate blocks of 1 byte. Instead, a minimum block size of 16 bytes is common. The block sizes in this paper can be interpreted as either bytes or multiples of the minimum.

cluster as a set of nested virtual clusters. We name this 'Virtual Cluster Allocation' (VCA). VCA improves both the randomness and space utilization. When the number of block sizes allocated from each cluster is increased to 2, the randomization of larger blocks improves by 25% compared to existing techniques while the size of the reserved area required decreases by 37.5%.

In the rest of this paper, we first show why a naive implementation of mixed block size allocations results in poor randomization. Next, we describe the intuition and the algorithm for VCA. We derive and prove the reserved space requirement for VCA. Finally, we describe the limitations and conclusions.

Related Works. Randomization is one of the major countermeasures against buffer overflow attacks. Our paper focuses on the randomization of memory blocks returned by the `libc` `malloc` function. Project similar in scope include the OpenBSD [8] allocator and the Diehard series of randomized allocators [5, 6]. Randomization may also involve other parts of the memory structure such as the location of stack or shared libraries [1–4, 7, 9], the instruction set encoding [10–13], and even the data [14].

2   Naive Implementation

In a naive implementation, when a block needs to be allocated, the corresponding cluster is first identified. Next, all available slots meeting the alignment and size constraints are identified. A slot is then chosen randomly to fulfil the allocation request. We demonstrate in this section, through an example, the techniques that an attacker can use to place blocks to ensure a high probability of achieving a particular relative ordering. This attack requires an attacker who is able to control the heap evolution. Scenarios where this is possible include Javascript based malware [15].

For our example, there is a cluster of size 16 which is initially free. The allocator handles requests for blocks of size 1, 2 and 4. The attacker is able to request allocation for 3 types of blocks: type A, type B and type C, each of size 1, 2 and 4 respectively. The steps used by the attacker are: (a) allocate three type C objects: C1, C2, C3, (b) allocate one type B objects: B1, and (c) allocate two type A objects: A1 and A2. Figure 2 illustrates a possible memory layout.

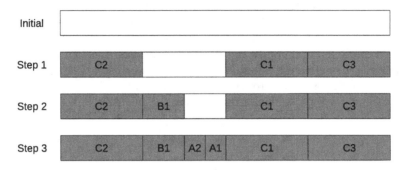

Fig. 2. Example showing how an attacker can control the sequence of allocations to ensure a high probability of achieving a desired placement order

Fig. 3. Possible permutations in the placement of B1, A1 and A2

In step (a), there are 4 available slots to place C1, C2 and C3, given the alignment restrictions. The allocator picks 3 of the slots randomly, leaving a single free slot of size 4. A single size 4 free slot can be divided into 2 size 2 free slots, each of which can in turn be divided into 2 size 1 free slots. To allocate a block for B1, since there are only 2 availble size 2 slots, the allocator picks 1 of the 2 slots randomly, leaving only a single slot of size 2. In step (c), the allocator places the objects A1 and A2 randomly into the remaining free area of the cluster.

To calculate the probability that A1 will be followed by A2, we refer to Figure 3. There are 4 possible permutations, each equiprobable. In 2 of the 4 permutations, A1 is followed by A2. The probability of this occurring is therefore $2/4 = 50\%$. Similarly, in 1 of the 4 permutations, B1 is followed by A2. The probability of this occurring is therefore $1/4 = 25\%$. A naive implementation of randomization where more than 1 block size can be allocated from a single cluster therefore does not guarantee high entropy.

3   Intuition

In Figure 1, so long as the attacker's total allocation size is limited to a maximum quota of 16, all possible permutations of block locations are equally likely.

This equiprobable property holds regardless of the order of allocation and deallocation made by the attacker. Intuitively, the problem with the naive implementation of Section 2 is that by varying the order of his allocation, an attacker can violate the equiprobable property.

We illustrate our solution to this problem using a simple example which involves only type A blocks (of size 1) and type B blocks (of size 2). To allocate a type B block, the allocator picks a free type B slot randomly (similar to the naive implementation). To handle allocations of type A blocks, the allocator chooses available type B slots randomly and uses them to form a *virtual* cluster. A free type A slot is then chosen randomly from the virtual cluster. Figure 4 shows the formation of a virtual cluster (of size 16) from an empty cluster (of size 20) and the allocation of a type A block from this virtual cluster.

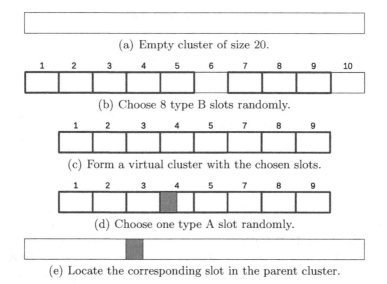

(a) Empty cluster of size 20.

(b) Choose 8 type B slots randomly.

(c) Form a virtual cluster with the chosen slots.

(d) Choose one type A slot randomly.

(e) Locate the corresponding slot in the parent cluster.

Fig. 4. Allocating type A blocks using a virtual cluster

Note that a new virtual cluster is formed for every allocation. When there are prior allocations of either type A or type B blocks, dummy type B slots may be added to the virtual cluster. A cluster can therefore contain up to 5 different types of type B slots (see Figure 5):

1. Dummy slots.
2. Type B slots from which 1 type B block has been allocated. We name them type B_B slots. The number of such slots is denoted by s_B.
3. Type B slots from which 2 type A blocks has been allocated. We name them type B_2 slots. The number of such slots is denoted by s_2.

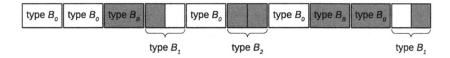

Fig. 5. Different types of type B slots. In this example, $s_0 = 4$, $s_1 = 2$, $s_2 = 1$, $s_B = 3$.

4. Type B slots from which exactly 1 type A block has been allocated. We name them type B_1 slots. The number of such slots is denoted by s_1.
5. Free (unused) type B slots. We name them type B_0 slots. The number of such slots is denoted by s_0.

Figure 6 shows the allocation process when there are prior allocations. From the virtual cluster, one type A slot is chosen randomly from among the dummy and available slots. If a dummy slot is chosen, the selection process is repeated. However, the repeated selection can only be made from the B_0 slots in the virtual cluster and not from the B_1 slots. The rest of the process is similar to that of Figure 4.

The use of a virtual cluster within a cluster ensures that all possible permutations of block locations are equiprobable, because the randomization within each cluster is similar in principle to that of Figure 1. The random formation of the virtual cluster from the slots of the parent cluster ensures that there is no correlation between the location of slots of different sizes. The concept of nesting a virtual cluster within a parent cluster can be extended to more than 2 block sizes.

4   Computation of Cluster Size

In this section, we show how the cluster size c can be chosen when the total amount of allocated memory is constrained by a quota q. The choice of c primarily involves a space-randomness tradeoff. The smaller the reserved space, the better the virtual and physical address space utilization efficiency; but it is also easier for an attacker to guess the absolute and relative location of each block. However, even if small space is desired, the reserved space cannot be as small as q. That is because fragmentation may result in available space that cannot be used. Figure 7 shows an example where c and q are 20 and 16 respectively. Even though the total allocation is only 14, this cluster can not handle any further request for type B blocks (type A blocks can still be allocated). A lower bound therefore exists for c.

For VCA, the theoretical lower bound depends on how the size of the virtual cluster, v, is chosen. Note that v must be even because the virtual cluster contains type B slots which are of size 2. For simplicity, we also assume q is even. If $v \geq 2q$, c, in theory, must be at least $2q$. Otherwise, there is at least 1 fragmentation pattern which the allocator cannot handle. If $v = q$, c must be at least $1.5q$. The reason is because, in a problem involving only 2 block sizes, the worst fragmentation occurs with B_1 blocks. If $v \geq 2q$, the worst fragmentation occurs

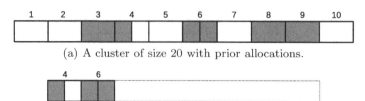

(a) A cluster of size 20 with prior allocations.

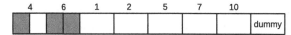

(b) Include all B_1 and B_2 slots in the virtual cluster. B_2 slots cannot be used for allocation. However, their inclusion affects the selection probabilities.

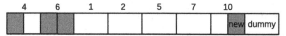

(c) Include all B_0 slots. If there are more slots than available space, a subset of B_0 slots is chosen randomly for inclusion.

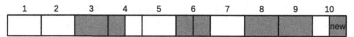

(d) If there are more space than B_0 slots, dummy slots are added.

(e) Choose a new type A slot randomly from the free slots and dummy slots.

(f) Locate the corresponding slot in the parent cluster.

Fig. 6. Allocating type A blocks when there are prior allocations

when the cluster consists entirely of B_1 blocks, resulting in a cluster size of $2q$. If $v = q$, the worst fragmentation occurs when the cluster contains a mix of B_1 and B_B blocks. Let a be the number of type A blocks that has been allocated. Let b be the number of type B blocks that has been allocated. Figure 8 shows the maximum number of B_1, B_2 and B_B slots that can be created as a varies. The maximum of $1.5q$ occurs when $a = 0.5q$ and $b = 0.25q$.

When q is large, some fragmentation patterns are so rare that they are virtually impossible. This suggests that a probabilistic bound for c exists and can be lower than $1.5q$. In such a case, the tradeoff involves not just space and randomness, but also the chance of failure. If c is chosen carefully, the chance of failure may be low enough that it is inconsequential. In the remainder of this section, we show that this intuition is correct.

Let s be the total number of type B_1 and B_2 slots (that is, $s = s_1 + s_2$). For ease of implementation, the procedure in Figure 6 can be simplified as follows:

1. Compute the ratio $r_{a,s} = (2s - a)/(v - a)$.
2. Compute a random number r' between 0 and 1.

Fig. 7. Fragmentation reduces usable space. For ease of analysis, VCA has a constraint that adjacent free type A slots in neighbouring type B slots (such as A1 and A2) cannot be merged and used for allocating type B blocks.

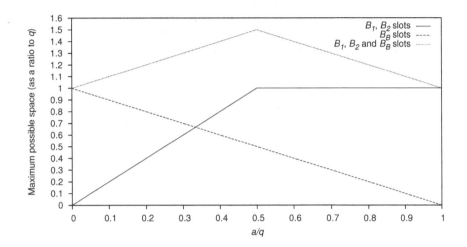

Fig. 8. Maximum space usage due to fragmentation when $v = q$

3. If $r' < r_{a,s}$ choose a type A slot from among the B_1 slots randomly.
4. If $r' >= r_{a_s}$ choose a B_0 slot from the parent cluster randomly and choose one of the two available type A slots (within the chosen B_0 slot) randomly.

We now prove some allocator properties. Let $p_{a,s}$ be the probability that when a type A blocks has been allocated, the total number of type B_1 and B_2 slots is s. Figure 9 shows an example of the distribution of $p_{a,s}$ when $v = q = 10$. Note that $p_{a,s}$ does not depend on b, the number of type B blocks allocated.

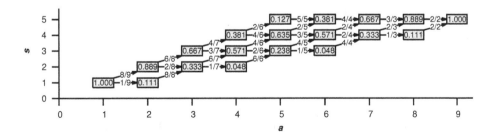

Fig. 9. The value of $p_{a,s}$ (in shaded boxes) as a function of s and a when $v = q = 10$

In Figure 9, the labels on the horizontal arrows equal $r_{a,s}$ and indicate the probability that s remains unchanged when a is incremented by 1 (because a B_1 slot was used, resulting in a B_2 slot). The labels on the diagonal arrows equal $1 - r_{a,s}$ and indicate the probability that s increases by 1 when a is incremented by 1 (because a B_0 slot was used, resulting in a B_1 slot).

Let the most likely value of s be denoted by s_{max}. We will show that the probability density function of s is unimodal and the further s is from s_{max}, the lower the probabililty. Next, we show that the larger the quota q, the larger the probability $\Pr[s_{max}(1 - \epsilon) < s < s_{max}(1 + \epsilon)]$ where ϵ is a small constant. In other words, the larger q is, the less likely s differs significantly from s_{max}. Figure 10 illustrates this property. The lower probabilistic bound of c is then given by the solution of an optimization problem.

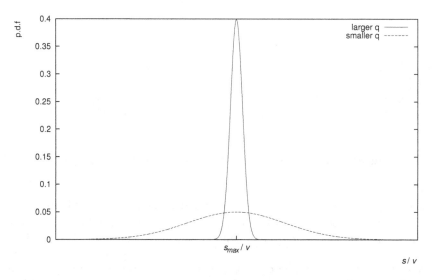

Fig. 10. The larger q is, the more likely s is close to s_{max}. Note that unlike a normal distribution, the probability density function of s is asymmetrical about the mode. The asymmetry generally diminishes as q becomes larger.

4.1 Computation of s_{max}

Theorem 1. *If $p_{a,s} \neq 0$ and $p_{a,s+1} \neq 0$, then the ratio between them is given by:*

$$h_{a,s} = \frac{p_{a,s+1}}{p_{a,s}} = \frac{2(v - 2s)(a - s)}{(2s - a + 1)(2s - a + 2)} \tag{1}$$

Proof. The proof is by induction. The base case can be shown to be true for $p_{2,1}$ and $p_{2,2}$. In the inductive step, it can be shown that Equation 1 holds for $p_{a+1,s}$ and $p_{a+1,s+1}$ whenever any of the following conditions are true:

1. $p_{a,s-1} = 0, p_{a,s} \neq 0, p_{a,s+1} \neq 0$ and Equation 1 holds for $p_{a,s}$ and $p_{a,s+1}$.
2. $p_{a,s-1} \neq 0, p_{a,s} \neq 0, p_{a,s+1} = 0$ and Equation 1 holds for $p_{a,s-1}$ and $p_{a,s}$.
3. $p_{a,s-1} \neq 0, p_{a,s} \neq 0, p_{a,s+1} \neq 0$ and Equation 1 holds for $p_{a,s-1}$ and $p_{a,s}$ as well as for $p_{a,s}$ and $p_{a,s+1}$.

Conditions 1 and 2 are corner cases while condition 3 is the general case. Condition 1 occurs when a is odd, $1 < a < v - 1$ and $s = (a + 1)/2$. Condition 2 occurs when $1 < a < v/2$ and $a = s$. Due to brevity of space, we only provide the proof for the general case:

$$
\begin{aligned}
p_{a+1,s} &= p_{a,s-1}(1 - r_{a,s-1}) + p_{a,s}r_{a,s} \\
&= p_{a,s-1}\frac{v - 2s + 2}{v - a} + p_{a,s}\frac{2s - a}{v - a} \\
&= p_{a,s}\frac{(2s - a - 1)(2s - a)}{2(v - 2s + 2)(a - s + 1)}\frac{v - 2s + 2}{v - a} + p_{a,s}\frac{2s - a}{v - a} \\
&= p_{a,s}\frac{2s - a}{v - a}\left(\frac{2s - a - 1}{2(a - s + 1)} + 1\right) \\
&= p_{a,s}\frac{2s - a}{v - a}\left(\frac{a + 1}{2(a - s + 1)}\right)
\end{aligned}
\tag{2}
$$

$$
\begin{aligned}
p_{a+1,s+1} &= p_{a,s}(1 - r_{a,s}) + p_{a,s+1}r_{a,s+1} \\
&= p_{a,s}\frac{v - 2s}{v - a} + p_{a,s+1}\frac{2s - a + 2}{v - a} \\
&= p_{a,s}\frac{v - 2s}{v - a} + p_{a,s}\frac{2(v - 2s)(a - s)}{(2s - a + 1)(2s - a + 2)}\frac{2s - a + 2}{v - a} \\
&= p_{a,s}\frac{v - 2s}{v - a}\left(1 + \frac{2(a - s)}{2s - a + 1}\right) \\
&= p_{a,s}\frac{v - 2s}{v - a}\left(\frac{a + 1}{2s - a + 1}\right)
\end{aligned}
\tag{3}
$$

Dividing (3) by (2) yields the desired result for $h_{a+1,s}$.   □

Theorem 2. *There is exactly 1 turning point for the probability density function of s within the problem domain.*

Proof. A turning point occurs when the gradient equals 0. Since s is discrete, the turning point occurs when $p_{a,s}$ equals $p_{a,s+1}$, or equivalently, when $h_{a,s} = 1$. From (1), we have

$$\frac{2(v - 2s)(a - s)}{(2s - a + 1)(2s - a + 2)} = 1$$

$$2(v - 2s)(a - s) = (2s - a + 1)(2s - a + 2)$$

$$2(va - vs - 2sa + 2s^2) = 4s^2 - 2sa + 4s - 2sa + a^2 - 2a + 2s - a + 2$$

$$2va - 2vs = 6s + a^2 - 3a + 2$$

$$-6s - 2vs = -2va + a^2 - 3a + 2$$

$$s = \frac{-2va + a^2 - 3a + 2}{-6 - 2v}$$

$$= \frac{2a - \frac{a^2}{v} + 3\frac{a}{v} - \frac{2}{v}}{\frac{6}{v} + 2} \tag{4}$$

Theorem 3. *The turning point for the probability density function of s is a maximum turning point.*

Proof. We only need to show that $h_{a,s+1} < h_{a,s}$ for all s. Since $h_{a,s_{max}} = 1$, $h_{a,s+1} < h_{a,s}$ implies that when $s < s_{max}$, $h_{a,s} > 1$. Similarly, when $s > s_{max}$, $h_{a,s} < 1$. In other words, the gradient is positive before the turning point and negative after the turning point, implying a maximum turning point. From 1:

$$h_{a,s+1} = \frac{2(v - 2s - 2)(a - s - 1)}{(2s - a + 3)(2s - a + 4)}$$

$$< \frac{2(v - 2s)(a - s)}{(2s - a + 3)(2s - a + 4)}$$

$$< \frac{2(v - 2s)(a - s)}{(2s - a + 1)(2s - a + 2)}$$

$$= h_{a,s} \quad \square$$

The probability density function therefore has the shape of Figure 10.

Theorem 4. *When q is large,*

$$s_{max} = a - \frac{a^2}{2v} \tag{5}$$

Proof. When q is large, v is also large. (5) is obtained from (4) by eliminating the insignificant terms when v is large. $\square$

4.2   Lower bound for c

The lower bound for the cluster size c depends on the worst case value of $s_1 + s_2 + s_B$ for all possible attacker allocation[1] strategies. We have shown that for large

---

[1] We need only consider the set of allocation only strategies because due to VCA's equiprobable property (see Section 3), each strategy that involves allocation and deallocation can be mapped to an equivalent strategy involving only allocation.

q (and therefore v), s_{max} is a good approximation for s, which equals $s_1 + s_2$. Also, since one B_B slot is created whenever one type B block is allocated, $b = s_B$. The lower bound of c therefore corresponds to the upper bound of $s_{max} + b$. For a 2 block size problem, this can be obtained from the following optimization problem:

> Determine a, the number of type A blocks, and b, the number of type B blocks, so as to maximize $s_{max}+b$, subject to the constraints:

1. $a \geq 0$
2. $b \geq 0$
3. $a + b \leq q$

The solution to this problem is:

$$a = \frac{v}{2} \tag{6}$$

$$b = \frac{2q - v}{4} \tag{7}$$

Substituting (6) and (7) into (5), the lower probabilistic bound for c is given by:

$$
\begin{aligned}
c_{min} &= s_{max} + s_B \\
&= a - \frac{a^2}{2v} + b \\
&= \frac{v}{2} - \frac{(\frac{v}{2})^2}{2v} + \frac{2q - v}{4} \\
&= \frac{v}{2} - \frac{v}{8} + \frac{2q - v}{4} \\
&= \frac{3v}{8} + \frac{2q - v}{4}
\end{aligned}
\tag{8}
$$

If v is chosen to be the minimum possible (i.e. q), then (8) simplifies to:

$$c_{min} = \frac{3q}{8} + \frac{2q - q}{4} = \frac{5q}{8} \tag{9}$$

Note that (9) is expressed in units of type B slots. Each type B slot has a size of 2. So the minimum size is $5q/4$. Compared to existing techniques, which reserve 1 cluster of size q each for type A and B blocks respectively, the randomization of type B blocks improves by 25% (from q to $5q/4$) while the size of the reserved area required decreases by 37.5% (from $2q$ to $5q/4$).

It should be noted that, in practice, a probabilistic allowance ϵ is needed to ensure VCA has a low chance of failure even when the worst case allocation strategy is used (see Equations 6 and 7). In such a case, the larger ϵ is, the less likely $s > c_{min} + \epsilon$. As q becomes larger, the required allowance increases in absolute terms, but decreases relative to q. If the cluster size c is set at exactly c_{min}, then approximately 50% of the time, s will exceed c when the worst case strategy is used.

In dynamic storage allocation parlance, the lower bound of c is also known as the worst case external fragmentation (WCEF). Robson proved that, when only 2 block sizes are involved and without randomization, the WCEF will never be better (lower) than $1.5q$ [16]. Our work in this section adds 2 interesting contributions to the analysis of WCEF. Firstly, to the best of our knowledge, we are the first to show that it is possible to have a probabilistic bound through the use of randomness. Secondly, we show that, for problems involving large q, the probabilistic bound ($1.25q$) is lower than Robson's limit ($1.5q$).

4.3   Computation of $p_{a,s}$

Generally, $p_{a,s}$ can be computed by applying the following formula recursively:

$$p_{a,s} = p_{a-1,s-1}(1 - r_{a-1,s-1}) + p_{a-1,s}r_{a-1,s} \qquad (10)$$

Referring to Figure 9, it can be seen that calculating $p_{a,s}$ using this method involves summing the probabilities along all possible paths starting from $p_{1,1}$ and ending with the desired $p_{a,s}$. There are 2 observations which help in simplifying the computation. Firstly, it can be observed in Figure 9, that there exists a symmetry about the line $a = v/2 = 5$. Secondly, there is a repetitive structure such that certain common numerator and denominator terms appear in all paths. All numerator and denominator terms on the diagonal arrows are common, while the denominator terms on the horizontal arrows are common. As an example, for all paths leading to $p_{4,3}$ in Figure 9, the common denominator terms are 9, 8 and 7, while the common numerator terms are 8 and 6.

In general, the common denominator terms on the paths to $p_{a,s}$ depend only on a and v (but not s). They are:

$$v - 1, v - 2, \ldots, v - a + 1$$

On the other hand, the common numerators terms on the paths to $p_{a,s}$ depend only on s and v (but not a). They are:

$$v - 2, v - 4, \ldots, v - 2(s - 1)$$

As an example, if all common terms are removed from Figure 9, the remaining numerator terms are shown in Figure 11. The product of the remaining numerator terms along each path can be characterised using a sequence $T(x, y)$, where:

1. Each term of T is formed from the multiplication of x sub-terms
2. All sub-terms are positive integers
3. The first sub-term never exceeds y and
4. Each sub-term never exceeds the preceding sub-term by more than 1.

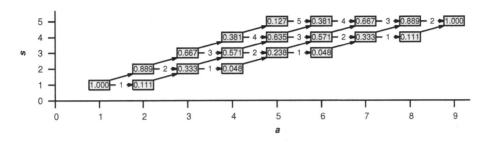

Fig. 11. Figure 9 with the common terms removed

For example,

$$
\begin{aligned}
T_{2,4} =&\; 1{\cdot}1,\ 1{\cdot}2, \\
&\; 2{\cdot}1,\ 2{\cdot}2,\ 2{\cdot}3, \\
&\; 3{\cdot}1,\ 3{\cdot}2,\ 3{\cdot}3,\ 3{\cdot}4, \\
&\; 4{\cdot}1,\ 4{\cdot}2,\ 4{\cdot}3,\ 4{\cdot}4,\ 4{\cdot}5 \\
=&\; 1,2,2,4,6,3,6,9,12,4,8,12,16,20 \\
T_{3,2} =&\; 1{\cdot}1{\cdot}1,\ 1{\cdot}1{\cdot}2, \\
&\; 1{\cdot}2{\cdot}1,\ 1{\cdot}2{\cdot}2,\ 1{\cdot}2{\cdot}3, \\
&\; 2{\cdot}1{\cdot}1,\ 2{\cdot}1{\cdot}2, \\
&\; 2{\cdot}2{\cdot}1,\ 2{\cdot}2{\cdot}2,\ 2{\cdot}2{\cdot}3, \\
&\; 2{\cdot}3{\cdot}1,\ 2{\cdot}3{\cdot}2,\ 2{\cdot}3{\cdot}3,\ 2{\cdot}3{\cdot}4 \\
=&\; 1,2,2,4,6,2,4,4,8,12,6,12,18,24
\end{aligned}
$$

These sequence are unique and not found in the OEIS database of integer sequences [17]. Note that $T_{0,y} = 1$, by definition. Let $S_{x,y}$ be the summation of all terms in $T_{x,y}$. Then $p_{a,s}$ can be computed from the product of $S_{a-s,2s-a+1}$ and the common numerators divided by the common denominators:

$$
p_{a,s} = S_{a-s,2s-a+1}\left(\frac{[v-2][v-4][\ldots][v-2(s-1)]}{[v-1][v-2][\ldots][v-a+1]} \right) \tag{11}
$$

4.4 Alternative Method for Computing $p_{a,s}$

There exists an alternative way to compute $p_{a,s}$. From Equation 2, we have a relation between $p_{a+1,s}$ and $p_{a,s}$. We can rewrite this equation as:

$$
p_{a,s} = p_{a-1,s}\left(\frac{2s-a+1}{v-a+1} \right)\left(\frac{a}{2(a-s)} \right) \tag{12}
$$

Similarly from Equation 3, we have a relation between $p_{a+1,s+1}$ and $p_{a,s}$. We can rewrite this equation as:

$$
p_{a,s} = p_{a-1,s-1}\left(\frac{v-2s+2}{v-a+1} \right)\left(\frac{a}{2s-a} \right) \tag{13}
$$

We also know that $p_{1,1} = 1$ for all v. To compute $p_{a,s}$, we can choose *any* path from $p_{1,1}$ to the desired $p_{a,s}$ and apply Equations 12 and 13. If $a = s$, there is only 1 path:

$$p_{1,1}, \quad p_{2,2}, \quad p_{3,3}, \quad \cdots, \quad p_{s,s} \tag{14}$$

The formulas for this path are:

$$p_{2,2} = p_{1,1}\left(\frac{v-2}{v-1}\right)\left(\frac{2}{2}\right)$$
$$= \left(\frac{v-2}{v-1}\right)$$

$$p_{3,3} = p_{2,2}\left(\frac{v-4}{v-2}\right)\left(\frac{3}{3}\right)$$
$$= \left(\frac{v-2}{v-1}\right)\left(\frac{v-4}{v-2}\right)$$

$$p_{4,4} = p_{3,3}\left(\frac{v-6}{v-3}\right)\left(\frac{4}{4}\right)$$
$$= \left(\frac{v-2}{v-1}\right)\left(\frac{v-4}{v-2}\right)\left(\frac{v-6}{v-3}\right)$$

$$\cdots$$

$$p_{n,n} = \left(\frac{v-2}{v-1}\right)\left(\frac{v-4}{v-2}\right)\left(\frac{v-6}{v-3}\right)\cdots\left(\frac{v-2(n-1)}{v-(n-1)}\right) \tag{15}$$

If $a > s$, for simplicity, we choose (14) for the first part of the path, then continue with

$$p_{s+1,s}, \quad p_{s+2,s}, \quad \cdots, \quad p_{a,s} \tag{16}$$

We have:

$$p_{a,s} = p_{a-1,s}\left(\frac{2s-a+1}{v-a+1}\right)\left(\frac{a}{2(a-s)}\right)$$
$$p_{a-1,s} = p_{a-2,s}\left(\frac{2s-a+2}{v-a+2}\right)\left(\frac{a-1}{2(a-s-1)}\right)$$
$$p_{a-2,s} = p_{a-3,s}\left(\frac{2s-a+3}{v-a+3}\right)\left(\frac{a-2}{2(a-s-2)}\right)$$
$$p_{s+1,s} = p_{s,s}\left(\frac{s}{v-s}\right)\left(\frac{s+1}{2(1)}\right) \tag{17}$$

Together, Equations 15 and 17 provide an alternative method of computing $p_{a,s}$. Interestingly, Equations 15, 17 and 11 also allow us to derive an expression for $S_{x,y}$. Substituting Equations 15 and 17 into 11 and simplifying, we get:

$$S_{a-s,2s-a+1} = \frac{(2s-a+1)(2s-a+2)(\ldots)(a)}{2^{a-s}(a-s)!} \tag{18}$$

Substituting $x = a - s$ and $y = 2s - a + 1$, we get:

$$S_{x,y} = \frac{(y)(y+1)(\ldots)(2x+y-1)}{2^x x!} \tag{19}$$

5   Limitations

Randomly allocating blocks from a large cluster results in poor spatial locality, which depending on the size of the cache and the application usage may affect cache performance. This problem affects all randomized allocators including VCA. This tradeoff however results in improved security against heap based buffer overflow attacks.

In practice, a probabilistic allowance, ϵ needs to be added to the cluster size. For a 2 block size problem, this increases the cluster size beyond the probabilistic bound of $1.25q$ (but never beyond the theoretical bound of $1.5q$). For a fixed probability of failure, the lower q is, the greater the magnitude of this allowance (relative to q).

To extend VCA to more than 2 block sizes, one way is to use multiple clusters with power of 2 block sizes. For example, on a platform with a page size of 4096 bytes, VCA would use 4 types of clusters, each handling block sizes of (i) 16 bytes and 32 bytes, (ii) 64 bytes and 128 bytes, (iii) 256 bytes and 512 bytes (iv) 1024 bytes and 2048 bytes. Requests greater than or equal to the page size can be allocated from the system directly (e.g. using the mmap system call). The rounding of allocation sizes to power of 2 may lead to wastage of storage known as internal fragmentation. This weakness is however shared by existing randomized allocators as well as the binary buddy allocator.

A second way of extending VCA to more than 2 block sizes is by nesting virtual clusters recursively. This results in a multi-variable optimization problem. It can be shown that a unique solution exists for the extended problem. The analysis of this problem is however omitted due to brevity of space.

Yet another possible way of extending VCA is to consider nesting more than 1 virtual cluster within a single parent cluster. For example, if the size of the parent cluster is a multiple of 6, then the cluster may support allocations of block size 6 directly, and allocations of block sizes 1, 2 and 3 using 3 virtual clusters. We have not analysed the feasibility of this approach and leave it as future work.

6   Conclusions

In this paper, we show that it is possible to improve the randomization while reducing the space requirement of randomized heap allocators by allocating more than 1 block size from a single cluster. With 2 block sizes, compared to existing randomized allocators, the randomization of larger blocks improves by 25% while the size of the reserved area required decreases by 37.5%.

References

1. The PaX Team: Homepage of the PaX Team, http://pax.grsecurity.net
2. Android community: Android security overview,
   http://source.android.com/tech/security/index.html
3. Otto Moerbeek: A new malloc(3) for OpenBSD,
   http://www.openbsd.org/papers/eurobsdcon2009/otto-malloc.pdf
4. Ollie Whitehouse: An Analysis of Address Space Layout Randomization on Windows Vista, http://www.symantec.com/avcenter/reference/Address_Space_Layout_Randomization.pdf.
5. Berger, E.D., Zorn, B.G.: Diehard: probabilistic memory safety for unsafe languages. In: Proceedings of the 2006 ACM SIGPLAN Conference on Programming Language Design and Implementation, PLDI 2006, pp. 158–168. ACM, New York (2006)
6. Novark, G., Berger, E.D.: Dieharder: securing the heap. In: Proceedings of the 17th ACM Conference on Computer and Communications Security, CCS 2010, pp. 573–584. ACM, New York (2010)
7. Li, L., Just, J.E., Sekar, R.: Address-space randomization for windows systems. In: Proceedings of the 22nd Annual Computer Security Applications Conference, pp. 329–338 (2006)
8. OpenBSD: The OpenBSD project, http://www.openbsd.org
9. Bhatkar, S., DuVarney, D.C., Sekar, R.: Address obfuscation: An efficient approach to combat a broad range of memory error exploits. In: Proceedings of the 12th USENIX Security Symposium, Washington, DC, vol. 120 (2003)
10. Barrantes, E.G., Ackley, D.H., Palmer, T.S., Stefanovic, D., Zovi, D.D.: Randomized instruction set emulation to disrupt binary code injection attacks. In: Proceedings of the 10th ACM Conference on Computer and Communications Security, pp. 281–289. ACM (2003)
11. Barrantes, E.G., Ackley, D.H., Forrest, S., Stefanović, D.: Randomized instruction set emulation. ACM Transactions on Information and System Security (TISSEC) 8(1), 3–40 (2005)
12. Boyd, S.W., Kc, G.S., Locasto, M.E., Keromytis, A.D., Prevelakis, V.: On the general applicability of instruction-set randomization. IEEE Transactions on Dependable and Secure Computing 7(3), 255–270 (2010)
13. Kc, G.S., Keromytis, A.D., Prevelakis, V.: Countering code-injection attacks with instruction-set randomization. In: Proceedings of the 10th ACM Conference on Computer and Communications Security, pp. 272–280. ACM (2003)
14. Cadar, C., Akritidis, P., Costa, M., Martin, J.P., Castro, M.: Data randomization. Technical report, Microsoft Research (2008) Technical Report MSR-TR-2008-120
15. Daniel, M., Honoroff, J., Miller, C.: Engineering heap overflow exploits with javascript. In: Proceedings of the 2nd Conference on USENIX Workshop on Offensive Technologies, WOOT 2008, pp. 1:1–1:6. USENIX Association, Berkeley (2008)
16. Robson, J.M.: An estimate of the store size necessary for dynamic storage allocation. J. ACM 18(3), 416–423 (1971)
17. OEIS: The On-Line Encyclopedia of Integer Sequences (August 2013),
    http://oeis.org/

VTOS: Research on Methodology of "Light-Weight" Formal Design and Verification for Microkernel OS

Zhenjiang Qian[1,2,3,*], Hao Huang[1,2], and Fangmin Song[1,2]

[1] State Key Laboratory for Novel Software Technology,
Nanjing University, Nanjing 210046, China
[2] Department of Computer Science and Technology,
Nanjing University, Nanjing 210046, China
[3] Department of Informatics, King's College London,
London WC2R 2LS, United Kingdom
zhenjiang.qian@gmail.com, {hhuang,fmsong}@nju.edu.cn

Abstract. The correctness of the operating systems is difficult to be described with the quantitative methods, because of the complexity. Using the rigorous formal methods to verify the correctness of the operating systems is a recognized method. The existing projects of formal design and verification focus on the validation of code level. In this paper, we present a "light-weight" formal method of design and verification for OS. We propose an OS state automaton model (OSSA) as a link between the system design and verification, and describe the correctness specifications of the system based on this model. We implement the trusted operating system (verified trusted operating system, VTOS) as a prototype, to illustrate the method of consistency verification of system design and safety requirements with formalized theorem prover Isabelle/HOL. The result shows that this approach is feasible.

Keywords: Microkernel OS, Formal Design, Formal Verification, System Correctness.

1 Introduction

Operating system (OS), as a significant system software or platform, provides services and security protection for a variety of other applications. The correctness of OS is the core issue of information security, and how to elaborate or ensure the correctness of OS is the direction of industry and academia efforts. Because of the enormous size and complexity of OS, the accuracy is not easy

* This work is supported by the National High Technology Research and Development Program (863 Program) of China under grant No. 2011AA01A202, the National Science Foundation of China under grant No. 61021062, the "Six Talents Peak" High-Level Personnel Project of Jiangsu Province under grant No. 2011-DZXX-035, University Natural Science Research Program of Jiangsu Province under grant No. 12KJB520001.

S. Qing et al. (Eds.): ICICS 2013, LNCS 8233, pp. 17–32, 2013.

to be described and illustrated. Despite intensive testing, the bugs in OS do occur over time, which can be seen from the fact that the current mainstream commercial OSs continually release the update patches.

For low-assurance application environment, using test to ensure the correctness of underlying OS can be considered sufficient. The situation is quite different for high-assurance application environment, in which even as complete as possible coverage of test cases cannot guarantee that OS is correctly implemented.

An apparently better approach is to use a more rigorous mathematical approach to do formal description and verification, e.g. code analysis, model checking [1] and theorem proving. Formal methods can guarantee the correctness of the software program. But in the actual application process, the developers often shun it due to the division of abstraction levels, and the complexity and scale of the program, as well as the difference between programming and formal logic. Therefore, many scholars try the "light-weight" [2-4] tools to do formal description and design, which have powerful expressiveness ability and can be applied easily. At present, many scholars do verification in the code level for the implemented OS. The OS codes (usually written with C language) are transformed into the input syntax for interactive mechanized verification using the theorem prove tools, e.g. Isabelle [5] or Coq [6]. There are two problems for the work: the investment of time and persons is great, such as seL4 [7] and Verisoft XT [31] projects, and for system maintenance and upgrade work, the updated OS codes still need to be transformed and verified with the existing OS modules merged.

In this paper, we argue that in order to design and implement the OS with formal methods, and illustrate the correctness of the system and ensure the system's security, we need to verify whether the design of OS meets the requirements of system security, and thereby verify whether the implementation meets the requirements of design. We propose that not only the verification for system implementation (code level) needs the formal methods, but also the system design (design level) requires the use of formal logic to ensure the correctness of the design, to the greatest extent of the correctness of system.

In this paper, we present a "light-weight" formal method for the design and verification of OS. We propose an OS state automaton model (OSSA) as a link between the system design and verification, and describe the correctness conditions of the system based on this model. We implement the trusted operating system (verified trusted operating system, VTOS) as a prototype, to illustrate the method of consistency verification of the system design and safety requirements with formalized theorem prover Isabelle/HOL.

The rest of this paper is organized as follows. Section 2 reviews the related work of formal design and verification for OS. Section 3 describes the state automaton model (OSSA). Section 4 illustrates the method of formal verification for VTOS in Isabelle/HOL. Section 5 explains the concrete verification of VTOS in Isabelle/HOL. Section 6 concludes this paper and makes prospect for the future work.

2   Related Work

In 1978, UCLA developed UCLA Secure UNIX [8] for PDP-11 machine. In this system, developers gave multi-layer specification. Top-level specification described permission access control model of the kernel. The specification of the abstraction layer included abstract data structures. The low-level specification contained all the variables and objects used in the kernel call interface. The lowest level is the Pascal codes of the kernel. The authors verified the consistency of specifications inside several parts of the abstraction levels, but did not prove the consistency between all the kernel levels, and consistency of implementation.

Provably Secure Operating System (PSOS) was developed by SRI international during 1973-1980, aiming at providing a generic OS with provable security. PSOS proposed multi-level hierarchical abstraction, and used a specification language (SPECIAL) [9] for precisely defining modules of all levels as well as abstraction mapping between layers. PSOS provided only some simple examples to illustrate the consistency of its implementation and specification, and did not process the formal design and verification from strict sense.

In 1995, Charlie Landau led the EROS [10] project, which focused its formal verification mainly on the correctness of the address translation and the security of usage of kernel memory. The Coyotos project, led by Hopkins in 2006, as the successor of the EROS, proposed a low-level programming language (BitC) [11] and defined the corresponding formal semantics.

VFiasco project [12] organized by the Technical University of Dresden, verified the microkernel compatible with L4. VFiasco used the SPIN model checker to verify the IPC mechanism, and used the PVS [13] verification system as an assistive theorem prover to build system model and verify the correctness of the code. VFiasco modified the C++ language to enhance security of the programming language. In 2008, they reported the Nova Hypervisor project [14] as the continuation of VFiasco, proposed formal models for IA32 processor and memory, and implemented a tool directly converts C++ code to corresponding PVS semantic code.

The seL4 project [7] was initiated by the Laboratory of National ICT Australia (NICTA) during 2004-2006. The project mainly focused on verifying L4 microkernel of the ARM architecture with Isabelle/HOL prover [5]. In the report [15] Klein illustrated the validation work. The objective of formalization was to verify that the implementation was consistent with the expected definition of the abstract model. They are dedicated to the reliability [16] and integrity [17] of OS with the formal methods and improving the efficiency of the real systems [18].

From beginning of the 1990s to the present, the Flint team led by Professor Shao at Yale University has done significant work on formal verification [19][20]. In safe language, they designed a new programming language (VeriML) [21], which introduces the inductive definition of data types in the logic system λHOL^{ind} based on λHOL logic [22], and provides strong formal description capacity as well as features of type security. The open logical framework OCAP [23] developed by Feng et al successfully combined the validation logics of different modules in OS, to form a complete verification system, and to ensure the scalability of the verification model. Meanwhile, the Flint team also studies the methodology of verifying the concurrent management [24] and uses the hierarchical abstraction method to validate the various functional modules in the OS [25]. The Flint team cooperates with the group led by Professor Chen in University of Science and Technology of China. They are committed to program verification technology in high trusted software, and studies how to effectively integrate the form of program verification, proof-carry-code (PCC) and domain-specific language, in order to form new methods for improving productivity of writing robust software, correctness and security [26-30].

Verisoft is a project of large computer system design from 2003 to 2007, to provide formal verifications for the entire computer system from hardware to application layer, i.e., from bottom up (Pervasive Formal Verification) [31][32]. In 2007, its successor Verisoft XT project was officially launched. In Verisoft XT project, pervasive formalization means that the entire project focuses on not only the compiler, or the correctness of the model of machine instructions, but that the design of the entire system must undergo the rigorous formal verification, and form a complete verification chain of software and hardware [33-36].

3   State Automaton Model of VTOS (OSSA)

In this section, we illustrate the functionality of our self-implemented secure microkernel OS (VTOS), and analyse the elements of the state automaton model, i.e., software/hardware computing entities, system object states, and events. Based on these elements, we explain the state automaton model of VTOS (OSSA).

3.1   Architecture and Functionality of VTOS

VTOS is our self-implemented secure and trusted OS. The kernel of VTOS provides the most general services, e.g., process/thread schedule, interrupt handling, message service and simple I/O service, etc. Other functionality services including file management (FM), process management (PM), and memory management (MM), etc, are implemented as user mode processes. The architecture VTOS is shown in the Figure 1.

VTOS adopts the microkernel architecture, in which the inter-process communication (IPC) is realized with message mechanism. From the aspect of functionality, the message processing copies the messages in the message buffer of sender to the one of receiver. The message processing needs to check the legality of the target process, and look up message buffers. Meanwhile, the microkernel converts the hardware and software interrupts into messages. The hardware interrupts are generated by hardware, and the software interrupts are the only way for the user-level applications to request system services delivered to the kernel.

The microkernel handles the process scheduling, responsible for state transitions of the processes in ready, running, and blocking.

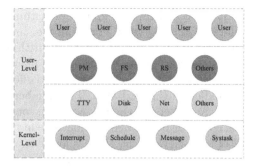

Fig. 1. The architecture of VTOS

Due to isolation, the processes outside the microkernel are prohibited to perform the actual I/O operations, manipulate kernel tables or complete the functionality as in monolithic-kernel OS. The microkernel works in the sealed condition, and modules outside the microkernel execute as independent processes and their codes are kept unchanged. Because of these limitations, the microkernel should provide a set of services for system drivers and functionality servers. These special services are handled by the system task, which is scheduled as a separate process, and is responsible for receiving all of request messages from system drivers and functionality servers, and forwarding these messages to the microkernel.

For interrupt handling, microkernel stores the process context, e.g. information of registers, and do procedure of interrupt handling, and restore the interrupted processes.

The principal reason for us to choose the microkernel architecture is that the microkernel is the only execution object running in highest privileged level and it is isolated. The device drivers are all implemented as user mode programs. The new OS service modules, if needed, are added in user mode. Therefore the user mode programs can not damage the microkernel directly. And the microkernel OS is adequate for multi-cores or many-cores platforms [37].

3.2 Hardware and Software Computing Entities

Modern computer system consists of memory, arithmetic units, and control units, etc. The memory includes registers in the CPUs, caches, main memory, registers in the device controllers, and exchange area in hard disks. The required instruction sequence and data for each arithmetic unit, and the results calculated are all stored in the memory. There is little trivial difference between these concepts and normal ones in computer organization, and these concepts are more convenient for introducing the following abstract model of OS.

The objects that can affect the data in the memory include arithmetic units in the CPU cores, and device controllers with DMA mechanism. All of these objects read and write the data in memory in parallel, and we call these objects as *hardware computing entities*.

The control units in the CPU control the running of arithmetic unit according to the values of the data in the memory. For example, in the Intel CPU, if CPL bit in the $EFLAG$ register is not equal to 0, the arithmetic unit may not execute the $SETGDT$ instruction. Because data in the memory (as $EFLAGS$ in Intel CPU) contains the mask bits of interrupt, it also affects the selection of interrupt events to be handled in the next step. The number of clock cycles for different instructions vary. At the end of each clock cycle, some instructions may happen to complete exactly, while others need to continue in the next clock cycle. Meanwhile, at the end of each clock cycle, there may be a number of events to arrive. According to the current value of each memory location and the hardware computing entities that have just finished an instruction, the control units select a number of events to be handled in these hardware computing entities from the beginning of the next clock cycle. Therefore, the value of each memory location is the key part of the system state. We call the object that consists of a sequence of instructions and can independently run in a hardware computing entity, as a **software computing entity**, e.g., processes, threads, and function objects.

We suppose U is a software computing entity. The read-only data object set of U is denoted by $R(U)$. And the modified data object set of U is denoted by $W(U)$. We call the object set $R(U) \cup W(U)$ as a **working object set** of U, which is denote by $RW(U)$. Because of interrupt mechanism, the software computing entity U may be interrupted during execution, and it may wait in the waiting queue. During the waiting period of U, any other software computing entity do not access its working object set. We can divide all the current software computing entities in the system into two categories. One is the set of **running software computing entities** denoted by A_r, in which all the entities are running on respective hardware computing entities. The other is the set of **waiting software computing entities** denoted by A_w, in which all the entities do not possess the hardware computing entities, thus in the waiting queue. The set of all the software computing entities is denoted as A, i.e., $A = A_r \cup A_w$.

3.3 System Object State

In this subsection, we use the notation in [38] to describe the system state.

Suppose $A_r = \{a_1, a_2, \cdots, a_t\}$, $A_w = \{a_{t+1}, a_{t+2}, \cdots, a_n\}$, and the working object set of a_i is $RW(a_i) = \{x_{ij} \mid j = 1, 2, \cdots, n_i; \ i = 1, 2, \cdots, n\}$. We denote the value range of object x_{ij} by V_{ij}. The initial value of the object x_{ij} is s_{ij}^0. We suppose that a_i has m_i instructions, and after running k instructions, the value of the object x_{ij} in $RW(a_i)$ will be $s_{ij}^k, k = 1, 2, \cdots, m_i$. The value space of the working object set $RW(a_i)$ is

$$\prod_{j=1}^{n_i} V_{ij} \tag{1}$$

which we denote as $VRW(a_i)$. The semantics of the software computing entity a_i may be expressed as the mapping: $\prod_{j=1}^{n_i} V_{ij} \to \prod_{j=1}^{n_i} V_{ij}$.

We call the Cartesian product

$$\prod_{i=1}^{n}\prod_{j=1}^{n_i} V_{ij} \tag{2}$$

as the **system object state set** denoted by S_D.

Sometimes, the software computing entity a_i may create or release objects during its execution process. In this case, its working object set $RW(a_i)$ may vary and so is its value space $\prod_{j=1}^{n_i} V_{ij}$.

In the system memory, in addition to the objects in the equation (2), there are a lot of fragments of free storage space. The positions and number of these fragments vary constantly. In order to analyze the system object state, we make unified numbering for all the data storage units including register, cache, memory, etc. These numbers as whole is a subset of the natural number set $\mathcal{N}$, and we denote this subset as N, $N \subset \mathcal{N}$.

3.4   Events

During each clock cycle, one device may generate hardware interrupt, that possible changes the set A_r. The process may generate the software interrupt and change A_r. And the exceptions of CPU may also change set A_r. We call the hard interrupt, software interrupt, and exceptions generated during the clock cycle as **current arrival events** denoted by E_a. The events that arrive before or are waiting to be handled are called as **waiting events** denoted by E_w. And the events being handled are called as **running events** denoted by E_r. Obviously, the system object state S_D, the current arrival events E_a, the waiting events E_w, the running software computing entities A_r, and the waiting software computing entities A_w, determine the next E_r, E_w, A_r and A_w.

3.5   State Model of VTOS

Base on the above analysis, the running of modern computer system can be described as the progress in which several computing entities manipulate a series of data objects in the memory in parallel.

From the point of view of the software, the factors affecting the system running are the data and instruction sequences in the memory and the arrival events. So the computer system can be described as a state automaton (OSSA) as follows.

1. The set of the accepted events corresponds to the alphabet of OSSA.
2. The events handled during the period from power on to system halt correspond to a sentence accepted by OSSA.
3. At the end of a clock cycle, the values of each memory location and the arrival events correspond to the current state of OSSA.
4. The modification actions to the memory units by hardware computing entities correspond to the state transitions of OSSA.

5. The state in which the CPU executes the *halt* instruction corresponds to the termination state of OSSA.

We build the OSSA model of VTOS as follows.

Definition 1 (VTOS OSSA Model). *VTOS OSSA model is a state automaton,*

$$A_{OS} = (S, \Sigma, \delta, s_0, \Gamma) \tag{3}$$

and the definitions of $S, \Sigma, \delta, s_0, \Gamma$ are as follows:

1. The system state: $S = (S_D, A_r, A_w, E_r, E_w)$
   (a) The object state S_D: the system object state.
   (b) The running software computing entities A_r: the software computing entities that are running in hardware computing entities;
   (c) The waiting software computing entities A_w: the software computing entities that are waiting for running;
   (d) The running events E_r: the events that are chosen to be handled;
   (e) The waiting events E_w: the events that wait to be handled;
2. Σ is the set of all kind of events that the OS accepts.
3. The set of state transfer functions denoted $\delta : \delta(s, E_a) = s'$.
4. s_0 is the initial state of VTOS.
5. Γ is the termination state set, $\Gamma \subseteq S$. Whenever the system reaches a state in Γ, the system terminates.

The architecture of VTOS OSSA model is shown as in Figure 2.

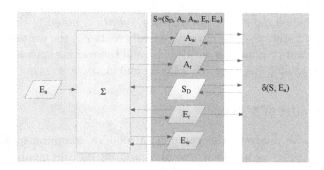

Fig. 2. OSSA model of VTOS

4   Method of Formal Verification for VTOS in Isabelle/HOL

In section 3, we explain how to use the OSSA model to describe the design of VTOS. Based on the OSSA model, in this section, we illustrate the method of how to use Isabelle/HOL theorem proving tools to verify the consistency of the design and implementation of VTOS.

4.1   Introduction of Isabelle/HOL Theorem Proving

Isabelle [5] is a theorem prover tool for validation of the abstract problems described by the logic systems. Isabelle can rigorously verify the program logics in the computer system. Isabelle/HOL supports for Higher-Order Logic in Isabelle, and provide the interactive verification platform with the form of functional programming.

Isabelle/HOL is a type system, and has predefined series of basic types, e.g., *nat*, *int* and *list*. Users can also define new types by keywords *record* and *datatype*, data objects by keyword *definition*, functions by keywords *primrec* and *fun*, and formulae by *lemma* and *theorem*. The special domain is established by building the theory in Isabelle/HOL. In general, each theory is a collection of types, definitions, functions, theorems and proofs.

Isabelle/HOL provides many rules for proving theorems. Meanwhile, we can quote existing theories that contain one or more proven theorems.

4.2   Domain of VTOS in Isabelle/HOL

As described in section 3 above, it is obvious that the system object state can be represented as the elements of the special domain[38][39], that is a mathematical system. The system states, the operations of the hardware and software computing entities, and the properties of the system shown in the form of propositions constitute the domain of VTOS, denoted by $\mathbf{M}_{Computer}$. Relatively, the domain of VTOS in Isabelle/HOL is denoted by $\mathbf{M}_{Isabelle/HOL}$. According to the design and implementation of VTOS, we construct the domain $\mathbf{M}_{Isabelle/HOL}$. There is the isomorphism[39] relation between $\mathbf{M}_{Computer}$ and $\mathbf{M}_{Isabelle/HOL}$, i.e., the proposition in $\mathbf{M}_{computer}$ is true if and only if the corresponding proposition is true in the $\mathbf{M}_{Isabelle/HOL}$.

According to the above described, we establish the relationship between VTOS and Isabelle/HOL logic reasoning system. First, we construct the OSSA model, and based on this model, we design and implement VTOS. With the implementation of VTOS, we describe the domains $\mathbf{M}_{computer}$, and $\mathbf{M}_{Isabelle/HOL}$ in Isabelle/HOL that is isomorphic to the $\mathbf{M}_{computer}$. Thereafter, the properties about the functionality or security of VTOS can be mapped to logic formulae in $\mathbf{M}_{Isabelle/HOL}$. On this basis, we verify the consistency of design and implementation of VTOS through reasoning in the Isabelle/HOL logic system.

4.3   OSSA Model of VTOS in Isabelle/HOL

We regard OS as a server that provides its services whenever a user-level program claims the requests. After finishing the service, the OS gets ready to receive another request. As described in subsection 3.5, an OS works like an OSSA $A_{OSSA} = (S, \Sigma, \delta, s_0, \Gamma)$. The principal elements of OSSA are the system state set S and the set of state transfer functions δ. Each element in S is a vector that consists of values of the data objects of all the current processes. All the functions of event handling and functionality constitute the set of state transfer functions δ. What each function in δ does is that it transfer the initial values of the data objects to new ones according to the functionality semantics.

For describing the OS domain, there are two principal works, i.e., design of the working object set, and of the functions of event handling and functionality that operate on the working object set. The processing of functions in OS corresponds to the transitions of values of the working object set. Therefore, in order to show that VTOS accomplishes all its functions correctly, we prove that VTOS correctly transfer the initial values of the data objects according to the functionality semantics whenever it handles the events and service requests. Relatively, in order to illustrate the security of VTOS, we prove that the system states satisfy the security specifications at any time.

Now we explain how to describe VTOS as an OSSA. As mentioned in subsection 3.1, VTOS is a microkernel OS for general purpose, consisting of microkernel, file manage management, process management, memory management, and device drivers. Firstly, we design the working object set $\{x_{ij} \mid j = 1, 2, \cdots, n_i\}$ for each computing object M_i, i.e., the software computing entity. Suppose the object x_{ij} takes value on the set $\{V_{ij} \mid j = 1, 2, \cdots, n_i\}$, the possible states for M_i is the space $\prod_{j=1}^{n_i} V_{ij}$. Then we design the function set $\{f_{ij} \mid j = 1, 2, \cdots, m_i\}$ for M_i. This function set is the subset of state transfer functions δ. The semantics of the function f_{ij} can be expressed as the mapping from S to S. In order to illustrate the correctness of the function f_{ij}, we prove that the running of the function f_{ij} complies with the expected functionality semantics.

4.4   State Transition Functions of OSSA in Isabelle/HOL

From the aspect of view of composition, the functions implemented in VTOS has two aspects, i.e., the working objects and the instruction sequences. In order to illustrate the correctness of functions, we describe the working objects and the instruction sequences in Isabelle/HOL. As shown in the following definitions of *Instr*, *PCinc* and *NextS*, we define the type of instructions as *Instr*, that contains all kind of assembly instructions, e.g., *mov*, *add*, *push*, *pop*, *leave*, etc. Due to the space limitations, we introduce some of them. The case *movrr Register Register*, whose type is *Instr*, corresponds to the instruction "*movl Register Register*". The function *PCinc* adds 1 to the program counter register *PC*. The semantics of the function *NextS* is that for "$s' = NextS\ s\ instr$", after executing the instruction *instr*, the system state s is converted into s'. Similarly, by applying *NextS* to the sequences of the functionality instructions, we can calculate the state transitions for multi-steps.

Definitions of Instr, PCinc and NextS in Isabelle/HOL

```
datatype Instr =
          movrr   Register Register
        | movir   int      Register
        | addrr   Register Register
          . . .
```

```
fun PCinc :: "state => state"
where
"PCinc s = s (| R:=((R s) (pc:=((R s) pc)+1)) |)"

fun NextS :: "state => Instr => state"
where
"NextS s (movrr y x) = PCinc (s (| R:=((R s) (x:=((R s) y)))|))"
...
```

4.5 Proving the Integrity Property in Isabelle/HOL

The running OS is a collection of several processes. Each process provides designated services. Can these processes always provide the services during the running of system? How can we describe and judge that these processes provide the services correctly? These questions confuse many researchers. As illustrated above, we regard that VTOS corresponds to an OSSA model. We prove the immutability of the corresponding OSSA model of VTOS to demonstrate the integrity of VTOS.

As illustrated in section 3, the current values of all working objects of the processes in the OS correspond to the system state of OSSA. It is obvious that if the accepted alphabet and transition functions of the OSSA remain unchanged, the OSSA is immutable. In order to prove this characteristic conveniently, during the design of VTOS, we guarantee that the working objects of any two processes do not intersect, and that the possible target address set of the branch points in the functions is identified and will not be changed by user applications and inputs. Because the services provided by VTOS are identified, this objective is reasonable. With these criteria We design and implement VTOS, and the result shows that it is feasible. Therefore we need only to prove that the accepted events and the semantics of functions in the microkernel are kept unchanged, i.e., that all memory units occupied by the codes of microkernel remain unchanged, and that the selection of target address in each branch point is consistent with the semantics of the functionality. This actually proves that all the factors that may affect the integrity of VTOS are kept unchanged during the running of system.

5 Verification of VTOS in Isabelle/HOL

In this section, we take the module of message processing service as the example to describe the method of proving the correctness of event handling and state transitions.

For building the model or structure in Isabelle/HOL, the significant work is to construct the domain and define the mapping or interpretation from Isabelle/HOL to the domain.

While we design the working object set for the modules of the VTOS, we have designed the state set of OSSA actually. And while we design the system call functions, we have designed the state transition functions of OSSA actually, and while we establish the integrity conditions, we have constructed the relations on domain actually. So when we complete VTOS design, we also complete the construction of the domain.

As illustrated in subsection 3.4, whenever the events occur, the OS select the corresponding event handlers to execute. The events may be interrupts, and service requests, etc. It is important to prove the correctness of the execution of event handlers and the corresponding state transitions.

In the microkernel of VTOS, the module of message processing service mainly includes the functions of *sys_send*, and *sys_receive*, etc. The working objects of these functions are components of the PCBs (process control block) of the sender and receiver processes.

In the following sections, we illustrate the correctness proof of the function *sys_send* in VTOS, which sends message from one process to another process. The main part of the C codes for *sys_send*, the corresponding assembly codes and definition in Isabelle/HOL are shown as follows.

sys_send in C

```
int sys_send(struct proc *caller_ptr, int dst, message *m_ptr,
             unsigned flags)
{
    struct proc *dst_ptr = get_proc_from_pid(dst);
    ...
    copy_mess(m_ptr, dst_ptr->p_messbuf, sizeof(message));
    ...
}
```

sys_send in ASM

```
<sys_send>:
push    %ebp
movl    %esp,%ebp
subl    $0x28,%esp
movl    0xc(%ebp),%eax
movl    %eax,(%esp)
call    c0101128
...
movl    %eax,0x4(%esp)
movl    0x10(%ebp),%eax
movl    %eax,(%esp)
call    c010116d <copy_mess>
...
```

sys_send in Isabelle/HOL

```
definition sys_send :: "Code"
where
  "sys_send =
    pushr      ebp;
    movrr      esp ebp;
    subir      10 esp;
    movirr     3 ebp eax;
    movrir     eax 0 esp;
    call   get_proc_from_pid;
    ...
    movrir     eax 1 esp;
    movirr     4 ebp eax;
    movrir     eax 0 esp;
    call       copy_mess;
    ..."
```

It is the key point for us to establish the formulae to describe the specifications for the correctness of the event handlers and the state transition functions whenever the event handlers are called, because these conditions should fit to any starting state for the state transition functions. For example, we illustrate the correctness specification for sys_send as follows.

$$\forall s.\ Q(s) \wedge (s' = NextnS\ s\ sys\_send) \longrightarrow P(s, s') \tag{4}$$

in which "$NextnS\ s\ sys\_send$" means the state after execution of the functionality semantics of sys_send, i.e., the state for multi-steps. The formula 4 means when the starting state s satisfies the condition Q, the function sys_send can correctly send designated messages to target process, i.e., that the starting state s and the subsequent state s' satisfy condition P. We regard that not all the states are security states. Therefore, there are some states that the VTOS may not reach, and we need not consider these cases for the starting states. In the formula 4, the condition P is considered as the semantic formula of the function sys_send, and Q as the initial condition.

From the aspect of view of the working object set, we consider the starting state condition Q. The working object set of the function sys_send includes the actual parameters in the stack, and the accessibility of the corresponding components of the PCBs of the sender and receiver processes. So the condition Q is defined as follows:

$$\begin{aligned} Q(s) : (s.regs.sp + 1 = caller\_ptr)\ \wedge \\ (s.regs.sp + 2 = dst)\ \wedge \\ (s.regs.sp + 3 = m\_ptr) \end{aligned} \tag{5}$$

The formula 5 states that the actual parameters that the function sys_send needs are located in the stack at proper location and possess the correct values.

When the sender process requires to send the message to the receiver process, the target process may be waiting for this message, or in dealing with other messages. Here we explain the case that the target process is waiting for this message. In this case, the handler sys_send copies the designated length of bytes from the sender's message buffer to the receiver's. Therefore, the correctness condition for sys_send is that the values in the two relevant memory location interval, i.e., the message buffers of the sender and receiver, are equivalent. The semantic formula P is defined as follows.

$$\begin{aligned} P(s, s') = CmpM(s', s.M(s.regs.sp + 3), \\ s'.M(proc + sizeof\_proc\ * \\ s.M(s.regs.sp + 2) + p\_messbuf), \\ sizeof\_msg) \end{aligned} \tag{6}$$

in which the auxiliary formula $CmpM$ is defined as follows.

$$\begin{aligned} CmpM(s, p, q, n) = (i \geq 0 \wedge i \leq (n - 1)) \\ \longrightarrow (s.M(p + i) = s.M(q + i)) \end{aligned} \tag{7}$$

The amount of the verification codes in Isabelle/HOL for the whole VTOS is about 56K SLOC. The result shows that VTOS achieves the desired safety.

6 Conclusion and Future Work

In this paper, we present a "lightweight" formal method to design and implement a safe and reliable OS. We propose a state automaton (OSSA) model as the basis of the system design. With this model, we describe the system states and state transition functions. We use Isabelle/HOL theorem proving tool to establish its corresponding formal model, and define the specifications of the system, to prove that the system design and implementation comply with these specifications. With this method we achieve a safe and trusted operating system (VTOS). The results show that this approach is feasible.

Various functional modules in the OS are often designed using a variety of program logics, and involved in different levels of abstraction, such as C language, assembly codes, and hardware layers, etc. For the correctness of the whole system integrated with these functional modules, it is not simply the conjunction of the correctness of each module. For the future work, we will study how to combine the verification of the separated modules to illustrate the correctness of the whole system, from the aspect of view of the domain and type theory.

References

1. Clarke, E.M., Grumberg, O., Peled, D.A.: Model Checking. The MIT Press, Cambridge (1999)
2. Jackson, D.: Alloy: A lightweight object modelling notation. ACM Transactions on Software Engineering and Methodology 11(2), 256–290 (2002)
3. Denney, R.: Succeeding with Use Cases: Working Smart to Deliver Quality. Addison-Wesley Professional Publishing, Boston (2005)
4. Agerholm, S., Larsen, P.G.: A lightweight approach to formal methods. In: Hutter, D., Stephan, W., Traverso, P., Ullmann, M. (eds.) FM-Trends 1998. LNCS, vol. 1641, pp. 168–183. Springer, Heidelberg (1999)
5. Nipkow, T., Paulson, L.C., Wenzel, M.T.: Isabelle/HOL: A Proof Assistant for Higher-Order Logic. LNCS, vol. 2283. Springer, Heidelberg (2002)
6. Bertot, Y., Casteran, P.: Interactive Theorem Proving and Program Development. Springer, Heidelberg (2004)
7. Klein, G., Andronick, J., Elphinstone, K., et al.: seL4: Formal verification of an operating system kernel. Communications of the ACM 53(6), 107–115 (2010)
8. Walker, B.J., Kemmerer, R.A., Popek, G.J.: Specification and verification of the UCLA Unix security kernel. Communications of the ACM 23(2), 118–131 (1980)
9. Robinson, L., Roubine, O.: Special: A Specification and Assertion Language. Technical Report, Stanford Research Institute (1977)
10. Shapiro, J.S., Smith, J.M., Farber, D.J.: EROS: A fast capability system. In: 17th SOSP, pp. 170–185. ACM, New York (1999)
11. Shapiro, J.S., Sridhar, S., Doerrie, M.S.: BitC Language Specification. Technical Report (1996)
12. Hohmuth, M., Tews, H., Stephens, S.G.: Applying source-code verification to a microkernel: the VFiasco project. Technical Report (2002)
13. Owre, S., Rushby, J.M., Shankar, N.: PVS: A prototype verification system. In: Kapur, D. (ed.) CADE 1992. LNCS, vol. 607, pp. 748–752. Springer, Heidelberg (1992)

14. Tews, H., Weber, T., Volp, M., Poll, E., Eekelen, M., Rossum, P.: Nova Micro-Hypervisor Verification Formal, machine-checked verification of one module of the kernel source code. Technical Report (2008)
15. Klein, G., Elphinstone, K., Heiser, G., et al.: seL4: Formal verification of an OS kernel. In: 22nd SOSP, pp. 207–220. ACM, New York (2009)
16. Heiser, G., Murray, T., Klein, G.: It's time for trustworthy systems. In: 33rd S & P, pp. 67–70. IEEE Computer Society, Washington (2012)
17. Sewell, T., Winwood, S., Gammie, P., Murray, T., Andronick, J., Klein, G.: seL4 enforces integrity. In: Van Eekelen, M., Geuvers, H., Schmaltz, J., Wiedijk, F. (eds.) ITP 2011. LNCS, vol. 6898, pp. 325–340. Springer, Heidelberg (2011)
18. Blackham, B., Shi, Y., Chattopadhyay, S., Roychoudhury, A.: Timing analysis of a protected operating system kernel. In: 32nd RTSS, pp. 339–348. IEEE Computer Society, Washington (2011)
19. Shao, Z.: Certified Software. Communications of the ACM 53(12), 56–66 (2010)
20. Stampoulis, A., Shao, Z.: Static and User-Extensible Proof Checking. In: 39th POPL, pp. 273–284. ACM, New York (2012)
21. Stampoulis, A., Shao, Z.: VeriML: Typed Computation of Logical Terms inside a Language with Effects. In: 15th ICFP, pp. 333–344. ACM, New York (2010)
22. Barendregt, H.P., Geuvers, H.: Proof-assistants using dependent type systems. Elsevier, Amsterdam (1999)
23. Feng, X.: An Open Framework for Certified System Software. Ph.D. dissertation. Yale University, New Haven (2007)
24. Guo, Y., Feng, X., Shao, Z., Shi, P.: Modular Verification of Concurrent Thread Management. In: Jhala, R., Igarashi, A. (eds.) APLAS 2012. LNCS, vol. 7705, pp. 315–331. Springer, Heidelberg (2012)
25. Vaynberg, A., Shao, Z.: Compositional Verification of a Baby Virtual Memory Manager. In: Hawblitzel, C., Miller, D. (eds.) CPP 2012. LNCS, vol. 7679, pp. 143–159. Springer, Heidelberg (2012)
26. Liang, H.J., Feng, X., Fu, M.: A Rely-Guarantee-Based Simulation for Verifying Concurrent Program Transformations. In: 39th POPL, pp. 455–468. ACM, New York (2012)
27. Tan, G., Shao, Z., Feng, X., Cai, H.X.: Weak Updates and Separation Logic. New Generation Comput. 29(1), 3–29 (2011)
28. Fu, M., Li, Y., Feng, X., Shao, Z., Zhang, Y.: Reasoning about Optimistic Concurrency Using a Program Logic for History. In: Gastin, P., Laroussinie, F. (eds.) CONCUR 2010. LNCS, vol. 6269, pp. 388–402. Springer, Heidelberg (2010)
29. Ferreira, R., Feng, X., Shao, Z.: Parameterized Memory Models and Concurrent Separation Logic. In: Gordon, A.D. (ed.) ESOP 2010. LNCS, vol. 6012, pp. 267–286. Springer, Heidelberg (2010)
30. Feng, X., Shao, Z., Dong, Y., Guo, Y.: Certifying low-level programs with hardware interrupts and preemptive threads. In: 30th PLDI, pp. 170–182. ACM, New York (2008)
31. Alkassar, E., Hillebrand, M.A., Leinenbach, D., Schirmer, N.W., Starostin, A.: The Verisoft Approach to Systems Verification. In: Shankar, N., Woodcock, J. (eds.) VSTTE 2008. LNCS, vol. 5295, pp. 209–224. Springer, Heidelberg (2008)
32. Daum, M., Dorrenbacher, J., Bogan, S.: Model stack for the pervasive verification of a microkernel-based operating system. In: 5th VERIFY, pp. 56–70. CEUR-WS.org, Aachen (2008)
33. Alkassar, E., Cohen, E., Hillebrand, M.A., Kovalev, M., Paul, W.J.: Verifying shadow page table algorithms. In: 10th FMCAD, pp. 267–270. IEEE Press, New York (2010)

34. Alkassar, E., Cohen, E., Hillebrand, M.A., Pentchev, H.: Modular specification and verification of interprocess communication. In: 10th FMCAD, pp. 167–174. IEEE Press, New York (2010)
35. Baumann, C., Beckert, B., Blasum, H., Bormer, T.: Ingredients of operating system correctness. In: Embedded World 2010 Conference (2010)
36. Baumann, C., Bormer, T., Blasum, H., Tverdyshev, S.: Proving memory separation in a microkernel by code level verification. In: 14th ISORCW, pp. 25–32. IEEE Computer Society, Washington (2011)
37. Wentzlaff, D., Agarwal, A.: Factored Operating Systems (FOS): The Case for a Scalable Operating System for Multicores. ACM SIGOPS Operating Systems Review 43(2), 76–85 (2009)
38. Li, W.: Mathematical Logic: Basic Principles and Formal Calculus. Science China Press, Beijing (2007) (in Chinese)
39. Marker, D.: Model Theory An Introduction. Oxford University Press, Oxford (1990)

Defeat Information Leakage from Browser Extensions via Data Obfuscation

Wentao Chang and Songqing Chen

Department of Computer Science
George Mason University
Fairfax, VA 22030
U.S.A.
{wchang7,sqchen}@gmu.edu

Abstract. Today web browsers have become the de facto platform for Internet users. This makes browsers the target of a lot of attacks. With the security considerations from the very beginning, Chrome offers more protection against exploits via benign-but-buggy extensions. However, more and more attacks have been launched via malicious extensions while there is no effective solution to defeat such malicious extensions. As user's sensitive information is often the target of such attacks, in this paper, we aim to proactively defeat information leakage with our iObfus framework. With iObfus, sensitive information is always classified and labeled automatically. Then sensitive information is obfuscated before any IO operation is conducted. In this way, the users' sensitive information is always protected even information leakage occurs. The obfuscated information is properly restored for legitimate browser transactions. A prototype has been implemented and iObfus works seamlessly with the Chromium 25. Evaluation against malicious extensions shows the effectiveness of iObfus, while it only introduces trivial overhead to benign extensions.

Keywords: Browser Extension, Chrome, Data Obfuscation, Information Leakage Threats.

1   Introduction

The web browser has become the de facto platform for everyday Internet users, and unarguably the driving force of the recent years' Internet revolution. Modern web browsers, such as Chrome, Firefox, and IE, are no longer simple static data renderers but complex networked operating systems that manage multiple facets of user online experiences[1][3].

   To help browsers handle various emerging files and events, functionalities of web browsers are constantly enhanced. Most often such functionalities are extended by third-party code that customizes user experience and enables additional interactions among browser-level data and events. As of today, all major commodity web browsers support extensions. For example, Chrome has a list of over 10,000 extensions on Chrome Web Store by Dec 2010 [13].

S. Qing et al. (Eds.): ICICS 2013, LNCS 8233, pp. 33–48, 2013.

However, the fact that web browsers have become the most popular vehicle for Internet surfing attracts more and more attacks. Among them, an increasingly popular attack is via browser extensions [7][8][10]. Commonly, these attacks are launched by exploiting existing extensions' weakness or by tricking user to install malicious extensions that can take over the web browser, steal cookies or user sensitive information without users' knowledge. For example, one of the earliest Firefox malicious extensions, FFsniFF [14] hides itself from the extension manager after it has been installed, monitors all form submissions in the browser for passwords and sends an email with gathered data to the attacker, and many Trojans disguise themselves as legitimate browser helper objects (BHO) for IE, but once installed they change user Internet settings and redirect users to random websites.

To deal with such threats, Google Chrome, one of the most popular web browsers, has made significant efforts by introducing several new security features to its extension framework [4][5]. It enforces strong isolation between web browsers and extensions, separates privileges among different components of extension, and uses a fine-grained permission system [11]. Recent studies [6][7] indicate that the Google Chrome extension framework is highly effective in preventing and mitigating security vulnerabilities in benign-but-buggy extensions that can be leveraged by web attackers. However, even Chrome does not cover all the bases, and most importantly it is defenseless to information dispersion or harvesting attacks launched by malicious extensions. For example, as these days online social networks are very popular, a rogue extension, Adobe Business Flash Player [15], fetches and executes arbitrary JavaScript code from network once it has detected that the user has landed to certain social media websites. Users' social media accounts are then hijacked to post feeds or "like"s without users' consent. Other attacks can be launched to steal bank account information when users conduct online transactions as discussed in [7][12]. Existing work on extensions made little progress on the detection or protection of such attack vector.

To mitigate such an imperative threat, in this paper we design and implement iObfus. As users' sensitive information is the most critical asset, iObfus aims to defeat sensitive information leakage through browser extensions. It automatically classifies sensitive information on the web page with different default protection levels. Based on the protection policy, sensitive information will be automatically and passively obfuscated before any IO operations are performed. In this way, the users' sensitive information is always protected even information leakage happens (under this case only obfuscated information is leaked). To ensure the proper function of normal browser transactions, iObfus restores the context-aware sensitive information for legitimate transactions.

To demonstrate the effectiveness of iObfus, we build a proof-of-concept prototype on top of web browser Chromium 25. Experiments conducted against several malicious extensions in the wild show that iObfus can effectively protect user information from leaking. Further tests show that Chromium with iObfus does not interfere with normal daily transactions, and the data obfuscation/de-obfuscation cause trivial delay on users' experience.

The rest of the paper is organized as follows. Section 2 introduces some background information on Chrome extensions followed by an analysis of the information leakage threats from Chrome extensions in Section 3. We describe iObfus design and implementation in Section 4. An evaluation is conducted in Section 5. We discuss some related work in Section 6 and make concluding remarks in Section 7.

2   Security of Chrome Extensions

Chrome uses a multi-process architecture, where the browser core process runs in the privileged mode to access system resources and performs I/O tasks and the renderer process is responsible for displaying web content. The single instance of the browser core process handles the browser UI and manages all tab and plugin processes, while each renderer process corresponds to a single tab in the browser and runs in a sandboxed environment. To perform any task that needs additional privileges, the renderer process simply sends messages to the browser core process via IPC.

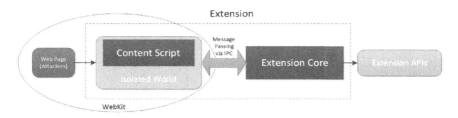

Fig. 1. Chrome Extension Security Architecture

Chrome also relies on various extensions to extend its functionality. Chrome extension consists of Content Scripts and extension core components. Figure 1 shows an example. A Content Script is a piece of JavaScript code that can be injected into a web page before/after the page is loaded. It is executed in the same process of the tab but in its separate JavaScript engine (called isolated world). Content Scripts cannot access any objects except for the DOM tree of the web page and cannot use any Chrome extension APIs. To communicate with the extension core or Content Scripts across tabs, a Content Script relies on the message passing mechanism of Chrome's inter-process communication (IPC). The extension core contains background web pages and their associated JavaScript code, and it runs in a separate sandboxed renderer process and has no privileges to access system resources or perform I/O. The message passing mechanism is also needed by the extension core to dispatch I/O tasks to the browser core process. Optionally, an extension can have binary code such as NPAPI plugins, which have the same set of privileges as the browser. Note that binary plugins are native executable and not protected by the Chrome extension security framework so we do not include these in our research.

The goal of Chrome extension security architecture is not to defend the browser process against malicious extensions but to protect benign-but-buggy extensions from being compromised. The most common attack against Chrome extensions is through malicious JavaScript codes that are either bundled with web pages or fetched from the network. Thus the security model is an effort to defeat attacks launched from malicious web pages that target vulnerabilities of buggy extensions. To minimize the potential damages caused to the browser process if the extension is exploited, Chrome also uses a multi-component architecture with fine-grained privilege separation strategies. Security features of Chrome extension framework mainly include four security mechanisms: a permission mechanism that governs access control to privileged browser extension APIs and web contents, privilege separation between extension components that protects extension core from attackers in case that Content Script has been compromised by a malicious website, isolated runtime environments for Content Script that prevent tampering of extension's JavaScript objects and the Content Security Policy (CSP) that disables certain dangerous JavaScript functions and features.

3   Information Leakage Threats from Chrome Extensions

In this section, we discuss the information leakage threats from Chrome extensions, and we further classify the sources of information leakage through Chrome extensions into two categories: per-tab user data from open web pages and browser user data exposed by extension APIs.

3.1   Threat Analysis

Security concerns that online transactions could be hijacked or tampered with malicious extensions have arisen in recent years [7][12]. Password or financial information sniffing is one form of security attacks that malicious extensions could launch against web surfers. To access sensitive information such as the bank account number or login credentials, extensions need to inject Content Scripts to the victim web page. The injected Content Script will search in the DOM tree for elements of their interests, for example, *<input>* elements with type or name equal to "password" where user password is usually stored. To steal this information, attackers also need to establish a communication channel to the IP address where they hide. Thus malicious extensions also request cross-origin *XHR* permissions.

The recently popular attacks against Social Media accounts do not even need to steal users' login credentials. Instead, the attackers try to masquerade as the users to engage social interactions stealthily. Such malware instances will check browser cookies to determine whether users have landed to certain social websites. If they have, another piece of JavaScript code will be fetched and executed, via which, the account can be used to spam your friends, post malicious links on news feed or follow/like other people or pages. This type of attacks seemingly acts like users' normal behavior, thus they are unlikely to be detected by anti-virus programs. Once infected, this threat tends to persist in user's browser. As a matter of fact, this type of malicious extensions is the most common ones in the wild because attackers could gain monetary benefits and users are often not aware of the fact that they become victims.

The root causes of these attacks are: 1) Content Scripts have full access privileges to the DOM tree of the web page they are injected to, regardless of the fact that certain elements contain more sensitive information. If a fine-grained access control policy is enforced, we could control the source of information leakage. 2) The cross-origin *XHR* permission often grants access privileges to more origins than necessary. Each origin specified in the extension manifest file expands the target set of origins that the extension can leak information to. Since the extension core and the Content Script share the same set of origins, the potential sink points could scatter anywhere in Content Scripts or the extension core, making it difficult to track leakages.

3.2   Sources of Information Leakage through Browser Extensions

To defeat information leakage attacks, we need to first define the scope of "sensitive information" in the context of web surfing. The term "sensitive information" often differs in different research fields. In a broad sense, sensitive information includes but not limited to:

- Any information that can reveal users' true identities or can be used to uniquely identify users, for instance, names, social security numbers, profile images, etc.
- Financial information or monetary equivalence such as bank account number, credit card number, digital currency, and so on.
- Any information from which others can infer users' tendency or personal preferences, for example, users' recent shopping list can indicate his/her lifestyle and be used for marketing purpose.

In general any data that users wish to withhold from others should be considered as sensitive and shall be protected cautiously by venders or service providers. The scope of sensitivity is so wide that in reality without a meaningful context of the term, there is little to be done to protect sensitive information practically. To defeat information leakage, it is essential to define the scope of sensitivity precisely in the context of browser extensions.

Based on our extensive study of possible leaking sources that are accessible to browser extensions, we classify sensitive information into two categories:

Per-Tab User Data from Open Web Pages

When a user opens and views web pages, the multi-process Chrome browser will fetch each web page along with its resource files from the web server and render them in sandboxed render processes respectively. The extension core runs in its own process and does not have direct access to the memory space of sandboxed render process, however, Chrome allows extensions to inject Content Scripts to any web pages as long as the origin of the web pages match Content Scripts' injection patterns. The injected Content Script has full access to the DOM tree of the targeted web page, thus sensitive information from per-tab user data becomes exposed to Content Script component of the extension.

Before Chrome 13, cross-origin *XHR* was not supported in Content Scripts, so that information leakage can only happen in the extension core. The message passing mechanism of Chrome extensions framework enables Content Scripts to send collected information back to the extension core. With proper message passing and receiving code implemented in the Content Script and the extension core, any user sensitive information on the web page is no longer local to its containing browser tab, and they are shared with the extension core, via which they can be further shared with other tabs.

We build our own set of privacy rules with the basis of HIPPA's 18 rules [18] to identify candidates of sensitive per-tab data. The scope of set is dynamic depending on different websites; easy to expand/update and even let users choose their own tolerance level (The configurable level of sensitive information will be further studied). Besides HIPPA rules, we also add to the scope DOM nodes with sensitive information specific to the browser, for example, sessions cookies, anti-forgery tokens that prevent Cross-Site Request Forgery (CSRF) attacks, etc.

Browser User Data Exposed by Extension APIs

Modern browsers are allowed to maintain certain state information about their users aiming to remember user preferences and facilitate user actions. Such state information includes bookmarks of websites, download history, browsing history, cache of visited web pages, the chosen theme of browser UI, list of installed extensions, geolocation of browser, etc. The Chrome browser even offers its users to back up aggregated user settings via cloud services to their centralized Google account, so that the state information is synchronized across different Chrome instances.

The state information together is called browser user data and security measures should be taken by browsers to protect them from tampering and stealing by web and local attackers. In Chrome's approach, browser extensions are executed in a sandboxed environment and a permission system is used to regulate permissions assigned to extensions. If the principle of least privilege is strictly enforced, even they are taken over by attackers the damage to the browser should be contained.

However, Chrome's rich extension APIs and rough privilege definition make this situation complicated. In addition to all the APIs that web pages and Apps can use, Chrome also provides its own set of extension APIs to allow tight integration with the browser. While these APIs vastly enrich extension features, it also permits unfettered accesses to browser user data by extensions. Browser user data that are inherently safe in other browsers suffer from information leakage threats in the Chrome extension framework [26].

4   Design and Implementation of iObfus

In this paper, we focus on protecting sensitive information that could be leaked through browser extensions. For this purpose, we design iObfus. We do not try to defeat information attacks launched by malicious websites in our system. We also assume malicious extensions discussed in this paper are written following the content security policy and are not easily detected by static analysis. Hence iObfus does not consider information leakage via *src* attributes of *img* tags, *iframe* tags, etc.

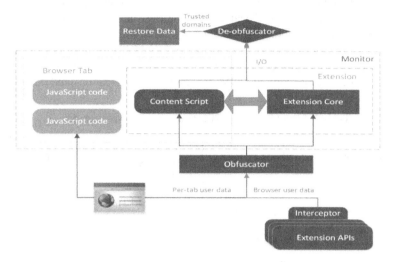

Fig. 2. iObfus architecture

Figure 2 sketches the architecture of iObfus and its working flow. We build the prototype on the open source Chromium project. Our prototype is compatible with all extensions developed for Chromium 25 and plus. What motivates us to build our pro-totype on Chromium is: (a) the Chrome browser is by far the most secure browser in the market and already has a comprehensive security model in place. (b) Building the prototype based on a platform that commercial browsers share the source code with also indicates that the security enhancement we propose can be easily transported to its commercial counterpart.

iObfus consists of four major components: Monitor, Interceptor, Obfuscator and De-obfuscator.

4.1 Monitor

This component monitors the execution of Content Scripts and JavaScript code in the extension core. Our system must be able to distinguish the execution of regular JavaScript code in web pages from JavaScript code introduced by extensions, which includes Content Scripts and JavaScript code running in background pages of the extension core. The ability to separate the execution of JavaScript code is important for two reasons. Firstly, limiting the scope of monitoring could reduce performance overhead of our system. Because iObfus aims to mitigate information leakage threats incurred by extensions in a cost effective manner, we can disregard attacks launched by JavaScript code of malicious websites and rely on the existing security model of Chrome extension framework to defeat them. Therefore, it is critical to identify origins of JavaScript code at runtime and enable/disable iObfus features on demand. Secondly, disabling obfuscation and restoration of sensitive per-tab data accessible to regular JavaScript code can avoid breaking the functionality of websites. For example, some normal behaviors in the web page such as the input validation of user login could be identified as a potential leakage and be obstructed by iObfus if we cannot exclude these JavaScript actions from our active monitoring.

We modify *compileAndRunScript()* method of *WebKit*'s *ScriptController* class to check whether the execution of JavaScript code is within isolated world. Only if it is, iObfus marks the separate copy of DOM documents as obfuscation candidates.

Table 1. List of Extension APIs that access browser user data

Extension API name	Methods/Property	Return Value (property/type)	Taint source
Bookmarks	get getChidlren getRecent getTree getSubtree	BookmarkTree-Node	url, title
contentSettings	get getResourceIdentifi-er	ResourceIdentifier	Id
Cookies	get getAll getAllCookieStore	Cookie	value, domain, path, storied
History	search getVisit	HistoryItem VistItem	url, title, lastVist-Time
pageCapture	saveAsMHTML	MHTML	details(object)
Permissions	getAll contains	Permissions Boolean	permissions, origins
pushMessage	getChannelId	ChannelIdResult	channelId
Storage	get getBytesInUse	Sync Local	Items(object)
Tabs	get getCurrent query	Tab	url, title
Topsites	Get	MostVistedUrl	url, title
Windows	get getCurrent getLastFocused getAll	Window	Tabs

4.2   Interceptor

This component intercepts the subset extension APIs we identify that can expose browser user data to the extension core. As we discussed in the Section 3, the browser user data is the second source of leakage, thus iObfus must be capable of instrumenting the subset extension APIs and obfuscating the browser user data before they are read by the extension core. Since the Chrome extension APIs are under active development, it is common that more experimental APIs become supported APIs in future releases.

We perform the identification of leaking APIs from all extension APIs currently available in Chromium 25, and the list of APIs that iObfus intercepts is shown in Table 1. The data in the fourth column of the Table 1 are required to be properly processed before they enter the isolated world of the Content Script.

4.3   Obfuscator

The goal of Obfuscator is to protect user sensitive information without breaking the normal functionalities of extensions. The values of those potential leakage sources are obfuscated before they enter the memory space of extensions. Extensions can still access those data objects and use their values for actions as if they are regular Java-Script objects.

Table 2. Regular expression of some common data formats

SSN #	\d{3}-\d{2}-\d{4}$
Email Address	\b[A-Z0-9._%+-]+@[A-Z0-9.-]+\.[A-Z]{2,4}\b
Url	^(http|https|ftp)\://([a-zA-Z0-9\.\-]+(\:[a-zA-Z0-9\.&%\$\-]+)*@)*((25[0-5]|2[0-4][0-9]|[0-1]{1}[0-9]{2}|[1-9]{1}[0-9]{1}|[1-9])\.(25[0-5]|2[0-4][0-9]|[0-1]{1}[0-9]{2}|[1-9]{1}[0-9]{1}|[1-9]|0)\.(25[0-5]|2[0-4][0-9]|[0-1]{1}[0-9]{2}|[1-9]{1}[0-9]{1}|[1-9]|0)\.(25[0-5]|2[0-4][0-9]|[0-1]{1}[0-9]{2}|[1-9]{1}[0-9]{1}|[0-9])|localhost|([a-zA-Z0-9\-]+\.)*[a-zA-Z0-9\-]+\.(com|edu|gov|int|mil|net|org|biz|arpa|info|name|pro|aero|coop|museum|[a-zA-Z]{2}))(\:[0-9]+)*(/($\|[a-zA-Z0-9\.\,\?'\\\+&%\$#\=~_\-]+))*$

iObfus only obfuscates sensitive information derived from DOM documents that have a marked sensitivity flag by the Monitor or browser user data from intercepted extension APIs by the Interceptor. According to HIPAA and Chesapeake Research Review, Inc. [19], from the security perspective there are 18 types of individual identifiers including name, telephone number, social security number, account number, etc. Based on our observation and previous research [7], DOM elements containing sensitive information often have name, type or ID attributes with values correlating to these individual identifiers. For example, the HTML input element for password in

Google account sign-in page has attributes of type="password", name="Passwd" and id="Passwd". Hence, a set of regular expression patterns is defined in iObfus to locate the first source of leakage – sensitive per-tab user data.

Due to the fact that the regular JavaScript code and the Content Script are executed intermittently, to avoid repetitive processing, iObfus also assigns an "isProcessed" Boolean flag to candidate DOM documents marked by the Monitor. Only if the value of "isProcessed" is false, iObfus begins to iterate every element of the DOM tree to find a pattern match for names, types and IDs. For matched DOM elements, iObfus processes them differently depending on their element type. For text node, iObfus applies the obfuscation algorithm to convert the text content into its obfuscated form and then call *replaceEntireText()* method to substitute the entire content of text node; for element node, iObfus only replaces the content of "value" attribute with obfuscated data.

A context-aware obfuscation algorithm is the key to the success of the Obfuscator. The "obfuscated" form has to be syntactically equivalent to its original form so that the evaluation of these DOM objects at runtime does not fail. In the current prototype, iObfus defines regular expressions for some most common data formats as known contexts, and they are listed in Table 2. Before applying a randomization-based generic obfuscation, iObfus examines the input for known contexts. If a pattern match is detected, it will instead perform a context-aware transformation. For example, if iObfus detects an email address smith@gmail.com in its input, it will transform the email address into a fake one such as hnrgs@ymail.com, which can be restored later for legitimate I/O operations.

4.4   De-obfuscator

The De-obfuscator is responsible for URL and payload inspection of cross-origin *XMLHTTPRequests* and it also restores obfuscated data if requests are sent to trusted domains. Some extensions heavily rely on the communication with their own servers to demonstrate features, for example, an extension that synchronizes users' bookmarks across multiple browser instances requires saving un-obfuscated bookmarks to its server. To add this domain to the trusted list, extension developers need to explicitly declare this specific domain in *manifest.json* file, and users' approvals are also required at the installation time for iObfus to trust this domain. Trusted domains also include the resource URI of extension such as "*chrome-extension://<extension-id>*".

To capture all cross-origin *XHRs*, iObfus instruments both the *open()* and *send()* methods of *XMLHttpRequest* class because sensitive information can either be leaked in the parameters of the target URLs or in the body of *send()* method. To restore sensitive information if necessary, iObfus first determines what domain each specific *XHR* is sent to. If the request URL matches any one of trusted domains, a de-obfuscation algorithm is then applied to the parameters and the body of *XHRs* in an effort to reverse the transformation done in the Obfuscator. iObfus also de-obfuscates messages that are written to disk via *LocalStorage*.

5   Evaluation

To evaluate the effectiveness of iObfus, we first test whether the prototype could defeat some known attacks via malicious extensions and then we assess iObfus's capability to protect users' sensitive information from leaking. At last, the performance overhead introduced by iObfus is studied.

Table 3. Experiment results of 20 popular extensions

Name	Description	Functioning in iObfus	Has Cross-origin *XHRs*	Leakage mitigated
AdBlock 2.5.63	Blocks ads all over the web	✓	✗	–
Google Mail Checker 4.4.0	Displays the number of un-read messages in your Google Mail inbox.	✓	✓	–
Stylish 1.1	A user styles manager that lets you easily install themes and skins for Google, Face-book, etc.	✓	✓	–
Fastest-Chrome Browse Fast-er 7.1.7	Get quick definitions, auto-load next pages, search fast-er, and more	✓	✗	–
Bookmark Sentry 1.7.13	A bookmark scanner that checks for duplicate and bad links.	✗	–	–
Google Voice 2.4.1	Make calls, send SMS, pre-view Inbox, and more	✓	✗	–
Webpage & WebCam Screenshot 8.0	Capture whole page, save PNG, edit, annotate and share to your favorite social network	✓	✗	–
Google Translate 1.2.4	Translates entire webpages into a language of your choice with one click.	✓	✓	✓
Turn Off the Lights 2.2	The entire page will be fad-ing to dark, so you can watch the video as if you were in the cinema	✓	✗	–
SpellChecker 2.76	Prevent spelling, grammar and punctuation mistakes when you write emails and post to social media sites	✓	✓	✓
Xmarks Bookmark Sync 1.0.24	Backup and sync your bookmarks, passwords and open tabs across computers and browsers.	✗	–	–

Table 3. (*Continued*)

SmartVideo for YouTube 0.9926	Provides 'Smart Buffer' for slow connections; auto loop; buffer preferences; quality selection and more	✓	✗	–
WOT 1.4.12	Helps you find trustworthy websites based on millions of users' experiences	✓	✓	–
Google Chrome to Phone Extension 2.3.1	Enables you to send links and other information from Chrome to your Android device	✓	✓	–
PanicButton 0.14.2.2	Hide all your tabs at once with one single button and restore them later	✗	–	–
Google Dictionary 3.0.17	View definitions easily as you browse the web.	✓	✓	✓
Amazon 1 Button App for Chrome 3.2013.530.0	Get special offers and features from Amazon	✓	✗	–
Google Quick Scroll 2	Let you jump directly to the relevant bits of a Google search result	✓	✓	✓
Similar Sites Pro 3	Instant access to the best sites related to the one you are browsing	✓	✓	–
Fabulous 27.2	Customize your Facebook with this free app. Block ads, change colors, zoom photos and more	✓	✓	–

Fig. 3. Failed stealthy actions of Business Adobe Flash Player

5.1   Mitigate Attacks That Hijack Social Media Accounts

Many rogue extensions that hijack Social Media accounts manifest similar attack behaviors. They are either derived from the same open-source attack toolkit [2] or its variants. Such rogue extensions include Adobe Flash Player 12.1.102.55, Business Adobe Flash Player [17], Chrome Guncellemesi, Facebook Black, etc.

We have tested all these social hijacking extensions in our experiments and iObfus can defeat all of them. Figure 3 shows a screenshot when Business Adobe Flash Player was tested in our experiment. Basically, we installed the malicious extension, landed to Facebook.com website and signed in as the test user "iObfus Leakage". The Monitor of iObfus accurately detected the execution of Content Script injected by rogue extension to Facebook.com, and then the Obfuscator processed the DOM document before it was accessed by the Content Script. We observed that the "c_user=100006040261082" in *cookie* (the Facebook user id of "iObfus Leakage") was replaced with its syntactic equivalence by our obfuscation algorithm. Moreover, since privacy rules defined in Section 3.2 contain anti-forgery token keyword "name=fb_dtsg", the value of token "AQBtosAv" was also obfuscated. Hence, the stealthy actions performed by Business Adobe Flash Player failed due to invalid cookie/anti-forgery token as shown in Figure 3.

5.2   Protect Sensitive Information from Leaking

We test iObfus prototype against 20 popular extensions from Chrome Web Store. The experiment results in Table 3 show that the obfuscation of sensitive information does not hinder the normal execution of most extensions with the exception of several extensions whose features are built on browser user data such as bookmarks or browsing history. These include bookmark sentry, Xmarks Bookmark Sync and PanicButton. We also observed that 7 of 20 extensions in our study do not initiate any cross-origin *XHRs*. For extensions that do make cross-origin *XHRs*, the sensitive information classified in Section 3.2 was properly obfuscated before it was read by extensions. Some extensions such as Google Translate and SpellChecker, did leak obfuscated information via *XHRs*, but it was not comprehensible to attackers.

However, in our experiments we also noticed that iObfus blocked certain features of extensions that heavily depend on interactions with their own servers, for instance, Similar Sites Pro and WOT. This is because by design the De-obfuscator only attempts to restore the obfuscated data when the request was sent to safe origins declared specifically by developers, but in reality extension developers often specify excessive web origins with wildcards such as http://*/*. Thus to ensure the data restoration, a set of whitelisted origins are required to be listed in *manifest.json* file. After adding the whitelist, the iObfus works with the browser seamlessly.

5.3   Performance Evaluation

We also evaluate the performance of iObfus prototype. The browser version is Chromium 25.0.1347.0 and our test platform is an Intel Core2 Quad 2.66GHz machine with 8GM memory running 64-bit Windows Server 2008R2. The SunSpider 1.0, V8 JavaScript benchmark suites 7.0 and Browsermark 2.0 online tools are used to measure the performance of an iObfus-enabled browser versus unmodified browser.

Table 4. Performance comparison between iObfus and unmodified browser

Benchmarks	iObfus	Unmodified browser	Overhead percentages
SunSpider 1.0	393ms	387ms	1.55%
V8 JavaScript benchmark suites 7.0	9422pts	9736pts	3.33%
Browsermark 2.0	4431pts	4695pts	5.96%

The final result is averaged over 5 runs and shown in Table 4. Compared to the unmodified browser, the performance overhead introduced by iObfus is indeed negligible.

6   Related Work

Browser extensions can pose significant threats to the security of the browser platform and privacy of browser users [24]. Vulnerabilities in extension platforms have been investigated [6][20], and attacks launched via malicious extensions have been found and reported [25].

Google Chrome has enforced several security policies to protect the browser from attacks via browser extensions. The security model of Chrome is found to be very effective against benign-but-buggy extensions [6], however, it does not consider threats from malicious extensions. Liu et al [7] demonstrated several possible attack scenarios that be achieved by malicious extensions including email spamming, DDOS attacks, password sniff, etc. A refined extension security framework has also been proposed with micro-privilege management and fine-grained access control to DOM elements. Compared to this work, iObfus focuses on defeating the most common and dangerous information leakage attack so that we consider not only the DOM elements in web pages but also browser user data as leakage sources.

Several capacity leaks have been found in JetPack[9], the new Firefox extension framework, via a thorough static analysis [21], many of which can be utilized by attackers to steal user sensitive information. Static analysis techniques are utilized to analyze JavaScript-based extensions. For example, VEX [22] applied a high-precision static information analysis on JavaScript code to identify potential security vulnerabilities in browser extensions automatically. Gatekeeper [23] is another static analysis framework that enforces the security and reliability policy for JavaScript program.

A number of researchers also explored the use of information flow for browser extension security. SABRE [16] is a framework that analyzes browser extensions via tracking in-browser information flows. Djeric et al [8] proposed a framework that is capable of tracking taint propagation at runtime not only in the script interpreter but also in browser's native code. Compared to static techniques, dynamic information flow techniques usually introduce significant performance and/or memory overhead.

Our work combines static analysis with dynamic JavaScript instrumentation. iObfus performs a static analysis to mark sensitive DOM elements first, and obfuscates the source or inspects the sink of leakage at runtime. The performance overhead is minimal when compared with traditional dynamic information flow approaches.

7   Conclusion and Future Work

Attacks via web browsers pose immense threats to Internet users as web browsers are the most commonly used platform for web surfing. Despite various efforts made, attacks via browser extensions are continuously emerging. In this paper, we seek to protect Internet users from information leakage via browser extension attacks. For this purpose, we have designed and implemented a system called iObfus that can seamlessly work with Chrome. The core of iObfus is to obfuscate sensitive information when there is IO operation pending. We have built a proof-of-concept prototype on Chromium project. Our experiments show that iObfus can effectively mitigate the information leakage threats without degrading users' browsing experience.

To bypass iObfus, attackers could deliberately devise a malicious extension that performs a transformation of sensitive data so that it can circumvent the pattern matching when we inspect network messages. In our next step, we will design and implement new techniques to overcome these attacks.

Acknowledgment. We appreciate constructive comments from anonymous referees. The work is partially supported by U.S. National Science Foundation under grants CNS-0746649 and CNS-1117300.

References

1. Firefox web browser,
   http://www.mozilla.com/en-US/firefox/firefox.html
2. QhaoserHq, an open-source attack toolkit for Facebook,
   http://userscripts.org/scripts/review/140659
3. Chrome browser features, https://www.google.com/intl/en/chrome/brow
   ser/features.html
4. Barth, A., Jackson, C., Reis, C., Team, T.G.C.: The security architecture of the chromium browser. In Stanford Technical Report (2008)
5. Barth, A.: More secure extensions, by default (February 2012), http://blog.chro
   mium.org/2012/02/more-secure-extensions-by-default.html
6. Carlini, N., Felt, A.P., Wagner, D.: An Evaluation of the Google Chrome Extension security architecture. In: Proc. of the 21st USENIX Security Symposium (2012)
7. Liu, L., Zhang, X., Yan, G., Chen, S.: Chrome Extensions: Threat Analysis and Countermeasures. In: Network and Distributed System Security Symposium, NDSS (2012)
8. Djeric, V., Goel, A.: Securing script-based extensibility in web browsers. In: Proc. of the 19th USENIX Security Symposium (2010)
9. Jetpack, https://jetpack.mozillalabs.com/

10. Barth, A., Felt, A.P., Saxena, P., Boodman, A.: Protecting browsers from extension vulnerabilities. In: Proc. of Network and Distributed System Security Symposium, NDSS (2010)
11. Felt, A.P., Greenwood, K., Wagner, D.: The Effectiveness of Application Permissions. In: USENIX Conference on Web Application Development, WebApps (2011)
12. Chrome extensions flaw allows password theft, http://www.pcpro.co.uk/news/security/359362/chrome-extensions-flaw-allows-password-theft
13. Chromium blog. A year of extensions, http://blog.chromium.org/2010/12/year-of-extensions.html
14. Wuest, C., Florio, E.: Firefox and Malware: When Browsers Attack (2009), http://www.symantec.com/content/en/us/enterprise/media/security_response/whitepapers/firefox_and_malware.pdf
15. Assolini, F.: Think twice before installing Chrome extensions, http://www.securelist.com/en/blog/208193414/Think_twice_before_installing_Chrome_extensions
16. Dhawan, M., Ganapathy, V.: Analyzing information flow in JavaScript-based browser extensions. In: Proc. of Annual Computer Security Applications Conference (2009)
17. Rogue Chrome Extension racks up Facebook "likes" for online bandits, http://www.pcworld.com/article/2028614/rogue-chrome-extension-racks-up-facebook-likes-for-online-bandits.html
18. Health information privacy, http://www.hhs.gov/ocr/privacy/
19. Chesapeake irb, http://chesapeakeirb.com/
20. Liverani, R.S., Freeman, N.: Abusing Firefox extensions. In Defcon 17 (2009), https://www.defcon.org/images/defcon-17/dc-17-presentations/defcon-17-roberto_liverani-nick_freeman-abusing_firefox.pdf
21. Karim, R., Dhawan, M., Ganapathy, V., Shan, C.-C.: An Analysis of the Mozilla Jetpack Extension Framework. In: Noble, J. (ed.) ECOOP 2012. LNCS, vol. 7313, pp. 333–355. Springer, Heidelberg (2012)
22. Bandhakavi, S., King, S.T., Madhusudan, P., Winslett, M.: Vex: Vetting browser extensions for security vulnerabilities. In: Proc. of the 19th USENIX Security Symposium (2010)
23. Guarnieri, S., Livshits, B.: GATEKEEPER: mostly static enforcement of security and reliability policies for JavaScript code. In: Proc. of the 18th Conference on USENIX Security Symposium (2009)
24. Martin Jr., D.M., Smith, R.M., Brittain, M., Fetch, I., Wu, H.: The privacy practices of web browser extensions. Communications of the ACM (2001)
25. Facebook scammers host Trojan horse extensions on the Chrome web store, http://www.pcworld.com/article/252533/facebook_scammers_host_trojan_horse_extensions_on_the_chrome_web_store.html
26. Kotowicz, K., Osborn, K.: Advanced Chrome extension exploitation leveraging API powers for better evil. Black Hat, USA (2012)

Rating Web Pages Using Page-Transition Evidence

Jian Mao[1], Xinshu Dong[2], Pei Li[1], Tao Wei[3], and Zhenkai Liang[2]

[1] School of Electronic and Information Engineering, BeiHang University
[2] School of Computing, National University of Singapore
[3] Institute of Computer Science and Technology, Peking University

Abstract. The rating of web pages is an important metric that has wide applications, such as web search and malicious page detection. Existing solutions for web page rating rely on either subjective opinions or overall page relationships. In this paper, we present a new solution, SnowEye, to decide the trust rating of web pages with evidence obtained from browsers. The intuition of our approach is that user-activated page transition behaviors provide dynamic evidence to evaluate the rating of web pages. We present an algorithm to rate web pages based on page transitions triggered by users. We prototyped our approach in the Google Chrome browser. Our evaluation through real-world websites and simulation supports our intuition and verifies the correctness of our approach.

1 Introduction

The rating of a web page is an important metric that has broad applications in the World Wide Web, ranging from web search to the detection of malicious web pages involving phishing or malware. A common way to rate web pages' trustworthiness is to rely on users to provide subjective opinions on web sites [1]. However, this is not a scalable approach. Moreover, the accuracy of such ratings depends on users' knowledge and experience, which might be biased.

Alternative solutions infer web page ratings using page relationships. For example, PageRank [2] used by Google leverages the link citation relationships among web pages to decide their ranking in search results. Such static link citations provide the necessary information to evaluate the overall popularity of web pages, yet they do not indicate the trustworthiness of these pages. Malicious pages could be cited frequently by another popular website, such as a web forum, which may give them relatively high rankings. PageRank also cannot access internal links, such as pages in a banking site that require customer login. Although such internal banking pages are highly trustworthy, they would usually have low ranking under algorithms such as PageRank.

Our Intuition: In this paper, we leverage user-activated page transition behaviors to infer trust propagation among web pages. Our intuition is that page transitions resulting from user clicks play an important role in deciding the trustworthiness of the destination page given the trustworthiness of the source one. Such page transition behaviors provide dynamic evidence to derive more objective page ratings on their trustworthiness.

To understand the intuition, consider a new benign URL and a URL from a malicious site. The benign URL is usually visited by following links from other trustworthy pages. In contrast, malicious web sites are much less likely to be visited from links in

S. Qing et al. (Eds.): ICICS 2013, LNCS 8233, pp. 49–58, 2013.

trustworthy web pages. Of course, page content from social networking sites and public web forums should not be considered as trustworthy, although such sites are not malicious. Therefore, the user-activated page transition to a web page is a form of evidence to indicate how trust propagates from the source site to the destination one. At the client side, web browsers can observe the dynamic behaviors of the non-public internal web pages and Ajax-based websites as well, long before they are available, if at all, in search engines.

Our intuition is based on an assumption that the vast majority of trustworthy web pages, such as banking pages, will not include links to arbitrary websites, and users are mindful in clicking links apparently leading to their intended destinations. It does not apply to cases where a large fraction of banking websites have already been compromised and thus containing links to malicious web pages. Addressing such devastating attack scenarios goes beyond the capability of rating-based security solutions.

Our Solution: In this paper, we develop a novel approach, *SnowEye*, to evaluate the trust rating of web pages. The core component of our solution is a *dynamic-evidence-based algorithm* to quantify the rating of a web site. We use user-activated page transitions as the evidence to propagate the trust between original and destination web pages. Our solution propagates ratings from a (presumably small) pool of blacklisted and whitelisted web pages whose rating are pre-assigned by security experts. Note that malicious JavaScript can simulate user interactions with links in web pages; our approach is able to distinguish page transitions from such malicious scripts and those from genuine user behaviors, and only take page transitions by user clicks as the evidence for trust propagation.

We prototyped SnowEye in the Google Chrome browser, we evaluated it using a real-world dataset, and showed that our intuition is consistent with real-world scenarios.

In summary, we made the following contributions in this paper: *a)* we summarize the basic requirements for the page trust rating system based on page behaviors, *b)* we propose a novel algorithm to compute the trust of a web page based on dynamic evidences from browsers, and *c)* we prototype our solution in the Google Chrome browser and evaluated it with real-world data and simulation.

2   Problem and Approach

We define the problem we are targeting in this paper as follows.

Problem 1. *Given a network of browsers, denoted as the set $\mathcal{N}$, using the set of past surfing behaviors $\mathcal{B} = \{b_i\}$ gathered from the browser set, how to calculate the trust rating of a target web page Url_{Target}, denoted as $R(Url_{Target})$?*

In this work, we focus on a basic scenario where we trust the browsers in reporting their behaviors. Note that a web page with high trust rating is conceptually different from a benign page. A benign page does not intentionally include malicious contents, or imitate other pages, but may include untrusted contents. Instead, a page with high trust rating indicates a benign page with probably only trusted content. Thus, web forums or social network sites that allow users to freely upload content may be benign sites, but their pages usually have low trust ratings.

2.1   Basic Requirements

In this paper, we treat browser page transition behaviors as the dynamic evidence to infer trust among web pages, where the source page transferring its trust to the target web page.

Given The *behavior* tuple $b = (Url_{original}, click, Url_{target}) \in B$, where the $Url_{original}$ means the original Url before the event *click* and the Url_{target} represents the Url of the target page after *click*. the *rating* of the target page corresponding to this page transition triggered by the browser behavior b should satisfy the following requirements:

R1: Transition Property. That means a web page transited from a high rating up-flow web page should be assigned a relatively high rating. At least, it should get the same rank as the original page.

R2: Non-degradation Property. This requirement claims that browser behaviors will not cause the decrease of the target page's rating.

R3: Feedback Property. If $Url_{Target} \in Blacklist$, then $R(Url_{Original})$ should be degraded sharply. The web page should be responsible for the trustworthiness of the links it cites. If a web page cites a fake page, it will be punished by our algorithm accordingly. To fulfill the property, the feedback function should be employed in the transition based rating algorithm.

The requirement *R1* is provided to match our algorithm's intuition that the page transition causes a rating transition consistent with its backward linked pages. Requirement *R2* is presented to prevent the *Malicious Citation Attack*, that is, malicious pages cite benign web pages to degrade the rating of the benign on. Even if there exist low rating websites citing the other pages in an attempt to degrade target page's rating, the benign page's rating will not be affected if it is pointed to by a relatively high rating web page (trustworthy page). In other words, the malicious citation is filtered out by the benign one. Requirement *R3* aims at the *False Citation Attack*, that is, attackers trick high-trust web sites to transit to malicious pages or arrange malicious websites to cite each other's pages to promote the rating of low-trust pages. It comes from the basic assumption that web page developers should audit the content inside their web sites carefully.

2.2   Rating Algorithm Based on Dynamic Evidence

We use an iterative algorithm to compute the rating of the target URL based on the given behavior set B. The whole algorithm includes three parts: *Rating initialization*, *Rating computation*, and *Rating feedback & update*.

Rating Initialization. In our algorithm, we whitelist a set of pre-trusted web pages, blacklist a set of known malicious web pages, and we use them as a starting point to initialize the page rating. That is, if the target URL is a new page that has no rating before, it will get an initial rating R^0 according to the record of the whitelist and blacklist. If the target URL belongs to the whitelist, then it should be a good web page and gets the highest rating (e.g., 1). If the target URL belongs to the blacklist, then it should be a malicious page and obtains the lowest rating (e.g.,0). If the page is published by a known developer who provided her/his technical confidence (or Reputation value, t_{ic} for a node N_i) as the guarantee of the target page, then its rating value depends on the technical confidence of its publisher/developer and for some practical consideration, we use a relative technical confidence to initialize the rating of the new page. Otherwise, we assign a relatively small value δ (where $0 < \delta < \epsilon$, and ϵ is the threshold for the future decision making) to the new page as its initial rating.

$$R^0(url) = \begin{cases} 1, & \text{if } url \in whitelist; \\ 0, & \text{if } url \in blacklist; \\ \frac{t_{pc}}{max_{\{N_i\}}t_{ic}}, & \text{if } url \text{ is published by node } N_p; \\ 0 < \delta < \epsilon, & \text{Otherwise.} \end{cases}$$

Rating Computation. After the initialization part, The rating of the target url confirmed by current page transition behavior $R^i(url|b_i)$ is quantified as follows
    $R^i(url|b_i) = R^{i-1}(url_{original})$
Then we compute the final rating of the Target page Url_{Target}. The final rating of the url should be the maximum value of behavior based ratings obtained so far corresponding to the target url.
    $R^i(url) = max\{R^i(url|b_i), R^{i-1}(url)\}$

Rating Feedback and Update. After getting the rating of the target page, if $R^i(url) < \epsilon$, where ϵ is a relatively low value depends on the effectiveness requirement, it means the target page might be a malicious page. It is necessary to review the target page and give a feedback to update (somehow, it means to degrade) the rating of its original link.

    Then we set $R^i(url) = 0$ and $R^i(url_{original}) = R^{i-1}(url_{original}) \times e^{-k}$, where k is the number of faulty citations found inside the web page $url_{original}$ by now.

    From Algorithm 1 we can see that *Step 3* corresponds to the intuitive requirement *R1 Rating transition property*, in which web pages will get corresponding ratings according to page transition behaviors and at least obtain the same ratings as the original pages. *Step 4* corresponds to the intuitive requirement *R2 Non-degradation property* that new behavior will not cause the degrade of rating. Thus, if there exists a malicious citation attack in order to degrade the rating of the benign site, such a citation will be ignored. *Step 6* corresponds to the intuitive requirement *R3 Feedback property* that we will degrade the rating of a web page if it cites a malicious page.

3   Implementation and Evaluation

To evaluate the algorithms we propose for web page trustworthiness rating, we have prototyped SnowEye. In this section, we describe the implementation and evaluation results of our prototype.

3.1   Implementation

Our prototype of SnowEye uses a server to maintain a database of collaborative ratings to the hash values of target web site URLs, which are contributed from the browser

Algorithm 1. Basic Dynamic-Evidence-Based Rating Algorithm

Input: Page transition behavior $b = (Url_{original}, click, Url_{target})$, and Rating Database DB, which is initialized to the blacklist and whitelist.

Output: Trust rating of $R^i(Url_{target})$.

Rating Initialization

1: For $url = b.d = Url_{Target} \notin DB_{url}$, computes

$$R^0(url) = \begin{cases} 1, & \text{if } url \in \textit{whitelist}; \\ 0, & \text{if } url \in \textit{blacklist}; \\ \frac{t_{pc}}{max_{\{N_i\}} t_{ic}}, & \text{if } url \text{ is published by } N_p; \\ 0 < \delta < \epsilon, & \text{Otherwise.} \end{cases}$$

Rating compute

2: Computes Target page rating confirmed by current behavior b_i

$R^i(url|b_i) = R^{i-1}(url_{original})$

3: Computes final rating of Target page Url_{Target}

$R^i(url) = max\{R^i(url|b_i), R^{i-1}(url)\}$

Rating Feedback& Update

4: Review the web page, if $Url_{Target} \in Blacklist$, then

$R^i(url) = 0$, and

$R^i(url_{org}) = R^{i-1}(url_{org}) \times e^{-k}$

Where, k is the faulty citations found inside the $url_{original}$ by now.

5: Update the *Rating DataBase DB_{url}*.

6: Output $R^i(url)$

clients. The server records the ratings under each client's profile, and computes a client's technical confidence according to its rating history. The server also maintains a database of blacklists and whitelists based on existing solutions and manual reviews. The server is not necessarily a single node. It can be replaced by a set of distributed servers to enhance the responsiveness and reliability. In our current prototype, we implemented the server functionality in Perl.

We implemented the client side of SnowEye as an extension to Google Chrome. The extension monitors Chrome's internal behaviors about page transitions. The UI of the Chrome extension is implemented based on BlockUI [3]. In the extension, we inject content script to every page, which listens to page load and users' click behaviors and passes them to the extension core. When a page is loaded, the extension uses the corresponding page transition information to calculate the rating to the current page. If the rating is below the threshold, it will display a warning to the user. Optionally, such a warning can only be displayed when the extension detects that the current web page requests privacy information from users. In current implementation, the detection of web pages requesting privacy information is based on the heuristics that the web page contains `password` fields.

Fig. 1. A Sample Scenario

3.2   Experience with SnowEye

Now we present a sample working scenario of SnowEye, which demonstrates that web pages that were new to our system in the beginning would obtain higher trust values after being navigated to from a high trust pages. For example, in Figure 1, with a single client SnowEye browser, when the user first visits the page from *www.blackberryworld.com*, it only had the trust value 0.1, as SnowEye had no knowledge about this page, nor did it appear in the whitelist. But later when the user clicked on the link to it from the high-trust page *www.networkworld.com/topics/security.html*, according to Algorithm 1, such a click-triggered page transition propagated its trust value to the destination page, so *www.blackberryworld.com* also obtained the trust value 0.7.

3.3   Evaluation of Trust Propagation in URL Transitions

As our algorithm is based on one intuition that web pages with higher trust values are unlikely to link to malicious web pages, we performed the following experiment to verify this intuition with a phishing page as an example. Subsequently, we will also demonstrate how our algorithms automatically degrade the trust values of *"good"* web pages that link to malicious web pages.

We performed a crawling on 10 seed URLs shown in Table 1 by following the links on web pages we have crawled, and obtained 1388 unique URLs after 3-level crawling, i.e., web pages that were within 3 links away from the seed pages..

1. We further investigate the number of cross-site links from each of the seed site. Here cross-site links are loosely defined as links to a completely different domain other than the same domain or the subdomain of the original page. In another word, we use such cross-site links to investigate the links that cross the boundary of the seed web sites. Shown in Table 1, although all of the 10 seed web sites contain cross-site

Table 1. Seed Web Sites and the Number of Cross-site Links

Seed Web Site	#Cross-site Links	#Malicious/Phishing
www.paypal.com	253	0
www.bankofamerica.com	54	0
www.chase.com	55	0
www.wellsfargo.com	62	0
www.americanexpress.com	182	0
www.hdfcbank.com	18	0
www.hsbc.com	51	0
www.citibank.com	4	0
www.capitalone.com	7	0
www.commbank.com.au	32	0

links, none of the links point to a malicious or phishing web site. Therefore, as the seed sites serve as whitelist, according to our algorithm, all benign web sites linked from them will obtain good rating in our algorithm.

2. However, some of them point to benign web sites with untrusted contents, such as *www.twitter.com*, *www.google.com*, *www.facebook.com* and *myspace.com*, etc. In our crawling dataset, these sites will also obtain good ratings according to our algorithm. This is not expected as those sites contain untrusted content posted by users that may contain links to malicious or phishing web sites, and their high ratings may be transferred to those malicious or phishing web sites. To solve this issue, we simulate the rating feedback mechanism in our algorithm by introducing another dataset, which is obtained by performing backward searching for web pages citing phishing pages. This verified that bringing the rating feedback is critical in our algorithms. As these benign sites also have links to phishing sites [4], our algorithm degraded their trust values, although they may obtain high values in the beginning.

3.4   Trust Value Degrading

Now we show a concrete example of how SnowEye degrades web page originally with high trust values after their links to phishing web pages are detected. As illustrated in Figure 2, in the beginning, the page had a high trust value 0.80. However, it had links to three phishing pages. When later the user clicked on the first link, such a page transition was captured by SnowEye. As the destination page was in the phishing page blacklist, the destination page was given the trust value 0.00. Besides, according to the feedback step in Algorithm 1, this page transition also degraded the trust value of the page *blog.sina.com.cn/s/blog_75b798e501012vb7.html* according to number of faulty citations detected in that page. So in this round, its trust value was degraded to $0.80 * e^{-1} = 0.29$. Similarly, when the user clicked on the second link, as it also redirected to a phishing page, the trust value of *blog.sina.com.cn/s/blog_75b798e501012vb7.html* was further degraded to $0.29 * e^{-2} = 0.04$. In the figure, we omitted the similar step after the user clicked on the third link, which degraded the trust value of *blog.sina.com.cn/s/blog_75b798e501012vb7.html* to 0.00. This example demonstrated

Fig. 2. Degrading Trust Values of Pages Linking to Phising Pages

that the basic algorithm of SnowEye automatically degrades the trust values of pages that made faulty citations to phishing pages.

4   Related Work

4.1   Page Relationship Based Solutions

Google uses PageRank [2], a method for rating Web pages objectively and mechanically, effectively measuring the human interest and attention devoted to them. It produces a global *"importance"* ranking of every web page based on the link structure. Actually, the simplicity of creating and publishing web pages results a large fraction of low quality web pages that user are unlikely to read. Attackers can make use of this to promote the rating of their malicious pages. This kind of approaches based on static linkage are not suitable to evaluate the trust rating of the web pages.

4.2   Subjective Feedback Based Solutions

WOT [1] and iTrustPage [5, 6], provide the solutions to rate the phishing possibility of a given page by using reputation scores either reported from the anti-phishing community or computed from the given web page. However, these two approaches are user-assisted.

WOT's rating algorithm is based on the comments subjectively submitted by the users. Nettrust [7] tries to connect people with each other by social network. In their framework, people make some interaction with the server to get some sharing experience (some kind of subjective comments and ranks) released by other nodes/members. The approach tries to defend the attack based on some kinds of common sense among the social peers. Nettrust proposes an e-mail based model to establish a security-related community, and mentions some privacy problems briefly. But there is no practical model or approach was presented to defend a specific attack and does concern about the malicious information posted by tricky members. The final score is the average of negative ranks and positive ranks separately.

4.3   Webpage Feature Based Solutions

SpoofGuard [8] is a browser plug-in that users domain name, URL, link and image check to determine if a given page is a part of a spoof attack. It applies three methods and combines the result using a scoring mechanism: a stateless method to determine whether a downloaded page is suspicious; a stateful method to evaluate downloaded page in the light of user's history and a method to evaluate outgoing HTML post data.

CANTINA [9] uses a content-based approach to detect phishing web sites. It combines a term frequency-inverse document frequency (TF-IDF) algorithm with other heuristics to determine whether a given web site is phishing one. The method uses five words with the highest TF-IDF weight on a given web sites as a signature and then submits those five words to the Google search engine. If the URL of the site is found within top results, then that URL is classified as legitimate, otherwise phishing. An attacker could bypass CANTINA using several approaches. Such as, use image instead of words in a given page, add invisible text that is tiny or matches background color of the page, or change a lot of words in order to confuse TF-IDF.

4.4   Black/White-List Solutions

EBay Toolbar [10] The eBay toolbar is an extension to Microsoft Internet Explorer and combines a tool named *AccountGuard* to protect against spoofed eBay or PayPal web sites. The tool can identify if any particular URL which is trying to phish ebay.com, but it cannot handle the phishing URL targeting some other web sites. Bayesian Antiphishing toolbar [11] is a whitelist based approach using DOM analyzer to check if the given URL is a legitimate web-site listed in the whitelist. If the URL is not in the pre-set whitelist, DOM analyzer labels the given web site and sends it to a scoring module. If the score exceeds a selected threshold, the URL is classified as malicious. Cloudmark [12] rates the web sites based on the system maintained blacklist. When the user surfs to the malicious web-site in blacklist, Cloudmark will direct the user to a specific page that illustrates the security risk. The blacklist database is partly maintained by the users in the way that user can report the malicious web-site. The system also contains a user rating scheme based on users' behavior to prevent users submitting fake report. the blacklist and the rating database are managed and audited manually. The effectiveness totally depends on the users and the system operators' experience and honesty.

Unlike the web page rating solutions discussed above, SnowEye monitors the dynamic features of web page transitions in the browser. The corresponding information is treated as critical metrics in web page trust rating evaluation. In addition, this objective information is verifiable and cannot be forged. The trust rating generated by SnowEye is more reliable. Attackers may mimic the static features of a web page somehow (e.g., URL, web page layout, content, etc.), but they cannot forge users' surfing behavior successfully without being detected.

5   Conclusion

In this paper, we present a novel trust rating approach for web pages, which is based on dynamic evidence captured by web browsers. Our approach, SnowEye, treats user-activated page transitions as an objective and dynamic evidence for the trust rating of web pages. Based on this intuition, we developed an algorithm to compute the suspicious ratings of the target web-pages. We prototyped our approach in the Google Chrome browser and evaluated it using real-world examples and simulation. Our evaluation verified our intuition and showed the effectiveness of SnowEye.

Acknowledgment. The authors thank anonymous reviewers for their insightful comments. This work was supported in part by the Beijing Natural Science Foundation (No. 4132056), the National Key Basic Research Program (NKBRP) (973 Program) (No. 2012CB315905), the Beijing Natural Science Foundation (No.4122024), and the National Natural Science Foundation of China (No. 61272501, 61173154, 61003214), and the Ministry of Education of Singapore via Tier-1 grant R-252-000-460-112.

References

1. WOT, http://www.mywot.com
2. Page, L., Brin, S., Motwani, R., Winograd, T.: The pagerank citation ranking: Bringing order to the web. Stanford InfoLab, Technical Report 1999-66 (November 1999)
3. BlockUI, jquery blockui plugin, http://jquery.malsup.com/block/
4. Report: Bank of melbourne's twitter feed used for phishing, http://www.thetechherald.com/article.php/201138/7633/Report-Bank-of-Melbourne-s-Twitter-feed-used-for-Phishing
5. Ronda, T., Saroiu, S., Wolman, A.: itrustpage: A user-assisted anti-phishing tool. In: Proceedings of Eurosys 2008. ACM (April 2008)
6. iTrustPage, http://www.cs.toronto.edu/~ronda/itrustpage/
7. Camp, L.J.: Net trust: Signaling malicious web sites (2007)
8. Boneh, D.: Spoofguard (2011), http://crypto.stanford.edu/SpoofGuard
9. Zhang, Y., Hong, J., Cranor, L.: Cantina: A content-based approach to detecting phishing web sites. In: Proceedings of the International World Wide Web Conference (WWW) (May 2007)
10. eBay Inc., ebay toolar (2011), http://www.pages.ebay.com/ebay_toolbar/
11. Likarish, P., Jung, E., Dunbar, D., Hansen, T.E., Hourcade, J.P.: B-apt: Bayesian anti-phishing toolbar. In: Proceedings of IEEE International Conference on Communications, ICC 2008. IEEE Press (May 2008)
12. C.Inc., Couldmark toolbar, http://www.cloudmark.com/desktop/ie-toolbar

OSNGuard: Detecting Worms
with User Interaction Traces in Online Social Networks

Liang He, Dengguo Feng, Purui Su, Lingyun Ying, Yi Yang,
Huafeng Huang, and Huipeng Fang

Trusted Computing and Information Assurance Laboratory
Institute of Software, Chinese Academy of Sciences, Beijing 100190, China
{heliang,feng,supurui,yly,yangyi,huanghuafeng,
fanghuipeng}@tca.iscas.ac.cn

Abstract. In the last few years we have witnessed an incredible development of online social networks (OSNs), which unfortunately causes new security threats, e.g., OSN worms. Different from traditional worms relying on software vulnerabilities, these new worms are able to exploit trust between friends in OSNs. In this paper, a new worm propagation model was proposed, named EP-Model, to find out the common characteristics of OSN worms including XSS-based JavaScript worms and Social-Engineering-based Executable worms. And then we designed OSNGuard, a client-side defense mechanism which could prevent the propagation of OSN worms conforming to the EP-Model. Particularly, starting from tracing relevant user interactions with client processes visiting OSNs, our system could identify and block malicious payload-submissions from worms by analyzing these traced user activities. To prove the effectiveness of OSNGuard, we presented a prototype implementation for Microsoft Windows platform and evaluated it on a small-scale OSN website. The system evaluations showed that OSNGuard could sufficiently protect users against OSN worms in a real-time manner and the performance tests also revealed that our system introduced less than 2.5% memory overhead when simultaneously monitoring up to 10 processes.

Keywords: Worm Detection, Online Social Networks, User Interaction Trace.

1 Introduction

Since its first appearance in 2005, OSN worm has become one of the most serious security issues on the Internet. Although the purpose of Samy, the first OSN worm, was just to propagate across the MySpace without any malicious payload [1], it did infect more than one million users within 20 hours, surpassing traditional worms such as Code Red, Slammer and Blaster [2]. Now numerous new OSN worms released for the purpose of getting privacy and profit have emerged in popular OSN websites, e.g., Twitter and Facebook. In fact, at the time of writing this article, a new OSN worm, named Ohaa, is spreading in Twitter by posting a message containing a shortened malicious URL on user's behalf: "Ohaa habere bak :O goo.gl/VbpzM".

S. Qing et al. (Eds.): ICICS 2013, LNCS 8233, pp. 59–74, 2013.

Owing to the popularity of Social-Engineering-based infection methods adopted by the new worms, conventional countermeasure methods [3,4] which mainly rely on the successful detection of the unique scanning patterns all become insufficient. Furthermore, systems [5,6] that focus on traffic anomaly detection also fail to protect users in that they can find no anomaly but only ordinary HTTP stream data.

Considering the ineffectiveness of traditional methods and the severity of impact of these new worms, the security community has proposed some preliminary solutions to mitigate the new threats. PathCutter [7], with view separation and request authentication, does better in JavaScript worm prevention than Spectator [8], which is the first server-side solution, and Sun's first pure client-side system [9], which is based on string comparison. Unfortunately, as the authors have mentioned, their systems are incapable of preventing the drive-by download executable worms. While Xu proposed an early warning OSN worm detection system [10] which is based on the deployment of decoy nodes collecting the malicious messages, their server-side system works only if the infection rate exceeds an empirical threshold which will cause an inevitable delay.

The aforementioned analysis naturally leads to the questions: *Can we propose a generic approach to effectively prevent current (or future) forms of OSN worms? If yes, how can we prevent them in real-time manner?* In this paper, we address these questions through a detailed study of OSN worms and their propagation model. First, we classify the worms into JavaScript worm (J-worm) and Executable worm (E-worm). Next, we propose a novel worm propagation model, named EP-Model which can describe these new worms. Finally, we find out and extract a common characteristic that can be used to detect and block OSN worms effectively. Sepcifically, we find that although different worms adopt various enticements to trick users, they propagate by submitting payload to servers with forged or without user's confirmations, which means the chance that we can prevent OSN worms if we are able to analyze the relevant user interaction traces to detect those automatic submissions.

In this paper, we propose OSNGuard as a complementary approach that addresses some of the limitations of existing systems. Particularly, OSNGuard correlates submissions from a client with relevant user interaction traces to identify propagation of OSN worms. To this end, OSNGuard introduce several functional modules: *Social Traffic Monitor*, *Social Interaction Tracer* and *OSN Worm Detector*. And to estimate our system, we further implement a system prototype for Windows platform and conduct experimental evaluations on a real but small-scale OSN website built on Elgg [11]. The evaluation results demonstrate that OSNGuard can effectively prevent OSN worms in real-time manner. Moreover, the performance test reveals that delays and memory overhead introduced by OSNGuard can be negligible.

The remainder of this paper is organized as follows. We first discuss classification and motivation in Section 2. Section 3 introduces our OSNGuard system and its components. We present the experimental evaluation results in Section 4. Section 5 discusses some limitations and potential future work. In Section 6 and Section 7, we discuss related work and conclude this paper.

2 Classification and Motivation

2.1 Worm Classification

By their existence forms and infection manners, OSN worms can be classified into two categories, XSS-based JavaScript worms (J-worms) and Social-Engineering-based Executable worms (E-worms).

J-worms. All J-worms exhibit similar behavior in propagating themselves as they all inject malicious script-based payload into HTML pages in which there exist XSS vulnerabilities. However, the J-worms can also be divided into passive and active according to their enticements. For instance, a passive worm such as the Samy propagates itself only to users who visit a victim's infected page by accident. In contrast, an active worms such as the HelloSamy spread more quickly by tricking users (e.g., posting attractive wall posts) to browse an infected page.

E-worms. In terms of E-worms, they all rely on various social engineering techniques to entice normal users to download and install their copies. However, we are able to classify them by their forms of existence. Particularly, the Koobface is a Windows worm that it is only able to propagate among Windows machines. And the Boonana is a Mac worm that is able to only infect clients running Mac OS. From the Figure 1, we can see that although E-worms are usually OS-specific due to the limitation of executable file formats, they can spread in different OSN websites as there is no need for any XSS vulnerability except trust between friends.

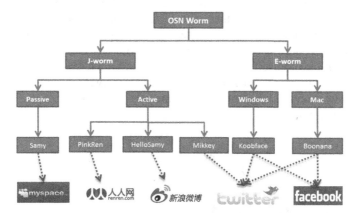

Fig. 1. Classifications of OSN worms and its representative samples

2.2 Case Study

Considering the similarities of propagation methods applied by various worms, in this work, we only present Samy and Koobface as the representative samples for J-worm and E-worm respectively. Actually, based on our bulk analysis of all known worms, for each kind of worms, they all present similar propagation behaviors with Samy (or Koobface). The similarity can also be seen in Cao's survey work [7].

Samy Worm. Figure 2(a) illustrates the propagation of Samy worm. Basically, the worm will first entice users to browse an infected web page in which the worm is embedded (step 1-3). And then when loaded in client browsers, the worm will run to inject itself into victims' pages (step 4-5).

To find out how these J-worms propagate, we also delve into their source code. It is obvious that we can directly analyze the Samy's source code as it is usually embedded into the victims' web pages presented in client browsers. Although there are various forms of existence for J-worms, e.g., Flash or Java Applet, they would ultimately inject the source script code into the HTML pages. Figure 2(b) reveals the pseudo code of the propagation function of Samy who replicates itself by operating an XMLHTTPRequest object to post payload to servers without user's confirmations.

Koobface Worm. Instead of relying on Updating Messages, Koobface will actively send to each of the victim's friends a disguised message usually containing shorten malicious URLs linked to compromised servers in which the worm copies are stored, as shown in Figure 3(a). Based on skilled social engineering techniques and vulnerable trust among friends, the worm is able to infect a large number of users in a very short time.

Similarly, we also intend to analyze the Koobface's source code to chase down how it propagates. However, the Koobface consists of various standalone function modules to accomplish its indispensable tasks, e.g., Downloader, Social Network Propagator, CAPTCHA breaker and Data stealer. As our aim is to prevent its propagation, here we just put our focus on the Propagator which is responsible for sending out worm messages in OSN websites. Figure 3(b) summaries our two-week disassemble analysis result of the executable module which accomplishes its propagation by operating an IWebBrowser2 object offered by Windows platform. From the pseudo code, we can see that Koobface submits the payload with forged user click to propagate itself. Although it may be a simpler method to submit the payload by directly using Socket API functions, we will provide a reasonable explanation why Kobbface dose not do it in this way based on our experiment results provided in Section 4.

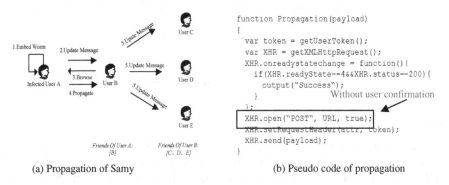

(a) Propagation of Samy   (b) Pseudo code of propagation

Fig. 2. Details of Samy worm

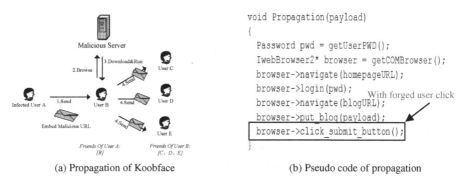

(a) Propagation of Koobface   (b) Pseudo code of propagation

Fig. 3. Details of Koobface worm

2.3 EP-Model and Assumptions

EP-Model. According to the analysis of OSN worms, we propose a new worm propagation model, named EP-Model, as shown in Figure 4. And our goal is to prevent all worms that confirm to this model. Basically, the model is based on the fact that OSN worms propagate themselves with two common sequential steps as follows:

(1) Enticement: Instead of exploiting any software vulnerabilities, OSN worms adopt various enticements to trick users to directly run their payloads. In this sense, these new worms rely on exploiting trust of friends. Specifically, the J-worms usually trick friends to visit one's malicious script-embedded pages and then run themselves in client browsers. For E-worms, they prefer to utilize social engineering-based enticements to trick users to directly download their copies. Once installed in client machines, a worm will run as a single process.

(2) Payload-Submission: To successfully propagate themselves, OSN worms have to try every means to submit their payloads to OSN servers without user's awareness. Based on our aforementioned analysis, the J-worms directly POST their payload without any user's confirmation, whereas the E-worms mimic user's confirmation by firing the button click.

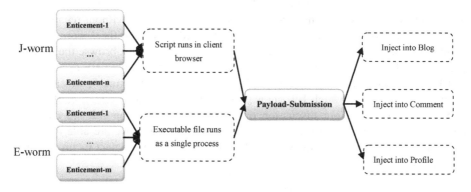

Fig. 4. EP-Model for OSN worms

Assumptions. In this work, all our assumptions are derived from an observed fact that users even equipped with the most advanced anti-viruses can still be infected by OSN worms. So while they are downloaded and run in client machines, we assume that OSN worms should not install any kernel-level rootkits, as otherwise they would have been detected by existing OS-oriented defense mechanisms. Second, we assume the worms do not present any high-risk behaviors in application-level such as adding or modifying Registry entries, tampering with system files and injecting application processes. Obviously, modern anti-viruses can easily notify and prevent these suspicious acts for users. In fact, OSN worms especially for E-worms will run as normal applications to avoid raising any doubt except a popup window for file download request.

2.4   Motivation and Basic Concept

Concerning the existence of overwhelming social engineering technologies nowadays and the vulnerable friendships, there is little work to be deployed to prevent all Enticements from attackers. However, from the EP-Model, we can see that OSN worms share common Payload-Submissions which provide the chance to detect and prevent all of them.

Before our basic idea, we first introduce several relevant concepts used in our following description. Specifically, we refer to any client process connecting OSN websites as a suspicious process. And we use user interaction trace (UIT) to refer to a collected sequence of user actions, such as browse, edit and confirm, which are related to a suspicious process. Finally, we use the term content-submission to broadly refer to submissions conducted by users or OSN worms.

To explain the basic idea, let us consider two real-world scenarios depicted in the top half of Figure 5. Here the Initial Page represents the first web page where a user will meet when she starts to login to the OSN website. Medial Pages are the pages a user has to browse first before she gets into his/her own Blog Page, such as news feed or profile. Next, before the user posts any blog, she should edit the content first and then confirms the blog posting usually by clicking a Submit button. Finally, the user will get a Return Page which indicates the success of posting. In contrast, let us consider a J-worm's propagation which is also shown in the top half of Figure 5. Here we assume the J-worm is just embedded in the infected Blog Page without regard to the concrete locations, e.g., post body or comment board. And then the J-worm will silently POST itself into Blog Page of the victim's friends who just browse the infected pages. Therefore, if we compare the two UITs for the content-submissions from user and J-worm, which have been presented in the bottom half of Figure 5, we can easily identify the scenario in which J-worm is propagating as there is no edit or confirm.

Similarly, based on our discussion of E-worm in the Section 2.2, we can only detect the forged confirm for a suspicious process. Hence, if we are able to collect the related UIT for E-worm's payload-submission, we can also detect its propagation effectively.

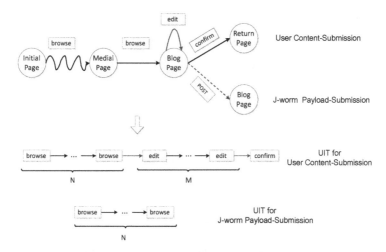

Fig. 5. User interaction traces involved in different conten-submissions

3   The OSNGuard System Architecture

In this section, we will introduce OSNGuard, a pure client-side system which aims to detect all OSN worms in real-time manner. In the following subsections, after providing an overview of the system, we elaborate the design of its components.

3.1   Overview

Figure 6 illustrates the fundamental architecture of OSNGuard system which consists of four functional modules and an extra configuration module. The Supervisor is responsible for configuring the entire system, e.g., loading all the possible locations for the content-submissions. Meanwhile, the Supervisor also manages to load or unload other modules in order to collect the relevant social traffic or user activities. The Social Traffic Monitor (STM) is in charge of sniffing network traffic to find suspicious process connecting the OSN website. Besides, the STM is also designed to trigger worm detection once the social traffic involved in a content-submission is detected. To collect the interaction traces, our Social Interaction Tracer (SIT) will capture every interaction generated from the client user when visiting OSN websites. For each collected user activity, the SIT will directly send it to our OSN Worm Detector (OWD) module which will ultimately record the activities to construct the corresponding UIT. Furthermore, the OWD will also accept normal interaction traces from the external configuration module as the user behavior model. To detect the propagation of OSN worms, our system will compare the configured traces with the collected ones.

Now we will describe the components of OSNGuard in the order of the OSN worm detection work-flow as presented in Figure 6.

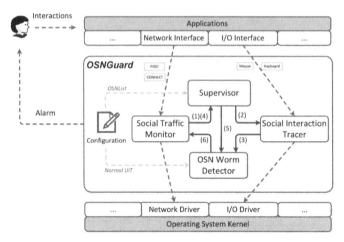

Fig. 6. Overview of OSNGuard system architecture

3.2　Social Traffic Monitor

To successfully detect OSN worms, we will first find suspicious processes by which the worms will propagate their payload. And then, we also need to identify the specific social traffic involved in a content-submission to trigger the worm detector.

Find Suspicious Processes. While it is straightforward to sniff the host traffic to find the suspicious processes that are connecting to OSN websites from the client Network Interface Card, however in OSNGuard, the STM is designed as a dynamic loadable module which will be loaded into the suspicious process space in order to precisely collect the involved information, such as the process id (PID) which will be used by the SIT to trace the corresponding user interactions.

Particularly, through Windows SPI technology, we design the STM as a service provider which will timely monitor each CONNECT intention of applications and precisely collect the process information, i.e., PID. Once finding any CONNECT to OSN website, STM will immediately signal the Supervisior upon the appearance of a suspicious process.

Identify Content-Submission. To detect any submission from a client, we need to do more works. Basically, our current STM will only filter any outbound HTTP POST request from suspicious processes as a content-submission. However, adding support for HTTP GET request as a content-submission should be straightforward. Besides, considering the popularity of SSL/HTTPS, all HTTP stream data may be encrypted and we have to be able to deal with this encrypted traffic.

Based on our thorough investigation, encrypted strategies vary from one OSN website to another. Accordingly, we use a configurable number, named EL, to refer to the encrypted level of website and it will be configured in the OSNList described in the next subsection. Specifically, for OSNs such as RenRen and Weibo, we will configure their ELs to 0 as they do not adopt any encrypting methods at all. And for OSNs such as Twitter, we will set their ELs to 2 as they encrypt all HTTP content with SSL/TLS. Finally, we will set their ELs to 1 for OSNs such as Facebook as they only encrypt user name and password for login and do not encrypt other content such as blog or comment posts. As OSN worms only embed themselves into ordinary content, we will adopt the same SPI technology to identify POST packages outbound to OSNs whose EL<2. And for OSNs such as Twitter, we will enable an extra parsing routing that is used to intercept all contents before they are encrypted. And we have implemented current parsing routines based on Detours lib to hook the relevant encrypting functions (e.g., *cryptencrypt* for Windows XP and *SslEncryptPacket* for Windows 7).

In summary, once intercepting any content-submission by STM, the Supervisor will immediately trigger OSN Worm Detector. And if any abnormal UIT is detected, the STM will discard all relevant packages as malicious payload, which will sufficiently block the propagation of OSN worms.

3.3 Supervisor

As the administrative module of OSNGuard, the Supervisor is mainly responsible for configuration and communication. Once the system starts up, the Superviors will load all the necessary information from the extra Configuration module. Furthermore, the Supervisor is also in charge of maintaining the communications between different modules, which is fundamental component in our system.

Configuration. When OSNGuard is launched, the Supervisor will sequentially load the configurable information consisting of two parts. One is the user-defined information which mainly includes OSNList. Particularly, the OSNList includes all websites to be monitored with some attributes such as encrypted level EL and the accepted HTTP request methods.

The other configurable information is the normal behavior model which will be utilized by the worm detector to compare with the collected UITs. In this paper, we will use regular-expression-based UIT, called Normal UIT, to summarize the patterns of interactions involved in content-submissions confirmed by users.

Communication. In our system, the Supervisor is also mainly in charge of maintaining internal communications among all the components, which enables it to coordinate their executions. For instance, once it receives the notification of the appearance of a suspicious process, the Supervisor initiates the tracing communications between the SIT and the OWD. Furthermore, the Supervisor will immediately trigger the worm detection when it is notified about a new content-submission.

3.4 Social Interaction Tracer

Once a suspicious process is found by STM, SIT will be notified by the Supervisor to collect all the relevant user activities. In our system, we only need to focus on several kinds of user actions as follows:

Browse or Edit: mainly includes user interactions related to the mouse or keyboard device, such as mouse-click and keystroke. For the convenience of description, in this paper, we refer to each mouse or keyboard activity involved in the suspicious process as a user browse or edit action respectively. Hence, we can directly capture these actions through collecting operating system input messages. Specifically, in our current implementation, we use the SetWindowsHookex function to trace all the input messages such as WM_LBUTTONDOWN and WM_KEYDOWN on Windows.

Confirm: represents a confirmation to the content-submission. Different from the activities above, confirm activity cannot be identified by system input message. Although the method proposed in BLADE [12] is able to obtain confirmations on a popup button, it is not efficient for our web applications. Basically, some time-consuming computations have to be introduced to correlate the mouse-click positions with the areas of a download dialog.

Instead of obtaining any position of mouse-click or UI element, we propose a novel approach to fetch the user confirm activities in OSN web pages. The basic idea is to find and hook the HTML BUTTON element, and add an extra handler to notify the user click as a confirmation. Specifically, we can get from the handle of current window, by which we can traverse to find the HTML submit button element and add the extra handler which enables us to fetch all the confirm activities from client user. In fact, this hook-based method is inspired by our code analysis of the Koobface.

3.5   OSN Worm Detector

The OSN Worm Detector (OWD) is the critical module of OSNGuard which is mainly in charge of worm detection. It has two working modes that one is UIT-Tracing and the other is UIT-Comparing. Usually, the OWD changes its working mode based on the messages received from other modules. Figure 7 illustrates the details of detection work-flow.

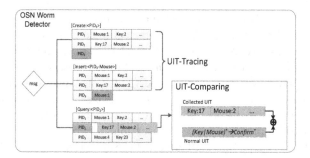

Fig. 7. The details of worm detection

UIT-Tracing. Before it receives any message, the OWD is initialized to create an empty structured table[1] which will be used to store all the UITs collected by the SIT. When receiving the first Create message from the Supervisor notified of the appearance of suspicious process, the OWD will run in UIT-Tracing mode. Usually, the PID included in the Create message will be used as the index item of a record. And then, if

---

[1] We use a tuple (PID, UIT) to form a complete record in a table and all the records are ordered and indexed by its PID.

a user action is found, the SIT will directly send to the OWD an Insert message which includes the PID and a collected action e.g., mouse-click, keystroke or Confirm. Once receiving this message, the OWD will immediately insert the action into the corresponding record in the table.

UIT-Comparing. The OWD will run in UIT-Comparing mode when it receives a Query message from the Supervisor indicating the appearance of the content-submission. In this working mode, the OWD will fetch the corresponding UIT according to the PID included in the message and compare it with the Normal UIT loaded from the configuration. Furthermore, the result will be set to true, indicating a confirmation from user, if the collected UIT matches the Normal UIT. Otherwise, the submission will be discarded as a payload-submission from OSN worms.

4 Experimental Evaluation

In this section, we first introduce our evaluation environment, an experimental OSN website based on an open source framework. And then, we show the effectiveness of our OSNGuard system against OSN worms. Finally, we provide test results for the performance overhead introduced by OSNGuard.

4.1 Expeirmental Environment

Considering the security threats caused by the real OSN worms, it is inconvenient to directly conduct the evaluations in a popular OSN websites. Accordingly, we build a real but small-scale OSN website, MyOSN, which is based on Elgg and deployed on a Windows machine with WampServer installed. Figure 8(a) reveals the MyOSN's news feed with various contents, e.g., newest members, latest upload files and blog posts. Furthermore, two kinds of OSN worms are also planted into several initial users' pages, e.g., blog, comment and profile. Figure 8(b) illustrates the results when worms propagate among the users without the deployment of OSNGuard. To collect real-world interaction data, more than 50 users are involved in the whole process of our evaluations.

(a) MyOSN website   (b) Propagations of OSN worms

Fig. 8. MyOSN website and two worms

4.2   System Effectiveness

In this section, we will evaluate the effectiveness of our system. Experiment 1 reveals the real-time defense against the typical Samy worm. Experiment 2 offers strong evidence that our system is also able to effectively block the propagation of E-worms such as the Koobface.

Experiment 1. OSNGuard against Samy

To evaluate the effectiveness of OSNGuard against J-worms, we plant into MyOSN the Samy worm that is provided by its author on his blog site [13]. We only modify a minimum of codes to make it infect users in various locations in MyOSN, such as the profile, blog post and comment board. From the bottom of Figure 8(b), we can see the results when the worm propagates among user blog posts without the deployment of OSNGuard.

To detect and contain this worm, we only need to configure the OSNGuard with a very simple but efficient Normal UIT:

$$(mouse\text{-}click \mid keystroke)^+ \rightarrow confirm^+$$

which means that a legitimate submission should be resulted from one or more confirm activities following one or more mouse-click or keystroke activities.

Table 1 provides the results of the worm detections. Due to space limit, we only presented several representative interaction traces of five users who had visited the infected pages and received the worm alerts from OSNGuard. As shown in the detected results for the worm propagation, only several mouse and/or key activities were traced when we identified the content-submissions which were actually resulted from the POST activities of the worm.

Table 1. Results of Samy detection based on user interaction traces (M=Mouse-click, K=Keystroke, C=Confirm, superscript denotes the number of repeats)

User	UIT	Result	Description	User	UIT	Result	Description
	$K^3\text{-} M^1\text{-}K^{24}\text{-} M^1\text{-}K^{14}\text{-} M^1\text{-} C^1$	√	login		$K^{28}\text{-} M^1\text{-}C^1$	√	login
	$M^1\text{-}K^2\text{-} M^1\text{-}K^2\text{-}K^{15}\text{-} M^1\text{-}C^1$	√	profile		$K^2\text{-}M^4\text{-}K^{126}\text{-}M^1\text{-} C^1$	√	comment
10001	$M^1\text{-}K^6\text{-} M^1\text{-}K^6\text{-}M^2\text{-}K^{78}\text{-} M^1\text{-}C^1$	√	blog		$K^4\text{-}M^3\text{-}K^{12}\text{-} M^1\text{-} C^1$	√	upload
	$M^{13}\text{-}K^{32}\text{-}M^1\text{-} C^1$	√	comment	10037	$M^4\text{-}K^{164}\text{-} M^1\text{-} C^1$	√	comment
	M^1	✗	**infection**		$M^4\text{-}K^{132}\text{-} M^1\text{-}C^1$	√	comment
	$M^1\text{-}K^{14}\text{-} M^1\text{-}K^{18}\text{-} M^1\text{-} C^1$	√	blog		$M^4\text{-}K^{48}\text{-}M^1\text{-}C^1$	√	search
	$M^7\text{-}K^{30}\text{-} M^1\text{-} C^1$	√	comment		$M^3\text{-}K^{16}\text{-}M^1$	✗	**infection**
10013	$M^3\text{-} C^1$	√	profile		$M^2\text{-} C^1$	√	login
	$M^6\text{-}K^{53}\text{-}M^2\text{-} C^1$	√	search		$M^6\text{-}K^{53}\text{-}M^2\text{-} C^1$	√	comment
	$M^1\text{-}K^7\text{-}M^5$	✗	**infection**		$M^1\text{-}K^7\text{-}M^5\text{-}C^1$	√	upload
	$K^3\text{-} M^1\text{-}K^{42}\text{-} M^1\text{-} C^1$	√	login	10045	$K^3\text{-} M^1\text{-}K^{42}\text{-} M^1\text{-} C^1$	√	search
10025	$M^1\text{-}K^3\text{-}M^6\text{-}K^{24}\text{-} M^1\text{-}K^{100}\text{-} M^1\text{-} C^1$	√	blog		$M^4\text{-}K^{12}\text{-}M^1\text{-}K^{12}\text{-} C^1$	√	upload
	$M^4\text{-}K^9\text{-} M^1\text{-}K^{16}\text{-}M^3\text{-} C^1$	√	comment		$M^1\text{-}K^3\text{-} K^{12}\text{-} M^1\text{-} C^1$	√	comment
	$K^3\text{-} M^1$	✗	**infection**		$K^3\text{-}M^1$	✗	**infection**

Experiment 2. OSNGuard against Koobface

As illustrated in Figure 3(b), to launch the worm propagation, the Koobface only forges confirmation happened without any other user interaction activities, such as mouse or keyboard inputs. Accordingly, OSNGuard can also effectively identify the worm with the same Normal UIT used in the Experiment 1.

However, while it can detect the propagation of the Koobface worm, we admit that our current OSNGuard is not able to locate the stored path of the original file on client host. We need to consider the suspicious process OSNGuard can detect. In fact, it is the IWebBrowser2 COM component that will run in a standalone process and visit the OSN website, which means OSNGuard can only detect this component process. Moreover, as we investigate it with other tools such as Process Explorer, the COM component process is started up by svchost.exe process which implies that we cannot find out the original main process according to the COM component process. This finding may also explain why the attackers would like to choose the COM component as an infection vector which can be used to hide their main process.

4.3   Performance Overhead

We conduct two additional experiments to measure the delay and memory consumption of OSNGuard. And both of the experiments were conducted on a Window XP client with two 2.5GHz Xeon processors and 2GB of memory.

Experiment 3. Delays on POST

Figure 10(a) shows the delays of submitting content when processing different numbers of user interaction activities. The delay for detecting a UIT containing up to 550 activities is no more than 20ms (19.8ms). Based on our practical observations, there are little users whose activity number exceeds 500 before an content-submission, which means the delay can be negligible even in a worst case scenario.

Experiment 4. Memory overhead of OSNGuard

The memory overhead introduced by OSNGuard mainly depends on the number of suspicious processes running on client system. When running without any suspicious process, OSNGuard only introduce 0.16% memory overhead, as shown in Figure 10(b). Although the overhead increases near-linearly when monitoring more suspicious processes, OSNGuard introduces less than 2.5% (2.035%) memory overhead in total when simultaneously detecting 10 suspicious processes.

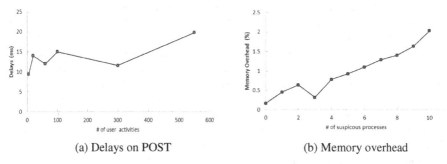

(a) Delays on POST   (b) Memory overhead

Fig. 9. POST delay and memory overhead introduced by OSNGuard

5   Discussion

Limitations. While the OSNGuard is designed to defend current OSN worms, we have not yet intended to prevent all current socwares [14], such as the reflected XSS and the Clickjacking. For the reflected XSS [15] attack, it usually tricks users to click on a malicious link in an e-mail message, which implies the relevant browse and confirm activities, so our OSNGuard can be ineffective in this attack scenario. For the Clickjacking [16] attack, the adversary will entice users to click a hidden button on a web page in which our OSNGuard will be also insufficient.

Future Worms. Although current OSN worms have not mainly focused on forging user interactions, we cannot ensure the effectiveness of current system when our scheme is published and especially the adversaries begin to adopt the relevant mimicking techniques. We assume that the capable attackers can forge a number of UITs. However, the personal specific behavioral biometric still cannot be forged, such as the keystroke dynamics and mouse dynamics. Hence, we argue the effectiveness of OSNGuard integrated with biometric-based authentication [17, 18] when coping with future OSN worms.

6   Related Work

OSN Worm Detection. There have been several systems proposed to deal with the J-worms in OSNs. Livshits et al. [8] provided the first automatic server-side solution, Spectator, to defend the XSS-based J-worms. They find the propagation path of the worms by tagging any HTTP request and response. If the length of the tag-path exceeded the threshold, the system would send alarms to the administrators. Sun et al. [9] proposed the first pure client side defending system which is depending on the content comparison implemented as a plugin on Firefox. By introducing view separation and request authentication, Cao et al. [7] proposed PathCutter approach which can effectively sever the paths of the propagation of J-worms.

Xu et al. [10] provided a satellite decoy network which can collect malicious messages spreading among the whole network. When the frequency of monitored messages exceeded a preset threshold, the system would notify the administrators of the propagation of malicious information. However, as we described in Section 1, their server-side system cannot protect users in real-time manner.

Drive-by Download Detection. There have been several works aiming at the drive-by download attacks, which are conceptually close to ours. Lu et al. [12] have developed BLADE, which is a system kernel extension designed to eliminate Drive-by malware installations. It asserts that all executable files delivered through browser downloads must result from explicit user consent and transparently redirects every unconsented browser download into a nonexecutable secure zone on disk.

Xu et al. [19] also provided a similar behavior based detection system, DeWare, for detecting the onset of infection delivered through vulnerable applications. It enforces the dependencies between user actions and system events, such as file-system access and process execution. Although these schemes are effective to detect drive-by downloads, they are not able to detect any Social-Engineering-based E-worms as the worms are downloaded and installed by users themselves. In fact, the authors have admitted this limitation in their papers.

User Interactoins in OSNs. The design of OSNGuard is extremely inspired by those researches on user interactions in OSNs. Wilson et al. [20] proposed the use of interaction graphs to impart meaning to online social links by quantifying user interactions. Benevenuto et al. [21] analyzed the collected clickstream dataset to characterize user behavior in OSNs. Their analysis reveals key features such as the types and sequences of activities that users conduct on these sites. Jiang et al. [22] focused on the latent interactions such as profile browsing that cannot be observed by traditional measurement techniques.

7   Conclusions

In this paper, we have presented a UIT-based approach to prevent the propagation of OSN worms in real-time manner. To achieve this challenging goal, we divide OSN worms into two categories and summary their commonalities. It is our primary findings that OSN worms propagate themselves by accomplishing the payload-submissions with forged or without the confirmations from users. Instead of focusing on these worms, we trace all the relevant user activities and compare these to the normal behavior model to prevent malicious propagation. We have designed a client-side defending system and implemented it upon Windows platform to prove the effectiveness of our approach. Finally, we have conducted various experimental evaluations on our own OSN website and the results suggest that our client-side system can be deployed to detect and prevent OSN worms effectively.

Acknowledgements. This work was supported by the National Program on Key Basic Research Project (2012CB315804), the Major Research Plan of the National Nature Science Foundation of China (91118006), the National Nature Science Foundation of China (61073179) and the Beijing Municipal Nature Science Foundation (4122086).

References

1. Samy, http://en.wikipedia.org/wiki/Samy_(computer_worm)
2. Cross-site scripting worms and viruses, https://www.whitehatsec.com/reso urce/whitepapers/XSS_cross_site_scripting.html
3. Schechter, S.E., Jung, J., Berger, A.W.: Fast Detection of Scanning Worm Infections. In: Jonsson, E., Valdes, A., Almgren, M. (eds.) RAID 2004. LNCS, vol. 3224, pp. 59–81. Springer, Heidelberg (2004)
4. Weaver, N., Staniford, S., Paxson, V.: Very Fast Containment of Scanning Worms. In: Proceedings of 13th USENIX Security Symposium, pp. 29–44 (2004)
5. Wang, K., Cretu, G.F., Stolfo, S.J.: Anomalous Payload-Based Worm Detection and Signature Generation. In: Valdes, A., Zamboni, D. (eds.) RAID 2005. LNCS, vol. 3858, pp. 227–246. Springer, Heidelberg (2006)

6. Ellis, D.R., Aiken, J.G., Attwood, K.S., Tenaglia, S.D.: A Behavioral Approach to Worm Detection. In: Proceedings of the 2nd ACM workshop on Rapid Malcode (WORM), pp. 43–53 (2004)

7. Cao, Y., Yegneswaran, V., Porras, P., Chen, Y.: PathCutter: Severing the Self-Propagation Path of XSS JavaScript Worms in Social Web Networks. In: Proceedings of the 19th Network and Distributed System Security Symposium, NDSS (2012)

8. Livshits, B., Cui, W.: Spectator: Detection and Containment of JavaScript Worms. In: Proceedings of the USENIX Annual Technical Conference, pp. 335–348 (2008)

9. Sun, F., Xu, L., Su, Z.: Client-Side Detection of XSS Worms by Monitoring Payload Propagation. In: Backes, M., Ning, P. (eds.) ESORICS 2009. LNCS, vol. 5789, pp. 539–554. Springer, Heidelberg (2009)

10. Xu, W., Zhang, F., Zhu, S.: Toward Worm Detection in Online Social Networks. In: Proceedings of the 26th Annual Computer Security Applications Conference (ACSAC), pp. 11–20 (2010)

11. Elgg, http://www.elgg.org

12. Lu, L., Yegneswaran, V., Porras, P., Lee, W.: BLADE: An Attack-Agnostic Approach for Preventing Drive-by Malware Infections. In: Proceedings of the 17th ACM Conference on Computer and Communications Security (CCS), pp. 440–450 (2010)

13. Technical explanation of The MySpace Worm, http://namb.la/popular/tech.html

14. Rahman, M.S., Huang, T., Madhyastha, H.V., Faloutsos, M.: Efficient and Scalable Socware Detection in Online Social Networks. In: USENIX Security Symposium, pp. 663–678 (2012)

15. Cross-site scripting, http://en.wikipedia.org/wiki/Cross-site_scripting

16. Clickjacking, http://en.wikipedia.org/wiki/Clickjacking

17. Monrose, F., Rubin, A.D.: Keystroke Dynamics as A Biometric for Authentication. Future Generation Computer Systems 16, 351–359 (2000)

18. Jorgensen, Z., Yu, T.: On Mouse Dynamics as A behavioral Biometric for Authentication. In: Proceedings of the 6the ACM Symposium on Information, Computer and Communications Security (ASIACCS), pp. 476–482 (2011)

19. Xu, K., Yao, D., Ma, Q., Crowell, A.: Detecting Infection Onset with Behavior-based Policies. In: Proceedings of the 5th International Conference on Network and System Security (NSS), pp. 57–64 (2011)

20. Wilson, C., Boe, B., Sala, A., Puttaswamy, K.P.N., Zhao, B.Y.: User Interactions in Social Networks and Their Implications. In: Proceedings of the 4th ACM European Conference on Computer Systems (EuroSys), pp. 205–218 (2009)

21. Benevenuto, F., Rodrigues, T., Cha, M., Almeida, V.: Characterizing User Behavior in Online Social Networks. In: Proceedings of the 9th Internet Measurement Conference (IMC), pp. 49–62 (2009)

22. Jiang, J., Wilson, C., Wang, X., Huang, P., Sha, W., Dai, Y., Zhao, B.Y.: Understanding Latent Interactions in Online Social Networks. In: Proceedings of the 10th Internet Measurement Conference (IMC), pp. 369–382 (2010)

A Secure and Efficient Scheme for Cloud Storage against Eavesdropper

Jian Liu, Huimei Wang, Ming Xian, and Kun Huang

State Key Laboratory of Complex Electromagnetic Environment Effects on
Electronics and Information System, National University of Defense Technology,
Changsha, 410073, China
ljabc730@nudt.edu.cn

Abstract. Cloud storage system, which can be viewed as a large collection of individually unreliable storage nodes, is potential to be faced with the threat of data loss and leakage, due to node failure and eavesdropped by an intruder. As a solution, secret sharing scheme stores the data redundantly across the distributed storage system(DSS) and it is able to protect data security against ℓ-eavesdropper without need of secret key management mechanism, however, it do not provide regeneration property. Combining the regenerating code with the secret sharing scheme is an effective approach to address this drawback, yet all the schemes that have been proposed in previous work are conducted under the perfect-security criterion and leads to an unaffordable loss of the storage capacity while the number of observed nodes ℓ get close to threshold k. In this paper we adopt the weak-security criterion and give a formal description of "Secure DSS against an ℓ-eavesdropper". Applying a secure hash function and concatenated with the Product-Matrix minimum bandwidth regenerating(PM-MBR) code, our scheme significantly improves the secrecy capacity and keeps the loss of data rate constantly in a low level with any ℓ. As the analysis result indicates, our scheme, which provides sufficient security, repair efficiency and storage efficiency, is more suitable for practical systems. Moreover, we introduce another approach as an extension, which combines the All-Or-Nothing Transform with PM-MBR, and finally achieves a secure storage against ℓ-eavesdropper without loss of data rate.

Keywords: Cloud Storage, Eavesdropper, PM-MBR, Data Confidentiality, Hash Function, All-Or-Nothing Transform, Secrecy Capacity.

1 Introduction

Cloud storage system is now increasing attracting individuals and organizations to outsource their data from local to remote cloud servers. However, many consumers are still feel hesitant, since they lose their control on the data which maybe lost and leaked by incidents. To deal with node failure and compromised by an attacker, which leads to data loss and leakage, the system is desired to provide both storage reliability and confidentiality. In general, a cloud storage

S. Qing et al. (Eds.): ICICS 2013, LNCS 8233, pp. 75–89, 2013.

system is considered as a large-scale distributed storage system(DSS) which consists of many independent storage nodes.

For reliable storage, DSS stores the data redundantly(e.g., by using (n, k)RS code) on a collection of individually unreliable storage nodes, such that the data can be recovered from active nodes even if a small set of nodes fails. However, the repair-bandwidth is so high up to the size of original file when only one node fails in this scenario. A repair-efficient scheme, called *regenerating codes(RC)*, was proposed in [1], where the tradeoff between the storage capacity of single node and the repair-bandwidth was studied, furthermore codes that achieve two extreme points, which are known as *minimum storage regenerating* (MSR) codes and *minimum bandwidth regenerating* (MBR) codes, were introduced. Moreover, explicit construct methods for MBR and/or MSR codes that allow *exact repair*[24] were presented in [2–4].

Besides reliability, storage confidentiality is also a significant property for DSS. Paulo *et al.*[5] considered a scenario in which a large, private file is to be stored securely and there exists an *intruder* may gain access to some storage nodes in the DSS, but not all. Assuming that the *intruder* only can eavesdrop on compromised nodes but cannot modify the data stored on them, it's desirable to ensure that the *intruder* is unable to recover the whole file or any of its parts. A straightforward solution is that, first encrypt the file using a secret key and then partition the resulting cryptogram into multiple shares that can be spread over the storage nodes. However, such cryptographic solution introduces the need for secret key management mechanism[6], which increases the overall complexity and the resources demanded by the system. The secret sharing scheme provides an effective solution without secret key management. In a secret sharing scheme, one divides a secret into shares, and a threshold number of shares is sufficient to recover the original secret but any number of shares(obtained by the intruder) smaller than the threshold reveal no information about the secret[5, 7, 8, 16]. Some other practical application of the combination of secret sharing scheme and erasure codes was proposed in [9, 10], these schemes applied cryptography but without need of key management and distribution. Even though all the schemes above provide reconstruction and security of data shares, they do not provide the property of regenerating the share as was stored in the failed node.

To address this drawback, combining RC with the secret sharing scheme is an effective way. It is noted that schemes following this way have been also studied in [11–14]. S.Pawar *et al.*[11] gave the upper bound of secrecy capacity for secure (n, k, d)-DSS against passive eavesdroppers and proposed achievable approach, based on nested MDS and RSKR-repetition codes, in the bandwidth-limited regime for repair degree $d = n - 1$. Further more, literature [13, 14] proposed *information-theoretically secure* MBR and/or MSR codes that achieve the secrecy capacity in [11]. Moreover, Rawat *et al.*[12] gave tighter bound on the secrecy capacity of a DSS at the MSR point, and presented an approach based on Gubidulin precoding to achieve the upper bound for certain system parameters. However, all these schemes achieve the *perfect-security criterion*, that is, intruder eavesdropping $\ell < k$ nodes gets *no information* of the original file stored.

By mixing a certain number of random symbols with original data before encoded by RC, these schemes lead to a decrease of the file size that can be securely stored in the DSS and the loss of secrecy capacity is unaffordable when ℓ get close to k. Take [13] for example, a $(n = 6, k = 3, d = 4)$ PM-MBR is applied, the storage capacity is 9β, in the presence of an intruder that can eavesdrop the data on two nodes, we need the ratio of random symbols up to $7/9$ of the storage capacity to be added to achieve the *perfect-security*, and thus the data rate $2/9$ is unbearable. Considering the fact that *perfect security criterion* is too strict and leads to above disadvantages, we adopt the *weak-security criterion*[15] in our work instead. In case of *weak-security criterion*, intruder cannot get any *"meaningful"* information of the stored data symbols when eavesdropping $\ell(< k)$ storage nodes.

In this paper, we focus on designing an efficient scheme for DSS, which provides not only data reliability but also data security against passive eavesdroppers. Taking the PM-MBR code[3] as the basis of our scheme, it satisfies the *regeneration property*(i.e., can regenerate a lost share with low bandwidth). Using a hash function or AONT[22] as the preprocessing procedure before data symbols are encoded by minimum bandwidth regenerating code, our scheme achieves the *weak security criterion*, which is sufficient in practical distributed storage scenario. Simultaneously the data capacity securely stored in the DSS is significantly improved, and the loss of data rate is kept constantly in a low level(equal to zero in case of AONT) for any $\ell(< k)$ with fixed (n, k, d).

Similar problem has been considered in the research field of multicast-network applying network coding[19]. [15, 22, 23] showed that weakly secure network coding can achieve the security with a higher multicast rate compared with perfect secure network coding[20, 21]. Inspired by the achievement of [15, 22, 23], their ideology is introduced into our research for building a secure distributed storage system against eavesdropper with high secrecy capacity. However, we use totally different models and methods in our work. To our best knowledge, few papers strived in this direction applying weak security criterion to DSS.

Contributions: Our main contribution in this paper is to provide a secure and efficient scheme, which exploits the Product-Matrix framework[3], for DSS. The proposed scheme provides the following guarantees:

- *Weak-Security Property:* We assure that an intruder who can eavesdrop any $\ell(< k)$ out of n storage nodes is unable to recover any individual original data symbol. To be viewed as a secret sharing scheme, however, our scheme does not apply secret key management and distribution mechanism.
- *Reconstruction Efficiency:* Since the regenerating code utilized by us satisfies MDS property, our proposed scheme is resilient to node failures, that is, a data collector is able to reconstruct the original data file as long as there are k out of n storage nodes active.
- *Regeneration Efficiency:* We combine minimum bandwidth regenerating code with secret sharing scheme, thus ensure that our scheme not only provides security guarantees, but also satisfies regeneration efficiency, i.e., low repair-bandwidth when node failure happens.

– *Secure Storage Efficiency(High Secure Data Rate):* We apply a secure hash function in the preprocessing procedure, and then concatenated with PM-MBR code. This approach is effective to improve secure data capacity, and keep the loss of data rate constantly in a low level. Moreover, another construction method with All-Or-Nothing Transform(AONT) is presented, which can achieve the secure storage without loss of data rate.

Organization: The rest of this paper is organized as follows. In Section 2 we introduce the system model, intruder model and some preliminaries for our scheme. Our proposed scheme is detailed described in Section 3 and evaluated in Section 4. In Section 5 we briefly present another construction method and analyze the essence of its security. Finally, we conclude this paper Section 6.

2 Model and Preliminaries

2.1 System Model

We consider the cloud storage to be a large-scale DSS, which consists of three components, i.e., the source node s, n active storage nodes and data collector DC. There's an incompressible data file $\mathcal{F}$ of $\mathcal{M}$ symbols(each belonging to a finite field $\mathbb{F}_q$) in the source node s. We assume that each storage node has a storage capacity of α symbols and is individually unreliable and may fail over time.

The source node s split, encode the file $\mathcal{F}$ and then distribute the coded result to the n connected storage nodes $\{v_1, v_2, ...v_n\}$. Any DC who can connect to any k out of n active nodes should be able to retrieve the $\mathcal{M}$ symbols and reconstruct the original file $\mathcal{F}$. We term this the *MDS property* of the DSS. To maintain the k-out-of-n MDS property, failed node must be immediately replaced by newcomer with same storage capacity α. In our work, we focus on the case of symmetrical repair, where the newcomer connects to arbitrary d active nodes out of the remaining active nodes and downloads equal amount of symbols, say β, from each. The repair degree d is a system parameter satisfying $k \leq d \leq n - 1$. The corresponding repair bandwidth of the system is defined as $\gamma = d\beta$ in this paper. Thus we define such a DSS as $\mathcal{D}(n, k, d)$. For instance, the DSS depicted in Fig.1 corresponds to $\mathcal{D}(4, 2, 3)$ which is operating at $(\alpha, \gamma) = (2, 3)$ with *functional repair*, the failed node v_1 is replaced by the newcomer v_5 in this scenario.

Moreover, for the reason that the *functional repair*[24] has some inherent security shortcomings for DSS in the presence of an eavesdropper, in this paper our presented scheme employs the *exact repair* where the newcomer regenerates an exact copy of the lost data and thus $\alpha = d\beta$. Specifically, the *PM-MBR code* proposed by Rashmi *et al.*[3] is applied. Besides, we denote the storage capacity of the DSS as $\mathcal{L}$, which was derived by [1] and:

$$\mathcal{L} = \sum_{i=1}^{k} \min\{(d - i + 1)\beta, \alpha\} \tag{1}$$

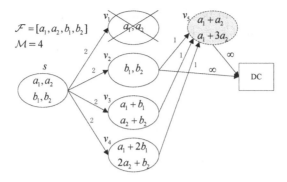

Fig. 1. $\mathcal{D}(4, 2, 3)$ under repair

Note that the right-hand side of Eq.(1) can be reduced to $\sum_{i=0}^{k}[(d - i + 1)\beta]$ in case where PM-MBR code is applied[3].

2.2 Intruder Model

We consider an (ℓ_1, ℓ_2) eavesdropper, which can access the stored data of nodes in set ε_1, and additionally can access both the stored and downloaded data of the nodes in set ε_2, with $|\varepsilon_1| = \ell_1$ and $|\varepsilon_2| = \ell_2$. The eavesdropper is passive and can only read the data on the observed nodes without modifying it. This is the same eavesdropper model considered in [12]. For the MBR code used in this paper, we have $d\beta = \alpha$, i.e., a replacement node stores all the data that it downloads during its repair. Thus an eavesdropper does not obtain any extra information from the data that is downloaded for repair. Without loss of generality, we can assume that $\ell_1 = \ell(\ell < k), \ell_2 = 0$, and then the intruder model is simplify to the ℓ-eavesdropper. In addition, the eavesdropper is assumed to have complete knowledge of the storage and coding schemes employed by the DSS. As a result, the intruder can choose any ℓ nodes from the initial storage nodes and/or the replacement nodes. For example in Fig.1 with $\ell = 1$, the replacement node v_5 is compromised by the intruder and shown in grey background.

2.3 Security Criterion

Here we first introduce *perfect security criterion* and then present our definition of the secure DSS against the ℓ-eavesdropper in this subsection.

Let $S = [s_1, s_2, s_3, ..., s_L]^T$ be a random vector uniformly distributed over $\mathbb{F}_q^L$, representing the incompressible data file at the source node. Each symbol of S denoted by $s_i(i = 1, 2, ..., L)$ is independent random variable uniformly distributed over $\mathbb{F}_q$. Let $H(S)$ denotes the entropy of the random variable S. The S is encoded into n shares $c_i \in \mathbb{F}_q^{\alpha}$. For each $i \in \{1, 2, .., n\}$, a share c_i is stored in node v_i. Let B be a collection of k active nodes randomly chosen from all n storage nodes, and define $C_B := \{c_i : v_i \in B\}$. Similarly, we let E be the collection of nodes that can be observed by the eavesdropper, and $|E| = \ell < k$ in our work, thus define $C_E := \{c_i : v_i \in E\}$.

Then the reconstruction property (or k-out-of-n MDS property) of the DSS, can be written as:

$$H(S|C_B) = 0, \qquad |B| = k. \tag{2}$$

and the perfect security condition implies:

$$H(S|C_E) = H(S), \qquad |E| = \ell < k. \tag{3}$$

The Eq.(3) can be interpreted that the eavesdropper cannot get any information about the original vector $S = [s_1, s_2, s_3, ..., s_L]^T$, even she is able to obtain the data shares on ℓ compromised nodes. As mentioned above, this security criterion is too strict and unnecessary in practical scenario. Notice the fact that an intruder who get the $s_i \oplus s_j (i \neq j)$ is also unable to recover the symbols s_i and s_j, i.e., $I(s_i; s_i \oplus s_j) = I(s_j; s_i \oplus s_j) = 0$, because these symbols are uniformly, independently and randomly distributed over $\mathbb{F}_q$. Therefore, it is sufficient that an intruder cannot get any *"meaningful"* information of each symbol in original vector S to guarantee the data secure against the ℓ-eavesdropper($\ell < k$), which is called the *weak-security* criterion[15]. We present the definition of a secure DSS following such criterion:

Definition 1. *(Secure DSS against an ℓ-eavesdropper): A DSS is said to be secure against an ℓ-eavesdropper, if, for any set E of size $\ell < k$,*

$$I(s_i; C_E) = 0, (i = 1, 2, ..., L_s) \tag{4}$$

Where s_i denotes the symbol of the data file S, and C_E represents data observed by the eavesdropper. Besides, we denote the file size that can be secure stored in the DSS as L_s.

Under the *weak-security* condition[15], our proposed scheme can achieve a higher secure data capacity as discussed in Section 4.

2.4   Product-Matrix MBR Code

Rashmi *et al.*[3] proposed the first construction of general and optimal exact-regenerating code such as (a)(n, k, d) MBR code for all values of (n, k, d), and (b)(n, k, d) MSR code for all values of (n, k, d) where $d \geq 2k - 2$. In general, in order to obtain a lower repair bandwidth, all n, k, d should satisfy $k \leq d \leq n - 1$. As the basis of our work, we briefly review the Product-Matrix MBR code here.

As assumed in [13], we set $\beta = 1$. It is reasonable since that any higher value of β can be obtained by a simple concatenation of the $\beta = 1$ code. Thus the PM-MBR code with $\beta = 1$ and $\alpha = d$ can be interpreted as an $(n \times \alpha)$ code matrix C, where each row corresponds to one storage node of the DSS, i.e., the α elements in the ith row represent the α symbols stored in node $v_i (i = 1, 2, ..., n)$. The code matrix C is a product of two matrices: a fixed encoding matrix $\Psi_{n \times d}$ and a message matrix $M_{d \times \alpha}$, i.e., $C_{n \times \alpha} = \Psi_{n \times d} \cdot M_{d \times \alpha}$.

The encoding matrix $\Psi_{n\times d}$ has the form as $\Psi_{n\times d} = [\Phi_{n\times k} \quad \Delta_{n\times(d-k)}]$ where the matrices $\Phi_{n\times k}$ and $\Delta_{n\times(d-k)}$ are chosen to satisfy (i)any k rows of Φ are linearly independent, and (ii)any d rows of Ψ are linearly independent, thus, a Vandermonde or Cauchy Matrix is applicable.

The message matrix $M_{d\times\alpha}$ contains the symbols of the data file to be stored in a redundant fashion. From Eq.(1) we get that the stored symbols amount to $\mathcal{L} = \frac{k(2d-k+1)}{2} = \frac{k(k+1)}{2} + k(d-k)$ in the DSS employing the PM-MBR code. The message matrix $M_{d\times\alpha}$ is of the following form

$$M_{d\times\alpha} = \begin{bmatrix} U_{k\times k} & V_{k\times(d-k)} \\ V^t_{k\times(d-k)} & O_{(d-k)\times(d-k)} \end{bmatrix}$$

The $U_{k\times k}$ in the above expression denotes a symmetric matrix, thus the $\frac{k(k+1)}{2}$ components in the upper-triangular half of the matrix are filled up by $\frac{k(k+1)}{2}$ distinct message symbols drawn from the $\mathcal{L}$ message symbols. The remaining $k(d-k)$ message symbols are used to fill up the matrix $V_{k\times(d-k)}$. The V^t denotes the transpose of matrix $V_{k\times(d-k)}$, and the $O_{(d-k)\times(d-k)}$ denotes the zero matrix with all zero components. To keep things simple, we use these denotations without the subscript in the rest of this paper.

3   Our Proposed Scheme

3.1   Notation and Definition

The original data file of size L is represented by a vector $S = [s_1, s_2, ..., s_L]^T$, with $s_i \in \mathbb{F}_q, i = 1, 2, ..., L$. Supposing that the file has been optimally compressed, then the symbols $s_i(i = 1, 2, ..., L)$ are independent random variables uniformly distributed over the finite field $\mathbb{F}_q$. Let K denotes a set of random symbols and $|K| = L_r$, and each symbol is chosen independently and uniformly across the elements of $\mathbb{F}_q$. In addition, we make use of suitable one-way function, i.e., a secure hash function defined as follow, in our scheme.

Definition 2. *(Secure Hash Function): The function $h(key, \bullet) : key \times X \to Y$ where $key \in \mathbb{F}_q$, for $\forall X \in \mathbb{F}^r_q(r \in \mathbb{N}^*)$, the result $Y \in \mathbb{F}_q$, is secure if the following conditions satisfy:*

(1)Given a hash value $y \in \mathbb{F}_q$, it's hard to find any $x \in \mathbb{F}^r_q(r \in \mathbb{N}^*)$ in polynomial time such that $y = h(key, x)$;

(2)Given any $x \in \mathbb{F}^r_q(r \in \mathbb{N}^*)$, the hash value $y = h(key, x)$ can be easily got in polynomial time;

(3)Given any $x \in \mathbb{F}^r_q(r \in \mathbb{N}^*)$, it's hard to find $x' \in \mathbb{F}^r_q(r \in \mathbb{N}^*)$ that have the same hash value in polynomial time, i.e., $h(key, x') = h(key, x)$.

To keep things simple, we define that $h(x) = h(x, x)$ with $x \in \mathbb{F}_q$ in the following subsection.

Besides, we denote the ith row of the encoding matrix Ψ as ψ_i. In order to meet the requirement of Ψ, we adopt the Vandermonde matrix to be the encoding matrix. The message matrix is represented by M. All the elements of matrix Ψ belong to the finite field $\mathbb{F}_q$, thus, $q \geq n$. Further, we set $\beta = 1$ in the scenario of $\mathcal{D}(n, k, d)$ in which our scheme executes.

3.2   Detailed Scheme

Our scheme is consisted of four procedures shown as follows:

1) Preprocessing Procedure:

step 1: Generate a set K that contains $L_r = d - k + 1$ random symbols $\{k_1, k_2, ...k_{L_r}\}$, where each symbol is independently, randomly and uniformly distributed over $\mathbb{F}_q$;

step 2: Let S' be a set with cardinality $L_s(< L)$, and the elements of S' are the symbols drawn from the incompressible data file $S = [s_1, s_2, ..., s_L]^T$, here we set $S' = \{s_1, s_2, ...s_{L_s}\}$ without loss of generality. In the scenario of $\mathcal{D}(n, k, d)$, $L_s = \mathcal{L} - L_r = \frac{k(2d-k+1)}{2} - (d - k + 1)$;

step 3: Let $sk = h(k_1, k_2||k_3||...||k_{L_r})$, where $k_2||k_3||...||k_{L_r}$ denotes the concatenation of the random symbols $k_i(i = 2, 3, ...L_r)$. Utilizing the hash value sk to preprocess the original data symbols, we get the result $P = \{p_1, p_2, ...p_{L_s}\}$ where $p_1 = s_1 \oplus h(sk)$, $p_i = s_i \oplus h(sk, s_1||s_2||...||s_{i-1})(i > 1, i \in \mathbb{N}^*)$;

2) Encoding and Distributing Procedure:

step 1: Note that $L_s + L_r = \mathcal{L}$, we populate the message matrix M with elements in P and K. To be specific, place the symbols of P into the first $k - 1$ rows and hence first $k - 1$ columns of the symmetric matrix M, the rest position of submatrix U and V of M is filled with L_r random symbols of K(an example is shown in Fig.2);

step 2: Choose n elements from $\mathbb{F}_q$ and then generate a Vandermonde matrix to be the encoding matrix Ψ. According to the encoding method of PM-MBR, we multiply the matrix Ψ and M to get the Product-Matrix $C = \Psi \cdot M$.

step 3: Extracting each row(denoted by c_i) of the Product-Matrix C as a share(of size d) of encoded data, the source node distributes them to the corresponding storage node v_i, $i = 1, 2, ...n$.

3) Regeneration Procedure:

Supposing that node $v_f(f \in [n])$ fails at a time, the regeneration process of our scheme is the same as that in traditional PM-MBR code[3]:

step 1: Notice that the share stored on the node v_f is $c_f = \psi_f M$. The replacement for the failed node f connects to an arbitrary set $\{h_i | 1 \leq i \leq d\}$ of d remaining nodes.

step 2: Each of these d nodes passes on the inner product $(\psi_{h_i} M)\psi_f^t$ to the replacement node. Thus from these d nodes, the replacement node obtains the $d = \alpha$ symbols, i.e., $C_{rev} = \Psi_{rev} M \psi_f^t$, where $\Psi_{rev} = [\psi_{h_1}, \psi_{h_2}, ..., \psi_{h_d}]$ is invertible by construction.

step 3: Replacement node performs matrix inversion on Ψ_{rev} and multiplies Ψ_{rev}^{-1} with C_{rev}. Thus $M\psi_f^t$ can be recovered, since M is symmetric, $(M\psi_f^t)^t = \psi_f M$ is precisely the data stored in the node prior to failure.

4) Reconstruction Procedure:

When a data collector try to reconstruct the original data file stored in the (n, k, d)-DSS, it firstly perform the same action as traditional PM-MBR code[3], then recover original symbols:

step 1: Data collector connects to k out of n active storage node, let $\Psi_{DC} = [\Phi_{DC} \quad \Delta_{DC}]$ be the corresponding k rows of Ψ. Thus the data collector gains the symbols $\Psi_{DC}M = [\Phi_{DC}U + \Delta_{DC}V^t \quad \Phi_{DC}V]$. Being a submatrix of Vandermonde matrix, Φ_{DC} is nonsingular. Hence, by multiplying the matrix $\Psi_{DC}M$ on the left by Φ_{DC}^{-1}, one can recover first the matrix V and subsequently the matrix U. Thus, all symbols in set K and P are gained by data collector;

step 2: Compute the $sk = h(k_1, k_2||k_3||...||k_{L_r})$ from K, and then the original symbols in set $S' = \{s_1, s_2, ...s_{L_s}\}$ can be got in the way: $s_1 = p_1 \oplus h(sk)$, $s_i = p_i \oplus h(sk, s_1||s_2||...||s_{i-1})$, $(2 \leq i \leq L_s$ and $i \in \mathbb{N}^*)$. Finally, the original data file stored in the system is reconstructed.

3.3   An Example

Detailed description of our scheme above should be tedious and stuffy, however, in order to make our scheme seems more concrete, we illustrate it with an example similar to [13] in this subsection.

Example 1. Let $(n, k, d) = (6, 3, 4)$, then with $\beta = 1$, we get $\alpha = d = 4$, $L_r = 2$, $L_s = 7$ and $\mathcal{L} = 9$. Our scheme is designed over the finite field $\mathbb{F}_7$. The (6×4) encoding matrix Ψ is chosen as a Vandermonde matrix with its ith row as $\psi_i = [1 \quad i \quad i^2 \quad i^3]$.

As depicted in Fig.2, the original data symbols $s_1, s_2, ..., s_7$ drawn from the incompressible data file F are first preprocessed with the random symbols in K, and then placed into the first two rows and first two columns of the message matrix $M_{4\times4}$. In the end, the matrices U and V are populated by the preprocessed symbols in $P = \{p_i\}_{i=1}^7$ and random symbols in $K = \{k_1, k_2\}$:

$$U = \begin{bmatrix} p_1 & p_2 & p_3 \\ p_2 & p_4 & p_5 \\ p_3 & p_5 & k_1 \end{bmatrix}, \qquad V = \begin{bmatrix} p_6 \\ p_7 \\ k_2 \end{bmatrix}$$

Further, $M_{4\times4}$ is multiplied on the left with the Vandermonde matrix $\Psi_{6\times4}$ and thus product-matrix $C_{6\times4}$ can be generated. Each row of $C_{6\times4}$ denoted by $\psi_i M$ corresponds to the share c_i stored on storage node $v_i(i = 1, 2, ..., 6)$.

4   Discussion

In this section, we evaluate the security property of $\mathcal{D}(n, k, d)$ applying our scheme, as well as its advantages in the aspects of secure data capacity and repair bandwidth over previous work. Then the computation cost of the proposed solution is compared against original PM-MBR scheme.

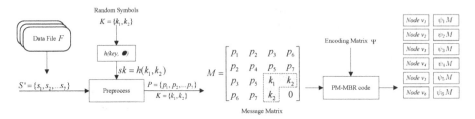

Fig. 2. An example with $(n, k, d) = (6, 3, 4)$

4.1 Security Analysis

To prove that our presented scheme is secure against an ℓ-eavesdropper($\ell < k$) in the (n, k, d)-DSS, we make use of the method appeared in [13] at first.

Lemma 1. *For any C_E representing the shares $\{c_i : v_i \in E\}$ stored on the node collection $E(|E| = \ell < k)$ eavesdropped by the intruder, no information about the random symbols set K is revealed, i.e., the mutual information between the random symbols and the eavesdropped shares is zero, that is*

$$I(K; C_E) = 0 \tag{5}$$

Proof. To prove Eq.(5), our scheme can be interpreted as a particular case of the construction method in [13], where $\ell = k - 1$, $\mathcal{E} = C_E$, and $\mathcal{U} = K$. Since original data symbol $s_i(i = 1, 2, ..., L_s)$ in S is independently, randomly and uniformly distributed over $\mathbb{F}_q$, and so is the hash value, thus $p_1 = s_1 \oplus h(sk)$ and $p_i = s_i \oplus h(sk, s_1||s_2||...||s_{i-1})(2 \le i \le L_s, i \in \mathbb{N}^*)$ all satisfy independent, random and uniform distribution over $\mathbb{F}_q$ as well. Then the preprocessed symbols set $P = \{p_i\}_{i=1}^{L_s}$ can be equivalent to the random symbols set $R = \{r_i\}_{i=1}^{L_s}$ denoted in previous literature[13].

Based on the above analysis, our proof proceeds in the same manner as [13](Section II), that is, $H(P|C_E, K) = 0$, $H(C_E) \le L_s$ proved firstly, and finally $I(K; C_E) = 0$ can be obtained. We do not present the details here due to lack of space.

Thus the ℓ-eavesdropper cannot obtain any information about the set K.   □

Theorem 1. *The ℓ-eavesdropper($\ell < k$) cannot get any "meaningful" information of the original data symbols from C_E, i.e., the mutual information between each $s_i(i = 1, 2, ...L_s)$ and eavesdropped shares set C_E, that is*

$$I(s_i; C_E) = 0, (i = 1, 2, ..., L_s) \tag{6}$$

Proof. As shown in *Lemma 1*, the ℓ-eavesdropper cannot obtain any information of the K, the mutual information between $sk = h(k_1, k_2||...||k_{L_r})$ and C_E comes to zero. This is determined by the property(3) of the function $h(key, \bullet)$ defined in *Definition 2*. Similarly, we can get $I(h(sk); C_E) = 0$;

Next, we will show that the mutual information between original symbol $s_i(i = 1, 2, ...L_s)$ and C_E is zero. We use the inductive method here, and take

$i = 1$ in the beginning, $s_1 = p_1 \oplus h(sk)$, since p_1 is an independent and random variable uniformly distributed in $\mathbb{F}_q$,

$$I(s_1; C_E) = I(p_1 \oplus h(sk); C_E) = 0 \tag{7}$$

can be obviously obtained. For $i \geq 2$, assuming that $I(s_{i-1}; C_E) = 0$, since s_i and s_j are independent for $i \neq j$, and that the hash function is secure against collision(property(3) in *Definition 2*), thus we see that $I(h(sk, s_1||s_2||...||s_{i-1}); C_E) = 0$. Finally we get that

$$I(s_i; C_E) = I(p_i \oplus h(sk, s_1||s_2||...||s_{i-1}); C_E) = 0, \quad (2 \leq i \leq L_s, i \in (N)^*) \tag{8}$$

since p_i satisfies independent, random and uniformly distribution over $\mathbb{F}_q$.

Thus, equation(6) can be achieved for any $i \in [L_s]$, i.e., and the $\mathcal{D}(n, k, d)$ applying our scheme is secure against ℓ-eavesdropper as shown in *Definition 1*.   □

In essence, notice that the input parameter of the secure hash function $p_i = h(key, \bullet)$ differs from each other for any $i = 1, 2, ...L_s$, and each element of $P = \{p_1, p_2, ...p_{L_s}\}$ is "encrypted" with different key(similar to *one-time pad*). Thus an intruder is unable to obtain any information of each original data symbol s_i without knowledge about the hash value sk(see *Lemma 1*), even though she has obtained some preprocessed symbols $p_i(i \in [L_s])$.

4.2 Repair-Bandwidth and Secrecy Capacity Analysis

Obviously, our scheme satisfies the MDS property(see Section 1), thus we analyze its repair and storage performance in such scenario: an $\mathcal{D}(n, k, d)$ with each storage node capacity up to α, the *newcomer* connects to d nodes out of the active ones when node failure happens, thus repair-bandwidth $\gamma = d\beta$. In such scenario, user accessing any k out of n storage nodes can recover the original data file, however, access to any $\ell < k$ does not leak any information about each original data symbol. So our proposed method can be viewed as a secret sharing scheme.

Before the analysis, we define data rate as follows at first:

$$\mathcal{R} = \frac{\mathcal{L}_{sec}}{\mathcal{L}} = \frac{\mathcal{L}_{sec}}{\sum_{i=0}^{k} \min\{(d - i + 1)\beta, \alpha\}} \tag{9}$$

where $\mathcal{L}_{sec}$ denotes the secrecy capacity of the system, and $\mathcal{L}$ denotes the storage capacity of $\mathcal{D}(n, k, d)$ using symmetrical repair.

Firstly, we will show that our scheme is repair efficiently compared to previous secret sharing schemes. Paulo F. Oliveira *et al.*[5] present a coding method and realize multi-secret sharing scheme, their schemes improved the secrecy capacity compared to Shamir's (k, n)-threshold scheme[16] and Bessani's (k, L, n)-threshold scheme[8]. As shown in Fig.3, Paulo's scheme provides an secrecy capacity up to the storage capacity. However, all their repair-bandwidth is so high up to the same as the Reed-Solomon coding scheme, that $\gamma = d\alpha = k\alpha$. Combined with MBR code, our secret sharing scheme provides the repair-bandwidth the same as minimum bandwidth regenerating code, that is, $\gamma = d\beta = \alpha$, which is much lower than schemes in [5, 8, 16]. Even though both the secrecy capacity and storage capacity of our scheme is slightly lower than Paulo's scheme $et\ al.$[5], as well as data rate is lower than 1, that is affordable and allowable in practise.

Various Schemes	Repair Bandwidth γ	Secrecy Capacity $\mathcal{L}_{sec}$	Storage Capacity $\mathcal{L}$	Secure Data Rate $\mathcal{R}$	Security Criterion
RS code	$k\alpha$	0	$k\alpha$	0	No
MBR code	α	0	$\left[kd - \binom{k}{2}\right]\beta$	0	No
Paulo's Scheme [5]	$k\alpha$	$k\alpha$	$k\alpha$	1	Weak
Shah's Scheme [13]	α	$\left[kd - \binom{k}{2}\right]\beta - \left[ld - \binom{\ell}{2}\right]\beta$	$\left[kd - \binom{k}{2}\right]\beta$	$1 - \frac{\ell^2 - (2d+1)\ell}{k^2 - (2d+1)k}$	Perfect
Ours	α	$\left[kd - \binom{k}{2}\right]\beta - (d-k+1)\beta$	$\left[kd - \binom{k}{2}\right]\beta$	$1 - \frac{2(d-k+1)}{k(2d-k+1)}$	Weak

Fig. 3. Comparison of repair-bandwidth and secure storage performance

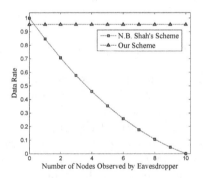

Fig. 4. An example with $(n, k, d) = (15, 10, 13)$

Next we will show that our scheme provides secure storage efficient(i.e., Higher Data Rate) guarantee relative to other similar work. [11–14] gave methods to construct schemes providing both the regenerating property and secure storage against eavesdroppers. But all these techniques provide $perfect\text{-}security$ with expense of storage capacity so high, even unbearable. Taking N.B.Shah's work on secure MBR [13] for example without loss of generality, the random symbols amount to $[\ell d - \binom{\ell}{2}]\beta$ need to be mixed with the original symbols, and the data rate $\mathcal{R} = \frac{\mathcal{L}_{sec}}{\mathcal{L}} = \frac{[kd - \binom{k}{2}]\beta - [\ell d - \binom{\ell}{2}]\beta}{[kd - \binom{k}{2}]\beta} = 1 - \frac{\ell^2 - (2d+1)\ell}{k^2 - (2d+1)k}$ decrease rapidly when the intruder can eavesdropped more nodes for $\ell < k$. Fig.4 shows an example for $(n, k, d) = (15, 10, 13)$, we can see that the data rate is lower than 20%

and intolerable to us when $\ell \geq 7$. However, our scheme achieve a higher data rate (approximate 95% in Fig.4) and it does not vary with $\ell(< k)$ when the parameters (n, k, d) are fixed. Although this comes at the expense of reduced security, the *weak-security* is enough in practical scenario.

4.3 Computation Cost Analysis

Comparing with the PM-MBR scheme[3], our solution leads to additional computation cost for the purpose of security. Taking (n, k, d) as the design parameters, we could get the overhead of our scheme. The Preprocessing Procedure takes $O(d^2)$ Hash operations and $O(d^2)$ Xor operations in order to obtain the set P from the original symbol set S. The number of operations taken by the second and third procedure is equal to that of the original PM-MBR scheme. Especially in the Regeneration Procedure, where the Ψ_{rev} is chosen to be a Vandermonde matrix, $O(d) + O(d^2) + O(d \log d^2)$ arithmetic operations are needed to repair the failed node. The Reconstruction Procedure firstly perform the same recover action as conventional PM-MBR and then recover original symbols, as a inverse precess of the first procedure, *step 2* of this procedure takes the same amount of operations as the first procedure. Totally, our scheme takes $2O(d^2)$ Hash operations and $2O(d^2)$ Xor operations more than traditional PM-MBR codes, but this overhead is rather smaller than schemes exploit encryption mechanism.

5 Divergent Thinking

As is mentioned above, we utilize the secure hash function and PM-MBR code, and finally achieve the *weak security* guarantee with the loss of data capacity kept in a low level. As shown in Fig.3, data rate of our scheme is a constant(close to 100%) when the parameters (n, k, d) are fixed. A natural question arises: is it possible to achieve the storage security against ℓ-eavesdropper without loss of the data capacity? The answer is yes, now we briefly introduce a construct method below. Here the AONT(All-Or-Nothing Transform) [17] $\mathcal{T}$ is introduced first.

$\mathcal{T}$: $(X_1, X_2, ..., X_n) \rightarrow (Y_1, Y_2, ..., Y_n)$ with $X_i, Y_i(i = 1, 2, ..., n)$ drawn from a finite field $\mathbb{F}_q$. The work in [18] considers AONT and addresses unconditional security with respect to a single block of the original message. In other words, someone who have obtained the symbols $Y_1, Y_2, ..., Y_m$ is unable to invert the transform $\mathcal{T}$ and recover each X_i when $m < n$, if and only if $m = n$ the transform is invertible, this is an important property of the AONT.

Replace the preprocessing procedure in our scheme with an AONT, and take the original data symbols $s_1, s_2, ..., s_{L_s}$ as input of the AONT, then we can get result symbols $P = \{p_1, p_2, ..., P_{L_s}\}$. Next, fill the result symbols into the message matrix M. Denoting a subset of P as $\hat{P}$, and each symbol of $\hat{P}$ is placed into the first $k - 1$ rows and first $k - 1$ columns of the symmetric matrix M, thus $|\hat{P}| = \frac{k(2d-k+1)}{2} - (d - k + 1)$. Reviewing the conclusion of *Lemma 1*, we know that the intruder who eavesdrops $\ell < k$ nodes cannot obtain any information of the subset $P \setminus \hat{P}$. As a result, the eavesdropper is impossible to recover each single original symbol s_i because she did not obtain all the result symbols in $P = \{p_1, p_2, ..., p_{L_s}\}$, i.e., $I(s_i; C_E) = 0$. Obviously, without using the random symbols(as K in above scheme), we can also achieve a secure storage against ℓ-eavesdropper with $L_s = \mathcal{L}$ and thus $\mathcal{R} = 1$, i.e., without loss of data capacity.

We must recognize the fact that the security of both the two schemes, respectively utilizing secure hash function and AONT, relies on the perfect security of K and partial elements of P (these elements are placed in the position of massage matrix M except that in the first $k-1$ rows and first $k-1$ columns, we denote these elements as a set $\mathcal{Q}$). Thus, making full use of the set $\mathcal{Q}$, we believe that various schemes with good properties can be constructed. In the future, we will make an intensive research in this aspect.

6 Conclusion

In this paper, we proposed an efficient scheme which provides not only data reliability but also data security against passive ℓ-eavesdroppers in DSS, based on the Product-Matrix framework. To be viewed as a combination of minimum bandwidth regeneration code with secret sharing scheme, our scheme offers more advantages over previous work. Other than data security against eavesdropper, it satisfies both the MDS property and regeneration property (the repair-bandwidth is as low as the MBR code).

Considering the fact that similar repair efficient scheme all provide perfect security criterion for data stored in the system, however, this criterion is too strict to be practical, because it leads to an unaffordable loss of the storage capacity while ℓ get closer to k. In contrast, we adopt the weak security criterion instead, and give a definition of "Secure DSS against an ℓ-eavesdropper". Utilizing a secure hash function and Product-Matrix framework, our scheme finally achieves a high secrecy capacity and constant data rate close to 1 with fixed (n, k, d). The analysis result indicates that, our scheme is sufficiently secure, repair efficient, storage efficient and suitable for practical systems.

Furthermore, another approach was introduced, which combines the All-Or-Nothing Transform with PM-MBR code, thus achieving a secure storage against ℓ-eavesdropper without loss of data rate.

References

1. Dimakis, A.G., Godfrey, P.G., Wu, Y., Wainwright, M.J., Ramchandran, K.: Network Coding for Distributed Storage Systems. IEEE Trans. on Information Theory 56, 4539–4551 (2010)
2. Suh, C., Ramchandran, K.: Exact Regeneration Codes for Distributed Storage Repair Using Interference Alignment. In: Proc. IEEE International Symposium on Information Theory (ISIT), Austin (2010)
3. Rashmi, K., Shah, N.B., Kumar, P.V.: Optimal Exact-regenerating Codes for Distributed Storage at the MSR and MBR Points via a Product-Matrix Construction. IEEE Trans. on Information Theory 57(8), 5227–5239 (2011)

4. Tamo, I., Wang, Z., Bruck, J.: Zigzag Codes: MDS Array Codes with Optimal Rebuilding. IEEE Trans. on Information Theory 59, 1597–1616 (2013)
5. Oliveira, P.F., Lima, L., Vinhoza, T.T.V., Barros, J., Médard, M.: Coding for Trusted Storage in Untrusted Networks. IEEE Trans. on Information Forensics and Security 7(6) (2012)
6. Bloch, M., Barros, J.: Physical-Layer Security: From Information Theory to Security Engeering. Cambridge Univ. Press, Cambridge (2011)
7. Oliveira, P.F., Lima, L., Vinhoza, T.T.V., Médard, M., Barros, J.: Trusted Storage Over Untrusted Networks. In: Proc. IEEE Global Communications Conference (GLOBECOM2010), Miami, FL (2010)
8. Yamamoto, H.: Secret Sharing System Using (k, l, n) Threshold Scheme. Electronics and Communications in Japan (Part I: Communications) 69, 46–54 (1986)
9. Bessani, A., Correia, M., Quaresma, B., André, F., Sousa, P.: DepSky: Dependable and Secure Storage in a Cloud-of-Clouds. In: Proc. EuroSys 2011, Salzburg, Austria (2011)
10. Krawczyk, H.: Secret Sharing Made Short. In: Stinson, D.R. (ed.) CRYPTO 1993. LNCS, vol. 773, pp. 136–146. Springer, Heidelberg (1994)
11. Pawar, S., El Rouayheb, S., Ramchandran, K.: Securing Dynamic Distributed Storage Systems Against Eavesdropping and Adversarial Attacks. IEEE Trans. on Information Theory 57(10), 6734–6753 (2012)
12. Rawat, A.S., Koyluoglu, O.O., Silberstein, N., Vishwanath, S.: Optimal Locally Repairable and Secure Codes for Distributed Storage Systems. In arXiv:1210.6954 (2013)
13. Shah, N.B., Rashmi, K.V., Kumar, P.V.: Information-Theoretically Secure Regenerating Codes for Distributed Storage. In: Proc. IEEE Global Communications Conference, GLOBECOM (2011)
14. Kurihara, M., Kuwakado, H.: Secret sharing Schemes Based on Minimum Bandwidth Regenerating Codes. In: 2012 International Symposium on Information Theory and its Applications (ISITA), pp. 255–259 (2012)
15. Bhattad, K., Narayanan, K.R.: Weakly Secure Network Coding. In: Proc. First Workshop on Network Coding, Theory, and Applicat. (NetCod), Riva del Garda, Italy (2005)
16. Shamir, A.: How to Share a Secret. Commun. ACM 22(11), 612–613 (1979)
17. Rivest, R.L.: All-or-Nothing Encryption and the Package Transform. In: Biham, E. (ed.) FSE 1997. LNCS, vol. 1267, pp. 210–218. Springer, Heidelberg (1997)
18. Stinson, D.R.: Something About All or Nothing (Transforms). Designs, Codes and Cryptography 22(2), 133–138 (2001)
19. Cui, T., Ho, T., Kliewer, J.: On Secure Network Coding Over Networks with Unequal Link Capacities and Restricted Wiretapping Sets. In: Proc. IEEE International Symposium on Information Theory, ISIT (2010)
20. Cai, N., Yeung, R.W.: Secure network coding. In: Proc. IEEE International Symposium on Information Theory (ISIT), Lausanne, Switzerland (2002)
21. El Rouayheb, S., Soljanin, E., Sprintson, A.: Secure network coding for wiretap networks of type II. IEEE Trans. on Information Theory 58(3), 1361–1371 (2012)
22. Luo, M.X., Yang, Y.X., et al.: Secure Network Coding Against Eavesdropper. Science In China Series F-Information Sciences 40(2), 371–380 (2010)
23. Adeli, M., Liu, H.: Secure Network Coding with Minimum Overhead Based on Hash Functions. IEEE Communications Letters 13(12), 956–958 (2009)
24. Dimakis, A.G., Ramchandran, K., Wu, Y., Suh, C.: A Survey on Network Codes for Distributed Storage. Proceedings of the IEEE 99(3) (2011)

Secure and Private Outsourcing
of Shape-Based Feature Extraction

Shumiao Wang[1,*], Mohamed Nassar[2], Mikhail Atallah[1],
and Qutaibah Malluhi[2]

[1] Computer Science Department, Purdue University, West Lafayette, USA
wang845@purdue.edu, mja@cs.purdue.edu
[2] Computer Science and Engineering, Qatar University, Doha, Qatar
meb.nassar@gmail.com, qmalluhi@qu.edu.qa

Abstract. There has been much recent work on secure storage outsourcing, where an organization wants to store its data at untrusted remote cloud servers in an encrypted form, such that its own employees can query the encrypted data using weak devices (both computationally and storage-wise). Or a weak client wants to outsource an expensive computational task without revealing to the servers either the inputs or the computed outputs. The framework requires that the bulk of the computational burden of query-processing be placed on the remote servers, without revealing to these servers anything about the data. Most of the existing work in this area deals with non-image data that is keyword based, and the present paper is to deal with raw image data (without any keyword annotations). We demonstrate that shape-based image feature extraction, a particularly computationally intensive task, can be carried out within this framework, by presenting two schemes for doing so, and demonstrating their viability by experimentally evaluating them. Our results can be used in a number of practical situations. In one scenario the client has images and wants to securely outsource shape-based feature extraction on them, in another the server has encrypted images and the client wants a feature-extracted representation of those that are feature-rich.

Keywords: Secure Outsourcing, Feature Extraction, Cloud Service.

1   Introduction

One of the major impediments to larger-scale use of cloud services is concern for confidentiality of the data and the queries carried out on it. This has motivated much of the recent work on secure storage and computational outsourcing. In the storage outsourcing setting that interests us, a data owner wants to store its

* Portions of this work were supported by National Science Foundation Grants CPS-1329979, CNS-0915436, CNS-0913875, Science and Technology Center CCF-0939370; by an NPRP grant from the Qatar National Research Fund; and by sponsors of the Center for Education and Research in Information Assurance and Security. The statements made herein are solely the responsibility of the authors.

S. Qing et al. (Eds.): ICICS 2013, LNCS 8233, pp. 90–99, 2013.

data in encrypted form at untrusted remote cloud servers, after which trusted clients can query it using weak devices (both computationally and storage-wise) in such a way that the bulk of the computational burden of the query-processing is placed on the remote servers without leaking the data to the servers. The main technical challenges are (i) how to get the untrusted servers to do the query-processing and associated computational work without leaking the data to them (the security issue), and (ii) how to lighten the clients' computational burden and lessen the number of rounds in the client-server interaction (the efficiency issue). Many problems have been considered in previous work, for text, numerical data, spatial data, etc (as we will review later), there has been almost no work that deal with raw image data. The present paper addresses the problem of secure and private outsourcing of feature extraction of image data. Feature extraction from an image is a fundamental operation in image processing, and has the goal of producing a reduced representation of the image that is more computationally tractable than working with the raw image. In shape-based feature extraction, the image is reduced to a collection of based shapes (line segments, circles, etc) for subsequent processing, and namely, these shapes (represented by their parameters) are a set of features of the input image. It is a computationally expensive operation, especially for massive image data (such as satellite images), and is therefore an ideal candidate for outsourcing. To be specific, we are outsourcing the Hough Transform method, which is a widely used shape-based feature extraction method in computer vision [9]. The essential idea of this method is that parametric shapes in an image are detected by looking for accumulation points in the parameter space (the detailed detection process will be reviewed in Section 3). The input images are used to produce a set of features in each by the servers, after which any trusted client can query images at the servers for the features.

We assume honest-but-curious untrusted servers (as is done in most of the research work in the secure outsourcing setting). And our privacy model is that the nature of the basic shapes (line segment, circle, etc) is not hidden from the servers, and what is confidential is the positions at which they occur and how they fit together to form complex patterns. Two approaches based on the Hough Transform method are proposed in this paper: the preliminary approach is simple, easy to implement, and has good performance, while it may leak some minor information about the input image; the second approach is provably secure, but it needs the implementation of more expensive cryptographic tools, such as the garbled circuit protocol [15]. The performances of the two approaches are evaluated by experiments, that quantify their security/efficiency trade-offs.

2   Related Work

There is much previous work in the area of secure outsourcing, and we lack the space for a comprehensive review of all the related research problems, so we give examples of what has been achieved. Paper [14] presents an implementation of Oblivious RAM which allows clients with limited (logarithmic) local storage to store their data on untrusted storage and retrieve it securely without leaking either the data or the access pattern to the server. Paper [5] shows how to securely outsource modular exponentiation with two untrusted servers. Papers [1] and [2] deal with the problem of securely outsourcing matrix computations.

In the area of secure image processing, related work exists in outsourcing of feature extraction in images directed towards face recognition. [11] and [13] address the problem of comparing subject faces with a database of faces and, at the same time, preserving the privacy of the subject faces and the confidentiality of the database. They are based on specific algorithms to extract features from face images, e.g, Eigenfaces. [7] works on extracting another kind of features, namely scale-invariant feature transform (SIFT). While these contributions are similar to ours, they are not shape-based and thus cannot be used to identify and analyze the structural components of images.

3   Building Blocks

Hough Transform. The Hough Transform (HT) method was introduced by P.V.C. Hough in [6]. One input to HT is a binary image with each pixel either 1 or 0, where 1 is the pixel representing data and 0 is the background pixel. Another input is the based shape (the nature of the features to be extracted), which can be represented using a number of parameters in cartesian coordinates. Generally, any parameterized shape can be represented by a vector of parameters as $\overrightarrow{p}$ in the equation of the form $f(\overrightarrow{p}, \overrightarrow{x}) = 0$, where $\overrightarrow{x}$ is the coordinates vector in cartesian coordinates.

Given the based shape (e.g, straight line), HT first quantizes the parameters and initializes an array with a cell for each possible parameter vector of the shape in the quantized parameter space (e.g, we use a two dimension array for the ρ-θ space of straight lines, described in Table 1). In the rest of the paper, we may use the index of a cell to represent its corresponding parameter vector. Then for each parameter vector in the parameter space, HT counts how many data pixels are lying on its corresponding shape instance, and records this count in the corresponding cell in the array. This is the accumulation process, and the resulting array is called the accumulation array or accumulation matrix. The cells in the accumulation array with high counts, *and* which are local maxima, correspond to shape instances. If a $\overrightarrow{p}$'s cell in the accumulation array is (i) a local maximum, and (ii) greater than a pre-determined threshold value t, then that cell is considered to be the parameter vector of an instance of the based shape. The set of all the indexes of such cells gives all the parameter vectors of occurrences of the based shape in the image, which are the features extracted.

Paillier's Homomorphic Encryption. The Paillier's Homomorphic Encryption[12] possesses the following properties. (i) It's a public key scheme. (ii) It's probabilistic. (iii) It possesses the homomorphic property that $E(M_1) * E(M_2) = E(M_1 + M_2)$ holds for any M_1 and M_2, where E denotes the encryption, $+$ is modular addition, and $*$ is modular multiplication.

Gaussian Blur. Gaussian blur [4] is a technique to blur an image by a Gaussian function. In this work, we do *not* use such blurring on any image, but we do use it *on the accumulation matrix* in computing the local maxima, which preserves local maxima with high probability. A Gaussian Blurring function specifies a group of integer weights $w_0, w_1, \ldots, w_8$ to compute a weighted average of a cell (with weight w_0) and its 8 neighbors (with weight $w_1, \ldots, w_8$ respectively), and the weights satisfy the constraint $w_0 \geq \sum_{i=1}^{m} w_m$. And by blurring an accumulation matrix, we mean to compute the weighted sum of each cell and its neighbors with the weights specified in the function as the resulting cell.

Blind and Permute. The input to the Blind and Permute (BP) protocol is a sequence of data items $S = (s_1, s_2, \cdots, s_n)$ whose values are component-wise additively split between party A who has $S' = (s'_1, s'_2, \cdots, s'_n)$ and party B who has $S'' = (s''_1, s''_2, \cdots, s''_n)$, where $s_i = s'_i + s''_i$ for $i = 1, \cdots, n$. The output is a sequence $\hat{S}$ (also additively split between A and B) obtained from S by (i) permuting the entries of S according to a random permutation π that is known to neither A nor B; and (ii) modifying the additive split of the entries of S so that neither A nor B can use their share of it to gain any information about π. A BP protocol (adapted from [3]) is used in the our secure approach.

Garbled Circuits. Garbled Circuits, first presented by Yao in [15], is a cryptographic technique for securely evaluating two-party functionalities. A two-party functionality can be written as $f(x, y) = (f_1(x, y), f_2(x, y))$, where x and y are the private inputs from the two parties, and after the evaluation of the function, one party receives $f_1(x, y)$ and the other one receives $f_2(x, y)$ as the outputs. Neither of the two parties should learn anything about the other's input other than what can be inferred from his own input and output. We refer to [10] for a review of Yao's protocol and a rigorous security proof.

4   Approaches

A preliminary approach using blurring method is provided to prevent possible leakage of information in Section 4.1 with a provably secure approach provided in Section 4.2. The outsourcing framework consists of four parties: the Data Owner DO, the Clients C, the first and second cloud server S_1 and S_2.

4.1   A Preliminary Approach with Homomorphic Encryption and Blurring

We first give an overview of this approach. For each image, DO specifies the shape(s) to be based on, encrypts each pixel in the image by the homomorphic encryption scheme whose decryption key is shared with S_2, and then sends the encrypted image to S_1 for analysis. With the homomorphic property, S_1 generates an encrypted accumulation array for each shape under detection without decryption, and associates each cell in the array with its encrypted index and some neighboring information in order to allow S_2 to check whether it's a local maximum cell, then permutes the cells and sends them to S_2. S_2 decrypts the cells by the homomorphic encryption key, finds out the local maxima after thresholding, and stores the qualified indexes(encrypted) as the set of features.

(The main challenge here is that S_2 should find the local maxima without knowing the index information.) The scheme is described in detail in the following, using straight line as an example of the based shape(s)to simplify the description.

Initialization. DO initializes the scheme by specifying the shape(s) to be based on and the global parameters (e.g, the ρ-θ space) to be used by the servers. DO generates a public and private key pair (K_E, K_D) for Paillier's homomorphic encryption scheme, publishes the public key K_E, and sends the private key K_D only to S_2. DO generates a key K for a symmetric encryption scheme (e.g. AES), and shares it with S_1 and C, which is used to encrypt the indexes of cells in the accumulation array as mentioned in the overview. In addition, if DO wants to hide the image id or to share more information of the images with C which are not supposed to be seen by the servers, he generates another symmetric key K_{DC} shared only to C, and uses it to encrypt the image id and other information.

Analyzing a New Image. To analyze a new image I with id and add it to the existing database, DO encrypts its id into $E_{K_{DC}}(id)$ to hide it, encrypts the image pixel by pixel with K_E, and gets an encrypted image, denoted by $E_{K_E}(I)$. DO sends $(E_{K_{DC}}(id), E_{K_E}(I))$ to S_1.

Accumulation. In this step, S_1 uses the homomorphic property of the Pallier's scheme, to generate the encrypted accumulation array ACC for the shape of interest, and we only consider the straight line here. Recall that HT counts the pixels with value 1 on a straight line for the cell in ACC corresponding to its parameter vector. In this scheme, for every possible parameter vector in ρ-θ space, S_1 calculates the sum of every pixel value on its corresponding straight line by multiplying the encryptions of them. After this step, the encrypted counts for all possible parameter vectors are obtained in the matrix ACC.

Processing Local Information and Permutation. Before sending ACC to S_2, S_1 should randomly permute all the cells and associate each cell $ACC[i][j]$ with its encrypted index $E_K(i, j)$, and provide enough information for S_2 to find the local maxima without seeing the indexes. S_1 computes the gradients for each cell in ACC before permutation and associate them with the cell, so that S_2 could check whether it is a local maximum cell after decryption. Here we define the gradients of a cell $ACC[i, j]$ as the difference value between it and its neighbors, and subtractions on the plaintexts could be performed by divisions on the ciphertexts according to the homomorphic property. In order to break the symmetry of the gradients between two neighbors, before computing the gradients, S_1 chooses two different simplified Gaussian functions, performs the two Gaussian blurring processes separately on ACC and gets ACC_1 and ACC_2 as the resulting matrices respectively. Gaussian blur preserves the local maxima with overwhelming probability due to the heavy weight of the central cell, so the local maxima in ACC will be preserved in ACC_1 and ACC_2 very likely. To compute the gradients for each cell $ACC[i][j]$, instead of using the exact values from ACC and performing the subtractions, if $i + j$ is odd, S_1 uses the values from corresponding cells of ACC_1; otherwise, uses the values from ACC_2. For each cell $ACC[i][j]$, S_1 creates a tuple $(E_K(i, j), ACC[i, j],$ its Gradients), and permutates all the tuples in the array randomly. S_1 sends all the tuples in an array along with $E_{K_{DC}}(id)$ to S_2.

Detection and Storage. In this step, S_2 receives the data, and for each tuple, he decrypts the gradients and checks whether it's a local maximum. If not, just discard it; otherwise, he decrypts $ACC[i,j]$ and if it's also beyond a pre-fixed threshold, the index is corresponding to an occurrence of the based shape. S_2 saves all the qualified indexes of occurrences of the based shape detected in I, and stores them with $E_{K_{DC}}(id)$.

Querying Phase. C queries S_2 with the encrypted image id $E_{K_{DC}}(id)$, gets back all the encrypted indexes of occurrences of the based shape, and decrypts them to recover the parameters as the features of the image.

4.2 Secure Approach with Additive Splitting and Garbled Circuit

The overall idea of this approach is that DO additively splits the image randomly into two shares, and sends one share to S_1, the other to S_2, so that the two servers can perform the accumulation process locally, and then collaborate to detect the parameters for the occurring based shapes without seeing any information about the original image. To add an image in this approach, instead of encrypting each pixel by encryption as in the preliminary approach, the DO additively splits each pixel into two secret shares: DO first chooses a modulo m, say 2^{32}, which should be larger than any value in the accumulation array; then for each pixel value v, DO randomly chooses v_1 over $[0, m-1]$, and splits v as v_1 and $v_2 = v - v_1 \bmod m$. And it can be proved that if I' and I'' are the two shares obtained by pixel-wise additive splitting of an image I, which means $I = I' + I'' \bmod m$, then the accumulation matrices produced by I' and I'' are a pair of additive splitting shares of the accumulation matrix produced by I. With this property, S_1 and S_2 could perform the accumulation process for I' and I'' separately without knowing I. Then they work together to detect the local maximum cells in the accumulation matrix of I, and which is the main challenge when designing this scheme and will be handled later. After the detection, one server could store the results in encrypted form and serve the clients for queries.

We first present our solution for the problem that two parties share an additive splitting of an accumulation matrix $M = M' + M'' \bmod m$, say A has M' and B has M'', and they want to compute the indexes of local maximum cells in M which are also beyond a given threshold t. In this protocol, we consider local maximum cells as those which are greater than its 8 neighbors within the radius equal to 1, while this radius can be adjusted as discussed in Table 1, and so is the protocol. The computation should not leak one party's share to the other and neither should see the result indexes.

Let M, M' and M'' be matrices of size $p \times q$, and the size is public known to A and B. For each cell in M' (resp, M''), A (resp, B) constructs a 3×3 square matrix which is the 3×3 submatrix of M' (resp, M'') centering at this cell (for those cells who do not have 8 neighbors, pad 0's to make a square matrix). A (resp, B) orders all the square matrices sequentially as a sequence $S' = s'_1, \cdots, s'_n$

(resp, $S'' = s_1'', \cdots, s_n''$), where s_i' (resp, s_i'') is the square matrix corresponding to the cell $M'[j][k]$ (resp, $M''[j][k]$) with $j = \lfloor i/q \rfloor, k = i - q * j$.

Note that now A and B together have the local information for each cell to determine whether it's a local maximum cell in M, and both of them know the indexes of the cells. We start with a variation of the BP protocol to allow them to permute their sequences of square matrices with the same permutation, which is known to neither of them but could be recovered by the clients.

Initialization. Both of A and B initialize a public homomorphic encryption scheme, denoted by E_A and D_A (resp, E_B and D_B) in this protocol. (The decryption key of B should be shared with the clients, and we will explain this later.) We use $E_A(s_i)$ or $D_A(s_i)$ to denote encrypting/decrypting a 3×3 square matrix s_i cell by cell.

One Direction Blind and Permute.

1. A computes and sends $E_A(s_1'), \cdots, E_A(s_n')$ to B.
2. B generates n 3×3 random matrices $r_1, \cdots, r_n$, and for $i = 1, \cdots, n$ he computes $E_A(-r_i)$ and cell-wisely multiplies it to $E_A(s_i')$, thereby obtaining $E_A(s_i' - r_i)$. B associates $E_B(i)$ to the matrix $E_A(s_i' - r_i)$ as an index field.
3. B generates a random permutation π_B and applies it to the sequence of $E_A(s_i' - r_i)$'s computed in the previous step, obtaining a sequence of the form $E_A(v_1'), \cdots, E_A(v_n')$ that he sends to A. He also applies π_B to the sequence $s_1'' + r_1, \cdots, s_n'' + r_n$, obtaining a sequence $V'' = v_1'', \cdots, v_n''$ as his new share.
4. A decrypts the n items $E_A(v_1'), \cdots, E_A(v_n')$ received from B, obtaining the sequence $V' = v_1', \cdots, v_n'$ as the new share.

The Other Direction Blind and Permute. A and B repeat the one direction BP protocol by changing their roles with their new sequences V' and V'' as inputs instead of S' and S''. The result of this step is they both possess a sequence which two together form an additive splitting of the original sequence S after permutation $\pi_A(\pi_B)$. Now each square matrix in A's sequence is associated with an index filed which is the encryption of its original index in S as $E_B(i)$, and each one in B's sequence is associated with $E_A(\pi_B(i))$.

Detection of Local Maxima. For each aligned pair of square matrices in their sequence, A and B perform the garbled circuit protocol to determine (i) whether its central cell in the original matrix M is greater than all its neighbors and (ii) is beyond the given threshold t, and reveal the answer to party A. If it satisfies the two conditions, A adds the encrypted index to a result set. Let s_i', held by A, and s_i'', held by B, be a pair of aligned square matrices, which are a pair of additive splitting shares modulo by m. Let

$$s_i' = \begin{pmatrix} a_1 & a_2 & a_3 \\ a_4 & a_5 & a_6 \\ a_7 & a_8 & a_9 \end{pmatrix}, s_i'' = \begin{pmatrix} b_1 & b_2 & b_3 \\ b_4 & b_5 & b_6 \\ b_7 & b_8 & b_9 \end{pmatrix}. \tag{1}$$

We define the functionality to check the two conditions as:

$$f(s_i', s_i'') = equal(add(a_5, b_5), \max_{j=1}^{9}(add(a_j, b_j))) \wedge gt(add(a_5, b_5), t) \tag{2}$$

A and B perform a garbled circuit protocol for f on each pair of the input square matrices, and enable A to learn the result. If the result is 1, which means the cell of the input square matrix is a local maximum point and beyond t, A stores the associated encrypted index for later queries. Now we are ready to present the main scheme for outsourcing feature extraction.

Initialization. DO initializes the scheme by specifying the shape(s) to be based on and the global parameters (e.g, the ρ-θ space) to be used by the servers. DO generates the homomorphic key pairs for S_1 and S_2 to be used in the BP protocol and shares the decryption key with the clients.

Analyzing a New Image.

1. To add a new binary image I to the database, DO additively splits it as $I = I' + I''$, and shares I' (resp, I'') to S_1 (resp, S_2).
2. S_1 (resp, S_2) performs Hough accumulation on I' (resp, I'') for the based shape specified by DO, obtaining the accumulation matrix M' (resp, M'').
3. S_1 and S_2 collaborate to detect the indexes (encrypted) for local maxima in $M = M' + M''$ which are also beyond a threshold, using the method described above. WLOG, assume S_1 plays the role of A.
4. S_1 stores the set of indexes (encrypted) of occurrences of the based shape in the image as the extracted features.

Querying Phase. The query part of this scheme is similar to the preliminary approach, except that the clients interact with S_1 for querying, and decrypt the results with the key of S_2.

Analysis. From the view of S_1 and S_2, either is receiving a random image due to the property of additive splitting secret sharing. They perform accumulation on their own share, which gives them no more information, after that they perform the provable secure BP protocol as used in [3], and then interact for detection under the garbled circuit protocol, the security of which has been proved in [10].

5   Experiment

In this section we evaluate the performance of the two approaches per party and per activity. All the parties are run on a local machine having Windows OS, Intel i5 four cores 2.67 GHz CPU, 4GB memory. For secure circuit evaluation, we adopt the approach in [8] and the tool (GCParser) from http://www.mightbeevil.com. The performance measurements included next are only indicative.

The most important input parameters are shown in Table 1. For this experiment we use the image shown in Fig. 1(a). The detected lines in Fig. 1(b) show a good accuracy example. However, a standalone study of the accuracy of the Hough transform is outside the scope of this paper (as it is an image processing issue). We focus more on the trade off between the accuracy and the computational demand.

For the preliminary approach, we show the breakdown by party in Fig. 2(a) and by activity in Fig. 2(b); and for the secure one, we show the breakdown by

Table 1. Discussion on the Input Parameters

Parameter	Description
ρ-θ space size	Sampling of the ρ dimension and the θ dimension. Large size means better accuracy but is more performance demanding.
Local maximization radius	Choosing a large radius may enhance the accuracy because it helps detecting only one line for a group of line segments that are close in the ρ-θ space.
Threshold	Since the parties are agnostic of the real votes for the lines, we can not filter a subset of the lines based on the threshold.

(a)   (b)

Fig. 1. The image used for experiments (a) and the extracted line-based features of the image shown as the detected lines (b)

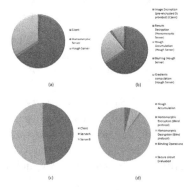

(a)   (b)

(c)   (d)

Fig. 2. Computation Break Down - First Approach by Party (a) and by Activity (b); Second Approach by Party (c) and by Activity (d)

party in Fig. 2(c) and by activity in Fig. 2(d). The second approach runs about 50 times slower than the first approach on the same set of parameters. This big difference is mainly caused by the secure circuit evaluation and the blind protocols in the second approach. Note that the time taken by both approaches are mainly dependent on the ρ-θ space size, which is the size of the ACC matrix and independent of how complex the original image is.

For the first approach Fig. 2(a) shows that the homomorphic server carries more load than the Hough server. This is due to the homomorphic cryptography operations as perceived in Fig. 2(b). For the second approach Fig. 2(c) shows that the load is distributed symmetrically between the two servers (Still the server starting the BP protocol does less homomorphic cryptography). The main bottleneck is the use of garbled circuits as perceived in Fig. 2(d).

6   Conclusion

In this paper, we presented two schemes for the secure outsourcing of shape-based feature extraction of images, one is more practical and easier to implement, while the other is provable secure, and experimentally demonstrated their viability and quantified their security and efficiency trade-offs.

References

1. Atallah, M.J., Frikken, K.B.: Securely outsourcing linear algebra computations. In: ASIACCS, pp. 48–59 (2010)
2. Atallah, M.J., Frikken, K.B., Wang, S.: Private outsourcing of matrix multiplication over closed semi-rings. In: SECRYPT, pp. 136–144 (2012)
3. Atallah, M.J., Kerschbaum, F., Du, W.: Secure private sequence comparisons. In: Proceedings of the 2003 ACM Workshop on Privacy in the Electronic Society (WPES 2003), pp. 39–44 (2003)
4. Ballard, D., Brown, C.: Computer Vision. Prentice Hall (1982)
5. Hohenberger, S., Lysyanskaya, A.: How to securely outsource cryptographic computations. In: Kilian, J. (ed.) TCC 2005. LNCS, vol. 3378, pp. 264–282. Springer, Heidelberg (2005)
6. Hough, P.: Method and means for recognizing complex patterns (1962)
7. Hsu, C.-Y., Lu, C.-S., Pei, S.-C.: Image feature extraction in encrypted domain with privacy-preserving sift. IEEE Transactions on Image Processing 21(11), 4593–4607 (2012)
8. Huang, Y., Evans, D., Katz, J., Malka, L.: Faster secure two-party computation using garbled circuits. In: USENIX Security Symposium (2011)
9. Leavers, V.F.: Shape Detection in Computer Vision Using the Hough Transform. Springer-Verlag New York, Inc., Secaucus (1992)
10. Lindell, Y., Pinkas, B.: A proof of security of yao's protocol for two-party computation. J. Cryptol. 22(2), 161–188 (2009)
11. Osadchy, M., Pinkas, B., Jarrous, A., Moskovich, B.: Scifi - a system for secure face identification. In: 2010 IEEE Symposium on Security and Privacy (SP), pp. 239–254 (2010)
12. Paillier, P.: Public-key cryptosystems based on composite degree residuosity classes. In: Stern, J. (ed.) EUROCRYPT 1999. LNCS, vol. 1592, pp. 223–238. Springer, Heidelberg (1999)
13. Sadeghi, A.-R., Schneider, T., Wehrenberg, I.: Efficient privacy-preserving face recognition. In: Lee, D., Hong, S. (eds.) ICISC 2009. LNCS, vol. 5984, pp. 229–244. Springer, Heidelberg (2010)
14. Williams, P., Sion, R.: Single round access privacy on outsourced storage. In: Proceedings of the 2012 ACM Conference on Computer and Communications Security, CCS 2012, pp. 293–304. ACM, New York (2012)
15. Yao, A.C.-C.: How to generate and exchange secrets. In: SFCS 1986, pp. 162–167. IEEE Computer Society, Washington, DC (1986)

Time-Stealer: A Stealthy Threat
for Virtualization Scheduler and Its Countermeasures

Hong Rong, Ming Xian, Huimei Wang, and Jiangyong Shi

State Key Laboratory of Complex Electromagnetic Environment Effects on Electronics and
Information System, National University of Defense Technology, Changsha, China
ronghong01@gmail.com, qwertmingx@tom.com,
{freshcdwhm,fangtuo90}@163.com

Abstract. Third-party Cloud Computing, Amazon's Elastic Compute Cloud
(EC2) for instance, provides Infrastructure as a Service (IaaS) solutions that
pack multiple customer virtual machines (VMs) onto the same physical server
with hardware virtualization technology. Xen is widely used in virtualization
which charges VMs by wall clock time rather than resources consumed. Under
this model, manipulation of the scheduler vulnerability may allow theft-of-
service at the expense of other customers.

Recent research has shown that attacker's VM can consume more CPU time
than fair share on Amazon EC2 in that Xen 3.x default Credit Scheduler's resolution was rather coarse. Although considerable changes have been made in
Xen 4.x Credit Scheduler to improve the performance in case of such stealing
attacks, we've found another alternative attack called Time-Stealer which can
obtain up to 96.6% CPU cycles stealthily under some circumstances on Xen-
Server6.0.2 platform by analyzing the source code thoroughly. Detection methods using benchmarks as well as a series of countermeasures are proposed
and experimental results have demonstrated the effectiveness of these defense
techniques.

Keywords: Cloud Computing, Virtualization, Xen, Credit Scheduler
vulnerability.

1 Introduction

Cloud Computing provides high efficiency mainly by multiplexing multiple customer
workloads onto a single physical machine to host data and deploy software and services. For instance, Amazon's Elastic Compute Cloud (EC2) [1] offers this sort of
service. In other words, Cloud Computing is used to refer to a new business model
where heavy computing and software capabilities are outsourced on demand to share
third-party infrastructure, not only providing a number of advantages, such as scalability, dynamic provisioning, and low cost maintenance, but also introducing a great
deal of new risks [2-4].

In virtualization which is fundamental technology of Cloud Computing, a hypervisor (also called Virtual Machine Monitor, VMM) schedules and manages different

S. Qing et al. (Eds.): ICICS 2013, LNCS 8233, pp. 100–112, 2013.
© Springer International Publishing Switzerland 2013

VMs. Operating system scheduler's vulnerabilities may result in inaccurate or unfair scheduling and such malicious behavior has been proved in the past operating systems—DoS (Denial of Service) attack on BSD4.4 [5] and similar attack more recently on Linux 2.6 [6]. F. Zhou, et al [7-8] have demonstrated that Xen hypervisor is vulnerable to timing-based manipulation and a VM using their attack method can obtain up to 98% (on lab experiments) and 85% (on modified EC2 scheduler) of total CPU cycles despite how many VMs running on the same core. Such attacks typically take advantage of the use of periodic sampling or a low-precision clock to measure CPU usage. An attacking process just needs to conceal itself whenever a scheduling tick occurs.

However, since Xen moves onto latest version Xen 4.x, a lot of improvements have been made to ensure scheduler's fairness, meanwhile experiments show the former attack can't reach its theoretic point. In spite of these changes, we discover another attack form: Time-Stealer which turns out to be useful on some conditions. An attacking VM can acquire 96.6% CPU cycles regardless of the number of VMs on the same pinned core, breaching fairness principle once again.

This paper presents a novel analysis of what variations are made in Xen 4.x scheduler and Time-Stealer's attack scheme while some conditions have to be sufficed to guarantee its success. In terms of its stealth, a detection method without CP support is proposed and a series of countermeasures utilizing Xen 4.x' features are discussed afterwards.

The rest of this paper is organized as follows: Section 2 describes details of Xen 4.x scheduling mechanism and potential vulnerabilities. Section 3 explains Time-Stealer attack mechanism and shows experimental consequences in the lab. Next, Section 4 illustrates our detection scheme and countermeasures. Section 5 presents related work and we draw a conclusion in Section 6.

2   Xen 4.x Scheduling Mechanism and Vulnerabilities

In this section, we start with a brief introduction of Xen hypervisor, and then give an analysis of how does Xen 4.x Credit Scheduler work and what improvement are made compared with previous versions. Finally, we present a novel illustration of its potential vulnerabilities that may be exploited by malicious Cloud customers.

2.1   Xen Hypervisor

Xen is an open-source VMM, or hypervisor, for both 32- and 64-bit processor architectures. It runs as software directly on top of the bare-metal, physical hardware and enables you to run several virtual guest operating systems on the same host computer at the same time. The VMs are executed securely and efficiently with near-native performance [9]. Xen hypervisor is split into two parts: A hypervisor core, which runs directly on the physical hardware and a privileged guest Domain0 (domain means VM in Xen) that provides device drivers. The hypervisor core is responsible for basic management functions, such as CPU scheduling, interrupt handling and memory management. It runs with ring0 privileges, whereas DomainUs are only allowed to run in the rings 1-3. Therefore, the hypervisor can trap all sensitive processor instructions and remains in full control of the physical machine [10-11].

Many enterprises are making tremendous investments in promoting Xen project, to name a few: Citrix, Amazon AWS, AMD, CA technologies, Cisco, Google, Intel, Oracle and so forth. Motivated by consolidation, reliability and security, a growing demand of server virtualization in industry boosts Xen's step towards Cloud Computing for its opening and excellent performance.

2.2   Inner Workings of Credit Scheduler

As with a multitasking operating system, scheduling in Xen is a tradeoff between achieving fairness for running domains and achieving good overall throughput [9][12]. Xen allows a VM to have one or more VCPUs (virtual CPUs) which are determined to run on which PCPU (Physical CPU) by scheduler. The design and tuning of the scheduler is one of the most important factors in keeping Xen system running well.

On the latest versions of Xen, the Credit Scheduler is used by default [13]. Each domain has two properties associated with it, a weight and a cap. The weight determines the share of the PCPU time that the domain gets, whereas the cap represents the maximum. Weights are relative to each other and decide the initial credits of the VCPU. Each VCPU's credits ensure its runtime compared to other VCPUs. There are five priority states in Credit Scheduler: BOOST (with positive credits, capable of preempting other VCPU if I/O comes to achieve better I/O latency), UNDER (with positive credits, capable of being scheduled), OVER (with negative credits and only can be scheduled in work-conserving mode) and IDLE (represent no VCPU running). The VCPUs marked with Priority States on a PCPU are kept in an ordered queue, with those in BOOST state ahead of those in UNDER state and those in UNDER state ahead of OVER state. Apart from these, BLOCKED state is another VCPU state which means that the current VCPU is not runnable any more, probably awaiting a timing event like I/O response with remaining credits.

The Credit Scheduler uses a fixed-size 30ms quantum. At the end of each quantum, it recalculates all VCPU's credits and priorities and selects a new VCPU to run from a list of those that have not already exceeded their fair allotment. If a PCPU has no UNDER-state VCPUs, it tries to pull some from other PCPUs. The scheduler ticks every 10ms, subtracting 100 credits from the running VCPU and restricting the maximum credits.

Recently, some changes have been made to improve Credit Scheduler performance in Xen 4.1.2, with 195 lines added in source code compared to version 3.1.2. For both, the default weight is 256 and cap is 0. To explain how the new Credit Scheduler behaves, we analyze the source code in detail.

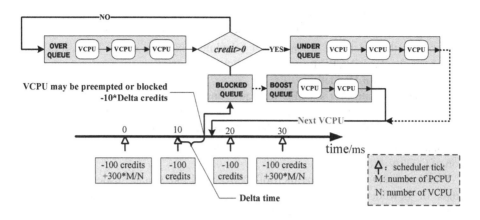

Fig. 1. Xen 4.1.2 Credit Scheduling Procedures

From Fig. 1, the scheduling process can be summarized as follows: a VCPU with adequate credits first goes to UNDER queue waiting to be scheduled; as long as it's on the top of the queue, it can be executed on PCPU, in the meantime its credits will be debited every 10ms; whenever it leaves the PCPU to enter OVER queue or BLOCKED queue, its credits corresponding to the running-time less than 10ms will also be debited. On each 30ms interval, all VCPUs' credits are recalculated and more credits are added. In this way, those in OVER queue can move onto UNDER queue and the whole process will repeat.

The most significant improvement in Xen 4.1.2 Credit Scheduler is smaller granularity in credit calculating. To illustrate further, one of the core scheduler functions called csched_schedule() in */xen/common/sched_credit.c* determines the next runnable VCPU and its duration. A primary advance is that when this function executes, the current VCPU's credits has to be burned regardless of whether clock ticks comes or not, as shown in Fig. 1. This kind of design restricts effectiveness of "Cycle Stealer" [8] which attempts to sleep before scheduler tick arrives to avoid credit deduction and wakes up later with BOOST state to obtain more CPU cycles, because its credits are inevitably deducted by Xen.

2.3 Potential Vulnerabilities

Although Credit Scheduler's resolution has been increased a great deal, as we describe in the following section, this adoption still allows attacker to steal CPU cycles under some conditions and degrade the other VMs performance because of frequent context switches. There are three major vulnerabilities in current Xen version:

(a) Boosting Mechanism

Boosting in Xen Credit Scheduler aims to achieve better I/O latency, simply by prioritizing VCPUs executing I/O work. When a VCPU sleeps waiting for I/O, it will still hold its remaining credits; when it wakes with positive credits, it enters BOOST state and may instantly   preempt running VCPU with lower priorities. This mechanism, however, gives attacker's VCPU chances to deprive of other VCPUs' execution by deliberately sleeping first and waking afterwards.

(b) Fixed Scheduling Rate

Each VCPU can run on the PCPU at most 30ms by default, which renders attacker to recognize the exact time when csched_schedule() executes easily. Thus, it is feasible for the attacker's VCPU to evade being scheduled away.

(c) Fixed Credit Deduction

In some cases, attacker's VCPU may quit running just before the debit tick comes, that is, it's quite unfair that the next VCPU can merely run on the PCPU for less than $\varepsilon(\varepsilon < 10)$ ms while its credits are reduced by 100 compared to those who execute for complete 10ms. This gives an opportunity to breach the justice and launch a Reduction of Quality Attack.

What's more, to achieve the theft-of-service goal like Cycle Stealer, there are two kinds of bewilderments needs to be solved: one is whether VCPU can enter BLOCKED state; the other is whether attacker's VCPU can be aroused apart from I/O events.

Both problems have been perfectly resolved with help of Xen hypervisor. Firstly, when a VM sleeps on the run, an idle process occurs in it. Under of model of paravirtualization, VM's idle process is supposed to be replaced by a hypercall named do_sched_op(), making its VCPU blocked and raising a soft-interrupt-request to Xen. Credit Scheduler then processes the request and reschedules next VCPU. Secondly, instead of hardware timer, VM OS (Operating System) uses a singleshot_timer provided by hypervisor to complete timing events. When VCPU is about to go to sleep for a period, a hypercall named do_set_timer_op() is invoked to set a timer. The moment timer expires, a software interrupt is released to hypervisor. In the end, attacker's VCPU is unblocked. Moreover, it will preempt current VCPU in BOOST priority with positive credits.

3   Time-Stealer Attack

Previous work F. Zhou [8] did has already proven a successful attack that every 10ms the scheduler tick fires and schedules the malicious VM which runs for $10 - \varepsilon$ ms and then calls halt() to briefly go idle to ensure another VM will be running at the next tick. Later, the attacker wakes in BOOST priority and preempts the current running VM, namely, it can execute for $10 - \varepsilon$ ms out of every 10ms tick debit cycle. On account of improvements in Xen 4.x, the former attack cannot reach up to its threatening impact. In this section, a similar attack scheme is proposed and experiments show Time-Stealer attack is more effective than Cycle Stealer.

3.1   Time-Stealer Attack Description

Time-Stealer attack mainly relies on the fixed scheduling rate used by Xen Credit Scheduler, not only in version 3.1.2, but also in 4.1.2 as well as newest 4.2.1, the default scheduling period is always 30ms. When this schedule tick arrives, no matter how many credits current VCPU may have, it has no choice but to leave the PCPU while next VCPU on the head of UNDER queue is probably scheduled at next time slice.

Since any VCPU credits are inevitably debited, attackers might as well choose to execute on the PCPU for $30 - \varepsilon$ ms and then go to sleep to prevent be scheduled away as shown in Fig. 2. After a little while, it just wakes up again to consume CPU cycles. Via this scheme, attackers can acquire more CPU time than fair share on conditions described as follows.

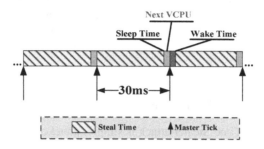

Fig. 2. Time-Stealer scheme

According to scheduling policy, attacker's VCPU can't wake up in BOOST state without positive credits. Here's a critical question: can Time-Stealer still work if its VCPU credits are burned? The answer is affirmative. Through theoretical analysis, the probability of attacker's VCPU running out of credits is relatively small, whereas in contrast, the probability of other VCPUs' being preempted is rather large.

To illustrate, consider a simplified scenario consisting of n identical VMs on a Xen host server. Each VM has only one VCPU and the server has m PCPU cores. Let Ra denote the minimum periods that attack's VCPU runs continually and let Rn denote the maximum scheduling periods that other VCPUs executes. We assume attacker's VCPU runs for 29ms then sleep 1ms in every scheduling period and its initial credits is set to be 300. As has been mentioned earlier, each active VCPU will get $300m / n$ credits every 30ms. Thus, the total credits of attacker's VCPU within Ra are given by:

$$Ca = 300 - 290Ra + (300m / n) \bullet Ra \qquad (1)$$

When attacker's credits are negative, it will wake up in OVER state; that is, by $Ca < 0$, we can get Ra:

$$Ra = ceil(\frac{300}{290 - 300m / n}) \qquad (2)$$

The function "$ceil(x)$" means the smallest integer which is larger than x.

When attacker's VCPU enters OVER queue, there are at most $n - 1$ VCPUs ahead waiting for execution, thus: $Rn = n - 1$.

As long as the attacker's VCPU credits return to positive (300 supposed) and stays on the top of UNDER queue, the whole process above will just repeat. Then, the probability of attacker's occupation of PCPU can be defined as:

$$Pa = \frac{Rn}{Rn + Ra} \tag{3}$$

Normally, the fair share probability of every VCPU is supposed to be $1/n$. On the condition that $Pa > 1/n$, attacker's purpose of obtaining more CPU cycles can be achieved. Notice that this sort of attack is closely related to number of PCPUs and VCPUs. When $n \leq m$, Ca will remain positive forever. Usually, this is not the case. When $n > m$, for instance, $n = 6, m = 4$, then Pa is 32.3% greater than normal rate 16.7%. Once taking the credits loss of other VCPUs into account, this proportion will be magnified incredibly.

3.2   Implementation and Evaluation

Our implementation of Time-Stealer attack is simple: attacker' VM chooses to run on one PCPU for $30 - \varepsilon$ ms and then invokes a systemcall—usleep() to go into BLOCKED state, hoping to be scheduled away from the PCPU. On the next scheduler tick, another victim VM is charged by 100 credits, and immediately the attacker' VM wakes up in BOOST state and preempts the victim VCPU. TSC hardware register is applied to provide precise time sampling.

To examine the performance of our attack scenario in practice, we evaluate in Citrix XenServer6.0.2 (Free) which is an enterprise-level complete virtualization platform delivering uncompromised performance, scale, and flexibility at no cost [14]. XenServer allows a deployment of virtual x86 computers based on Xen hypervisor. Time-Stealer effectiveness is testified in two ways: one tested is by a simple loop; the other is tested by a CPU benchmark. Experiment configurations are given in Table 1.

Table 1. Experiment Setup

ITEMS	CONIFGURATIONS
Type	Dell PowerEdge T410
CPU	Intel Xeon E5606@2.13GHz
RAM	16GB
Platform	XenServer6.0.2
Kernel	Xen 4.1.2
Guest OS	CentOS 5.8_32bit (paravirtualized)

As our CPU has 4 cores, we intentionally separate our testing instances in order to prevent interferences: 2 cores for test instances and the other 2 for Domain0. Eight identical VMs are setup by Xen "VM copy" function and every VM has only one VCPU. Note that sleep time cannot go beyond ε to make sure waking up timely, meanwhile, ε should be as small as possible to obtain maximum stealing cycles. However, too small ε increases the risks to be ticked by the scheduler. In the overall tests, sleep time is set to be 0.5ms.

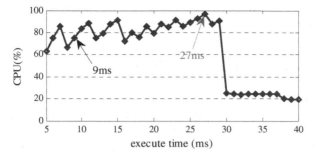

Fig. 3. Attack performance vs. execute time

Our first test concerns about the effect of Time-Stealer execute time on CPU utilization. Fig. 3 shows that there's unstable growth of attacker's VM CPU utilization before 30ms execution while a dramatic drop appears at exact 30ms point, after which the usage remains to be around 20%. This figure demonstrates our attack effectiveness, whereas the curve reaches its top at 27ms instead of 29ms probably because of tick timing jitter. In addition, execution of 9ms proposed in [7-8] cannot reach its theoretical point (98%).

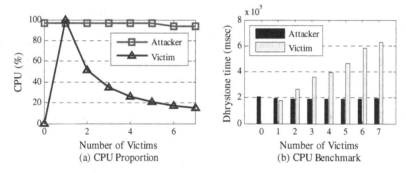

Fig. 4. XenServer experiments- CPU and application performance for attackers and victims

In Fig. 4 (a), we can see attacker and victim CPU utilization on two-pinned-core scenario. As with an increase of victim VM numbers, attacker can obtain up to 96% CPU of a single core all the time while resource contentions of other VMs are getting worse and worse.

Fig. 4 (b) presents consequence of CPU benchmark. In this test, we modified the source code of a famous CPU benchmark—Dhrystone 2.1, by adding Time-Stealer's control part that runtime interval is checked every 9,000 iterations of Dhrystone runs. Via comparing the time the modified VM and unmodified VMs takes to complete 1.0×10^9 runs of Dhrystone operation, the performance of Time-Stealer can be further testified. The touchstone measurement was achieved by a VM using unmodified Dhrystone without CPU usage competition; it finished the total iterations in 177,105ms compared with 207,935ms recorded by mere one VM with modified benchmark. From Fig. 4 (b), it's quite obvious to see that time costs have a steady growth with growth of victim VMs while attacker's time keeps rather low and stable; in the severest situation; the cost of victim VMs is 3 times higher than attacker's.

4   Time-Stealer Detection and Mitigation Measures

The theft-of-service attack on Credit Scheduler mainly takes advantage of BOOST mechanism and fixed scheduler timing. It's rather easy and feasible to launch a similar attack on Xen 3.x platform proven by earlier work [7-8]. Due to more changes has been made to Xen scheduler, especially, right before attacker's VCPU chooses to sleep, its credits will be subtracted even if credit tick does not arrive yet. In this section, we propose some countermeasures to detect and mitigate Time-Stealer attack.

4.1   Detection Measures

Generally, it's a little bit difficult to detect Time-Stealer attack, since it has no collateral effect except for performance degradation like lowering CPU usage as well as cache polluting because of frequent context switches. If users of victim VMs paid more attention to their CPU utilization and time gap of finishing the same job, theft-of-service evidences would be collected to detect attacker's existence.

For our detection method, we take Dhrystone CPU benchmark as our detection tool. Support from CP is not basically required. Specifically, it involves continual surveillance on benchmark data and judgment on whether a turning point might come. Assume that T_i means the time Dhrystone takes in i th round; T_{ave} shown in (4) is the average time tested many times starting from the very beginning of purchasing service from CP like Amazon EC2; T_{curr} shown in (5) is the average time tested recently ($m \gg n$). Note that the quantity of samples should be large enough to be precise.

$$T_{ave} = (1/m)\sum\nolimits_{i=1}^{i=m} T_i \tag{4}$$

$$T_{curr} = (1/n)\sum\nolimits_{i=1}^{i=n} T_i \tag{5}$$

$$|T_{curr} - T_{ave}| < \delta \tag{6}$$

(6) can be used as a judgment formula where $\delta(\delta > 0)$ is the judgment factor set by VM owner's before the test. There might be Time-Stealer attack if the time difference were larger than δ .

In our experiments, we also apply more simple strategy that it's more efficient to detect abnormity by observation of VM CPU usage under CPU-bound workloads like Dhrystone. Generally, CPU-bound workloads consume a large proportion of CPU (82% on average through various tests) while only 2~3% under Time-Stealer attack cases. This can be considered as an alert that attacks like Time-Stealer may exist, but more accurate judgments and forensics require longer observations using the method we mentioned earlier.

4.2   Mitigation Measures

A. Be Careful to Pin

In the experimental scenario, pinning method is exploited on purpose of excluding the interferences of Domain0. However, we find that results can be various with different CPU affinity. Fig. 4 presents a test VMs sharing 2 cores and Fig. 5 shows CPU usage under 3 different conditions. From Fig. 5 (a), it can be concluded that Time-Stealer attack has no obvious effect under No-CPU-Affinity condition since they experience the same drop as with the growing number of VMs. From Fig. 5 (b), we can see that on 3 cores condition, attacker still occupies more CPU cycles though its plot drops when the number of VM increases. From Fig. 5 (c), the competition seems worse for victim VCPUs than (a) and (b), because the total CPU resources is restricted to one PCPU, however, this does not affect attacker's VCPU much. Obviously, CPU affinity does have some relations with Time-Stealer performance. A primary reason for this is that affinity restricts VCPU floating among the cores, offering a good chance for launching the attack, whereas in no affinity case, each PCPU's queue constantly changes and load can be balanced among all cores.

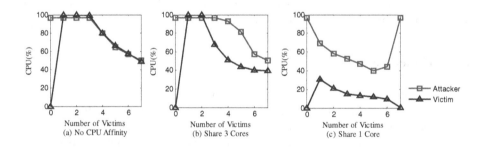

Fig. 5. Attack performance vs. CPU affinity

B. Take Care of Default Parameters

As Xen has made a great deal of improvement in VCPU scheduling, we should make the most of it to secure customer's VM. For example, Xen 4.1 provides a feature called cpupools, which allows users to divide PCPU into distinct groups [15]. Each pool has its entirely separate scheduler, which can protect our CPU cycles from be stolen by attackers from other cpupools.

In Xen 4.2, parameters like Schedule Rate Limiting (ratelimit_us) and Timeslice (tslice_ms) were added for easier control and customization. "ratelimit_us" is used to restrict the schedule rate to ensure the minimum amount of time which a VM is allowed to run without being preempted [15]. The default value is 1000 (that is, 1ms). This kind of parameter helps a lot to constrain Time-Stealer activities which depends on BOOST priority.

"tslice_ms" is Credit Scheduler timing period which is fixed at 30ms for the Xen4.1.2 Credit Scheduler. Remember that our attack scheme relies a lot on this fixed period. If this parameter can be changed, it'll take much longer before attackers find the real Timeslice. However, since its default setup is 30ms, we'd better not to use the default parameter.

5   Related Work

A lot of security analyses have been conducted on the traditional operating system scheduler; meanwhile, proof of concepts of timing attack were not received enough focus until recently. McCanne and Torek [5] showed the timing attack on BSD4.4 and created a uniform randomized sampling clock to estimate CPU utilization. Effectiveness of a similar attack on the Linux 2.6 scheduler has been proven by Tsafrir [6], which brought about receiving higher priority without consumption of CPU.

As I/O performance comes as a bottleneck for most hypervisors, researchers dedicate great efforts on improving I/O [16-20]. Most of them handle the problems like long-term fairness between various VMs such as CPU-bound, I/O bound, but malicious VM's activities are not taken into consideration. Recently, hypervisor security is attached a great importance [21]. Hosting many VMs onto one physical server brings various security threats to Cloud Computing, such as performance isolation violation [22-29], scheduler timing attacks [7-8], and side-channel attacks [30-31]. Several projects have demonstrated side-channel attacks through the shared LLC that can be used to extract information from co-resident VMs.

6   Conclusion

Scheduling processes in hypervisors like Xen, VMware ESXi, KVM play a significant role in multiplexing VMs as well as ensuring the fair share of CPU resources, which should be considered carefully in commercial services like Cloud Computing. Owing to vulnerabilities of schedulers, ordinary customers couldn't get the service they paid for if CPU cycles were stolen by a co-resident malicious VM.

We have demonstrated that this vulnerability still exists on the platform of Xen-Server6.0.2. Under our test scenario, a malicious VM using Time-Stealer scheme obtained up to 96.6% cycles of a PCPU regardless of competitions from other VMs and effects were more obvious with modified Dhrystone CPU benchmark. In addition, a feasible method to detect Time-Stealer existence without support of CP is proposed. Finally, we further illustrate that this kind of attack can be mitigated if proper configurations are made like changing the default parameters.

References

1. Amazon Elastic Compute Cloud, EC2 (2013), http://aws.amazon.com/ec2/
2. Vaughan-Nichols, S.J.: Virtualization Sparks Security Concerns. IEEE Computer Society 41, 13–15 (2008)

3. Ristenpart, T., Tromer, E., Shacham, H., Savage, S.: Hey, You, Get Off of My Cloud: Exploring Information Leakage in Third-Party Computer Clouds. In: ACM CCS, pp. 199–212 (2009)
4. Tanzim Khorshed, M., Shawkat Ali, A.B.M., et al.: A Survey on Gaps, Threat Remediation Challenges and Some Thoughts for Proactive Attack Detection in Cloud Computing. In: Future Generation Computer System, vol. 28, pp. 833–851 (2012)
5. McCanne, S., Torek, C.: A Randomized Sampling Clock for Cpu Utilization Estimation and Code Profiling. In: USENIX, pp. 387–394 (1993)
6. Tsafrir, D., Etsion, Y., Feitelson, D.G.: Secretly Monopolizing the CPU without Superuser Privileges. In: The 16th USENIX Security Symposium, pp. 239–256 (2007)
7. Zhou, F., Goel, M., Desnoyers, P.: Scheduler Vulnerabilities and Coordinated Attacks in Cloud Computing. In: IEEE International Symposium on Network Computing and Applications, pp. 123–130 (2011)
8. Zhou, F., Goel, M., Desnoyers, P.: Scheduler Vulnerabilities and Attacks in Cloud Computing. In: Distributed, Parallel, and Cluster Computing, pp. 1–23 (2011)
9. Williams, D.E., Garcia, J.: Virtualization with Xen, pp. 43–91. Syngress Publishing (2007)
10. Barham, P., Dragovic, B., Fraser, K., et al.: Xen and the Art of Virtualization. In: ACM SOSP, pp. 164–177 (2003)
11. Jaeger, D., Krentz, K.-F., Richly, M.: Xen Episode IV: The Guests still Strike Back. In: Cloud Computing Security Summer Term, pp. 1–15 (2011)
12. Chisnall, D.: The Definitive Guide to the Xen Hypervisor, pp. 217–223. Prentice Hall PTR (2007)
13. Cherkasova, L., Gupta, D., Vahdat, A.: Comparison of the Three CPU Schedulers in Xen. SIGMETERICS Performance Evaluation Reviews, 42–51 (2007)
14. Citix, Inc.: Citrix XenServer 6.0 Administrator's Guide. 1.1 Edition (2012)
15. Credit Scheduler (2013), http://wiki.xensource.com
16. Kim, H., Lim, H., Jeong, J., Jo, H., et al.: Task-aware Virtual Machine Scheduling for I/O Performance. In: ACM VEE, pp. 101–110 (2009)
17. Govindan, S., Nath, A., Das, A., Urgaonkar, B., Sivasubramaniam, A.: Xen and Co.: Communication-aware Cpu Scheduling for Consolidated Xen-based Hosting Platforms. In: ACM VEE, pp. 126–136 (2007)
18. Ongaro, D., Cox, A.L., Rixner, S.: Scheduling I/O in a Virtual Machine Monitor. In: ACM VEE, pp. 1–10 (2008)
19. Weng, C., Wang, Z., Li, M., et al.: The Hybrid Scheduling Framework for Virtual Machine Systems. In: ACM VEE, pp. 111–120 (2009)
20. Gulati, A., Merchant, A., Varma, P.J.: Mclock: Handling Throughput Variability for Hypervisor IO Scheduling. In: OSDI, pp. 1–7. USENIX, CA (2010)
21. Luo, S., Lin, Z., Chen, X., et al.: Virtualization Security for Cloud Computing Service. In: International Conference on CSC, pp. 174–179. CSC, Hong Kong (2011)
22. Bhadauria, M., McKee, S.A.: An Approach to Resource-aware Co-scheduling for CMPs. In: ICS, pp.189-199. ACM (2010)
23. Merkel, A., Stoess, J., Bellosa, F.: Resource-conscious Scheduling for Efficiency on Multicore Processors. In: EuroSys, pp. 153–166. ACM (2010)
24. Zhuravlev, S., Blagodurov, S., Fedorova, A.: Addressing Shared Resource Contention in Multicore Processors via Scheduling. In: ASPLOS, pp. 129–142. ACM (2010)
25. Raj, H., Nathuji, R., Singh, A., England, P.: Resource Management for Isolation Enhanced Cloud Services. In: CCSW, pp. 77–84. ACM, Chicago (2009)
26. Shieh, A., Kandula, S., Greenberg, A., Kim, C.: Seawall: Performance Isolation for Cloud Datacenter Networks. In: HotCloud, p. 1. USENIX (2010)

27. Verghese, B., Gupta, A., Rosenbum, M.: Performance Isolation: Sharing and Isolation in Share-memory Multiprocessors. In: ASPLOS, pp. 181–192. ACM (1998)
28. Cardenas, C., Boppana, R.V.: Detection and Mitigation of Performance Attacks in Multi-tenant Cloud Computing. In: ICACON (2012)
29. Varadarajan, V., Kooburat, T., et al.: Resource-Freeing Attacks: Improve Your Cloud Performance (at Your Neighber's Expense). In: ACM CCS, pp. 281–292 (2012)
30. Xu, Y.J., Bailey, M., Jahanjan, F., Joshi, K., Hiltunen, M., Schlichting, R.: An Exploration of L2 Cache Covert Channels in Virtualized Environments. In: CCSW, pp. 29–40. ACM, Chicago (2011)
31. Zhang, Y., Juels, A., Oprea, A., Reiter, M.K.: Homealone: Co-residency Detection in the Cloud via Side-channel Analysis. In: Security and Privacy IEEE Symposium, Berkeley, CA, pp. 313–328 (2011)

Detecting Malicious Co-resident Virtual Machines Indulging in Load-Based Attacks

Smitha Sundareswaran and Anna C. Squcciarini

College of Information Sciences and Technology
Pennsylvania State University
University Park, PA 16802

Abstract. Virtualization provides many benefits for Cloud environments, as it helps users obtain dedicated environments abstracted from the physical layer. However, it also introduces new vulnerabilities to the Cloud such as making it possible for malicious VMs to mount cross-VM attacks through cache based side channels. In this paper, we investigate load-based measurement attacks born specifically as a result of the virtualization in Cloud systems. We develop a framework to identify these attacks based on the observation that the events taking place during the attacks lead to an identifiable sequence of exceptions. We test the accuracy of our framework using the Microsoft Azure infrastructure.

1 Introduction

Cloud computing provides great benefits to the consumers through effective and efficient services in the form of infrastructure, platform, and software. These types of services are offered by all leading Cloud Computing Service Providers (CSPs), including Microsoft Azure, Amazon EC2, and Rackspace [1,3,15]. The advantages of such a service model are exemplified in the reduced operational costs, and efficient resource allocation and usage.

To date, security issues have remained the biggest thorns in the full blown adoption of these services [6,8,19]. Most of the current and recent work on Cloud computing security focuses on ensuring the privacy of general outsourcing techniques (e.g. [20]). Furthermore, recently there has been a interest in attacks which particularly target the weaknesses of the Cloud Computing architecture's general design [5,10], particularly due to the use of virtualization [8,9]. Virtualization of computing resources is a prominent feature of the Cloud providers, regardless of the type of service being offered (i.e. infrastructure, platform, and software). However, virtualization also produces unique side-channels for attacks, which cannot be controlled by usual information flow procedures. The virtual machines (VMs) may be malicious themselves [22] or the VMs' image may be compromised [23]. Precisely, recent work [2,16,25] found that Cloud systems leak information about location of the Cloud instances, letting attackers collocate an instance with another specific instance. Thus, if an attacker can cause a victim's Cloud instance to leak information covertly, and if covert channels with sufficient bandwidth exist, unauthorized leakage might be possible.

S. Qing et al. (Eds.): ICICS 2013, LNCS 8233, pp. 113–124, 2013.

In this paper, we focus on load-based measurement attacks, which are covert side-channel attacks born specifically as a result of the virtualization in Cloud systems [16]. In general, a covert channel attack is an attack which takes place when two entities or processes communicate with each other via channels that are hidden and therefore not subject to the general access control techniques. These channels can be formed by relying on time-based operations [2], such as opening and closing a file at a certain time, or can rely on techniques such as port knocking [24]. In the context of Clouds, these attacks are based on shared physical resources, such as the physical host's cache to create a side-channel in VMs that are otherwise segregated. Attacks based on covert-channels not only exploit co-residence, but also cover the basic requisites of identifying a particular VM, instantiating a VM co-resident with the VM of interest, and communicating data about the VM of interest. Other attacks, such as the VM conflicts arising due to competitors sharing a physical host described in [17], and the adversarial VMs presented in [25] are extensions on the same theme.

We design our attack detection framework based on empirical observations on the attacks patterns and behavior. We observe that by identifying the patterns of exceptions, and whether the number of exceptions in a given time period crosses a carefully crafted threshold, one can identify on-going attacks, and with further analysis, zoom in on the types of attacks being carried out. Our solution therefore relies on extracting and detecting event-based patterns, where the events are comprised of exceptions, and on establishing a baseline frequency for the total number of events occurring in an allotted time.

We test our system's accuracy using Windows' Azure architecture, where we co-host multiple VMs. We show our achieved accuracy even in increasing noise of busy VMs, which have a large number of active programs and tasks.

The paper is organized as follows. We discuss the related work in Section 2. Our threat model is discussed in Section 3. Section 4 describes the attacks we handle. The design of our framework is described in Section 5. Experimental results are discussed in Section 6. Finally, we conclude in Section 7.

2   Related Work

Since Ristenpart's seminal work [16], there has been a lot of interest in side-channel attacks. Accordingly, many have introduced new extensions of the original attacks and tackled some of them, or their variations [7, 11–13, 17, 25].

Cleemput [7] discusses compiler based mitigations for timing attacks. Similar to the approach discussed in this paper, the authors solution uses compiler instructions to look for attacks, in as much that some exceptions are issued by the compiler. The authors' proposed solution however does not consider VMs or co-resident systems, instead it focuses on loss of cryptographic secrets by timing attacks. A possible solution to load-measurement attacks is offered by Sun et al. [11], who consider the load sharing between co-resident virtual machines in a Cloud. They observe that two co-resident VMs may pose a "threat" to each other due to a need for common resources, which may enable each to learn secrets of the others. Kong et al [12] suggests a combination of hardware and software approaches to provide a solution to side-channel attacks. While they do not consider VMs or Clouds in particular, they propose using a special set of Load instructions that inform the software when the load-misses in the cache. As we show in the next sections, although all similar to our work in their intention, existing approaches are vastly different from ours. We are similar to Sun's work in terms of objective, but their primary focus is on conflict resolution through negotiation, rather than on detection. Kong's proposal also shares some similarities with our work, i.e. it seeks to eliminate cache based interferences, but yet differs vastly. Our idea is to exploit existing instructions as signals of an attack as opposed to Kong's approach, that is based on forming new ones.

A variation on this theme is offered by Choi and colleagues [4]. The authors discuss an authentication scheme which may be used for Cloud Computing systems. An authentication scheme of this kind is useful in providing the attacker with an identity, but it does nothing to prevent such attacks, and is therefore complementary to the scheme proposed in our work. In addition, side-channel analysis has been often used to mitigate problems due to co-residency, such as competitive organizations' VMs being co-resident or high loads on shared physical resources [13, 17, 25]. Also related to our methodology is work on software component thefts [21] from Wang. Wang and colleagues exploit the notion of dependencies among system calls to detect various attacks. We do not analyze system calls' dependencies in our approach, so as to focus on the events which lead to the system calls.

3   Threat Model

Our architecture is built to identify the attacks launched between tenants of co-existing VMs. We assume that all the VMs are compatible on a physical level, and they may run any applications intended by the tenant. The provider and its infrastructure are assumed to be trusted. That is, we do not consider attacks that rely on subversion of the Cloud's administrative functions. This in turn means that we trust any software that is run on the physical machines or the VMs that the Cloud hosts. Our threat model considers non-insider adversaries, who manage to get a VM hosted on the same physical machine as their victim's by chance or intentionally [16, 17]. We assume that a malicious party can run and control many instances in the Cloud, simply by leasing the required storage space. The targeted victims are tenants who run confidential services in the Cloud. Any data leakage, including data about the usage of the VMs, can breach the confidentiality of the victim. From the victims' point of view, the co-existing VMs on the physical machine could be benign, or malicious by attempting to find information about other co-existing VMs through the cache-based side-channel. Although a tenant can trust that his VM is not willfully malicious, the attacker can manipulate all shared physical resources at his own gain. Shared resources include CPU caches, branch target buffers, and network queues. By properly controlling and observing information gathered from these resources, information may be leaked unwittingly to the attacker. In particular, we focus on load-based co-residence detection as this type of attack is a common and well-know example of network probing attacks.

Notice that our model is a generalization of the threats discussed in the seminal works [16, 17], which discussed the load-variation attacks tackled in this work. In our threat model, however, we do not require an existing VM to have a conflict with a newly migrated VM, for the existing VM to be malicious (as in [17]). Further, different from [16], we do not differentiate between attackers who are interested in simply attacking any known hosted service, and attackers interested in attacking a particular victim service. Due to these differences, we no longer can depend on shared services to point out possible conflicts.

4   Covert Attacks

4.1   Attack Description

Load-based attacks require two steps: placement and extraction. Placement refers to the attacker placing their malicious VMs on the same physical machine as that of a victim. Extraction refers to extracting confidential information via a cross-VM attack using side-channels. Cross-VM information leakage is due to the sharing of physical resources (e.g., the CPU's data caches). In this work, we focus on extraction, assuming placement is given. A malicious VM can detect co-residence in many ways [16]. When the attacker has some knowledge of computational load variation on the target instance, no network-based detection techniques are needed. The attacker can actively cause load variation due to a publicly-accessible service running on the target (for example, HTTP, POP3 or FTP services). Publicly-accessible services are not suspect for an intrusion detection system as they normally are not access restricted. Hence, any accesses or measurements on these public services often remain unnoticed. In our work, we consider the existence of such publicly-accessible services as the primary condition for an attack. The attacker may also be able to detect co-residence without resorting to actively creating any load variations if he has a priori information about some relatively unique load variation on the target. For example, knowing that a certain website experiences heavy traffic from 9 am to 5 pm, and in the remaining time, no traffic or negligible traffic is experienced on a daily basis can provide useful a priori information for the attacker. In this case, based on the time of the day, an attacker can detect the co-residence of a VM by identifying the physical hosts which experience a similar load variation. The difficulty (or ease) of detection would be based on the comprehensiveness of the apriori information.

One of the best known ways for accurate measurement of cache usage is based on three main functions: *prime, probe and trigger* [16]. *Priming* consists of reading a contiguous buffer B of size b. The buffer B is located on the CPU cache of the physical host. b is large enough that a significant portion of one of the lower level caches (L1, L2 or L3) on the physical host is filled by the contents of buffer B. The buffer B is read in s-byte offsets where s is the size of the cache.

The next step of load measurement is *trigger*, which is busy looping. Busy looping is a technique in which a process repeatedly checks if a condition is true. The attacking VM busy loops until the CPU counter cycle jumps by a large value, so that is allows enough time for the processes of the other VMs to run. Thus, the cache is filled by data accessed by the victims. The final step is *probing*, which consists of reading B again at s-byte offsets. When carrying out the probe by reading b/s memory locations of B, the attacker uses a pseudorandom order, and the pointer-chasing technique described in [18], as using the pseudorandom order prevents the CPU's hardware prefetcher from hiding the access latency. The time of the final step's read gives the load sample, where the load sample is measured in number of CPU cycles.

Identifying whether or not a VM is co-located prepares the ground for the attacker to mount more intrusive attacks, such as colluding with a rogue program on the co-resident VM even if other channels of communications are stopped. Further, knowing that a specific VM is co-resident allows the attacker to find some meta data about the owner of the VM: an attacker can correlate the service hosted on the VM with the name of a company running the service. This not only tells the attacker the victim's preferred Cloud provider, it also allows her to identify the regions in which the victim is running certain services.

4.2   Preliminary Evaluation

In order to gauge a better understanding of the attacks' dynamics, we recreated the scenario required for co-residence detection. The testbed consisted of 5 Windows Server 2008R2 SP1 based VMs [1], where each of the VMs had their TCP ports 80 enabled to allow HTTP services. Out of these 5 VMs, 3 of them were simply bystanders used to create noise. One of the VMs functioned as the attacker VM, while another was the victim VM. The victim additionally hosted an Apache Tomcat application server, with a single webpage. Because load-based detection can occur in many ways, we executed the attacks under various settings. First, to detect whether two VMs were co-resident, we created a high load on one of the VMs (the target VM) using the LoadUI tool [14]. LoadUI is a utility commonly used for load testing, and is being used to to simulate the attacker VM in a systematic and rigorous fashion. The attacker VM collected 100 load samples on a public HTML page of size 10KB both during the load variation and when the load variation was not done. It tracked the variation in size of the load samples: if the target and the attacker VM were co-resident the load samples taken during the load induced by the LoadUI tool were larger.

To communicate with a co-resident VM (assuming all other communication channels are closed), we rely on the simple cache-covert channel attack wherein the attacker sending the message idles while transmitting "0", but frantically access the memory to transmit "1". The receiver checks the latencies by collecting a load sample or accessing a memory block of his own. While communicating

---

[1] We ensured that the VMs were co-resident by checking their PhysicalHostName through their registry keys.

with a rogue program can be done simply by using load variations, where a high
load indicates a "1" and a low load indicates a "0", a noisy channel can reduce
the efficiency of this method of transmission. To overcome the effects of noise,
the rogue program needs to be able to cause a sufficiently high load to be "heard"
over the channel by the colluding attacker. Empirically, we can see that a load
spike above 100000 CPU cycles is necessary for a clear co-residence detection.
Further, a process generally crashes when the process has a utilization of 67%-
70%. Our systems crashed upon reaching 8100000 CPU cycles, when channel
noise was created by loading 3 other VMs. The noise was measured by taking
load samples from the cache at any one of these VMs. So long as the load spike
of over 100000 CPU cycles can be achieved without crashing the loaded process,
the simple method of load variations to transmit a message works well.

In case of a high probability of crash due to noisy channels, the use of the
prime+probe+trigger method is preferable. To test the detection of co-residence
on a noisy channel, we simulated a channel with high noise by having 5 co-
resident VMs, out of which one was the attacker VM, and one was the victim,
while the others were just meant to create noise. We had the co-resident VMs
performing I/O operations, while the attacker VM measured took 100 load samples on a public HTML pages varying in size from 1Kb to 10 KB over a period of
time varying from 12 seconds (for the 1KB page) to 120 seconds (for the 10KB
pages). The measurements were then paused for a period of 30 sec. after which
they were repeated while simultaneously making numerous HTTP get requests
from a third system to the target. The attack was successful in that the malicious
VM was able to detect the co-residence when the HTTP requests were made.

These initial tests provided us with insights on the scope and effectiveness of
each of these attacks. We observed that there is always a pre-set sequence of
events that yields to an attack. All the events are observable from the physical
host in the form of exceptions.

5   Design of Co-residency Attack Detector

Our initial experiments confirmed that each attack instance incur into a notable
load increase accompanied by a given pattern of system calls and exceptions.
Accordingly, our solution consists of few main steps: (1) collection of system
calls occurring at the physical host, and the exceptions which may be specific to
the attacks, to (a) identify the VM causing the exception, and the process that
spawned the exception, and (b) identify whether conditions sufficient for the
attack exist, and (2) processing of these exceptions to detect the load-variation
attacks discussed in Section 4. Each of the steps is associated with a logic module,
which we refer to as **Observer** and **Defender**, in what follows. The **Observer**
and **Defender** are implemented as part of a trusted VM.

5.1   Observer

The Observer component is designed to dynamically collect metrics indicative of
suspicious load variations. We specifically focus on tracking network processes,

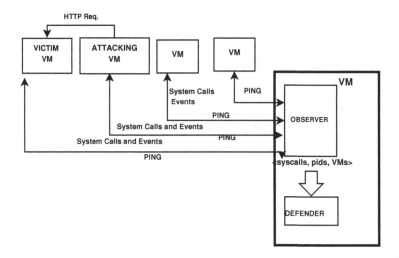

Fig. 1. System Design

their CPU loads and spawned system calls. Hence, the Observer has three main tasks: (1) extract systems calls and interrupts of monitored processes, (2) map the identified system calls and interrupts to specific programs from the specific VMs which generated them, and (3) determine whether the conditions necessary for an attack to be carried out co-exist. In order to extract and map the system calls, the Observer spawns multiple tracing threads, instantiated by means of debugging tools, such as Linux strace and WinGB in Windows.

To quantify the necessary conditions for an attack, the Observer uses some baseline system metrics on CPU utilization by processes observed in absence of attacks, as well as the expected number of system calls experienced by any given process. Specifically, a training phase is performed first, during which processes are monitored under minimum activity for over 72 hours (or more), such that each process activity remains lower than 1%. We observe the number of system calls per second for each process, denoted as $SysC_t^{PID}$, with PID denoting a specific process. Obviously, the base number of system calls per second is unique to each process. Nevertheless, we observed the following pattern. Given a process PID, let $SysC_t$ be the base rate per second, and let CPU_UT its percentage of CPU utilization.

$$AVG_t^{PID} = \begin{cases} SysC_t + 0.02 * SysC_t & \text{if } CPU\_UT < 20\% \\ SysC_t + (SysC_t * 2^{(CPU\_UT-0.2)/5})\frac{CPU\_UT}{5} & \text{if } CPU\_UT > 20\% \end{cases}$$
$$(1)$$

The above equation indicates that a general 2% rate increase exists when the process activity increases up to 20%. Above 20% CPU utilization, the rate starts exponentially increasing, for each 5% increase in process activity. When the number of system calls increases exponentially, the monitoring becomes exponentially difficult too. Based on the above, we determine CPU utilization threshold, denoted as τ, which ranges from 10% to 20% for a given process. τ denotes the point to start the monitoring and is chosen so that the attack cannot be hidden in the explosion of system calls. In addition, the system calls generated by each process are then averaged over a time interval T according to Equation 1, to AVG_T^{PID}. The gathered data is stored with the trusted VM where the observer is hosted.

Upon gathering sufficient training data on all possible network processes triggered by the VMs, the Observer labels as suspicious each process PID if (a) the CPU activity is above a given threshold τ, and (b) PID is a network process. Specifically, with respect to (b), upon crossing the τ CPU threshold activity, the Observer checks the event logs which are downloaded from the monitored VM to the trusted VM hosting the Observer and Defender, to identify if a particular external host or a group of hosts has been trying to ping or otherwise activate the process. If the increase in activity is indeed caused by external systems, the Observer alerts the Defender to check for possible attack patterns.

5.2 Defender

Once it receives the IDs of the VMs, the corresponding suspected processes and the exceptions from the Observer, the Defender starts searching for attack-specific patterns. It specifically starts monitoring for patterns if the network processes reach a high load due to network events, per the information obtained from the Observer. Each pattern consists of a particular sequence of exceptions, wherein both the type of exceptions observed, their order, as well as the frequency of particular system calls within the sequence matter. Of course, system calls may be suppressed by a sophisticated attacker at the originating VM. Hence, before searching for such patterns the Defender completes a sanity check, by verifying whether the observed $AVG_{\overline{T}}^{PID}$ over a normalized time interval $\overline{T}$ matches the corresponding $AVG_{\overline{T}}^{PID}$ stored in the system during training, per each suspicious PID. If no system calls are suspected suppressed, the pattern search starts. Otherwise, the process halts and a suspicious activity is detected.

As discussed in Section 4, load-variation attacks can be carried out in multiple ways, all of which result in different patterns of system calls. Due to this "polymorphic" nature of load-variation attacks a single approach may not suit all the possible ways according to which the load-variation is measured. Therefore, similar to an intrusion detection system, it is possible to implement various pattern recognition methods or security policies, zeroing-in the different forms of these attacks. We provide the discussion of two sample patterns that can be detected. The selected examples are representative of (1) the load-variation technique which requires the least effort from the attacker end, and (2) the most well-known load variation, based on prime, probe and trigger.

Load Variations by simple HTTP requests The Defender checks for patterns that involve socket creation, connection acceptance and socket deletion. These calls include **sys_accept** (Accepts 3-way TCP handshake), **sys_poll** (waits for http request), and **sys_read** (reads payload). **sys_socketcall** is often seen during various stages of a socket based connection as it supports a number of sub-commands to create, open and close the socket. **sys_accept** and **sys_poll** are

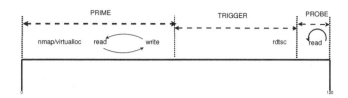

Fig. 2. Typical pattern of a Probe, Prime, Trigger Load-based attack

seen early on during the socket creation stage. In case of an attack, these calls are repeated multiple times in quick succession within a short time period due to the large number of sockets created for causing a load variation. In particular, the larger the number of sockets created in a given time unit (roughly 120 seconds), the greater the chance of an attack.

Probe-Prime-Trigger Method The Defender uses the mapping provided by the Observer to identify the suspicious exceptions generated in the prime, probe or trigger phases of load measurement. The pattern followed by load-based attacks includes a combination of system calls and interrupts generated during load measurement. Precisely, `mmap` for Linux, `virtualloc` for Windows, `read()`, `write()`, `malloc` and `rdtsc` are used. No additional interrupts or system calls are needed. When load measurement is being carried out, these exceptions occur continuously over a time period of 90 to 120 seconds depending on the attack duration: the `mmap` call or the `virtualloc`, followed by the `read()`, and then the `write()` occur repeatedly (the sequence occurs over 5 to 10 times due to repeated priming) during the first half, followed by a long gap after which another `rdtsc` calls occur to signal the trigger. The `rdtsc` is then followed by repeated `read()` to signal the probe phase. This pattern is shown in Fig. 2

Note that the challenge of pattern detection lies in the fact that these system calls generated in any variant of the attacks occur during normal operations of the VM also. The detection of some variants, such as the one using prime probe and trigger is more accurate (see Section 6) because the attacker has to carry out these steps within a set time and in a given order, generating a more recognizable pattern, than say just HTTP (or FTP or POP3) requests. While HTTP requests occur every day, the probability of seeing the steps of prime probe and trigger in the wild are lesser than seeing a HTTP request.

6   Experimental Evaluation

In this Section we discuss the tests performed to validate our framework's accuracy, and scalability. The tests were performed on Azure's infrastructure [3]. The testbed includes 5 Windows Servers, and is described in Section 4.2. One of server implemented the Observer and Defender, and is assumed trusted. The main goal of evaluation on Azure was to ascertain the detection accuracy during an attack in a noisy channel. The channel noise was varied roughly in steps of about 50000 CPU cycles (it is not possible to accurately control the noise level) from 200000 to 900000 cycles. Channel noise was created by loading 3 out of the 5 co-hosted VMs. The noise was measured by taking load samples from the cache at any one of these 3 VMs.

First, we conducted two experiments: The first set of experiments was aimed at detecting the accuracy of co-residence detection using the simple load-variation technique. Channel noise was generated by the 3 co-hosted VMs by running multiple subsequent programs on each VM. In the first 346 ms in CPU time, the VMs execute in parallel a program which performed route finding algorithm, so as to cause excessive file reads and writes. In the following 346 ms of CPU time, in each of the 3 VMs, using LoadUI we simulate 100 users' activities on a 10KB Web page. Finally, both the route algorithm and the LOADUI users activities were executed for the remaining 346 ms/CPU. We varied the threshold of detection τ from 20% to 10%. For each set threshold, we increased the channel noise as described above. In all of our experiments, we had no false positives, but rather had a decreasing number of false negatives as we decreased the threshold. Precisely, with τ set at 20% and 18%, we reported 5 false negatives when then channel noise was higher than 620000 CPU cycles. Henceforth, the overall accuracy was low, only 58%. With τ set at 16% and 14% the accuracy increased to 66.7%. Our best results are obtained when $\tau = 10\%$, wherein 83.3% accuracy was achieved.

The second set of experiments used the prime+probe+trigger to carry out the load variations. The same experimental settings were used. As for the experiment above, we tested various detection thresholds, from 20% to 10%. The overall accuracy is consistently higher than the simple load variation attack, for all cases. Accuracy ranges from 66.7% for $\tau = 20\%$ to over 90% (for $\tau = 10\%$). All of the errors were false negative, and reported when the noise was 670000 or above. The only false negative reported with $\tau = 10\%$ was experienced when the channel was at its highest, above 880000. The improvement in detection accuracy occurs due to the unique pattern of system calls that occurs during the prime, probe and trigger phases (see Figure 2).

We then executed a final experiment wherein we tested how sensitive our mechanism is to high volume of noise, and whether and to what extent this can lead to false positives. The final test was conducted on a similar set up as the other two tests, except this time there was no attacking VM. We had three executions: in one run the load variations were caused using LoadUI, in the second run they were caused using the route planning algorithm, and in the third run either the LoadUI or the route planning algorithm were used. The load was again varied from 2000000 to 8800000 over an average of 346 ms in CPU cycles. τ was varied too, between 10% and 20%. Results are reported in Table 1. We notice that the higher τ, the lower the rate of false positives. Intuitively, this is explained as one of the VMs causes a load variation, meeting one of the conditions for a probable attack earlier in case of a low threshold. Therefore, there is always a tradeoff between the number of false positive and false negatives, and the percentage above minimum must be decided according to which is more tolerable.

Table 1. Deceptive loads: load variation was divided amongst all the 4 co-resident VMs. 1 denotes a correct true negative, 0 denotes a false positive.

CPU/Threshold	20%	18%	16%	14 %	12%	10%
200,000	1	1	1	1	1	1
230,000	1	1	1	1	1	1
300,000	1	1	1	1	1	1
340,000	1	1	1	1	1	1
420,000	1	1	1	1	1	1
480,000	1	1	1	1	1	1
520,000	1	1	1	1	1	1
570,000	1	1	1	1	1	1
620,000	1	1	1	1	1	1
670,000	1	1	1	0	0	0
740,000	1	1	0	0	0	0
790,000	0	0	0	0	0	0
840,000	0	0	0	0	0	0

7 Conclusion

In this paper, we studied covert side-channel attacks that arise as a consequence of virtualization in Cloud systems. We proposed a framework to identify load-based attacks according to our analysis of system calls generated by the attacker and the victim. Our evaluation, conducted on a real Cloud testbed, demonstrates the accuracy of our approach. We plan to extend our architecture to extract more probing patterns, and additional polymorphic forms of existing attacks.

Acknowledgement. The work from Squicciarini was partly funded under the auspices of the National Science Foundation Project # 1250319.

References

1. Amazon Web Services, http://aws.amazon.com/
2. Aviram, A., Hu, S., Ford, B., Gummadi, R.: Determinating timing channels in compute clouds. In: Proceedings of the 2010 ACM Workshop on Cloud Computing Security Workshop, CCSW 2010, pp. 103–108. ACM (2010)
3. Chappell, D.: Windows Azure (2009),
   http://www.microsoft.com/windowsazure/resources/
4. Choi, T., Acharya, H.B., Gouda, M.G.: Is that you? Authentication in a network without identities. Int. J. Secur. Netw. 6(4), 181–190 (2011)
5. Christodorescu, M., Sailer, R., Schales, D.L., Sgandurra, D., Zamboni, D.: Cloud security is not (just) virtualization security: a short paper. In: Proceedings of the 2009 ACM Workshop on Cloud Computing Security, pp. 97–102. ACM (2009)
6. Cisco. Cloud Security: Choosing the right email security deployment (2010)
7. Cleemput, J.V., Coppens, B., De Sutter, B.: Compiler mitigations for time attacks on modern x86 processors. ACM Trans. Archit. Code Optim. 23, 1–23 (2012)

8. Cochrane, N.: Security experts ponder the cost of cloud computing (2010), http://www.itnews.com.au/news/174941,security-experts-ponder-the-cost-of-cloud-computing.aspx

9. Hay, B., Nance, K., Bishop, M.: Storm clouds rising: Security challenges for iaas cloud computing. In: Hawaii International Conference on System Sciences, pp. 1–7 (2011)

10. Kandukuri, B.R., Paturi, V.R., Rakshit, A.: Cloud security issues. In: IEEE International Conference on Services Computing, pp. 517–520 (2009)

11. Kong, J., Aciicmez, O., Seifert, J.-P., Zhou, H.: Deconstructing new cache designs for thwarting software cache-based side channel attacks. In: Proceedings of the 2nd ACM Workshop on Computer Security Architectures, pp. 25–34. ACM (2008)

12. Kong, J., Aciicmez, O., Seifert, J.-P., Zhou, H.: Hardware-software integrated approaches to defend against software cache-based side channel attacks. In: High Performance Computer Architecture, pp. 393–404. IEEE (February 2009)

13. Okamura, K., Oyama, Y.: Load-based covert channels between xen virtual machines. In: Proceedings of the 2010 ACM Symposium on Applied Computing, SAC 2010, pp. 173–180. ACM (2010)

14. Ole: loadui: A uniquely cool approach to interactive distributed load testing. In: DevoXX - The Java Community Conference (2010)

15. Rackspace, http://www.rackspace.com/

16. Ristenpart, T., Tromer, E., Shacham, H., Savage, S.: Hey, you, get off of my cloud: exploring information leakage in third-party compute clouds. In: Proceedings of the 16th ACM Conference on Computer and Communications Security, pp. 199–212. ACM (2009)

17. Sun, P., Shen, Q., Chen, Y., Wu, Z., Zhang, C., Ruan, A., Gu, L.: Poster: LBMS: load balancing based on multilateral security in cloud. In: Proc. of the 18th ACM Conference on Computer and Communications Security, pp. 861–864. ACM (2011)

18. Tromer, E., Osvik, D.A., Shamir, A.: Efficient cache attacks on aes, and countermeasures. J. Cryptol. 23(2), 37–71 (2010)

19. VanTil, S.: Study on cloud computing security: Managing firewall risks (2011), http://resource.onlinetech.com/study-on-cloud-computing-security-managing-firewall-risks/

20. Wang, Q., Wang, C., Li, J., Ren, K., Lou, W.: Enabling public verifiability and data dynamics for storage security in cloud computing. In: ESORICS, pp. 355–370 (2009)

21. Wang, X., Jhi, Y.-C., Zhu, S., Liu, P.: Behavior based software theft detection. In: Proceedings of the 16th ACM Conference on Computer and Communications security, CCS 2009, pp. 280–290. ACM (2009)

22. Wang, Y., Wei, J.: Viaf: Verification-based integrity assurance framework for mapreduce. In: Proc. of the 2011 IEEE 4th International Conference on Cloud Computing, CLOUD 2011, pp. 300–307. IEEE Computer Society (2011)

23. Wei, J., Zhang, X., Ammons, G., Bala, V., Ning, P.: Managing security of virtual machine images in a cloud environment. In: Proceedings of the 2009 ACM Workshop on Cloud Computing Security, CCSW 2009, pp. 91–96. ACM (2009)

24. Zander, S., Armitage, G., Branch, P.: A survey of covert channels and countermeasures in computer network protocols. Commun. Surveys Tuts. 9(3), 44–57 (2007)

25. Zhang, Y., Juels, A., Oprea, A., Reiter, M.K.: Homealone: Co-residency detection in the cloud via side-channel analysis. In: Proceedings of the 2011 IEEE Symposium on Security and Privacy, SP 2011, pp. 313–328. IEEE Computer Society (2011)

A Covert Channel Using Event Channel State on Xen Hypervisor*

Qingni Shen[1,2,**], Mian Wan[1,2], Zhuangzhuang Zhang[1,2], Zhi Zhang[1,2],
Sihan Qing[1,2,3], and Zhonghai Wu[1,2]

[1] School of Software and Microelectronics, Peking University, Beijing 102600, China
[2] MoE Key Lab of Network and Software Assurance, Peking University,
Beijing 100871, China
[3] Institue of Software, Chinese Academy of Sciences, Beijing 100190, China
qingnishen@ss.pku.edu.cn

Abstract. Covert channel between virtual machines is one of serious threats to cloud computing, since it will break the isolation of guest OSs. Even if a lot of work has been done to resist covert channels, new covert channels still emerge in various manners. In this paper, we introduce event channel mechanism in detail. Then we develop a covert channel called CCECS(Covert Channel using Event Channel State) and implement it on Xen hypervisor. Finally we quantitatively evaluate CCECS and discuss the possible mitigation methods. Results show that it can achieve larger bit rate than most existing covert channels.

Keywords: Covert Channel, Virtualization, Event Channel.

1 Introduction

Thanks to the resource sharing, both cloud computing and virtualization give the users an illusion of "occupying resources independently".Nevertheless, resource sharing is a double-edged sword. It makes virtualization have a inherent feature - multitenancy, placing multiple virtual machines(VM) of distinct customers upon the same physical hardware. Therefore, the privacy and security of customers' information may be compromised[1]. Isolation, one important function of virtualization, is designed to eliminate this kind of threat. Due to isolation, a VM cannot access the resources of others. Even if a VM is exploited or manipulated by an attacker, it will not affect the other VMs within the same host.

However, this isolation has been proved not strong enough(e.g. covert and side channels)[2]. Covert Channel[3] is a mechanism that is not intended to transfer sensitive message, violating security policies specified by system . Covert channel is actively sending data, while side channel[4] is passively observing information. At present, several covert channels have been discovered, but the mediums they used are not the same.

---

* This work is supported by National Natural Science Foundation of China (No. 61232005, 61073156, 61170282).
** Corresponding author.

S. Qing et al. (Eds.): ICICS 2013, LNCS 8233, pp. 125–134, 2013.

Ristenpart et al. [5] first exposed cloud computing to covert channel attacks. They had implemented an L2 cache covert channel in Amazon EC2. The bit rate of it was just 0.2 bps(bit-per-second), a mere fraction above the minimum standard of 0.1 bps [3]. Xu et al. [6] refined the communication model of L2 Cache Covert Channel and the channel arrived at considerably higher bandwidth(3.20 bps) in EC2. On the basis of previous work, Wu et al. [7] redesigned the data transmission scheme and exploited the memory bus as medium. At last, their new covert channel achieved a transmission rate of 107 plus or minius 39 bps in EC2, and 700bps in house. Except for covert channels using CPU cache, there were some other covert channels using other resource(such as CPU load [8], core alternation [9], sharing memory [10],[11], *mfn2pfn* table [12], network [13]) as medium. None of the covert channel above had considered event channel as a vehicle. In fact, the channel via event channel states is feasible and even more dangerous than most of the covert channels in virtualized environment.

In this paper, we analyze the event channel mechanism in Xen and develop a reliable covert channel to transfer information between two virtual machines. We verify the feasibility and effectiveness of the covert channel using event channel state(CCECS) for data leakage through a set of experiments. The bandwidth can achieve about 13Kbps. Then we discuss the method to mitigate the threat.

2   Background

Xen is an open-source VMM(Virtual Machine Monitor), also called *hypervisor*[14], that widely used in the cloud computing industry. For example, Amazon's EC2 (Elastic Compute Cloud)[15] adopts Xen as its virtualization technology. It is a software layer that sits between the host hardware and the VMs(Virtual Machine). It partitions hardware resources and offers them to the VM as virtual resource. Aside from that, it also controls access to I/O devices.

In Xen, VMs is also called *domains*. When Xen boots, it first create a special domain called Dom0, which has elevated privileges. It helps Xen to create, destroy, configure, migrate, save and restore VMs, and controls VM's access to I/O devices.

DomU, VMs created by Dom0, is more restrictive. Since Xen is a kind of paravirtualization, DomU cannot perform any privileged operations. For instance, instead of accessing the devices directly, DomU has to transmit device request through the front-end driver to the back-end driver in Dom0. Then Dom0 access the real devices as an agent. Unlike Dom0, users can have an arbitrary number of domU guests.

As a hypervisor, Xen has to track and control the running situation of each domain. And in some cases such as migration, communication between domains is necessary. Xen hypervisor offers 3 communication mechanisms. They are hypercall, sharing memory and event channel. Since our channel uses event channel, thus we will just introduce event channel mechanism in next section.

2.1   Event Channel Mechanism in Xen

Event channel is an asynchronous notifications mechanism within Xen. Event channels cooperate with ring buffers in shared memory pages to accomplish the message transmission between the front and back ends of split device drivers. In Xen, events are notifications that are delivered from hypervisor to domains, or between domains. Each event's content is one bit of information that indicates its occurrence. Events can divide into 4 categories: *physical IRQ, virtual IRQ(VIRQ), interprocessor interrupts(IPIs), interdomain events.* Physical IRQ is used for the communicating with hardware. Guest in Dom0 or domain that is authorized to access device will set up physical IRQs to event channel mapping for diverse devices. Because of its paravirtualization, this is done by a hypercall instead of BIOS calls. Virtual IRQs resemble physical IRQs, but are related to virtual devices. Interdomain events involve two domains and include two stages. First, Domain A allocates a new event channel(port) as an unbound channel and grants Domain B with the permission to bind to it. Then, Domain B allocates a new channel and binds it to the remote domain(Domain A)'s port. When the connection is built, either domain can send an event to the local port. Moreover, the connection is duplex. The fourth kind of events, the interprocessor interrupts, are equivalent to *intradomain events*. It can be viewed as a special case of interdomain events where both local and remote domain are the same one. It can be used to communicate between vCPUs in the same guest.

In Xen, every domain can own its own event channels. when a event channel is allocated, a port is used to identify the channel. Besides port, a event channel has some other attributes, mainly including the state and other variables related to certain state. All the possible states of event channels is listed in Table 1.

Table 1. States and Statuses of Event Channels

State Constant	Status Constant	Comments
ECS_FREE	EVTCHNSTAT_closed	Not in use now
ECS_RESERVED	EVTCHNSTAT_closed	Not in use now
ECS_UNBOUND	EVTCHNSTAT_unbound	Waiting inter-dom connect
ECS_INTERDOMAIN	EVTCHNSTAT_interdomain	Connected to a remote Dom
ECS_PIRQ	EVTCHNSTAT_pirq	Bound to a physical IRQ
ECS_VIRQ	EVTCHNSTAT_virq	Bound to a virtual IRQ
ECS_IPI	EVTCHNSTAT_ipi	Bound for IPC

Like other operations of event channels, building interdomain event channels is done by calling the hypercall **HYPERVISOR_event_channel_op**. When DomA wants to communicate with DomB, DomB initially acquires an unbound event channel by calling the operation "**EVTCHNOP_alloc_unbound**" in the hypercall. During the allocating, its state is set as **ECS_UNBOUND**. And its port is stored in XenStore where DomA can consult. Besides, the channel creator specifies which domain is authorized to bind to it. Next, DomA will also obtain an allocated channel. After that, DomA accesses XenStore and retrieves the port number, then binds itself by calling the operation "EVTCHNOP_bind_interdomain" in the hypercall. Then the two event channels will constitute a duplex connection. If Dom A wants to send events to Dom B, it will just send them to local event channel. Both channels' state changes to ECS_INTERDOMAIN. Either of the channels has *remote_dom* and *remote_port* attributes pointing to each other.

As long as interdomain communication is complete, either domain can close its own event channel. Specifically, DomA decides to close its channel by calling the operation "EVTCHNOP_close" in the hypercall. During the closing process, DomB's event channel's state restores as ECS_UNBOUND. Moreover, DomA's state alters as ECS_FREE. The state change of event channel during a connection life cycle between DomA and DomB is described in figure 1.

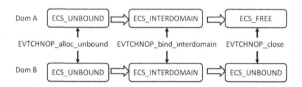

Fig. 1. State Change of Event Channel during Connection Life Cycle

During the use of event channels, it might be necessary to retrieve the state of them. However, the *state* variable cannot be accessed by guests directly. Guests have to inquire the *status* by calling the operation "EVTCHNOP_status" in the hypercall. From Table 1, we can see the differences between state and status.

3   Covert Channel Using Event Channel State

3.1   Threat Scenario

In a host of cloud environment where Xen is installed, any domain may store some sensitive information such as the user's password and identity information. We assume that an attacker is capable of injecting a spyware such as Trojan into the guest in a domain. According to the isolation between domains, other domains do not have the ability to access it or eavesdrop it. Thus, the user or the VMM administrator usually adopts network traffic monitoring software that monitor how the data stream transmit, specific-configured firewall or IDS(Intrusion Detection Systems) that inspect the data packets transport in the network, VPN(Virtual Private Network)that encrypts the data, to prevent data leakage. Since the presence of these facilities, the spyware could not send the sensitive data through Internet. Once there is abnormal data stream sent to outside, the VMM administrator will notice or receive an alert. However, we find that there is still a special information transmission path the attacker can make use of. In our scenario, this domain owns sensitive information is called *Sender Domain*. Like the normal users, the spyware owner can rent(having not controlled

Dom0) or create(having controlled Dom0) a domain beside the *Sender Domain* on the same hypervisor, that is to say, co-resident with the *Sender Domain*. We presume the co-residence is always possible[16]. In most cases, *Receiver Domain* is controlled by the attacker, so it doesn't enable the additional facilities like *Sender Domain*. The spyware in *Sender Domain* sends user's private or secret information to an unrecognized covert channel(e.g. CCECS, covert channel using event channel state), through which a program in *Receiver Domain* can acquire the data and send it to the attacker's host through Internet.

3.2 A New Kind of Covert Channel

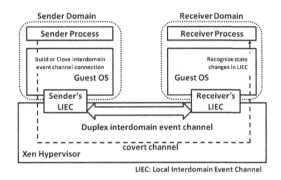

Fig. 2. Structure of CCECS

As depicted in Figure 2, the new CCECS(Covert Channel using Event Channel State) is different from duplex interdomain event channel(see section 2.2).

According to the event channel mechanism mentioned above, the sender process runs a spyware program in the *sender domain* which can read the sensitive information that attackers are interested in. But the receiver process in the *receiver domain* of the attacker is not granted to share the secrets, though the event channel is permitted between guests. In order to construct the CCECS, the sender process would send sensitive information by building or closing interdomain event channel connection to local end of the connection, which will change the state of local end. Meanwhile, the receiving end of the connection could change its state synchronously. So the receiver process could acquire the secrets by recognizing the changes of the local end's state(see figure 1).This covert channel exists between guests independently of the domain(dom0 or domU).

3.3 Request Hypercall from DomU

In most cases, OS kernel runs in Ring 1 can use the hypercall services directly. However, the guest application running in Ring 3 may need to request hypercalls.

Fortunately, Xen kernel offers a privileged command driver `/proc/xen/privcmd`[1] to invoke hypercalls. Applications in user space can request hypercalls by calling *ioctl* function with necessary parameters. Thus, it is feasible for process in DomU to operate event channels.

3.4   Communication Protocol

In this section, we describe the communication protocol of CCECS. The sender and the receiver need to act in a synchronized manner. Therefore, both processes must synchronize the timing of communication before sending bit-streams. When an interdomain connection is constituted by calling hypercall, both end's state is `ECS_INTERDOMAIN`. When one end closes, remote end is set to `ECS_UNBOUND` and its own state is `ECS_FREE`. After analyzing the source code of Xen, we know that the state-setting instructions are separated by a few lines of instructions. Thus, in terms of the powerful computing capability of host CPUs, the time interval is so short that it is negligible. Once the sender end's state changes, the receiver's alters correspondingly. We can see the process in Figure 3.

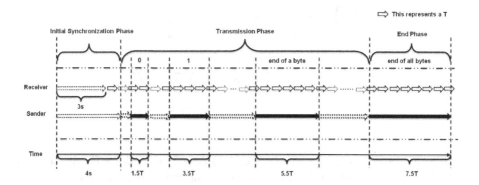

Fig. 3. Communication Protocol of CCECS

Initial Synchronization Phase. In Figure 3, the initial synchronization phase shows our timing setting for the sender and receiver. Because building interdomain event channel is done by hypercall, so it takes longer time than normal function calls, which execution time is about `1s`. Empirically, we let the receiver dectect its own state every `ns`(e.g. `3s`) to ensure that the synchronization request from the sender is always not missed. And we let the sender wait `(n+1)s`(e.g. `4s`) before sending data to ensure enough time to switch receiver's console to the process of receiving data. During the phase, it includes three operations in order: First, the receiver domain should request an event channel and let the sender domain be its remote end, and then its initial state is

---

[1] The driver have been re-engineered as /dev/xen/privcmd since the Linux 3.3 was released.

ECS_UNBOUND,that is the EVTCHNSTAT_unbound for the process in the end. Second, the sender should request a event channel for the interdomain connection with the remote end of receiver domain. When the new event channel is allocated, it will retrieve the remote port number and bind itself to the local port. Once the binding is finished, both end's state becomes ECS_INTERDOMAIN, that is the EVTCHNSTAT_interdomain for the processes in both ends. Third, the receiver would check whether the state of its local event channel is EVTCHNSTAT_interdomain. If that is the case, it indicates both ends share the same timing of the following operations and the transimission phase starts out.

Transmission Phase. After synchronization, the sender and receiver enter the communication phase, in which they communicate $8n(n \geq 1)$ bits information. To stimulate the common situation, the transmission includes file operations. Apart from that, to be flexible, we let both entities share a value T(T μs is configured by an attacker, we test some minimal value of T in section 4). The protocol require a short timespan to convey one bit. The timespan is determined by how long some state of event channel lasts. As long as the local end does the operation EVTCHOP_close(or EVTCHOP_bind_interdomain) of HYPERVISOR_event_channel_op succesfully, it means the sender has sent the bit data '1'(or '0'). Meanwhile, if sending bit '0', the sender suspends its process for 1.5T μs, which is more than 1 time but less than 2 times of T. Otherwise, if sending bit '1', the sender suspends its process for 3.5T μs, which is more than 3 times but less than 4 times of T. We let the receiver measure the state of local event channel every T μs. If the detected times is 1(supposing the previous state has emerged) or 2 for the "EVTCHNSTAT_interdomain" state, it receives bit '0'. If the detected times is 3 or 4 for the "EVTCHNSTAT_UNBOUND" state, it receives bit '1'. Thus, during the transmission phase, no extra waiting time or synchronization time is needed between two bit-sending.

To observe the transmission result more directly, we collects the bits and combine them into text printed on the console. Thus, when the sender finishes the transmission of one byte, we let it suspend 5.5T μs, which is more than 5 time but less than 6 times of T. Afterwards the receiver will detect one state more than 4 times. If the condition is met, the receiver will print the 1 byte data.

End Phase. When communication of all bits finishes, the sender simply stops changing the state of the event channel without doing extra operations. Considering recycling the event channel resources, if the channel is not closed, the sender closes the channel and last the state for 7.5T. Afterward, the receiver will detect the state more than 6 times. And they end the data communication. After that, if both entities try to communicate more information, they have to resume from the initial synchronization phase.

4   Evaluation

Our experimental platform is a HP Compaq 8100 Elite CMT PC with an Intel Core i7-870 running at 2.93 GHz and We use Xen version 4.1.1 as the base hypervisor. The domain0 in Xen's terminology runs 32-bit Ubuntu 12.04.2 Linux and the two guest domains(DomUs) that make use of the covert channel run para-virtualized 32-bit Ubuntu 12.04.2. Xen assigns two virtual CPUs and 512 MB RAM to each guest VM while domain0 owns four virtual CPUs and 2048 RAM. Every domain uses the kernel 3.5.0-23.

And we conduct the experiments based on the CCECS ommunication protocol mentioned above. There are 1023 Byte secret data stored as a file in the sending end. Our first test target is to show that if the choice of T changes, the receiving end could always get these information at very high bit rate. That is to say, we will test if minimal T exists. Our second test target is to show that if the usage of vCPU changes, the minimal T will increase and the maximal transmission rate will decrease.

First, to get to know the minimal value of T at the error rate less than 5%, we tested the value of T from 100-20000μs in 100μs intervals. Second, we developed a small tool to simulate different execution environment with different usage of vCPU. This tool will run two processes in each DomU to occupy their vCPUs, each process binding itself to one vCPU in the local DomU using CPU affinity. Considering the existed preempted core scheduling algorithm, we also assign each process the highest priority to run in the individual vCPU and then keep them staying on the core as long as possible. With the help of this tool, we simulate the usage of vCPUs from 0%-100% and test the minimal T and maximal bit rate.

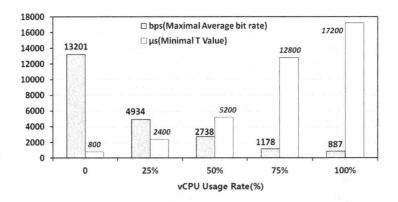

Fig. 4. Maximal Bit Rate and Minimal T at Different Usage Rate of vCPU

The execution results with the error bit rate limited to 5% are shown in figure 4. From 4, we can see that the minimal value of T is directly proportional to vCPU usage. When the vCPU usage is about 0%, the T should not be smaller than 800 μs. But when the usage is about 100%, the T should not be smaller than 17200 μs. Correspondingly, the average bit rates is inversely proportional to vCPU usage. When the vCPU usage is about 0%, the average rate is up to 13201bps, and when the usage is about 100%, the rate is also about 887bps.

As a result, if the T is not smaller than the minimal T, two guests could always share large information using CCECS even though the vCPU is busy.

5   Discussion

Since the exclusiveness of interdomain event channels, the accuracy rate is steadily high if the minimal T is adequate. To lower the danger of the covert channel, two possible solutions are discussed here. First, adding security checks to the operations of creating, binding, closing and quering event channels between domains. As we know, if the XSM(Xen Security Module) is enabled in Xen hypervisorte[14] and the restriction policy is adequately enforced, this covert channel can be controlled to some extent. The second solution is to reset all event channels randomly in each domain. This will affect the time of state change and state query in CCECS, and thus the accuracy of bits transimission will be decreased.

Furthermore, intradomain threat scenario using CCECS may exist when two processes running in the same domain. In this case, the guest OS does not permit them to communication with each other because of the mandatory policy enforced in the operating system. But if the Xen hypervisor does not restrict the event channel between them, the CCECS communication between them may happen and will result in the data leakage from one process to another process. We had evaluated the bit rate also, which is also very high but obviously lower than the interdomain scenario. This is because the interferences between two processes in the same domain is more often than those in the different domains.

6   Conclusion and Future Work

In this paper, we first demonstrate the danger of existing covert channels. Then we introduce the event channel mechanisms of Xen. After that, we design a protocol for CCECS(Covert Channel using Event Channel State) and implement it on Xen hypervisor. Then we do a series of experiments to evaluate CCECS, which can arrive at average 13210bps with error rate less than 5%. Additionally, the state event channels is only impacted by either end of the channel, so the channel is high noise-tolerant. In a word, CCECS is a perilous threat to Xen, its bit rate is larger than most existing covert channel till now.

Our future job is mainly to do some experiments in Amazon EC2 and check if the CCECS still works in the real world. The second aspect is to optimize the transmission scheme because there may be new encoding method to improve the transmission rate of CCECS. The third aspect is to analyze some new communication method introduced in Xen's latest release(e.g. Xen4.3), check if some other factors will downgrade the threat of CCECS.

References

1. Chen, Y., Paxson, V., Katz, R.H.: What's New About Cloud Computing Security? Technical report, UCB/EECS-2010-5, EECS Department, University of California, Berkeley (2010)

2. Reuben, J.S.: A survey on virtual machine security. In: Security of the End Hosts on the Internet, Seminar on Network Security Autumn 2007. Helsinki University of Technology Telecommunications Software and Multimedia Laboratory (2007)

3. U. D. of Defense: Trusted Computing System Evaluation Criteria. DoD 5200.28-STD, Washington (1985)

4. Wang, Z., Lee, R.B.: Covert and Side Channels Due to Processor Architecture. In: Proceedings of the 22nd Annual Computer Security Applications Conference, Washington, pp. 473–482 (2006)

5. Ristenpart, T., Tromer, E., Shacham, H., Savage, S.: Hey, you, get off of my cloud: exploring information leakage in third-party compute clouds. In: Proceedings of the 16th ACM Conference on Computer and Communications Security, New York, pp. 199–212 (2009)

6. Xu, Y., Bailey, M., Jahanian, F., Joshi, K., Hiltunen, M., Schlichting, R.: An exploration of L2 cache covert channels in virtualized environments. In: Proceedings of the 3rd ACM Workshop on Cloud Computing Security Workshop, New York, pp. 29–40 (2011)

7. Wu, Z., Xu, Z., Wang, H.: Whispers in the hyper-space: high-speed covert channel attacks in the cloud. In: Proceedings of the 21st USENIX Conference on Security Symposium, Berkeley, p. 9 (2012)

8. Okamura, K., Oyama, Y.: Load-based covert channels between Xen virtual machines. In: Proceedings of the 2010 ACM Symposium on Applied Computing, New York, pp. 173–180 (2010)

9. Li, Y., Shen, Q., Zhang, C., Sun, P., Chen, Y., Qing, S.: A Covert Channel Using Core Alternation. In: Proceedings of the 2012 26th International Conference on Advanced Information Networking and Applications Workshops, Washington, pp. 324–328 (2012)

10. Wu, J., Ding, L., Wang, Y., Han, W.: Identification and Evaluation of Sharing Memory Covert Timing Channel in Xen Virtual Machines. In: Proceedings of the 2011 IEEE 4th International Conference on Cloud Computing, Washington, pp. 283–291 (2011)

11. Xiao, J., Xu, Z., Huang, H., Wang, H.: POSTER: A covert channel construction in a virtualized environment. In: Proceedings of the 2012 ACM Conference on Computer and Communications Security, New York, pp. 1040–1042 (2012)

12. Salaün, M.: Practical overview of a xen covert channel. J. Comput. Virol. 6, 317–328 (2010)

13. Ranjith, P., Priya, C., Shalini, K.: On covert channels between virtual machines. J. Comput. Virol. 8, 85–97 (2012)

14. Barham, P., Dragovic, B., Fraser, K., Hand, S., Harris, T., Ho, A., Neugebauer, R., Pratt, I., Warfield., A.: Xen and the art of virtualization. In: Proceedings of the Nineteenth ACM Symposium on Operating Systems Principles, New York, pp. 164–177 (2003)

15. Amazon Elastic Compute Cloud (EC2), http://aws.amazon.com/ec2/

16. Zhang, Y., Juels, A., Oprea, A., Reiter, M.K.: Homealone: Co-residency detection in the cloud via side-channel analysis. In: Proceedings of the 2011 IEEE Symposium on Security and Privacy, Washington, pp. 313–328 (2011)

Type-Based Analysis of Protected Storage in the TPM

Jianxiong Shao, Dengguo Feng, and Yu Qin

Trusted Computing and Information Assurance Laboratory,
Institute of Software, Chinese Academy of Sciences
{shaojianxiong,feng,qin_yu}@tca.iscas.ac.cn

Abstract. The Trusted Platform Module (TPM) is designed to enable trustworthy computation and communication over open networks. The TPM provides a way to store cryptographic keys and other sensitive values in its shielded memory and act as *Root of Trust for Storage* (RTS). The TPM interacts with applications via a predefined set of commands (an API). In this paper, we give an abstraction model for the TPM 2.0 specification concentrating on Protected Storage part. With identification and formalization of their secrecy properties, we devise a type system with asymmetric cryptographic primitives to statically enforce and prove their security.

Keywords: TPM, Trusted computing, Type system, API analysis.

1 Introduction

The Trusted Platform Module (TPM) is a system component designed to establish trust in a platform by providing protected storage, robust platform integrity measurement, secure platform attestation and other security mechanisms. The TPM specification is an industry standard [12] and an ISO/IEC standard [11] coordinated by the Trusted Computing Group. The TPM is separate from the system on which it reports (the host system) and the only interaction is through the interface (API) predefined in its specification.

In the last few years, several papers have appeared to indicate vulnerabilities in the TPM API designs. These attacks highlight the importance of formal analysis of the API commands specifications. A number of efforts have analyzed secrecy and authentication properties of protocols using model checkers, theorem provers, and other tools. Backes *et al.* used ProVerif to obtain the first mechanized analysis of DAA protocol[2]. In [6], a TPM impersonation attack was discovered when sharing authdata between users are allowed. Lin described an analysis of various fragments of the TPM API using Otter and Alloy[10]. In [9], an analysis of the TPM API was described by using finite state automata. Delaune *et al.* used the tool ProVerif to analyze the API commands and rediscover some known attacks and some new variations on them[7].

Most of the established work on formal analysis of TPM API commands and protocols focus on original TPM 1.2 specification, whose latest revision [12] is in

S. Qing et al. (Eds.): ICICS 2013, LNCS 8233, pp. 135–150, 2013.

2006. However, Trusted Computing Group (TCG) has published the TPM 2.0 specification on their website in 2012. The new version of the TPM specification has several changes from previous versions especially on the protected storage part. In this paper, we conduct a formal analysis of the protected storage part of API commands in the TPM 2.0 specification w.r.t secrecy property. A formal security proof of secrecy, in the presence of a Dolev-Yao attacker who have complete control over all the existent sessions, is first proposed based on a core type system statically enforcing API security.

Our present work extends the line of research by exploring a language-based, static analysis technique that allows for proving the security of key management API commands. In [4], Centenaro *et al.* devise a language to specify PKCS#11 key management APIs at a fine granularity. We utilize their abstraction of key templates in our model but devise a new type system to check information flow properties for cryptographic operations in security APIs. Moreover, we devise a new set of assignment commands to specify the internal functions according to Trusted Platform Module Library (TPML) 2.0, Part 4: Supporting Routines.

For the core type system, although Centenaro *et al.* considered the integrity (they call it trust) for keys, the key with high integrity in their model must be with high confidentiality. It cannot be used to formalize asymmetric cryptographic primitives since the public key should be with high integrity but low confidentiality. In our model, we devise a new type system with more specific types for asymmetric cryptographic primitives. Actually in this sense our result is more in the line of [13], in which Keighren *et al.* proposed a type system based on the principles of information flow to investigate a much stronger property *noninterference* for a general model. Yet they gave no language to express the internal commands and did not consider the integrity level. We apply the types of keys from [8,1,14], in which the types of the payload are determined by the types of the key. We also consider the integrity level, which is different from [13].

The paper is organized as follows. In section 2 we give a brief introduction to the protected storage part of the TPM 2.0 specification and describe the simple language for modeling TPM commands. In section 3 we introduce the core type system statically enforcing API security. In section 4 we apply the type system to our model of the TPM API commands, which we prove to be secure. We conclude in section 5.

2   Overview of the TPM Protected Storage

Trusted Platform Module (TPM) is defined as the Root of Trust for Storage (RTS) by TCG, since the TPM can be trusted to prevent inappropriate access to its memory, which we call Shielded Locations. TPM protections are based on the concept of Protected Capabilities and Protected Objects. A Protected Capability is an operation that must be performed correctly for a TPM to be trusted. A Protected Object is data (including keys) that can be accessed to only by using Protected Capabilities. Protected Objects in the TPM reside in Shielded Locations. The size of Shielded Locations may be limited. The effective memory of the TPM is expanded by storing Protected Objects outside of the TPM memory with cryptographic protections when they are not being used and reloading if necessary.

2.1   Protected Storage Hierarchy

In the TPM 2.0 specification, the TPM Protected Objects are arranged in a tree structure, which is called Protected Storage Hierarchy. A hierarchy is constructed with storage keys as the connectors to which other key objects or connectors may be attached. A Storage Key, acting as a parent, protects its children when those objects are stored out of the TPM. Storage keys should be used in the process of creation, loading, duplication, unsealing, and identity activation. However, such keys cannot be used in the cryptographic support functions.

When creating a new object on the device, two commands are needed. In the command TPM2_Create(), a loaded storage key should be provided as the parent and a loadable creation blob protected by it is created. The keys used in this protection are derived from a seed in the sensitive area of the parent object. Then the command TPM2_Load() may load the creation blob into the TPM with a handle returned. The new key can be used by reference to its handle.

We focus on the process of duplication, which needs three commands. Duplication allows an object to be a child of an additional parent key. In the command TPM2_Duplicate(), a loaded object for duplication and its new parent handle should be provided and a duplication blob is returned. The duplication blob is protected in a similar way to the creation blob except that the seed is random and protected by new parent's asymmetric methods to guarantee that only the new parent may load it. In this way, the storage key must be asymmetric. In the command TPM2_Import(), the duplication blob is transformed to a loadable blob, which can be loaded in TPM2_Load().

An object might be connected to another hierarchy by two ways. One is to duplicate it directly by the process above. The other is to duplicate one of its ancestors and it can be loaded by its creation blob. The hierarchy attributes of an object, *FixedParent* and *FixedTPM*, indicate how the object can be connected to another hierarchy. An object with *FixedParent* SET means it cannot be duplicated directly and with *FixedTPM* SET means all of its ancestors have *FixedParent* SET. Thus an object with *FixedParent* CLEAR must have *FixedTPM* CLEAR. The attribute *FixedTPM* of an object depends on *FixedTPM* in its parent and *FixedParent* in itself. The hierarchy attributes setting matrix is in Table 1

The consistency of the hierarchy settings is checked by internal function PublicAttributesValidation() in object templates (when creating) and in public areas for loaded objects (when loading) or duplicated objects (when importing). The root of a hierarchy is denoted as the Primary Object which is protected by keys derived from a Primary Seed and its attributes. The Primary Object can be seen as a child object of a virtual object with *FixedTPM* SET.

Table 1. Allowed Hierarchy Settings

Parent's *FixedTPM*	Object's *FixedParent*	Object's *FixedTPM*
CLEAR	CLEAR	CLEAR
CLEAR	SET	CLEAR
SET	CLEAR	CLEAR
SET	SET	SET

2.2   Object Structure Elements

According to the TPM 2.0 specification, each object has two components: public area and sensitive area. The former contains the fields `objectAttributes` and `type`. For an asymmetric key object, the public key should also be contained in the public area. The sensitive area includes an authorization value (`authValue`), a secret value used to derive keys for protection of its child (`seedValue`), and the private key (`sensitive`) dependant on the type of the object.

For the public area, the attributes of the object (`objectAttributes`) are in 5 classes: hierarchy, usage, authorization, creation, and persistence. The hierarchy attributes have been discussed above.

The usage of an object is determined by three attributes: *restricted*, *sign*, and *decrypt*. An object with only *decrypt* SET may use the key in its sensitive area to decrypt data blobs that have been encrypted by that key (for symmetric key) or the public portion of the key (for asymmetric key). Thus we call it Decryption Key Object. An object with both *decrypt* and *restricted* SET is used to protect the other objects when they are created or duplicated. A restricted decryption key is often referred to as a Storage Key Object. An object with *sign* SET may perform signing operation and with both *sign* and *restricted* SET may only sign a digest produced by the TPM. This two kinds of objects corresponds to the secure platform attestation. On the viewpoint of the protected storage, they act the same way as the Decryption Key Objects and could not be used as the Storage Key Objects. It is the same case for a legacy key with both *sign* and *decrypt* SET. It is not allowed for an object with all the three attributes SET. Thus we divide all the objects into two groups: `Decryption Key Object` and `Storage Key Object` which correspond to the leaf node and the branch node.

For the sensitive area, `seedValue` is required for `Storage Key Objects`. It is an obfuscation value for `Decryption Key Object`.

3   Modeling the TPM APIs

3.1   A Language for Modeling TPM Commands

In this section, we extend the work of [4] to get an imperative language which is more suitable to specify the protected storage part of TPM 2.0 APIs.

Values and Expressions. Let $\mathcal{C}$ and $\mathcal{F}$ respectively denote the set of atomic constant and fresh values with $\mathcal{C} \cap \mathcal{F} = \emptyset$. The former specifies any public data, including the templates of the key objects and the usage of the key derivation function (kdf). The latter is used to model the generation of new fresh values such as the sensitive values and the seed values of the key objects. We introduce the extraction operator $f \leftarrow \mathcal{F}$ in [4] to represent the extraction of the first 'unused' value f from $\mathcal{F}$. It is obvious that the extracted values are always different. We define the values in Table 2. For the sake of readability, we let $\tilde{v}$ denote a tuple $(v_1, \cdots, v_k)$ of values.

Table 2. Definition of Values and Expressions

$v, v', h ::=$	values	$e ::=$	expressions
val	atomic fresh value	x, y	variables
tmp	template	$kdf(usg, x)$	key diversification
usg	$\{STORAGE, INTEGRITY\}$	$ek(x)$	encryption key
$kdf(usg, v)$	key diversification	$senc(x, \tilde{y})$	sym encryption
$senc(v', \tilde{v})$	sym encryption	$aenc(x, \tilde{y})$	asym encryption
$ek(v)$	encryption key	$hmac(x, \tilde{y})$	hmac computation
$aenc(v', \tilde{v})$	asym encryption		
$hmac(v', \tilde{v})$	hmac computation		

We use template to describe the properties of the key objects. Denoted by tmp, a template is represented as a set of attributes. Set an attribute for a key object is to include such an attribute in its template set. Formally, a template tmp is a subset of $\{W, E, A, S, N, F\}$. First, two attributes are used to identify the groups of key objects: W (wrap) for **Storage Key Object**; E (encryption) for **Decryption Key Object**. Second, we use A (Asymmetric) and S (Symmetric) to specify the field **type** in the public area of the key object. Third, for the hierarchy attributes *FixedTPM* and *FixedParent*, we use N (*Non-FixedParent*) to denote *FixedParent* CLEAR and F to denote *FixedTPM* SET. We do not specify the other attributes since they are irrelevant to the protected storage hierarchy. As in section 2, (W, E), (A, S), (N, F), and (W, S) are on the list of conflicting attribute pairs. Actually, the allowable combination of the attributes can only be of the form $\{W, A, N/F\}$, $\{E, A, N/F\}$, and $\{E, S, N/F\}$ where N/F means N, F or neither. We have 3 kinds of key objects which is denoted by **mode**: the Storage Key Object, the Symmetric Decryption Key Object, and the Asymmetric Decryption Key Object. We abstract such restrictions and focus on a particular set of all allowable templates of keys denoted by $\wp$, which we call the security policy. In our model, $\wp$ contains the above 9 possible templates.

Constant value $usg \in \{STORAGE, INTEGRITY\}$ is a label to specify the usage of the key derived from the *Seed* stored in a Storage Key Object. $STORAGE$ means a symmetric key and $INTEGRITY$ means an HMAC key. We use $kdf(usg, v)$ to denote a new key obtained via key derivation function from label usg and a seed value v. $senc(v', \tilde{v})$ performs symmetric encryption on a tuple of values $\tilde{v}$. $ek(v)$ denotes the public encryption key value corresponding to the private key v and can be published. Notice that we model a cryptographic scheme where the encryption key can be recovered from the corresponding decryption key, which means decryption keys should be seen as key-pairs themselves. $aenc(v', \tilde{v})$ and $hmac(v', \tilde{v})$ denote, respectively, the asymmetric encryption and the HMAC computation of the tuple $\tilde{v}$ with the key v'.

As in [4], we use a set of expressions to manipulate the above values. Table 2 gives the formalization of expressions which are similar to those of values. Expressions are based on a set of variables $\mathcal{V}$. We introduce the memory environment $\mathbf{M} : x \mapsto v$ in [4] to denote the evaluation of variables. For simplicity, we let $\tilde{x}$ denote a tuple $(x_1, \cdots, x_n)$ of variables and $\mathbf{M}(\tilde{x}) = \tilde{v}$ the evaluation $\mathbf{M}(x_1) = v_1, \cdots, \mathbf{M}(x_n) = v_n$. Expression e in an environment $\mathbf{M}$ evaluating to v is denoted by $e \downarrow^{\mathbf{M}} v$. It is trivial to derive the semantics of evaluation for the expressions in Table 2.

Handle-Map. In the TPM 2.0 specification, objects are referenced in the commands via handles. We use a key handle-map $\mathbf{H} : h \mapsto (tmp, v_s, v_k)$ from a subset of atomic fresh values $\mathcal{F}$ to tuples of templates, seed values and key values. We do not consider the Authentication mechanisms in the TPM. This corresponds to a worst-case scenario in which attackers may gain access to all keys available in the TPM without knowing their values. Thus, for the sensitive area, we only need to model the field `seedValue` by v_s and `sensitive` by v_k. The type of sensitive values v_k and v_s is dependant on the template tmp.

API Commands and Semantics. We devise a set of internal functions according to the supporting routines in Trusted Platform Module Library 2.0 for object and hierarchy.

An API is specified as a set $\mathcal{A} = \{c_1, \cdots, c_n\}$ of commands. Each command contains a binding of values to variables and a sequence of inner execution of clauses as follows:

$c ::= \lambda \tilde{x}.p$

$p ::= \varepsilon|\ x := e|\ \mathtt{return}\ \tilde{y}|\ p_1; p_2|\ (x_t, x_s, x_k) := \mathtt{checkTemplate}\ (y_h, tmp)|$
$\quad \mathtt{x_k} := \mathtt{genKey}\ (y_t)|x_s := \mathtt{genSeed}\ (y_t)|x_h := \mathtt{ObjectLoad}\ (y_s, y_k, y_t)|$
$\quad (x_{pA}, x_{inA}) := \mathtt{PAV}\ (y_{pA}, y_{inA})|\tilde{x} := f$

$f ::= \mathtt{sdec}\ (y_k, y_c)|\ \mathtt{adec}\ (y_k, y_c)|\ \mathtt{checkHMAC}\ (y_k, y_{hmac}, \tilde{y}_v).$

All of the free variables (variables that have no evaluation) in clauses p appear in input parameters $\tilde{x} = (x_1, \cdots, x_n)$. We will only focus on the API commands in which `return` $\tilde{y}$ can only occur as the last clause. Intuitively, ε denotes the empty clause; $x := e$ is an evaluation of variable x; $p_1; p_2$ recursively specifies the sequential execution of clauses. `chechTemplate` retrieves k_s, k_v, and tmp' of a key object loaded on the device, given its handle by requiring the template to match some pattern tmp. `genKey` and `genSeed` generate a new key value or seed value, given its template y_t. `ObjectLoad` loads a new key object with its sensitive values and an allowable template. `PAV` checks the hierarchy attributes in the template

y_{pA} of the parent object should be compatible with that in the template y_{inA} of an input object according to Table 1. The other three internal functions f are cryptography operations provided by the TPM and cannot be used directly by user applications. $\mathtt{sdec}$ and $\mathtt{adec}$ respectively specify the symmetric and asymmetric decryption. The decrypting function fails (ie. is stuck) if the given key is not the right one. $\mathtt{checkHAMC}$ checks whether $y_{hmac} = hamc(y_k, \tilde{y}_v)$ and if so, $\tilde{y}_v$ is evaluated to $\tilde{x}$, or otherwise, it fails. A call to an API command $c = \lambda(x_1, \cdots, x_k).p$, written as $c(v_1, \cdots, v_k)$, binds variables $x_1, \cdots, x_k$ to values $v_1, \cdots, v_k$, executes p and outputs the value given by $\mathtt{return}\ \tilde{y}$.

For convenience, it is required that all the variables on the left side of the assignment clauses may appear only once. This does not limit the capability of our model since the repeated variables can be rewrite to different names.

An API command c working on a configuration contains a memory environment $\mathbf{M}$ and a key handle-map $\mathbf{H}$, which is denoted as $\langle \mathbf{M}, \mathbf{H}, p \rangle$. Operation semantics are expressed as follows.

$$\frac{e{\downarrow}_M v}{\langle M,H,x{:=}e\rangle \rightarrow \langle M\cup[x{\mapsto}v],H,\varepsilon\rangle}$$

$$\frac{H(M(y_h)){=}(v_t,v_s,v_k),tmp{\subseteq}v_t}{\langle M,H,(x_t,x_s,x_k){:=}checkTemplate(y_h,tmp)\rangle \rightarrow \langle M\cup[x_t{\mapsto}v_t,x_s{\mapsto}v_s,x_k{\mapsto}v_k],H,\varepsilon\rangle}$$

$$\frac{v_k{\leftarrow}\mathcal{F},M(y_t){\in}\wp}{\langle M,H,x_k{:=}genKey(y_t)\rangle \rightarrow \langle M\cup[x_k{\mapsto}v_k],H,\varepsilon\rangle}, \quad \frac{v_s{\leftarrow}\mathcal{F},M(y_t){\in}\wp}{\langle M,H,x_s{:=}genSeed(y_t)\rangle \rightarrow \langle M\cup[x_s{\mapsto}v_s],H,\varepsilon\rangle}$$

$$\frac{v_h{\leftarrow}\mathcal{F},M(y_t){\in}\wp}{\langle M,H,x_h{:=}ObjectLoad(y_s,y_k,y_t)\rangle \rightarrow \langle M\cup[x_h{\mapsto}v_h],H\cup[v_h{\mapsto}(M(y_t),M(y_s),M(y_k))],\varepsilon\rangle}$$

$$\frac{y_k{\downarrow}_M k,y_c{\downarrow}_M senc(k,\tilde{v})}{\langle M,H,\tilde{x}{:=}sdec(y_k,y_c)\rangle \rightarrow \langle M\cup[\tilde{x}{\mapsto}\tilde{v}],H,\varepsilon\rangle}, \quad \frac{y_k{\downarrow}_M k,y_c{\downarrow}_M aenc(ek(k),\tilde{v})}{\langle M,H,\tilde{x}{:=}adec(y_k,y_c)\rangle \rightarrow \langle M\cup[\tilde{x}{\mapsto}\tilde{v}],H,\varepsilon\rangle}$$

$$\frac{M(y_{pA}),M(y_{inA}){\in}\wp,F{\in}M(y_{pA}){\Rightarrow}N/F{\in}M(y_{inA}),F{\notin}M(y_{pA}){\Rightarrow}F{\notin}M(y_{inA})}{\langle M,H,x_{inA}{:=}PAV(y_{pA},y_{inA})\rangle \rightarrow \langle M\cup[x_{inA}{\mapsto}M(y_{inA})],H,\varepsilon\rangle}$$

$$\frac{y_k{\downarrow}_M k,\tilde{y}_v{\downarrow}_M \tilde{v},y_{hmac}{\downarrow}_M HMAC(k,\tilde{v})}{\langle M,H,\tilde{x}{:=}checkHMAC(y_k,y_{hmac},\tilde{y}_v)\rangle \rightarrow \langle M\cup[\tilde{x}{\mapsto}\tilde{v}],H,\varepsilon\rangle}$$

$$\frac{\langle M,H,p_1\rangle \rightarrow \langle M',H',\varepsilon\rangle}{\langle M,H,p_1;p_2\rangle \rightarrow \langle M',H',p_2\rangle}, \quad \frac{\langle M,H,p_1\rangle \rightarrow \langle M',H',p'_1\rangle}{\langle M,H,p_1;p_2\rangle \rightarrow \langle M',H',p'_1;p_2\rangle}$$

$$\frac{a{=}\lambda\tilde{x}.p,\langle M_e\cup[\tilde{x}{\mapsto}\tilde{v}],H,p\rangle \rightarrow \langle M',H',return\ e\rangle,e{\downarrow}_{M'} v}{a(\tilde{v}){\downarrow}_{H,H'} v}$$

We explain the second rule and the other rules are similar. For the function $\mathtt{checkTemplate}$, it evaluates y_h in $\mathbf{M}$, finds the key referenced by the handle $\mathbf{M}(y_h)$, and checks whether $tmp \subseteq v_t$. If so, it may store the key object in the tuple variables (x_t, x_s, x_k), noted $\mathbf{M} \cup [x_t \mapsto v_t, x_s \mapsto v_s, x_k \mapsto v_k]$. The last rule is standard for API calls on a configuration. The API command are executed and the returned value is given as the output value of the call. Notice that we cannot observe the memory used internally by the device. The only exchanged data are input parameters and the returned value. This is the foundation for the attacker model.

3.2   Attacker Model and API Security

The attacker is formalized in a classic Dolev-Yao style. The knowledge of the attacker is denoted as a set of values derived from known values V with his capability. Let V be a finite set of values, The knowledge of the attacker $\mathcal{K}(V)$ is defined as the least superset of V such that $v, v' \in \mathcal{K}(V)$ implies

(1) $(v, v') \in \mathcal{K}(V)$
(2) $senc(v, v') \in \mathcal{K}(V)$

(3) $aenc(v, v') \in \mathcal{K}(V)$
(4) if $v = senc(v', v'')$, then $v'' \in \mathcal{K}(V)$
(5) if $v = aenc(ek(v'), v'')$, then $v'' \in \mathcal{K}(V)$
(6) $kdf(v, v') \in \mathcal{K}(V)$
(7) $hmac(v, v') \in \mathcal{K}(V)$

API commands can be called by attackers in any sequences and with any parameters in his knowledge. The returned values will be added to his set of known values and enlarge his knowledge. Formally, An attacker configuration is denoted as $\langle \mathbf{H}, V \rangle$ and has a reduction as follows:

$$\frac{c \in \mathcal{A}, v_1 \cdots v_k \in \mathcal{K}(V), c(v_1, \cdots, v_k) \downarrow^{\mathbf{H}, \mathbf{H}'} v}{\langle \mathbf{H}, V \rangle \rightarrow_{\mathcal{A}} \langle \mathbf{H}', V \cup \{v\} \rangle}$$

The set of initial known values V_0 contains all the atomic constant values in $\mathcal{C}$. For all Asymmetric key value $v'' \in \mathcal{F}, ek(v'') \in V_0$. The set of initial handle-map $\mathbf{H}_0$ is empty. In our model, $\rightarrow_{\mathcal{A}}^*$ notes multi-step reductions.

The main property of the Protected Storage Hierarchy required by TPM 2.0 specifications is secrecy. More specifically, the value of private keys loaded on a TPM should never be revealed outside the secure device, even when exposed to a compromised host system.

Formally, the sensitive keys available on the TPM should never be known by the attacker, as well as the seed in a Storage Key. The definition of *Secrecy of API commands* follows.

Definition 1 (Secrecy). Let $\mathcal{A}$ be an API. $\mathcal{A}$ is secure if for all reductions of attacker configuration $\langle \emptyset, V_0 \rangle \rightarrow_{\mathcal{A}}^* \langle \mathbf{H}, V \rangle$, we have

Let g be a handle in $\mathbf{H}$ such that $\mathbf{H}(g) = (tmp, v_s, v_k)$ and $F \in tmp$. Then, $v_s, v_k \notin \mathcal{K}(V)$.

The language in section 2.2 can be used to model the TPM 2.0 API commands of protected storage part. We give a brief specification on them and conclude they preserve secrecy in section 4.

4   Type System

4.1   A Core Type System

In this section, we present a type system to statically enforce secrecy in API commands. At first, we introduce the concept of security level [8], a pair $\sigma_C \sigma_I$, to specify the levels of confidentiality and integrity. We consider two levels: $High(H)$ and $Low(L)$. Intuitively, values with high confidentiality cannot be read by the attackers while data with high integrity should not be modified by the attackers.

While it is safe to consider a public value as secret, low integrity cannot be promoted to high integrity. Otherwise, data from the attackers may erroneously be considered as coming from a secure device. Therefore, we have the confidentiality and integrity preorders: $L \sqsubseteq_C H$ and $H \sqsubseteq_I L$. We let σ_C and σ_I range over $\{L, H\}$, while we let σ range over the pairs $\sigma_C \sigma_I$ with $\sigma_C \sigma_I \sqsubseteq \sigma_C' \sigma_I'$ iff

$\sigma_C \sqsubseteq_C \sigma'_C$ and $\sigma_I \sqsubseteq_I \sigma'_I$. It gives the standard four-point lattice. Formally, type syntax T is as follows:

$$T ::= \sigma | \rho^\sigma | SeedK^\sigma[] | \phi K^\sigma[\tilde{T}],$$

where

$$\sigma ::= \sigma_C \sigma_I = LL | LH | HL | HH$$
$$\rho ::= Unwrap | Dec | Sym | Any$$
$$\phi ::= \rho | Wrap | Enc | hmac.$$

Each type has an associated security level denoted by $\mathcal{L}(T)$. For basic types we trivially have $\mathcal{L}(\sigma) = \sigma$. As expected, we have $\mathcal{L}(\rho K^\sigma[\tilde{T}]) = \sigma$ and $\mathcal{L}(\rho^\sigma) = \sigma$. It is nature to define $\mathcal{L}_C(T)$ and $\mathcal{L}_I(T)$ for confidentiality and integrity levels.

In type syntax T, σ is the type for general data at such level. ρ^σ is the type of templates. label ρ specifies the **mode** of the key object which depends on its template. $Unwrap$ denotes the Storage Key Object; Dec denotes the Asymmetric Decryption Key Object; Sym denotes the Symmetric Decryption Key Object; Any is the top mode including all the three modes. All templates are public. Yet the templates with F are generated by the TPM and cannot be forged. Thus they have a security level LH. The other templates with attribute N or without any hierarchy attributes may be forged by the attackers via the process of duplication or loading. Thus they have a security level LL. The types are as follows:

$$\frac{W, A, F \in tmp}{\vdash tmp : Unwrap^{LH}}, \frac{E, A, F \in tmp}{\vdash tmp : Dec^{LH}}, \frac{E, S, F \in tmp}{\vdash tmp : Sym^{LH}},$$

$$\frac{W, A \in tmp, F \notin tmp}{\vdash tmp : Unwrap^{LL}}, \frac{E, A \in tmp, F \notin tmp}{\vdash tmp : Dec^{LL}}, \frac{E, S \in tmp, F \notin tmp}{\vdash tmp : Sym^{LL}}.$$

The type $\phi K^\sigma[\tilde{T}]$ describes the key values at security level σ which are used to perform cryptographic operations on payloads of type $\tilde{T}$. For the sake of readability, we let $\tilde{T}$ denote a sequence $T_1, \cdots, T_n$ of types and use $\tilde{x} : \tilde{T}$ to type a sequence $x_1, \cdots, x_n$ of variables. Label ϕ specifies the usage of the key values. Intuitively, $Seed$ value is stored as v_s in a Storage Key Object to be used for the derivation of HMAC key and symmetric key which are used for the protection of the other objects; $Wrap$ and $Unwrap$ are a pair of asymmetric keys stored as v_k in a Storage Key Object used in the process of duplication; Enc and Dec are similar but stored in a Decryption Key Object; Sym is used in symmetric encryption and decryption; $hmac$ is used in the computation of HMAC for the protection of integrity.

Based on security level of types, we have *subtyping* relations. Formally, $\leq$ is defined as the least preorder such that:
(1) $\sigma_1 \leq \sigma_2$ iff $\sigma_1 \sqsubseteq \sigma_2$;
(2) $LL \leq \phi K^{LL}[LL, \ldots, LL], LL \leq \rho^{LL}, LL \leq SeedK^{LL}[]$;
(3) $\phi K^\sigma[\tilde{T}] \leq \sigma, SeedK^\sigma[] \leq \sigma, \rho^\sigma \leq \sigma$;
(4) $\rho K^\sigma[\tilde{T}] \leq AnyK^\sigma[\tilde{T}], \rho^\sigma \leq Any^\sigma$.

It is obvious that subtyping relationship does not compromise the security, since $T \leq T'$ implies $\mathcal{L}(T) \sqsubseteq \mathcal{L}(T')$.

Typing Expressions. After the definition of types, we introduce a typing environment $\Gamma : x \mapsto T$, namely a map from variables to their respective types. Type judgement for expressions is written as $\Gamma \vdash e : T$ meaning that expression e is of type T under Γ. The typing rules for expressions are described as follows.

$$[\text{var}] \frac{\Gamma(x) = T}{\Gamma \vdash x : T}, [\text{sub}] \frac{\Gamma \vdash e : T', T' \leq T}{\Gamma \vdash e : T}, [\text{tuple}] \frac{\Gamma \vdash \tilde{x}_1 : \tilde{T}_1, \Gamma \vdash x_2 : T_2}{\Gamma \vdash (\tilde{x}_1, x_2) : (\tilde{T}_1, T_2)},$$

$$[\text{kdfSH}] \frac{\Gamma \vdash x : SeedK^{HH}[],usg=STORAGE}{\Gamma \vdash kdf(usg,x):SymK^{HH}[\tilde{T}]}, [\text{kdfSL}] \frac{\Gamma \vdash x : SeedK^{LL}[],usg=STORAGE}{\Gamma \vdash kdf(usg,x):SymK^{LL}[LL,\cdots,LL]},$$

$$[\text{kdfIH}] \frac{\Gamma \vdash x : SeedK^{HH}[],usg=INTEGRITY}{\Gamma \vdash kdf(usg,x):hmacK^{HH}[\tilde{T}]}, [\text{kdfIL}] \frac{\Gamma \vdash x : SeedK^{LL}[],usg=INTEGRITY}{\Gamma \vdash kdf(usg,x):hmacK^{LL}[LL,\cdots,LL]},$$

$$[\text{wrapK}] \frac{\Gamma \vdash x : UnwrapK^{\sigma_C \sigma_I}[\tilde{T}]}{\Gamma \vdash ek(x):WrapK^{L\sigma_I}[\tilde{T}]}, [\text{encK}] \frac{\Gamma \vdash x : DecK^{\sigma_C \sigma_I}[\tilde{T}]}{\Gamma \vdash ek(x):EncK^{L\sigma_I}[\tilde{T}]},$$

$$[\text{Sym}] \frac{\Gamma \vdash x : SymK^{\sigma_C \sigma_I}[\tilde{T}], \Gamma \vdash \tilde{y} : \tilde{T}}{\Gamma \vdash senc(x,\tilde{y}):L\sigma_I}, [\text{hmac}] \frac{\Gamma \vdash x : hmacK^{\sigma_C \sigma_I}[\tilde{T}], \Gamma \vdash \tilde{y} : \tilde{T}, \sigma'_I = \sigma_I \cup_{T \in \tilde{T}} L_I(T)}{\Gamma \vdash HMAC(x,\tilde{y}):L\sigma_I},$$

$$[\text{Wrap}] \frac{\Gamma \vdash x : WrapK^{\sigma_C \sigma_I}[\tilde{T}], \Gamma \vdash \tilde{y} : \tilde{T}}{\Gamma \vdash aenc(x,\tilde{y}):L\sigma_I}, [\text{Enc}] \frac{\Gamma \vdash x : EncK^{\sigma_C \sigma_I}[\tilde{T}], \Gamma \vdash \tilde{y} : \tilde{T}}{\Gamma \vdash aenc(x,\tilde{y}):L\sigma_I}.$$

Rules [var], [sub], and [tuple] are standard to derive types directly from Γ or via subtyping relationship. Rules [kdfSH], [kdfSL], [kdfIH], and [kdfIL] states that given a seed and its usage, we may derive a new key of the security level inherited from the seed. The security level of the seed value can only be HH (Trusted) or LL (Untrusted). Rules [wrapK] and [encK] says that if an asymmetric decryption key k_x is of type $\rho K^{\sigma_C \sigma_I}[\tilde{T}]$ where ρ ranges over $\{Unwrap, Dec\}$, then the corresponding encryption key $ek(k_x)$ is of type $\rho K^{L\sigma_I}[\tilde{T}]$. Notice that the confidentiality level is L(Low), since public keys are allowed to be known to the attacker, while the integrity level is the same with its decryption key. Rules [Sym], [Wrap], and [Enc] state the encryption of data. The type of the operand e is required to be compatible with that of the payload which is specified by the type of the key. The integrity level of the ciphertext should be the same with that of the key. Rules [hmac] requires that the integrity level of the HMAC should be $\sigma_I \bigsqcup_{T \in \tilde{T}} \mathcal{L}_I(T)$, which represents the lowest integrity level of σ_I and each level of $\mathcal{L}_I(T)$ while $T \in \tilde{T}$. The reason for it is the fact that if the attacker may generate either the HMAC key or the plaintext, he could modify the computation of HMAC. Ciphertexts and the HMAC can be returned to the caller and consequently their confidentiality level is L.

Typing API Commands. Type judgement for API commands is denoted as $\Gamma \vdash p$ meaning that p is well-typed under the typing environment Γ. For simplicity, we write $\Gamma(\tilde{x}) = \tilde{T}$ or $\tilde{x} \mapsto \tilde{T}$ for the binding of variables $\tilde{x} = (x_1, \cdots, x_n)$ respectively to their types $\tilde{T} = (T_1, \cdots, T_n)$. The judgement for API commands is formalized as follows.

$$[API] \frac{\forall c \in A \quad \Gamma \vdash c}{\Gamma \vdash A}, [assign] \frac{\Gamma \vdash e:T \quad \Gamma, x \mapsto T \vdash p}{\Gamma \vdash x:=e;p}, [seq] \frac{\Gamma \vdash p_1 \quad \Gamma \vdash p_2}{\Gamma \vdash p_1;p_2},$$

$$[checktmp] \frac{\Gamma \vdash y_h:LL \quad \forall \tilde{T} \in PTS(tmp, \wp) \Rightarrow \Gamma, \tilde{x} \mapsto \tilde{T} \vdash p}{\Gamma \vdash \tilde{x}:=checkTemplate(y_h, tmp);p}, [sdec] \frac{\Gamma \vdash y_k:SymK^\sigma[\tilde{T}] \quad \Gamma, \tilde{x} \mapsto \tilde{T} \vdash p}{\Gamma \vdash \tilde{x}:=sdec(y_k, y_c);p},$$

$$[genKey - H] \frac{\Gamma \vdash y_t:Any^{LH} \quad \Gamma, x_k \mapsto AnyK^{HH}[\tilde{T}] \vdash p}{\Gamma \vdash x_k:=genKey(y_t);p}, [genKey - L] \frac{\Gamma \vdash y_t:LL \quad \Gamma, x_k \mapsto LL \vdash p}{\Gamma \vdash x_k:=genKey(y_t);p},$$

$$[genSeed - H] \frac{\Gamma \vdash y_t:Any^{LH} \quad \Gamma, x_s \mapsto SeedK^{HH}[] \vdash p}{\Gamma \vdash x_s:=genSeed(y_t);p}, [genSeed - L] \frac{\Gamma \vdash y_t:LL \quad \Gamma, x_s \mapsto LL \vdash p}{\Gamma \vdash x_s:=genSeed(y_t);p},$$

$$[ObjLoad - H] \frac{\Gamma \vdash y_s:SeedK^{HH}[] \quad \Gamma \vdash y_k:\rho K^{HH}[\tilde{T}] \quad \Gamma \vdash y_t:\rho^{LH} \quad \Gamma, x_h \mapsto LL \vdash p}{\Gamma \vdash x_h:=ObjectLoad(y_s, y_k, y_t);p},$$

$$[ObjLoad - L] \frac{\Gamma \vdash y_s:LL \quad \Gamma \vdash y_k:LL \quad \Gamma \vdash y_t:LL \quad \Gamma, x_h \mapsto LL \vdash p}{\Gamma \vdash x_h:=ObjectLoad(y_s, y_k, y_t);p},$$

$$[Dec] \frac{\Gamma \vdash y_k:DecK^\sigma[\tilde{T}] \quad \Gamma \vdash y_c:T \quad \Gamma, \tilde{x} \mapsto \tilde{T} \vdash p \quad L_I(T)=L \Rightarrow \Gamma, \tilde{x} \mapsto (LL, \cdots, LL) \vdash p}{\Gamma \vdash \tilde{x}:=adec(y_k, y_c);p},$$

$$[Unwrap] \frac{\Gamma \vdash y_k:UnwrapK^\sigma[\tilde{T}] \quad \Gamma \vdash y_c:T \quad \Gamma, \tilde{x} \mapsto \tilde{T} \vdash p \quad L_I(T)=L \Rightarrow \Gamma, \tilde{x} \mapsto (LL, \cdots, LL) \vdash p}{\Gamma \vdash \tilde{x}:=adec(y_k, y_c);p},$$

$$[PAV - H] \frac{\Gamma \vdash (y_{pA}, y_{inA}):(Unwrap^{LH}, LL) \quad \Gamma, x_{inA} \mapsto Any^{L\sigma_I} \vdash p}{\Gamma \vdash x_{inA}:=PAV(y_{pA}, y_{inA});p},$$

$$[PAV - L] \frac{\Gamma \vdash (y_{pA}, y_{inA}):(LL, LL) \quad \Gamma, x_{inA} \mapsto LL \vdash p}{\Gamma \vdash x_{inA}:=PAV(y_{pA}, y_{inA});p},$$

$$[chkHMAC] \frac{\Gamma \vdash y_k:hmacK^\sigma[\tilde{T}] \quad \Gamma, \tilde{x} \mapsto \tilde{T} \vdash p}{\Gamma \vdash \tilde{x}:=checkHMAC(y_k, y_{hmac}, \tilde{y}_v);p},$$

$$[return] \frac{\Gamma \vdash \tilde{x}:(LL, \cdots, LL)}{\Gamma \vdash return \; \tilde{x}}, [command] \frac{\Gamma \vdash x_1:LL \quad \cdots \quad \Gamma \vdash x_k:LL \quad \Gamma \vdash p}{\Gamma \vdash \lambda x_1, \cdots, x_k.p}$$

Most of the above rules are standard. We just explain [checktmp] and [PAV]. The details of the others are in full version [16]. Rule [checktmp] is adapted form the same rule in [4]. We have to type-check all the permitted templates tmp' in $\wp$ matching the checked template tmp, such that $tmp \subseteq tmp'$. The Permitted Templates Set is denoted as

$$PTS(tmp, \wp) = \{(\rho^{L\sigma_I}, SeedK^{\sigma_I\sigma_I}[], \rho K^{\sigma_I\sigma_I}[\tilde{T}])|$$
$$\exists tmp' \in \wp, tmp \subseteq tmp' \wedge \vdash tmp' : \rho^{L\sigma_I}\}.$$

For example, if $tmp = \{W\}$, the permitted templates matching with tmp are $\{W, A\}$, $\{W, A, N\}$, and $\{W, A, F\}$. The corresponding types are $(\rho^{LL}, SeedK^{LL}[], \rho K^{LL}[\tilde{T}])$ and $(\rho^{LH}, SeedK^{HH}[], \rho K^{HH}[\tilde{T}])$, where $\rho = Unwrap$. We need to type-check the following clauses under the assumption that $\tilde{x}$ may have all the types in PTS. Meanwhile, $PTS(\{W, F\}, \wp) = (Unwrap^{LH}, SeedK^{HH}[], Unwrap^{HH}[\tilde{T}])$. The rules $[PAV - H]$ and $[PAV - L]$ are used for public hierarchy attributes validation. The purpose for PAV is to check the consistency of hierarchy attributes between the parent object and the child. The former rule says that if the parent object has the attribute $FixedTPM$ (F), then any allowable combination of the hierarchy attributes would be fine for the child. The latter rule states that if the template of the parent object does not include the attribute F, then F cannot be in the template of the child.

4.2   Properties of the Type System

In this section, some properties of our Type System are introduced, including the main result, well-typed APIs are secure. The proof of the main theorem can be found in the full version [16]. Centenaro, et al.[4] have proposed the notion of value well-formedness in their type system in order to track the value integrity at run-time. Their judgement was based on a mapping Θ from atomic values to types. We follow this method but lay more restriction on the foundation of this typing environment for values to obtain more valuable properties. Rules for typing values are given in Table. They are close to those for typing expressions.

$$[empty]\ \phi \vdash \emptyset,$$

$$[Env]\ \frac{\Theta\vdash\emptyset, v\notin dom(\Theta), T=\varphi K^{\sigma}[\tilde{T}], SeedK^{\sigma}[]\Rightarrow(\varphi\in\{Sym,Dec,Unwrap,hmac\}\wedge\sigma=HH)}{\Theta\cup\{val\mapsto T\}\vdash\emptyset},$$

$$[atom]\ \frac{\Theta(val)=T}{\Theta\vdash val:T},\ [sub]\ \frac{\Theta\vdash v:T',T'\leq T}{\Theta\vdash v:T},\ [tuple]\ \frac{\Theta\vdash\tilde{v}:\tilde{T},\Theta\vdash v':T'}{\Theta\vdash(\tilde{v},v'):(\tilde{T},T')},$$

$$[kdfSH]\ \frac{\Theta\vdash v:SeedK^{HH}[],usg=STORAGE}{\Theta\vdash kdf(usg,v):SymK^{HH}[\tilde{T}]},\ [kdfSL]\ \frac{\Theta\vdash v:SeedK^{LL}[],usg=STORAGE}{\Theta\vdash kdf(usg,v):SymK^{LL}[LL,\cdots,LL]},$$

$$[kdfIH]\ \frac{\Theta\vdash v:SeedK^{HH}[],usg=INTEGRITY}{\Theta\vdash kdf(usg,v):hmacK^{HH}[\tilde{T}]},\ [kdfIL]\ \frac{\Theta\vdash v:SeedK^{LL}[],usg=INTEGRITY}{\Theta\vdash kdf(usg,v):hmacK^{LL}[LL,\cdots,LL]},$$

$$[wrapK]\ \frac{\Theta\vdash v:UnwrapK^{\sigma}C^{\sigma}I[\tilde{T}]}{\Theta\vdash ek(v):WrapK^{L\sigma}I[\tilde{T}]},\ [encK]\ \frac{\Theta\vdash v:DecK^{\sigma}C^{\sigma}I[\tilde{T}]}{\Theta\vdash ek(v):EncK^{L\sigma}I[\tilde{T}]},$$

$$[Sym]\ \frac{\Theta\vdash v':SymK^{\sigma}C^{\sigma}I[\tilde{T}],\Theta\vdash\tilde{v}:\tilde{T}}{\Theta\vdash senc(v',\tilde{v}):L\sigma_I},\ [HMAC]\ \frac{\Theta\vdash v':hmacK^{\sigma}C^{\sigma}I[\tilde{T}],\Theta\vdash\tilde{v}:\tilde{T},\sigma'_I=\sigma_I\cup_{T\in\tilde{T}}L_I(T)}{\Theta\vdash HMAC(v',\tilde{v}):L\sigma_I},$$

$$[Wrap]\ \frac{\Theta\vdash v':WrapK^{\sigma}C^{\sigma}I[\tilde{T}],\Theta\vdash\tilde{v}:\tilde{T}}{\Theta\vdash aenc(v',\tilde{v}):L\sigma_I},\ [Enc]\ \frac{\Theta\vdash v':EncK^{\sigma}C^{\sigma}I[\tilde{T}],\Theta\vdash\tilde{v}:\tilde{T}}{\Theta\vdash aenc(v',\tilde{v}):L\sigma_I}$$

However, two additional rules [empty] and [env] are set to define the well-formedness of our typing environment Θ. The rule [env] requires that Θ does not contain multiple bindings for the same value. Moreover, only atomic fresh keys at a security level of HH are allowable. It is sound because in operation semantics for commands in section 2.2, atomic fresh keys can only be generated by genKey and genSeed, which are internal functions that cannot be touched by the attackers. On the basis of these rules, some properties for the types of key values can be obtained by easy induction on the derivation of $\Theta \vdash v : \phi K^{\sigma}[\tilde{T}]$.

Proposition 1 (Private Keys). If $\Theta \vdash \emptyset$, $\Theta \vdash v : \phi K^{\sigma}[\tilde{T}]$, and $\phi \in \{Seed, Sym, Dec, Unwrap, hmac\}$, then $\sigma \in \{HH, LL\}$.

Proposition 2 (Low Keys). If $\Theta \vdash \emptyset$, then $\Theta \vdash v : \phi K^{LL}[\tilde{T}]$ implies $\tilde{T} = LL, \cdots, LL$.

Proposition 3 (Public Keys). If $\Theta \vdash \emptyset$, $\Theta \vdash v : \phi K^{\sigma}[\tilde{T}]$, and $\phi \in \{Wrap, Enc\}$, then $\sigma \in \{LH, LL\}$.

The next proposition says the type of private key is unique, if it has a security level of HH.

Proposition 4 (Uniqueness of Key Types). Let $\Theta \vdash \emptyset$. If $\Theta \vdash k : \phi K^{\sigma}[\tilde{T}]$ and $\Theta \vdash k : \phi'K^{\sigma'}[\tilde{T'}]$ with $\phi, \phi' \in \{Seed, hamc, Sym, Unwrap, Dec\}$, then $\sigma = \sigma'$. If $\sigma = \sigma' = HH$, we also have $\phi = \phi'$.

The notion of well-formedness for memory environment follows the definition 3 in [4] except that we add item (1), which requires Θ is well formed. With this requirement, we may apply proposition 1 to 4.

Definition 2 (Well-formedness). The judgement of well-formedness for memory environment and key handle-map is denoted as $\Gamma, \Theta \vdash \mathbf{M}, \mathbf{H}$ if
(1) $\Theta \vdash \emptyset$, ie., the typing environment Θ is well formed by the typing rules [empty] and [Env];

(2) $\Gamma, \Theta \vdash \mathbf{M}$, ie., $\mathbf{M}(x) = v, \Gamma(x) = T$ implies $\Theta \vdash v : T$;

(3) $\Theta \vdash \mathbf{H}$. Let $\mathbf{H}(h) = (tmp, v_s, v_k)$. $\vdash tmp : \rho^{LH}$ implies $\Theta \vdash v_s : SeedK^{HH}[]$, $\Theta \vdash v_k : \rho K^{HH}[\tilde{T}]$; $\vdash tmp : LL$ implies $\Theta \vdash v_s : LL, \Theta \vdash v_k : LL$.

As we have mentioned above, the security level σ restrict the capability of attackers such that they can read from LL, LH and modify LL, HL. Due to $\rho K^{LH}[\tilde{T}] \leq LH \leq LL$ and the subtyping rule, we may assume the knowledge of attackers has a security level of LL. Proposition 5 proves that if we only give the attacker atomic values of type LL, all the values that can be derived from his capability are of a security level LL. In the proof of this proposition, we may use proposition 2 (Low Keys) in some cases.

Proposition 5 (Attacker typability). Let $\Theta \vdash \emptyset$, $\Theta \vdash \mathbf{H}$ and V be a set of atomic values. Suppose $\forall v \in V, \Theta(v) = LL$. Then, $v' \in \mathcal{K}(V)$ implies $\Theta \vdash v' : LL$ if v' is an atomic values, and $\Theta \vdash v' : (LL, \cdots, LL)$ if v' is a tuple.

Lemma 1 states that in a well-formed memory, each expression has a type matched with its evaluation. Lemma 2 states that well-typed commands remain well-typed at run-time and preserve well-formedness of typing environment.

Lemma 1. If $\Theta \vdash \emptyset$, $\Gamma, \Theta \vdash \mathbf{M}$, $\Gamma \vdash e : T$, and $e \downarrow^{\mathbf{M}} v$, then $\Theta \vdash v : T$.

Lemma 2. Let $\Gamma, \Theta \vdash \mathbf{M}, \mathbf{H}$ and $\Gamma \vdash p$. If $\langle \mathbf{M}, \mathbf{H}, p \rangle \to \langle \mathbf{M}', \mathbf{H}', p' \rangle$ then we have

(1) if $p' \neq \varepsilon$ then $\Gamma \vdash p'$;

(2) $\exists \Theta' \supseteq \Theta$ such that $\Gamma, \Theta' \vdash \mathbf{M}', \mathbf{H}'$.

With Lemma 1 and 2 above, we finally prove our main result that well-typed API commands are secure.

Theorem 1. If $\Gamma \vdash \mathcal{A}$, then $\mathcal{A}$ is secure.

5 Type-Based Analysis of TPM 2.0 Specification Commands

In this section, we show that the TPM 2.0 Specification commands such as TPM2_Duplicate, TPM2_Import, TPM2_Create and TPM2_Load are secure in the framework of our model (It is expected to include more commands). We will prove that these commands guarantee the secrecy of the key object with its *FixedTPM* SET, even in case of the worst scenario in which the attacker may access all loaded key objects via API commands to perform operations corresponding to the protected storage hierarchies rooted in the TPM.

The API is defined in Trusted Platform Module Library (TPML) Family 2.0, Part 3: Commands [15], which specifies the input parameters, the response, and the detailed actions of each command. We may translate the detailed actions to our language introduced in section 2.2. The commands that need to be formalized include Object Commands in Chapter 14 and Duplication Commands in Chapter 15 of TPML 2.0, Part 3. As we have discussed in section 2.1, we focus on these commands since they decide how an object might be connected to the protected storage hierarchy rooted in the TPM.

The detailed actions in these commands contain internal functions specified in section 7.6 of TPML 2.0, Part 4: Supporting Routines. These internal functions should be called by Protected Capabilities. We have transferred these functions to our language. Now we give an example of `AreAttributesForParent()`, which decides whether the input handle refers to a parent object. It can be implemented by (ObjTemplate, ObjSeed, ObjSensitive):= `checkTemplate`(ObjHandle, {W}); In a similar way, we could formalize a set of internal functions in section 7.6 of Part 4.

After this formalization, we could translate to our language the protected storage API commands such as `TPM2_Create()`, `TPM2_Load()`, `TPM2_Duplicate()`, and `TPM2_Import()` in Part 3. We give an example of `TPM2_Load()`. The detailed translation is in the full version.

Command `TPM2_Load` takes as input the handle of the parent object (parentH), the public area of the loaded object (inAttributes), an HMAC to check the integrity (inHMAC), and the encrypted sensitive area of the loaded object (LoadPrivate). The execution of the command depends on whether the loaded object has *FixedTPM* SET in its template ($F \in$ inAttributes) since it decides whether *FixedTPM* is needed in the parent object. In the detailed actions of Part 3, it is expressed by a standard if/else statement. For the former case, F is needed to be included in the template of the parent object. The latter is not. Thus we have different requirements for the first `checkTemplate`. There are no differences in the following clauses. Then, the public attributes of the loaded object should be checked to be consistent with the parent's by `PAV`. If passed, a symmetric key (symKeyP) for secure storage and an HMAC key (HMACkeyP) for integrity are derived from the secret seed (parentSeed) in the parent object. After checking the integrity of the public area (inAttributesC) and the encrypted sensitive area (LoadPrivate), the command will decrypt the sensitive area by `sdec`. At last, new object are loaded and its handle (ObjH) is returned.

In a similar way, we have translated the Object Commands and Duplication Commands in Trusted Platform Module Library (TPML) Family 2.0, Part 3: Commands. In the following, we need to type-check these API commands by our type system in section 3.1 to enforce the security of API commands. We will give an example of the command `TPM2_Load`. The detailed specification is in the full version [16].

Since the command `TPM2_Load` requires a branch, we need to devise two typing environment Γ respectively to type these two cases. For both cases, it is required that all the input parameters have type LL (line 00 and line 10). For the former case, when `checkTemplate` requires a handle for a parent key object with W, F SET. Then the type returned is $(Unwrap^{LH}, SeedK^{HH}[], UnwrapK^{HH}[\tilde{T}])$ according to section 3.1. Then by the rule $[PAV - H]$, we get the input attributes after check should have type Any^{LH} because $F \in$ inAttributes. By `kdf`, we get two keys derived from the seed value in the parent sensitive area with types $SymK^{HH}[SeedK^{HH}[], AnyK^{HH}]$ and $hmacK^{HH}[LH, Any^{LH}]$. The payload type is decided by the usage of the parent key object. Then after checking the HMAC and symmetric decryption, the returned sensitive area types are

$(SeedK^{HH}[\,], AnyK^{HH}[\tilde{T}])$. With appropriate types of sensitive area and public area, `ObjectLoad` could load the object into the TPM. Then the type of the returned handle value is LL, which could be returned as the response. For the latter case, `checkTemplate` requires a handle for a parent key with just W SET and the returned type is in $PTS(\{W\}, \wp)$. There are two types in this set, (LL, LL, LL) and $(Unwrap^{LH}, SeedK^{HH}[\,], UnwrapK^{HH}[\tilde{T}])$. We have to type-check the continuation clauses twice, under these two assumptions. The two typing derivations are the same for `PAV` since $F \notin$ inAttributes. The input template (inAttributes: LL) after `PAV` has type LL. For `kdf`, since the types of payloads are decided by the usage of the parent key object, they both have type LL, LL for the payloads. Thus these two cases are the same for checking HMAC, decryption and loading the object. We finally type-check `return` ObjH by $[return]$.

We have shown that the command `TPM2_Load` is well-typed. By Theorem 1, we know that `TPM2_Load` is secure. In a similar way, we could type-check the other commands that have been formalized in our model and enforce the security of protected storage APIs of the TPM 2.0 specification. We have Theorem 2 to state the security of the TPM 2.0 API commands concentrating on Protected Storage part.

Theorem 2. For the protected storage API $\mathcal{A} = \{$`TPM2_Create()`, `TPM2_Load()`, `TPM2_Duplicate()`, `TPM2_Import()`$\}$ defined by TPM 2.0 specification, $\mathcal{A}$ is secure.

6 Conclusion

We have prososed a type system to statically enforce the security of storage part of the TPM 2.0 API commands. Our type system consumes type-checks for asymmetric cryptographic primitives. A formal proof has been proposed that the commands can guarantee the secret of key values in security devices under the worst scenario where the attackers in Delov-Yao style may gain access to all keys loaded on the device and the API commands can be called by any sequence with any parameters. This has not been proved before.

As future work, we foresee extending our model with more commands such as those involved in Credential Management. We also plan to model the TPM's platform configuration registers (PCRs) which allow one to condition some commands on the current value of a register. Moreover, more security properties such as *integrity* and *noninterference* will be the subject of future work.

Acknowledgments. The research presented in this paper is supported by the National Basic Research Program of China (No. 2013CB338003) and National Natural Science Foundation of China (No. 91118006, No.61202414).

References

1. Abadi, M., Blanchet, B.: Secrecy types for asymmetric communication. Theoretical Computer Science 298(3), 387–415 (2003); In: Honsell, F., Miculan, M. (eds.) FOSSACS 2001. LNCS, vol. 2030, pp. 25–41. Springer, Heidelberg (2001)
2. Backes, M., Maffei, M., Unruh, D.: Zero-knowledge in the applied pi-calculus and automated verification of the direct anonymous attestation protocol. In: IEEE Symposium on Security and Privacy 2008, pp. 202–215 (2008)
3. Bruschi, D., Cavallaro, L., Lanzi, A., Monga, M.: Replay attack in TCG specification and solution. In: Proceedings of ACSAC 2005, Tucson, AZ (USA), vol. 10, pp. 127–137. ACSA, IEEE Computer Society (December 2005)
4. Centenaro, M., Focardi, R., Luccio, F.L.: Type-based analysis of PKCS#11 key management. In: Degano, P., Guttman, J.D. (eds.) Principles of Security and Trust. LNCS, vol. 7215, pp. 349–368. Springer, Heidelberg (2012)
5. Chen, L., Ryan, M.: Offline dictionary attack on TCG TPM weak authorisation data, and solution. In: Gawrock, D., Reimer, H., Sadeghi, A.-R., Vishik, C. (eds.) Future of Trust in Computing, pp. 193–196. Vieweg Teubner (2009)
6. Chen, L., Ryan, M.: Attack, solution and verification for shared authorisation data in TCG TPM. In: Degano, P., Guttman, J.D. (eds.) FAST 2009. LNCS, vol. 5983, pp. 201–216. Springer, Heidelberg (2010)
7. Delaune, S., Kremer, S., Ryan, M.D., Steel, G.: A formal analysis of authentication in the TPM. In: Degano, P., Etalle, S., Guttman, J. (eds.) FAST 2010. LNCS, vol. 6561, pp. 111–125. Springer, Heidelberg (2011)
8. Focardi, R., Maffei, M.: Types for Security Protocols. In: Formal Models and Techniques for Analyzing Security Protocol, vol. 5, ch. 7, pp. 143–181. IOS Press (2010)
9. Gürgens, S., Rudolph, C., Scheuermann, D., Atts, M., Plaga, R.: Security evaluation of scenarios based on the TCG's TPM specification. In: Biskup, J., López, J. (eds.) ESORICS 2007. LNCS, vol. 4734, pp. 438–453. Springer, Heidelberg (2007)
10. Lin, A.H., Rivest, R.L., Lin, A.H.: Automated analysis of security APIs. Technical report, MIT (2005)
11. ISO/IEC PAS DIS 11889: Information technology –Security techniques – Trusted Platform Module
12. Trusted Computing Group. TPM Specification version 1.2. Parts 1–3, revision, http://www.trustedcomputinggroup.org/resources/tpm_main_specification
13. Keighren, G., Aspinall, D., Steel, G.: Towards a Type System for Security APIs. In: Degano, P., Viganò, L. (eds.) ARSPA-WITS 2009. LNCS, vol. 5511, pp. 173–192. Springer, Heidelberg (2009)
14. Centenaro, M., Focardi, R., Luccio, F.L., Steel, G.: Type-based analysis of PIN processing APIs. In: Backes, M., Ning, P. (eds.) ESORICS 2009. LNCS, vol. 5789, pp. 53–68. Springer, Heidelberg (2009)
15. Trusted Computing Group. TPM Specification version 2.0. Parts 1–4, revision, http://www.trustedcomputinggroup.org/resources/tpm_main_specification
16. Shao, J., Feng, D., Qin, Y.: Type-Based Analysis of Protected Storage in the TPM (full version). Cryptology ePrint Archive (2013), http://eprint.iacr.org/2013/501

Remote Attestation Mechanism
for User Centric Smart Cards
Using Pseudorandom Number Generators

Raja Naeem Akram[1], Konstantinos Markantonakis[2], and Keith Mayes[2]

[1] Cyber Security Lab, Department of Computer Science, University of Waikato,
Hamilton, New Zealand
[2] ISG Smart card Centre, Royal Holloway, University of London
Egham, Surrey, United Kingdom
rnakram@waikato.ac.nz, {k.markantonakis,keith.mayes}@rhul.ac.uk

Abstract. User Centric Smart Card Ownership Model (UCOM) gives
the "freedom of choice" of respective applications to the smart card users.
The user-centric architecture requires a trusted entity to be present on
the smart card to provide security assurance and validation to the requesting application providers. In this paper, we propose the inclusion of
a trusted computing platform for smart cards that we refer as the Trusted
Environment & Execution Manager (TEM). This is followed by the rationale behind the changes to the traditional smart card architecture to
accommodate the remote security assurance and validation mechanism.
We propose an attestation protocol that provides an on-demand security
validation of a smart card by its respective manufacturer. Finally, the
attestation protocol is informally analysed, and its test implementation
and performance measurements are presented.

1 Introduction

The ecosystem of the User Centric Smart Card Ownership Model (UCOM) [1]
in centred around smart cards that have to implement adequate security and
operational functionality to support a) enforcement of security policies stipulated
by the card platform and individual Service Providers (SPs) for their respective
applications, and b) operational functionality that enables an SP to manage its
application(s), and a cardholder to manage her ownership privileges. The smart
card architecture has to represent this change in ownership architecture. For this
purpose, we require a trusted module as part of the smart card architecture. The
module would validate the current state of the platform to requesting entities in
order to establish the trustworthiness of a smart card in the UCOM ecosystem.

In the UCOM, the card manufacturers make sure that smart cards have
adequate security and operational functionality to support user ownership. In
addition, the cardholder manages her relationship with individual SPs. These
relationships enable her to request installation of their applications. Before leasing an application, SPs will require an assurance of the smart card's security and

S. Qing et al. (Eds.): ICICS 2013, LNCS 8233, pp. 151–166, 2013.
© Springer International Publishing Switzerland 2013

reliability. This assurance will be achieved through a third party security evaluation of the smart cards before they are issued to individual users. Furthermore, to provide a dynamic security validation [2], the evaluated smart cards implement an attestation mechanism. The attestation mechanism should accommodate remote validation, as in the UCOM an SP will not always have physical access to the smart card. In addition, the attestation mechanism will certify that the current state of the smart card is as evaluated by the independent third party. Therefore, the trust architecture in the UCOM is based on the adequacy of the third party evaluation, and the security and reliability of the remote attestation mechanism.

1.1   Contributions

In this paper, we propose a smart card remote attestation mechanism based on Pseudorandom Number Generators. The paper also proposes an attestation protocol, both the protocol and attestation mechanism is implemented, and evaluated, along with presenting the underlying performance measurements.

1.2   Organisation

Section 2, discusses the major component that provides security and reliability assurance to (remote) requesting entities: attestation handler and self-test manager. Subsequently, we extend the discussion to the remote attestation mechanism in section 3 and propose two attestation algorithms based on pseudorandom number generators. In section 4 we propose an attestation protocol; in section 5 we detail an informal analysis and test implementation results of the attestation protocol.

2   Proposed Components to Support Attestation Mechanism

The crucial components that support the attestation mechanism are discussed below. Both of these are part of the TEM, and for an indepth discussion on TEM and Security Assurance & Validation Mechanism for UCOM please consult [2,3]. The difference between these two modules (i.e. the attestation handler and the self-test manager) of the TEM is that one focuses on the software and the other on the hardware. However, in the proposed attestation mechanism (section 3) they complement each other to provide proof that a smart card is secure, reliable and trustworthy.

2.1   Attestation Handler

During the application installation process, the attestation handler will verify the current state of the platform runtime environment (e.g. security and operationally sensitive parts of the Smart Card Operating System) and affirm to the appropriate SP that the platform is as secure and reliable as it is claimed to be by the (third party) evaluation certificate [2]. Once the application is installed the relevant SP can ask the TEM to generate its state validation (e.g. signed hash of the downloaded application), ensuring that the application is downloaded without any errors onto the platform. This function of the TEM is similar to the GlobalPlatform's DAP mechanism [4,5].

2.2   Self-test Manager

The self-test mechanism checks whether the smart card is tamper-resistant as certified by a trusted third party evaluation. The aim of the self-test mechanism is to provide a remote hardware validation framework in a way that enables a requesting entity (e.g. an SP) to independently verify it. As our focus is not the hardware end of the smart card, we do not propose any (pure) hardware-based mechanism in this paper, which is one of the possible directions for future research.

A self-test mechanism in the UCSC should provide the properties that are listed below:

1. Robustness: On input of certain data, it should always produce associated output.
2. Independence: When the same data is input to a self-test mechanism implemented on two different devices, they should output different (random) values.
3. Pseudo-randomness: The generated output should be computationally difficult to distinguish from a pseudo-random function.
4. Tamper-evidence: Any attack aiming to access the function should cause irreversible changes which render the device dead.
5. Unforgeable: It should be computationally difficult to simulate the self-test mechanism and mimic the actual deployed function on a device.
6. Assurance: the function should provide assurance (either implicitly or explicitly) based on independent evaluation (e.g. Common Criteria) to requesting entities. The mechanism should not (always) require an active connection with the device manufacturer to provide the assurance.

There are several possibilities for a self-test mechanism in a UCSC including using active (intelligent) shield/mesh [6], the Known Answer Test (KAT) [7], and the Physical Unclonable Function (PUF) [8].

To provide protection against invasive attacks, smart card manufacturers implement an active shield/mesh around the chip. If a malicious user removes the active shield then the chip will be disabled. The self-test mechanism can be associated with this shield to provide a limited assurance that the protective measures of the chip are still in place and active.

Furthermore, Hash-based Message Authentication Code (HMAC) can be deployed with a hard-wired key that would be used to generate a checksum of randomly selected memory addresses that have non-mutable code related to the

Smart Card Operating System (SCOS). This mechanism requires the involvement of the device manufacturer, as the knowledge of the correct HMAC key would be a secret known only to the card manufacturer and its smart cards.

Another potential protection strategy is to utilise Physical Unclonable Functions (PUFs) [8] to provide hardware validation [9]. It is difficult to find a single and consistent definition of PUF in the literature [10]. However, a property description definition of the PUF is provided by Gassend et al. in [8].

Based on the above listed features, table 1 shows the comparison between different possible functions that can act as the self-test mechanism. Although the debate regarding the viability, security, and reliability of the PUFs is still open in both academic circles and industry [11]; for completeness, we consider them as a possible self-test mechanism in table 1. Similar to the PUF, Psuedorandom Number Generators (PRNG) [12] might also be used to implement the self-test mechanism.

Table 1. Comparison of different proposals for self-test mechanism

Features	Active-Shield	Keyed-HMAC	PRNG	PUF
Robustness	Yes	Yes	Yes	Yes
Independence	No	No	Yes	Yes
Pseudo-randomness	No	Yes	Yes	Yes
Tamper-evidence	Yes	–	Yes*	Yes
Unforgeable	No	Yes	Yes*	Yes
Assurance	Yes	No	Yes	Yes*

Note. "Yes" means that the mechanism supports the feature. "No" indicates that the mechanism does not support the required feature. The entry "Yes*" means that it can supports this feature if adequately catered for during the design.

If a manufacturer maintains separate keys for individual smart cards that support the HMAC then it can provide the independence feature. However the HMAC key is hard-wired and this makes it difficult for it to be different on individual smart cards of the same batch. Furthermore, it requires other features to provide tamper evidence, like active-shield. On the other hand, PUFs and adequately designed PRNGs can provide assurance that the platform state and the tamper-resistant protections of a UCSC are still active. In this paper, we propose the PRNG based design for the self-test mechanism that is detailed in section 3.1.

Before we discuss how a self-test manager and an attestation handler can be implemented based on PRNG, we first discuss the overall framework that is responsible for providing security assurance and validation of a smart card.

3   Attestation Mechanisms

In this section, we discuss the attestation mechanism based on PRNGs that combine the functionality of attestation handler and self-test manager discussed in section 2.

3.1   Pseudorandom Number Generator

In this section, we propose the use of a Pseudorandom Number Generator (PRNG) to provide the device authentication, validation, and implicit anti-counterfeit functionality. Unlike (non-simulatable) PUFs, PRNGs are emulatable and their security relies on the protection of their internal state (e.g. input seed values, and/or secret keys, etc.).

The PRNGs implemented in one device will be the same as they are in other devices of the same batch and given the same input, they will produce the same output. Therefore, the manufacturer will populate the PRNG seed file with unique values in each smart card (no two smart cards from the same batch should have the same seed file).

Algorithm 1. Self-test algo for offline attestation based on a PRNG

Input   : l; list of selected memory addresses.
Output: S; signature key of the smart card.
Data:
$seed$; temporary seed value for the PRNG set to zero.
n; number of memory addresses in the list l.
i; counter set to zero.
a; memory address.
k; secret key used to encrypt the signature key of the smart card.
S_e; encrypted signature key using a symmetric algorithm with key k.

```
1   SelfTestOffline (l) begin
2       while i < n do
3           a ⟵ ReadAddressList (l,i)
4           seed ⟵ Hash (ReadMemoryContents (a), seed)
5           i ⟵ i+1
6       if seed ≠ ∅ then
7           k ⟵ GenPRNG (seed)
8       else
9           return testfailed
10      S ⟵ DecryptionFunction (k, Se)
11      return S
```

The seed file is a collection of inputs that is fed to the PRNG to produce a random number, and it is updated constantly by the PRNG [12]. This will enable a card manufacturer to emulate the PRNG and generate valid Chanllenge-Response Pairs (CRPs: discussed in section 3.2) for a particular device. The PRNG mechanism is not tamper-evident and it relies on the tamper-resistant mechanisms of the smart card to provide physical security. Based on the PRNG, algorithms 1 and 2 show the offline and online attestation mechanism, respectively.

The `SelfTestOffline` takes a list of selected memory addresses l that is illustrated in algorithm 1. The function iterates through the l reading one memory address at a time, and then generating a hash of the contents stored at the given memory address. In the next step at line six, the function `SelfTestOffline` checks the value of *seed* and if it is not zero it will proceed; otherwise, it will throw a test fail exception. If the *seed* value is not zero then the *seed* is input to the PRNG and a sequence k is generated. The k is used to encrypt the smart card signature key, and if the input to the PRNG at line seven is as expected the signature key will be correctly decrypted.

Algorithm 2. Self-test algo for online attestation based on a PRNG

    Input   : c; randomly generated challenge sent by the card
                 manufacturer.
    Output: r; hash value generated on selected memory addresses.
    Data:
    seedfile; seed file that has a list of non-zero values.
    seed; temporary seed value for the PRNG set to zero.
    ns; number of entries in a seed file.
    s; unique reference to an entry in the *seedfile*.
    nc; number of bytes in the c.
    i; counter set to zero.
    l; upper limit of memory address defined by the card manufacturer.
    m; memory address.
    mK; HMAC key shared between a smart card and respective card manufacturer

```
1  SelfTestOnline (c) begin
2  |   while i < nc do
3  |   |   s ⟵ ReadChallenge(c, i) % ns
4  |   |   seed ⟵ ReadSeedFile(seedfile, s)
5  |   |   m ⟵ GenPRNG(seed) % l
6  |   |   r ⟵ r ⊕ Hash(ReadMemoryContents(m), mK)
7  |   |_  i ⟵ i + 1
8  |_  return r
```

The algorithm returns the signature key, which is used by the attestation handler to sign a message. The requesting entity will verify the signed message and if the state of the platform is in conformance with the evaluated state then the signature will be verified; otherwise, it will fail. The signature verification will fail because the decrypted signature key will be different as the input to the PRNG at line seven of the algorithm was different. Therefore, we can assume that if the state is changed, the signature key will change, and the generated signature will not verify.

The PRNG-based online attestation mechanism is illustrated in algorithm 2. The function SelfTestOnline takes the challenge c from the card manufacturer as input. The received challenge is treated as an array of bytes and individual bytes of the challenge c are used to generate indexes to the *seedfile*; values stored on these indexes are used to generate memory addresses (within the range specified by the card manufacturer). The contents of the generated memory addresses are then HMACed and the result is securely sent to the card manufacturer. The SP can use the same process described in algorithm 2 to generate the HMAC result and if the result matches with the one sent by the smart card, then the card manufacturer can ascertain that the current state of the card is trustworthy. At line six of the algorithm 2, we update the *seedfile* with the value stored in 'm'. This update is necessary to avoid generation of the same 'r' if the card manufacturer sends the same challenge 'c'.

In the implementation of the attestation protocol (section 4), we implement the online online attestation based on a PRNG illustrated in the algorithm 2.

3.2   Challenge-Response Pair (CRP) Generation

In the case of the mechanism based exclusively on the PRNG as depicted in algorithm 2, the card manufacturer will provide a set of seed values that is referred to as the seed file. This file is internally updated by the PRNG; however, as the card manufacturer knows the initial seed file it does not need to communicate CRPs with the smart card as it can generate the correct response independently (using the seed file and the PRNG associate with the respective smart card).

3.3   Keys Generation

Individual smart cards have a unique set of cryptographic keys that the card uses for different protocols/mechanisms during its lifetime. Therefore, after the hardware fabrication and masking of the SCOS is completed [13] the card manufacturer initiates the key generation process.

Each smart card will generate a signature key pair that does not change for the lifetime of the smart card. The smart card signature key pair is certified by the card manufacturer, and it is used to provide offline attestation (section 3). Furthermore, in the certificate hierarchy shown in figure 1, the smart card signature key pair is linked with the Platform Assurance Certificate (PAC) [2] via the card manufacturer's certificate. The reason for this is that a malicious user might copy a PAC that belongs to a genuine device and put it on his tampered device and when an SP requests security assurance from the tampered device, it provides the (copied) PAC of a (trusted) genuine device. By ensuring the PAC is tied to genuine devices by the certificate hierarchy shown in figure 1 we can avert such scenarios.

The evaluation authority (e.g. Common Criteria evaluation laboratory) issues a certificate (e.g. a PAC) [2], which certifies that the signature key of the card manufacturer is valid only for the evaluated product. If an adversary can get hold of the manufacturer's signature key pairs then he can successfully masquerade

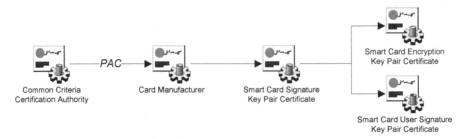

Fig. 1. Certificate hierarchy in the UCOM

as the smart card; either as a dumb device or by simulating the smart card on a powerful device like a computer.

The smart card will also generate a public encryption key pair that is certified by the smart card signature key. The smart card user signature key pair is used to identify the owner of the device and to provide "proof of ownership" that is beyond the scope of this paper. This signature key is unique to the individual user and it is generated on the successful completion of ownership acquisition process.

Finally, the smart card and card manufacturer share an encryption key for symmetric algorithms (e.g. TDES, AES) and a MAC key. These keys will be used to encrypt and MAC communication-messages between the smart card and the card manufacturer.

4   Attestation Protocol

The attestation protocol, referred as Attestation Protocol (ATP), involves the card manufacturer in the security assurance and validation framework by using the online attestation mechanisms. The aim of the protocol is to provide an assurance to a remote SP that the current state of the smart card is not only secure but also (dynamically and on-demand) attested by the card manufacturer. The card manufacturer generates a security validation message that testifies to the requesting SP that its product is safe and still in compliance with the security evaluation indicated by the associated PAC.

4.1   Protocol Goals

The goals for the attestation protocol are listed as below:

PG-1 Secrecy: During the attestation protocol, the communication messages are adequately protected.
PG-2 Privacy: In the attestation protocol, the identity smart card owner (user) should not be revealed to any eavesdropper or the card manufacturer.

4.2 Intruder's Capabilities

The aim of an adversary $\mathcal{A}$ could be to retrieve enough information to enable him to successfully masquerade as a card manufacturer or as a smart card. Therefore, we assume an adversary $\mathcal{A}$ is able to intercept all messages communicated between a smart card and its manufacturer. In addition, $\mathcal{A}$ can modify, change, replay, and delay the intercepted messages.

If $\mathcal{A}$ is able to masquerade as a card manufacturer then $\mathcal{A}$ can issue fake attestation certificates to individual smart cards, which might compromise the security and privacy of the user and related SPs. On the other hand, if $\mathcal{A}$ is able to compromise the smart card then he can effectively simulate the smart card environment. This will enable him to reverse engineer the downloaded applications and retrieve sensitive data related to the user and application (e.g. intellectual property of the SP).

4.3 Protocol Notation and Terminology

Table 2 summarises the notation used in the proposed attestation protocol.

Table 2. Protocol notation and terminology

Notation	Description
$\mathcal{SC}$	Denotes a smart card.
$\mathcal{SP}$	Denotes a Service Provider.
$\mathcal{CM}$	Denotes the respective card manufacturer of the SC.
$\mathcal{CC}$	Denotes the respective Common Criteria evaluation laboratory that evaluates the $\mathcal{SC}$.
X_i	Indicates the identity of an entity X.
N_X	Random number generated by entity X.
$h(Z)$	The result of applying a hash algorithm (e.g. SHA-256) on data Z.
K_{X-Y}	Long term encryption key shared between entities X and Y.
mK_{X-Y}	Long term MAC key shared between entities X and Y.
B_X	Private decryption key associated with an entity X.
V_X	Public encryption key associated with an entity X.
$e_K(Z)$	Result of encipherment of data Z with symmetric key K.
$f_K(Z)$	Result of applying MAC algorithm on data Z with key K.
VM	The Validation Message (VM) issued by the respective CM to a SC representing that the current state of the SC is as secure as at the time of third party evaluation, which is evidenced by the PAC.
$Sign_X(Z)$	Is the signature on data Z with the signature key belonging to an entity X using a signature algorithm like DSA or based on the RSA function.
$CertS_{X \leftarrow Y}$	Is the certificate for the signature key belonging to an entity X, issued by an entity Y.
$CertE_{X \leftarrow Y}$	Certificate for the public encryption key belonging to an entity X, issued by an entity Y.

Notation	Description
$X \rightarrow Y : C$	Entity X sends a message to entity Y with contents C.
$X \| Y$	Represents the concatenation of data items X and Y.
SID	Session identifier that is used as an authentication credential and to avoid Denial of Service (DoS) attacks. The SID generated during the protocol run 'n' is used in the subsequent protocol run (i.e. n+1).

4.4 Protocol Description

In this section, we describe the attestation protocol, and each message is represented by ATP-n, where n represents the message number.

ATP-1. $\qquad SC : mE = e_{k_{SC-CM}}(SC_i \| N'_{SC} \| CM_i \| ReqVal)$
$\qquad SC \rightarrow CM : SC_{i'} \| mE \| f_{mk_{SC-CM}}(mE) \| SID$

Before issuing the smart card to the user, the SC and CM will establish two secret keys; encryption key K_{SC-CM} and MAC key mK_{SC-CM}. The SC and CM can use these long-term shared keys to generate the session encryption key k_{SC-CM} and the MAC key mk_{SC-CM}. The method deployed to generate session keys is left to the sole discretion of the card manufacturer. Each SC has a unique identifier SC_i that is the identity of the smart card. To provide privacy to each smart card (and its user) the identity of the SC is not communicated in plaintext. Therefore, the psuedo-identifier $SC_{i'}$ is used in the ATP-1, which is generated by the SC and corresponding CM on the successful completion of the previous run of the attestation protocol. We will discuss the generation of $SC_{i'}$ and SID in subsequent messages, as the generated $SC_{i'}$ and SID during this message will be used in the next execution of the attestation protocol. A point to note is that for the very first execution of the attestation protocol, the smart card uses the pseudo-identifier ($SC_{i'}$) that was generated by the card manufacturer and stored on the smart card before the card was issued to the user. The SID is used for two purposes: firstly to authenticate the SC and secondly, to prevent a Denial of Service (DoS) attack on the attestation server. The $ReqVal$ is the request for attestation process.

On receipt of the first message, the CM will check whether it has the correct values of $SC_{i'}$ and SID. If these values are correct, it will then proceed with verifying the MAC. If satisfied, it will then decrypt the encrypted part of the message.

ATP-2. $CM \qquad : mE = e_{k_{SC-CM}}(CM_i \| N'_{SC} \| N_{CM} \| Challenge)$
$\qquad CM \rightarrow SC : mE \| f_{mk_{SC-CM}}(mE) \| SID$

The CM generates a random number N_{CM} and a $Challenge$. In case of the PRNG-based attestation mechanism, the $Challenge$ would also be a random number.

ATP-3. $SC \qquad : mE = e_{k_{SC-CM}}(N'_{SC} \| N_{CM} \| N_{SP} \| N_{SC} \| Resp \| Opt)$
$\qquad SC \rightarrow CM : mE \| f_{mk_{SC-CM}}(mE) \| SID$

After generating the *Resp* using the PRNG-based algorithm discussed in section 2, the $\mathcal{SC}$ will proceed with message three. It will concatenate the random numbers generated by the $\mathcal{SC}$, $\mathcal{CM}$, and $\mathcal{SP}$, with the *Resp*. The rationale for including the random number from the SP in message three is to request $\mathcal{CM}$ to generate a validation message that can be independently checked by the $\mathcal{SP}$ to ensure it is fresh and valid. The function of the *Opt* element is to accommodate the CRP updates if other algorithms are used (e.g. PUF-based attestation).

While the $\mathcal{SC}$ was generating the *Resp* based on the *Challenge*, the $\mathcal{CM}$ also calculates the correct attestation response. When the $\mathcal{CM}$ receives message three, it will check the values and if they match then it will issue the validation message. Otherwise the attestation process has failed and $\mathcal{CM}$ does not issue any validation message (VM).

ATP-4. $\mathcal{CM} : VM = Sign_{CM}(CM_i||SC_i||N_{SP}||N_{SC}||PAC)$
$\mathcal{CM} : mE = e_{k_{SC-CM}}(N'_{SC}||VM||SC_{i'}^+||SID^+||CertS_{CM})$
$\mathcal{CM} \rightarrow \mathcal{SC} : mE||f_{mk_{SC-CM}}(mE)||SID$

If the attestation response is successful then the $\mathcal{CM}$ will take the random numbers generated by the $\mathcal{SP}$ and the $\mathcal{SC}$ and include the identities of the $\mathcal{SC}$ and $\mathcal{CM}$. All of these items are then concatenated with the $\mathcal{SC}$'s evaluation certificate PAC and then signed by the $\mathcal{CM}$. The signed message is then communicated to the $\mathcal{SC}$.

In the ATP-4, the $\mathcal{CM}$ will also generate a SID and $SC_{i'}$ that will be used in the subsequent execution of the attestation protocol between the $\mathcal{SC}$ and $\mathcal{CM}$. The SID and $SC_{i'}$ for the subsequent run of the attestation protocol is represented as SID^+ and $SC_{i'}^+$. The SID^+ is basically a (new) random number that is associated with the pseudo-identifier of the smart card that it will use to authenticate in the subsequent attestation protocol. Furthermore, the $SC_{i'}^+$ is generated as $SC_{i'}^+ = f_{mK_{CM}}(CM_i||N_{SC}||N_{CM}||SID)$, where mK_{CM} is the MAC key that the $\mathcal{CM}$ does not share.

5   Protocol Analysis

In this section, we analyse the proposed attestation protocol for given goals and provide details of the test performance results.

5.1   Informal Analysis

In order to meet the goals PG-1 and PG-2, all messages communicated between the $\mathcal{SC}$ and $\mathcal{CM}$ are encrypted and MACed using long term secret encryption and MAC keys; k_{SC-CM} and mK_{SC-CM}, respectively. The $\mathcal{A}$ has to compromise these keys in order to violate the PG-1. If we consider that the symmetric algorithm used (e.g. AES) is sufficiently strong to avert any exhaustive key search and robust enough to thwart any cryptanalysis then it is difficult for the $\mathcal{A}$ to break the protocol by attacking the used symmetric algorithms. A possibility can be to perform side-channel analysis of the smart card and attempt to retrieve the cryptographic keys; however, most modern smart cards have adequate security to prevent this attack, which are evaluated and certified by the third party evaluation (e.g. Common Criteria evaluation). Nevertheless, these assurances can only be against the state-of-the-art attack methodologies at the time of manufacturing/evaluation. Any attacks which surface after manufacture and evaluation may render both the assurance and validation mechanisms useless.

The smart card identity is not used as plaintext during the communication between the $\mathcal{SC}$ and the $\mathcal{CM}$. Instead of using the $\mathcal{SC}_i$, the $\mathcal{SC}$ uses a psuedo-identity $\mathcal{SC}_{i'}$ which changes on every successful completion of communication with the respective $\mathcal{CM}$. Therefore, a particular $\mathcal{SC}$ will only use $\mathcal{SC}_{i'}$ once during its lifetime.

5.2   Protocol Verification by CasperFDR

The CasperFDR approach is adopted to test the soundness of the proposed protocol under the defined security properties. In this approach, the Casper compiler [14] takes a high-level description of the protocol, together with its security requirements. It then translates the description into the process algebra of Communicating Sequential Processes (CSP) [15]. The CSP description of the protocol can be machine verified using the Failures-Divergence Refinement (FDR) model checker [16]. A short introduction to the CasperFDR approach to mechanical formal analysis is provided in appendix A. The intruder's capability modelled in the Casper script (appendix A) for the proposed protocol is as: 1) An intruder can masquerade as any entity in the network. 2) It can read the messages transmitted by each entity in the network. 3) An intruder cannot influence the internal process of an agent in the network.

The security specifications for which the CasperFDR evaluates the network are as shown below. The listed specifications are defined in the # Specification section of appendix A: 1) The protocol run is fresh and both applications are alive. 2) The key generated by a smart card is known only to the card manufacturer. 3) Entities mutually authenticate each other and have mutual key assurance at the conclusion of the protocol. 4) Long term keys of communicating entities are not compromised.

The CasperFDR tool evaluated the protocol and did not find any attack(s). A point to note is that in this paper, we provide mechanical formal analysis using CasperFDR for the sake of completeness and we do not claim expertise in the mathematical base of the formal analysis.

5.3   Implementation Results and Performance Measurements

The test protocol implementation and performance measurement environment in this paper consists of a laptop with a 1.83 GHz processor, 2 GB of RAM running on Windows XP. The off-card entities execute on the laptop and for on-card entities, we have selected two distinct 16bit Java Cards referred as C1 and C2. Each implemented protocol is executed for 1000 iterations to adequately take into account the standard deviation between different protocol runs, and the time taken to complete an iteration of protocol was recorded. The test Java

Cards (e.g. C1 and C2) were tested with different numbers of iterations to find out a range, which we could use as a common denominator for performance measurements in this paper. As a result, the figure of 1000 iterations was used because after 1000 iterations, the standard deviation becomes approximately uniform.

Regarding the choice of cryptographic algorithms we have selected Advance Encryption Standard (AES) [17] 128-bit key symmetric encryption with Cipher Block Chaining (CBC) [18] without padding for both encryption and MAC operations. The signature algorithm is based on the Rivest-Shamir-Aldeman (RSA) [18] 512-bit key. We use SHA-256 [19] for hash generation. For Diffie-Hellman key generation we used a 2058-bit group with a 256-bit prime order subgroup specified in the RFC-5114 [20]. The average performance measurements in this paper is rounded up to the nearest natural number.

The attestation mechanism implemented for emulating the practical performance is based on the PRNG design. The PRNG for our experiments was based on the AES [12] and it has been implemented such that it allows us to input the seed file. The performance measures taken from two different 16-bit Java Cards are listed in table 3. The offline attestation mechanism based on PRNG take in total (excluding PRNG seed file) 2084 bytes. Similarly, the online attestation mechanism and associated attestation protocol based on PRNG take in total (excluding PRNG seed file) 5922 bytes.

Table 3. Test performance measurement (milliseconds) for the attestation protocol

Measures	Offline Attestation		Online Attestation	
Card Specification	C1	C2	C1	C2
Average	408.63	484.55	1008	1284
Best time	367	395	930	1075
Worse time	532	638	1493	1638
Standard Deviation	41.82	59.43	87.68	92.29

5.4   Related Work

The basic concept of remote attestation and ownership acquisition came from the TCG's specifications [21]. The user takes the ownership of the Trusted Platform Module (TPM) and in return, the TPM generates a unique set of keys that are associated with the respective user. The remote attestation mechanism described in the TPM specification [22] provides a remote system attestation (only software). The attestation mechanism is designed so that if the software state is modified, the TPM cannot generate a valid report.

The TPM does not provide an attestation that includes the hardware state. Furthermore, the attestation defined in the TPM specification is more like the offline attestation. However, the offline attestation mechanism (algorithm 1) is different to the one used by TPM, whereas the online attestation is not part of the TPM specifications.

Similarly, other proposals concentrate on the software attestation without binding it to a particular hardware. Such proposals include SCUBA [23], SBAP [24], and SWATT [25]. These protocols utilise execution time as a parameter in the attestation process. This is difficult to guarantee remotely, even with the delegation of time measurement to neighbouring trustworthy nodes [23]. Other mechanisms that use trusted hardware are proposed by Schellekens et al. [26] and PUF-based protocols [27,28,29].

There is no such proposal for remote attestation in smart card frameworks like Java Card, Multos, or GlobalPlatform. The nearest thing is the DAP in the GlobalPlatform card specification that checks the signature on the downloaded application (if the application provider chooses this option). Furthermore, we have opted out of having execution measurement as part of the attestation process as it is difficult to ascertain the trustworthiness of the remote device that measures it. However, unlike other proposed protocols we have an explicit requirement that third party evaluation is used to provide an implicit trust in the attestation process. Furthermore, our proposal binds the software attestation with the hardware protection (tamper-evident) mechanism to provide added assurance.

6   Conclusion

In this paper, we briefly discussed the generic architecture of the UCSC and its components. Later, we extended the discussion to the security assurance and validation framework that requires a third party evaluation and an attestation process. The attestation process includes hardware validation with the traditional software attestation. We proposed two modes for the attestation process: offline and online attestation. In designing the attestation processes, we based our proposal on the PRNG algorithms. To have an online attestation, we proposed the attestation protocol that communicates with the card manufacturer to get a dynamic certificate of assurance (a signed message from the card manufacturer) that the smart card is still secure and reliable. We implemented offline and online attestation mechanisms, along with an attestation protocol on 16-bit Java Cards. We also detailed the performance measurements of the implemented mechanisms and protocols.

References

1. Akram, R.N., Markantonakis, K., Mayes, K.: A Paradigm Shift in Smart Card Ownership Model. In: Apduhan, B.O., Gervasi, O., Iglesias, A., Taniar, D., Gavrilova, M. (eds.) Proceedings of the 2010 Intl. Conf. on Computational Science and Its Applications (ICCSA 2010), pp. 191–200. IEEE Computer Society, Fukuoka (2010)
2. Akram, R.N., Markantonakis, K., Mayes, K.: A Dynamic and Ubiquitous Smart Card Security Assurance and Validation Mechanism. In: Rannenberg, K., Varadharajan, V., Weber, C. (eds.) SEC 2010. IFIP AICT, vol. 330, pp. 161–172. Springer, Heidelberg (2010)

3. Akram, R.N., Markantonakis, K., Mayes, K.: Coopetitive Architecture to Support a Dynamic and Scalable NFC Based Mobile Services Architecture. In: Chim, T.W., Yuen, T.H. (eds.) ICICS 2012. LNCS, vol. 7618, pp. 214–227. Springer, Heidelberg (2012)
4. The GlobalPlatform Proposition for NFC Mobile: Secure Element Management and Messaging, GlobalPlatform, White Paper (April 2009)
5. GlobalPlatform: GlobalPlatform Card Specification, Version 2.2 (March 2006)
6. Eagles, K., Markantonakis, K., Mayes, K.: A comparative analysis of common threats, vulnerabilities, attacks and countermeasures within smart card and wireless sensor network node technologies. In: Sauveron, D., Markantonakis, K., Bilas, A., Quisquater, J.-J. (eds.) WISTP 2007. LNCS, vol. 4462, pp. 161–174. Springer, Heidelberg (2007)
7. FIPS 140-2: Security Requirements for Cryptographic Modules, Online, National Institute of Standards and Technology (NIST) Federal Information Processing Standards Publication, Rev. Supercedes FIPS PUB 140-1 (May 2005)
8. Gassend, B., Clarke, D., van Dijk, M., Devadas, S.: Silicon Physical Random Functions. In: Proceedings of the 9th ACM Conf. on Computer and Communications Security, CCS 2002, pp. 148–160. ACM, New York (2002)
9. Tuyls, P., Schrijen, G.-J., Škorić, B., van Geloven, J., Verhaegh, N., Wolters, R.: Read-Proof Hardware from Protective Coatings. In: Goubin, L., Matsui, M. (eds.) CHES 2006. LNCS, vol. 4249, pp. 369–383. Springer, Heidelberg (2006)
10. Busch, H., Sotáková, M., Katzenbeisser, S., Sion, R.: The PUF promise. In: Acquisti, A., Smith, S.W., Sadeghi, A.-R. (eds.) TRUST 2010. LNCS, vol. 6101, pp. 290–297. Springer, Heidelberg (2010)
11. Merli, D., Schuster, D., Stumpf, F., Sigl, G.: Side-Channel Analysis of PUFs and Fuzzy Extractors. In: McCune, J.M., Balacheff, B., Perrig, A., Sadeghi, A.-R., Sasse, A., Beres, Y. (eds.) Trust 2011. LNCS, vol. 6740, pp. 33–47. Springer, Heidelberg (2011)
12. Akram, R.N., Markantonakis, K., Mayes, K.: Pseudorandom Number Generation in Smart Cards: An Implementation, Performance and Randomness Analysis. In: Mana, A., Klonowski, M. (eds.) 5th Intl. Conf. on New Technologies, Mobility and Security (NTMS), IEEE CS, Istanbuls (2012)
13. Rankl, W., Effing, W.: Smart Card Handbook, 3rd edn. John Wiley & Sons, Inc., NY (2003)
14. Lowe, G.: Casper: a compiler for the analysis of security protocols. J. Comput. Secur. 6, 53–84 (1998)
15. Hoare, C.A.R.: Communicating sequential processes, vol. 21(8). ACM, New York (1978)
16. Ryan, P., Schneider, S.: The Modelling and Analysis of Security Protocols: the CSP Approach. Addison-Wesley Professional (2000)
17. Daemen, J., Rijmen, V.: The Design of Rijndael: AES - The Advanced Encryption Standard. Springer, Heidelberg (2002)
18. Menezes, A.J., van Oorschot, P.C., Vanstone, S.A.: Handbook of Applied Cryptography. CRC (October 1996)
19. FIPS 180-2: Secure Hash Standard (SHS), National Institute of Standards and Technology (NIST) Std. (2002)
20. Lepinski, M., Kent, S.: RFC 5114 - Additional Diffie-Hellman Groups for Use with IETF Standards. Tech. Rep. (January 2008)
21. Trusted Computing Group, TCG Specification Architecture Overview, The Trusted Computing Group (TCG), Oregon, USA, revision 1.4 (August 2007)

22. Trusted Module Specification 1.2: Part 1- Design Principles, Part 2- Structures of the TPM, Part 3- Commands, TCG Std., Rev. 103 (July 2007)
23. Seshadri, A., Luk, M., Perrig, A., van Doorn, L., Khosla, P.: SCUBA: Secure Code Update By Attestation in sensor networks. In: Proceedings of the 5th ACM Workshop on Wireless Security, WiSe 2006, pp. 85–94. ACM, NY (2006)
24. Li, Y., McCune, J.M., Perrig, A.: SBAP: Software-based attestation for peripherals. In: Acquisti, A., Smith, S.W., Sadeghi, A.-R. (eds.) TRUST 2010. LNCS, vol. 6101, pp. 16–29. Springer, Heidelberg (2010)
25. Seshadri, A., Perrig, A., van Doorn, L., Khosla, P.: SWATT: SoftWare-based AT-Testation for Embedded Devices. In: IEEE Symposium on Security and Privacy, p. 272 (2004)
26. Schellekens, D., Wyseur, B., Preneel, B.: Remote attestation on legacy operating systems with trusted platform modules. Sci. Comput. Program. 74, 13–22 (2008)
27. Schulz, S., Wachsmann, C., Sadeghis, A.-R.: Lightweight Remote Attestation using Physical Functions. Technische Universitat Darmstadt, Darmstadt, Germany, Technical Report (July 2011)
28. Suh, G.E., Devadas, S.: Physical Unclonable Functions for Device Authentication and Secret Key Generation. In: Proceedings of the 44th Annual Design Automation Conf. ACM Press, USA (2007)
29. Busch, H., Katzenbeisser, S., Baecher, P.: PUF-Based Authentication Protocols – Revisited. In: Youm, H.Y., Yung, M. (eds.) WISA 2009. LNCS, vol. 5932, pp. 296–308. Springer, Heidelberg (2009)

A   Attestation Protocol

The Casper script in this section corresponds to the attestation protocol described in section 4.

```
#Free variables
SC, CM : Agent
ns, nsp, nt, c, r : Nonce
S1, S2 : Num
VKey: Agent -> PublicKey
SKey: Agent -> SecretKey
InverseKeys = (sKey, skey), (VKey,
SKey)

#Protocol description
0.  -> SC : CM
1. SC -> CM : S1,{SC, ns, CM,}{sKey}
2. CM -> SC : {CM, ns, nm, c, S2}{sKey}
3. SC -> CM : {ns,nm,nsp,r}{sKey}
4.  CM -> SC : {ns,{CM,SC,ns,nsp}
            {Skey{CM}}}{sKey}

#Actual variables
SmartCard, CardManufacturer, MAppl :
Agent
Ns, Nsp, Nt, Nm, Challenge, Response :
Nonce
SOne, STwo : Num

#Processes

INITIATOR(SC, CM, ns, nsp, r) knows
skey, VKey
RESPONDER(CM, SC, nm, c) knows    sKey,
SKey(CM), VKey

#System
INITIATOR(SmartCard, CardManufacturer,
Ns, Nsp, Response)
RESPONDER(CardManufacturer, SmartCard,
Nm, Challenge)

#Functions
symbolic VKey, SKey

#Intruder Information
Intruder = MAppl
IntruderKnowledge = {SmartCard,
CardManufacturer, MAppl, MAppl, Nm,
Nsp, SKey(MAppl), VKey}

#Specification
StrongSecret(SC, sKey, [CM])
StrongSecret(SC, r, [CM])
Aliveness(SC, CM)
Aliveness(CM, SC)
```

Direct Construction of Signcryption Tag-KEM from Standard Assumptions in the Standard Model

Xiangxue Li[1,2], Haifeng Qian[1,*], Yu Yu[3], Jian Weng[4], and Yuan Zhou[5]

[1] Department of Computer Science and Technology, East China Normal University
hfqian@cs.ecnu.edu.cn
[2] National Engineering Laboratory for Wireless Security, Xi'an University of Posts and Telecommunications
[3] Institute for Interdisciplinary Information Sciences, Tsinghua University
[4] Department of Computer Science, Jinan University
[5] Network Emergency Response Technical Team/Coordination Center, China

Abstract. The paper presents a direct construction of signcryption tag-KEM under the standard DBDH and CDH assumptions in the standard model, without using strongly unforgeable signature schemes as building blocks. We prove its confidentiality and unforgeability with respect to adversarially-chosen keys where the adversary is given more advantageous attack environment than existing models in the literature. The performance of our construction is comparable to existing signcryption tag-KEM schemes.

1 Introduction

Signcryption [13] provides confidentiality and non-repudiation simultaneously for the messages sent over an insecure channel, at lower costs of computation and communication than those required in both signature-then-encryption and encryption-then-signature approaches. At Eurocrypt 2005, Abe et al. [1] introduced tag-KEM (tKEM) scheme which has an extra input τ as a tag in KEM scheme[6]. Bjørstad and Dent [3] extended tag-KEM scheme with an authentication by proposing signcryption tag-KEM (SC-tKEM).

This paper focuses on both security model and concrete construction of signcryption tKEM schemes. We summarize our results in each of these areas, and relate them to prior work.

Constructions. Concrete constructions for signcryption tag-KEM may be evaluated according to the following perspectives: (1) the complexity assumptions on which the security of the construction is based; (2) the operational assumption of setting up the construction practically; etc.

The constructions in [3] are proven secure in the random oracle model [4]. Although those in [9] and [11] are without random oracles, yet 'generic': they

---

* Corresponding author.

S. Qing et al. (Eds.): ICICS 2013, LNCS 8233, pp. 167–184, 2013.
© Springer International Publishing Switzerland 2013

involve running standard strongly unforgeable signature schemes as building blocks. The construction in [9] is based on non-standard GHDH assumption [7]. We present in the paper a direct construction of signcryption tag-KEM which is provably secure under the standard complexity assumptions (DBDH and CDH) in the standard model. The idea of our construction follows the Waters signature[12] and the public key encryption by Lai et al.[8]. Our trick allows us to prove its security w.r.t. adversarially-chosen keys (see below).

Security. The security requirements of a signcryption tag-KEM scheme are confidentiality and authenticity [3,9,11]. In the game that defines confidentiality in [9], the challenger produces the challenge private/public key pairs of the sender and the receiver, hands the key pair of the sender and the public key of the receiver to the adversary $\mathcal{A}$, who outputs a tag τ of which he receives an encapsulation of some symmetric key. $\mathcal{A}$ wins if it succeeds in guessing a bit. Thus, the definition of confidentiality [9] only considered the case of honestly chosen challenge key of the sender.

In real-world applications, however, the keys are usually chosen by the users themselves. It seems thus natural to let the adversary choose the keys in the security experiment to reflect this fact. Furthermore, the adversary should be allowed to choose the challenge key of the sender in an adaptive manner, i.e., it can make multiple queries containing a public key of some sender and a tag to the key decapsulation oracle, where future queries (especially, the challenge query) can depend on the results of previous queries. Like the definition of confidentiality, the unforgeability models in [9,11] did not consider the case of adversarially-chosen challenge key of the receiver.

Hence, we define confidentiality and unforgeability with new adversarial powers such that the adversary can choose its challenge keys in the games that define confidentiality and unforgeability. These games give the adversary more advantageous attack environment which is indeed quite natural as the adversary is given all the possible resources, except those that allow it to trivially win the game. We also notice that there do exist some signcryption schemes which consider adversarially chosen keys in their security models [10,5,2].

In a nutshell, our signcryption tag-KEM achieves the following desirable features simultaneously, compared with the previous constructions [3,9,11].

1. *Full insider security w.r.t. adversarially-chosen keys*: Our SC-tKEM provides full insider security with respect to adversarially-chosen keys in the standard model (in definitions 5 and 6). Whereas, there exist in the prior work on SC-tKEM [3,9,11] the failure to consider the possibility of adversarially-chosen challenge keys (for confidentiality and unforgeability).

2. *Standard complexity assumptions*: Security of our SC-tKEM relies on the well-established Decisional Bilinear Diffie-Hellman and the Computational Diffie-Hellman assumptions. Prior to our work, the SC-tKEM schemes [9] require non-standard assumption (i.e., the Gap Hashed Diffie-Hellman assumption [7]) to prove security in the standard model. And the schemes in [11] partially relies on the strong unforgeability of the underlying signature.

3. *Operational assumption*: Our construction enjoys *simple setup operation* since only one key generation algorithm is needed to generate the keys of both the sender and the receiver. Whereas, two different key generation algorithms are required in [9,11] respectively for the entities, e.g., RSA-like for the sender and DLP-like for the receiver. Thus, the setup process of these SC-tKEM schemes is more complicate than that of ours.

2   Preliminaries

2.1   Bilinear Group

Let $\mathbb{G}$ and $\mathbb{G}_T$ be two multiplicative cyclic groups of prime order p, g a generator of $\mathbb{G}$; $e : \mathbb{G} \times \mathbb{G} \to \mathbb{G}_T$ an efficiently computable map with the following properties: i) bilinear: for all $u, v \in \mathbb{G}$ and $a, b \in \mathbb{Z}_p$, $e(u^a, v^b) = e(u, v)^{ab}$; ii) efficiently computable: $e(u, v)$ is efficiently computable for any input pair $(u, v) \in \mathbb{G} \times \mathbb{G}$; iii) non-degenerate: $e(g, g) \neq 1$. We say that $\mathbb{G}$ is a bilinear group if it satisfies these requirements.

2.2   Complexity Assumptions

Let $\mathbb{G}$ be a bilinear group of prime order p and g be a generator of $\mathbb{G}$.

Definition 1 (DBDH). *Let a, b, c and z be random from $\mathbb{Z}_p$, g the generator of $\mathbb{G}$. The (t, ε)-DBDH assumption says that there is no algorithm $\mathcal{A}$ that can distinguish the tuple $(g^a, g^b, g^c, e(g, g)^{abc})$ from the tuple $(g^a, g^b, g^c, e(g, g)^z)$ in time t with advantage ε, where the advantage of $\mathcal{A}$ is defined as the probability*

$$\text{Adv}_{\mathcal{A}}^{\text{DBDH}} = \left| \Pr[\mathcal{A}(g^a, g^b, g^c, e(g, g)^{abc}) = 1] - \Pr[\mathcal{A}(g^a, g^b, g^c, e(g, g)^z) = 1] \right|.$$

Definition 2 (CDH). *In a bilinear group $\mathbb{G}$, the computational Diffie-Hellman problem is: given $(g, g^a, g^b) \in \mathbb{G}^3$ for some $a, b \xleftarrow{R} \mathbb{Z}_p$, to find $g^{ab} \in \mathbb{G}$.*

The success probability of an algorithm $\mathcal{A}$ in solving the CDH problem on $\mathbb{G}$ is defined as $\text{Adv}_{\mathcal{A}}^{\text{cdh}} \stackrel{\text{def}}{=} \Pr\left[\mathcal{A}(g, g^a, g^b) = g^{ab} : a, b \xleftarrow{R} \mathbb{Z}_p \right]$. The probability is over the random choice of g from $\mathbb{G}$, of a, b from $\mathbb{Z}_p$, and the coin tosses of $\mathcal{A}$. If there is no adversary $\mathcal{A}$ which can break the CDH problem on $\mathbb{G}$ in time at most t, and $\text{Adv}_{\mathcal{A}}^{\text{cdh}} \geq \varepsilon$, we say the CDH problem on $\mathbb{G}$ is (t, ε)-secure.

2.3   Collision Resistance

Definition 3 (Collision Resistance). *Let $\ell, \ell' : \mathbb{N} \leftarrow \mathbb{N}$ be such that $\ell(n) > \ell'(n)$ and let $I \subseteq \{0, 1\}^*$. A collection of functions $\{H_s : \{0, 1\}^{\ell(n)} \to \{0, 1\}^{\ell'(n)}\}_{s \in I}$ is called collision-resistant hash family (with index-set I) if the following holds: 1) There exists a probabilistic polynomial-time evaluation algorithm that on input $s \in I, x \in \{0, 1\}^{\ell(k)}$ computes $H_s(x)$; 2) Collisions are hard to find. Formally, a pair x, x' is called a collision for a function H_s if $x \neq x'$*

but $H_s(x) = H_s(x')$. *Collision resistance requires that given input s, every PPT algorithm succeeds in finding a collision for the function H_s with a negligible probability.*

We say $\{H_s\}_{s \in I}$ is (t, ε_{cr})-collision resistant hash function indexed by $s \in I$, if no probabilistic t-polynomial time algorithm $\mathcal{A}$, which outputs x, x' such that $H_s(x) = H_s(x')$ and $x \neq x'$ for chosen $s \in I$, is of probability at least ε_{cr}:
$$\Pr[H_s(x) = H_s(x') \wedge x \neq x' : \text{given}\ \ s \in I; (x, x') \leftarrow \mathcal{A}(H_s)] < \varepsilon_{cr}.$$

3   Definition of Signcryption Tag-KEM

3.1   Syntax

Unlike an encryption algorithm, the tag-KEM's encapsulation algorithm does not take any plaintext as input but rather randomly generates its own "message" – the symmetric key K [1]. A signcryption tag-KEM is defined by direct analogy to the definition of tag-KEM [1]. The following definition is borrowed from [9,11] which is a simplified version of the original one defined by Bjørstad and Dent[3].

Definition 4 (SC-tKEM). *A signcryption tag-KEM consists of the following algorithms:*

Setup(1^λ): *setup algorithm, on input a security parameter λ, outputs the common parameters used in the scheme.*

tKeyGen(1^λ): *key generation algorithm, on input a security parameter λ, outputs the sender's public/private key pair (pk_s, sk_s) and the receiver's public/private key pair (pk_r, sk_r). We write $(pk, sk) = $ tKeyGen(1^λ).*

tKeyEnc(sk_s, pk_r, τ): *key encapsulation algorithm, on input the sender's private key sk_s, the receiver's public key pk_r, and a tag τ, outputs a symmetric key K, and a ciphertext C which is an encapsulation of the key K. We write $(K, C) = $ tKeyEnc(sk_s, pk_r, τ).*

tKeyDec(pk_s, sk_r, C, τ): *key decapsulation algorithm, on input the sender's public key pk_s, the receiver's private key sk_r, the encapsulation C of some symmetric key K, and the tag τ, outputs either the symmetric key K or the error symbol $\perp$ in case C is not valid. We write $K = $ tKeyDec(pk_s, sk_r, C, τ).*

The correctness of a SC-tKEM requires that $K = $ tKeyDec(pk_s, sk_r, C, τ), for all $(K, C) = $ tKeyEnc(sk_s, pk_r, τ), and public/private key pairs $(pk_s, sk_s), (pk_r, sk_r)$.

3.2   Definition of Confidentiality

The confidentiality condition requires, informally, that an adversary should not be able to distinguish a real key output by the encapsulation algorithm from a random key. As in the scenario of signcryption [10,5,2], we consider the confidentiality with respect to adversarially-chosen keys for signcryption tKEM.

Definition 5. *Given a SC-tKEM scheme, the attack model of confidentiality w.r.t. adversarially-chosen keys is defined in terms of a game, termed the IND-CCA2-SCtKEM game, played between a hypothetical challenger $\mathcal{C}$ and an attacker $\mathcal{A}$. For a given security parameter λ:*

- **Setup**: *The challenger C runs the key generation algorithm* $\mathsf{tKeyGen}(1^\lambda)$ *(as in definition 4) to produce the receiver's key pair* $(pk_r^\star, sk_r^\star)$, *and sends* $pk_r^\star$ *to the attacker A, while keeping $sk_r^\star$ secret.*
- **Phase 1**: *During this phase, A may make the polynomially bounded queries of key decapsulation. In a key decapsulation query, A submits to the challenger C a ciphertext C associated with the sender's public key pk_s and a tag τ. Herein, the public key pk_s and the tag τ may be generated by A as it wishes. The challenger C performs key decapsulation operations for A in the algorithm $\mathsf{tKeyDec}$ by using the private key $sk_r^\star$ and then sends the result $K = \mathsf{tKeyDec}(pk_s, sk_r^\star, C, \tau)$ or $\bot$ (if C is not valid) to A.*
- **Challenge**: *At the end of Phase 1, A generates and sends a sender's key pair $(pk_s^\star, sk_s^\star)$ and a tag $\tau^\star$ to C. The challenger performs the key encapsulation algorithm $\mathsf{tKeyEnc}$ by using the private key $sk_s^\star$, the public key $pk_r^\star$ and the tag $\tau^\star$, and obtains the result $(K_0^\star, C^\star) = \mathsf{tKeyEnc}(sk_s^\star, pk_r^\star, \tau^\star)$. C also chooses a random bit $b \in \{0, 1\}$ and a random symmetric key $K_1^\star$ with the requirement that $K_1^\star$ and $K_0^\star$ are of the same length. Lastly, C gives A the tuple $(K_b^\star, C^\star)$ as the challenge.*
- **Phase 2**: *During this phase, A may make the queries as in **Phase 1**, while differently we do not allow A to query the key decapsulation for the ciphertext $C^\star$ under the sender's public key $pk_s^\star$ and the tag $\tau^\star$. However, A is allowed to make a key decapsulation query on the challenged ciphertext $C^\star$ with a different sender's public key or a different tag.*
- **Guess**: *Eventually, A outputs a bit b', and it wins the game if $b = b'$.*

The advantage of the adversary A is defined as the probability $\mathsf{Adv}_{A, \mathsf{SC-tKEM}}^{\mathsf{IND}} = |2\Pr[b = b'] - 1|$. *We say A (t, q_d, ε)-breaks the IND-CCA2 security of the signcryption tag-KEM, if A wins the* IND-CCA2-SCtKEM *game with the advantage ε in time t after making q_d key decapsulation queries. A signcryption tag-KEM is said to achieve the IND-CCA2 security if no polynomially bounded adversary has a non-negligible advantage in winning the* IND-CCA2-SCtKEM *game.*

3.3 Definition of Unforgeability

Similarly, existing unforgeability definition of SC-tKEM defined in the literature [3,9,11] does not take into account the possibility of adversarially-chosen challenge keys of the receiver. This induces the following definition.

Definition 6. *The security model of strongly existential unforgeability for a signcryption tag-KEM is defined by the so-called* SUF-SCtKEM *game, played between a hypothetical challenger C and an attacker F described below. For a given security parameter λ:*

- **Setup**: *The challenger C runs the key generation algorithm $\mathsf{tKeyGen}(1^\lambda)$ (as in definition 4) to produce the sender's key pair $(pk_s^\star, sk_s^\star)$, and sends $pk_s^\star$ to the attacker F, while keeping $sk_s^\star$ secret.*
- **Attack**: *During this phase, F may make the polynomially bounded queries of key encapsulation. In a key encapsulation query, the attacker F chooses a*

receiver's key pair (pk_r, sk_r) and a tag τ, and sends pk_r, τ to the challenger $\mathcal{C}$. Then $\mathcal{C}$ performs key encapsulation operations for $\mathcal{F}$ by the algorithm tKeyEnc on input the private key $sk_s^\star$, the public key pk_r and the tag τ, obtains the result $(K, C) = \mathsf{tKeyEnc}(sk_s^\star, pk_r, \tau)$, sends C to $\mathcal{F}$, and appends (C, pk_r, τ) to a list Σ (which is initially empty).

- **Forgery:** Eventually, the attacker $\mathcal{F}$ outputs a receiver's key pair $(pk_r^\star, sk_r^\star)$, a tag $\tau^\star$ and a ciphertext $C^\star$ with the requirement that $(C^\star, pk_r^\star, \tau^\star)$ is a fresh forgery, i.e., $(C^\star, pk_r^\star, \tau^\star) \notin \Sigma$. Then, we say $\mathcal{F}$ wins the game if $(C^\star, pk_r^\star, \tau^\star)$ is valid under $pk_s^\star$, i.e., $\mathsf{tKeyDec}(pk_s^\star, sk_r^\star, C^\star, \tau^\star) \neq \bot$.

The advantage of the attacker $\mathcal{F}$ is defined as the probability of success in winning the SUF-SCtKEM game: $\mathrm{Adv}_{\mathcal{F}, \mathsf{SC-tKEM}}^{\mathsf{SUF}} = \Pr[\mathsf{Win}]$.

We say the signcryption tag-KEM is (t, q_e, ε)-forgeable if $\mathcal{F}$ wins the SUF-SCtKEM game with the advantage ε in time t after making q_e key encapsulation queries. A signcryption tag-KEM has strongly existential unforgeability if no polynomially-bounded adversary can win the SUF-SCtKEM game with non-negligible advantage.

4   The Proposed Construction

Now we are ready to present our construction of SC-tKEM.

Setup(1^λ): Let $\mathbb{G}$ be a group of prime order p, for which there exists an efficiently computable bilinear map into $\mathbb{G}$. The size of the group is determined by the security parameter. Additionally, let $e : \mathbb{G} \times \mathbb{G} \to \mathbb{G}_T$ denote the bilinear map and g be the corresponding generator, along with $u', u_1, \ldots, u_n, f, h, v, w, z \in_R \mathbb{G}$. Let $G : \{0,1\}^* \to \{0,1\}^n$, $H : \{0,1\}^* \to \mathbb{Z}_p$ be two collision resistant hash functions.

tKeyGen(1^λ): A probabilistic polynomial-time sender/receiver key generation algorithm, chooses $x_s, x_r \xleftarrow{R} \mathbb{Z}_p$, sets $sk_s = x_s$, $pk_s = g^{x_s}$, $sk_r = x_r$, $pk_r = g^{x_r}$, and outputs the public/private key pair (pk_s, sk_s) for the sender and the public/private key pair (pk_r, sk_r) for the receiver.

tkeyEnc(sk_s, pk_r, τ): A probabilistic polynomial-time key encapsulation algorithm, takes as input the private key sk_s of the sender, the public key pk_r of the receiver and a tag τ, and outputs a key K and a ciphertext $C = (\sigma_1, \sigma_2, \sigma_3, \sigma_4)$ of (K, τ).

1. Randomly choose $k, r, \sigma_4 \xleftarrow{R} \mathbb{Z}_p$.
2. Compute $K = e(h, pk_r)^k$, $\sigma_1 = g^k$, $\sigma_2 = g^r$, $t_1 = G(\sigma_1, \tau, \sigma_4, pk_s, pk_r)$, $t_2 = H(\sigma_1, \sigma_2, \tau, pk_s, pk_r)$, and

$$\sigma_3 = f^{x_s} \cdot \left(u' \prod_{i \in \mathcal{T}} u_i \right)^r \cdot \left(z \cdot v^{t_2} w^{\sigma_4} \right)^k \tag{4.1}$$

where $\mathcal{T} \subset \{1, \ldots, n\}$ is the set of indices s.t. $t_1[i] = 1$, letting $t_1[i]$ is the i-th bit of t_1.

3. Let $C = (\sigma_1, \sigma_2, \sigma_3, \sigma_4)$ and return (K, C).

tKeyDec(pk_s, sk_r, C, τ): A deterministic polynomial-time decapsulation algorithm, takes as input an encapsulation $C = (\sigma_1, \sigma_2, \sigma_3, \sigma_4)$, the public key pk_s of the sender, the private key sk_r of the receiver and a tag τ, and outputs either a key K or the error symbol $\bot$.

1. Compute $t_1 = G(\sigma_1, \tau, \sigma_4, pk_s, pk_r)$, $t_2 = H(\sigma_1, \sigma_2, \tau, pk_s, pk_r)$.
2. Return $K = e(\sigma_1, h^{x_r})$ (and $\bot$ otherwise) if

$$e(g, \sigma_3) = e(f, pk_s) \cdot e\left(\sigma_2, u' \prod_{i \in \mathcal{T}} u_i\right) \cdot e\left(\sigma_1, z \cdot v^{t_2} w^{\sigma_4}\right).$$

The correctness of the proposed signcryption tag-KEM can be easily verified.

4.1 Unforgeability

Our signcryption tag-KEM satisfies the security model of SUF-SCtKEM in definition 6. The following theorem formally proves the unforgeability of our signcryption tag-KEM. Note that we can conclude that the proposed construction is unforgeable under the CDH assumption asymptotically if the underlying hash function is collision-resistant, as security of the Waters signature [12] itself can be reduced to the CDH problem(see [12] and the appendix A).

Theorem 1 (Unforgeability). *Our signcryption tag-KEM is (t, q_s, ε)-strongly unforgeable assuming the Waters signature is $(t + \mathcal{O}(q_s), q_s, \varepsilon/2)$-existentially unforgeable, the CDH assumption $(t + \mathcal{O}(q_s), (\varepsilon - \varepsilon_{cr})/2q_s)$-holds in $\mathbb{G}$, and H is (t, ε_{cr})-collision resistant.*

Proof. Suppose there is an adversary $\mathcal{A}$ which can win the SUF-SCtKEM game in time t with probability ε. $\mathcal{A}$ is first equipped with the public parameters and the keys $pk_s^\star$. Meanwhile $\mathcal{A}$ can make q_s key encapsulation queries and will be given $\Sigma = \{(C_i, pk_r, \tau_i) | i = 1, \ldots, q_s\}$ on these queries where $C_i = (\sigma_{i1}, \sigma_{i2}, \sigma_{i3}, \sigma_{i4})$ is a valid encapsulation ciphertext with respect to $(pk_s^\star, pk_r, \tau_i)$.

Let $\Sigma_1 = \{(\sigma_{i1}, \tau_i, \sigma_{i4}, pk_s^\star, pk_r) | i = 1, \ldots, q_s\}$, and let $C^* = (\sigma_1^*, \sigma_2^*, \sigma_3^*, \sigma_4^*)$ associated with $(pk_s^\star, pk_r^\star, \tau^\star)$ be the forgery $\mathcal{A}$ eventually produces. As $(C^*, pk_r^\star, \tau^\star) \notin \Sigma$, we can then distinguish between two types of forgeries:

Type I. A forgery where $(\sigma_1^*, \tau^\star, \sigma_4^*, pk_s^\star, pk_r^\star) \notin \Sigma_1$. In this case we denote the adversary as type I forger $\mathcal{A}_I$.

Type II. A forgery where $(\sigma_1^*, \tau^\star, \sigma_4^*, pk_s^\star, pk_r^\star) = (\sigma_{l1}, \tau_l, \sigma_{l4}, pk_s^\star, pk_r)$ but $\sigma_2^* \neq \sigma_{l2}$ for some $l \in \{1, \ldots, q_s\}$. In this case we denote the adversary as type II forger $\mathcal{A}_{II}$.

Note that if $(\sigma_1^*, \tau^\star, \sigma_4^*, pk_s^\star, pk_r^\star) = (\sigma_{l1}, \tau_l, \sigma_{l4}, pk_s^\star, pk_r)$ and $\sigma_2^* = \sigma_{l2}$ for some $l \in \{1, \ldots, q_s\}$, then $\sigma_3^* = \sigma_{l3}$ because given $(pk_s^\star, pk_r^\star, \tau^\star)$, σ_1^*, σ_2^* and σ_4^* (resp., $(pk_s^\star, pk_r, \tau_i)$, σ_{l1}, σ_{l2} and σ_{l4}) uniquely determines σ_3^* (resp., σ_{l3}) that implies $(C^*, pk_r^\star, \tau^\star) = (C_l, pk_r, \tau_l) \in \Sigma$ is not a valid forgery.

A successful adversary $\mathcal{A}$ must output a forgery of either Type I or Type II. We will show that $\mathcal{A}_I$ can be used to break the existential unforgeability of the Waters signature, and $\mathcal{A}_{II}$ can be used to solve the CDH problem if H is collision resistant. The simulator can flip a coin at the beginning of the simulation to guess which type of forgery the adversary will produce and set up the simulation appropriately. In both cases the simulation is perfect. We start by describing how to use a Type II forgery which is the more interesting case.

Type II Forgery. Suppose $\mathcal{A}_{II}$ is a Type II adversary which (t, q_s, ε)-breaks the strong unforgeability of our signcryption tag-KEM, producing a Type II forgery. We will construct an adversary $\mathcal{B}_{II}$ that can $(t, \frac{1}{q_s}(\varepsilon - \varepsilon_{cr}))$-break the Computational Diffie-Hellman problem if the hash function is (t, ε_{cr})-collision resistant. Details are described as follows:

Suppose $\mathcal{B}_{II}$ is given (g, g^a, g^b) associated with the bilinear group parameters $\mathsf{pp} = (\mathbb{G}, \mathbb{G}_T, e, g)$ and its goal is to output g^{ab}. To utilize the forger $\mathcal{A}_{II}$, the simulator $\mathcal{B}_{II}$ simulates the environment of the SUF-SCtKEM game:

Setup. $\mathcal{B}_{II}$ generates the parameters, the public key of the sender:

1. Randomly chooses $\alpha_0, \alpha_1, \ldots, \alpha_n, \alpha_v, \alpha_w, \alpha_z, \beta_v, \beta_w, \beta_z, \gamma$ and x_s from $\mathbb{Z}_p$, then sets $u' = g^{\alpha_0}, u_1 = g^{\alpha_1}, \ldots, u_n = g^{\alpha_n}, f = g^b, h = g^\gamma$, $v = g^{\alpha_v} f^{\beta_v}, w = g^{\alpha_w} f^{\beta_w}, z = g^{\alpha_z} f^{\beta_z}, pk_s^\star = g^{x_s}$.
2. Give $\mathcal{A}_{II}$ the parameters $u', u_1, \ldots, u_n, f, h, v, w, z$ and the public key $pk_s^\star$ of the sender.

   All the parameters and keys here we give have the same distribution as those used in our construction. Therefore, in this phase, we get a perfect simulation.

Encapsulation Queries. Suppose $\mathcal{A}_{II}$ issues q_s key encapsulation queries. $\mathcal{B}_{II}$ first picks up $j^\star \in \{1, \ldots, q_s\}$ randomly, then on receiving (pk_r, τ) from $\mathcal{A}_{II}$, $\mathcal{B}_{II}$ responds to the i-th query as follows $(i = 1, \ldots, q_s)$:

1. If $i \neq j^\star$, select k, η, δ randomly from $\mathbb{Z}_p$, compute $\sigma_{i1} = g^k$, $\sigma_{i2} = g^\eta$, $\sigma_{i4} = \delta$, $t_1 = G(g^k, \tau, \delta, pk_s^\star, pk_r)$, $t_2 = H(g^k, g^\eta, \tau, pk_s^\star, pk_r)$,

$$\sigma_{i3} = (g^b)^{x_s} \cdot \left(u' \prod_{i \in \mathcal{T}^\star} u_i \right)^\eta \cdot (z \cdot v^{t_2} w^\delta)^k, \text{ and return } C_i = (\sigma_{i1}, \sigma_{i2}, \sigma_{i3}, \sigma_{i4});$$

2. Otherwise $i = j^\star$, let $\sigma_{j^\star 1} = g^a$, randomly choose s from $\mathbb{Z}_p$, compute $\sigma_{j^\star 2} = g^s$, $t_2 = H(g^a, g^s, \tau, pk_s^\star, pk_r)$, $\sigma_{j^\star 4} = \delta^\star = -\frac{\beta_z + t_2 \beta_v}{\beta_w}$, and $t_1 = G(g^a, \tau, \delta^\star, pk_s^\star, pk_r)$,

$$\sigma_{j^\star 3} = (g^b)^{x_s} \cdot \left(u' \prod_{i \in \mathcal{T}^\star} u_i \right)^s \cdot (g^a)^{\alpha_z + \alpha_v t_2 + \alpha_w \delta^\star},$$

eventually return $C_i = (\sigma_{j^\star 1}, \sigma_{j^\star 2}, \sigma_{j^\star 3}, \sigma_{j^\star 4})$.

3. Update $\Sigma = \Sigma \bigcup \{(C_i, pk_r, \tau)\}$ (where we let Σ be initially empty). Indeed, the ciphertext $C_{j*} = (\sigma_{j*1}, \sigma_{j*2}, \sigma_{j*3}, \sigma_{j*4})$ is valid because

$$\sigma_{j*1} = g^a, \quad \sigma_{j*2} = g^s, \quad \sigma_{j*4} = \delta^*,$$

$$\sigma_{j*3} = (g^b)^{x_s} \cdot \left(u' \prod_{i \in \mathcal{T}^*} u_i \right)^s \cdot (g^a)^{\alpha_z + \alpha_v t_2 + \alpha_w \delta^*}$$

$$= (g^b)^{x_s} \cdot \left(u' \prod_{i \in \mathcal{T}^*} u_i \right)^s \cdot (g^a)^{\alpha_z + \alpha_v t_2 + \alpha_w \delta^*} (f^a)^{\beta_z + t_2 \beta_v + \beta_w \delta^*}$$

$$= (g^b)^{x_s} \cdot \left(u' \prod_{i \in \mathcal{T}^*} u_i \right)^s \cdot \left(g^{\alpha_z + \alpha_v t_2 + \alpha_w \delta^*} f^{\beta_z + t_2 \beta_v + \beta_w \delta^*} \right)^a$$

$$= (g^b)^{x_s} \cdot \left(u' \prod_{i \in \mathcal{T}^*} u_i \right)^s \cdot \left(z \cdot v^{t_2} w^{\delta^*} \right)^a.$$

Output. $\mathcal{A}_{\mathrm{II}}$ eventually outputs its forgery $(C^*, pk_r^*, \tau^*) \notin \Sigma$ of Type II where $C^* = (\sigma_1^*, \sigma_2^*, \sigma_3^*, \sigma_4^*)$. Then, it follows $(\sigma_1^*, \tau^*, \sigma_4^*, pk_s^*, pk_r^*) = (\sigma_{l1}, \tau_l, \sigma_{l4}, pk_s^*, pk_r)$ and $\sigma_2^* \neq \sigma_{l2}$ for some $l \in \{1, ..., q_s\}$. If $l \neq j^*$, $\mathcal{B}_{\mathrm{II}}$ aborts; otherwise $l = j^*$ implies $(\sigma_1^*, \tau^*, \sigma_4^*, pk_s^*, pk_r^*) = (\sigma_{j*1}, \tau_{j*}, \sigma_{j*4}, pk_s^*, pk_r^*)$ and $\sigma_2^* \neq \sigma_{j*2}$, $\mathcal{B}$ does the following.

1. Compute $t_1 = G(\sigma_1^*, \tau^*, \sigma_4^*, pk_s^*, pk_r^*)$, and $t_2^* = H(\sigma_1^*, \sigma_2^*, \tau^*, pk_s^*, pk_r^*)$, $t_2 = H(\sigma_{j*1}, \sigma_{j*2}, \tau_{j*}, pk_s^*, pk_r^*)$.
2. If $t_2 = t_2^*$, abort (we denote this event ColF); otherwise return

$$(\Delta)^{\frac{1}{\beta_z + t_2^* \beta_v + \delta^* \beta_w}}, \text{ where } \Delta = \frac{\sigma_3^*}{(g^b)^{x_s} \cdot (\sigma_2^*)^{\alpha_0 + \sum\limits_{i \in \mathcal{T}} \alpha_i} \cdot (\sigma_1^*)^{\alpha_z + t_2^* \alpha_v + \delta^* \alpha_w}}.$$

Note that $t_2 \neq t_2^*$ implies that $\beta_z + t_2^* \beta_v + \delta^* \beta_w \neq 0$. As $C^* = (\sigma_1^*, \sigma_2^*, \sigma_3^*, \sigma_4^*)$ is a valid forgery, we have, for some $s \in \mathbb{Z}_p$:

$$\sigma_1^* = g^a, \quad \sigma_2^* = g^s, \quad \sigma_4^* = \delta^*, \sigma_3^* = (g^b)^{x_s} \cdot \left(u' \prod_{i \in \mathcal{T}} u_i \right)^s \cdot (z \cdot v^{t_2^*} w^{\delta^*})^a,$$

$$\Delta = \frac{\sigma_3^*}{(g^b)^{x_s} \cdot (\sigma_2^*)^{\alpha_0 + \sum\limits_{i \in \mathcal{T}} \alpha_i} \cdot (\sigma_1^*)^{\alpha_z + t_2^* \alpha_v + \delta^* \alpha_w}}$$

$$= \frac{(g^b)^{x_s} \cdot \left(g^{\alpha_0 + \sum\limits_{i \in \mathcal{T}} \alpha_i} \right)^s \cdot (g^{\alpha_z + t_2^* \alpha_v + \delta^* \alpha_w} f^{\beta_z + t_2^* \beta_v + \delta^* \beta_w})^a}{(g^b)^{x_s} \cdot (g^s)^{\alpha_0 + \sum\limits_{i \in \mathcal{T}} \alpha_i} \cdot (g^a)^{\alpha_z + t_2^* \alpha_v + \delta^* \alpha_w}} \qquad (4.2)$$

$$= (f^{\beta_z + t_2^* \beta_v + \delta^* \beta_w})^a = (g^{ab})^{\beta_z + t_2^* \beta_v + \delta^* \beta_w}$$

Therefore, $\Delta^{\frac{1}{\beta_z + t_2^* \beta_v + \delta^* \beta_w}} = g^{ab}$.

For all, when $\mathcal{A}_{II}$ outputs a valid forgery C^* of Type II (denoted event ASuc), $\mathcal{B}$ can successfully solve the CDH problem if $l = j^*$ holds and the event ColF doesn't happen.

Since j^* is information theoretically hidden from $\mathcal{A}_{II}$, both event ASuc and event ColF are independent from event $l = j^*$. Then we have $\Pr[l = j^*] \geq \frac{1}{q_s}$, and

$$
\begin{aligned}
\Pr[g^{ab} &\leftarrow \mathcal{B}(g, g^a, g^b)] \\
&= \Pr[\mathsf{ASuc} \bigwedge \neg \mathsf{ColF} \bigwedge l = j^*] = \Pr[\mathsf{ASuc} \bigwedge \neg \mathsf{ColF}] \cdot \Pr[l = j^*] \\
&\geq \frac{\Pr[\mathsf{ASuc} \bigwedge \neg \mathsf{ColF}]}{q_s} \\
&\geq \frac{\Pr[\mathsf{ASuc}] - \Pr[\mathsf{ColF}]}{q_s} \\
&= \frac{\varepsilon - \Pr[\mathsf{ColF}]}{q_s}
\end{aligned}
\tag{4.3}
$$

If event ColF happens, then we can find a collision for H, i.e., $(\sigma_1^*, \sigma_2^*, \tau^*, pk_s^*, pk_r^*) \neq (\sigma_{j*1}, \sigma_{j*2}, \tau_{j*}, pk_s^*, pk_r^*)$ is a pair of collision of H. Thus $\Pr[\mathsf{ColF}] \leq \varepsilon_{cr}$. From Equation (4.3), we have

$$
\Pr[g^{ab} \leftarrow \mathcal{B}(g, g^a, g^b)] \geq \frac{\varepsilon - \varepsilon_{cr}}{q_s}.
$$

The running time of $\mathcal{B}$ is close to that of $\mathcal{A}_{II}$ except for $(4q_s + 12) \cdot T_e$ in simulation where T_e is the running time of the exponentiation in $\mathbb{G}$.

Type I Forgery. Suppose $\mathcal{A}_I$ is a Type I forger which (t, q_s, ε)-breaks the strong unforgeability of our signcryption tag-KEM, producing a Type I forgery. We can construct an adversary $\mathcal{B}_I$ that (t, ε)-breaks (existential unforgeability of) the Waters signature [12]. The readers may refer to [12] for more details on the Waters signatures. Suppose $\mathcal{B}_I$ is given a public key $g_1 = g^a$ associated with a signing oracle $\mathcal{O}_w$ that returns the Waters signatures on requested messages and the parameters $\mathsf{pp} = (\mathbb{G}, \mathbb{G}_T, e, g, u', u_1, \ldots, u_n, g_1, g_2, G)$. Its goal is to output a Waters signature on a fresh message which is not any of queried message. To utilize the forger $\mathcal{A}_I$, the adversary $\mathcal{B}_I$ simulates the environment of the SUF-SCtKEM game.

Setup. In this phase, $\mathcal{B}_I$ generates the remaining parameters and the public key of the sender and the private/public key pair of the receiver:
1. Randomly choose α_z, α_v, α_w, γ and x_r from $\mathbb{Z}_p$.
2. Set $f = g_2$, $h = g^\gamma$, $z = g^{\alpha_z}$, $v = g^{\alpha_v}$, $w = g^{\alpha_w}$, $pk_s^* = g_1$.
3. Give $\mathcal{A}_I$ the parameters u', $u_1, \ldots, u_n$, f, h, z, v, w and the sender's public key pk_s^*.

Encapsulation Queries. When $\mathcal{A}_I$ makes a key encapsulation query on (τ, pk_r), $\mathcal{B}_I$ simulates the encapsulation oracle as follows:
1. Select k, δ randomly from $\mathbb{Z}_p$, and compute $\sigma_1 = g^k$.
2. Submit $M = (g^k, \tau, \delta, pk_s^*, pk_r)$ to the oracle $\mathcal{O}_w$ and obtain the signature $(\sigma_{w1}, \sigma_{w2})$ on the message M.

3. Set $t_2 = H(g^k, \sigma_{w1}, \tau, pk_s^\star, pk_r)$, $\sigma_1 = g^k$, $\sigma_2 = \sigma_{w1}$, $\sigma_4 = \delta$.
4. Compute $\sigma_3 = \sigma_{w2} \cdot (\sigma_1)^{\alpha_z + \alpha_v t_2 + \alpha_w \delta} = \sigma_{w2} \cdot (z \cdot v^{t_2} w^\delta)^k$.
5. Return $C = (\sigma_1, \sigma_2, \sigma_3, \sigma_4)$.
6. Update $\Sigma_1 = \Sigma_1 \bigcup \{M\}$ (where we let Σ_1 initially be empty).

Output. Eventually $\mathcal{A}_\mathrm{I}$ outputs its forgery $(C^*, pk_r^\star, \tau^\star)$ of Type I, where $(\sigma_1^*, \tau^\star, \sigma_4^*, pk_s^\star, pk_r^\star) \notin \Sigma_1$ and $C^* = (\sigma_1^*, \sigma_2^*, \sigma_3^*, \sigma_4^*)$. Then, $\mathcal{B}_\mathrm{I}$ does the following to obtain its own forgery for the Waters signature:

1. Set $M^\star = (\sigma_1^*, \tau^\star, \sigma_4^*, pk_s^\star, pk_r^\star)$, $t_2^* = H(\sigma_1^*, \sigma_2^*, \tau^\star, pk_s^\star, pk_r^\star)$ and $\sigma_{w1}^\star = \sigma_2^*$;
2. Compute $\sigma_{w2}^\star = \sigma_3^* \cdot (\sigma_1^*)^{-\alpha_z - \alpha_v t_2^* - \alpha_w \sigma_4^*}$, and return $(M^\star, (\sigma_{w1}^\star, \sigma_{w2}^\star))$.

Here $M^\star \notin \Sigma_1$ implies that $(\sigma_{w1}^\star = \sigma_2^*, \sigma_{w2}^\star)$ is a valid Waters signature as

$$\sigma_{w2}^\star = \sigma_3^* \cdot (\sigma_1^*)^{-\alpha_z - \alpha_v t_2^* - \alpha_w \sigma_4^*} = \sigma_3^* \cdot (z \cdot v^{t_2^*} w^\delta)^{-k} = g_2^a \cdot \left(u' \prod_{i \in \mathcal{T}^\star} u_i \right)^s,$$

where $k = \log_g \sigma_1^*$, $s = \log_g \sigma_2^*$, and $\mathcal{T}^\star \subset \{1, \ldots, n\}$ is the set of indices such that $G(M^\star)[i] = 1$, and $G(M^\star)[i]$ is the i-th bit of $G(M^\star)$. .

The probability of $\mathcal{B}_\mathrm{I}$'s success in forging a Waters signature is the same as that of $\mathcal{A}_\mathrm{I}$'s success in outputting a forgery of Type I. The running times of $\mathcal{A}$ and $\mathcal{B}$ are almost the same except for the $2q_s T_e$ exponentiation computations in simulation.

This completes the whole proof.   □

4.2   Confidentiality

We can also show that the proposed construction achieves confidentiality w.r.t. adversarially-chosen keys (definitions 5) based on the standard DBDH assumption in the standard model (unlike existing constructions [3,9,11]). Our signcryption tag-KEM achieves IND-CCA2 security (in definition 5) under the Decisional Bilinear Diffie-Hellman assumption.

Theorem 2 (Confidentiality). *If there exists an adversary $\mathcal{A}$ that can (t, q_d, ε)-break the IND-CCA2 security of our signcryption tag-KEM (where q_d is the total number of queries to the key decapsulation oracle), then it can be utilized to construct an algorithm $\mathcal{B}$ that (t', ε')-breaks the Decisional Bilinear Diffie-Hellman problem assuming that H is (t, ε_{cr})-collision resistant, where*

$$\varepsilon' \geq \frac{\varepsilon}{2} - \varepsilon_{cr} - \frac{q_d}{p}, \quad t' \leq t + \mathcal{O}(6 \cdot q_d + n + 12) T_e + \mathcal{O}(6 \cdot q_d) T_p, \qquad (4.4)$$

and T_e, T_p are the running-time of the exponentiation in $\mathbb{G}$ and the pairing respectively.

Proof. Our idea of the proof is to utilize the adversary $\mathcal{A}$ that (t, q_d, ε)-breaks the IND-CCA2 security of our signcryption tag-KEM, to construct an algorithm $\mathcal{B}$

that first simulates the environment of the IND-CCA2-SCtKEM game, and then uses the output of $\mathcal{A}$ to solve the DBDH problem.

Assume that algorithm $\mathcal{B}$ is given as input a random 5 tuple (g, g^a, g^b, g^c, Z) where $Z = e(g,g)^{abc}$ or $e(g,g)^z$ for a, b, c, z sampled in $\mathbb{Z}_p$. Algorithm $\mathcal{B}$'s goal is to output 1 if $Z = e(g,g)^{abc}$ and 0 otherwise. $\mathcal{B}$ does the following to achieve the goal.

Setup. $\mathcal{B}$ randomly chooses $\alpha_0, \alpha_1, \ldots, \alpha_n, \alpha_v, \alpha_w, \alpha_z, \beta_v, \beta_w, \beta_z, \gamma$ from $\mathbb{Z}_p$, then sets $u' = g^{\alpha_0}, u_1 = g^{\alpha_1}, \ldots, u_n = g^{\alpha_n}, h = g^b, f = g^\gamma, v = g^{\alpha_v} h^{\beta_v}, w = g^{\alpha_w} h^{\beta_w}, z = g^{\alpha_z} h^{\beta_z}, pk_r^\star = g^a$. $\mathcal{B}$ gives $\mathcal{A}$ the parameters $u', u_1, \ldots, u_n, f, h, v, w, z$ and the public key $pk_r^\star$ of the receiver.

All the parameters and keys here we give have the same distribution as those used in our construction. Therefore, in this phase, $\mathcal{B}$ provides a perfect simulation.

Phase 1. When $\mathcal{A}$ submits a query $(pk_s, C = (\sigma_1, \sigma_2, \sigma_3, \sigma_4), \tau)$ to the key decapsulation oracle, $\mathcal{B}$ responds as follows:

1. Compute $t_1 = G(\sigma_1, \tau, \sigma_4, pk_s, pk_r^\star)$, $t_2 = H(\sigma_1, \sigma_2, \tau, pk_s, pk_r^\star)$.
2. Return $\perp$ if

$$e(g, \sigma_3) \neq e(f, pk_s) \cdot e\left(\sigma_2, u' \prod_{i \in \mathcal{T}} u_i\right) \cdot e(\sigma_1, z \cdot v^{t_2} w^{\sigma_4}). \tag{4.5}$$

3. Randomly choose λ from $\mathbb{Z}_p$ and compute $\Omega_g = \alpha_z + t_2 \alpha_v + \sigma_4 \alpha_w$, $\quad \Omega_h = \beta_z + t_2 \beta_v + \sigma_4 \beta_w$. Note that we have $z \cdot v^{t_2} w^{\sigma_4} = g^{\Omega_g} h^{\Omega_h}$.
4. If $\Omega_h = 0$ (denoted by Event DecFail), abort; otherwise compute:

$$\begin{aligned} D_1 &= (g^a)^{-\frac{\Omega_g}{\Omega_h}} \cdot \left(z \cdot v^{t_2} w^{\sigma_4}\right)^\lambda = h^a \cdot (h^a)^{-\frac{\Omega_h}{\Omega_h}} \cdot (g^a)^{-\frac{\Omega_g}{\Omega_h}} \cdot \left(z \cdot v^{t_2} w^{\sigma_4}\right)^\lambda \\ &= h^a \cdot \left(g^{\Omega_g} h^{\Omega_h}\right)^{-\frac{a}{\Omega_h}} \cdot \left(z \cdot v^{t_2} w^{\sigma_4}\right)^\lambda \\ &= h^a \cdot \left(z \cdot v^{t_2} w^{\sigma_4}\right)^{-\frac{a}{\Omega_h}} \cdot \left(z \cdot v^{t_2} w^{\sigma_4}\right)^\lambda \\ &= h^a \cdot \left(z \cdot v^{t_2} w^{\sigma_4}\right)^{\lambda - \frac{a}{\Omega_h}}, \\ D_2 &= g^\lambda \cdot (g^a)^{-\frac{1}{\Omega_h}} = g^{\lambda - \frac{a}{\Omega_h}}. \end{aligned}$$

Let $\eta = \lambda - \frac{a}{\Omega_h}$, we have $D_1 = h^a \cdot (z \cdot v^{t_2} w^{\sigma_4})^\eta$, $\quad D_2 = g^\eta$. Herein, we use the random λ to generate random D_1, D_2 for each query of $\mathcal{A}$.
5. Compute

$$\Delta = \sigma_3 \cdot (pk_s)^{-\gamma} \cdot (\sigma_2)^{-\alpha_0 - \sum\limits_{i \in \mathcal{T}} \alpha_i}. \tag{4.6}$$

Since $C = (\sigma_1, \sigma_2, \sigma_3, \sigma_4)$ can pass the verification equation (4.5), we have

$$pk_s = g^x, \ \sigma_1 = g^k, \ \sigma_2 = g^r, \ \sigma_3 = f^x \cdot \left(u' \prod_{i \in \mathcal{T}} u_i\right)^r \cdot (z \cdot v^{t_2} w^{\sigma_4})^k,$$

for some $x, k, r \in \mathbb{Z}_p$. Thus, we know that

$$
\begin{aligned}
\Delta &= \sigma_3 \cdot (pk_s)^{-\gamma} \cdot (\sigma_2)^{-\alpha_0 - \sum\limits_{i \in \mathcal{T}} \alpha_i} \\
&= \sigma_3 \cdot (g^x)^{-\gamma} \cdot (g^r)^{-\alpha_0 - \sum\limits_{i \in \mathcal{T}} \alpha_i} \\
&= \sigma_3 \cdot (g^\gamma)^{-x} \cdot \left(u' \prod_{i \in \mathcal{T}} u_i \right)^{-r} \\
&= (z \cdot v^{t_2} w^{\sigma_4})^k.
\end{aligned}
$$

6. Return $K = e(\sigma_1, D_1)/e(D_2, \Delta)$.
   Note that K is correct because

$$
\begin{aligned}
e(\sigma_1, D_1) &= e\left(\sigma_1, h^a \cdot (z \cdot v^{t_2} w^{\sigma_4})^\eta \right) \\
&= e(\sigma_1, h^a) \cdot e\left(g^k, (z \cdot v^{t_2} w^{\sigma_4})^\eta \right) \\
&= K \cdot e\left(g^\eta, (z \cdot v^{t_2} w^{\sigma_4})^k \right) \\
&= K \cdot e(D_2, \Delta).
\end{aligned}
$$

Challenge. At the end of Phase 1, $\mathcal{A}$ sends a pair of keys $(pk_s^\star = g^x, sk_s^\star = x)$ and a tag $\tau^\star$ to $\mathcal{B}$. Then $\mathcal{B}$ generates the challenge ciphertext for the adversary $\mathcal{A}$:

1. Randomly choose s from $\mathbb{Z}_p$, compute $\sigma_2^\star = g^s$;
2. Let $\sigma_1^\star = g^c$, compute $t_2^\star = H(\sigma_1^\star, \sigma_2^\star, \tau^\star, pk_s^\star, pk_r^\star)$;
3. Compute $\sigma_4^\star = -\frac{\beta_z + t_2^\star \beta_v}{\beta_w}$, $t_1^\star = G(\sigma_1^\star, \tau^\star, \sigma_4^\star, pk_s^\star, pk_r^\star)$, and

$$
\sigma_3^\star = (g^\gamma)^x \cdot \left(u' \prod_{i \in \mathcal{T}^\star} u_i \right)^s \cdot (g^c)^{\alpha_z + \alpha_v t_2^\star + \alpha_w \sigma_4^\star};
$$

4. Set $K_0^\star = Z$, $C^\star = (\sigma_1^\star, \sigma_2^\star, \sigma_3^\star, \sigma_4^\star)$;
5. Choose a random bit $\theta \in \{0, 1\}$ and a random key $K_1^\star \in \mathbb{G}_T$;
6. Return $(K_\theta^\star, C^\star)$ as the challenge.

The ciphertext $C^\star$ is valid and can pass the Equation (4.5) since

$$
\begin{aligned}
\sigma_3^\star &= (g^\gamma)^x \cdot \left(u' \prod_{i \in \mathcal{T}^\star} u_i \right)^s \cdot (g^c)^{\alpha_z + \alpha_v t_2^\star + \alpha_w \sigma_4^\star} \\
&= f^x \cdot \left(u' \prod_{i \in \mathcal{T}^\star} u_i \right)^s \cdot (g^{\alpha_z + \alpha_v t_2^\star + \alpha_w \sigma_4^\star} h^0)^c \\
&= f^x \cdot \left(u' \prod_{i \in \mathcal{T}^\star} u_i \right)^s \cdot (g^{\alpha_z + \alpha_v t_2^\star + \alpha_w \sigma_4^\star} h^{\beta_z + t_2^\star \beta_v + \sigma_4^\star \beta_w})^c \\
&= f^x \cdot \left(u' \prod_{i \in \mathcal{T}^\star} u_i \right)^s \cdot \left(z \cdot v^{t_2^\star} w^{\sigma_4^\star} \right)^c
\end{aligned}
$$

Note that $C^\star$ has the same distribution as the real ciphertext generated by the proposed scheme, due to the selection pattern of the parameters generated in the setup phase and used to compute the challenge ciphertext $C^\star$.

Phase 2. $\mathcal{B}$ responds to the queries of $\mathcal{A}$ as it does in Phase 1, except denying to answer the query of the challenge ciphertext $C^\star$ with respect to $(pk_s^\star, \tau^\star)$.

Guess. Eventually $\mathcal{A}$ outputs a bit θ' as its guess for θ.

Algorithm $\mathcal{B}$ outputs 1 if $\theta' = \theta$ (denoted by ASuc) and 0 otherwise.

Analysis. In the following, we analyze $\mathcal{B}$'s probability of success in solving the Decisional Bilinear Diffie-Hellman problem. According to Claim 4.2 (see below), the bound of the probability that $\mathcal{B}$ aborts is: $\Pr[\mathsf{DecFail}] \leq \varepsilon_{cr} + \frac{2q_d}{p}$.

Now we can compute the probability that in the above game $\mathcal{B}$ outputs 1 given Z with either $Z = e(g,g)^{abc}$ or $Z = e(g,g)^z$ where a, b, c, z are random chosen from $\mathbb{Z}_p$. Let ASuc be the event that adversary $\mathcal{A}$ succeeds in guessing θ (i.e., $\theta' = \theta$).

Due to the simulation, it follows that if $Z = e(g,g)^{abc}$ then the challenge ciphertext $C^\star = (\sigma_1^\star, \sigma_2^\star, \sigma_3^\star, \sigma_4^\star)$ is a valid key encapsulation of $K_0^\star = Z$ and $\tau^\star$ with respect to $(sk_s^\star, pk_r^\star)$. Therefore, $\mathcal{B}$ provides a perfect simulation unless event DecFail happens and then $\mathcal{A}$'s view is identical to that in the real attack game unless event DecFail happens. So we have the following result.

$$
\Pr\left[\mathcal{B}(g^a, g^b, g^c, Z = e(g,g)^{abc}) = 1\right]
$$
$$
= \Pr\left[(\mathsf{ASuc}|Z = e(g,g)^{abc}) \bigwedge (\neg\mathsf{DecFail})\right]
$$
$$
\geq \Pr\left[\mathsf{ASuc}|Z = e(g,g)^{abc}\right] - \Pr\left[\mathsf{DecFail}\right]
$$
$$
\geq \Pr\left[\theta = \theta'|Z = e(g,g)^{abc}\right] - \varepsilon_{cr} - \frac{2q_d}{p} \tag{4.7}
$$
$$
= \frac{\mathrm{Adv}_{\mathcal{A}}^{\mathrm{IND}} + 1}{2} - \varepsilon_{cr} - \frac{2q_d}{p}
$$
$$
= \frac{\varepsilon + 1}{2} - \varepsilon_{cr} - \frac{2q_d}{p}.
$$

If $Z = e(g,g)^z$, then the challenge ciphertext $C^\star = (\sigma_1^\star, \sigma_2^\star, \sigma_3^\star, \sigma_4^\star)$ is an invalid key encapsulation of $K_0^\star = Z$ and $\tau^\star$ with respect to $(sk_s^\star, pk_r^\star)$. In this case, both $K_0^\star = Z$ and $K_1^\star$ are random. Therefore, $\mathcal{A}$ succeeds in guessing θ with probability at most $\frac{1}{2}$. Thus, we have

$$
\Pr\left[\mathcal{B}(g^a, g^b, g^c, Z = e(g,g)^z) = 1\right]
$$
$$
= \Pr\left[(\mathsf{ASuc}|Z = e(g,g)^z) \bigwedge (\neg\mathsf{CRFail})\right]
$$
$$
\leq \Pr\left[\mathsf{ASuc}|Z = e(g,g)^z\right] \tag{4.8}
$$
$$
= \Pr\left[\theta = \theta'|Z = e(g,g)^z\right]
$$
$$
= \frac{1}{2},
$$

herein, the event CRFail can be found in the following claim 4.2.

Combining Equation (4.7) and Equation (4.8), we conclude that

$$\varepsilon' = \mathrm{Adv}_{\mathcal{B}}^{\mathsf{DBDH}} = \left| \Pr[\mathcal{A}(g^a, g^b, g^c, e(g,g)^{abc}) = 1] - \Pr[\mathcal{A}(g^a, g^b, g^c, e(g,g)^z) = 1] \right|$$

$$\geq \frac{\varepsilon + 1}{2} - \varepsilon_{cr} - \frac{2q_d}{p} - \frac{1}{2} = \frac{\varepsilon}{2} - \varepsilon_{cr} - \frac{2q_d}{p}.$$

Finally, for the running-time of $\mathcal{B}$, we mainly take into account the running-time t of $\mathcal{A}$, the exponentiations and the pairings in the key decapsulation queries, and n exponentiation in setup phase. This takes time at most $t + \mathcal{O}(6 \cdot q_d + n + 12)T_e + \mathcal{O}(6 \cdot q_d)T_p$, where T_e is the running-time of the exponentiation in $\mathbb{G}$, T_p is the running-time of the pairing and q_d is the number of key decapsulation queries.

Claim. $\Pr[\mathsf{DecFail}] \leq \varepsilon_{cr} + \frac{2q_d}{p}$.

Proof. For any valid ciphertext $C = (\sigma_1, \sigma_2, \sigma_3, \sigma_4)$ with respect to (pk_s, τ), event CRFail happens only when one of the following two events takes place:

1. Event CR, $(\sigma_1, \sigma_2, \tau, pk_s, pk_r^\star) \neq (\sigma_1^\star, \sigma_2^\star, \tau^\star, pk_s^\star, pk_r^\star) \bigwedge t_2 = t_2^\star \bigwedge \sigma_4 = \sigma_4^\star$.
   In this case, $(\sigma_1, \sigma_2, \tau, pk_s, pk_r^\star) \neq (\sigma_1^\star, \sigma_2^\star, \tau^\star, pk_s^\star, pk_r^\star)$ and $t_2 = t_2^\star$ happen simultaneously, thus $\mathcal{B}$ can find a collision for hash function H. And it follows

$$\Pr[\mathsf{CR}] = \Pr\left[(\sigma_1, \sigma_2, \tau, pk_s, pk_r^\star) \neq (\sigma_1^\star, \sigma_2^\star, \tau^\star, pk_s^\star, pk_r^\star) \bigwedge t_2 = t_2^\star \bigwedge \sigma_4 = \sigma_4^\star\right]$$

$$\leq \Pr\left[(\sigma_1, \sigma_2, \tau, pk_s, pk_r^\star) \neq (\sigma_1^\star, \sigma_2^\star, \tau^\star, pk_s^\star, pk_r^\star) \bigwedge t_2 = t_2^\star\right] \leq \varepsilon_{cr}.$$

2. Event Fail, $(\sigma_1, \sigma_2, \tau, pk_s, pk_r^\star) = (\sigma_1^\star, \sigma_2^\star, \tau^\star, pk_s^\star, pk_r^\star) \bigwedge \sigma_4 = \sigma_4^\star$. In this case the query $C = (\sigma_1, \sigma_2, \sigma_3, \sigma_4)$ with respect to (pk_s, τ) is almost identical to the challenge ciphertext except the third part σ_3. Indeed, $(\sigma_1, \sigma_2, \tau, pk_s, pk_r) = (\sigma_1^\star, \sigma_2^\star, \tau^\star, pk_s^\star, pk_r^\star) \bigwedge \sigma_4 = \sigma_4^\star$ implies $\sigma_3 = \sigma_3^\star$ since σ_3 (or $\sigma_3^\star$) is uniquely determined by all the other parts of the ciphertext. Thus, $C = (\sigma_1, \sigma_2, \sigma_3, \sigma_4) = C^\star$ with respect to $(pk_s, \tau) = (pk_s^\star, \tau^\star)$ is not allowed to be queried in **Phase 2**. It follows that event Fail may happen in **Phase 1,** but it is impossible to happen in **Phase 2.**
   However, the adversary can't know the challenge ciphertext in **Phase 1** because it is information-theoretically hidden in **Phase 1.** Then, $\mathcal{A}$ submits a ciphertext identical to the challenge ciphertext with the same sender's public key and tag happens with probability at most $\frac{1}{p}$. Thus we know event Fail happens with probability at most $\frac{q_d}{p}$ for the q_d queries in **Phase 1,** i.e., $\Pr[\mathsf{Fail}] \leq \frac{q_d}{p}$.

3. Event DiPart4, $\sigma_4 \neq \sigma_4^\star \bigwedge \Omega_h = 0$. For any pair $(t_2 = H(\sigma_1, \sigma_2, \tau, pk_s, pk_r^\star), \sigma_4)$, and randomly chosen $\beta_v, \beta_w, \beta_z$, it follows that $\Omega_h = \beta_z + t_2\beta_v + \sigma_4\beta_w = 0$ (for $\sigma_4 \neq \sigma_4^\star$) with probability at most $\frac{1}{p}$. Thus, $\Pr[\mathsf{DiPart4}] \leq \frac{q_d}{p}$.

Since $(\sigma_1, \sigma_2, \tau, pk_s, pk_r^\star) = (\sigma_1^\star, \sigma_2^\star, \tau^\star, pk_s^\star, pk_r^\star)$ implies $t_2 = t_2^\star$, thus

$$
\begin{aligned}
&\Pr\left[(\sigma_1, \sigma_2, \tau, pk_s, pk_r^\star) = (\sigma_1^\star, \sigma_2^\star, \tau^\star, pk_s^\star, pk_r^\star) \bigwedge t_2 = t_2^\star \bigwedge \sigma_4 = \sigma_4^\star\right] \\
&= \Pr\left[(\sigma_1, \sigma_2, \tau, pk_s, pk_r^\star) = (\sigma_1^\star, \sigma_2^\star, \tau^\star, pk_s^\star, pk_r^\star) \bigwedge \sigma_4 = \sigma_4^\star\right]
\end{aligned}
\tag{4.9}
$$

Therefore, we know $\mathcal{B}$'s abortion probability is bounded as follows:
$\Pr[\mathsf{DecFail}]$

$$
\begin{aligned}
&= \Pr\left[\sigma_4 \neq \sigma_4^\star \bigwedge \Omega_h = 0\right] + \Pr\left[\sigma_4 = \sigma_4^\star \bigwedge \Omega_h = 0\right] \\
&= \Pr[\mathsf{DiPart4}] + \Pr\left[\sigma_4 = \sigma_4^\star \bigwedge t_2 = t_2^\star\right] \\
&= \Pr[\mathsf{DiPart4}] + \Pr\left[(\sigma_1, \sigma_2, \tau, pk_s, pk_r^\star) \neq (\sigma_1^\star, \sigma_2^\star, \tau^\star, pk_s^\star, pk_r^\star) \bigwedge t_2 = t_2^\star \bigwedge \sigma_4 = \sigma_4^\star\right] \\
&\quad + \Pr\left[(\sigma_1, \sigma_2, \tau, pk_s, pk_r^\star) = (\sigma_1^\star, \sigma_2^\star, \tau^\star, pk_s^\star, pk_r^\star) \bigwedge t_2 = t_2^\star \bigwedge \sigma_4 = \sigma_4^\star\right] \\
&= \Pr[\mathsf{DiPart4}] + \Pr[\mathsf{CR}] + \Pr\left[(\sigma_1, \sigma_2, \tau, pk_s, pk_r^\star) = (\sigma_1^\star, \sigma_2^\star, \tau^\star, pk_s^\star, pk_r^\star) \bigwedge \sigma_4 = \sigma_4^\star\right] \\
&= \Pr[\mathsf{DiPart4}] + \Pr[\mathsf{CR}] + \Pr[\mathsf{Fail}] \leq \varepsilon_{cr} + \frac{2q_d}{p}.
\end{aligned}
$$

$\square$

5   Conclusion

We present a direct construction of signcryption tag-KEM from standard assumptions without random oracles. When proving its security, we equip the insider adversaries with the power such that they can choose their key pairs of possibly ill-formed, rather than generated by the challenger [3,9,11]. As in the signcryption schemes, such models give the adversary more advantageous attack environment which is indeed quite natural as the adversary is given all the possible resources, except those that allow it to trivially win the game.

Acknowledgement. This work has been supported by the National Natural Science Foundation of China (Grant Nos. 61272536, 61172085, 61103221, 61021004, 61070249, U1135004, 61170080, 11061130539 and 60703031) and Key Program of Natural Science Foundation of Shaanxi Province(Grant No.2013JZ020).

References

1. Abe, M., Gennaro, R., Kurosawa, K., Shoup, V.: Tag-KEM/DEM: A new framework for hybrid encryption and A new analysis of kurosawa-desmedt KEM. In: Cramer, R. (ed.) EUROCRYPT 2005. LNCS, vol. 3494, pp. 128–146. Springer, Heidelberg (2005)

2. Arriaga, A., Barbosa, M., Farshim, P.: On the joint security of signature and encryption schemes under randomness reuse: Efficiency and security amplification. In: Bao, F., Samarati, P., Zhou, J. (eds.) ACNS 2012. LNCS, vol. 7341, pp. 206–223. Springer, Heidelberg (2012)
3. Bjørstad, T., Dent, A.W.: Building better signcryption schemes with Tag-KEMs. In: Yung, M., Dodis, Y., Kiayias, A., Malkin, T. (eds.) PKC 2006. LNCS, vol. 3958, pp. 491–507. Springer, Heidelberg (2006)
4. Canetti, R., Goldreich, O., Halevi, S.: The random oracle methodology, revisited. In: STOC 1998, pp. 209–218 (1998)
5. Chiba, D., Matsuda, T., Schuldt, J.C.N., Matsuura, K.: Efficient generic constructions of signcryption with insider security in the multi-user setting. In: Lopez, J., Tsudik, G. (eds.) ACNS 2011. LNCS, vol. 6715, pp. 220–237. Springer, Heidelberg (2011)
6. Cramer, R., Shoup, V.: Design and analysis of practical public-key encryption schemes secure against adaptive chosen ciphertext attack. SIAM J. on Computing 33(1), 167–226 (2004)
7. Kiltz, E.: Chosen-ciphertext secure key-encapsulation based on gap hashed Diffie-Hellman. In: Okamoto, T., Wang, X. (eds.) PKC 2007. LNCS, vol. 4450, pp. 282–297. Springer, Heidelberg (2007)
8. Lai, J., Deng, R.H., Liu, S., Kou, W.: Efficient CCA-secure PKE from identity-based techniques. In: Pieprzyk, J. (ed.) CT-RSA 2010. LNCS, vol. 5985, pp. 132–147. Springer, Heidelberg (2010)
9. Li, F., Shirase, M., Takagi, T.: Efficient signcryption key encapsulation without random oracles. In: Yung, M., Liu, P., Lin, D. (eds.) Inscrypt 2008. LNCS, vol. 5487, pp. 47–59. Springer, Heidelberg (2009)
10. Matsuda, T., Matsuura, K., Schuldt, J.C.N.: Efficient constructions of signcryption schemes and signcryption composability. In: Roy, B., Sendrier, N. (eds.) INDOCRYPT 2009. LNCS, vol. 5922, pp. 321–342. Springer, Heidelberg (2009)
11. Tan, C.: Insider-secure signcryption KEM/tag-KEM schemes without random oracles. In: ARES 2008, pp. 1275–1281 (2008)
12. Waters, B.: Efficient identity-based encryption without random oracles. In: Cramer, R. (ed.) EUROCRYPT 2005. LNCS, vol. 3494, pp. 114–127. Springer, Heidelberg (2005)
13. Zheng, Y.: Digital signcryption or how to achieve cost (signature & encryption) $<<$ cost(signature) + cost(encryption). In: Kaliski Jr., B.S. (ed.) CRYPTO 1997. LNCS, vol. 1294, pp. 165–179. Springer, Heidelberg (1997)

A   The Waters Signature

In [12], Waters showed an elegant technique to build a signature scheme that is secure under the computational Diffie-Hellman assumption without random oracles.

Let $\mathbb{G}$ and $\mathbb{G}_T$ be two groups of prime order p, $e : \mathbb{G} \times \mathbb{G} \to \mathbb{G}_T$ the bilinear map and g the corresponding generator of $\mathbb{G}$. Additionally, $G : \{0,1\}^* \to \{0,1\}^n$ is a collision resistant hash function which maps the messages of arbitrary length to the messages of n bits. Waters's scheme consists of the following three algorithms.

KeyGen The algorithm generates the signer's public/private keys.
1. Choose $\alpha \in \mathbb{Z}_p$ randomly and set the value $g_1 = g^\alpha$;
2. Choose $g_2, u' \in_R \mathbb{G}$ and a random n-length vector $U = (u_i)$, whose elements are chosen at random from $\mathbb{G}$.
3. The public key is published as g, g_1, g_2, u', and U, and the secret key is g_2^α.

Sign Given a message $m \in \{0,1\}^*$ and the private key g_2^α of the signer, the algorithm does the following.
1. Compute $M = H(m)$;
2. Let M_i denote the i-th bit of M, and $\mathcal{M} \subset \{1, ..., n\}$ be the set of all i for which $M_i = 1$;
3. Choose $r \in \mathbb{Z}_p$ randomly;
4. Compute $\sigma_1 = g^r$, $\sigma_2 = g_2^\alpha \left(u' \prod_{i \in \mathcal{M}} u_i \right)^r$;
5. Output $\sigma = (\sigma_1, \sigma_2)$ as the signature on m.

Verify Given a signature $\sigma = (\sigma_1, \sigma_2)$ on the message m, the signature σ is accepted if

$$e(g, \sigma_2) = e(g_1, g_2) e \left(\sigma_1, u' \prod_{i \in \mathcal{M}} u_i \right).$$

The Waters signature is existentially unforgeable under a chosen-message attack (EUF-CMA, existential unforgeability under a chosen message attack, the standard notion of signature security), but not strongly unforgeable.

Theorem 3. *The Waters signature scheme is (t, q, ε) existentially unforgeable assuming the Computational Diffie-Hellman problem is $(t + \mathcal{O}(q), 4nq\varepsilon)$-secure.*

Efficient eCK-Secure Authenticated Key Exchange Protocols in the Standard Model

Zheng Yang

Horst Grtz Institute for IT Security
Ruhr-University Bochum, Germany
zheng.yang@rub.de

Abstract. The extended CanettiKrawczyk (eCK) security model, is widely used to provide security arguments for authenticated key exchange protocols that capture leakage of various kinds of secret information like the long-term private key and session-specific secret state. In this paper, we study the open problem on constructing eCK secure AKE protocol without random oracles and NAXOS like trick. A generic construction GC-KKN satisfying those requirements is first given relying on standard cryptographic primitives. On the second a concrete protocol is proposed which is the first eCK secure protocol in the standard model under both standard assumptions and post-specified peer setting. Both proposed schemes can be more efficiently implemented with secure device than previous eCK secure protocols in the standard model, where the secure device might be normally used to store the long-term private key and implement algorithms of protocol which require to be resilience of state leakage.

Keywords: eCK model, authenticated key exchange, standard model, key encapsulation mechanism, non-interactive key exchange.

1 Introduction

Authenticated Key Exchange (AKE) is a fundamental cryptographic primitive which forms a crucial component in many network protocols. The security model for two party AKE and associated definitions have been evolved over years subjecting to increasing security requirements. Recently the extended Canetti-Krawczyk (eCK) [9] model is widely used to provide security arguments for AKE protocols. The eCK model is known to be one of the strongest AKE models that covers the most desirable security attributes for AKE including resistance to key compromise impersonation (KCI) attacks, leakage of secret states and chosen identity and public key (CIDPK) attacks and provision of weak perfect forward secrecy (wPFS). Nevertheless the eCK model leaves out the definition of session state or ephemeral key to specific protocols. Since it is hard to define session state in a general approach, which is independent of any protocols and corresponding implementation scenarios. However the ambiguities on session state may yield a lot of potential problems in either the protocol construction or its security

S. Qing et al. (Eds.): ICICS 2013, LNCS 8233, pp. 185–193, 2013.

analysis. If any implementer realizes a specific AKE protocol in a *careless* way allowing it to leak non-trivial session state to attackers, then it would trivially invalidate the security proof in such strong model. On the other hand, to our best of knowledge, no AKE protocol is secure in the eCK model if *all* session states can be revealed. Namely some session states of AKE protocols should be leakage resilience.

IMPLEMENTATION MODEL VS. SESSION STATES. In order to fulfil the gap that often exists between formal models and practical security, Sarr et al. [12] introduced two implementation scenarios for the situation that at each party an untrusted host machine is used together with a secure device such as tamper-proof smart card. A secure device may usually be used to store long-term cryptographic authentication keys and at least be able to fulfil a library of mathematical functions which are necessary to implement cryptographic operations or primitives. Hence based on secure device we are able to adopt a 'All-and-Nothing' strategy to define the states that can be revealed without leaving any ambiguity. General speaking we could assume that all intermediate states and ephemeral keys generated on host machine are susceptible to the maximum state leakage (MSL) attacks, but we treat the secure device as a black-box which is immune to leakage of internal states. On the other side, our goal is to define the maximum states that can be leaked. As those secure devices might be short in both storage capacity and computational resource, the algorithm on secure device is often causing performance bottleneck of systems. In addition, the communication round between host machine and secure device (which is called *HS-round* for short) might cause another efficiency problem, since the serial I/O bus of most secure devices is too slow. Due to those facts, it is necessary to optimize AKE protocols when they are realized involving secure device.

Motivating Problem. So far there are only few AKE protocols which are provably secure without random oracles in the eCK model. Although the protocols [11,10] have been proven to be eCK secure in the standard model, they require a rather strong class of pseudo-random function family with pairwise independent random sources (which is referred to as πPRF) as key derivation function (KDF). Most recently, Fujioka et al. [7] introduced a generic construction for two-message AKE from key encapsulation mechanism (KEM) which is generalized from BCNP [3]. Although the FSXY scheme [7] has been shown to be CK+ (eCK) secure in the standard model, it is built relying on a special twisted-PRF trick (which is a variant of NAXOS trick and is first used in [11]).[1] However to securely implement the FSXY protocol, one might need to distribute all computations related to NAXOS trick on secure device in order to resist with the leakage of corresponding states (see detail discussion in [13]). This would lead to inefficiencies in the implementation of the FSXY protocol with secure device. Another drawback of FSXY protocol is not a one-round AKE protocol. Since two session participants cannot execute the FSXY protocol instances

---

[1] The CK+ model can be seen as a variant of eCK model in which the StateReveal query is used instead of EphemeralKeyReveal query to model MSL attacks.

simultaneously. To our best of knowledge it is still an open question to construct eCK secure one-round AKE protocols without random oracles and NAXOS trick, and under standard assumptions (e.g. without πPRF).

Contributions. We first present a one-round authenticated key exchange protocol (named GC-KKN) to solve the above open problem. As opposed to FSXY scheme, GC-KKN does not rely on any NAXOS like trick that yields a more efficient solution when it is implemented with secure device. We give compact game-based proofs reducing eCK security of GC-KKN to break the used cryptographic primitives without random oracles.

On the second we present a concrete and practical AKE protocol (P1) that is eCK secure under standard assumptions (e.g. without πPRF). The proposed protocol is based on bilinear pairings, target collision resistant hash function family, and pseudo-random function family. To be of independent interesting, P1 is able to run under post-specified peer setting [5] (i.e. without knowing any information of communication peer at session activation), unlike FSXY scheme and our GC-KKN scheme which might be executed under only pre-specified peer setting. Our construction idea of P1 is inspired by the GC-KKN. In order to securely implement P1, only one exponentiation is required on secure device that is the more efficient than any previous eCK secure protocols without random oracles.

2   Preliminaries

Notations. We let $\kappa \in \mathbb{N}$ denote the security parameter and 1^κ the string that consists of κ ones. Let a 'hat' on top of a capital letter denote an identity; without the hat the letter denotes the public key of that party. Let $[n] = \{1, \ldots, n\} \subset \mathbb{N}$ be the set of integers between 1 and n. If S is a set, then $a \xleftarrow{\$} S$ denotes the action of sampling a uniformly random element from S. Let $\mathcal{IDS}$ be an identity space. Let $\mathcal{K}_{\mathsf{AKE}}$ be the key space of session key, and $\{\mathcal{PK}, \mathcal{SK}\}$ be key spaces for long-term public/private key respectively. Those spaces are associated with security parameter κ.

In our constructions, we will make use of one-round passively secure key exchange protocols KE, IND-CCA secure key encapsulation mechanism schemes KEM, CKS-light secure [6] non-interactive key exchange protocols NIKE, strong randomness extractor SEXT, pseudo-random function family PRF, symmetric bilinear groups and Bilinear Decisional Diffie-Hellman (BDDH) assumption.

Meanwhile, a one-round KE = (KE.Setup, KE.EGen, KE.SKGen) protocol consists of three algorithms, where KE.EGen is the ephemeral key generator and KE.SKGen is the session key generator. In our construction should satisfy the following two conditions: (i) the protocol is executed without any long-term keys; (ii) all ephemeral public/secret key are chosen freshly and randomly from corresponding key spaces for each protocol instance. A KEM = (KEM.Setup, KEM.Gen, KEM.EnCap, KEM.DeCap) scheme consists of four polynomial time algorithms, where KEM.Setup is the initiation algorithm used to generate the system parameters, KEM.Gen is the key generation which outputs a pair of long-term keys, KEM.EnCap is the encryption algorithm and KEM.DeCap is the decryption algorithm. Furthermore, a NIKE = (NIKE.Setup, NIKE.KGen, NIKE.ShKey) scheme consists of three algorithms , where NIKE.KGen is the long-term key generation algorithm and NIKE.ShKey is the algorithm that is used to compute the long-term shared secret key between two parties. The corresponding security definitions are detailed in the full version of this paper [13].

3   Security Model

In this section we present the eCK security model for two party PKI-based authenticated key-exchange (AKE) protocol. We provide an 'execution environment' for active adversaries following an important research line research [2,4,9,8] which is initiated by Bellare and Rogaway [1].

EXECUTION ENVIRONMENT. In the execution environment, we fix a set of honest parties $\{\mathsf{ID}_1, \ldots, \mathsf{ID}_\ell\}$ for $\ell \in \mathbb{N}$, where ID_i ($i \in [\ell]$) is the identity of a party which is chosen uniquely from space $\mathcal{IDS}$. Each identity is associated with a long-term key pair $(sk_{\mathsf{ID}_i}, pk_{\mathsf{ID}_i}) \in (\mathcal{SK}, \mathcal{PK})$. Each honest party ID_i can sequentially and concurrently execute the protocol multiple times with different intended partners, this is characterized by a collection of oracles $\{\pi_i^s : i \in [\ell], s \in [d]\}$ for $d \in \mathbb{N}$. Moreover, we assume each oracle π_i^s maintains a list of independent internal state variables with following semantics: (i) Ψ_i^s – storing the identity of its communication partner; (ii) Φ_i^s – denoting the decision $\Phi_i^s \in \{\texttt{accept}, \texttt{reject}\}$; (iii) K_i^s – recording the session key $K_i^s \in \mathcal{K}_{\mathsf{AKE}}$; (iv) st_i^s – storing the maximum secret states that allow to be revealed; (v) sT_i^s – recording the transcript of messages sent by oracle π_i^s; (vi) rT_j^t – recording the transcript of messages received by oracle π_i^s. All those variables of each oracle are initialized with empty string which is denoted by the symbol $\emptyset$. At some point, each oracle π_i^s may complete the execution always with a decision state $\Phi_i^s \in \{\texttt{accept}, \texttt{reject}\}$. Furthermore, we assume that the session key is assigned to the variable K_i^s (such that $K_i^s \neq \emptyset$) iff oracle π_i^s has reached an internal state $\Phi_i^s = \texttt{accept}$.

ADVERSARIAL MODEL. An adversary $\mathcal{A}$ in our model is a PPT Turing Machine taking as input the security parameter 1^κ and the public information (e.g. generic description of above environment), which may interact with these oracles by issuing the following queries.

- Send(π_i^s, m): The adversary can use this query to send any message m of his own choice to oracle π_i^s. The oracle will respond the next message m^* (if any) to be sent according to the protocol specification. Oracle π_i^s would be initiated as *initiator* via sending the oracle the first message $m = (\top, \widetilde{\mathsf{ID}}_j)$ consisting of a special initialization symbol $\top$ and a value $\widetilde{\mathsf{ID}}_j$, where the $\widetilde{\mathsf{ID}}_j$ is either the identity ID_j of intended partner or empty string $\emptyset$. After answering a Send query, the internal state variables of π_i^s will be updated depending on the specific protocol.

- RevealKey(π_i^s): Oracle π_i^s responds with the contents of variable K_i^s.
- StateReveal(π_i^s): Oracle π_i^s responds with the contents of variable st_i^s.[2]
- Corrupt(ID_i): Oracle π_i^1 responds with the long-term secret key sk_{ID_i} of party ID_i if $i \in [\ell]$; otherwise a failure symbol $\bot$ is returned.
- EstablishParty(ID_τ, pk_{ID_τ}): This query allows the adversary to register an identity ID_τ ($\ell < \tau < \mathbb{N}$) and a static public key pk_{ID_τ} on behalf of a party ID_τ, if ID_τ is unique.
- Test(π_i^s): If the oracle has state $\Phi_i^s = \texttt{reject}$ or $K_i^s = \emptyset$, then the oracle π_i^s returns some failure symbol $\bot$. Otherwise it flips a fair coin b, samples a random element K_0 from key space $\mathcal{K}_{\mathsf{AKE}}$, and sets $K_1 = K_i^s$. Finally the key K_b is returned.

SECURE AKE PROTOCOLS. To formalize the notion that two oracles are engaged in an on-line communication, we define the partnership via *matching sessions*.

Definition 1. *We say that an oracle π_i^s has a* matching session *to oracle π_j^t, if π_i^s has sent all protocol messages and all the following conditions hold: (i) $\Psi_i^s = ID_j$ and $\Psi_j^t = ID_i$, (ii) $sT_i^s = rT_j^t$ and $rT_i^s = sT_j^t$.*

CORRECTNESS. We say an AKE protocol Σ is correct, if two oracles π_i^s and π_j^t accept with matching sessions, then both oracles hold the same session key, i.e. $K_i^s = K_j^t$.

Definition 2. *Let π_i^s be an accepted oracle with $\Psi_i^s = ID_j$. Let π_j^t be an oracle (if it exists), such that π_i^s has a matching session to π_j^t. Then the oracle π_i^s is said to be* fresh *if none of the following conditions holds: (i) $\mathcal{A}$ queried EstablishParty(ID_j, pk_{ID_j}); (ii) $\mathcal{A}$ queried either RevealKey(π_i^s) or RevealKey(π_j^t) (if π_j^t exists); (iii) $\mathcal{A}$ queried both Corrupt(ID_i) and StateReveal(π_i^s); (iv) If π_j^t exists, $\mathcal{A}$ queried both Corrupt(ID_j) and StateReveal(π_j^t); (v) If π_j^t does not exist, $\mathcal{A}$ queried Corrupt(ID_j).*

SECURITY EXPERIMENT $\mathsf{EXP}_{\Sigma,\mathcal{A}}^{\mathsf{AKE}}(\kappa)$: On input security parameter 1^κ, the security experiment is proceeded as a game between a challenger $\mathcal{C}$ and an adversary $\mathcal{A}$ based on an AKE protocol Σ, where the following steps are performed:

1. At the beginning of the game, the challenger $\mathcal{C}$ implements the collection of oracles $\{\pi_i^s : i \in [\ell], s \in [d]\}$, and generates ℓ long-term key pairs (pk_{ID_i}, sk_{ID_i}) for all honest parties ID_i for $i \in [\ell]$ where the identity $ID_i \in \mathcal{IDS}$ of each party is chosen uniquely. $\mathcal{C}$ gives adversary $\mathcal{A}$ all identities, public keys $\{(ID_1, pk_{ID_1}), \ldots, (ID_\ell, pk_\ell)\}$ as input.
2. $\mathcal{A}$ may issue polynomial number of Send, StateReveal, Corrupt, EstablishParty and RevealKey queries. At some point, $\mathcal{A}$ may issue a Test(π_i^s) query to an oracle π_i^s during the game with only once.

---

[2] We stress that the exact meaning of the StateReveal must be defined by each protocol separately, and each protocol should be proven secure to resist with such kind of state leakage as its claimed, i.e., the content stored in the variable st during protocol execution. In other word, each protocol should define the protocol steps processed on secure device. Our goal is to define the maximum states that can be leaked.

3. At the end of the game, the $\mathcal{A}$ may terminate with returning a bit b' as its guess for b of Test query. Finally, 1 is returned if all following conditions hold: (i) $\mathcal{A}$ has issued a Test query to a fresh oracle π_i^s without failure, and (ii) $\mathcal{A}$ returned a bit b' which equals to b of Test-query; Otherwise 0 is returned.

Definition 3. *A correct AKE protocol Σ is called (t,ϵ)-secure if probability bound $|\Pr[\mathsf{EXP}_{\Sigma,\mathcal{A}}^{\mathsf{AKE}}(\kappa) = 1] - 1/2| \leq \epsilon$ holds for all adversaries $\mathcal{A}$ running within time t in the above security experiment and for some negligible probability $\epsilon = \epsilon(\kappa)$ in the security parameter κ.*

4 A Generic One-Round AKE Construction from KE, KEM and NIKE

In this section, we present a generic one-round authenticated key exchange protocol (denoted by GC-KKN), that is more suitable to be implemented for providing eCK security than previous works.

PROTOCOL DESCRIPTION. In our generic construction, the following building blocks are required: (i) One-round key exchange scheme KE; (ii) Key encapsulation mechanism scheme KEM; (iii) Non-interactive key exchange scheme NIKE; and (iv) Strong randomness extractor SEXT; and (v) Pseudo-random function family PRF.

Set-up: To initiate the system, the public system parameters $pms := (pms^{ke}, pms^{kem}, pms^{nike}, k_{\mathsf{SEXT}})$ are firstly generated via performing
$pms^{ke} \leftarrow \mathsf{KE.Setup}(1^\kappa)$, $pms^{kem} \leftarrow \mathsf{KEM.Setup}(1^\kappa)$, $pms^{nike} \leftarrow \mathsf{NIKE.Setup}(1^\kappa)$
and $k_{\mathsf{SEXT}} \xleftarrow{\$} \mathcal{S}_{\mathsf{SEXT}}$ where k_{SEXT} is the secret key of SEXT and $\mathcal{S}_{\mathsf{SEXT}}$ is a key space.

Long-term Key Generation: A party $\hat{A}$ may run algorithms $(pk_{\hat{A}}^{kem}, sk_{\hat{A}}^{kem}) \xleftarrow{\$} \mathsf{KEM.Gen}(pms^{kem})$ and $(pk_{\hat{A}}^{nike}, sk_{\hat{A}}^{nike}) \xleftarrow{\$} \mathsf{NIKE.KGen}(pms^{nike}, \hat{A})$ to generate the long-term key pair.

Protocol Execution: On input pms, the protocol between party $\hat{A}$ and party $\hat{B}$ is depicted in Fig. 1.

Session States and Implementaton Senario. We now define the session states in terms of implementation model with secure device. Basically, all states of KE.EGen, KE.SKGen and KEM.EnCap algorithms would be stored in the state variable st. However, we assume no secret states related to KEM.DeCap and NIKE.ShKey algorithms can be revealed. This can be realized by doing all computations involving long-term private key of KEM.DeCap and NIKE.ShKey algorithms, and final session key generation on secure device.

SECURITY ANALYSIS. We assume without loss of generality that the maximum probability for the event that two oracles output the same ciphertext C or ephemeral public key epk, is a negligible fraction $1/2^\lambda$ where $\lambda \in N$ is a large

$$\hat{A} \qquad\qquad\qquad\qquad\qquad \hat{B}$$

$(epk_{\hat{A}}, esk_{\hat{A}}) \overset{\$}{\leftarrow} \mathsf{KE.EGen}(pms^{ke}) \qquad\qquad (epk_{\hat{B}}, esk_{\hat{B}}) \overset{\$}{\leftarrow} \mathsf{KE.EGen}(pms^{ke})$

$(K_{\hat{A}}, C_{\hat{A}}) \overset{\$}{\leftarrow} \mathsf{KEM.EnCap}(pk_{\hat{B}}^{kem}) \qquad\qquad (K_{\hat{B}}, C_{\hat{B}}) \overset{\$}{\leftarrow} \mathsf{KEM.EnCap}(pk_{\hat{A}}^{kem})$

$$\xrightarrow{\hat{A}, epk_{\hat{A}}, C_{\hat{A}}}$$

$$\xleftarrow{\hat{B}, epk_{\hat{B}}, C_{\hat{B}}}$$

Each party has $\mathsf{sid} := \hat{A}||\hat{B}||epk_{\hat{A}}||C_{\hat{A}}||epk_{\hat{B}}||C_{\hat{B}}$

$eK := \mathsf{KE.SKGen}(esk_{\hat{A}}, epk_{\hat{B}}) \qquad\qquad eK := \mathsf{KE.SKGen}(esk_{\hat{B}}, epk_{\hat{A}})$

$K_{\hat{B}} := \mathsf{KEM.DeCap}(sk_{\hat{A}}^{kem}, C_{\hat{B}}) \qquad\qquad K_{\hat{A}} := \mathsf{KEM.DeCap}(sk_{\hat{B}}^{kem}, C_{\hat{A}})$

$ShK_{\hat{A},\hat{B}} := \mathsf{NIKE.ShKey}(\hat{A}, \qquad\qquad ShK_{\hat{A},\hat{B}} := \mathsf{NIKE.ShKey}(\hat{B},$

$\qquad sk_{\hat{A}}^{nike}, \hat{B}, pk_{\hat{B}}^{nike}) \qquad\qquad\qquad sk_{\hat{B}}^{nike}, \hat{A}, pk_{\hat{A}}^{nike})$

$eK'' := \mathsf{PRF}(\mathsf{SEXT}(eK), \mathsf{sid}) \qquad\qquad eK'' := \mathsf{PRF}(\mathsf{SEXT}(eK), \mathsf{sid})$

$K_{\hat{A}}'' := \mathsf{PRF}(\mathsf{SEXT}(K_{\hat{A}}), \mathsf{sid}) \qquad\qquad K_{\hat{B}}'' := \mathsf{PRF}(\mathsf{SEXT}(K_{\hat{B}}), \mathsf{sid})$

$K_{\hat{B}}'' := \mathsf{PRF}(\mathsf{SEXT}(K_{\hat{B}}), \mathsf{sid}) \qquad\qquad K_{\hat{A}}'' := \mathsf{PRF}(\mathsf{SEXT}(K_{\hat{A}}), \mathsf{sid})$

$ShK_{\hat{A},\hat{B}}'' := \qquad\qquad\qquad\qquad ShK_{\hat{A},\hat{B}}'' :=$

$\mathsf{PRF}(\mathsf{SEXT}(ShK_{\hat{A},\hat{B}}), \mathsf{sid}) \qquad\qquad \mathsf{PRF}(\mathsf{SEXT}(ShK_{\hat{A},\hat{B}}), \mathsf{sid})$

$k_e := \qquad\qquad\qquad\qquad\qquad k_e :=$

$eK'' \oplus K_{\hat{A}}'' \oplus K_{\hat{B}}'' \oplus ShK_{\hat{A},\hat{B}}'' \qquad\qquad eK'' \oplus K_{\hat{A}}'' \oplus K_{\hat{B}}'' \oplus ShK_{\hat{A},\hat{B}}''$

Fig. 1. Generic One-round AKE Protocol from KE, KEM and NIKE

enough integer in terms of the security parameter κ. Let $\mathsf{MAX}(X_1, X_2, X_3)$ denote the function to obtain the maximum values from variables X_1, X_2 and X_3.

Theorem 1. *Suppose that the* SEXT *is* $(\kappa, \epsilon_{\mathsf{SEXT}})$-*strong randomness extractor, the* KEM *is* $(q_{kem}, t, \epsilon_{\mathsf{KEM}})$-*secure (key indistinguishable) against adaptive chosen message attacks and* KE *is* $(t, \epsilon_{\mathsf{KE}})$-*passively secure, and the* PRF *is* $(q_{prf}, t, \epsilon_{\mathsf{PRF}})$-*secure, and the* NIKE *is* $(t, \epsilon_{\mathsf{NIKE}})$-*CKS-light-secure. And we assume that either* KE *key or* KEM *key or* NIKE *key has* κ-*min-entropy. Then the proposed protocol is* (t', ϵ)-*secure in the sense of Definition 3 with* $t' \leq t$, $q_{kem} \geq d$ *and* $q_{prf} \geq d+1$, *and* $\epsilon \leq \frac{(d\ell)^2}{2^\lambda} + 3(d\ell)^2 \cdot (\mathsf{MAX}(\epsilon_{\mathsf{KE}}, \epsilon_{\mathsf{KEM}}, \epsilon_{\mathsf{NIKE}}) + \epsilon_{\mathsf{SEXT}} + \epsilon_{\mathsf{PRF}}).$ [3]

The proof of this theorem can be found in [13].

5   An Efficient One-Round AKE Protocol under Standard Assumptions

In this section we present a concrete eCK secure AKE protocol P1 in the standard model.

---

[3] The integer q_{kem} and q_{prf} are the numbers of oracle queries that can be issued in corresponding security experiment.

PROTOCOL DESCRIPTION. The proposed protocol relies on standard bilinear pairings $\mathcal{PG} = (\mathbb{G}, g, \mathbb{G}_T, p, e)$ [13] along with random values $(u_1, u_2, u_3, u_4) \xleftarrow{\$} \mathbb{G}$, target collision resistant hash function family TCR and pseudo-random function family PRF. The variable pms stores the public system parameters $pms :=$ $(\mathcal{PG}, \{u_i\}_{1 \le i \le 4}, hk_{\mathsf{TCR}})$ where hk_{TCR} is the hash key of TCR and is chosen uniformly at random.

$\hat{A}$

$x \xleftarrow{\$} \mathbb{Z}_p^*, X := g^x$
$h_X := \mathsf{TCR}(X)$
$t_X := (u_4^{h_X^2} u_3^{h_X} u_2)^x$

$\hat{B}$

$y \xleftarrow{\$} \mathbb{Z}_p^*, Y := g^y$
$h_Y := \mathsf{TCR}(Y)$
$t_Y := (u_4^{h_Y^2} u_3^{h_X} u_2)^y$

$$\xrightarrow{\hat{A}, X, t_X}$$
$$\xleftarrow{\hat{B}, Y, t_Y}$$

$h_Y := \mathsf{TCR}(Y), h_B := \mathsf{TCR}(B)$
reject if either

$e(t_Y, g) \ne e(u_4^{h_Y^2} u_3^{h_Y} u_2, Y)$ or
$e(t_B, g) \ne e(u_4^{h_B^2} u_3^{h_B} u_2, B)$

$h_X := \mathsf{TCR}(X), h_A := \mathsf{TCR}(A)$
reject if either

$e(t_X, g) \ne e(u_4^{h_X^2} u_3^{h_Y} u_2, X)$ or
$e(t_A, g) \ne e(u_4^{h_A^2} u_3^{h_A} u_2, A)$

Each party has $\mathsf{sid} := \hat{A}||A||t_A||X||t_X||\hat{B}||B||t_B||Y||t_Y$
Each party rejects if some values recorded in sid are identical

$\beta_{\hat{A}} := e(u_1, BY), k := \beta_{\hat{A}}^{a+x}$
accept $k_e := \mathsf{PRF}(k, \mathsf{sid})$

$\beta_{\hat{B}} := e(u_1, AX), k := \beta_{\hat{B}}^{b+y}$
accept $k_e := \mathsf{PRF}(k, \mathsf{sid})$

Fig. 2. Pairing-based AKE Protocol under Standard Assumptions

Long-term Key Generation: A party $\hat{A}$ may run an efficient key generation algorithm to generate the long-term key pair as: $sk_{\hat{A}} = a \xleftarrow{\$} \mathbb{Z}_p^*, pk_{\hat{A}} = (A, t_A)$ where $A = g^a$, $t_A := (u_4^{h_A^2} u_3^{h_A} u_2)^a$ and $h_A = \mathsf{TCR}(A)$.[4]

Protocol Execution: On input pms, the protocol between parties $\hat{A}$ and $\hat{B}$ is depicted in the Fig. 2.

Implementation and Session States: We assume that only the ephemeral private key x (resp. y) would be stored in the state variable st. This can be guaranteed by performing the computations of key material k and session key k_e on secure device.

SECURITY ANALYSIS. We show the security result of proposed protocol in our strong security model via the following theorem.

Theorem 2. *Assume each ephemeral key chosen during key exchange has bit-size* $\lambda \in \mathbb{N}$. *Suppose that the* BDDH *problem is* $(t, \epsilon_{\mathsf{BDDH}})$-*hard in the symmetric*

---

[4] Please note that we allow arbitrary key registration.

bilinear groups $\mathcal{PG}$, *the* TCR *is* $(t, \epsilon_{\mathsf{TCR}})$*-secure, and the* PRF *is* $(q_{prf}, t, \epsilon_{\mathsf{PRF}})$*-secure. Then the proposed protocol is* (t', ϵ)*-secure in the sense of Definition 3 with* $t' \approx t$ *and* $q_{prf} \geq 2$ *and* $\epsilon \leq \frac{(d\ell)^2}{2^\lambda} + \epsilon_{\mathsf{TCR}} + 3(d\ell)^2 \cdot (\epsilon_{\mathsf{BDDH}} + \epsilon_{\mathsf{PRF}})$.

The proof of this theorem can be found in [13].

References

1. Bellare, M., Rogaway, P.: Entity authentication and key distribution. In: Stinson, D.R. (ed.) CRYPTO 1993. LNCS, vol. 773, pp. 232–249. Springer, Heidelberg (1994)
2. Blake-Wilson, S., Johnson, D., Menezes, A.: Key agreement protocols and their security analysis. In: Darnell, M. (ed.) Cryptography and Coding 1997. LNCS, vol. 1355, pp. 30–45. Springer, Heidelberg (1997)
3. Boyd, C., Cliff, Y., Gonzalez Nieto, J.M., Paterson, K.G.: Efficient one-round key exchange in the standard model. In: Mu, Y., Susilo, W., Seberry, J. (eds.) ACISP 2008. LNCS, vol. 5107, pp. 69–83. Springer, Heidelberg (2008)
4. Canetti, R., Krawczyk, H.: Analysis of key-exchange protocols and their use for building secure channels. In: Pfitzmann, B. (ed.) EUROCRYPT 2001. LNCS, vol. 2045, pp. 453–474. Springer, Heidelberg (2001)
5. Canetti, R., Krawczyk, H.: Security analysis of IKE's signature-based key-exchange protocol. In: Yung, M. (ed.) CRYPTO 2002. LNCS, vol. 2442, pp. 143–161. Springer, Heidelberg (2002), http://eprint.iacr.org/2002/120/
6. Freire, E.S.V., Hofheinz, D., Kiltz, E., Paterson, K.G.: Non-interactive key exchange. In: Kurosawa, K., Hanaoka, G. (eds.) PKC 2013. LNCS, vol. 7778, pp. 254–271. Springer, Heidelberg (2013)
7. Fujioka, A., Suzuki, K., Xagawa, K., Yoneyama, K.: Strongly secure authenticated key exchange from factoring, codes, and lattices. In: Fischlin, M., Buchmann, J., Manulis, M. (eds.) PKC 2012. LNCS, vol. 7293, pp. 467–484. Springer, Heidelberg (2012)
8. Jager, T., Kohlar, F., Schäge, S., Schwenk, J.: On the security of TLS-DHE in the standard model. In: Safavi-Naini, R., Canetti, R. (eds.) CRYPTO 2012. LNCS, vol. 7417, pp. 273–293. Springer, Heidelberg (2012)
9. LaMacchia, B.A., Lauter, K., Mityagin, A.: Stronger security of authenticated key exchange. In: Susilo, W., Liu, J.K., Mu, Y. (eds.) ProvSec 2007. LNCS, vol. 4784, pp. 1–16. Springer, Heidelberg (2007)
10. Moriyama, D., Okamoto, T.: An eck-secure authenticated key exchange protocol without random oracles. TIIS 5(3), 607–625 (2011)
11. Okamoto, T.: Authenticated key exchange and key encapsulation in the standard model (invited talk). In: Kurosawa, K. (ed.) ASIACRYPT 2007. LNCS, vol. 4833, pp. 474–484. Springer, Heidelberg (2007)
12. Sarr, A.P., Elbaz-Vincent, P., Bajard, J.-C.: A new security model for authenticated key agreement. In: Garay, J.A., De Prisco, R. (eds.) SCN 2010. LNCS, vol. 6280, pp. 219–234. Springer, Heidelberg (2010)
13. Yang, Z.: Efficient eck-secure authenticated key exchange protocols in the standard model (full version). Cryptology ePrint Archive, Report 2013/365 (2013), http://eprint.iacr.org/

XLRF: A Cross-Layer Intrusion Recovery Framework for Damage Assessment and Recovery Plan Generation

Eunjung Yoon[1] and Peng Liu[2]

[1] Department of Computer Science and Engineering
Pennsylvania State University, PA, USA
eyoon@cse.psu.edu
[2] College of Information Sciences and Technology
Pennsylvania State University, PA, USA
pliu@ist.psu.edu

Abstract. Recovering mission-critical systems from intrusion is very challenging, where fast and accurate damage assessment and recovery is vital to ensure business continuity. Existing intrusion recovery approaches mostly focus on a single abstraction layer. OS level recovery cannot fully meet the correctness criteria defined by business process semantics, while business workflow level recovery usually results in *non-executable* recovery plans. In this paper, we propose a cross-layer recovery framework, called XRLF, for fast and effective post-intrusion diagnosis and recovery of compromised systems using the dependencies captured at different levels of abstraction; business workflow level and OS level. The goal of our approach is two-fold: first, to bridge the semantic gap between workflow-level and system-level recovery, thus enable comprehensive intrusion analysis and recovery; second, to automate damage assessment and recovery plan generation, thus expedite the recovery process, an otherwise time-consuming and error-prone task.

Keywords: cross-layer intrusion recovery, recovery plan, dependency graph, system calls.

1 Introduction

Intrusion, especially in mission-critical, enterprise systems, often results in the corruption of important data causing devastating effects to serious consequences such as significant financial loss. In fact, many mission critical systems have rather strict business continuity and availability requirements, and thus demand fast and efficient recovery from intrusion, which is essential for minimizing financial losses from cyber attacks.

Although a lot of effort has been devoted to the detection and prevention of malicious attacks, perfect prevention is still unobtainable. Intrusion detection can prevent the effects of the intrusion from spreading but cannot guarantee the integrity and availability of the compromised system. In some situations, an

S. Qing et al. (Eds.): ICICS 2013, LNCS 8233, pp. 194–212, 2013.

intrusion detection system (IDS) is also unable to discover all damage to the system and the damage can be spread without being detected by the IDS. We recognize that perfect intrusion detection is hard to achieve and some damage to the system even after the detection of the attack is always possible. To this end, we believe that an effective intrusion response and recovery scheme is essential for repairing compromised systems from the damage.

There has been growing interest in studies of intrusion recovery ([1], [8–10], [12], [14,15], [18], [20]), however most of intrusion recovery research has focused on a *single layer of abstraction*: Operating System (OS) level, Application level, or Business workflow level. None of them considered the problem of the *semantic gap* in infection diagnosis and recovery between high-level business workflow and the underlying infrastructure. Besides, there is a significant difference between *business workflow-level semantics* and *OS-level semantics*. Different abstraction layers may provide different granularity levels and different semantic views of the attack.

Due to the significant semantic gap between the two layers, an effective and comprehensive recovery may be very difficult. Most business-critical systems adopt the workflow management system with mission-critical processes [3] and thus, these systems, when intrusion detected either at workflow level or OS level, would require combined damage assessment and recovery by cooperation between the workflow layer and the underlying system layer.

In this paper, we present a *Cross-Layer Intrusion Recovery framework*, called XLRF, based on a combination of workflow-level and OS-level view. A cross-layer architecture allows us to have a global view about the intrusion and a more comprehensive understanding about recovery from the intrusion. Primary goal of our framework is to close the gap between business workflow-level and OS-level recovery semantics by focusing on two levels of abstraction in both, thus preserving workflow integrity, as well as system integrity. To the best of our knowledge, this is the first cross-layer recovery approach that focuses on both at business workflow level and OS level.

OS-level recovery approaches focus on low-level system events and do not take into account high-level business workflow implications. Due to the lack of higher workflow-level abstraction, OS-level intrusion recovery alone may cannot provide the comprehensive recovery solution, thus in many situations, needs manual work.

Similarly, *workflow-level recovery approaches* do not have enough information about low-level system activities that are very useful for fine grained intrusion analysis. Workflow-level recovery actions are generally performed at the granularity of business workflow tasks while OS-level recovery actions are generally performed at a granular file level, and thus workflow-level recovery approaches cannot handle the OS-level attacks (such as compromised processes, unauthorized data modification) properly. For example, workflow-level recovery performs task-level recovery actions (e.g., **undo** and **redo** of tasks), and thus task-level recovery actions cannot guarantee the removal of all the effects of the attack (compromised components) at the OS layer. As a result, workflow-level recovery often results in *non-executable* recovery plan. In order for a recovery plan to be effective, it must be *executable* in reality, which consists of low-level system recovery operations. Therefore, neither the *OS-level recovery* nor the *workflow-level recovery* can provide a comprehensive and effective recovery solution.

Our cross-layer recovery framework explores the association between two different levels of abstraction by extracting information about the relationships between a business workflow and system call invocations from system call traces. We perform an automated analysis of system call log to semantically map OS-level dependencies to workflow-level dependencies. The damage assessment and recovery plan generation using dependency information is performed in both a *top-down* and *bottom-up* fashion between OS layer and workflow layer by exploiting the hierarchical relationship between the two layers.

Another goal of our recovery framework is to maximize automation in damage assessment and recovery plan generation. Traditionally, the recovery from an attack is manually performed by system administrators, which is time-consuming and error-prone. Automated response to intrusions has become a major issue in defending mission-critical systems, in which it is important to know how fast a problem can be resolved after it is detected, and distributed systems, in which manual diagnosis and repair is difficult. To this end, we propose automated recovery plan generation framework for fast recovery.

This paper makes the following contributions:

- We develop a cross-layer recovery framework that bridges the semantic gap between business workflow-level recovery and OS-level recovery. To the best of our knowledge, this work is the first to develop a cross-layer recovery framework that considers business workflow layer and OS layer.
- We provide automated damage assessment and generation of recovery plan that is *executable*.
- We point out the inherent problems with single layer intrusion recovery schemes.

The remainder of the paper is organized as follows. We describe related work in Section 2. Section 3 describes our running workflow example. Section 4 presents an overview of our cross-layer recovery framework, called XLRF. We present the details of XLRF design and implementation of three phases in Section 5, and the evaluation of XLRF in Section 6. In Section 7, we briefly revisit the limitations of single layer recovery Finally, we conclude the paper in Section 8.

2   Related Work

Existing intrusion analysis and recovery approaches focus either on the OS layer or the workflow layer (*single-layered approach*), whereas our work focuses on both the OS layer and the workflow layer (*cross-layered approach*).

OS-level Recovery. OS-level recovery approaches only focus on low-level system events and do not take into account high-level abstraction of workflow-level recovery, which is essential for most business and mission-critical systems.

ReVirt [5] focuses on intrusion analysis by using Virtual Machine logging and replay. ReVirt provides recovery capability using checkpoint and roll back, however, it removes both affected and legitimate changes. BackTracker [13] provides intrusion analysis tool of tracking the sources of an intrusion. BackTracker captures and uses system calls for analyzing problems on the process and file system level. BackTracker uses previously recorded system calls and constructs the dependency graph by using system call dependencies from the detection point and traces affected system events on files or processes. XLRF is closely related to BackTracker for computation of system call dependencies and the dependency graph generation. Taser [8] is an intrusion recovery system that determines the set of tainted file system-operations and reverts the tainted operations but preserves legitimate operations. Taser logs all process, file and network operations to identify the file system modification after intrusion and provides selective redo of legitimate file-system operations after an attack occurs. RETRO [12] analyzes OS-level system events to determine the source of an intrusion by recording action history graph. RETRO tries to minimize re-execution (selective redo) by predicates, refinement, and shephered re-execution. SHELF [18] is a self-recovery system that leverages the Virtual Machine Monitor and taint-analysis for dynamic dependency tracking and quarantine. SHELF logs system-level events to track the dependencies among the events, maintains the dependency graph, and quarantine the infected and malicious objects.

Workflow-level Recovery. As discussed in Section 1, workflow-level recovery approaches often result in *non-executable* recovery plan. Yu et al. [20] introduced theories and analytical experiments for on-line attack recovery of workflows. Their recovery system identifies all damages caused by the malicious tasks that are detected by an IDS and automatically repairs the damages based on data and control dependencies among workflow tasks. Our *workflow-level* damage assessment using workflow-level dependencies are based on this work. Eder et al. [6] introduced workflow recovery concepts for reliable and consistent execution of business processes in the presence of failures and excetions. They integrate workflow transactions into WFMSs so that processes are treated as workflow transactions and in the event of failures, a running process is aborted and compensated. However, this approach mainly focuses on workflow failure recovery, which is different from the intrusion recovery that removes the effects of intrusions.

Other Recovery Approaches. Polygraph [14] is a software layer that extends the functionality of weakly consistent replication systems to support compromise recovery. Polygraph is based on the replication technique and tries to recover from data corruption in weakly consistent replicated storage systems. Ammann et al. [1] presented the recovery approch to the problem of removing undesirable but committed transactions from databases. They detect the flow of contaminated transactions through a database and roll back those transactions that are affected directly or indirectly by contaminated transactions. Solitude [10] is an application-level isolation and recovery system that uses a copy-on-write filesystem to limit attack propagation by sandboxing untrusted applications and providing an explicit file sharing.

3   Example

For our case study in this work, we develop a simplified version of *travel reservation system* running on the Apache web server. Our travel reservation system can be represented as a business workflow that consists of six tasks as follows.

T_1: Input travel information

T_2: Reserve a flight ticket and sign in or sign up

T_3: If the customer is signed as a member, reserve a hotel as a member.

T_4: If the customer is a member, apply any credit or promo code.

T_5: If the customer is a guest, reserve a hotel as a guest.

T_6: Make a payment

Figure 1 shows the workflow graph that represents our travel reservation system example. This model is based on [2] and [20]. The workflow has two choices of execution paths, P_1: $T_1 T_2 T_3 T_4 T_6$ and P_2: $T_1 T_2 T_5 T_6$, but in each execution, only one path can be selected by T_2. An attack can change the execution path of the workflow. In this example, P_1 is the execution path led by an attack, and P_2 is the normal execution path without an attack.

The workflow shows control and data dependencies between tasks. For example, if task T_1 is a malicious task, tasks T_2 and T_4 would be affected by T_1 as they will read corrupted data from task T_1, and thus calculating wrong results as T_2 is *data dependent* on T_1 and T_4 is *data dependent* on T_2. Consequently, T_2 would make a wrong decision to execute tasks on path P_1, resulting in changing the normal execution path as T_3 and T_5 are *control dependent* on T_2.

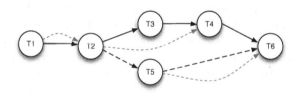

Fig. 1. Workflow of Travel Reservation System

4   XLRF Overview

We propose a *Cross-Layer Recovery framework*, called XLRF, an automated intrusion analysis and recovery plan generation framework. Our approach considers two different levels of abstraction: workflow level and OS level, and provides multi-level damage assessment and comprehensive recovery plan generation.

4.1   Assumptions

In this work, we assume the integrity of the system call log and checkpoints is preserved. We archive and send the system call logs collected on the web server to the trusted host that will investigate the effects of the intrusion and generate a recovery plan by using XLRF framework. We also assume that the administrator noticed an attack (i.e., system compromise) and identified at least one intrusion point before using XLRF, which is similar to the assumption of Backtracker [13] A sophisticated attacker may be able to successfully evade the IDS by manipulating a sequence of system calls (i.e., *mimicry attack* [17]). Recovery from mimicry or evasion attacks is out-of-scope for this paper, if these attacks have never been identified, as XLRF starts from the identified intrusion point.

4.2   Cross-Layer Recovery

Our cross-layer recovery framework (XLRF) is based on the analysis of workflow-level and OS-level control and data dependencies. We use the dependency information at each layer to analyze the effects of the intrusion and to automatically generate a recovery plan which consists of recovery actions that will revert the effects. XLRF takes inputs as a *workflow specification*, system call log recorded by the operating system, and the intrusion point identified by the administrator from IDS alerts. XLRF builds the association between workflow tasks and system calls based on the dependencies at the both layers. From the workflow-level perspective, each component at the OS layer has a corresponding task node at the workflow layer, and vice versa.

Damage assessment is performed in a combined *bottom-up* (from OS level to workflow level) and *top-down* (from workflow level to OS level) analysis. Once XLRF has completed damage assessment, it starts to generate a recovery plan with the result.

4.3   Workflow Level

A workflow typically represents a business process, which is composed of a sequence of tasks (i.e., business activities), and a set of dependencies that represent the relationships between the tasks.

Workflow Dependencies. The task dependencies in a business workflow is imperative to determine which tasks to recover and the order in which tasks are recovered. In this paper, we consider two types of dependencies between workflow tasks: *data dependency* and *control dependency*.

- *Data dependency.* Data dependencies (data flows) among tasks describe inputs and outputs of a task. Given a task T_i, we use $R(T_i, f)$ and $W(T_i, f)$ to denote a read operation and a write operation of task T_i on file f, respectively. Task T_j is data dependent on task T_i if $W(T_i, f)$ happens before $R(T_j, f)$ or $W(T_j, f)$.

  For example, if T_i modified file f and then T_j uses (reads or writes) the file for performing the task, task T_j is *data dependent* on task T_i. That is, the state of T_j would depend on the value of the input file f as T_i has modified the file f that is shared by the two tasks. In Figure 1, dotted red lines represent data dependencies between tasks.

– *Control dependency.* The control dependency specifies the control flow of the workflow. Given two tasks T_i and T_j within a workflow, the task T_j is *control dependent* on T_i if T_j can be activated depending on the outcome of T_i. The output value of T_i determines the execution path of the workflow, either to execute T_j or another task. Thus, control dependencies of a workflow decide the execution order of tasks. In our running example shown in Figure 1, T_3 and T_5 are *control dependent* on T_2.

Workflow Dependency Graph (WDG). A workflow can be represented as a directed graph G(V, E), called *workflow dependency graph* (WDG), comprising V a set of nodes and E a set of directed edges, in which each node represents a task and directed edges represent dependencies between tasks, as shown in Figure 1. The WDG also can be generated by using workflow mining technique [16].

4.4   Operating System Level

XLRF uses OS-level information to identify system-level causal events (i.e., information flow) that connect OS objects, such as processes and files. The OS-level information can provide finer grained auditing and view of underlying system activities. For OS-level analysis, we are particularly interested in system calls and the data dependencies among system calls, which is similar to the approach that is generally used for behavioral malware detection in [4] and [19]. XLRF records all or selected system call invocations at run-time to extract system call dependencies from the system call traces.

   System Call Dependencies. Every system call operation has a list of argument values and the return value, which we use for exploring *data dependencies* among system calls. We also use the timestamp of each system call to determine *the temporal order* of system calls. We extract dependencies among system calls for OS-level dependency analysis by analyzing each system call's arguments and the return value. In this paper, we only focus on *data dependencies* among system calls, which allow us to effectively identify data flows between system calls and to understand the semantics of the program and the effects of intrusion on system objects.

   Christodorescu et al. [4] describe three types of dependencies among system calls: *def-use, ordering,* and *value* dependence but we only focus on data dependency (same as their *def-use* dependency) in this paper.

– *Data dependency*: Data dependencies between system calls can be computed by arguments (i.e., input) and a return value (i.e., output) of each system call. The return value of a system call can be used as the argument of subsequent system calls. For example, given two system calls sc_i and sc_j, system call sc_j is *data dependent* on sc_i if sc_j uses the valid return value of sc_i as its argument.

System Call Dependency Graph (SCDG). The data dependencies that we extracted from system call traces are represented as a directed graph G(V, E), called *system call dependency graph* (SCDG), such that nodes are system calls and edges represent data dependencies among system calls. We compute the dependencies by analyzing relationships between system call arguments and return values.

5   Design and Implementation

The XLRF framework provides automated damage assessment and recovery plan generation by analyzing dependencies within and across at the workflow layer and at the OS layer, and by identifying affected workflow tasks and system objects using the observed dependencies.

The XLRF framework consists of three main phases (Figure 2): dependency analysis, damage assessment, and recovery plan generation. During the dependency analysis phase, XLRF analyzes the system call log to determine dependencies among system calls and workflow tasks and constructs a *cross-layer dependency graph*, called XDG. In the damage assessment phase, XLRF identifies all the malicious or affected workflow tasks and system objects by traversing XDG from initially identified, malicious system objects (i.e., intrusion point). In the recovery plan generation phase, XLRF automatically generates a recovery plan based on the malicious or affected tasks and system objects that have been identified.

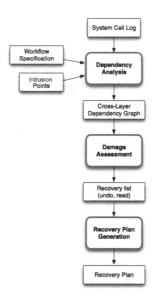

Fig. 2. The XLRF framework

5.1 Input

Workflow Specification. One of the inputs to XLRF is the *workflow specification*. The workflow specification contains the workflow type information that describes the workflow task structure (control flow) and information exchange between tasks (data flow) in a workflow. Each workflow is an instance of a workflow type. XLRF takes as input the workflow specification and system call traces to identify current running workflow instances.

System Call Log. The second input to XLRF is the system call log. System call traces are essential for XLRF to identify attack events and analyze dependencies between system calls. Logging mechanism will be discussed further in Section 5.3

Intrusion Point. Once an intrusion is detected by an IDS, the administrator can identify the intrusion point from the IDS alerts. XLRF takes as input the intrusion point and start to investigate the effects of the intrusion both at the OS layer and at the workflow layer to generate a recovery plan.

5.2 Output

Recovery Plan. The output of XLRF is a recovery plan that consists of a set of recovery actions. XLRF automatically generates a recovery plan which is very useful not only by reducing the system administrator's manual recovery process but also by minimizing human errors, and thus ultimately reducing the recovery time.

5.3 Logging

To build a proof-of-concept prototype of XLRF, we collect system call traces on the Apache HTTP server (`httpd`) using *DTrace* framework during normal execution of our *online travel reservation workflow* to track system events on OS-level objects such as processes, files and socket connections. *DTrace* is a dynamic tracing framework developed by Sun Microsystems. *DTrace* can dynamically instrument the running operating system kernel and running applications without rebooting the kernel or restarting applications. Gessiou et al. [7] also used *DTrace* framework for collecting data provenance information.

Each entry of the system call log contains detailed system object information such as process ID, file descriptor, and socket descriptor, the timestamp, and/or session ID of each system call invocation. During the dependency analysis phase, XLRF uses this information to construct a *system call dependency graph* (SCDG) and a *workflow dependency graph* (WDG). XLRF then constructs a *cross-layer dependency graph* (XDG) by associating the two graphs, SCDG and WDG; mapping of each node of SCDG (system call operation) and each node of WDG (workflow-level task).

XLRF can identify a user's workflow instance that corresponds to a particular system call and process. In our running example, once an authenticated session has been established, the session ID can be identified for all web page (`php` code file)

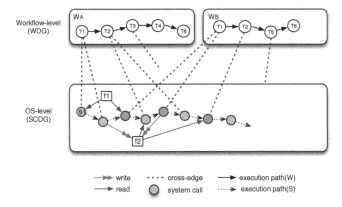

Fig. 3. Cross-Layer Depedency Graph

accesses. In addition, the entities involved in a workflow can be uniquely identified by a combination of a username and the workflow ID that is generated for every workflow of a user. This user identification allows us to observe whose workflow instance ID matches the current workflow instance (i.e., the origin of a system call and the corresponding workflow task), and thus enables selectively to recover only affected workflow instances. For example, in Figure 3, Alice's workflow instance (W_A) and Bob's workflow instance (W_B) at the workflow layer are mapped to each system call node at the OS layer based on our approach.

5.4 Dependency Analysis

Once an IDS has detected an intrusion, XLRF takes as input the intrusion point deduced by the administrator from the IDS alerts, the system call logs collected during normal execution, and the workflow specification. The system call log allows us to learn about the executed path of the workflow and dependencies among system calls. XLRF preprocesses the system call log by focusing particularly on file and process operations and extracts the data dependencies, and constructs *dependency graphs*. The dependency information is essential for our recovery framework to identify directly or indirectly affected objects from the intrusion which recovery is needed for. XLRF identifies current running workflow instances and their *workflow dependency graph* (WDG) with the workflow specification and the system call trace. Similarly, XLRF constructs the *system call dependency graph* (SCDG) with the dependencies among system calls extracted from the system call trace. XLRF then correlates and combines the two layers of dependency graphs as a single hierarchical graph, called *cross-layer dependency graph* (XDG), by associating semantic links between two graphs.

Cross-Layer Dependency Graph. *Cross-layer dependency graph* (XDG) enables cross-layer damage analysis, which allows us to identify the effects of

Table 1. Association of file information to workflow tasks

T_1	T_2	T_3	T_4	T_5	T_6
index.php (GET)	login.php (POST)	check.php (POST)	member.php (GET)	guest.php (POST)	payment.php (POST)
flight.dat (R)	guestinfo.php (POST)	users.dat (R)	hotel.dat (R)	hotel.dat(R)	invoice.dat (R)
	users.dat (R/W)		promo.dat (R)	discount.php (POST)	credit.dat (R/W)
			invoice.dat (W)	promo.dat (R)	payment.dat (W)
				invoice.dat (W)	

intrusion using dependencies collected both at the workflow layer and the OS layer.

After we constructed WDG and SCDG, we find the *semantic relationships (links)* between the two dependency graphs. Given WDG and SCDG, XLRF adds the edges that cross the two layers so that each *cross-edge* in the resulting XDG connects vertices of each graph at the two layers.

XLRF correlates the relationship between WDG and SCDG by analyzing the system call log and the workflow specification. Having a good criteria to associate each system call to a task of a particular workflow instance is challenging, as the system call log consists of multiple workflow instances involving multiple clients. XLRF separates the combined traces at the OS layer (SCDG) into separate *workflow instances* at the workflow layer (WDG) for each user. The *workflow specification* provides us information of interaction between a workflow task and its operations on some input and output data (e.g., data files). Therefore, XLRF takes both the workflow specification and system call logs as inputs and leverages the information to find out the semantic relationships between workflow-level and OS-level activities.

Table 1 shows the information obtained from the workflow specification used for our running workflow example. Our workflow example separates a workflow into a set of tasks with the semantic relationships between webpages, and data files specified in the workflow specification. Each workflow task basically comprises of program code files (**php** files) and data files. In this work, for the sake of simplicity, we use data files stored in file system instead of database. Using this information along with system call traces, XLRF can generate XDG, as shown in Figure 3, which is an integrated graph of WDG and SCDG, connected by the *cross-edges*.

5.5   Damage Assessment

During the damage assessment phase, XLRF identifies which tasks at the workflow layer and which system objects at the OS layer have been affected by malicious system objects. XLRF takes as inputs XDG that has been constructed in the dependency analysis phase, and the intrusion points (i.e., identified malicious objects) to create the *recovery list* of malicious or affected workflow tasks and system-level objects, as shown in Algorithm 1. This information is essential for deciding recovery actions that will be used for generating a recovery plan. The overview of recovery actions (**undo** and **redo**) will be given in the following section.

The analysis is performed on XDG, in both directions: *bottom-up* (SCDG→WDG) and *top-down* (WDG→SCDG):

Bottom-up Analysis. XLRF starts from the detection point to diagnose affected workflow tasks by using a bottom-up analysis.

At the OS layer (SCDG). Given the intrusion point, locate a malicious node of SCDG.

OS layer (SCDG) → Workflow layer (WDG). From the malicious node of SCDG, follow the *cross-edge* to locate the associated task node of WDG. Add the task to the *recovery list (workflow undo list)*.

At the workflow layer (WDG). From the malicious task node, identify all affected tasks by using data and control dependencies (*dependency edges*). Add all affected tasks to the *recovery list (workflow undo list or workflow redo list)*. For workflow-level analysis, we use the approach similar to Yu et al's workflow recovery [20] to determine which workflow tasks have been affected and need to be repaired.

We explain the analysis by using our workflow example and XDG, shown in Figure 1 and Figure 3. Suppose that file $f1$ has been identified as corrupted by an intrusion. From XDG shown in Figure 3, the first system call node s_1 of SCDG (**read f1**) will read the corrupted data (a). The system call node has a *cross-edge* to task node T_1 of Alice's workflow instance (W_A), and thus T_1 of WDG is marked as bad (malicious or affected) and added to Alice's workflow *undo list*, $WU_A = \{T_1\}$ because T_1 needs to be undone in the recovery (b). At the workflow layer (WDG), by the data dependencies shown in Figure 1, task T_2 is infected by task T_1 because it is *data dependent* on T_1, by reading a corrupted data ($f1$) from T_1 and then creating wrong results. Thus, T_2 is added to *undo list*, $WU_A = \{T_1, T_2\}$. Similarly, T_4 is *data dependent* on T_2, and thus added to the *undo list*, $WU_A = \{T_1, T_2, T_4\}$. Although task T_3 is not affected, it needs to be undone in case T_3 performed data write operations (**e.g.**, **write f**), because the data will be corrupted if the execution path is changed by $\text{redo}(T_2)$ and T_3 is not on the new execution path. XLRF adds T_3 to *candidate undo list*, $CU_A = \{T_3\}$. T_6 is also added to $CU_A = \{T_3, T_6\}$ because it will be *data dependent* on T_5 and get a wrong result from the current execution if the execution path is changed by $\text{redo}(T_2)$. From the $WU_A = \{T_1, T_2, T_4\}$ and $CU_A = \{T_3, T_6\}$, XLRF creates *redo list* $WR_A = \{T_1, T_2, T_6\}$, because the tasks are *not control dependent* on any malicious or affected tasks. If any task is not on the new executing path (T_3, T_4), it does not need to be redone because it can create corrupted data (c).

Top-down Analysis. XLRF refines the *workflow-level recovery list* at the high level of abstraction (WDG) and bottoms out in a set of directly *executable OS-level recovery actions* at the low level of abstraction (SCDG) by using a top-down analysis. This analysis allows us to derive a recovery plan from recovery goals. XLRF can create the *OS-level recovery list* of affected system objects given malicious or affected tasks of a particular workflow instance, which will be used in the recovery plan generation phase.

Algorithm 1. Damage Assessment

Input:
XDG: Cross-layer dependency graph
M: Malicious Objects (from IDS alerts)
Output:
WU: Workflow Undo list
WR: Workflow Redo list
CU: Candidate Undo list
SU: System-call Undo list

1: **if** SCDG node s of XDG is data-dependent
   on M **then**
2:     **if** cross-edge $e(s, t)$ exists **then**
3:         Follow $e(s, t)$ and locate task node t
4:         Add t to WU
5:         **while** $succ(t)$ exists **do**
6:             **for all** $succ(t)$ data-dependent on
               t **do**
7:                 Add $succ(t)$ to WU
8:                 $t \leftarrow succ(t)$
9:                 **if** $t_i \in succ(t)$, not data-
                   dependent on t **then**
10:                     Add t_i to CU
11: **for each** WDG node t_i of XDG **do**
12:     **if** t_i is control-dependent on t_j **then**
13:         **if** $(t_j \notin WU)$ **or** $(t_j \in WU, t_i \in$
           $succ(redo(t_j)))$ **then**
14:             Add t_i to WR
15: **for each** t_i of WU **do**   ▷ backward
16:     Follow cross-edge$e(s, t_i)$
17:     **for all** node s belongs to t_i **do**
18:         Add s to $SU[t_i]$

Workflow layer (WDG) → OS layer (SCDG). Given a malicious or affected task node of WDG, follow the *cross-edges* to identify the associated low-level system call nodes of SCDG.

At the OS layer (SCDG). From the identified system call nodes and dependencies among them, find all the affected system objects (files, in our example).

In our framework, redoing a workflow task will automatically re-execute all system calls associated with the task. Thus, XLRF only maintains *undo list* for system call-level operations (no *redo list*).

5.6 Recovery Plan Generation

The last phase of XLRF is to automatically generate a *recovery plan* based on the dependency information and the damage analysis results. Generated recovery plan describes *executable recovery actions* needed for reverting the effects of intrusion both at the workflow layer and at the OS layer.

Before discussing our recovery plan generation scheme, we briefly describe recovery actions.

Workflow Task Undo and Redo. To recover from intrusion, basically two operations: **undo** and **redo** are used. To remove all effects of intrusion, XLRF needs to **undo** malicious and affected tasks that have been identified during the damage assessment phase. XLRF creates *undo lists* for workflow tasks to revert all the effect and creates *redo lists* for tasks to restore legitimate but removed operations that have been affected by the attack.

System-Call Undo and Redo. As far as we know, there is no known way to actually **undo** the already executed system call. Alternatively, we could roll back the object (e.g., file) affected by the system call to the last checkpoint, which is commonly used for reverting **write** operation to a file, or we could ideally use an *inverse* operation if supported. Executing *inverse* operations can be substantially more efficient than checkpoint and rollback mechanism. A recent work [11] presents a new technique for *inverse* operations but their approach is still limited for linked data structures, which needs to be extended if it is to be used in real systems.

In fact, XLRF generates a recovery plan for leveraging checkpoint and rollback mechanism for system call undo and removing system-call level redo because the task-level redo operation will automatically re-execute system calls that belong to the specific task. From OS-level recovery perspective, the task-level redo is too coarse-grained, resulting in some unnecessary system call redo operations can be included in a recovery plan. However, we do not focus on efficient selective-redo approach for system calls in this work. Nevertheless, our recovery plan generation framework can be easily adapted to the advanced recovery technique as needed.

Algorithm 2. Recovery Plan Generation

Input:
WU: Workflow Undo list
WR: Workflow Redo list
CU: Candidate Undo list
SU: System-call Undo list
Output:
P: Recovery Plan

1: **while** WU is not empty **do**
2:     Get task T_i from WU ▷ backward
3:     Add undo(T_i) to P
4:     **while** $SU[T_i]$ is not empty **do**
5:         Get system call s_i from $SU[T_i]$
6:         **if** s_i is write(f) **then**
7:             Add rollback (f) to P
8: **while** WR is not empty **do**
9:     Get task T_i from WR ▷ forward
10:     Add redo(T_i) to P
11:     **if** redo(T_i) changes the execution path **then**
12:         **while** CU is not empty **do**
13:             Get task T_i from CU
14:             **while** $SU[T_i]$ is not empty **do**
15:                 **if** s_i is write(f) **then**
16:                     **if** s_i is the first write **then**
17:                         Add undo(T_i) to P
18:                         Add rollback (f) to P

The Order of Recovery Actions. To preserve correctness during the repair, the order of recovery actions needs to be correctly determined. The following rules describe the correct order of recovery actions from a workflow perspective.

- undo actions are performed in reverse order.
- redo actions are performed by following the original order of the task operations.
- For any task , its undo action should be done before its redo action.
- For any two tasks that modify the same file in order, the later task should be undone first before the earlier task is redone. For example, suppose that both task t_i and task t_j modify the same file f, $W(t_i, f)$ precedes $W(t_j, f)$. In this case, undo(t_j) should be done before redo(t_i).

XLRF automatically generates a recovery plan by the rules with *undo list* and *redo list* obtained during the damage assessment phase (see Algorithm 2).

5.7 Implementation

We implemented a proof-of-concept prototype of the XLRF framework on Linux based on the detailed design and algorithms that we have presented. We developed a simple web-based travel planning service in *PHP* running on Apache web server as our running example. Our implementation does not need to make any changes to existing software components.

For logging system-level activities, we use *DTrace* framework to record selected system call invocations (e.g., read(), write()) on `httpd` process. While we do not focus on performance degradation problem in this work, logging overhead using *DTrace* was not a big concern, as *DTrace* has been designed to operate with low overheads when enabled, and zero or near-zero overhead when not enabled (selective instrumentation). We store the logs collected from the web server on a trusted platform that is isolated from the web server and we run the XLRF framework on the trusted platform so it does not incur much overhead to the HTTP server. We do not invent the wheel to prevent the integrity of the XLRF framework in this work but it is also hard to compromise the XLRF framework by the intrusion on the web server.

We implemented XLRF in *Perl* and *XML* for log analysis and automated recovery plan generation. We selected *Perl* script language as *Perl* is powerful for regular expressions processing. We generate dependency graphs using the dependencies obtained in the dependency analysis phase. The dependency graphs can be visualized using *Graphviz* as desired. XRLF then generates a recovery plan as an *XML* file that is human-readable and machine-readable. *XML* provides a basic syntax that can be used for sharing information between different platforms and applications. Manual or automated execution of a recovery plan using scripts is also much easier with *XML*. *Perl* also provides the features of *XML parsing* and converting it to *Perl* data structures.

6 Evaluation of Recovery Plan

We evaluated the correctness of our *cross-layer recovery framework* using several intrusion scenarios. In this paper, we present the evaluation of two scenarios due to space limit. We ran XLRF for each scenario on a trusted platform and compared generated recovery plans with the manually derived dependencies and expected recovery actions. We argue that XLF correctly generates a recovery plan for each attack scenario based on the evaluation.

Scenario 1: Data File Compromise

In our running example, an attacker can modifty the content of an invoice file (*invoice.dat*), in order to intentionally change the price of a particular travel plan, for example, from \$2000 to \$1000. In this scenario, Alice's workflow tasks T_4 and T_6 will be affected by the compromise, and thus will lead to a financial loss.

Recovery Goals. Revert *invoice.dat* and all affected files by rolling back the file to the last checkpoint to remove the effect from compromise. Remove all the effects and restore operations (`undo` and `redo`).

1. *Generated Recovery Plan: (for Alice)*

⟨plan name=$"rW_A"$⟩
   ⟨action=$"uT_6"$⟩ undo(T_6)
      ⟨subaction=$"T_6w11"$⟩
         rollback(*payment.dat*)
      ⟨/subaction⟩
   ⟨/action⟩
   ⟨action=$"uT_4"$⟩ undo(T_4)
      ⟨subaction=$"T_4w12"$⟩
         rollback(*invoice.dat*)
      ⟨/subaction⟩
   ⟨ /action⟩
   ⟨action=$"rT_4"$⟩ redo(T_4) ⟨/action⟩
   ⟨action=$"rT_6"$⟩ redo(T_6) ⟨/action⟩
⟨/plan⟩

2. *Derived Dependencies (manual):*
by Attacker:
write (invoice.dat, *badInput*)→**invoice.dat/**
by Alice's workflow: from T_6
read(payment.php)→read(invoice.dat/)→ read(credit.dat)
→write(payment.dat/)
Workflow level:
undo(T6) → undo(T4) → redo(T4) → redo(T6)
OS level (system call):
* Need undo? (Y/N)
T_6: w(payment.dat):Y ⇒ rollback (payment.dat)
T_6: r(credit.dat),r(invoice.dat), r(payment.php): N
T_4: w(invoice.dat):Y ⇒ rollback(invoice.dat)
T_4: r(promo.dat), r(hotel.dat), r(member.php): N
* Need redo? (Y/N)
T_4: r(member.php), r(hotel.dat), w(invoice.dat): Y

System-call level `redo` actions are automatically performed by their task-level `redo`, thus do not need to be added to a recovery plan.

Scenario 2: Execution Path Change. An attacker modifies *login.php* file and changes the execution path, allowing a guest member to be redirected to the webpage that only registered member can access. All guest members can benefit from this attack by making her travel plan using a member-only promotion, but resulting in a financial loss to the travel agency (*workflow violation*). Suppose that Figure 3 shows Alice (guest member)'s new execution path after the attack. Her original execution is $T_1 \to T_2 \to T_5 \to T6$, but it has been changed to $T_1 \to T_2 \to T_3 \to T_4 \to T_6$, respectively.

Recovery Goals. Revirt all malicious (*index.php*) or affected files and operations from the attack and restore original execution path.

1. *Generated Recovery Plan: (for Alice)*

⟨plan name= $"rW_A"$⟩
   ⟨action=$"uT_6"$⟩ undo(T_6)
      ⟨subaction=$"T_6w11"$⟩
         rollback(*payment.dat*)
      ⟨/subaction⟩
   ⟨/action⟩
   ⟨action=$"uT_4"$⟩ undo(T_4)
      ⟨subaction=$"T_4w12"$⟩
         rollback(*invoice.dat*)
      ⟨/subaction⟩
   ⟨action=$"uT_2"$⟩ undo(T_2)
      ⟨subaction=$"T_2w11"$⟩
         rollback(*users.dat*)
      ⟨/subaction⟩
   ⟨ /action⟩
   ⟨action=$"rT_2"$⟩ redo(T_2) ⟨/action⟩
   ⟨action=$"rT_6"$⟩ redo(T_6) ⟨/action⟩
⟨/plan⟩

2. *Derived Dependencies (manual):*
by Attacker:
write (users.dat, *badInput*) → **users.dat/**
by Alice's workflow: from T_2
read(login.php)→read(guestinfo.php)→ **write**(users.dat/)
→read(check.php)→ **read**(users.dat/) →read(member.php)→
read(hotel.dat)→read(promo.dat)→ **write**(invoice.dat/)
→read(payment.php)→read(invoice.dat/)→read(credit.dat)
→ **write**(payment.dat)
Workflow level:
undo(T6) → undo(T4) → undo(T2) → redo(T2) →
redo(T6)
OS level (system call):
* Need undo? (Y/N)
T_6: w(payment.dat):Y ⇒ rollback (payment.dat)
T_6: r(credit.dat), r(invoice.dat), r(payment.php): N
T_4: w(invoice.dat):Y ⇒ rollback(invoice.dat)
T_4: r(promo.dat), r(hotel.dat), r(member.php): N
T_2: w(users.dat):Y ⇒ rollback (users.dat)
T_2: r(guestinfo.php), r(login.php): N
* Need redo? (Y/N)
T_2: r(login.php), r(guestinfo.php), r(users.dat): Y
T_6: r(payment.php), r(invoice.dat), r(credit.dat), w (payment.dat): Y

Task T_4 is not on the re-execution path, thus T_4 needs not to be redone. The generated recovery plan shows for each user after `rollback`(*login.php*) has been done. The file *login.php* is shared by all users, so need to recover separately, before recover any workflow instance. The comparison shows that the recovery plan for Scenario 2 generated by XLRF is correct.

In all the scenarios mentioned above, we show that our approach is effective in damage assessment and recovery plan generation for intrusion recovery.

7 Revisiting the Limitations of Single Layer Recovery

As we discussed earlier, single layer recovery approaches cannot provide the comprehensive damage assessment and recovery solution due to the semantic gap between the high-level workflow abstraction and the low-level OS-level abstraction. Here we revisit and discuss the limitations of single layer recovery approaches: workflow-level and OS-level recovery with our running example.

A host-based IDS can monitor system activities so the administrator can identify the intrusion point such as a corrupted file, from the IDS alerts, which is used for OS-level recovery. By using data dependencies among system calls, all the affected files can be identified and recovered using the checkpoint and roll-back scheme and some of system call `redo` operations. However, even after all the corrupted files are recovered at the OS layer, the recovery still cannot ensure the correctness in business workflow semantics.

Let's revisit Scenario 1, OS-level recovery will do: `rollback`(payment.dat), `rollback`(invoice.dat), and `redo` operations on the files, such as `read` (invoice.dat), and `write`(payment.dat), however at the end of this OS-level recovery, only part of task T_6 has been recovered; `read`(payment.php) of T_6 will not be redone. From a workflow perspective, the client's payment process needs to be cancelled and re-executed, thus the entire task needs to be undone and redone for the client's input (She can probably change her mind later due to the price increase), so we need to redo the entire task T_6. Without the association between OS-level semantics and workflow-level semantics, the identification of current workflow instances that are affected and need to be repaired, will be very challenging. Therefore, we argue that OS-level recovery approach cannot provide correct recovery actions for high-level business workflow as it cannot determine the damage in the business workflow semantics correctly.

Workflow-level recovery scheme does not have the semantic information about the low-level system activities such as system call invocations. Therefore, in Scenario 1, when *invoice.dat* file has been compromised, workflow-level recovery does not aware about the intrusion and the system-level damage until any anomalous task of a workflow (e.g., task abortion) has been detected. It could never been detected in case of normal execution of the task even with a malicious data. Workflow-level approach provides task-level recovery so may cannot perform fine-grained recovery actions such as single file operation. Most workflow-level recovery approaches use workflow-level checkpointing resulting in expensive coarse-grained recovery. Therefore, workflow recovery often results in *non-executable* recovery plan as it cannot perform recovery actions at the OS layer, which requires the system administrator's manual process.

8   Conclusion

In this paper, we have first presented a cross-layer recovery framework for automatically analyzing the damage caused by intrusion and generating a recovery plan. We addressed the problem of single layer recovery approaches and proposed a new cross-layer recovery approach that takes into account both business workflow-level and OS-level recovery for providing a comprehensive recovery. We developed a proof-of-concept prototype of our recovery framework, called XLRF, that comprises dependency analysis, damage assessment, and recovery plan generation phases. We evaluated the effectiveness of our cross-layer recovery framework with several attack scenarios. XLRF correctly identified the effects of the intrusion and generated recovery plans for reverting all the effects from intrusion both at the workflow layer and at the OS layer.

Acknowledgments. This work was supported by ARO W911NF-09-1-0525 (MURI), AFOSR FA9550-07-1-0527 (MURI), NSF CNS-0905131, and AFOSR W911NF1210055.

References

1. Ammann, P., Jajodia, S., Liu, P.: Recovery from malicious transactions. IEEE Trans. on Knowl. and Data Eng. 14(5), 1167–1185 (2002)
2. Atluri, V., Ae Chun, S., Mazzoleni, P.: Chinese wall security for decentralized workflow management systems. J. Comput. Secur. 12(6), 799–840 (2004)
3. Balzarotti, D., Cova, M., Felmetsger, V.V., Vigna, G.: Multi-module vulnerability analysis of web-based applications. In: Proceedings of the 14th ACM Conference on Computer and Communications Security, CCS 2007, pp. 25–35. ACM, New York (2007)
4. Christodorescu, M., Jha, S., Kruegel, C.: Mining specifications of malicious behavior. In: Proceedings of the 6th Joint Meeting of the European Software Engineering Conference and the ACM SIGSOFT Symposium on the Foundations of Software Engineering, ESEC-FSE 2007, pp. 5–14. ACM, New York (2007)
5. Dunlap, G.W., King, S.T., Cinar, S., Basrai, M.A., Chen, P.M.: Revirt: enabling intrusion analysis through virtual-machine logging and replay. SIGOPS Oper. Syst. Rev. 36(SI), 211–224 (2002)
6. Eder, J., Liebhart, W.: Workflow recovery. In: Proceedings of the First IFCIS International Conference on Cooperative Information Systems, COOPIS 1996, pp. 124–134. IEEE Computer Society, Washington, DC (1996)
7. Gessiou, E., Pappas, V., Athanasopoulos, E., Keromytis, A.D., Ioannidis, S.: Towards a universal data provenance framework using dynamic instrumentation. In: Gritzalis, D., Furnell, S., Theoharidou, M. (eds.) SEC 2012. IFIP AICT, vol. 376, pp. 103–114. Springer, Heidelberg (2012)
8. Goel, A., Po, K., Farhadi, K., Li, Z., de Lara, E.: The taser intrusion recovery system. In: Proceedings of the Twentieth ACM Symposium on Operating Systems Principles, SOSP 2005, pp. 163–176. ACM, New York (2005)
9. Hsu, F., Chen, H., Ristenpart, T., Li, J., Su, Z.: Back to the future: A framework for automatic malware removal and system repair. In: Proceedings of the 22nd Annual Computer Security Applications Conference, ACSAC 2006, pp. 257–268. IEEE Computer Society, Washington, DC (2006)

10. Jain, S., Shafique, F., Djeric, V., Goel, A.: Application-level isolation and recovery with solitude. In: Proceedings of the 3rd ACM SIGOPS/EuroSys European Conference on Computer Systems 2008, Eurosys 2008, pp. 95–107. ACM, New York (2008)
11. Kim, D., Rinard, M.C.: Verification of semantic commutativity conditions and inverse operations on linked data structures. In: Proceedings of the 32nd ACM SIGPLAN Conference on Programming Language Design and Implementation, PLDI 2011, pp. 528–541. ACM, New York (2011)
12. Kim, T., Wang, X., Zeldovich, N., Kaashoek, M.F.: Intrusion recovery using selective re-execution. In: Proceedings of the 9th USENIX Conference on Operating Systems Design and Implementation, OSDI 2010, pp. 1–9. USENIX Association, Berkeley (2010)
13. King, S.T., Chen, P.M.: Backtracking intrusions. In: Proceedings of the Nineteenth ACM Symposium on Operating Systems Principles, SOSP 2003, pp. 223–236. ACM, New York (2003)
14. Mahajan, P., Kotla, R., Marshall, C.C., Ramasubramanian, V., Rodeheffer, T.L., Terry, D.B., Wobber, T.: Effective and efficient compromise recovery for weakly consistent replication. In: Proceedings of the 4th ACM European Conference on Computer Systems, EuroSys 2009, pp. 131–144. ACM, New York (2009)
15. Paleari, R., Martignoni, L., Passerini, E., Davidson, D., Fredrikson, M., Giffin, J., Jha, S.: Automatic generation of remediation procedures for malware infections. In: Proceedings of the 19th USENIX Conference on Security, USENIX Security 2010, p. 27. USENIX Association, Berkeley (2010)
16. van der Aalst, W., Weijters, T., Maruster, L.: Workflow mining: Discovering process models from event logs. IEEE Trans. on Knowl. and Data Eng. 16(9), 1128–1142 (2004)
17. Wagner, D., Soto, P.: Mimicry attacks on host-based intrusion detection systems. In: Proceedings of the 9th ACM Conference on Computer and Communications Security, CCS 2002, pp. 255–264. ACM, New York (2002)
18. Xiong, X., Jia, X., Liu, P.: Shelf: Preserving business continuity and availability in an intrusion recovery system. In: Proceedings of the 2009 Annual Computer Security Applications Conference, ACSAC 2009, pp. 484–493. IEEE Computer Society, Washington, DC (2009)
19. Yin, H., Song, D., Egele, M., Kruegel, C., Kirda, E.: Panorama: capturing system-wide information flow for malware detection and analysis. In: Proceedings of the 14th ACM Conference on Computer and Communications Security, CCS 2007, pp. 116–127. ACM, New York (2007)
20. Yu, M., Liu, P., Zang, W.: Self-healing workflow systems under attacks. In: Proceedings of the 24th International Conference on Distributed Computing Systems (ICDCS 2004), pp. 418–4025. IEEE Computer Society, Washington, DC (2004)

PRIDE: Practical Intrusion Detection in Resource Constrained Wireless Mesh Networks

Amin Hassanzadeh[1], Zhaoyan Xu[1], Radu Stoleru[1],
Guofei Gu[1], and Michalis Polychronakis[2]

[1] Department of Computer Science and Engineering, Texas A&M University, USA
[2] Computer Science Department, Columbia University, USA
{amin,z0x0427,stoleru,guofei}@cse.tamu.edu, mikepo@cs.columbia.edu

Abstract. As interest in wireless mesh networks grows, security challenges, e.g., intrusion detection, become of paramount importance. Traditional solutions for intrusion detection assign full IDS responsibilities to a few selected nodes. Recent results, however, have shown that a mesh router cannot reliably perform full IDS functions because of limited resources (i.e., processing power and memory). Cooperative IDS solutions, targeting resource constrained wireless networks impose high communication overhead and detection latency. To address these challenges, we propose PRIDE (PRactical Intrusion DEtection in resource constrained wireless mesh networks), a non-cooperative real-time intrusion detection scheme that optimally distributes IDS functions to nodes along traffic paths, such that detection rate is maximized, while resource consumption is below a given threshold. We formulate the optimal IDS function distribution as an integer linear program and propose algorithms for solving it accurately and fast (i.e., practical). We evaluate the performance of our proposed solution in a real-world, department-wide, mesh network.

Keywords: wireless mesh network, intrusion detection, resource constraints, integer linear programming, real-world implementation.

1 Introduction

Wireless Mesh Networks (WMN) are self-managing networks that provide Internet, intranet, and other services to mobile and fixed clients using a multi-hop multi-path wireless infrastructure consisting of mesh nodes [1, 2]. They have emerged as a cost-effective broadband network technology for services in large remote areas where no networking infrastructure is available, e.g., rural connectivity in Zambia [3] and disaster response applications [4]. A wireless mesh network can serve as the backbone communication infrastructure among WiFi networks, ad hoc networks, sensor networks and the Internet [4]. It is important to remark the lack of a vantage point for the network traffic, due to the peer-to-peer nature of communication in WMN.

S. Qing et al. (Eds.): ICICS 2013, LNCS 8233, pp. 213–228, 2013.
© Springer International Publishing Switzerland 2013

As the interest in WMN grows, security issues, especially intrusion detection, become of paramount importance. Due to the *decentralized nature of WMN*, researchers have proposed distributed solutions for network wide intrusion detection. Distributed solutions do not rely on a single vantage point (e.g., gateways in traditional intrusion detection systems (IDS) in wired networks) as there always could be internal traffic (e.g., between two hosts[1]) in WMN to be monitored. The state-of-the-art distributed solutions can be categorized as: i) *monitoring node* solutions; and ii) *cooperative* solutions. *Monitoring node* solutions [5, 6] assign the same set of IDS functions (i.e., detection rules) to monitoring nodes (note: each monitoring node is responsible for a distinct part of the network). These solutions, however, have high false negative rates. This is because some IDS functions cannot be executed on monitoring nodes with limited resources (e.g., processing power and memory). A recent work [7] investigates challenges in applying off-the-shelf IDS (Snort and Bro) on mesh devices and proposes a lightweight (i.e., customized) IDS for WMN. The proposed IDS requires less memory and decreases the packet drop rate, when compared to off-the-shelf IDS. These achievements, however, are at the price of detecting fewer types of network attacks (smaller detection coverage), since most IDS functions are not implemented. *Cooperative* solutions (e.g., hierarchical [8] or group-based [9] cooperation) distribute IDS functions to multiple cooperative nodes, in order to achieve higher detection rate and lower IDS load. These solutions, however, incur high communication overhead and high latency in attack detection. This is because nodes have to exchange their local observations with other nodes running different IDS functions. Considering the relatively high traffic rates in WMN, caused by mesh clients and external hosts in WMN, the communication overhead of cooperative IDS [9, 10] degrades the network performance and delays intrusion response.

This research is motivated by the fact that neither monitoring nodes nor cooperative IDS techniques can practically solve the intrusion detection problem in WMN. As we will show in Section 2, the fact that WMN are resource constrained poses significant challenges for intrusion detection. Our idea is to use the knowledge a security administrator has about the WMN traffic to distribute IDS functions more efficiently. More precisely, a security administrator, knowing the routing paths of the traffic in the WMN, would employ a traffic-aware framework that optimally places IDS functions on the nodes along the routing paths. The information about the busiest and most frequently used paths in the WMN is obtained from routing algorithms (e.g., OLSR) and network monitoring tools (e.g., tcpdump). Furthermore, it is observed [4] that when deploying WMN for disaster response, the points of interest like physical locations of data sources (e.g., Search & Rescue Robots) and destinations, e.g., Command and Control Center, and consequently the traffic paths are always known.

A related idea for traffic-aware IDS deployments in wired networks was recently proposed [11], where different IDS responsibilities (i.e., different portions of network traffic) are assigned to each node along the traffic paths while

---

[1] A host inside the mesh is either a client or a local server (e.g., a local FTP server) connected to the mesh routers.

ensuring that no node is overloaded. However, that technique cannot be directly applied to WMN since it assumes that each node performs all IDS functions - infeasible for resource constrained mesh devices. Our proposed solution has no communication overhead, has no detection latency (i.e., it provides real-time intrusion detection, in contrast to cooperative IDS) and it has a higher detection rate, when compared with monitoring node solutions. In our proposed solution, *each node along a routing path, runs a distinct and customized IDS*. This *customized* IDS (technically a subset of IDS functions) allows resource conservation. The combination of *distinct* IDS along the path allows for a complete set of IDS functions to be applied to the entire network traffic. Our main concern in this paper is the reduction of RAM utilization as we will experimentally show that it also improves the CPU utilization in regular traffic rates. More precisely, our paper makes the following contributions: 1) demonstrates that distributing IDS functions along routing paths increases the intrusion detection rate and decreases the average memory load; 2) formulates a novel IDS function distribution problem, called Path Coverage Problem (PCP), with the objective to maximize the detection rate while ensuring that nodes are not overloaded by IDS functions; 3) presents PRIDE, a protocol implemented to solve PCP accurately and fast, based on an Integer Linear Program (ILP); 4) presents results obtained from a real prototype system implementation and an evaluation in a real-world, department-wide, deployed WMN.

2   Motivation and Background

The research presented in this paper is motivated by the challenges we faced when attempted to deploy a common off-the-shelf IDS with a full configuration (i.e., configured to detect the largest set of attacks) on existing WMN router hardware. When loading Snort with its full configuration on a Netgear WNDR3700 router, the router crashes because the RAM is not sufficiently large. In the remaining part of this section we describe the hardware capabilities of our mesh routers, background information on Snort, and experimental results that illustrate how Snort configuration (note: this is equivalent with trading off intrusion detection capabilities) impacts memory load of the router.

The Netgear WNDR3700 router has an Atheros AR7161 processor running at 680MHz, 64MB RAM, 8MB flash memory. It has two wireless cards with Atheros AR9223-bgn and Atheros AR9220-an chipsets, working on 2.4GHz and 5GHz, respectively. The operating system on the router is the most recent release of OpenWrt (i.e., Backfire 10.03.1), a Linux distribution for embedded networking devices, with kernel version 2.6.32.10. We emphasize that our mesh hardware is more powerful (in terms of processing and memory resources) than devices used in some existing real world deployments [2,3]. Although in this research we focus mainly on Netgear WNDR3700 router hardware, later in this section we present our experience and results with more sophisticated and expensive mesh hardware, e.g., Meshlium Xtreme which has a 500MHz CPU, 256MB RAM, 8/16/32GB disk memory and WiFi, Zigbee, and GPRS wireless interfaces.

The router runs Snort, an off-the-shelf intrusion detection system. Snort's detection engine is based on thousands of detection rules (categorized in multiple rule files, corresponding to known network threats) and several preprocessors. All files are listed in "snort.conf", a global configuration file. Upon activating each rule file in "snort.conf" and running Snort, all detection rules present in the rule file are loaded in memory and are used for packet investigation. A full Snort configuration activates all preprocessors and rule files. A customized configuration activates only some preprocessors and rule files (i.e., IDS functions), thus, the network traffic is analyzed by fewer detection functions.

The intrusion detection in Snort is performed by packet-level rule matching. Each packet is preprocessed, following preprocessing directives for extracting possible plain-text content. The preprocessed packet is then inspected by Snort detection rules, to expose whether it is an intrusion attempt or not. Preprocessors parse network packets and provide abstract data for some high-level detection rules in the rule files. It is important to note that a rule file that contains high-level detection rules has *preprocessor dependency*. This dependency means that the rule file cannot be activated (i.e., Snort generates an error message and stops) unless all the preprocessors required by its rules (usually one or two preprocessors) are also activated.

To understand how different Snort configurations impact the memory load on the Netgear WNDR3700 and Meshlium Xtreme, we performed several experiments. Running Snort causes two types of memory loads to the router: 1) *static*, the initial load imposed by packet capturing modules, preprocessors, detection rules, etc. when Snort is loaded; 2) *dynamic*, the variable load imposed by stateful preprocessors (e.g., Stream5) which is a function of the traffic load and some configuration parameters.

We first investigate the static memory load of Snort on the routers when no network traffic is applied. We have observed that a typical memory load on a Netgear WNDR3700 router is ~30% and on the Meshlium Xtreme router it is ~60%. This accounts for OS firmware and various services (OLSR, DHCP, etc.). Without preprocessors or rule files active, loading Snort on Netgear WNDR3700 increases memory load to 43% ("Snort(S)" in Figure 1). Memory load increases to 46% if preprocessor Stream5 is

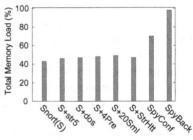

Fig. 1. Effect of Snort configuration on the memory load

activated ("S+str5" in Figure 1), and to 48% if preprocessors "http-inspect", "smtp" and "ftp-telnet" are also activated ("S+4Pre" in Figure 1).

The memory load of a rule file is a function of the number of detection rules in it and the pattern matching algorithm Snort uses (e.g., Aho-Corasick). For example, using "ac-bnfa-nq" search method, "dos.rules" which has 20 detection rules and requires the Stream5 preprocessor, increases memory load to 47% ("S+dos" in Figure 1). A very large file such as "spyware-put" ("SpyConf" in Figure 1) which contains ∼1,000 rule files increases the RAM load to 70%. The memory load caused by activating a set of rule files also depends on their sizes. For example, activating 20 small rule files (i.e., 10 rules per file on average) and the Stream5 preprocessor (which the rules require) increases memory load to 49%. Activating two large rule files, "spyware-put.rules" and "backdoor.rules" ("SpyBack" in Figure 1) increases memory load to 98%. We have experimentally verified that adding a few small rule files on top of "spyware-put.rules" and "backdoor.rules" causes the router to crash. *We have observed a similarly overloaded operation for the Meshlium Xtreme router, where a full configuration Snort increases the memory load to 98.5%, leaving almost no room for processes/services beyond stock deployment.* We also emphasize here the rapid increase in the number of Snort rule files (i.e., currently about 70 files) and their sizes as functions of the number of threats. Some rules might not be needed in a particular setting, but conversely, that setting might require many more rules of some other kind (e.g., custom signatures for suspicious or blacklisted domains, which can increase significantly).

Dynamic memory load, imposed by Stream5 when tracking traffic sessions, is the other considerable type of Snort memory load since almost all rule files require this preprocessor. Two configuration parameters of Stream5, "max_tcp" and "memcap", specify the maximum simultaneous TCP sessions it tracks (similarly, "max_udp", "max_icmp", and "max_ip") and the maximum buffer size for TCP packet storage, respectively. We have experimentally observed that the value of "max_tcp" affects both dynamic and static memory loads. When using the Snort version available on the OpenWrt development tree, the default configuration has max_tcp=8192. Choosing max_tcp=100,000, imposes ∼10% more static load than default "S+Str5" to the routers. Moreover, this value allows more simultaneous TCP sessions to be inspected which also imposes larger dynamic memory load and may cause the router to crash at high traffic rates (note: we observed that for max_tcp≥150,000 the router crashes if a simple HTTP request is sent using the Linux "wget" tool). Throughout this paper, we use the default setting, i.e., max_tcp=8192, and consider the maximum dynamic load this setting imposes on the router. Hence, the total memory load of Stream5 is assumed to be its static load plus its maximum allowable dynamic load. We note that although hardware improves, the fundamental challenge for a resource-limited node to handle *ever-increasing network traffic* still remains.

In addition to RAM, processing power (CPU) is also limited on current mesh hardware. Consequently, investigating the impact of Snort IDS on this limited resource might seem worthwhile. Experimentally we have found that network traffic, actually, has a much larger influence on CPU utilization than executing Snort IDS functions. Our experimental results are depicted in Figure 2 where we enabled "tcp_track" and "icmp_track" in Stream5 and used "hping3"

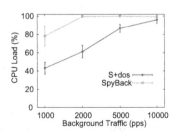

Fig. 2. Effect of Snort configuration on the CPU load

to generate TCP and ICMP traffic. As shown, for an extremely high traffic rate, both lightweight and heavy Snort configurations impose more than 95% CPU utilization. Similar with our result, it was shown [7] that even a lightweight IDS exhausted the CPU when traffic rate was extremely high. However, as shown in Figure 2, "S+dos", a lightweight IDS configuration, imposes less processing load than "SpyBack", a heavyweight IDS configuration, when the traffic rate is not high. *Consequently, we aim at reducing the memory utilization as we have experimentally observed that it also improves the CPU utilization in regular traffic rates (as shown in Figure 2).*

3   System and Security Models

The system we are considering in this paper is as specified by the IEEE 802.11s WLAN Mesh Standard [1]. The system consists of: i) *mesh access points (AP)* connecting mesh clients (from now on we will refer to them as "clients") to the mesh network; ii) a *wireless mesh backbone*; and iii) a *gateway*, connecting the mesh network to the Internet. The network traffic is either *external*, i.e., between clients and external hosts (external to the mesh), or *internal*, i.e., between two hosts inside the mesh network. Our system also requires the presence of a base station – a computer which periodically and securely collects, via a middleware, information about mesh nodes: *processing/memory* loads, traffic information, etc. Based on these information, the base station assigns IDS functions to nodes.

The IDS we are considering in this paper is Snort. We chose Snort because it is a mainstream off-the-shelf IDS that consumes less resources than other IDS, e.g., Bro (as it was shown recently [7]). Moreover, Snort is readily available for our mesh hardware, as part of the OpenWrt development tree. To the best of our knowledge, there is no port of Bro to the mesh hardware we have available. Assigning a Snort IDS function to a node is equivalent to activating a rule file in the Snort configuration file on that node. Activating a rule file imposes a specific amount of memory load to the device, thus, a limited number of rule files can be activated when running Snort on the device. We use the default search method of Snort, i.e., "ac-bnfa-nq", as we experimentally observed that it consumes the minimum memory among all *low memory* search methods, e.g., "lowmem."

We consider multi-hop attacks where the attacker and the target are connected to the mesh network at different APs. Thus, the attack traffic (malicious packet(s)) is routed across multiple nodes. The attacker can be either *insider* or *outsider*. An insider attacker is a client, connected to a mesh AP, running attacks against a target (a router or host) several hops away. An outsider attacker is an external host attacking a router or a host in the mesh network.

4   Problem Formulation

In this section, we formulate the optimal distribution of IDS functions as an optimization problem and propose a method to solve it. We use Figure 3 to support our formulation. Although Snort is our target IDS (and present a formulation that uses Snort terminology), we believe that other IDS (e.g., Bro) can be analyzed similarly, if their internals and functionality are publicly available.

We denote the number of nodes and number of links in the wireless mesh network by N and Q, respectively. Considering the information collected from the nodes, we denote the number of nodes and links actively contributing in traffic routing by n ($n \leq N$) and q ($q \leq Q$), respectively. Thus, we model the wireless mesh network (i.e., after removing *idle* nodes/links) as

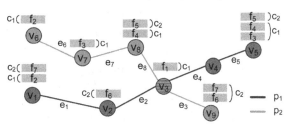

Fig. 3. An example graph for a WMN, consisting of 9 nodes, 8 links, and two paths (p_1 and p_2). The nodes run different configurations of Snort, e.g., node v_5 runs Snort functions f_3, f_4 and f_5, which require preprocessors c_1 and c_2.

a reduced graph $G = \{V, E\}$, where V is the set of nodes $\{v_1, v_2, \cdots, v_n\}$, and E is the set of links $\{e_1, e_2, \cdots, e_q\}$. An example of a reduced graph, in Figure 3, $V = \{v_1, v_2, ..., v_9\}$ and $E = \{e_1, e_2, ..., e_8\}$.

We denote the set of routing paths for the network traffic by $P = \{p_1, p_2, \cdots, p_l\}$, where $P_i = \{v_j \,|\, v_j$ is located in $p_i\}$ and $P_i \subseteq V$. In Figure 3 two paths are present: p_1 and p_2. Additionally, we denote by matrix $\mathbb{T}_{l \times n}$ the mapping between nodes and paths, i.e., $t_{ij} = 1$ iff node j is located on path i. For the example shown in Figure 3, the matrix $\mathbb{T}$ is as follows:

$$\mathbb{T} = \begin{bmatrix} 1\,1\,1\,1\,1\,0\,0\,0\,0 \\ 0\,0\,1\,0\,0\,1\,1\,1\,1 \end{bmatrix}.$$

We denote the set of IDS functions by $\mathcal{F} = \{f_k \,|\, f_k$ is a set of detection rules$\}$ with size K (i.e., $|\mathcal{F}| = K$). We denote the set of IDS preprocessors by $\mathcal{C} = \{c_r \,|\, \exists f_k \in \mathcal{F}$ that requires $c_r\}$ of size R (i.e., $|\mathcal{C}| = R$). For the example in Figure 3, $\mathcal{F} = \{f_1, f_2, ..., f_7\}$ and $\mathcal{C} = \{c_1, c_2\}$. The dependency between IDS functions and preprocessors is stored in matrix $\mathbb{D}_{K \times R}$ where $d_{kr} = 1$ means that activation of function f_k requires the activation of preprocessor c_r.

Let $w : \{\mathcal{F}, \mathcal{C}\} \longrightarrow [0, 1]$ be a cost function that assigns memory load w_k^f and w_r^c to IDS function f_k and IDS preprocessor c_r, respectively. Consequently, vectors $W^f = [w_1^f, w_2^f, \cdots, w_K^f]$ and $W^c = [w_1^c, w_2^c, \cdots, w_R^c]$ represent memory loads for the IDS functions in $\mathcal{F}$ and for the IDS preprocessors in $\mathcal{C}$, respectively (we remark that $w_{Stream5}^c$ in Snort is the summation of its static load and its maximum dynamic load). We denote by $B = [b_1, b_2, ..., b_n]$ the base memory load (i.e., without IDS functions loaded) of all nodes. Finally, we use vector $\Lambda = [\lambda_1, \lambda_2, \cdots, \lambda_n]$ (*i.e., Memory Threshold*) to represent the maximum allowable memory load after IDS functions are loaded. Memory threshold is an important parameter. It is typically set by a network administrator based on the number of active services in the mesh network and the memory space they require.

Definition 1. *An **IDS Function Distribution**, $A = \{(v_j, \mathcal{F}_j, \mathcal{C}_j) |\, v_j \in V, \mathcal{F}_j \subseteq \mathcal{F}, \text{ and } \mathcal{C}_j \subseteq \mathcal{C}\}$, is a placement of IDS functions in the network, such that node v_j only executes IDS functions $\mathcal{F}_j$ and their corresponding preprocessors $\mathcal{C}_j$.*

For example, the *IDS Function Distribution* in Figure 3 is:

$$A = \{(v_1, \{f_2, f_7\}, \{c_1, c_2\}), (v_2, \{f_6\}, \{c_2\}), (v_9, \{f_6, f_7\}, \{c_2\})\}.$$

We represent an *IDS Function Distribution* by matrices $\mathbb{X}_{n \times K}$ and $\mathbb{Z}_{n \times R}$, corresponding to IDS functions and preprocessors active on each node, respectively. For $\mathbb{X}$, $x_{jk} = 1$ iff IDS function f_k is activated on node v_j. For $\mathbb{Z}$, $z_{jr} = 1$ iff preprocessor c_r is activated on node v_j. Matrix $\mathbb{Z}$ for the network in Figure 3 is (we omit matrix $\mathbb{X}$ due to space constraints):

$$\mathbb{Z}^T = \begin{bmatrix} 1 & 0 & 1 & 0 & 1 & 1 & 1 & 1 & 0 \\ 1 & 1 & 0 & 0 & 1 & 0 & 0 & 1 & 1 \end{bmatrix}.$$

Considering the above mathematical formalism, the dependencies between IDS functions and preprocessors can now be represented more compactly as:

$$z_{jr} = \begin{cases} 1 & if \quad (\mathbb{X} \cdot \mathbb{D})_{jr} \geq 1 \\ 0 & if \quad (\mathbb{X} \cdot \mathbb{D})_{jr} = 0 \end{cases} \tag{1}$$

Equation 1 indicates that preprocessor c_r must be activated on node v_j if there exists at least an IDS function f_k requiring c_r, assigned to it. It is important to note that $z_{jr} = min\{1, \Sigma_{k=1}^{K} x_{jk} d_{kr}\}$ and $z_{jr} \in \{0, 1\}$.

After the *IDS Function Distribution*, the total memory load for node v_j becomes $L_j = b_j + \Sigma_{c_r \in \mathcal{C}_j} w_r^c + \Sigma_{f_k \in \mathcal{F}_j} w_k^f$, where $w_r^c \in W^c$ and $w_k^f \in W^f$. It is important to mention that an *IDS Function Distribution* in which $L_j > \lambda_j$, i.e., the load L_j is greater than threshold λ_j, for any node v_j, is deemed infeasible.

From a network security administrator point of view, we aim for an *IDS Function Distribution* where all IDS functions are activated on each path. This means that the entire network traffic will be investigated by all IDS functions (albeit at different times), eliminating the possibility of false negatives.

Definition 2. *For a given path p_i and its corresponding set of nodes P_i, **Coverage Ratio (CR)** is defined as $CR_i = |U_i|/K$, where $U_i = \bigcup_{v_j \in P_i} \mathcal{F}_j$ is the set of IDS functions assigned to nodes along the path. Path p_i is called **covered** if $CR_i = 1$ $(U_i = \mathcal{F})$, i.e., for $\forall f_k \in \mathcal{F}, \exists v_j$ assigned by $\mathcal{F}_j$ such that $f_k \in \mathcal{F}_j$.*

Considering the effect of *IDS Function Distribution* on the memory load of each node and the desired distribution of IDS functions to the nodes, in order to achieve higher intrusion detection rate, we define Path Coverage Problem (PCP) as follows:

Definition 3. *Path Coverage Problem (PCP)*
Given $G = \{V, E\}$, a set of paths P in WMN, the dependency matrix $\mathbb{D}$, and vectors W^f and W^c, find a distribution $A = \{(v_j, \mathcal{F}_j, \mathcal{C}_j) |\, v_j \in V \text{ and } \mathcal{F}_j \subseteq \mathcal{F} \text{ and } \mathcal{C}_j \subseteq \mathcal{C}\}$, such that $\frac{1}{l} \Sigma_{p_i \in P} CR_i$ is maximized and $L_j \leq \lambda_j \; \forall v_j \in V$.

PCP is an optimization problem which has the objective of maximizing the average coverage ratio while guaranteeing that memory loads on nodes are below a memory threshold. Although a lower memory threshold λ_j allows more additional processes to execute on node v_j, it makes solving PCP more difficult.

We formulate PCP as an Integer Linear Program (ILP) that can be solved by an ILP solver. The objective function is maximizing the average coverage ratio of all paths. Additionally, preprocessor dependency and memory threshold are considered as ILP constraints. To better understand

$$Max. \quad \frac{1}{l}(\mathbf{1}^T \cdot \mathbb{T})(\mathbb{X} \cdot \mathbf{1}) \tag{2}$$

$$s.t.: \quad B^T + \mathbb{Z} \cdot W^{cT} + \mathbb{X} \cdot W^{fT} \leq \quad \Lambda^T \tag{3}$$

$$(\mathbb{T} \cdot \mathbb{X})_{ik} \leq 1 \qquad\qquad ,\forall i,k \tag{4}$$

$$z_{jr} \geq \frac{(\mathbb{X} \cdot \mathbb{D})_{jr}}{K} \qquad\qquad ,\forall j,r \tag{5}$$

$$z_{jr} \leq (\mathbb{X} \cdot \mathbb{D})_{jr} \qquad\qquad ,\forall j,r \tag{6}$$

$$x_{jk}, z_{jr} \in \{0,1\} \qquad\qquad ,\forall j,k,r \tag{7}$$

the mathematical formulation of the objective function, one can expand the objective function as $\frac{1}{l}\Sigma_{i=1}^{l}\Sigma_{j=1}^{n}\Sigma_{k=1}^{K}t_{ij}x_{jk}$ where $t_{ij} = 1$ means node v_j is located on path p_i and $x_{jk} = 1$ means node v_j is assigned by function f_k. In other words, the average CR has to be maximized. Constraint 3 limits the memory load on every node v_j, i.e., $\Sigma_{r=1}^{R}z_{jr}w_r^c + \Sigma_{k=1}^{K}x_{jk}w_k^f$, to be less than its memory threshold λ_j. Most importantly, (*to ensure that we can formulate PCP as a linear program*), this constraint computes the total memory load as the sum of individual memory loads of preprocessors and rule files. Obviously, one needs to investigate if this linearity assumption always holds (we will discuss this in the next section). Constraint 4 ensures that only one copy of each function is assigned to the nodes along each path. Constraints 5 and 6 ensure that if an IDS function is assigned to a node, its required preprocessors are also assigned to the node. As presented in Equation 1, $z_{jr} = 1$ if at least one of the IDS functions assigned to node v_j requires preprocessor c_r, otherwise $z_{jr} = 0$. The maximum number of functions that require a specific preprocessor is at most K. Hence, Constraint 5 ensures that $0 < z_{jr} \leq 1$ if there is a function assigned to node v_j that requires preprocessor c_r. On the other hand, if none of the functions assigned to node v_j requires preprocessor c_r, then Constraint 6 enforces z_{jr} to be zero. Taking into account Constraint 7, i.e., z_{jr} has to be either 0 or 1, Constraint 5 enforces $z_{jr} = 1$ if preprocessor r is required on node j, otherwise, Constraint 6 enforces $z_{jr} = 0$.

5   PRIDE: Challenges and Solutions

Considering the aforementioned ILP formulation for PCP, we investigated two major challenges that impact the accuracy and time complexity of a solution. First, we experimentally observed that the total memory load of multiple Snort rule files is generally linear (i.e., it is equal to the sum of their individual memory loads), but not always (e.g., for some small rule files and certain rule types). This influences the accuracy of our proposed model for calculating the total memory load on each node (i.e., Challenge 1). Next, one can observe that the complexity of ILP depends on the number of paths in the network, the path lengths, the number of IDS functions, the number of preprocessors, and the memory threshold. For example, considering the number of Snort preprocessors (i.e., more than 20) and the number of Snort rule files (i.e., more than 60),

for single path p_i, the number of ILP constraints grows to more than 1400 ×
$|P_i|$, where $|P_i|$ is the path length. Additionally, a lower memory threshold λ_j
increases the number of infeasible solutions, thus requiring more iterations for
the ILP solver. Hence, the ILP performance degrades as network size increases or
memory threshold decreases (i.e., Challenge 2). In this section, we investigate the
aforementioned challenges and propose techniques to overcome them. Finally, we
present PRIDE protocol that distributes IDS functions to the nodes accurately
and fast (i.e., practical).

Experimentally, we observed that when activating multiple *small* rule files
(i.e., containing at most 50 detection rules), Snort memory load is much less
than the sum of individual memory loads. However, we observed that when
multiple *large* rule files (i.e., containing more than 250 detection rules) were activated, the memory load is closer to the sum of the rule file's individual memory
loads. When a rule file is activated, depending on: 1) the number of detection
rules it has; 2) the preprocessors it activates (if already not activated); and 3)
the Snort search method, a different amount of memory load will be imposed
to the node. In order to show how the aforementioned three factors impact our
assumption about memory load linearity (i.e., constraint 3), we performed extensive experiments (omitted here due to space constraints) on the Snort memory
consumption modeling in the absence of preprocessors. As the result, we observed *a linear behavior when adding blocks of 250 rules to the set of active rules
irrespective of rule order and search method.* We use this finding to address the
non-linearity of memory load for the variable-size rule files (i.e., Challenge 1) in
the following subsections.

5.1   Rule Files Modularization

To reduce the complexity of the problem the ILP solver faces (i.e., Challenge
2), we propose to reduce the number of individual preprocessors and IDS functions, which would result in a decrease in the number of constraints in ILP. Our
proposal is to group multiple IDS functions together and consider them as a
single function. *From here on, we refer to each group of rule files as a "detecting
module" and use the term "group" for a group of preprocessors.* If a detecting
module is assigned to a node, all rule files in that module will be activated. We
experimentally observed that grouping rule files not only reduces the problem
complexity (Challenge 2), but also decreases the variance in memory load estimation (Challenge 1). When several small rule files are grouped in a single
detecting module, it acts as a larger rule file (same as a block of 250 rules),
and the estimated memory load is more accurate. In addition, considering the
preprocessor dependency mentioned in Section 4, an efficient rule file grouping
reduces the number of preprocessor dependencies. For example, if two rule files
require the same preprocessor(s), they can be grouped in the same detecting
module. Similarly, multiple preprocessors required for the same rule files, can be
grouped together. Hence, when activating a new *detecting module*, the load imposed by rules' data structure dominates the load imposed by the new activated

preprocessor (that can be ignored). This is very similar to the behavior observed in memory consumption modeling experiments in the absence of preprocessors.

Grouping rule files together, however, has a disadvantage when the memory threshold set by the system administrator is very low. For low memory thresholds, we cannot assign larger modules to nodes, which results in low coverage/detection ratio. Consequently, despite the positive aspects of grouping small rule files together, memory threshold forces us to avoid large detecting modules. Unfortunately, there already exist large detecting modules. For example, the memory space required by the "backdoor" rule file is twice the memory space required by a detecting module with 25 small rule files. This illustrates the need to also split extremely large rule files into some smaller ones (i.e., creating several detecting modules out of a large rule file).

We thus define "modularization" as the procedure that, for a given set of IDS functions (e.g., Snort rule files), i) *groups* small IDS functions together in order to reduce the problem complexity and load estimation error, and ii) *splits* large IDS functions into several smaller functions so that they can be activated with low memory thresholds.

Rule File Splitting: When splitting a rule file, we consider the dependency between detection rules and the dependency between preprocessors and detection rules. This is to ensure that two dependent rules along with all of their essential preprocessing directives are included in the same split rule file. In order to split a rule file into several detecting modules, we first pre-parse each detection rule and specify its preprocessing dependency in advance (e.g., Stream5 preprocessor for HTTP-relevant rule files). We summarize all these preprocessing dependencies before splitting the rule files. In addition, rule dependency is expressed by the options' keywords, e.g., "flowbits." To meet the rule dependency requirements, we parse each detection rule and specify whether the rule contains such keywords or not, if it does, it must be relevant. For example, the "flowbits" options can help us maintain the stateful check in a set of Snort detection rules. When some keys are set by "flowbits" in a detection rule, every other detection rule which does not set the "flowbits," is dependent on that detection rule. Thus, using these two types of dependency, we split large rule files properly.

In addition, rule dependency is expressed by the options' keywords, e.g., "flowbits." To meet the rule dependency requirements, we parse each detection rule and specify whether the rule contains such keywords or not, if it does, it must be relevant. For example, the "flowbits" options can help us maintain the stateful check in a set of Snort detection rules. When some keys are set by "flowbits" in a detection rule, every other detection rule which does not set the "flowbits," is dependent on that detection rule. Similarly, the keyword "rev:VALUE" in a detection rule, that identifies revisions of Snort rules, denotes that it is related to a detection rule whose "sid" is "VALUE." Thus, using these two types of dependency, we split large rule files properly.

Proposed Modularizations: We propose three modularizations with different numbers of detecting modules and different sizes. We then compare the execution time of the solver, i.e., Matlab ILP solver, for each modularization.

In the first modularization, the entire set of Snort rule files is classified into 23 detecting modules where 6 different groups of preprocessors are required. The average memory load of the 23 detecting modules is 3.98% and the standard deviation is 1.68%. The second modularization consists of 12 detecting modules of average memory load 6.76% and standard deviation 2.31%, while the third modularization has only 6 detecting modules of average memory load 15.06% and standard deviation 1.88%. The second and the third modularizations require three groups of preprocessors.

Figure 4 shows the execution time of the ILP solver when solving the problem for different lengths of a single path. As depicted, 12-module and 6-module configurations are much faster than 23-module configuration, especially for longer paths (i.e., more complex problems). With these two modularizations, the ILP solver finds the optimal solution in less than 2 sec, which is very fast, thus practical in real deployments.

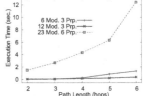

Fig. 4. Effect of modularizations on ILP execution time

The longer execution time for 6-module configuration, comparing to 12-module configuration, is because of its larger detecting modules that increase the number of infeasible solutions for a given memory threshold (increasing the solver's execution time). We use 6-module and 12-module configurations in our system evaluations.

5.2 PRIDE Protocol

Given a modularization chosen for the IDS configuration, PRIDE periodically collects the local information from the nodes, removes *idle* nodes from the network, i.e., those not contributing in the traffic routing, and optimally distributes IDS functions to the nodes along traffic paths. If the reduced graph is disconnected, each graph component is considered as a sub-problem and solved separately. Algorithm 1 presents PRIDE protocol.

Given the set of nodes, the protocol first collects information from nodes and then produces the reduced sets V and E by removing idle nodes/links. Next, the set of active routing paths P is extracted in Line 3. Given P, the Algorithm creates the set $\mathcal{P}$ of unvisited paths, and then defines variable g as the num-

Algorithm 1. PRIDE IDS Function Distribution

```
1: Data_Collection(V, E, N, Q)
2: Relaxation(V, E, n, q)
3: Path_Extract(V, E, P)
4: P = P
5: g = 0
6: while ∃ p_i ∈ P do
7:     g + +
8:     S_g = {p_i}
9:     P = P\{p_i}
10:    while ∃ p_j ∈ Q and
11:        ⋃    (P_j ∩ P_k) ≠ ∅ do
          p_k∈S_g
12:        S_g = S_g ∪ {p_j}
13:        P = P\{p_j}
14:    end while
15: end while
16: for ∀ S_g do
17:    V_g = {v_j|v_j ∈ P_i and p_i ∈ S_g}
18: for ∀ V_g do ILP(V_g, P)
```

ber of sub-problems. For every unvisited path p_i in set $\mathcal{P}$, the Algorithm first creates a new sub-problem S_g and marks it as a visited path. The Algorithm then searches $\mathcal{P}$ to find any unvisited path p_j which is *connected* (Two paths are *connected* if they are in the same component of the reduced graph) to at least one path in the current S_g. If so, the corresponding path p_j will be added to the current sub-problem S_g and removed from $\mathcal{P}$. When no more paths in $\mathcal{P}$ can be added to the current S_g, the Algorithm increases g and creates a new sub-problem. This process repeats until there is no unvisited path in $\mathcal{P}$. Next, for every sub-problem S_g, the Algorithm creates the corresponding set V_g as the set of nodes located on the paths of component S_g. Finally, the Algorithm runs ILP on the nodes and paths of each sub-problem S_g.

6   System Implementation and Evaluation

In this section, we evaluate the performance of PRIDE in a department-wide mesh network. Our mesh network consists of 10 Netgear WNDR3700 routers deployed in a $50 \times 30m^2$ rectangular area (Note: comparing with other testbeds, DistressNet [4] 8 nodes, SMesh [2] 14 nodes, PRIDE uses an average size testbed.). The routers use OLSR as the routing protocol and provide mesh connections on their 5GHz wireless interfaces and network access for the clients on the 2.4GHz wireless interfaces. PRIDE periodically (i.e., 5 minutes in the current setup) collects nodes/traffic information and runs ILP. This interval can be optimally chosen by administrator in dynamic networks. We use *bintprog* function in Matlab as the ILP solver.

We evaluate the *intrusion detection rate (coverage ratio)* and *average memory load* of nodes. The parameters that we vary are the *Path Length (PL)* and *memory threshold (λ)*. The attack traffic we use is based on *Rule 2 Attack* tool, as explained in [12]. In all our experiments, the memory thresholds of all nodes are equal and some of the preprocessors (e.g., perfmonitor) are not used as they are not activated by default or not required by rule files. Since the maximum path length in our mesh network is 4 hops, we consider 2-hop, 3-hop and 4-hop paths. The initial memory load on the routers is $\sim 30\%$ (as caused by DHCP, OLSR, and other services). We vary the Snort memory threshold from 30% to 60% (i.e., $60\% \leq \lambda \leq 90\%$). Since implementing the related traffic-aware solution [11] on the mesh devices is infeasible (the routers crash), we compare PRIDE with monitoring node solutions ([5,6]). We implement a monitoring node solution [5] to which we refer as "MonSol". A monitoring node loads detecting modules up to a given memory threshold based on the default order of rule files in Snort configuration file. If a monitoring node monitors at least one link of a given path, the entire path is considered as monitored.

6.1   Proof-of-Concept Experiment

When assigning IDS functions to multiple nodes on a path, each node can detect only a subset of attacks depending on the detecting modules it executes. As a proof-of-concept experiment, we show that distributing two IDS functions to two nodes generates exactly the same alerts as if both detecting modules were assigned to a single node (e.g., MonSol). For that purpose, we used two routers and one laptop connected wireless to each router (one laptop was the attacker

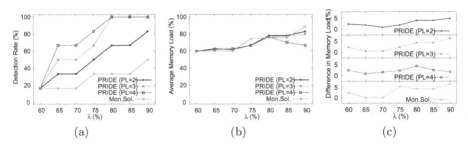

Fig. 5. 6-module configuration: effect of λ and PL on a) Detection rate. b) Average estimated memory load. c) The difference between estimated and actual memory load.

and the other was the target). We ran a customized Snort on each router (monitoring the mesh traffic) ensuring that every Snort rule file is activated on at least one of the routers. We then generated two R2A exploits such that their corresponding rule files, e.g., "dos.rules" and "exploit.rules", were activated on routers 1 and 2, respectively. When running attacks, the Snort on node 1 generated 4 alerts, while the one on node 2 generated 10 alerts (real-time detection, unlike cooperative IDS). We repeated the experiment where only node 1 was running Snort and both rule files were activated on node 1 (many other rule files were deactivated due to memory constraint). In this experiment, node 1 generated exactly the same 14 alerts upon launching the same exploits. Hence, we have shown that PRIDE can distribute IDS functions to nodes along a path such that network packets are inspected by all IDS functions.

6.2 Effects of Memory Threshold and Path Length

Given the network paths in our test-bed mesh network, we evaluate the intrusion detection rate of PRIDE and the average memory load on nodes, using 6-module and 12-module configurations. For each modularization, we change λ and PL as our evaluation parameters to see their effects on PRIDE performance. Given a λ, we show PRIDE can achieve higher detection rate than MonSol.

Figure 5 shows the effect of memory threshold and path length on intrusion detection rate and average memory load on the nodes when using the 6-module configuration. As depicted in Figure 5(a), maximum detection rate for MonSol is 50% which occurs when $\lambda = 90\%$. However, PRIDE can achieve 100% detection rate even in a lower memory threshold (e.g., at $\lambda = 80\%$ for $PL = 4$ and $PL = 3$). This is because more than one node is assigned with IDS functions and packets are inspected by more detecting modules. In this modularization, for a low memory threshold (e.g., $\lambda = 60\%$), only module 3 can be activated on the nodes, and thus, PRIDE cannot achieve a higher detection rate than MonSol. Figure 5(b) depicts the average estimated memory load on the nodes for different memory thresholds. It can be observed that PRIDE usually requires less memory load than MonSol, especially for the longer paths, since the modules are distributed to multiple nodes. We also compare the estimated memory loads and the actual memory loads of the two configurations in all of the experiments,

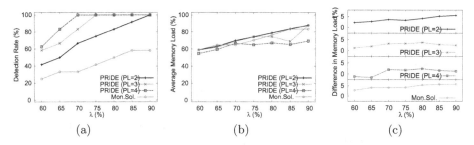

Fig. 6. 12-module configuration: effect of λ and PL on a) Detection rate. b) Average estimated memory load. c)The difference between estimated and actual memory load.

i.e., different memory thresholds and path lengths. Figure 5(c) shows the difference between estimated memory load and actual load measured on the routers when using 6-module configuration. One can see that the difference is below ~5%, thus giving confidence in our ILP formulation and memory consumption modeling. The results for the same evaluations performed on the 12-module configuration are shown in Figure 6. As depicted in Figure 6(a), the intrusion detection rate for the 12-module configuration is higher than the detection rate for the 6-module configuration (for the same memory threshold). This is because the size of the detecting modules in the 12-module configuration is smaller than for the 6-module configuration, which allows more modules to fit in the small free memory spaces. In contrast with the 6-module configuration, where at low memory thresholds the detection rate was similar to MonSol, in the 12-module configuration the detection rate at 60% (a low memory threshold) is higher than for MonSol. This is because more modules are activated on the nodes even at this low memory threshold. The average estimated memory loads for this modularization are shown in Figure 6(b). Similar to the 6-module configuration, it is observed that the 12-module configuration usually impose less memory load than MonSol solution for the longer paths. It is worth mentioning that the estimated values for the 12-module configuration, as shown in 6(c), are closer to the real values than the 6-module configuration because the modules are roughly the same size as 250-rule blocks.

Figure 7 shows the ILP solver execution time for $PL = 3$ and $PL = 4$, and for each modularization. As depicted, the execution time of the algorithm ranges from a few seconds to tens of seconds, thus making it practical for real world deployments. As shown, the lower the memory threshold is, the longer the execution time is. This is because lower memory thresholds increase the number of infeasible solutions and the solver requires more iterations to obtain feasible and optimal solutions. As shown in Figure 7, the execution time increases with the path length as well. As mentioned in Section 5, this is because

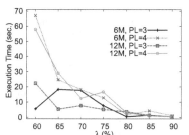

Fig. 7. ILP solver execution time for different problems and parameters

the number of ILP constraints (i.e., the problem complexity) is a direct function of path length.

7   Conclusions

In this paper, we have shown that intrusion detection in WMN requires significant resources, and traditional solutions are not practical for WMN. To address these challenges, we propose a solution for an optimal distribution of IDS functions. We formulate the optimal IDS function distribution as an integer linear program and propose algorithms for solving it accurately and fast. Our solution maximizes intrusion detection rate, while maintaining the memory load below a threshold set by network administrators. We have investigated the performance of our proposed solution in a real-world, department-wide, deployed WMN.

Acknowledgement. This work is based in part on work supported by Naval Surface Warfare Center, Grant No. N00164-11-1-2007.

References

1. Hiertz, G.R., Denteneer, D., Max, S., Taori, R., Cardona, J., Berlemann, L., Walke, B.: IEEE 802.11s: the WLAN mesh standard. Wireless Commun. (2010)
2. Amir, Y., Danilov, C., Musăloiu-Elefteri, R., Rivera, N.: The SMesh wireless mesh network. ACM Transactions on Computer Systems (September 2008)
3. Backens, J., Mweemba, G., van Stam, G.: A rural implementation of a 52 node mixed wireless mesh network in macha, zambia. In: Villafiorita, A., Saint-Paul, R., Zorer, A. (eds.) AFRICOM 2009. LNICST, vol. 38, pp. 32–39. Springer, Heidelberg (2010)
4. Chenji, H., Hassanzadeh, A., Won, M., Li, Y., Zhang, W., Yang, X., Stoleru, R., Zhou, G.: A wireless sensor, adhoc and delay tolerant network system for disaster response. LENSS-09-02, Tech. Rep. (2011)
5. Hassanzadeh, A., Stoleru, R., Shihada, B.: Energy efficient monitoring for intrusion detection in battery-powered wireless mesh networks. In: ADHOC-NOW (2011)
6. Shin, D.-H., Bagchi, S., Wang, C.-C.: Distributed online channel assignment toward optimal monitoring in multi-channel wireless networks. In: IEEE INFOCOM (2012)
7. Hugelshofer, F., Smith, P., Hutchison, D., Race, N.J.: OpenLIDS: a lightweight intrusion detection system for wireless mesh networks. In: MobiCom (2009)
8. Hassanzadeh, A., Stoleru, R.: Towards optimal monitoring in cooperative ids for resource constrained wireless networks. In: IEEE ICCCN (2011)
9. Krontiris, I., Benenson, Z., Giannetsos, T., Freiling, F.C., Dimitriou, T.: Cooperative intrusion detection in wireless sensor networks. In: Roedig, U., Sreenan, C.J. (eds.) EWSN 2009. LNCS, vol. 5432, pp. 263–278. Springer, Heidelberg (2009)
10. Hassanzadeh, A., Stoleru, R.: On the optimality of cooperative intrusion detection for resource constrained wireless networks. Computers & Security (2013)
11. Sekar, V., Krishnaswamy, R., Gupta, A., Reiter, M.K.: Network-wide deployment of intrusion detection and prevention systems. In: ACM CoNEXT (2010)
12. Hassanzadeh, A., Xu, Z., Stoleru, R., Gu, G.: Practical intrusion detection in resource constrained wireless mesh networks. Texas A&M University 2012-7-1, Tech. Rep. (2012)

Fingerprint Embedding: A Proactive Strategy of Detecting Timing Channels

Jing Wang[1,2,*], Peng Liu[3], Limin Liu[1], Le Guan[1,2], and Jiwu Jing[1]

[1] State Key Laboratory of Information Security,
Institute of Information Engineering, CAS, Beijing, China
{jwang,lmliu,lguan,jing}@lois.cn
[2] University of Chinese Academy of Sciences, Beijing, China
[3] Pennsylvania State University, University Park, PA, USA
pliu@ist.psu.edu

Abstract. The detection of covert timing channels is notoriously a difficult work due to the high variation of network traffic. The existing detection methods, mainly based on statistical tests, cannot effectively detect a variety of covert timing channels. In this paper, we propose a proactive strategy of detecting covert timing channels. The basic idea is that a timing fingerprint is embedded into outgoing traffic of the to-be-protected host in advance. The presence of a covert timing channel is exposed, provided that the fingerprint is absent from the traffic during transmission. As a proof of concept, we design and implement a detection system, which consists of two modules for fingerprint embedding and checking, respectively. We also perform a series of experiments to validate if this system works effectively. The results show that it detects various timing channels accurately and quickly, while has less than 2.4‰ degradation on network performance.

Keywords: timing channel, covert channel, fingerprint embedding, intrusion detection system.

1 Introduction

Covert timing channel is a mechanism that exploits timing intervals of transmitted packets to convey sensitive information. Due to a large volume of data over the Internet, network traffic has become an ideal medium for stealthy communication. A cyber attacker can utilize this mechanism for various purposes, e.g., exfiltrating secrets [25], launching DDoS attacks [13], and tracking network flows [30]. Under the cover of massive overt traffic, it is generally hard to reveal

* This work was supported by National Natural Science Foundation of China Grant 70890084/G021102 and 61003274, Strategy Pilot Project of Chinese Academy of Sciences Sub-Project XDA06010702, National High Technology Research and Development Program of China (863 Program, No.2013AA01A214), ARO W911NF-09-1-0525 (MURI), NSF CNS-0905131, NSF CNS-0916469, and AFOSR W911NF1210055.

S. Qing et al. (Eds.): ICICS 2013, LNCS 8233, pp. 229–244, 2013.
© Springer International Publishing Switzerland 2013

the presence of a covert timing channel. Sometimes, an attacker creates one in a victim machine even with no additional traffic, only by manipulating the timings of the existing traffic, under which circumstance the system administrator is practically unconscious of it. This kind of channels, referred to as passive timing channels, are more difficult to be detected than active ones.

The detection of covert timing channels is acknowledged as a difficult work all along. In the current literature, detection methods are mainly based on statistical tests, which differentiate covert traffic with irregular statistical properties from legitimate traffic. Empirically, these detection methods are over-sensitive to the high variation of network traffic, and thereby causes a unacceptable false alarm rate. Due to the inherent limitation, statistical-test-based detection methods are strongly dependent of encoding techniques applied in timing channels, and only accurate in detecting a specific timing channel. Furthermore, if covert traffic is designed to be statistically approximate to legitimate traffic, these methods are unable to detect it. In addition, the extraction of statistical properties requires large test samples. If a covert channel exists, a large amount of sensitive information (e.g., possibly, encryption keys or passwords) has already been leaked before it is detected. In brief, previous detection methods have limitations in detection effectiveness.

In this paper, we propose a proactive strategy of detecting covert timing channels. The basic idea is that a secret fingerprint is embedded into outgoing traffic of the to-be-protected host in advance. Meanwhile, a detector, which is located in the transmission path of the protected traffic, checks if the traffic still retains the fingerprint. The presence of a covert timing channel is exposed, provided that the fingerprint is absent.

To demonstrate the feasibility of the proactive strategy, we design and implement a detection system targeting passive timing channels, whose covert encoder resides on the intermediate routers/gateways or low-layer network protocol stack of the victim machine. The detection system consists of two modules: ADAPTOR and CHECKER. ADAPTOR is installed on the machine in protection, and the purpose is to embed a specific fingerprint shared with CHECKER into each flow of network traffic; CHECKER is located on the intrusion detection system (IDS) to examine the presence of the fingerprint in passing traffic. To evaluate the performance of our detection system, we also conduct a series of experiments to validate if the detection system works effectively. In the experiments, it can successfully detect existing timing channels and raw legitimate traffic with no fingerprint, which indicates that the performance of our detection method is independent of channel encoding methods. Moreover, the results show that our system can detect covert traffic not only accurately but also quickly, while has little influence on network performance.

The rest of the paper is organized as follows. In Section 2, we discuss the related work in timing channels. After that, we introduce the communication scenario, the system model and the adversary model. In Section 4, we describe the structure of our detection system. Then we validate the effectiveness of this system. Finally, we conclude the paper.

2   Related Work

The timing of some events can leak secret information in a manner that compromises security properties. In side timing channels, attackers exploit the fact that the time for executing a cryptographic algorithm is data dependent. Specifically, key information can be extracted through precise measurements of the time [17]. Side-channel timing attacks have also been proved to be practical over a network [4,3,7]. In addition, it has been shown that such attacks are effective not only on cryptosystems but also in other scenarios [8,27]. However, the focus of this paper is on deliberate information leakage from timing channels established by a premeditated adversary rather than unintentional leakage from side channels.

Inter-packet delays in network traffic can be used as a medium for data stealth transfer. This kind of communication channel, which is not intended for data transfer, is usually called "covert channel" [19]. Compared with network storage channel, which exploits the redundancy of network protocols, timing channel is more stealthy due to the cover of varying overt traffic.

The recent literature is not lack of practical exploitation of covert timing channels. Since the first IP covert timing channel came into being [6], channel exploitation has made great progress over the years. In [25], Shah et al. designed a device called Jitterbug, which can extract typed information and leak it through a timing channel. This is a typical example of real-world network timing channels. Gianvecchio et al. [10] proposed a model-based covert timing channel, which mimics the distribution of legitimate traffic. Liu et al. [20] introduced spreading codes to encode messages for the purpose of increasing the robustness of timing channel. Sellke et al. [24] proposed the "L-bits to N-packets" encoding scheme in order to build a high-capacity covert timing channel. In general, the research on network covert timing channel exploitation has been done from three aspects: undetectability [5,10,28,18], robustness [14,20], capacity [2,34,32].

Covert timing channel can be categorized into two types: active and passive. In an active channel, the sender generates additional network packets to embed covert information and needs to compromise the host for the total control over it. While in a passive channel, the sender just compromises the I/O device [25] or low-level network protocol stack [33], or resides in the middle nodes (e.g., routers or gateways) [21,34], manipulating the existing network traffic. In general, it is harder to discover passive channels due to their parasitism on overt ones. Additionally, in terms of encoding techniques, passive channels usually maintain the inter-packet dependencies of legitimate traffic, and thus, are hardly detectable. The detection of them has become a challenging work.

There is another form of passive timing channel, i.e., network flow watermark, intended for packet traceback. Wang et al. [31] develop a watermark, aiming to correlate "stepping stones", by means of sightly changing the timing of flow-based packets. This technique can also be used to correlate encrypted VoIP calls even in anonymous networks [30].

To eliminate the threat from covert timing channels, researchers have proposed a series of solutions: fuzzy time [15], jammers [11], pump [16], etc. The fundamental idea among them is to insert random interrupts in order to lower the channel capacity boundary. However, network suffers performance degradation therefrom. In addition, covert timing channel is still able to exist but with a poor bandwidth. By comparison, it might be preferable to adopt passive traffic analysis, namely channel detection, which aims to differentiate covert traffic from normal traffic. The research on this field has attracted a lot of attention in recent years, and meanwhile, a series of detection techniques have been developed [6,2,22,9]. The most noteworthy among these, supposedly, is the entropy-based method [9]. This method utilizes entropy and conditional entropy to detect the anomaly in first-order and high-order statistics, respectively. Compared with the others, empirically, it has a better performance in detecting various covert timing channels. Even so, it still can be defeated by some mimicry-based encoding techniques [28,18].

3   Preliminaries

3.1   Communication Scenario

A covert timing channel consists of a covert encoder sending secrets by modulating network event timings, and a decoder extracting secrets by observing the timings. In reality, the covert encoder is not necessarily the sender of network traffic. Specifically, it can be located in the transmission path, and manipulates the delays of passing-by packets. Sometimes, an attacker may choose to create such a passive channel instead of an active one, the reasons of which include: 1) sometimes the creation of a passive channel does not require a compromised host. 2) the generation of additional traffic is prone to exposing the presence of a covert channel, whereas a passive channel can avoid this risk. There has been recognized difficulty in mitigating the security threat from such channels. In this paper, we target passive channels to demonstrate the feasibility of our proactive strategy. For the sake of clarity, we elaborate that, in the scenario of covert communication we are concerned with, as shown in Figure 1, the covert encoder can reside on the intermediate routers/gateways near the overt sender, or even on the compromised output device or low-layer network protocol stack of the same machine as the overt sender. We note that the scenario of Jitterbug [25], which compromises an input channel, is not in the application scope of our proof-of-concept implementation.

3.2   System Model

In a general system model of network covert communication, there is another role besides a covert encoder and decoder, that is, a network warden, residing between the covert encoder and decoder and monitoring the passing messages [12]. There are mainly two types of wardens in the literature of covert timing channel:

- A *passive* warden can detect the presence of covert timing channels, but cannot alter the existing traffic.

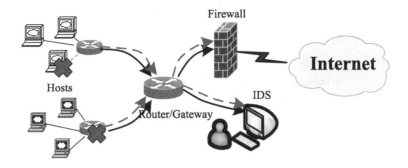

Fig. 1. Communication Scenario

- An *active* warden can alter the timings of existing traffic to eliminate or disrupt covert timing channels.

In this paper, we introduce a new type of warden, which is an *active* one but intended for detection. Specifically, the warden embeds a specific timing fingerprint into the newly generated traffic by slightly altering inter-packet delays, and meanwhile, he is located in the transmission path and detects if the transmitted packets still retain the specific fingerprint.

3.3 Adversary Model

In some cases of passive channels, the location of an adversary is physically separated from the overt sender, e.g., intermediate routers/gateways, so the adversary is unable to directly access secrets in the victim machine. On the other hand, an adversary might reside in some important components of the victim machine, e.g., the output device or low-layer network protocol stack, and thus, have an opportunity to steal secrets about fingerprint information. To consider the worst situation, we assume the adversary has the ability to compromise the host; then he can grab desirable information.

We also assume that virtualization technology is implemented in the to-be-protected machine. Such assumption is realistic because this technology has been widely applied in personal computers, servers, and workstations. The self-protection of secrets about specific fingerprints and fingerprint embedding code can be addressed by applying the SIM [26] framework. Even if an adversary compromises the OS kernel, he is unable to know about the fingerprints or disable the code.

4   Detection System

The detection system consists of two modules: ADAPTOR and CHECKER. ADAPTOR, which is installed on the to-be-protected machine, embeds a specific fingerprint into each flow of network traffic. CHECKER, installed on the IDS, which is located on the edge of the LAN, checks if the passing traffic still retains the fingerprint. Figure 2 shows the overview of our detection system.

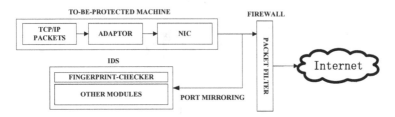

Fig. 2. System Overview

In the practical implementation, ADAPTOR and CHECKER agree a priori on the knowledge about fingerprint patterns, including the specific encoding/decoding method and the involved secrets (e.g., sensitive parameters or random number seeds). ADAPTOR can be installed on multiple to-be-protected machines in a LAN, but the fingerprint patterns may be distinct from each other. CHECKER is only required to be installed on the boundary between the LAN and the outside world, and thus, is responsible to check all the traffic generated from protected machines in the LAN. CHECKER should maintain a list of services in protection and corresponding fingerprint patterns in use. The pair of each ADAPTOR and CHECKER constitutes a trusted transmission path. If the timing interval pattern of a flow deviates from the expected one, a covert timing channel probably exits in the corresponding transmission path. A warning will be given to the security administrator once CHECKER detects such traffic anomaly. The ADAPTOR and CHECKER modules are detailed in the following subsections.

4.1 ADAPTOR

The main task of the ADAPTOR module is to change the timing characteristic of the original traffic, which is intended to leave its fingerprint on the transmitted traffic. As an exemplary implementation, we place ADAPTOR between the OS kernel and network interface card. ADAPTOR intercepts TCP/IP packets just generated from the OS. The original traffic is stored temporarily in a buffer, waiting to be forwarded at an elaborately planned time. ADAPTOR classifies the traffic into individual flows based on protocol, source and destination port and IP address, and then calculates intervals between adjacent packets of each flow. The transmission time of each packet is determined according to the original intervals and the fingerprint pattern. ADAPTOR finally forwards the manipulated packets to network interface card. Figure 3 shows the workflow of ADAPTOR.

Fingerprint Encoding. There is a basic principle regarding fingerprint encoding, that is, the timing of the original traffic cannot be altered a lot. If the

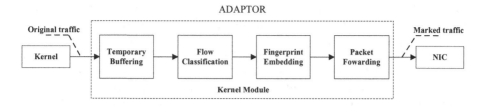

Fig. 3. The workflow of ADAPTOR

packets are delayed for a long time, the network performance will suffer penalty seriously. We note that, this is similar to the negative effect of current disruption techniques, which reduces covert channel capacity by adding random delays to traffic. For this reason, a slight change in packet intervals is only allowed when fingerprint information is encoded into the original traffic.

We develop a simple fingerprint encoding scheme for the detection system. The sequence of original times when packets are delivered from the kernel is denoted as $\{t_1, ..., t_n\}$ here. To mark the traffic generated from the to-be-protected machine, we add a slight delay noted by τ_i to each element of the sequence. So the new sequence of altered times when packets are forwarded by ADAPTOR turns out to be $\{t'_1, ..., t'_n\}$, where $t'_i = t_i + \tau_i$. The fingerprint of ADAPTOR is marked on the resulting inter-packet delays $IPD_i = t'_{i+1} - t'_i$, which satisfies the following equation:

$$IPD_i \ mod \ \omega \ = \ 0$$

where ω is a time parameter, referred to as the fingerprint pattern.

We can infer that the delay τ_i is less than ω all the time. Therefore, the parameter ω determines the maximum delay to packet transmission time, and hence, directly affects the network performance.

An example is given below to help the understanding of the fingerprint encoding scheme. We assume $\omega = 1000us$, and the sequence of original intervals is $\{375, 17790, 3889, 8456, 55322\}us$. To make each interval be an integral multiple of ω, ADAPTOR adds a delay to each packet, and consequently, the sequence of altered intervals turns out to be $\{1000, 18000, 4000, 9000, 56000\}us$.

Influencing Factors. As described above, the delays manipulated by ADAPTOR, which are bounded from above by the parameter ω, cannot be too long in consideration of user experience. On the other hand, if ω is small, the fingerprint will be wrongly decoded on the module CHECKER side although no intentional change occurs during transmission. There are several factors influencing the accuracy rate of fingerprint decoding.

The major one is jitter. In the context of computer networks, jitter, also referred to as packet delay variation, represents an average of the deviation from the packet mean latency over a network. From another perspective, it indicates that a network has inconstant latency, and there always exists a difference between an inter-packet delay on the sender side and that on the receiver side.

A packet forwarded later may even reach at an earlier time due to the large network jitter. The timing fingerprint cannot avoid the disturbance from network jitter during packet transmission.

To ensure CHECKER decodes the fingerprint correctly under the existence of jitter, ω must be at least two times larger than the largest jitter in a LAN. To demonstrate this, we assume that ADAPTOR sends the i-th packet at t'_i time, and the packet is transmitted with an average delay of θ and a random jitter of γ which is bounded by the inequality $-\gamma_{max} \le \gamma \le \gamma_{max}$, where γ_{max} denotes the longest jitter. Then the CHECKER observes the very packet at $t + \theta + \gamma$. Figure 4 shows two extreme cases in which the observed intervals are changed by $2\gamma_{max}$. Therefore, to counter network jitter, the parameter ω should be much larger than $2\gamma_{max}$.

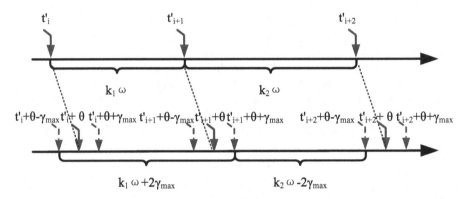

Fig. 4. Jitters involved in transmission

In addition, clock skew is another influencing factor. As a matter of fact, the clock frequencies of the protected machine and IDS where two modules are installed respectively may not be completely identical. Although the difference is rather small, it poses a non-ignorable obstacle to the precise fingerprint embedding. Empirically, there is indeed a *linear* relationship between the timing shifts and intervals. The asynchrony can be addressed by estimating the timing ratio between the clock of the protected machine and that of the IDS as follows. The protected machine transmits two packets with an interval of θ, and then the corresponding interval θ' in us is obtained on the IDS. The ratio is simply θ/θ'. The timing intervals observed in the IDS will be finally multiplied by this ratio so that the clocks are adjusted to be synchronous.

4.2   CHECKER

CHECKER is used in conjunction with ADAPTOR. It sits on the IDS of a LAN, and takes charge of all outbound traffic from protected hosts in the LAN. Firstly, the IDS monitors traffic of inside network via a mirroring port which carries a copy of outbound traffic. CHECKER then singles out the traffic in protection according to the maintained list. Sequently, since fingerprint embedding is flow based, CHECKER should classify the picked traffic into individual flows based on the traffic 5-tuple. Each flow will be examined for the presence of the expected fingerprint. If the fingerprint is absent, it implies that there is probably a covert timing channel in the transmission path. Figure 5 shows the workflow of CHECKER.

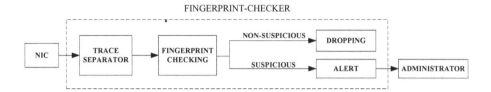

Fig. 5. The workflow of CHECKER

Fingerprint Decoding. CHECKER takes the reverse operation of fingerprint embedding to determine if packet intervals retain the expected fingerprint pattern. For decoding, we assume the sequence of packets reaches the IDS at the times of $\{T_1, ..., T_n\}$. Each inter-packet delay is then denoted as $\widehat{IPD}_i = T_{i+1} - T_i$. To remove the effect of network jitter detailed in Section 4.1, the decoding of the fingerprint allows each interval has small fluctuation. The decoding algorithm is given as follows: if $-\beta \leq \widehat{IPD}_i \leq \beta \ (mod \ \omega)$, where β is a tolerance parameter, then the fingerprint is identified as present; otherwise, the fingerprint is identified as absent. Obviously, the selection of β depends on the amount of network jitter in the LAN. To tolerate the worst cases, β should be no less than the double of the largest jitter γ_{max}.

In addition, to counter bad network conditions, we utilize a tolerant mechanism for determining whether a covert timing channel exits. If the fingerprint pattern is absent in an interval, the corresponding packet is flagged as illegitimate. When an illegitimate packet comes along, a burglar alert will not be immediately sent out. Actually, only a lot of illegitimate packets during a period will trigger the IDS to send an alert to system administrator. We use the density of illegitimate packets to indicate the health condition of the host in protection. More specifically, we record the number of illegitimate packets among the previous 10 ones. If this number exceeds a threshold, the trusted transmission path is identified to contain a covert timing channel.

4.3   Security Enhancement

There are some potential attacks against the naive fingerprint encoding method. To mitigate these attacks, two security-enhanced schemes based upon the naive one are presented hereinafter.

Potential Attacks. The fingerprint encoding method has some drawbacks that can be exploited by an attacker to forge the fingerprint pattern in use or evade fingerprint checking. We discuss potential attacks in the following paragraphs.

1. *Forging fingerprint* After the fingerprint is embedded, packet intervals turn into be multiples of the parameter ω. An attacker located on a router inside the LAN can eavesdrop the traffic delivered from the host in protection and extract the value of ω. If ω is not changed constantly, the attacker is able to forge ADAPTOR's fingerprint and embed it into covert traffic. CHECKER will identify covert traffic with forged fingerprint as legitimate, and thereby, covert traffic can pass through CHECKER undetected.

2. *Invalidating censorship* The parameter ω is generally much smaller than the mean intervals of legitimate traffic. Some simple encoding schemes of timing channels encode bit information in fixed and relatively long intervals, e.g., IP-PCTC [34] transmits 0-bit by a 5ms interval and 1-bit by a 12ms interval. Thus, the intervals of covert traffic happen to be multiples of ω. If those channels can manipulate packet delays exactly on the millisecond, CHECKER also fails to detect them.

Enhanced Schemes. One solution is to constantly change the parameter ω. ADAPTOR and CHECKER are assumed to negotiate a set of ω values in advance. For instance, there are 10 elements in the set, ranging from 1000us to 1900us with the gradient of 100us. The parameter values are indexed from 0 through 9, respectively. We also assume ADAPTOR and CHECKER share a pseudo-random sequence of integers that range from 0 to 9. The random seed and the set of values used by ADAPTOR can be protected by the hypervisor in the host from being stolen, as described in Section 3.3. For each inter-packet delay, ω value to be used in the encoding algorithm is determined according to the newly generated random number. Meanwhile, the same process is applied to decode the fingerprint.

Another solution is to introduce another more secure parameter in the encoding algorithm. We assume ADAPTOR and CHECKER share a pseudo-random bit stream $\{r_1, ..., r_n\}$. The random seed used by ADAPTOR can protected in the same way as hereinbefore. The encoding algorithm turns into be as follows:

$$IPD_i \bmod \omega = \begin{cases} 0, & \text{if } r_i = 0; \\ \frac{\omega}{2}, & \text{if } r_i = 1. \end{cases}$$

where IPD_i is the resulting inter-packet delay as before, and ω is also the same as before. To decode the fingerprint, the following algorithm is used:

$$r_i = \begin{cases} 0, & \text{if } -\beta \le \widehat{IPD}_i \le \beta \ (mod\ \omega); \\ 1, & \text{if } \omega/2 - \beta \le \widehat{IPD}_i \le \omega/2 + \beta \ (mod\ \omega); \\ invalid, & \text{otherwise.} \end{cases}$$

We note that this enhanced scheme is inspired by Jitterbug [25]. This solution can be combined with the former to achieve more secure properties.

5   Implementation and Evaluation

We implemented a prototype in a real network environment to validate the effectiveness of our detection strategy. In this section, we first describe the implementation details at a high level. Then, we measure the maximum network jitter, based on which we determine the parameter ω and β. Finally, our detection test is performed against two existing timing channels: MBCTC [10] and Jitterbug [25]. Furthermore, we test if the detection method works against legitimate traffic that has no fingerprint embedded.

The evaluation criterions include false positive rate, false negative rate, detection latency, and performance penalty. An ideal detection method achieves both low false positive and false negative rate, while has small detection latency and little influence on system performance. Generally, conventional detection tests are unable to satisfy the first three due to their inherent limitation that comes with statistical tests. The purpose of our proposed idea is to conquer this limitation, thereby achieving a high performance on detection regardless of encoding techniques used in covert timing channels.

5.1   Implementation Details

Our design goal is to be effective in detecting passive timing channels as much as possible. We implemented ADAPTOR in Linux environment as a kernel module, which can embed its fingerprint into a newly-generated packet. Netfilter [23] hooks were utilized to intercept packets. For fingerprint encoding, we used udelay() function to add delays to the original packets. This is because the manipulation of intervals when embedding a fingerprint needs to be very precise. Additionally, we disabled Large Segment Offload feature, which alleviates the burden of operating system by allowing it to assemble large packets and by transferring the task of disassembling large packets into smaller segments to NIC. This technology has been widely deployed in Linux since kernel 2.6.18. The host in our prototype runs a Linux OS with kernel version 2.6.35.

We implemented CHECKER as a module of an IDS in Windows environment. The IDS and the hosts in protection are located within the same LAN. For this reason, the switch of the IDS is configured to mirror all the outbound traffic to the IDS port. CHECKER only need to monitor the outbound traffic and record packet arriving times. This module was implemented using WinPcap [1].

5.2   Parameter Determination

In order to counter the ubiquitous existence of network jitter, the parameters ω and β are introduced in fingerprint encoding and decoding algorithms (detailed in Section 4.1 and 4.2). More specifically, β is set to tolerate bad network conditions and hence no less than jitter, while ω should be much larger than β so as to have a high detection effectiveness. From a statistical perspective, packet intervals with no fingerprint modulo ω uniformly fall in the range $[-\frac{\omega}{2}, \frac{\omega}{2}]$, so the probability that they fall in the tolerant range $[-\beta, \beta]$ is $\frac{2\beta}{\omega}$. When this value is small, the situation that an illegitimate packet is wrongly identified as legitimate occurs with a low probability. We set the ratio of $\frac{2\beta}{\omega}$ to be $\frac{1}{20}$. For example, when ω is $400us$, the fingerprint pattern is valid if an observed interval is in $[k * \omega - 10, k * \omega + 10]us$ $(k \in N_+)$.

Since ADAPTOR and CHECKER both reside in the LAN, the variation of network latency is intuitively rather small. To investigate the real jitter in a LAN, we conducted a series of experiments as follows. We sent from ADAPTOR 4 test sets of packets, whose intervals are multiples of $50us, 200us, 800us,$ and $1000us$, respectively. Each test set has 1027 packets (1026 intervals). On the CHECKER side, we calculated the mean and standard deviation of observed intervals modulo the respective parameter value, as shown in Table 1. Note that the count represents the number of intervals beyond the tolerant range. We can observe that when $\omega = 800us$, the false alarm rate is very low, only 0.19%, which is acceptable. In fact, approximately 85 percent of intervals modulo $800us$ gather within the range $[-10, 10]us$. We choose $\omega = 800us$ and $\beta = 20us$ in the following experiments.

Table 1. Timing Jitters

Parameter/us	Mean/us	StdDev/us^2	Count	Ratio
50	-0.3655	8.09576	908	88.50%
200	0.04191	7.9225	140	13.65%
800	0.14352	8.1617	2	0.19%
1000	0.16179	10.19637	2	0.19%

5.3   Detection

Real Timing Channels. To investigate the effectiveness of our detection system, we performed the detection test against existing timing channels: MBCTC [10] and Jitterbug [25]. We only concern about their encoding methods. We implement their encoding methods with ADAPTOR disabled, which means no fingerprint is embedded in their traffic. For MBCTC, we utilize HTTP traffic, which is extracted from NZIX-II data sets [29], as the modeling objective. We fit a set of 100 packets to a model and use the model to generate covert traffic. For Jitterbug, we use SSH traffic, also from NZIX-II data sets, to transfer covert information. The timing window is set at 20 milliseconds, and a pseudo-random sequence of integers is used to smooth out interval patterns, as suggested by Shah et al. [25].

As illustrated in Figure 6, the number of illegitimate packets among the previous 10 ones rises rapidly when the transmission of covert packets starts. We set the threshold to be 5. This indicates if the number exceeds 5, the traffic will be identified as illegitimate, and then an alert will be sent to the security administrator. Based on this given threshold, the detection latency and effect is given in Table 2. We can see that no more than 7 packets (6 intervals) have been sent out before the presence of a timing channel is detected. In addition, the test maintains both 0% false positive rate and false negative rate. Our detection method

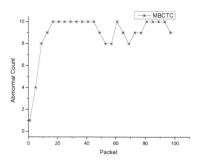 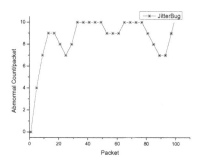

Fig. 6. Detection against real timing channels

achieves much higher detection performance compared to statistical-test-based detection methods, which not only require thousands of packets to analyze traffic behavior, but also have over sensitivity to the high variation of traffic [9].

Table 2. Detection latency and effect

	MBCTC	JitterBug
Latency/interval	6	6
Information Disclosure/bit	6	6
False Positive Rate	0%	0%
False Negative Rate	0%	0%

Raw Legitimate Traffic. To validate the effectiveness of our detection system further, we conducted the detection test against raw legitimate traffic which is legitimate but with no fingerprint. We replayed HTTP traces from NZIX-II data sets. During the experiment, we enabled and disabled ADAPTOR alternately, as shown in Figure 7. After ADAPTOR is disabled at the 16th packet, the abnormal count reaches up to 10 immediately and then stays around there. When ADAPTOR is enabled again at the 56th packet, the abnormal count decreases gradually to 0. This experimental result shows that even legitimate traffic can be detected by this test as long as it has no fingerprint. From another aspect, it indicates the effectiveness of our detection method is independent of encoding methods. That is to say, no matter how approximate covert traffic can be to legitimate overt traffic, this method is still successful in detecting it.

5.4   Network Performance

Since packets are delayed when ADAPTOR's fingerprint is embedded, network performance degrades more or less. To estimate the practical performance penalty,

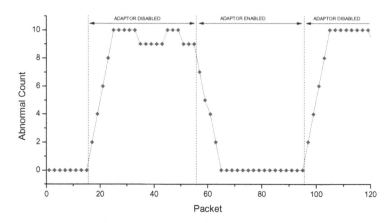

Fig. 7. Detection against raw legitimate traffic

the test machine sent 2 sets of HTTP packets, which are selected from the previous traffic. The first set consists of low-density traffic, while the second one is highly dense. We calculated the difference between the total transmission time with ADAPTOR and that without ADAPTOR. The penalty is set as the ratio of the difference and the transmission time without ADAPTOR, as given in Table 3. We consider the performance penalty of no more than 2.4‰ to be acceptable.

Table 3. Performance Penalty

Test set	Number of intervals	Mean	Sum(without adaptor)	Sum(with adaptor)	Penalty
1	10000	0.91s	9070.45s	9074.59s	0.46‰
2	10000	0.17s	1681.52s	1685.56s	2.40‰

6   Conclusion and Future Work

We introduced a proactive strategy of detecting covert timing channels. The basic idea is that a timing fingerprint is embedded into outgoing traffic of the to-be-protected host in advance. If a covert timing channel exits in the transmission path, the fingerprint will probably be disrupted, and thereby the presence of the timing channel can be detected. We described our detection system, a proof-of-concept implementation aiming at passive timing channels. This system consists of the ADAPTOR module and CHECKER module: the former is located on the machine in protection, and the purpose is to embed a specific fingerprint into each flow of network traffic; the latter resides on the IDS of the same LAN to examine if the passing traffic retains the fingerprint.

We then applied our detection system to detect covert timing channels. The experimental results show that it can detect various existing timing channels accurately and quickly. Even raw legitimate traffic with no fingerprint is also detectable by this system. This indicates that the performance of our detection techniques is independent of channel encoding methods. Finally, we showed that the penalty on network performance is acceptably small.

The arms race between covert timing channel design and detection techniques has been ongoing. In this paper, we suggested some simple ideas to the design of detection systems. We hope our proactive techniques can open a new perspective for researchers. To further improve the proactive detection scheme, we plan to investigate this direction in the future.

References

1. Winpcap: The windows packet capture library, http://www.winpcap.org
2. Berk, V., Giani, A., Cybenko, G., Hanover, N.: Detection of covert channel encoding in network packet delays. Tech. Rep. TR2005-536, Dartmouth College, Computer Science, Hanover (2005)
3. Brumley, B.B., Tuveri, N.: Remote timing attacks are still practical. In: Proceedings of the 16th European Symposium on Research in Computer Security, pp. 355–371 (2011)
4. Brumley, D., Boneh, D.: Remote timing attacks are practical. In: Proceedings of the 12th Conference on USENIX Security Symposium (2003)
5. Cabuk, S.: Network covert channels: design, analysis, detection, and elimination. PhD thesis (2006)
6. Cabuk, S., Brodley, C., Shields, C.: Ip covert timing channels: design and detection. In: Proceedings of the 11th ACM Conference on Computer and Communications Security, pp. 178–187 (2004)
7. Crosby, S.A., Wallach, D.S., Riedi, R.H.: Opportunities and limits of remote timing attacks. ACM Transactions on Information and System Security 12(3), 17 (2009)
8. Felten, E.W., Schneider, M.A.: Timing attacks on web privacy. In: Proceedings of the 7th ACM Conference on Computer and Communications Security, pp. 25–32 (2000)
9. Gianvecchio, S., Wang, H.: Detecting covert timing channels: an entropy-based approach. In: Proceedings of the 14th ACM Conference on Computer and Communications Security, pp. 307–316 (2007)
10. Gianvecchio, S., Wang, H., Wijesekera, D., Jajodia, S.: Model-based covert timing channels: Automated modeling and evasion. In: Lippmann, R., Kirda, E., Trachtenberg, A. (eds.) RAID 2008. LNCS, vol. 5230, pp. 211–230. Springer, Heidelberg (2008)
11. Giles, J., Hajek, B.: An information-theoretic and game-theoretic study of timing channels. IEEE Transactions on Information Theory 48(9), 2455–2477 (2002)
12. Handel, T., Sandford, M.: Hiding data in the OSI network model. In: Anderson, R. (ed.) IH 1996. LNCS, vol. 1174, pp. 23–38. Springer, Heidelberg (1996)
13. Henry, P.: Covert channels provided hackers the opportunity and the means for the current distributed denial of service attacks. CyberGuard Corporation (2000)
14. Houmansadr, A., Borisov, N.: CoCo: Coding-based covert timing channels for network flows. In: Filler, T., Pevný, T., Craver, S., Ker, A. (eds.) IH 2011. LNCS, vol. 6958, pp. 314–328. Springer, Heidelberg (2011)
15. Hu, W.M.: Reducing timing channels with fuzzy time. In: IEEE Symposium on Security and Privacy, pp. 8–20 (1991)

16. Kang, M., Moskowitz, I.: A pump for rapid, reliable, secure communication. In: Proceedings of the 1st ACM Conference on Computer and Communications Security, pp. 119–129 (1993)
17. Kocher, P.C.: Timing attacks on implementations of Diffie-Hellman, RSA, DSS, and other systems. In: Koblitz, N. (ed.) CRYPTO 1996. LNCS, vol. 1109, pp. 104–113. Springer, Heidelberg (1996)
18. Kothari, K., Wright, M.: Mimic: An active covert channel that evades regularity-based detection. Computer Networks (2012)
19. Lampson, B.: A note on the confinement problem. Communications of the ACM 16(10), 613–615 (1973)
20. Liu, Y., Ghosal, D., Armknecht, F., Sadeghi, A.-R., Schulz, S., Katzenbeisser, S.: Hide and seek in time — robust covert timing channels. In: Backes, M., Ning, P. (eds.) ESORICS 2009. LNCS, vol. 5789, pp. 120–135. Springer, Heidelberg (2009)
21. Lucena, N.B., Pease, J., Yadollahpour, P., Chapin, S.J.: Syntax and semantics-preserving application-layer protocol steganography. In: Fridrich, J. (ed.) IH 2004. LNCS, vol. 3200, pp. 164–179. Springer, Heidelberg (2004)
22. Peng, P., Ning, P., Reeves, D.: On the secrecy of timing-based active watermarking trace-back techniques. In: IEEE Symposium on Security and Privacy (2006)
23. Russell, R., Welte, H.: Linux netfilter hacking HOWTO (2002), www.netfilter.org/documentation/HOWTO/netfilter-hacking-HOWTO.html
24. Sellke, S., Wang, C., Bagchi, S., Shroff, N.: TCP/IP timing channels: Theory to implementation. In: INFOCOM 2009, pp. 2204–2212 (2009)
25. Shah, G., Molina, A., Blaze, M.: Keyboards and covert channels. In: Proceedings of the 15th Conference on USENIX Security Symposium, vol. 15 (2006)
26. Sharif, M.I., Lee, W., Cui, W., Lanzi, A.: Secure in-VM monitoring using hardware virtualization. In: Proceedings of the 16th ACM Conference on Computer and Communications Security, pp. 477–487 (2009)
27. Song, D.X., Wagner, D., Tian, X.: Timing analysis of keystrokes and timing attacks on SSH. In: Proceedings of the 10th USENIX Security Symposium, vol. 2, p. 3 (2001)
28. Walls, R., Kothari, K., Wright, M.: Liquid: A detection-resistant covert timing channel based on IPD shaping. Computer Networks 55(6), 1217–1228 (2011)
29. WAND Research Group: Waikato internet traffic storage, http://wand.net.nz/wits/nzix/2/
30. Wang, X., Chen, S., Jajodia, S.: Tracking anonymous peer-to-peer voip calls on the internet. In: Proceedings of the 12th ACM Conference on Computer and Communications Security, pp. 81–91 (2005)
31. Wang, X., Reeves, D.S.: Robust correlation of encrypted attack traffic through stepping stones by manipulation of interpacket delays. In: Proceedings of the 10th ACM Conference on Computer and Communications Security, pp. 20–29 (2003)
32. Wu, J., Wang, Y., Ding, L., Liao, X.: Improving performance of network covert timing channel through huffman coding. Mathematical and Computer Modelling 55(1), 69–79 (2012)
33. Zander, S., Armitage, G., Branch, P.: A survey of covert channels and countermeasures in computer network protocols. IEEE Communications Surveys & Tutorials 9(3), 44–57 (2007)
34. Zi, X., Yao, L., Pan, L., Li, J.: Implementing a passive network covert timing channel. Computers & Security 29(6), 686–696 (2010)

Comprehensive Evaluation of AES Dual Ciphers as a Side-Channel Countermeasure

Amir Moradi and Oliver Mischke

Horst Görtz Institute for IT Security, Ruhr University Bochum, Germany
{moradi,mischke}@crypto.rub.de

Abstract. Because of the isomorphisms in $GF(2^8)$ there exist 240 different non-trivial dual ciphers of AES. While keeping the in- and outputs of a dual cipher equal to the original AES, all the intermediate values and operations can be different from that of the original one. A comprehensive list of these dual ciphers is given by an article presented at ASIACRYPT 2002, where it is mentioned that they might be used as a kind of side-channel attack countermeasure if the dual cipher is randomly selected. Later, in a couple of works performance figures and overhead penalty of hardware implementations of this scheme is reported. However, the suitability of using randomly selected dual ciphers as a power analysis countermeasure has never been thoroughly evaluated in practice. In this work we address the pitfalls and flaws of this scheme when used as a side-channel countermeasure. As evidence of our claims, we provide practical evaluation results based on a Virtex-5 FPGA platform. We realized a design which randomly selects between the 240 different dual ciphers at each AES computation. We also examined the side-channel leakage of the design under an information theoretic metric as well as its vulnerability to different attack models. As a result, we show that the protection provided by the scheme is negligible considering the increased costs in term of area and lower throughput.

1 Introduction

From a mathematical point of view embedded systems can easily be protected by modern ciphers which are secure in a black-box scenario. However, since the late 90s the security of a cryptographic device relies not only on the use of a secure cryptographic algorithm but also on how this algorithm is implemented. Since sensitive information like encryption keys of an unprotected implementation can be recovered by observing so called side channels, the need of secure implementations of cryptographic primitives like AES is at an all-time high.

Many different kinds of countermeasures have been proposed either for protection of software and/or hardware platforms (see [18] for instance). Masking of sensitive values is one of the most considered solutions, and the community has shown a huge interest to different aspects of masking countermeasures, e.g., [2, 5, 8, 10, 11, 15, 22–24, 26, 28]. Because of sequential nature of the platform, masking in software is usually straight forward and effective. However, realizing

S. Qing et al. (Eds.): ICICS 2013, LNCS 8233, pp. 245–258, 2013.
© Springer International Publishing Switzerland 2013

the masking schemes in hardware is intricate since glitches in the circuit can cause otherwise theoretically secure schemes to leak [19–21].

Back to the early 2000s, there exist only few attempts to better understand the algebraic specification of AES-Rijndael. One is about how to make *dual ciphers* which are equivalent to the original Rijndael in all aspects [3]. By replacing all the constants in Rijndael, including the replacement of the irreducible polynomial, the coefficients of the MixColumns, the affine transformation in the S-box, etc, the idea is to make another ciphers which generate the same ciphertext as the original Rijndael for the given plaintext and key. As explained in [3], there exist 240 non-trivial Rijndael dual ciphers, and a comprehensive list of the matrices and coefficients is given in [4]. Later in [27], it has been shown that one can include field mappings from $GF(2^8)$ to $GF(2)^8$ as well as intermediate isomorphic mappings to $GF(2^2)$ and $GF(2^4)$ to build 61 200 similar Rijndael dual ciphers.

This idea was taken by the authors of [31], and by means of the gate count they investigated which of those 240 dual ciphers can be implemented in hardware using smaller area, and which ones can speed up the implementation. Since the intermediate values of the dual ciphers during encryption are different than Rijndael's, it is mentioned in [3] that one can randomly change the constants of the cipher thereby realizing different dual ciphers and provide security against power analysis attacks. This led to other contributions. For instance, a hardware-software co-design of a system based on an Altera FPGA where according to the randomly chosen parameters the content of the lookup tables are dynamically changed is presented in [16, 17][1]. Moreover, the authors of [12] and [13] represented a hardware implementation which can realize every selected dual cipher amongst those 240 ones. They reported the performance and area loss when the scheme is realized in order to increase the security against side-channel attacks.

In this work we examine this scheme, i.e., random selection of constants to choose a dual cipher out of 240, from a side-channel point of view. We address its flaws and weaknesses which can lead to easily breaking the corresponding implementation. In order to examine our findings in practice, we implemented the scheme on a Virtex-5 FPGA by means of precomputed matrices and constants and – in contrast to [17] – by avoiding the use of any lookup table. Our practical side-channel evaluations confirm our claims indicating that the protection provided by the scheme is negligible while having high area and performance overheads. We show that the implementation can be easily broken when a suitable attack model is taken by the adversary.

The next section restates the concept of Rijndael dual ciphers with respect to the original work [3]. Our design of the scheme considering our targeted FPGA platform in addition to its performance and area overhead figures are represented in Section 3. Our discussions about the side-channel resistance of the scheme and practical investigations are given by Section 4 while Section 5 concludes our research.

---

[1] In fact, the cipher which is realized by their design is not always equivalent to the original AES-Rijndael.

2   Dual Cipher Concept

Two ciphers E and E' are called dual ciphers, if they are isomorphic, i.e., if there exist invertible transformations $f(\cdot)$, $g(\cdot)$ and $h(\cdot)$ such that

$$\forall P, K \quad E_K(P) = f(E'_{g(K)}(h(P))),$$

where plaintext and key are denoted by P and K respectively.

The concept of dual ciphers for AES-Rijndael was first published in 2002 [3]. The authors demonstrate how to build a square dual cipher of the original AES and show that it is possible to again iterate this process multiple times creating more square dual ciphers. This way 8 dual ciphers for each possible irreducible polynomial in $GF(2^8)$ can be derived. Since it is also shown how to create dual ciphers by porting the cipher to use one of the other 30 irreducible polynomials in $GF(2^8)$, a total of 240 non-trivial dual ciphers for AES exist. Here non-trivial means that we are only considering those dual ciphers which actually change the inner core of AES and not only consist of invertible transformations of the input and output of the cipher.

As an example, closely following the explanation in [3], let us consider a square dual cipher of the original AES-Rijndael. In order to create this dual cipher one first has to multiply all AES constants by a matrix which performs the squaring operation under the original AES-Rijndael polynomial $0x11b$. These constants include the round constant of the key schedule, the coefficients of the MixColumns transformation, as well as the input data and the key. In this special example this matrix is generated by taking a generator a, in this case the polynomial x^2 in $GF(2^8)$, and building a matrix of the form $R = (a^0, a^1, a^2, a^3, a^4, a^5, a^6, a^7)$, where each of these elements represents a column of the matrix and the result of the exponentiation is reduced by the original AES reduction polynomial. The resulting matrix is

$$R = \begin{pmatrix} 1 & 0 & 0 & 0 & 1 & 0 & 1 & 0 \\ 0 & 0 & 0 & 0 & 1 & 0 & 1 & 1 \\ 0 & 1 & 0 & 0 & 0 & 1 & 0 & 0 \\ 0 & 0 & 0 & 0 & 1 & 1 & 1 & 1 \\ 0 & 0 & 1 & 0 & 1 & 0 & 0 & 1 \\ 0 & 0 & 0 & 0 & 0 & 1 & 1 & 0 \\ 0 & 0 & 0 & 1 & 0 & 1 & 0 & 0 \\ 0 & 0 & 0 & 0 & 0 & 0 & 1 & 1 \end{pmatrix}.$$

Furthermore, we also need to make changes to the SubBytes transformation. If we consider SubBytes to be pure a table look-up of constants $S(x)$, we can compute a new look-up table S^2 by applying the R matrix and its inverse R^{-1} as follows: $S^2 = RS(R^{-1}x)$. If we consider the SubBytes transformation as inversion in $GF(2^8)$ followed by a multiplication by the affine matrix A and addition of the constant b, then the inversion stays unchanged while the new affine matrix A^2 is computed as $A^2 = RAR^{-1}$ and the new constant b^2 is computed (similar to the other constants, i.e., those of MixColums and key schedule) by multiplying it with the transformation matrix R: $b^2 = Rb$. Note that in the case of S^2 or A^2 no actual squaring is taking place.

If we consider the original cipher as E and the above described square dual cipher as E^2, by applying the same squaring routines again we can create a total of 8 square dual ciphers (up to E^{128} since E^{256} is equal to E in $GF(2^8)$). These square dual ciphers all use different constants and SubBytes transformations. According to the dual cipher concept, if the R matrices are multiplied with all input data bytes and key bytes and the result is transformed back by multiplying each output byte with the inverse matrix R^{-1}, the results of all ciphers when given the same input data and key will be equal. The differences in the internal structure, like the different S-box in SubBytes or the different coefficients in the MixColumns, also translates into e.g., different power consumption and EM emanations of a circuit implementing this technique. As denoted in [3], these differences in the internal structure of the dual ciphers might be usable as some kind of side-channel countermeasure. If the used dual cipher is randomly chosen, this could be comparable to a normal masking countermeasure.

Besides using square dual ciphers of the original AES-Rijndael, one can use the same transformation techniques as above to change all constants by using different generators a and reducing the a^i by the new irreducible polynomial. If the SubBytes transformation is not implemented as table look-up but as inversion plus affine, the inversion as well as all field multiplications as in MixColumns are then also performed using the new irreducible polynomial not the original one. This works for all 30 irreducible polynomials in $GF(2^8)$. Since there exist 8 generators for all irreducible polynomials representing the 8 square dual ciphers, as stated previously a total of 240 different non-trivial dual ciphers in $GF(2^8)$ exist. All generators, polynomials and constants of each of the 240 dual ciphers can be found in [4]. Note that we consider only dual ciphers using mappings in $GF(2^8)$ not such where other composite field representations are utilized, e.g., those presented in [27].

3   Our Design

The first design decision one has to make is whether to implement the SubBytes transformation purely based on look-up tables or if a general inversion circuit is used together with the affine matrix multiplication and constant addition. Since the area overhead to store 240 different complete S-boxes is massive, similar to [12] and [13] we opted to implement a general inversion circuit. Since we want to analyze the side-channel resistance of the original submission of dual-ciphers [3], this requires the inversion to be implemented in $GF(2^8)$ without the option to save on resources by utilizing inversions in composite fields or using a tower field approach [25, 29]. In other words, the inversion circuit must be general and valid for all the 30 irreducible polynomials mentioned in Section 2.

In order to prevent leakage through the timing channel during the inversion it is important to make the circuit time invariant. To achieve this one can make use of the fact that in $GF(2^8)$ x^{256} is equivalent to x, which leads to $x^{-1} \equiv x^{254}$.

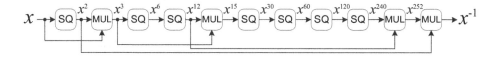

Fig. 1. Inversion circuit in $GF(2^8)$

Using addition chains this exponentiation can be implemented by a low number of modular multipliers and squaring circuits as depicted in Fig. 1. Note that the squaring step itself is free in $GF(2^8)$ and only requires hardware resources for the modular reduction.

For each possible dual cipher one needs to store the following parameters:

1. **Initial transformation matrix** R (64 bits), which is required to transform the original input data and key to the dual cipher representation.
2. **Inverse transformation matrix** R^{-1} (64 bits), required to transform the output of the AES computation from the dual cipher representation back to the original AES representation, precomputed as normal matrix inversion of R in $GF(2)$.
3. **Modular reduction polynomial** $\hat{p}$ (8 bits), to be used during all field multiplications (MixColumns) and the inversion steps (SubBytes).
4. **MixColumns coefficients** $\hat{mc}$ (2×8 bits). While the MixColumns coefficients originally are 8-bit elements of a 4×4 matrix, because the coefficients of each row are only a rotated variant of the first row and only two are not 01_x (in $GF(2^8)$), it is sufficient to store only these two transformed coefficients $(R(02_x), R(03_x))$.
5. **Affine matrix of SubBytes** $\hat{A}$ (64 bits), to apply the affine matrix multiplication step of the affine transformation. The matrix is computed as $\hat{A} = RAR^{-1}$, where A is the original affine matrix of the AES.
6. **Affine constant** $\hat{b}$ **of SubBytes** (8 bits), final addition step of the affine transformation. As for every other constant transformation this can be computed as $\hat{b} = Rb$, where b is the original affine constant, i.e., 63_x.
7. **Round constants (rcon) of the key scheduling** $\hat{rc}$ (10×8 bits). The rcons are constructed as $\hat{rc}(r) = (R\,02_x)^r \mod \hat{p}$, with r starting from 1 for the first round, $\hat{p}$ being the used irreducible polynomial, (02_x) the initial element, and R the transformation matrix. The rcons could also be computed on-the-fly which would only require the storage of the transformed $\hat{rc}_{init} = R\,02_x$ (8 bits). Since this would require another modular multiplier, we have opted to store all the precomputed rcons for each of the 240 dual ciphers.

The overall architecture of our evaluation circuit is depicted in Fig. 2. The initial transformations of the input data and key are performed prior to the general AES/dual cipher computation. After the full encryption is complete, the inverse transformation moves the result back to the original AES representation as described previously. The AES/dual cipher computation itself is implemented as round-based design, i.e., every round of AES requires one clock

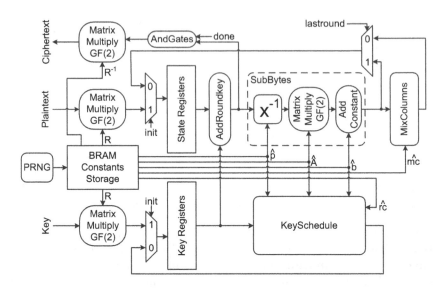

Fig. 2. Overall architecture of the AES dual ciphers circuit

cycle and the computation is finished after ten clock cycles excluding the initial and final transformations and data loading.

We chose to implement a round-based design because this is very common in real-world implementations when a hardware platform is targeted. The on-the-fly key scheduling seems to be the most suitable option since the roundkeys, which are different for each dual cipher, would otherwise require 41 kBytes of storage. We have implemented the whole design on a Virtex-5 LX50 FPGA mounted on a SASEBO-GII [1] (Side-channel Attack Standard Evaluation Board). In our implementation all the aforementioned parameters and constants are stored in block RAMs and are preloaded before every complete AES computation. The resource utilization is shown in Table 1. Compared to an unprotected design utilizing a more common S-box implementation based on look-up tables we require significantly more LUT resources. This is due to the 20 large general inversion circuits implemented in parallel (16 for the round function and 4 for the key scheduling) which are required to perform the inversion in every selectable dual cipher representation. The number of LUTs could be heavily reduced by using a composite field or tower field approach in the S-box design which, as stated

Table 1. Performance figures (excluding the PRNG)

Version	#LUTs	#FFs	#BRAMs	FREQ
Random Dual Cipher	13 481	651	6	21 MHz
General AES Enc Only	503	154	6	202 MHz

previously, we have not implemented at this point to enable a side-channel evaluation of the original dual cipher proposal. We should also highlight the very low maximum operation frequency of our design. It is due to the very long critical path of the inversion unit. Since it has to be general for any given irreducible polynomial, it could not be optimized with respect to both delay and area.

4 Evaluation

According to the explanation and the architecture figure given in the previous section, at the start of each encryption process the PRNG randomly selects one of the 240 dual ciphers and holds the outputs of the BRAM, i.e., constants and coefficients, until the whole of the encryption process is finished. If the selected dual cipher, whose index is denoted here by $1 \leq i \leq 240$, is unknown to the adversary, the intermediate values cannot be predicted. Therefore, it can be seen as a kind of a masking scheme on which certain side-channel attacks are supposed to be infeasible. However, below we address a few issues which significantly affect the robustness of the scheme.

Mask Reuse. All intermediate values and inputs are transformed to a new domain by means of the selected transformation matrix R_i. It means that all 16 plaintext bytes are transformed using the same transformation. It can be seen as similar as the *mask reuse* issue in masking schemes. In the case of e.g., a boolean masking when two S-boxes get the inputs masked by the same mask value, a classical linear collision attack [6] might be able to recover the corresponding key bytes difference [9]. The same holds for the dual ciphers case; all the S-boxes compute the inversion using the same parameters and their inputs have been transformed using the same matrix. By help of side-channel leakages once a collision between two S-boxes is detected

$$S_i(R_i(x^{(1)} \oplus k^{(1)})) = S_i(R_i(x^{(2)} \oplus k^{(2)})),$$

the linear key difference $k^{(1)} \oplus k^{(2)}$ is revealed as $x^{(1)} \oplus x^{(2)}$, where $x^{(j)}$ and $k^{(j)}$ denote the j-th byte of the given plaintext and key. However, in the case of our design, which realizes a round-based architecture, this issue can be ignored since the side-channel leakage of different S-boxes in a round cannot be separated making the collision detection infeasible.

Concurrent Processing of Mask and the Masked Data. In contrast to software implementations of masking, preventing univariate leakages when the target platform is hardware is a challenging task. It is due to the glitches of the circuit, e.g., a masked S-box, when processing both mask and the masked data at the same time. This issue has been seen in many different realizations of masking in hardware (see [19–21]). Our implementation of dual ciphers suffers from this problem as well. The SubBytes unit gets the transformed key-whitened input as well as the irreducible polynomial $\hat{p}$, affine matrix coefficients $\hat{A}$, etc.

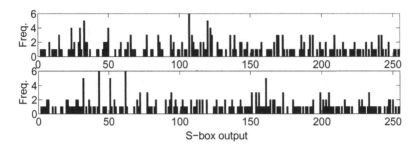

Fig. 3. Distributions of the S-box output for (top) 11_x and (bottom) 44_x as original input over all 240 dual ciphers

All these parameters are independent of the transformed input. Therefore, the side-channel leakage of e.g., the S-box circuit due to its glitches is not independent of its original (untransformed) input. Hence it is expected that a univariate attack, e.g., a CPA [7] with an appropriate power model or a MIA [14], will be able to recover the relation between the leakages and the secret materials.

Unbalance. Having the lemmas and properties given in [22, 23] in mind, we explain this issue as follows. For the sake of simplicity suppose a masking scheme which maps an input value x into its masked representation x_m for a given mask m as $x_m = x * m$. In order to guarantee the balance of the distributions the conditional probability

$$\Pr(x_m = X_M | x)$$

must be constant for $\forall x$ and the given X_M by which we mean a realization of x_m. In other words, if $f_x(x_m)$ represents the probability density function of x_m for the given x, each pair of probability distributions $f_{x=X^1}(x_m)$ and $f_{x=X^2}(x_m)$ must be equal, where X^1 and X^2 are two realizations of x. Otherwise, when two distributions are different, their corresponding side-channel leakages can be distinguished from each other. Therefore, it may lead to detecting whether X^1 or X^2 is processed. This property should hold for all intermediate values at all steps of the scheme. However, it is not true for the case of dual ciphers. For example, we considered the S-box output and computed the probability distributions for two original input values 11_x and 44_x over all 240 cases. Two different resulting histograms are shown by Fig. 3, clearly indicating the unbalance of intermediate values. Therefore, it is expected that a univariate side-channel attack can be successfully mounted.

Zero Value. There is a general problem in multiplicative masking schemes, i.e., masking the zero value. That is because regardless of the mask m, input value $x = 0$ never gets masked. Therefore, a CPA attack using the zero-value power model [15] can easily overcome the protection. The same problem holds for the dual cipher approach. Because of the linearity of the transformation, i.e.,

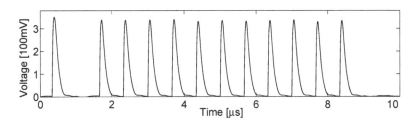

Fig. 4. A sample power trace, PRNG ON

multiplication by the matrix R in GF(2), the zero input is always transformed to itself in all 240 cases. It is indeed a special case of the unbalanced distributions. The distribution for the zero value $f_{x=0}(x_m)$ shows the certainty of x_m and is much different to all other distributions when $x \neq 0$. Therefore, a zero-value CPA attack targeting the S-box input should break the implementation.

Before moving toward practical results, we would like to comment on these issues when not only 240 AES dual ciphers are considered but also when one can take more from those 61 200 cases of [27]. Regardless of the existence and its difficulty one may find a set of 255 dual ciphers which satisfy the *balance* property. Note that because of the zero-value issue, a set of 256 dual ciphers can never satisfy the property. On the other hand, if the desired condition is fulfilled considering e.g., the S-box input, keeping the balance property for the S-box output cannot be certainly justified because each dual cipher employs a different S-box. Therefore, it seems that the balance property can never be fully satisfied. In short, for any selection of the dual ciphers all the aforementioned problems stay valid theoretically making the scheme vulnerable to certain attacks.

4.1   Practical Investigations

As stated before, our practical experiences are based on a SASEBO-GII [1] platform. The design was implemented on the crypto FPGA of the board, a Virtex-5 LX50. The crypto core receives the plaintext and by means of the stored key performs the whole of the encryption operation while the dual cipher index i is internally generated by a PRNG. A LeCroy HRO66Zi 600MHz digital oscilloscope at the sampling rate of 1GS/s was used to measure the power consumption of the crypto core over a 1Ω resistor in the VDD path (oscilloscope in AC mode). In order to reduce the electronic noise the bandwidth of the oscilloscope was set to 20MHz, and the crypto core was running at the clock frequency of 1.5MHz during the whole of our practical experiments.

A sample power trace clearly indicating the round computations is shown in Fig. 4. The first peak between 0 and $1\mu s$ is due to the selection of the dual cipher. At this clock cycle the corresponding parameters of the selected dual cipher appear at the BRAMs' output causing glitches and activities in whole of the circuit. We should also highlight the very high power consumption of the design resulting in more than 300 mV peak-to-peak power traces.

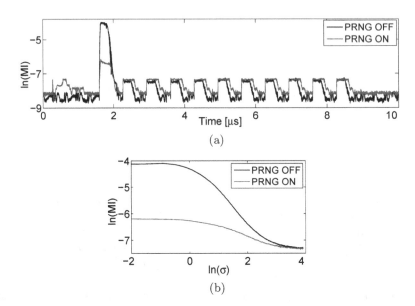

Fig. 5. Mutual information based on an S-box output, using 2 000 000 traces (a) curves over time, (b) over added noise standard deviation

Following the information theoretic metric of [30] to examine the amount of information available through the power traces we computed the mutual information based on the output of an S-box module in the first round. In order to examine the level of protection provided by the scheme, we also collected the power consumption traces of the design when the PRNG is OFF thereby selecting the original AES parameters. In both cases we used 2 000 000 traces to make the mutual information curves shown in Fig. 5(a). It indeed shows that compared to the unprotected case – considering the same amount of traces – the scheme can reduce information available to be recovered by an adversary. Figure 5(b) compares the mutual information of these two cases in presence of noise. In order to make this figure we artificially added Gaussian noise to the collected traces.

The shown figures confirm our theoretical discussions on the available univariate leakages which can be used by different attacks. In order to check the feasibility of a successful attack we mounted a correlation collision attack [21] making use of the first-order moments. We targeted two S-boxes of the first round and tried to recover their corresponding key difference. The result of the attacks is depicted in Fig. 6. As expected, the attack is successful though compared to the unprotected case the number of required traces increased from less than 5000 to 100 000.

We also examined the feasibility of a zero-value attack whose results are represented by Fig. 7. The graphics confirm our theoretical claims that a zero-value attack is amongst the weakest points of the scheme since using a very low number of traces of 10 000 one can overcome the provided protection.

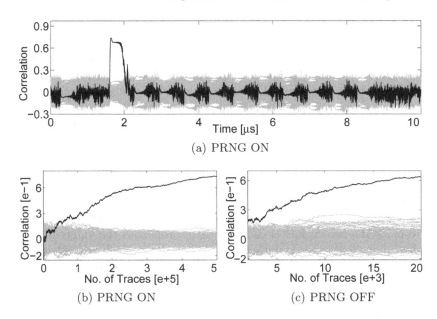

Fig. 6. Correlation Collision attack results, (a) using 500 000 traces, (b) and (c) over the number of traces

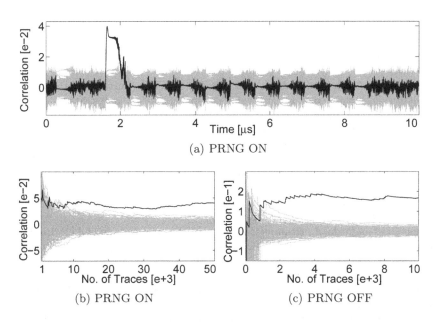

Fig. 7. Zero-value attack results, (a) using 100 000 traces, (b) and (c) over the number of traces

5   Conclusions

In this work we have taken an in-depth look at the AES-Rijndael dual cipher concept from a side-channel point of view. We have implemented an evaluation circuit which is able to perform AES computations using randomly chosen dual ciphers. The inversion part of the circuit operates in $GF(2^8)$, as in the original dual cipher contribution [3], giving a total choice of 240 different internal computations with correspondingly different side-channel leakage characteristics.

Besides providing practical evidence of the vulnerability of this original dual cipher implementation to several side-channel attacks, we have also described some of the general flaws of the scheme when considered as a side-channel countermeasure. This includes the mask reuse, the concurrent operations on both mask and the masked data, the violation of the *balance* property, and the inability to mask the zero value. Because of these properties the vulnerability of dual cipher implementations is not only limited to those which are restricted to a low amount of possible transformations by focusing on mappings in $GF(2^8)$. Even when one would be able to select between several thousand dual ciphers using composite fields, as given in [27], the described weaknesses still exist and would enable an attacker to successfully extract the secret key. In conclusion, even when ignoring the large area overhead of the circuit in comparison to other lighter masking schemes, AES-Rijndael dual ciphers are unsuitable as a side-channel countermeasure and can be broken using modest efforts and simple attack models.

References

1. Side-channel attack standard evaluation board (sasebo). Further information are available via, http://www.morita-tech.co.jp/SASEBO/en/index.html
2. Akkar, M.-L., Giraud, C.: An Implementation of DES and AES, Secure against Some Attacks. In: Koç, Ç.K., Naccache, D., Paar, C. (eds.) CHES 2001. LNCS, vol. 2162, pp. 309–318. Springer, Heidelberg (2001)
3. Barkan, E., Biham, E.: In How Many Ways Can You Write Rijndael? In: Zheng, Y. (ed.) ASIACRYPT 2002. LNCS, vol. 2501, pp. 160–175. Springer, Heidelberg (2002)
4. Barkan, E., Biham, E.: The Book of Rijndaels. Cryptology ePrint Archive, Report 2002/158 (2002), http://eprint.iacr.org/
5. Blömer, J., Guajardo, J., Krummel, V.: Provably Secure Masking of AES. In: Handschuh, H., Hasan, M.A. (eds.) SAC 2004. LNCS, vol. 3357, pp. 69–83. Springer, Heidelberg (2004)
6. Bogdanov, A.: Multiple-Differential Side-Channel Collision Attacks on AES. In: Oswald, E., Rohatgi, P. (eds.) CHES 2008. LNCS, vol. 5154, pp. 30–44. Springer, Heidelberg (2008)
7. Brier, E., Clavier, C., Olivier, F.: Correlation Power Analysis with a Leakage Model. In: Joye, M., Quisquater, J.-J. (eds.) CHES 2004. LNCS, vol. 3156, pp. 16–29. Springer, Heidelberg (2004)

8. Canright, D., Batina, L.: A Very Compact "Perfectly Masked" S-Box for AES. In: Bellovin, S.M., Gennaro, R., Keromytis, A.D., Yung, M. (eds.) ACNS 2008. LNCS, vol. 5037, pp. 446–459. Springer, Heidelberg (2008); the corrected version at Cryptology ePrint Archive, Report 2009/011 http://eprint.iacr.org/.
9. Clavier, C., Feix, B., Gagnerot, G., Roussellet, M., Verneuil, V.: Improved Collision-Correlation Power Analysis on First Order Protected AES. In: Preneel, B., Takagi, T. (eds.) CHES 2011. LNCS, vol. 6917, pp. 49–62. Springer, Heidelberg (2011)
10. Genelle, L., Prouff, E., Quisquater, M.: Secure Multiplicative Masking of Power Functions. In: Zhou, J., Yung, M. (eds.) ACNS 2010. LNCS, vol. 6123, pp. 200–217. Springer, Heidelberg (2010)
11. Genelle, L., Prouff, E., Quisquater, M.: Thwarting Higher-Order Side Channel Analysis with Additive and Multiplicative Maskings. In: Preneel, B., Takagi, T. (eds.) CHES 2011. LNCS, vol. 6917, pp. 240–255. Springer, Heidelberg (2011)
12. Ghellar, F., Lubaszewski, M.: A novel AES cryptographic core highly resistant to differential power analysis attacks. In: Integrated Circuits and Systems Design - SBCCI 2008, pp. 140–145. ACM (2008)
13. Ghellar, F., Lubaszewski, M.: A novel AES cryptographic core highly resistant to differential power analysis attacks. Journal Integrated Circuits and Systems 4(1), 29–35 (2009)
14. Gierlichs, B., Batina, L., Tuyls, P., Preneel, B.: Mutual Information Analysis. In: Oswald, E., Rohatgi, P. (eds.) CHES 2008. LNCS, vol. 5154, pp. 426–442. Springer, Heidelberg (2008)
15. Golić, J.D., Tymen, C.: Multiplicative Masking and Power Analysis of AES. In: Kaliski Jr., B.S., Koç, Ç.K., Paar, C. (eds.) CHES 2002, vol. 2523, pp. 198–212. Springer, Heidelberg (2003)
16. Jing, M.-H., Chen, J.-H., Chen, Z.-H., Chang, Y.: The Secure DAES Design for Embedded System Application. In: Denko, M.K., et al. (eds.) EUC-WS 2007. LNCS, vol. 4809, pp. 617–626. Springer, Heidelberg (2007)
17. Jing, M.-H., Chen, Z.-H., Chen, J.-H., Chen, Y.-H.: Reconfigurable system for high-speed and diversified AES using FPGA. Microprocessors and Microsystems 31(2), 94–102 (2007)
18. Mangard, S., Oswald, E., Popp, T.: Power Analysis Attacks: Revealing the Secrets of Smart Cards. Springer (2007)
19. Mangard, S., Pramstaller, N., Oswald, E.: Successfully Attacking Masked AES Hardware Implementations. In: Rao, J.R., Sunar, B. (eds.) CHES 2005. LNCS, vol. 3659, pp. 157–171. Springer, Heidelberg (2005)
20. Moradi, A., Mischke, O.: How Far Should Theory Be from Practice? In: Prouff, E., Schaumont, P. (eds.) CHES 2012. LNCS, vol. 7428, pp. 92–106. Springer, Heidelberg (2012)
21. Moradi, A., Mischke, O., Eisenbarth, T.: Correlation-Enhanced Power Analysis Collision Attack. In: Mangard, S., Standaert, F.-X. (eds.) CHES 2010. LNCS, vol. 6225, pp. 125–139. Springer, Heidelberg (2010)
22. Nikova, S., Rechberger, C., Rijmen, V.: Threshold Implementations Against Side-Channel Attacks and Glitches. In: Ning, P., Qing, S., Li, N. (eds.) ICICS 2006. LNCS, vol. 4307, pp. 529–545. Springer, Heidelberg (2006)
23. Nikova, S., Rijmen, V., Schläffer, M.: Secure Hardware Implementation of Nonlinear Functions in the Presence of Glitches. J. Cryptology 24(2), 292–321 (2011)
24. Oswald, E., Mangard, S., Pramstaller, N., Rijmen, V.: A Side-Channel Analysis Resistant Description of the AES S-Box. In: Gilbert, H., Handschuh, H. (eds.) FSE 2005. LNCS, vol. 3557, pp. 413–423. Springer, Heidelberg (2005)

25. Paar, C.: Efficient VLSI Architectures for Bit-Parallel Computation in Galois Fields. PhD thesis, Institute for Experimental Mathematics, University of Essen, Germany (1994)
26. Prouff, E., Roche, T.: Higher-Order Glitches Free Implementation of the AES Using Secure Multi-party Computation Protocols. In: Preneel, B., Takagi, T. (eds.) CHES 2011. LNCS, vol. 6917, pp. 63–78. Springer, Heidelberg (2011)
27. Raddum, H.: More Dual Rijndaels. In: Dobbertin, H., Rijmen, V., Sowa, A. (eds.) AES 2005. LNCS, vol. 3373, pp. 142–147. Springer, Heidelberg (2005)
28. Rivain, M., Prouff, E.: Provably Secure Higher-Order Masking of AES. In: Mangard, S., Standaert, F.-X. (eds.) CHES 2010. LNCS, vol. 6225, pp. 413–427. Springer, Heidelberg (2010)
29. Satoh, A., Morioka, S., Takano, K., Munetoh, S.: A Compact Rijndael Hardware Architecture with S-Box Optimization. In: Boyd, C. (ed.) ASIACRYPT 2001. LNCS, vol. 2248, pp. 239–254. Springer, Heidelberg (2001)
30. Standaert, F.-X., Malkin, T.G., Yung, M.: A Unified Framework for the Analysis of Side-Channel Key Recovery Attacks. In: Joux, A. (ed.) EUROCRYPT 2009. LNCS, vol. 5479, pp. 443–461. Springer, Heidelberg (2009)
31. Wu, S.-Y., Lu, S.-C., Laih, C.-S.: Design of AES Based on Dual Cipher and Composite Field. In: Okamoto, T. (ed.) CT-RSA 2004. LNCS, vol. 2964, pp. 25–38. Springer, Heidelberg (2004)

EMD-Based Denoising for Side-Channel Attacks and Relationships between the Noises Extracted with Different Denoising Methods

Mingliang Feng[1], Yongbin Zhou[1,*], and Zhenmei Yu[2]

[1] State Key Laboratory of Information Security,
Institute of Information Engineering, Chinese Academy of Sciences,
89-A, Mingzhuang Rd, Beijing, 100093, P.R. China
{fengmingliang,zhouyongbin}@iie.ac.cn
[2] School of Information Technology,
Shandong Womens University,
45, Yuhan Rd, Jinan, 250002, P.R. China
yuzhenmei@gmail.com

Abstract. In essence, side-channel leakages produced during the execution of crypto implementations are noisy physical measurements. It turns out that various noises contained in leakages have, in general, negative effects on the key-recovery efficiency of side-channel attacks. Therefore, in practice, frequency-based denoising methods are presented and in wide use nowadays. However, most of them for reducing noises of high-frequency are not always effective, and they sometimes do little or even no help. On the other hand, the relationship between noises extracted with different denoising methods that target different frequencies, in time-domain, is not being discussed, which in turn will determine the potential power of combining these denoising methods. Motivated by this, we present two empirical mode decomposition (EMD) based denoising methods for side-channel attacks, and study their effectiveness in reducing noises of high frequency in real power traces. Compared with their counterparts, EMD-based denoising methods achieve both effectiveness and stability. Furthermore, we investigate the relationships between the noises extracted with denoising methods that target different frequencies, by performing attacks on real power traces denoised by multiple combinations of different denoising methods. For this purpose, we define the notion of overlapping coefficient, which measures how much that noises are overlapped with each other. Our results and observations are evidently verified by correlation power analysis attacks on multiple real power traces sets.

Keywords: Side-channel Cryptanalysis, Correlation Power Analysis, Empirical Mode Decomposition, Noise Reduction, Overlapping Coefficient.

---

* Corresponding author.

S. Qing et al. (Eds.): ICICS 2013, LNCS 8233, pp. 259–274, 2013.
© Springer International Publishing Switzerland 2013

1   Introduction

Side-channel attack (SCA) aims at recovering the secret information embedded in a crypto devices from its physical leakages, including execution time[15], power consumption[1], and electromagnetic emanation[16]. Among those, power analysis attack which uses the instantaneous power consumption of crypto devices as its side-channel leakage is one of the most widely researched powerful side-channel attacks.

Generally, SCA consists of two stages: leakage acquisition and leakage exploitation. Concerning the latter, a number of power analysis attacks have been proposed so far, which are also referred to as distinguishers. Among them, differential power analysis (DPA) [1] is the most original one, which was then extended to other more powerful variants such as correlation power analysis (CPA) [2]. CPA is an effective method for finding the secret key based on the correlation between the hypothetical power consumption and the actual power consumption. Recent work [8] shows that side-channel distinguishers are not only asymptotically equivalent, but also can be rewritten one in function of the other only by modifying the power model. In particular, they have established one equivalence between most univariate side-channel distinguishers and CPA performed with different leakage models.

Even though the main focus of SCA is leakage exploitation, leakage acquisition also plays a critical role, as acquisition itself is the physical requisite for mounting power analysis attacks. The outputs of acquisition process are often referred to as power traces. Because of the electronic characteristics of the physical implementation, power traces always contain not only useful side-channel information which benefits cryptanalysts, but also a variety of noises which are found to have negative effects on side-channel attacks [14]. Therefore, to reduce noises inherent in power traces is commonly believed to be, in general, an effective approach enhancing the performance of power analysis attacks.

Up to now, a number of noise reduction methods have been proposed to reduce noises contained in power traces after sampling, i.e. to increase the signal-to-noise ratio (SNR). Generally speaking, those denoising methods can be roughly divided into two categories: frequency-based and non frequency-based. Frequency-based methods are the most popular one and in wide use in practice, which include wavelet-based methods [3] [4] and trend removal method (TR) [5]. Wavelet-based methods mainly target noise components of high frequency, while TR mainly targets that of low frequency. In [3], one applies wavelet transform to original power traces from a hardware implementation of unprotected DES on smart card, producing an approximation sub-signal. Afterwards, one performs DPA on the approximation sub-signal. In [4], one also applies wavelet transform into original power traces to obtain the approximation sub-signal and the detail sub-signal. The difference between [3] and [4] is that the latter sets a specific threshold value for the detail sub-signal, while the former sets the detail coefficients that dissatisfy the threshold to zero. Afterwards, one reconstructs the power traces and then performs power analysis attacks on the reconstructed power traces. Principal component analysis (PCA) [6] belongs to the non frequency-based method, because it identifies trends in a whole trace set instead of a single trace. In [6], one applies PCA to original power traces, and then performs a DPA attack on a PCA-transformed power traces. Actually, the effects of PCA in practical attacks against hardware crypto implementations like that used in DPA contest v2 are very limited, and sometimes even negative [5]. However, we focus on frequency-based methods only.Frequency-based methods are most frequently used, yet there is one technical drawback: they are not always effective, and sometimes they do little or even no help, in practice. This drawback is again confirmed by one recent work of [5]. Therefore, a very natural and pertinent question arises at this point, namely, is there any effectively stable and easy-to-use denoising method dealing with high frequency noises? Another problem relates to the combination of denoising methods that target different frequencies [5]. Noise components of different frequencies will locate at distinct places with frequency domain, and they will overlap to some extent with each other in time domain. Then, how much is this overlap? This problem makes sense, because power analysis attacks examine the leakages in time domain. And this also determines how best the combination of different denoising methods would be.

Main contributions of this paper are two-fold. Firstly, we present two empirical model decomposition (EMD) [9] based denoising methods that target noises of high frequency for SCA, and address some technical issues concerning their applications. Both of these methods achieve effectiveness and stability. Secondly, we study the relationship of the noises extracted with different denoising methods. For this purpose, we define the notion of overlapping coefficient, which measures how much that noises are overlapped with each other.

The rest of this paper is organized as follows. Section 2 briefly introduces some background knowledge. Section 3 presents EMD-based denoising Methods for power analysis attacks in practice. Section 4 discusses the relationship between noises extracted with different denoising methods. Section 5 presents our experiments against real power traces from two kind of typical crypto implementations. Section 6 concludes the whole paper.

2   Preliminaries

In this section, we will present some basic knowledge, including composition of power traces, the general relationship between SNR and CPA, and EMD-based denoising methods in signal processing.

2.1   Composition of Power Trace

Power analysis attacks exploit the fact that the power consumption of cryptographic modules is correlated to the operations performed and the data processed. For each single point of a power trace, we denote the operation-dependent component by P_{op}, the data-dependent component by P_{data}. Due to the characteristics of the physical implementation, the power measurements are not always the same even if the operation performed and data manipulated are fixed. We refer to this noise component of power consumption as $P_{el.noise}$. Besides these three components, each point in a power trace also has a constant component denoted by P_{const} (which is, for example, caused by leakage currents). Therefore, we can define each point of a power trace by (1).

$$P = P_{op} + P_{data} + P_{el.noise} + P_{const} \qquad (1)$$

Given the fact that different power analysis attacks often exploit different properties of P_{op} and P_{data}, we refer to the components that exploited by a given attack as P_{exp}. And we refer to the rest part that is not exploitable of P_{op} and P_{data} combined with $P_{el.noise}$ as P_{noise}. So we can rewrite (1) to (2) in a given attack scenario.

$$P = P_{exp} + P_{noise} + P_{const} \qquad (2)$$

2.2 General Relationship between SNR and CPA

SNR is the signal to noise ratio. Under our assumption and in a given attack scenario, SNR of a set of power traces at a fixed point is given by (3), in which $var(x)$ denotes the variance of x.

$$SNR = \frac{var(P_{exp})}{var(P_{noise})} \qquad (3)$$

SNR quantifies the amount of information that leaks from a point of a set of power traces. The equation $\rho(H_i, P) = \rho(H_i, P_{exp})/\sqrt{1 + 1/SNR}$ [14] shows the relationship among the correlation coefficient $\rho(H_i, P)$ between the hypothetical power consumption values and the real power consumption values, the correlation coefficient $\rho(H_i, P_{exp})$ between the hypothetical power consumption values and the real side-channel leakages and SNR. It can be seen that the increase of SNR can effectively enhance the value of $\rho(H_i, P)$ with a given power traces. Besides this, in [14] the number of power traces needed to break a cryptographic implementation by CPA which is referred to as n can be estimated by (4),

$$n = 3 + 8\frac{Z_{1-\alpha}^2}{ln^2\frac{1+\rho(H_{ck},P)}{1-\rho(H_{ck},P)}} \qquad (4)$$

where $Z_{1-\alpha}$ is a quintile of a normal distribution for a 2-sided confidence interval with error $1 - \alpha$. From the above formulas (3) and (4) it can be easily deduced that with the decrease of SNR, the traces number n will become bigger, and the attack will become more difficult. In order to improve the performance of power analysis attacks on given traces, attackers have to reduce the noise part P_{noise} in power traces as much as possible to enhance SNR.

2.3 Empirical Mode Decomposition and EMD-Based Denoising

In this section, we will introduce the empirical mode decomposition (EMD) method [9], and then describe two typical EMD based denoising methods: conventional EMD denoising and iterative EMD interval thresholding denoising.

Empirical Mode Decomposition in Signal Processing

The EMD method is an algorithm for the analysis of multicomponent signal [10] that breaks them down into a number of amplitude and frequency modulated (AM/FM) zero-mean signals, termed intrinsic mode functions (IMFs). In contrast to conventional decomposition methods such as wavelets, which perform the analysis by projecting the signal under consideration onto a number of predefined basis vectors, EMD expresses the signal as an expansion of basis functions that are signal-dependent and are estimated via an iterative procedure called sifting. Next we will give EMD a brief description and notation.

EMD [9] adaptively decomposes a multicomponent signal [10] $x(t)$ into a number L of the so-called IMFs $I^{(i)}(t)$ and a remainder $d(t)$ as formula (5). Here $d(t)$ is a remainder that is non-zero-mean slowly varying function with only few extrema. Each one of the IMFs, say, the ith one $I^{(i)}(t)$, is estimated with the aid of an iterative process, called sifting, applied to the residual multicomponent signal $x^{(i)}(t)$.

$$x(t) = \sum_{i=1}^{L} I^{(i)}(t) + d(t) \qquad 1 \le i \le L \tag{5}$$

$$x^{(i)}(t) = \begin{cases} x(t) & i = 1 \\ x(t) - \sum_{j=1}^{i-1} I^{(j)}(t) & i \ge 2 \end{cases} \tag{6}$$

The sifting process used in this paper is the standard one [9]. According to this, during the $(n+1)th$ sifting iteration, the temporary IMF estimate $I_n^{(i)}(t)$ is improving according to the following steps. [1]

1) Find the local maxima and mimima $I_n^{(i)}(t)$

2) Interpolate, using natural cubic splines, along the points of $I_n^{(i)}(t)$ estimated in the first step in order to form an upper and a lower envelope

3) Compute the mean of the two envelopes $m_n^{(i)}$

4) Obtain the refined estimate $I_{n+1}^{(i)}(t)$ of the IMF by subtracting the mean $m_n^{(i)}$ found in the previous step from the current IMF estimate $I_n^{(i)}(t)$.

5) Check whether a stopping criterion has been fulfilled. If not, proceed from 1) again

Supposing the procedure above runs N times before we getting the ith IMF $I^{(i)}(t)$, then the following formula must be fulfilled.

$$I^{(i)}(t) = x^{(i)}(t) - \sum_{j=1}^{N} m_j^{(i)} \tag{7}$$

What's more all IMFs have the following properties:
1) Zero mean
2) All the maxima and all the minima of $I^{(i)}(t)$ will be positive and negative respectively

---

[1] For the first iteration, $x^{(i)}(t)$ is used as temporary IMF estimate $I_1^{(i)}(t)$.

Often, but not always, the IMFs resemble sinusoids that are both amplitude and frequency modulated. By construction, the number of, say, $N(i)$ extrema of $I^{(i)}(t)$ positioned at time instances $r^{(i)} = [r_1^{(i)}, r_2^{(i)}, ..., r_{N(i)}^{(i)}]$ and the corresponding IMF points $I^{(i)}(r_j^{(i)}), j = 1, ..., N(i)$ will alternate between maxima and minima. As a result, in any pair of extrema, $z_j^{(i)} = [I^{(i)}(r_j^{(i)}), I^{(i)}(r_{j+1}^{(i)})]$ corresponds to a single zero-crossing interval. Whats more, each IMF occupies lower frequencies locally in the time-frequency domain than its preceding ones. Fig. 1 presents an example the EMD of a real noisy trace signal(Fig. 1(a)), and this EMD process results in seven IMFs and a final remainder(Fig. 1(b)-(i)).

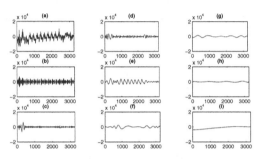

Fig. 1. A Real Noisy Trace(shown in (a)) and its EMD Components (shown in (b)-(i))

Conventional EMD Denoising

The conventional EMD denoising (EMD-Conv) method here refers to the method in [11]. The main idea is to discard the IMFs of which the main components are noises. And it is usually considered that noises exist mainly in the high frequency domain, In other words, it exists in the first few IMFs.

$$\widetilde{x}(t) = \sum_{i=M_1}^{L} I^{(i)}(t) + d(t) \qquad (8)$$

In the above formula, $\widetilde{x}(t)$ is the signal after the noise reduction, and M_1 can be determined in the way that used in [11], and it can be described as below.

1) Calculate the actual IMF energies using a robust estimator based on the components median [12]

$$E_k = \left(\frac{median(I^{(k)}(t))}{0.6745} \right)^2 \qquad k = 1, 2, 3 \ldots \qquad (9)$$

2) Calculate the noise-only IMF energies. And they can be approximated according to

$$\widetilde{E_k} = \frac{E_1}{\beta}\rho^{-k} \qquad k = 2,3,4\dots \tag{10}$$

where E_1 is the energy of the first IMF and β,ρ are parameters that for a specific EMD implementation, depend mainly on the number of sifting iterations used. It is suggested in [11] that setting β and ρ to be 0.719 and 2.01 respectively is a good choice. This paper also adopts this choice.

3) Compare the energies from the first IMF between the actual and the theoretical ones. If the energies significant diverge from each other at the ith IMF, indicating the presence of significant amounts of no-noise signal, then we can assign i to the parameter M_1.

Fig. 2 is an example of using conventional EMD denoising method on a noisy signal, where the blue line is the original noisy signal and the red line represents the denoised one.

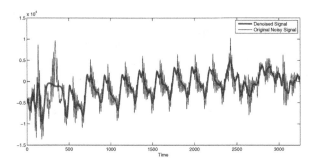

Fig. 2. Conventional EMD Denoising

Iterative EMD Interval Thresholding Denoising

The iterative EMD interval thresholding (EMD-IIT) denoising method was first introduced in [13]. The main idea of it is to enhance the tolerance against noise by averaging a number of denoised versions of the signal which are obtained iteratively. Before introducing the EMD-IIT method, we should get an understanding of the EMD interval thresholding method (EMD-IT), which is also introduced in [13]. The main idea of the EMD-IT is to reconstruct the denoised signal by

$$\widetilde{x}(t) = \sum_{i=M_1}^{M_2} \bar{I}^{(i)}(t) + \sum_{i=M_2+1}^{L} I^{(i)}(t) + d(t) \tag{11}$$

Here the $\bar{I}^{(i)}(t)$ is calculated as the formula (12)

$$\bar{I}^{(i)}(z_j^{(i)}) = \begin{cases} I^{(i)}(z_j^{(i)}) & |I^{(i)}(r_j^{(i)})| > T_i \\ 0 & |I^{(i)}(r_j^{(i)})| \leq T_i \end{cases} \tag{12}$$

where $T_i = C\sqrt{\tilde{E}_i 2lnN}$ and C is a constant. For consant C, choosing one value between 0.6 and 0.8 is usually a good choice [13]. $\tilde{E}_i$ is calculated using (10). N is the sample number of the signal. Now we can go to an in-depth study of EMD-IIT, it can be summarized as the following steps.

1) Perform an EMD expansion of the original noisy signal x.

2) Perform a partial reconstruction using the last $L - 1$ IMFs and the remainder only, $x_p(t) = \sum_{i=2}^{L} I^{(i)}(t) + d(t)$

3) Randomly alter the sample positions of the first IMF $I_a^{(1)}(t) = Alter(I^{(1)}(t))$.

4) Construct a different noisy version of the original signal $x_a(t) = x_p(t) + I_a^{(1)}(t)$

5) Perform EMD on the new altered noisy signal $x_a(t)$.

6) Perform the EMD-IT denoising using formula (12) on the IMFs of $x_a(t)$ to obtain a denoised version $\tilde{x}_1(t)$ of x

7) Iterate $K - 1$ times between 3)-6), where K is the number of averaging iterations in order to obtain K denoised versions of x , i.e., $\tilde{x}_1, \tilde{x}_2, , \tilde{x}_K$.

8) Average the resulted denoised signals $\tilde{x}(t) = (1/K)\sum_{k=1}^{K} \tilde{x}_k(t)$.

The altering function can take several forms, in this paper we use random permutation approach recommended by [13], in other words, the samples of the first IMF change their positions randomly.

3   EMD-Based Denoising Methods for SCA

Frequency-based denoising methods are in wide use nowadays. However, most of them for reducing noises of high-frequency are not always effective, and sometimes they do little or even no help. Therefore, for practical purpose, a more effectively stable method that target noise of high frequency is highly desirable. To address this problem, we introduce two EMD-based denoising methods into the filed of SCA. Applications of EMD-based denoising in power analysis attacks involves some technical issues and appear to be tricky, even though these methods are relatively mature in the field of signal processing.

Before talking about how to use two typical EMD-based denoising methods in power analysis attacks, we would define some key parameters concerned, which are summarized in Table 1. First of all, we present conventional EMD-Conv for SCA and show how it works. In this case, one applies EMD-Conv denoising to every single trace contained in the trace set, and then produce a new trace set. The corresponding process is shown in Algorithm 1.

Table 1. Definition of Parameters Used in EMD-Based Denoising Methods

Parameter Name	Description of Parameter
$Traceset$	a set of power traces
$Trace_i$	the i_{th} power trace in the traces set $Traceset$
$Tracenum$	the number of traces in the traces set
$Traceset'$	a set of new power traces that have been denoised
$Trace_i'$	a denoised trace that generated by $Trace_i$
M_1	the starting order of IMF that is used to reconstruct a denoised signal
IM_2	$M_2 = L - IM_2$, meaning the last $IM_2 - 1$ IMFs and the remainder do not get thresholded
C	it is a ocnstant coefficient of getting T_i, $T_i = C\sqrt{\widetilde{E_i}2\ln N}$
$Siftnum$	maximum number of the sifting progress to get an IMF in EMD
$Iteration$	the average number to get a denoised signal in EMD-IIT

Algorithm 1. EMD-Conv for SCA

Input: $Traceset, M_1, siftnum$
Output: $Traceset'$
1: **function** EMDCONVFORSCA($Traceset, M_1, siftnum$)
2:     $i \leftarrow 1$
3:     **while** $i <= Tracenum$ **do**
4:         $Trace_i' \leftarrow EMD - Conv(Trace_i, M_1, siftnum)$
5:     **end while**
6:     **return** $Traceset'$
7: **end function**

In Algorithm 1, M_1 can de determined according to the method introduced in section 2.3, and $siftnum$ is an optional parameter. If $siftnum$ is not set, the sifting progress will not end until a default stopping criterion has been fulfilled, which would be very time-consuming. Therefore, in practice, choosing one value between 10-16 of $siftnum$ is a good balance between effectiveness and time-efficiency.

Next, we will introduce more effective EMD-IIT method into SCA and show how it works. The EMD-IIT transformation from one original dataset of power traces into a new dataset, shown in Algorithm 2, is the same as that in EMD-Conv transformation. Contrary to the case of EMD-Conv, in this case,. according to [13], it has been empirically found that a very good choice of M_1 is given by $M_1 = max(1, J - 2)$, where J is the order that used in EMD-Conv as a starting order to reconstruct a denoised signal. Usually, a good choice of M_2 is $L - 1$. In other words, the last IMF and the remainder do not get thresholded. For parameter C, the values between 0.6 and 0.8 is often the best choice, but not always. In general, a balanced tradeoff between the number of sifting ($siftnum$) and the performance of EMD-IIT is realized with about eight sifting iterations. The final parameter $Iteration$ can be set to a value between 10 and 20. Note that, unlike using EMD-IIT in the field of signal processing, for EMD-IIT to be correctly used in SCA, all traces must use the same permutation matrix, or it will lead to a problem of power trace misalignment that would decrease the performance of the attack or even worse make it fail.

Algorithm 2. EMD-IIT for SCA

Input: $Traceset M_1 IM_2, C, Siftnum, Iteration$
Output: $Traceset'$
1: **function** EMDIITFORSCA($Traceset, M_1, IM_2, C, Siftnum, Iteration$)
2:     Generate a random permutation matrix $pm(Iteration * |trace|)$ according to the parameter iteration and the length of a Trace
3:     $i \leftarrow 1$
4:     **while** $i <= Tracenum$ **do**
5:         $Trace'_i \leftarrow EMD - IIT(Traceset, M_1, IM_2, C, Siftnum, Iteration, pm)$
6:     **end while**
7:     **return** $Traceset'$
8: **end function**

Unlike the wavelet based denoising methods [3] [4] where one has to choose a wavelet basis function that affects the performance of denoising greatly, EMD based denoising methods are nonparametric. So in this respect, compared with wavelet based denoising methods, EMD based denoising methods are more easily used. Then how about the actual performance of EMD-based methods? We will study this issue through a series of experiments in section 5.

4 Relationship between Noises Extracted with Different Denoising Methods

Intuitively, the combination of denoising methods that target different frequencies will be more effective than any one of them [5]. In this section, we will examine the overlap between these noise components. And the overlap could reflect how best the combination will be in practice. Actually, this problem could also be naturally extended into the case of noise components extracted with different methods that target similar frequencies, as those of Wavelet-based and EMD-based methods.

From the perspective of set theory, there are three kinds of relationships between two sets A and B. In order to measure the overlap between two sets, we can use the formula (13), where $|set|$ is the number of elements contained in the set. If $d = 0$, then A and B do not intersect; if $0 < d < 1$, then A and B intersect, but they do not have a containment relationship; if $d = 1$, then they have a containment relationship, namely, A contains B or B contains A.

$$d = \frac{|A \cap B|}{min(|A|, |B|)} \tag{13}$$

Inspired by formula (13), we will use a similar idea in analyzing the different parts of a noisy leakages as shown in Fig. 3, where P_{exp} is the exploitable component by a given attack, P_{noise1} is the noise extracted with a denoising method m_1, P_{noise2} is the noise extracted with another denoising method m_2. Then what is the relationship between P_{noise1} and P_{noise2}? In other words, how much the noises are overlapped with each other? Currently, there is no direct metric available to measure this overlap. Therefore, we try another indirect yet useful way. Specifically, we define the notation of overlapping coefficient, which could serve as a quantitative metric to measure the overlap rate between two noise components. The definition of overlapping coefficient is based on success rate (SR)[7], and is shown in formula (14), where ΔSR_1 is the improvement of SR achieved by m_1 on a given number of power traces compared with that acquired on the raw power traces; similarly, ΔSR_2 is achieved by m_2 and ΔSR_3 is achieved by the combination use of m_1 and m_2. In practice, this indirect quantitative metric could well reflect the relationship of the noises, which is verified by the experiments in Section 5.

$$oc = \frac{\Delta SR_1 + \Delta SR_2 - \Delta SR_3}{min(\Delta SR_1, \Delta SR_2)} \tag{14}$$

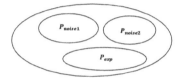

Fig. 3. Components of Noisy Side-Channel Leakages

As per its definition, it always holds that $0 \leq oc \leq 1$.Apprently, the smaller the value of oc is, the better the effect of the combination. If $oc \approx 1$, it indicates that the two denoising are almost of the same capability to remove the noise extracted with the method that generates a smaller ΔSR. In this case, using the method which makes a higher improvement of SR alone is enough, and using the combination of the two does not help.

5   Experiments

In this section, we will firstly examine the stability and effectiveness of the two EMD-based denoising methods for SCA(EMD-Conv and EMD-IIT respectively) in eliminating noise of high frequency, by performing a series of CPA attacks on real power traces from the second stage of DPA Contest and PowerSuite 4.0 (one software bechnark evalution board we designed and developed ourselves, and its CPU is an 8-bit microcontroller STC89C58RD+). And then we will explore the potential of combination of different denoising methods and study the overlapping relationship of the noises extracted with different denoising methods by performing CPA attacks on the DPA Contest v2 traces.

5.1   Settings

Hardware Implementation

The traces from the DPA Contest v2 are acquired with a sampling rate of 5G sample/s from a SASEBO-GII board, which implements an unprotected hardware AES implementation over a Xilinx Virtex-5 FPGA. Ideally, it is better to perform the denoising methods on all 32 traces sets from DPA Contest v2 public database to evaluate their performance. However, in actual cases, it is too time consuming to perform this. Therefore, we turn to another way of randomly choosing eight datasets of power traces from DPA Contest v2 public database. And then, we target the last round of the AES on these raw sets of power measurements to calculate SR on a given number of traces for the first S-box by mounting a CPA attack 500 times. The evaluation results are shown in Fig. 4. After these, we choose dataset1, which matches the average and median of the eight different SRs best, as the representative dataset to analyze.

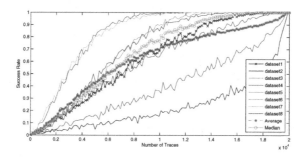

Fig. 4. Results of CPA Attacks on Eight Sets of Traces from DPA Contest v2

Software Implementation

The other three traces sets are acquired with a sampling rate of 50 M sample/s from PowerSuite 4.0 board, which contains an unprotected software AES implementation. For simulating different levels of SNR, the traces sets differ only in the average number during the sampling process. The average number is one time, four times and eight times, respectively.

Next, we will use SR to evaluate the stability and effectiveness of each denoising method or their combinations, by mounting CPA key recovery attacks 500 times for the traces set from DPA Contest v2 and 1,000 times for the traces sets from PowerSuite 4.0. For clarity, we name the denoising method in [3] as Wavelet and another denoising method in [4] as Wavelet1. And all the description of the experiments' labels are shown in Table 2. Note that our experiments' results shown that the combination order of different denoising methods has little influence on the final results.

Table 2. Description of Our Experiments

Experiment Label	Description of the Experiment
CPA	perform CPA attacks on the original power traces
EMD-Conv+CPA	perform EMD-Conv method to the original power traces, and then perform CPA attacks on the resultant power traces
EMD-IIT+CPA	perform EMD-IIT method to the original power traces, and then perform CPA attacks on the resultant power traces
Wavelet+CPA	perform wavelet transform in [3] to the original power traces, and then perform CPA attacks on the resultant power traces
Wavelet1+CPA	perform wavelet transform in [4] to the original power traces, and then per-form CPA attacks on the resultant power traces
TR+CPA	perform detrending method in [5] to the original power traces , and then perform CPA attacks on the resultant power traces
EMD-IIT+TR+CPA	remove noise in the original power traces using EMD-IIT, perform detrending method in [5] to the resultant power traces, and then perform CPA attacks on the final power traces.
EMD-IIT+Wavelet+CPA	remove noise in the original power traces using EMD-IIT, perform wavelet transform in [3] to the resultant power traces, and then perform CPA attacks on the final power traces.
EMD-IIT+Wavelet1+CPA	remove noise in the original power traces using EMD-IIT, perform wavelet transform in [4] to the resultant power traces, and then perform CPA attacks on the final power traces.

5.2 Results and Analysis

Firstly, we evaluate the stability and effectiveness of the two EMD-based denoising methods on the trace set from DPA Contest v2. The results are shown in Fig. 5(a). From Fig. 5(a), it is shown that both EMD-Conv and EMD-IIT denoising methods are capabale of improving the SRs of CPAs effectively. With repsect to achieving a partial stable SR of 80%, compared with CPA which needs 12,050 traces, EMD-Conv+CPA needs 9,350, which reduces the traces needed by 22.4%. EMD-IIT+CPA works even better than EMD+CPA, and it needs only 8,150 traces, gaining an improvement of 32.3%. Meanwhile, the Wavelet-Based methods used to remove noise of high frequency do little or even no help. Specifically, Wavelet reduces the trace number less than 10%, and Wavelet1 less than 1%. That is to say, in our case, the EMD-based methods are more effective than the Wavelet-based ones.

After the effectiveness of EMD-based methods have been proved, we would like to further study their stability and performance under different SNRs. Since under this scenario, the SNRs are relatively high compared with that of DPA Contest v2, the performances of EMD-Conv and EMD-IIT are almost the same. Therefore, in this part, we only focus on EMD-Conv which is more time efficient. As is shown in Fig. 5(b), with the increase of SNR (or average times), the percentage of the decrease of trace number to achieve a partial success rate of 80% becomes smaller and smaller, from 26.9% to 14.3% to less than 2%. This phenomena can be explained like this: with the increase of SNR, noises of high frequency also decrease. In this case, the performance decrease of the EMD-Based methods is reasonable. From another perspective, though the performance of EMD-Based methods is not always significant, they can always remove noises of high frequency, which is the evidence of their stability.

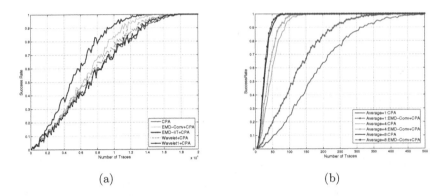

(a)   (b)

Fig. 5. (a)SRs of EMD-Based and Wavelet-based Denoising on Traces from DPA Contest v2 (b)SRs of EMD-Conv Denoising on Traces with Different Noise Levels

Next, we examine the potential power of combining denoising methods and study the relationship of the noises reduced with different denoising methods on the traces set from DPA Contest v2. Firstly, we make a combination of two denoising methods that target different frequencies: one is EMD-IIT which reduces mainly noise of high frequency, and another is TR [5] which reduces the trend noise of low frequency. The results are shown in Fig. 6(a). The SR is improved greatly on a given traces number when we make a combination of EMD-IIT and TR. In terms of achieving a partial success rate of 80%, this combination reduces as many as 58.5% of the traces that needed before denoising. To study the relationship between the noises reduced by EMD-IIT and TR, we choose three numbers, A, B and C, on the abscissa axis first. Given the number of each trace set, the SR of one denoising strategy reaches 80% or little more, i.e., the SR of EMD-IIT+TR+CPA reaches 80% when given A traces. Then we calculate the overlapping coefficient for using three different number of traces respectively, The results are shown in Table 3, where ΔSR_1 is for EMD-IIT, ΔSR_2 is for TR, and ΔSR_3 is for their combination. For more accuracy, we calculate the mean value of the three overlapping cofficients, and the result is 0.6136, meaning that about 61% noise that extracted by EMD-IIT can also be extracted by TR. Secondly we make a combination between denoising methods that target noises of high frequency and the results are shown in Fig. 6(b). Clearly, these combinations do little help in reducing noise, and the overlapping coefficient values calculated by (14) are both very close to zero, which means that EMD-IIT can remove almost all the noises extracted by the Wavelet-based methods. So in these cases, choosing a more effective one, i.e. EMD-IIT, will be more reasonable. Based on the analysis of the above experiments, combination of denoising methods that target noise of different frequencies, may improve the denoising performance a lot. As to the combination of denoising methods that target the same frequency domain, it usually makes little or no improvement in removing the noise. Therefore, in this scenario, choosing a better one alone is enough.

Table 3. Overlapping Coefficients for Different Number of Traces

ΔSR and oc — Traces number	ΔSR_1	ΔSR_2	ΔSR_3	oc
A	0.142	0.330	0.406	0.4648
B	0.206	0.364	0.408	0.7864
C	0.234	0.284	0.380	0.5897

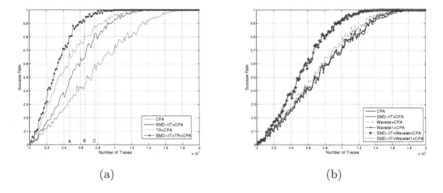

(a)   (b)

Fig. 6. (a)SRs of the Combination of EMD-IIT and TR on the Traces from DPA Contest v2 (b)SRs of the Combination of EMD-IIT and Wavelet-bsed Methods on Traces from DPA Contest v2

6   Conclusions and Future Work

Reducing noise serves an important way to enhance the performance of the side-channel attacks. Considering the fact that frequency-based denoising methods are dominant and in wide use in practice and that most of existing of these methods suffers instability in performance enhancement, stable and effective frequency-based denoising methods make a lot of sense. In this paper, we proposed EMD-based denoising methods for use in side-channel attacks. Results of practical attacks against real power traces from two kind of typical crypto implementations (i.e. hardware and software implementations of AES) proves that these methods are superior to their counterparts (say, for example, Wavelet-based approaches). On the other hand, through a series of experiments of combination, it proves that the combination of methods that dealing with noises of different frequencies may improve the denoising performance a lot. At the same time we define the notion of overlapping coefficient, which is an indirect yet helpful quantitative metric to measure to what extent that noises extracted with different methods are overlapped with each other.

Additionally, EMD-based denoising methods seem not so good at dealing with side-channel leakages with high SNR. Therefore, the study of improvements of EMD-based methods in this case would be one of the relevant future works.

Acknowledgments. This work was supported in part by National Natural Science Foundation of China (No. 61272478, 61073178 and 61170282), Beijing Natural Science Foundation (No. 4112064), Strategic Priority Research Program of the Chinese Academy of Sciences (No.XDA06010701).

References

1. Kocher, P., Jaffe, J., Jun, B.: Differential Power Analysis. In: Wiener, M. (ed.) CRYPTO 1999. LNCS, vol. 1666, pp. 388–397. Springer, Heidelberg (1999)
2. Brier, E., Clavier, C., Olivier, F.: Correlation Power Analysis with a Leakage Model. In: Joye, M., Quisquater, J.-J. (eds.) CHES 2004. LNCS, vol. 3156, pp. 16–29. Springer, Heidelberg (2004)
3. Charvet, X., Pelletier, H.: Improving the DPA attack using Wavelet transform. In: Non-Invasive Attack Testing Workshop 2005 (2005)
4. Souissi, Y., Aabid, M., Debande, N., Guilley, S., Danger, J.: Novel Applications of Wavelet Transforms based Side-Channel Analysis. In: Non-Invasive Attack Testing Workshop 2011 (2011)
5. Cao, Y., Zhou, Y., Yu, Z.: On the Negative Effects of Trend Noise and Its Applications in Side-Channel Cryptanalysis, http://eprint.iacr.org/2013/102.pdf
6. Batina, L., Hogenboom, J., van Woudenberg, J.G.J.: Getting More from PCA: First Results of Using Principal Component Analysis for Extensive Power Analysis. In: Dunkelman, O. (ed.) CT-RSA 2012. LNCS, vol. 7178, pp. 383–397. Springer, Heidelberg (2012)
7. Standaert, F., Malkin, T., Yung, M.: A Unified Framework for the Analysis of Side-Channel Key Recovery Attacks. In: Joux, A. (ed.) EUROCRYPT 2009. LNCS, vol. 5479, pp. 443–461. Springer, Heidelberg (2009)
8. Doget, J., Prouff, E., Rivain, M., Standaert, F.X.: Univariate side channel attacks and leakage modeling. Journal of Cryptographic Engineering 1, 123–144 (2011)
9. Huang, N.E., et al.: The empirical mode decomposition and the Hilbert spectrum for nonlinear and non-stationary time series analysis. Proc. Roy. Soc. London A 454, 903–995 (1998)
10. Cohen, L.: Time-Frequency Analysis. Prentice-Hall, Englewood Cliffs (1995)
11. Flandrin, P., Rilling, G., Goncalves, P.: EMD equivalent filter banks, from interpetation to applications. In: Huang, N.E., Shen, S. (eds.) Hilbert-Huang Transform and Its Applications, 1st edn. World Scientific, Singapore (2005)
12. Mallat, S.: A Wavelet Tour of Signal Processing, 2nd edn. Academic, New York (1999)
13. Kopsinis, Y., McLaughlin, S.: Development of EMD-Based Denoising Methods Inspired by Wavelet Thresholding. IEEE Transactions on Signal Processing 57(4) (April 2009)
14. Mangard, S., Oswald, E., Popp, T.: Power Analysis Attacks: Revealing the Secrets of Smart Cards. Springer (2007)
15. Kocher, P.C.: Timing Attacks on Implementations of Diffie-Hellman, RSA, DSS, and Other Systems. In: Koblitz, N. (ed.) CRYPTO 1996. LNCS, vol. 1109, pp. 104–113. Springer, Heidelberg (1996)
16. Agrawal, D., Archambeault, B., Rao, J., Rohatgi, P.: The EM side-channel(s). In: Kaliski Jr., B.S., Koç, Ç.K., Paar, C. (eds.) CHES 2002. LNCS, vol. 2523, pp. 29–45. Springer, Heidelberg (2003)

Accelerating AES in JavaScript with WebGL

Yang Yang[1,2,3], Zhi Guan[1,2,3,*], Jiawei Zhu[1,2,3],
Qiuxiang Dong[1,2,3], and Zhong Chen[1,2,3]

[1] Institute of Software, School of EECS, Peking University, China
[2] MoE Key Lab of High Confidence Software Technologies (PKU)
[3] MoE Key Lab of Network and Software Security Assurance (PKU)
{yangyang,guanzhi,chen}@infosec.pku.edu.cn

Abstract. Cryptography is a fundamental building block for security sensitive Web applications. Because the architecture of JavaScript can not provide sufficient performance, the client-side web applications still lacks high performance cryptography primitives. In this paper we studied the feasibility of a new Web standard, i.e., the WebGL API for accelerating AES in JavaScript by exploiting the ability of GPU. We design and implemented AES using 128-bit key length. We compared the performance of our approach to the currently reported fastest pure JavaScript implementation and found our approach runs more than ten times faster in major browsers on all platform. Our work showed the potential optimization of using GPU via WebGL to accelerate JavaScript code.

Keywords: AES, WebGL, GPGPU, JavaScript.

1 Introduction

Recent years, the fast development of cloud computing makes it much easier for users to synchronize their personal data with the cloud to access the data anywhere for convenience. Since the service provider are untrusted, the unencrypted users' privacy may leak to curious employees or even the government, according to the recent report from Guardians[1]. It is necessary for many applications to encrypt the data before uploading to the cloud to preserve the privacy of users, especially sensitive photos, documents, musics, etc. As web browser is becoming a universal tool for interacting with remote servers, almost all popular applications provides a web interface, it is important to provide efficient cryptographic primitives for web applications to enhance their security, especially symmetric cryptography such as AES.

Although the performance of JavaScript has been experienced a continuous increasing recent years, there is still a remarkable gap between the performance of JavaScript code and native code because of the nature of a untyped scripting language dynamically interpreted running in a virtual machine. Unless a prominent improvement on the architecture of JavaScript occurs in the future, the gap

---

[*] Corresponding author.

[1] http://www.guardian.co.uk/world/2013/jun/06/us-tech-giants-nsa-data

S. Qing et al. (Eds.): ICICS 2013, LNCS 8233, pp. 275–287, 2013.

may still exist for a long time. Another restriction for JavaScript is it doesn't support parallel computing. This means even the performance gap has been narrowed, pure JavaScript code can still not make full use of the processing power of the CPU. Since the performance of the single core has almost reached the limit, manufacturers tend to increase the performance mainly by increasing the number of cores in one CPU instead of increasing the performance of each core. This means unless there is a significant change in the architecture of JavaScript, the increasing of performance of JavaScript may be limited.

The poor performance of cryptographic primitives in JavaScript may deter potential users. In the experiment conducted by Chandra etc.[1], it takes more than 3 seconds to encrypt and transfer a file of 1MB in JavaScript, while about 90% of the time was consumed on encryption and decryption. Due to the existence of these restrictions in JavaScript, increasing the performance of cryptographic primitives in JavaScript is not simply a engineering problem, because the improvements is limited within the framework of pure JavaScript and the framework prevents the JavaScript code to make full use of the computation power of processors.

The emergence of WebGL(Web Graphics Library) provides us a choice to get rid of the restriction of JavaScript for more performance. WebGL is a web standard designed and maintained by the non-profit Khronos Group. It provides a JavaScript API based on OpenGL ES 2.0 for GPU accelerated rendering of 3D graphics within web browsers. The API is exposed through the HTML5 Canvas element as Document Object Model(DOM) interfaces. Developers can use WebGL to create shaders, textures, framebuffers in the graphics memory run shaders on GPUs directly. This indicates that we can run certain arithmetics on GPU directly by using WebGL APIs exposed in JavaScript. As GPU(Graphics Processing Unit) has been widely deployed as a de facto unit of personal computer and mobile devices, and provides highly parallel specialized processors the total throughput of which has surpassed CPU, the developers may gain great benefits on both performance and portability using WebGL for computation. This approach works similarly as the legacy GPGPU(General-Purpose Computation on Graphics Hardware)[2] technique which uses graphics APIs and shader language for general purpose programming and has been replaced by more dedicated GPGPU framework such as CUDA, OpenCL, etc. But in JavaScript, we found this technique showed us more advantages than it used to.

The aim of this work is to investigate how the WebGL can be used to accelerate browser side JavaScript cryptography computation. We selected the AES[2] as the focal algorithm to demonstrate the possibility and efficiency of WebGL acceleration. We made following contributions in this work:

- We analyzed the features provided by WebGL and discussed some issues that may lead to mistakes when using WebGL for GPGPU.
- We designed and implemented a WebGL version of AES that use the power of GPU for accelerating the AES encryption in JavaScript through WebGL API.

---

[2] http://www.gpgpu.org/

– We evaluated the performance of our implementation and compare the result with the leading AES implementation in pure JavaScript.

We found that our implementation runs several times faster than AES implementation in pure JavaScript on the platform with a powerful graphics card. Even on a machine with a low end integrated graphics card our implementation also runs well and performs almost as fast as the pure JavaScript Implementation. Our research demonstrates that it is possible and efficient to use WebGL to accelerate the general purpose computing in browsers, and provides a way to make the encryption and decryption practical in browsers.

The remainder of this paper is organized as follows. Section 2 gives a overview of related work. Section 3 gives a brief introduction to WebGL and detailed several important issues in general purpose computing using WebGL. Section 4 introduced the standard approach and the fast approach of AES algorithm. Section 5 describes how we design and implemented the WebGL version of AES. Section 6 shows how we conducted the experiment and the result of experiment. At last we conclude our paper and talk about our future work.

2   Related Work

There is no cryptographic primitives and high performance general computation APIs currently available in major browsers. Web cryptography API is trying to provide common cryptographic services in JavaScript through the object window.crypto, but there is only a draft at the moment and no browser has announced a time table to support this standard.

Some modern browsers also provide other ways to implement the logic of web applications besides JavaScript, such as programmable plug-ins and Java Applets, while all these techniques are not portable for browsers on all platform, such as smart phones, and the extra installations they require also bothers users.

Asm.js[3] provides a framework to compile the JavaScript code to a well defined subset of JavaScript instructions which are easier to optimize. It reduce the performance gap between JavaScript code and native code greatly, but it doesn't support parallel computing, either. WebCL[4] is a JavaScript binding to OpenCL for heterogeneous parallel computing, but there are only several prototypes at the moment. Native Client[3] gives browser-based applications the computational performance of native applications without compromising safety, but currently only Chrome on X86 platform is supported.

There has been several cryptography libraries implemented in pure JavaScript[5,6]. The most effective research previous published on accelerating symmetric cryptography in JavaScript was done by Stark et al.[4]. They studied a few optimizations and trade-offs for implementing AES effectively in JavaScript

---

[3] http://asmjs.org/
[4] http://www.khronos.org/webcl/
[5] http://people.eku.edu/styere/Encrypt/JS-AES.html
[6] https://code.google.com/p/crypto-js/

and built a highly optimized AES implementation in JavaScript. Their AES implementation is both faster and smaller than any other AES implementation in JavaScript before their work, but still dozens of times slower than native implementation.

D. Cook et al. [5] firstly implemented AES-128 on GPU by mapping the AES cipher to the standard fixed graphics pipeline using OpenGL, but their performance was only 184Kbps–1.53Mbps on Geforce3 Ti200, which was 40 to 100 times slower compared with CPU. Harrison et al.[6] used the shader-based programmable pipeline to implement AES and got a much better performance than Cook's research, but still under performed compared to some optimized implementations on standards CPU. Fleissner[7] accelerated the Montgomery exponentiation with OpenGL to more than 100 times faster than the standard algorithm. Moss[8] implemented RSA using an RNS based approach using OpenGL and gave results comparable to the fastest CPU implementation.

The emergence of dedicated GPGPU frameworks such as CUDA[9], Brooks[10] and OpenCL[11] inspired the research on accelerating crypto primitives with GPU. Manavski[12] implemented AES using CUDA and showed GPU can perform as an efficient cryptographic accelerator for the first time, their solution was 20 times faster than the native implementation. Szerwinski et al.[13] used CUDA to accelerated DSA, RSA and ECC. Zhang et al.[14] accelerated composite order bilinear pairing with CUDA.

3   WebGL Background

WebGL is a standard of graphics APIs based on OpenGL ES 2.0 developed by Khronos group, the version 1.0 of the WebGLspecification was released March 2011[15]. Until the time of this paper writing, most major desktop browsers and mobile browsers have supported WebGL officially or internally. This indicates our approach can be used in most browsers across platforms without modification.

WebGL is a shader-based API using OpenGL Shading Language(GLSL), which makes full use of programmable pipelines in GPUs and provides a great convenience for general purpose computing. As illustrated in Figure 1, using WebGL for general purpose computing works in similar as rending a frame in graphics computing: developer passes bunch of input data into graphics memory as textures, implements the computing logic in shaders, renders the computing result into framebuffers, then read the result back to the main memory or use the result as the input of the next iteration. These steps involves much glue code, how to launch these steps and what these steps mean can be found at WebGL tutorials and references books.

The key to general purpose computing in GPU via WebGL is how to map the computing procedure to graphics rendering precisely and effectively. Since WebGL is designed for graphics computing, it supports only limited data structures, especially for input and output, and it does not have full support of integer arithmetics until now. This indicates that developers sometimes have to map the unsupported arithmetics and data structures to supported ones in order

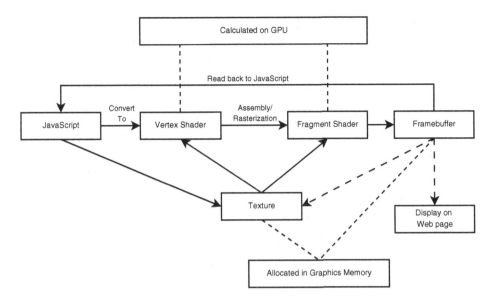

Fig. 1. A simplified view of WebGL pipeline model of computation

to leverage WebGL and GPU for computing. And any computing that is used in shaders must take the precision that shaders supported into consideration in order to prevent the unexpected truncation affect the result. As GPU is not effective at executing the serial control logic, the algorithm of the computing must be optimized for parallel. From our observation and experiments, the following concrete principles are helpful when using WebGL and GPU for general purpose computing.

Simplify the logic of shaders. As we have mentioned, GPU is not good at executing the control logics, such as the conditional branch. Another reason is complex logic may consume much longer time to compile. A possible mitigation is to complete the computing with multiple renders, and use CPU to execute the control flow between renders.

Reduce the number of data transfers on bus. As the bandwidth of the bus is limited, transfer data between the main memory and the graphics memory is time consuming.

Batch processing the data. Because of the executing model of GPU, computing with a block of input may take the same time as computing with 1,000 blocks.

Memory access pattern. As most circuits of GPU are used to implement the arithmetic units, the space of cache and registers is relatively small, there will be a great penalty on the performance if the cache miss occurs too much. It is important for the developer to optimize the memory access pattern, for example, try not to access a large part of data randomly.

Number conversion. In WebGL, the data supplied to the texture in JavaScript should be 8-bit integers, but the data got in GLSL are floating numbers in $[0, 1]$. In brief, the integers are linearly mapped to the floating number when they are transferred from main memory to graphics memory, and mapped in the reverse way when floating numbers are transferred back from graphics memory to main memory. So any linear transformations on the floating form in GLSL would be equally applied to the integer form in JavaScript. This is a feature or restriction in another word of GLSL, the developers must be conscious of this.

Texture coordinate. In shaders, the texel is accessed by function `texture2D()` using the coordinate (x, y). Each dimension of the coordinate is a floating number within the range of $[0, 1]$, which means there is not only one single value can be used to look up any texel, but a range of coordinates. Generally speaking, any coordinate within the scope of the texel can be used to look up the texel, but there is no guarantee for different hardware to behave totally the same for boundary values. For the texel at i-th column and j-th row in a texture whose width is w and height is h, using $(\frac{i}{w-1}, \frac{j}{h-1})$ as the coordinate is acceptable in most cases, but since accuracy is critical for general purpose computing, it is necessary to calculate the coordinate by $(\frac{2 \times i + 1}{2 \times w}, \frac{2 \times j + 1}{2 \times h})$ sometimes.

4 AES Background

AES(Advanced Encryption Standard) [2] is a symmetric block cipher that encrypt plain text blocks of 128 bits with various key length of 128 bits, 192 bits or 256 bits. It is a restricted version of Rijndael symmetric block cipher that can encrypt and decrypt blocks of 128 bits using a key size of 128-bit, 192-bit, and 256-bit length. The cipher is basically a series of round transformations on blocks with round keys expanded from the original key using a key schedule algorithm [16,2], the output of each round is the input of the next round. The number of the rounds is determined by the key length: 10 rounds for 128-bit, 12 rounds for 192-bit, and 14 rounds for 256-bit. The block is depicted as a 4×4 column-major order matrix of bytes, termed **state**.

The standard implementation of AES encryption starts with an AddRoundKey operation on the state, followed by 10/12/14 round transformations depending on the length of the key. Each round transformation includes 4 successive steps except the final round: SubBytes, ShiftRows, MixColumns and AddRoundKey. The final round is similar except the lack of the MixColumns step. Decryption is done by reversing each step of encryption using the same key.

SubBytes. Each byte of the state is substituted independently using a predefined substitution box(S-box) computed over the Galois Field $GF(2^8)$ [2].

ShiftRows. Rows are rotated by 0, 1, 2 and 3 bytes, respectively, to the left.

MixColumns. A substitution that makes use of arithmetic over the Galois Field $GF(2^8)$.

AddRoundKey. A simple bitwise XOR of the state with a piece of the expanded round key.

For processors supporting 32-bit or greater word length, Daemen and Rijmen detailed a fast implementation approach that combines the SubBytes, ShiftRows and MixColumns transformations into four 256-entry(each entry is 4 bytes) lookup tables("T-Table")[16,2]. The T-Table approach reduces the SubBytes, ShiftRows, MixColumns operations in round transformation to simply updating the j-th column of the state according to the Equation 1.

$$[s'^j_0, s'^j_1, s'^j_2, s'^j_3]^T = \overset{3}{\underset{i=0}{\oplus}} T_i[s_{i,j} + C_i], 0 \le j \le 3 \tag{1}$$

where $s_{j,k}$ is the byte in the j-th row and k-th column of the state, and C_i is a constant equivalently doing the ShiftRows in place. Each T_i is a rotation of the other. After the state is updated, the step AddRoundKey is performed to complete the round operation. As we can see from the equation, there are only XORs and table lookups needed in this technique.

The block cipher itself is not sufficient for the security of multiple blocks, a mode of operation is needed. The cipher mode is important for both performance and security for block ciphers. The CBC mode, OFB mode and other chained modes are secure but not efficient for parallel computing since the computation of the next block depends on the result of the previous one. The ECB mode is efficient for parallel computing but insecure. CTR mode is both secure and efficient for parallel computing as the counter can be precomputed efficiently and simple to implement. Another advantage for CTR mode is that only the encryption procedure of the cipher is needed for both encryption and decryption in CTR mode.

5   WebGL Version of AES

5.1   Overview

We implemented AES encryption using 128-bit key length using WebGL. The decryption and other key lengths can be implemented with minor modifications. We implemented the ECB mode for plain text of various length, and other modes such as CTR mode can be implemented simply with a extra shader. As our purpose here is to demonstrate the feasibility and efficiency of WebGL for cryptography, we just keep our implementation simple but convincing.

Specifically, the algorithm we implemented is the fast approach for 32-bit processors as mentioned in section 4, because this approach mainly involves two types of operation: table lookup and XOR. Since the arithmetic operation supported by GLSL is limited, this feature will facilitate our work. We did not implement the key scheduling in WebGL, because this procedure is a serial of limited operations that can be done in no time in JavaScript in CPU. And once the key schedule is expanded, it can be used repeatedly to encrypt message of any length. The key schedule, the plain text and other parameters would be packed into textures as input to shaders, the cipher text would be written to the framebuffer by shaders and read back into JavaScript. We can encrypt multiple blocks in the same time with GPU and WebGL in order to exert the power of high throughput of GPU. We denote the blocks we encrypt at the same time as a packet.

The multiple-target technique is not supported in WebGL, so the output of a shader could be only a texel which is no more than four bytes. As the size of one block is 16 bytes, it takes four shader instances to produce the result of one block. As each round operation requires the whole state output by the previous round operation, there should be a synchronization after each round, or each shader instance has to execute all the rounds completely before the final one. The too complex logic takes much more time to compile and run, therefore we decided to split the encryption logic into 3 independent shader programs: the first implemented the initial round which just combines the key with the state by a XOR operation, the second implemented the round operation between the state and a piece of round key that can be specific by a parameter, the third implemented the final round operation. In this case, we have to render for 11 times in total to encrypt a packet regardless of the size of the packet with a 128-bit key: 1 for the initial round, 9 for round operations, and 1 for the final round. As we don't want to read the intermediate result back into main memory, we used two framebuffers alternatively: the one holding the result of the previous round will be used as the input to the next round, since the framebuffer of one render can also be used as the texture to another render.

5.2   XOR Operation

The AES fast approach requires to calculate the XOR of two 32-bit unsigned integers, while both 32-bit integer and XOR operation are not supported in GLSL. Although each texel can hold up to 32-bit data, it actually consists of four 8-bit floating numbers in GLSL or four 8-bit integer in JavaScript. As XOR of two integers is just the combination or XOR of each bits at corresponding position, we can just hold the 32-bit integers in texels and calculate the XOR of two texels by just calculating each 8-bit component of them. Therefore we can construct a table whose element at i-th column and j-th row is $i \oplus j$, then the calculation of $i \oplus j$ can be transformed to looking up the element at i-th column and j-th row in the table. In GLSL, the situation is a little sophisticated: there is slightly difference between the mapped floating number and the texture coordinate as mentioned the Section 3, an integer i will be transformed to $i/255.0$ in GLSL, as the reliable coordinate to access the i-th column or row is $\frac{i \times 2 + 1}{256 \times 2}$, it is better to convert the floating form f_i of the integer i to the texture coordinate by $\frac{f_i \times 255.0 \times 2 + 1}{256.0 \times 2}$ for accuracy, especially on GPUs with lower precision.

For XOR of two 8-bit integers, there would be $256 \times 256 = 65536$ entries in the table. The random access to a table of this size in GPU may cause plenty of cache misses. An optimization has been proposed in the paper[17]: We can construct a table holding the XOR of any two 4-bit integers instead of for any two 8-bit integers. For any two 8-bit integers first we divide it equally into two 4-bit parts and calculate the XOR of each part, then combine the result to get the XOR of original 8-bit integer. This optimization reduces the table from 256×256 to 16×16 and has been proved to be much faster in the experiments[17].

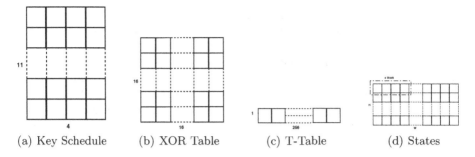

(a) Key Schedule   (b) XOR Table   (c) T-Table   (d) States

Fig. 2. The memory layout of the key schedule, the XOR table, the T-Table, and the state, each square in the figure stands for a texel

5.3 Memory Layout

We will discuss the memory layout of the input, output and parameters in graphics memory and how to access them in this part. As the texture and the framebuffer has two dimension, there could be many possibilities for memory layout and access pattern of the same piece of data, our purpose is to choose the most efficient and easy-to-use one.

The key schedule is common for all plain text blocks encrypted using the same key. For the key of the same length, there are 11 round keys including the original one, each round key is 16 bytes. Each texel holds 4 bytes at most, we use 4 continuous texels for one piece of round key, and each round key is held in a row in sequence in a texture as shown in Figure 2(a). In this layout, the coordinate used to access the i-th element of the j-th round key is easy to calculate as $(\frac{i \times 2+1}{2 \times 4}, \frac{j \times 2+1}{2 \times 11})$ as described in Section 3.

The original T-Table takes up 4KB memory in total. As the T-Table has to be accessed randomly, it is better if we can reduce the memory usage to reduce the cache miss. Since each T-Table is a rotation of the other, the Equation 1 can be optimized to the Equation 2:

$$[s'^j_0, s'^j_1, s'^j_2, s'^j_3]^T = \begin{aligned} &T_0[s_{0,j} + C_0] \oplus Rot(T_0[s_{1,j} + C_1] \oplus \\ &Rot(T_0[s_{2,j} + C_2] \oplus Rot(T_0[s_{3,j} + C_3]))) \end{aligned} \quad (2)$$

In this case, there is only one T-Table needed and takes up 1KB memory space only. Each entry of the T-Table is 32-bit long and can be packed into one texel, so we put the whole table in a texture whose size is 256 × 1. The layout of T-Table is shown in Figure 2(c) The i-th element of the table can be looked up with the coordinate $(\frac{i \times 2+1}{256 \times 2}, 0.5)$.

The XOR table is a 16 × 16 matrix as shown in Figure 2(b) and mentioned above, we use the alpha component of the texel to hold each XOR result.

The size of the state is 16 bytes, so we can keep it in sequence in a row in the texture. Since it is not effective to encrypt just one block at one time, we have to supply multiple blocks to the input texture. The difficulty is how to locate the right block of state for each shader instance when there are multiple blocks supplied. As the size of input and output of the encryption are same, we can construct the framebuffers holding the result and the texture holding the input of the same size, so there would be a one to one map between the input and the output. This corresponding relation can be constructed by rendering a rectangle to fill the viewport with a designed vertex shader program easily. A simple approach is to place only one block in a row in the texture or framebuffer, then for the shader instance outputting to (s, t) in the framebuffer, it can locate the input to it at the t-th row of the input texture easily. Since the side length of the texture and framebuffer that supported by GPU is limited to the order of thousands, this approach can encrypt only thousands of blocks at the same time, so it is necessary to put multiple blocks in each row as shown in Figure 2(d). In this case, for the shader instance outputting to (s, t) in the framebuffer whose size is $w \times h$, the coordinate of the i-th column$(0 \leq i < 4)$ can be calculated by Equation 3. In this approach, we can encrypt millions of blocks at the same time.

$$s_i = \frac{(floor(s \times w \times 2.0/8.0) \times 8.0 + 2.0 \times i + 1.0)}{(w \times 2.0)}$$
$$t_i = t \qquad\qquad (3)$$

6   Experiment

Table 1. The configuration of test machines

Machine	A	B	C
Platform	Desktop	Laptop	Pad
Model	Dell OptiPlex 990MT	Lenovo Y400N	Nexus 4
OS	Ubuntu 12.04	Windows 8 Pro	Android 4.2.2
CPU	i7 2660	i5 3230M	A5
GPU	NVIDIA 560TI	NVIDIA G750M	PowerVR SGX 543

We expected to find out how fast the WebGL AES can be, and the impaction of packet size on performance through the experiment. So we designed the experiment as follows: We launched the the implementation with different packet sizes, start from one block which is 16 bytes, up to 1M bytes, and the next packet size is always four times of the previous one. We used the implementation to encrypt the randomly generated plain text whose length is 3 times of the packet size, so the algorithm would run 3 times to finish the encryption. Then we get the time consumed during the encryption and calculate the throughput of the implementation. We also launched the experiment on SJCL(Stanford JavaScript Crypto Library)[4] which is the fastest pure JavaScript AES implementation currently reported in the same way for comparison.

We launched the experiment in different browsers on different platforms in order to have a comprehensive view of the implementation. We used two most popular browsers of their latest version: Chrome(27.0) and Firefox(23.0). The machines used belongs to different platforms: desktop, laptop and pad. The major configuration are summarized in Table 1 and indexed by characters.

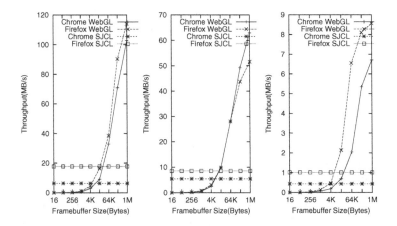

Fig. 3. The throughput of different approaches with different packet size

The result of experiment is shown in Figure 3. We found that the WebGL approach ran well on various operating systems and hardware platforms. The speed of pure JavaScript AES implementation is almost stable regardless of the packet size, while the speed of WebGL AES implementation continuously increased as the packet size increased. From the figure we can see that when the packet size is small, the WebGL version AES ran slowly, but when the packet size became larger (more than 16K), the WebGL version AES ran much faster than pure JavaScript version AES on all platforms. And when the packet size is large enough(greater or equal than 1MB), the speed of WebGL version AES could be more than 10 times of pure JavaScript version AES. Considering the size of pictures, songs or other multimedia files users daily use could all be several MBs or even dozens of MBs, the WebGL version AES could surely exert its full power in modern Web applications.

7 Conclusion

In this paper, we proposed a new approach to accelerate AES in JavaScript via WebGL. Our primary contribution is demonstrating the feasibility of using GPU via WebGL to provide much better performance than pure JavaScript since JavaScript is an untyped language and it doesn't support parallel computing.

Our approach was more than ten times faster than pure JavaScript implementation of AES. The performance is sufficient for most cryptographic operations in web applications to provide a smooth user interface. This also demonstrated that legacy techniques such as using graphics API for GPGPU can be very powerful in certain runtime environment.

Acknowledgement. I would like to thank my supervisor, Researcher Zhi Guan and Professor Zhong Chen for their excellent guidance throughout the writing of the paper.

References

1. Chandra, R., Gupta, P., Zeldovich, N.: Separating web applications from user data storage with BSTORE. MIT web domain (June 2010)
2. NIST. Specification for the Advanced Encryption Standard (AES). Technical Report Federal Information Processing Standards (FIPS) 197, National Institute of Standards and Technology (November 2001)
3. Yee, B., Sehr, D., Dardyk, G., Chen, J.B., Muth, R., Ormandy, T., Okasaka, S., Narula, N., Fullagar, N.: Native client: A sandbox for portable, untrusted x86 native code. In: 2009 30th IEEE Symposium on Security and Privacy, pp. 79–93 (2009)
4. Stark, E., Hamburg, M., Boneh, D.: Symmetric Cryptography in Javascript. In: ACSAC, pp. 373–381. IEEE Computer Society (2009)
5. Cook, D.L., Ioannidis, J., Keromytis, A.D., Luck, J.: cryptographics: Secret key cryptography using graphics cards. In: Menezes, A. (ed.) CT-RSA 2005. LNCS, vol. 3376, pp. 334–350. Springer, Heidelberg (2005)
6. Harrison, O., Waldron, J.: AES Encryption Implementation and Analysis on Commodity Graphics Processing Units. In: Paillier, P., Verbauwhede, I. (eds.) CHES 2007. LNCS, vol. 4727, pp. 209–226. Springer, Heidelberg (2007)
7. Fleissner, S.: GPU-accelerated montgomery exponentiation. In: Shi, Y., van Albada, G.D., Dongarra, J., Sloot, P.M.A. (eds.) ICCS 2007, Part I. LNCS, vol. 4487, pp. 213–220. Springer, Heidelberg (2007)
8. Moss, A., Page, D., Smart, N.P.: Toward acceleration of RSA using 3D graphics hardware. In: Galbraith, S.D. (ed.) Cryptography and Coding 2007. LNCS, vol. 4887, pp. 364–383. Springer, Heidelberg (2007)
9. C. CUDA. Programming guide. NVIDIA Corporation (July 2012)
10. Buck, I., Foley, T., Horn, D., Sugerman, J., Fatahalian, K., Houston, M., Hanrahan, P.: Brook for GPUs: stream computing on graphics hardware. ACM Trans. Graph. 23(3), 777–786 (2004)
11. Munshi, A. (ed.): Khronos OpenCL Working Group. The opencl specification (2008)
12. Manavski, S.A.: CUDA compatible GPU as an efficient hardware accelerator for AES cryptography. In: ICSPC 2007, pp. 65–68 (November 2007)
13. Szerwinski, R., Güneysu, T.: Exploiting the Power of GPUs for Asymmetric Cryptography. In: Oswald, E., Rohatgi, P. (eds.) CHES 2008. LNCS, vol. 5154, pp. 79–99. Springer, Heidelberg (2008)

14. Zhang, Y., Xue, C.J., Wong, D.S., Mamoulis, N., Yiu, S.M.: Acceleration of composite order bilinear pairing on graphics hardware. In: Chim, T.W., Yuen, T.H. (eds.) ICICS 2012. LNCS, vol. 7618, pp. 341–348. Springer, Heidelberg (2012)
15. Marrin, C.: Webgl specification. Khronos WebGL Working Group (2011)
16. Daemen, J., Rijmen, V.: The design of Rijndael: AES–the Advanced Encryption Standard. Springer, Berlin (2002)
17. Harrison, O., Waldron, J.: AES Encryption Implementation and Analysis on Commodity Graphics Processing Units. In: Paillier, P., Verbauwhede, I. (eds.) CHES 2007. LNCS, vol. 4727, pp. 209–226. Springer, Heidelberg (2007)

Analysis of Multiple Checkpoints in Non-perfect and Perfect Rainbow Tradeoff Revisited*

Wenhao Wang[1,2] and Dongdai Lin[1]

[1] State Key Laboratory Of Information Security,
Institute of Information Engineering, CAS, Beijing, China
[2] University of Chinese Academy of Sciences, Beijing, China
{wangwenhao,ddlin}@iie.ac.cn

Abstract. Time memory tradeoff (TMTO) attack has proven to be an effective cryptanalysis method against block ciphers and stream ciphers. Since it was first proposed in 1980s, many new ideas have come out to reduce the false alarms during the online phase, among which rainbow table introduced by Oechslin and perfect table introduced by Borst et al. are notable landmarks. Avoine et al. introduced the checkpoints technique to detect false alarms using little additional memory without regenerating the pre-computed chain. In this paper, we revisit the analysis of multiple checkpoints in rainbow tradeoff. For non-perfect table we give a new sight to the computation of the expected decreasing number of chain regenerations at the k-th iteration. This helps to better understand the real nature of false alarms and leads us to the same results as the work of Jung Woo Kim et al. at Indocrypt 2012. For perfect rainbow tradeoff we give the first way to find optimal positions of multiple checkpoints. The results are better than previous work of Avoine et al., which only applies when the perfect table has the maximum number of chains. All the results are verified through meticulous experiments.

Keywords: time memory tradeoff, rainbow tradeoff, multiple checkpoints.

1 Introduction

Inverting one-way functions is one of the fundamental problems in cryptography. Much of cryptanalysis of block ciphers and stream ciphers can be expressed as the process of computation of pre-images or inversion of one-way functions. A cryptanalytic time-memory tradeoff (TMTO) is a technique to quickly invert generic one-way functions with the help of pre-computation. After it was first introduced by Hellman to perform an attack over DES [7] TMTO has been applied to many cryptosystems, for example against the GSM algorithm A5/1

* Supported by the National 973 Program of China under Grant 2011CB302400, the National Natural Science Foundation of China under Grants 10971246, 60970152, and 61173134, and the Strategic Priority Research Program of the Chinese Academy of Sciences under grant XDA06010701.

S. Qing et al. (Eds.): ICICS 2013, LNCS 8233, pp. 288–301, 2013.

[5], LILI-128 [16] and Windows LM Hash [15]. There are also ongoing research projects dealing with the implementations, such as the RainbowCrack Project [1] and the TMTO-based A5/1 Cracking Project [14] etc..

Two common ways to find a pre-image under a one-way function are exhaustive search and table lookup. In an exhaustive search method, one simply tries all possible keys in order to find the pre-image. With the table lookup method, one precomputes a table containing all the values of the key and then perform a search to find a pre-image. Hellman's TMTO attack achieves a middle ground between the exhaustive key search and the massive pre-computation of all possible ciphertexts for a given plaintext. During the pre-computation phase the attacker precomputes sufficiently many chains and only stores the starting points and ending points in a table. This concise table is used to find the pre-image in time shorter than an exhaustive search during an online phase.

A major drawback of Hellman's tradeoff attack is that it is possible to cause false alarms, when the online chain merges with pre-computed chains. False alarms significantly decrease the tradeoff efficiency and can increase more than 50% of the cryptanalysis time. After the inspiring work of Hellman, a lot of work has been done to reduce the cost of false alarms. Perfect table, suggested by Borst, Preneel, and Vandewalle in 1998, cleans the tables by discarding the merging and cycling pre-computed chains [6]. Rainbow table, introduced by Oechslin et al. in 2003, uses a different reduction function for each column of a table [15] and two different chains can merge only if they have the same key at the same position of the chain.

In 2005, Avoine, Junod and Oechslin [3] proposed using checkpoints to rule out false alarms. Additional information on some intermediate points of a chain are stored in the pre-computed tables, besides the starting points and ending points. During the online phase the attacker regenerates the pre-computed chain only when a match of both the ending point and the checkpoints is found. Using the technique, the cost of false alarms is reduced with a minute amount of memory. In [4] Avoine et al. presented an analysis of the effects of checkpoints in perfect rainbow tables when the table contains the MAXIMUM number of chains. And they did not clearly figure out the way to obtain optimal positions of multiple checkpoints in these tables. In 2010, Jin Hong et al. established a theoretical framework of analyzing false alarms [8] and gave a fair comparison of existing tradeoff algorithms [10]. Related works include the analysis of parallel distinguished point tradeoff [9], non-perfect table fuzzy rainbow tradeoff [11], perfect rainbow tradeoff [13] etc.. Analysis of one checkpoint for a single non-perfect rainbow table was done also in [8]. Analysis of multiple checkpoints for a non-perfect rainbow table was performed in [12].

In this paper we revisit the analysis of multiple checkpoints in rainbow tradeoff. For non-perfect rainbow tradeoff, when computing the expected decreasing number of false alarms at the k-th iteration, [12] used the approximation of $z_0 \approx m(1 + k)$ and $z_u \approx m(1 + k - c_u)$. They applied the same reasoning approach as [8] to analyze false alarm costs, by simply ignoring collisions and treating the pre-computed chains as independent chains. However this might not be obvious[1]. We adopt a natural approach to compute the expected chains to be regenerated, with random selection of points at the k-th iteration. This leads us to identical results but explains the real nature of false alarms. For perfect rainbow tradeoff, considering that in most cases the perfect table has not the maximum number of chains due to the limit of pre-computation, we give the first way to find optimal positions of multiple checkpoints, even when the table is not maximum. All our results are verified through meticulous experiments.

The rest of the paper is organized as follows. We first introduce the theoretical framework of pre-image under function iteration and fix some notations in Section 2. In Section 3, we present our work on checkpoints for non-perfect rainbow tradeoff. In Section 4, we present our work on checkpoints for perfect rainbow tradeoff. In Section 5, we conclude the paper.

2   Theoretical Background

In this section we give some definitions that are used in the remainder of the paper.

2.1   Time Memory Tradeoff Attack

Let $F : \mathcal{N} \to \mathcal{N}$ be the one-way function to be inverted. In an off-line phase, we build m Hellman chains of length t with the form demonstrated in Fig. 1. A nice property of a chain is that we do not need to store all the elements in it. By knowing the starting point, we can recalculate the successive elements in the chain. So we just store the pairs of starting points and ending points $\{(SP_j, EP_j)\}_{j=1}^m$ in one table. Suppose l tables are constructed. A different reduction function r_i is used in the i-th table, and we denote $r_i(F(x))$ by $F_i(x)$. In the online phase, the goal is to find the unknown key by making use of the pre-computed tables. The attacker is given $y_0 = F(x_0)$ and has to find x_0. To search for x_0 in the i-th table, recursively he applies F_i to $r_i(y_0)$ and check if some $Y_k = (F_i)^k(x_0)$ appears as an ending point in the table. Whenever a match $Y_k = EP_j$ is found, he regenerates the corresponding pre-computed chain by computing $x = X_{j,t-k+1} = (F_i)^{t-k}(SP_j)$. There is a large chance that $(F_i)(x) = Y_1$, i.e. $F(x) = F(x_0)$.

Rainbow table uses a different reduction function for each column of a table. A rainbow chain is of the form

$$SP_j = X_{j,1} \xrightarrow{F} Y_{j,1} \xrightarrow{r_1} X_{j,2} \xrightarrow{F} Y_{j,2} \xrightarrow{r_2} \cdots \xrightarrow{F} Y_{j,t} \xrightarrow{r_t} EP_j,$$

and two different chains can merge only if they have the same key at the same position of the chain.

Checkpoint is a technique for resolving false alarms (false alarms occur if an online chain merges with pre-computed chains) without regenerating the chain,

---

[1] Note that the table becomes a perfect table if we treat the pre-computed chains as independent. And a perfect table is meant to cause less false alarms than a non-perfect table.

$$SP_1 = X_{1,1} \xrightarrow{F} Y_{1,1} \xrightarrow{r} X_{1,2} \xrightarrow{F} Y_{1,2} \xrightarrow{r} \cdots \xrightarrow{F} Y_{1,t} \xrightarrow{r} EP_1$$

$$\vdots \qquad\qquad\qquad\qquad\qquad\qquad\qquad\qquad\qquad \vdots$$

$$SP_j = X_{j,1} \xrightarrow{F} Y_{j,1} \xrightarrow{r} X_{j,2} \xrightarrow{F} Y_{j,2} \xrightarrow{r} \cdots \xrightarrow{F} Y_{j,t} \xrightarrow{r} EP_j$$

$$\vdots \qquad\qquad\qquad\qquad\qquad\qquad\qquad\qquad\qquad \vdots$$

$$SP_m = X_{m,1} \xrightarrow{F} Y_{m,1} \xrightarrow{r} X_{m,2} \xrightarrow{F} Y_{m,2} \xrightarrow{r} \cdots \xrightarrow{F} Y_{m,t} \xrightarrow{r} EP_m$$

Fig. 1. Structure of a Hellman table

applicable to both Hellman and rainbow tradeoffs. Besides the starting points and ending points, additional information on some intermediate points are also stored. During the online phase the attacker regenerates the pre-computed chain only when a match of both the ending point and the checkpoints is found. Suppose a 1-bit information b_j about the intermediate point $X_{j,t-c}$ is extracted by a function G, i.e. $b_j = G(X_{j,t-c})$. During the online phase at the k-th iteration if an alarm is encountered and $k \geq c$, then we have

$$Pr\{b_j = G(Y_{k-c})|X_{j,t-c} \neq Y_{k-c}\} \approx \frac{1}{2}.$$

Hence the comparison of checkpoint information can be used to filter out false alarms without regenerating the pre-computed chain.

2.2 Pre-image under Function Iteration

In this subsection we present previous results concerning the size of a pre-image set under an iteration of functions. The framework was established in [8] to analyze the cost of false alarms in Hellman tradeoff and rainbow tradeoff.

We consider a random one-way function $F : \mathcal{N} \to \mathcal{N}$, where $\mathcal{N}$ is a set of size N. Note that in Hellman tradeoff and rainbow tradeoff, the one-way function F is followed by a reduction function. Considering F as a random function, the following results are applicable to both Hellman tradeoff and rainbow tradeoff. We denote the k-times iteration of F by $F^k = F \circ \cdots \circ F$. It is well known that if m_0 distinct random inputs are subject to F^k, the expected image size denoted by m_k can be approximated by

$$m_k \approx \frac{N}{N/m_0 + k/2}. \tag{1}$$

Definition 1. *An i-node with respect to a mapping is an element of the range space with exactly i-many pre-images. For each non-negative integers i and k, let*

$$\mathcal{R}_{k,i}(F) = \{y \in \mathcal{N} | y \text{ is an } i\text{-node under } F^k\},$$

$$\mathcal{D}_{k,i}(F) = \{x \in \mathcal{N} | F^k(x) \in \mathcal{R}_{k,i}(F)\}$$

denote the set of i-nodes and pre-images of i-nodes, associated to the mapping F^k. An element of $\mathcal{R}_{k,i}(F)$ will be referred to as an (F^k, i)-node and the probability of a random point from the range space $\mathcal{N}$ to be an (F^k, i)-node is

$$p_{k,i} = \frac{|\mathcal{R}_{k,i}|}{N}.$$

For each non-negative integer k, fix a notation

$$\mathcal{P}_k(x) = \sum_{i=0}^{\infty} p_{k,i} x^i,$$

for the formal power series relating to (F_k, i)-node ratios.

A closed form approximation for function $\mathcal{P}_k(x)$ is given in [8].

Theorem 1.
$$\mathcal{P}_k(x) = 1 - \frac{2(1-x)}{2 + k(1-x)}.$$

The number of points that are F^k-equivalent to a set of points is formulated by the following theorem, given the image space size. The theorem is frequently used by our later analysis and will not be explicitly specified.

Theorem 2. *Let $D_0 \subset \mathcal{N}$ be a set of randomly chosen points. If the number of distinct elements in $D_t = F^t(D_0)$ is m_t, then the pre-image of D_t under F^k is expected to be of size*

$$m_t(1+k)(1 - \frac{m_t k}{4N}).$$

3   Checkpoints for Non-perfect Rainbow Tradeoff

In this section, we analyze the expected number of chains to be regenerated due to false alarms and the expected decreasing number of chain regenerations by checkpoints in a single non-perfect rainbow table. Note that if an online chain matches a common ending point of several pre-computed chains, then all these chains will have to be regenerated for false alarm verification. In [12] and [8], they compute the expected number of false alarms by simply ignoring the collisions in pre-computed chains and treating the pre-computed chains as independent chains. However the reasoning might not be obvious. We adopt a natural approach to compute the expected number of chains to be regenerated at the k-th iteration. This leads us to identical results but explains the real nature of false alarms.

We consider a non-perfect rainbow table constructed from $m_0 = m$ distinct starting points $RT_0 \subset \mathcal{N}$. Denote the chain length by t. For $1 \leq k \leq t$, denote the number of distinct elements in $RT_k = F^k(RT_0)$ by m_k, then we have $m_k \approx \frac{N}{N/m+k/2}$. We first study the expected number of pre-images of $F^k(x)$ under F^t that belongs to RT_0, with a random selection of $x \in \mathcal{N}$ at the k-th iteration.

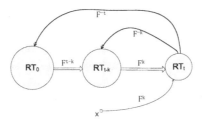

Definition 2. *If we randomly choose a point $x \in \mathcal{N}$ and assume $F^k(x) \in RT_t$, then denote the number of pre-images of $F^k(x)$ under F^k that belongs to RT_{t-k} by $\mathcal{C}(k,k)$, and denote the number of pre-images of $F^k(x)$ under F^t that belongs to RT_0 by $\mathcal{C}(k,t)$.*

Proposition 1.

$$
p_{k,i} =
\begin{cases}
\dfrac{k}{k+2} & i = 0 \\[2mm]
\dfrac{4}{k(k+2)} \cdot \left(1 - \dfrac{2}{k+2}\right)^i & i \geq 1
\end{cases}.
$$

Proof. Recall from Theorem 1 that

$$
\mathcal{P}_k(x) = \sum_{i=0}^{\infty} p_{k,i} x^i = 1 - \frac{2(1-x)}{2 + k(1-x)}.
$$

For $i \geq 1$,

$$
\mathcal{P}_k^{(i)}(x) = 4 \cdot i! \cdot k^{i-1} \cdot (2 + k(1-x))^{-(i+1)}.
$$

According to the Maclaurin Series Expansion, we have

$$
p_{k,i} = \frac{\mathcal{P}_k^{(i)}(0)}{i!} = \frac{4}{k(k+2)} \cdot \left(1 - \frac{2}{k+2}\right)^i,
$$

if $i \geq 1$. When $i = 0$, $p_{k,i} = \mathcal{P}_k(0) = \frac{k}{k+2}$.   □

Proposition 2.

$$
\mathcal{C}(k,k) = \frac{(\frac{m_{t-k} \cdot k}{N} + 2)^2}{\frac{m_{t-k} \cdot k}{N} + 4}, \quad \mathcal{C}(k,t) = \frac{(\frac{m_{t-k} \cdot k}{N} + 2)^2}{\frac{m_{t-k} \cdot k}{N} + 4} \cdot \frac{m}{m_{t-k}}.
$$

Proof. Randomly choose a point $x \in \mathcal{N}$, denote by random variable A the number of pre-images of $F^k(x)$ under F^k. Since $p_{k,i}$ is the proportion of i-nodes in the domain space and every i-node has i pre-images under F^k, then the probability of a random x to produce an (F^k, i)-node is

$$
Pr\{A = i\} = Pr\{F^k(x) \text{ is an } i\text{-node under } F^k\} = i \cdot p_{k,i}.
$$

Denote by random variable B the number of pre-images of $F^k(x)$ under F^k that belongs to RT_{t-k}. Then for $j \leq i$, we have

$$Pr\{B = j | A = i\} = C_i^j (1 - \frac{m_{t-k}}{N})^{i-j} (\frac{m_{t-k}}{N})^j,$$

$$Pr\{B \neq 0 | A = i\} = 1 - (1 - \frac{m_{t-k}}{N})^i.$$

By the law of total probability, for $j \geq 1$ we have

$$Pr\{B = j\} = \sum_{i=j}^{N} Pr\{B = j | A = i\} \cdot Pr\{A = i\}$$

$$= \sum_{i=j}^{N} C_i^j (1 - \frac{m_{t-k}}{N})^{i-j} (\frac{m_{t-k}}{N})^j \cdot \frac{4}{k(k+2)} \cdot i(1 - \frac{2}{k+2})^i,$$

$$Pr\{B \neq 0\} = \sum_{i=1}^{N} Pr\{B \neq 0 | A = i\} \cdot Pr\{A = i\}$$

$$= \sum_{i=1}^{N} [1 - (1 - \frac{m_{t-k}}{N})^i] \cdot \frac{4}{k(k+2)} \cdot i(1 - \frac{2}{k+2})^i.$$

Thus

$$C(k, k) = \sum_{j=1}^{m} j \cdot Pr\{B = j | B \neq 0\}$$

$$= \sum_{j=1}^{m} \frac{j \cdot \sum_{i=j}^{N} C_i^j (1 - \frac{m_{t-k}}{N})^{i-j} (\frac{m_{t-k}}{N})^j \cdot \frac{4}{k(k+2)} \cdot i(1 - \frac{2}{k+2})^i}{\sum_{i=1}^{N} [1 - (1 - \frac{m_{t-k}}{N})^i] \cdot \frac{4}{k(k+2)} \cdot i(1 - \frac{2}{k+2})^i}$$

$$= \frac{\sum_{j=1}^{m} j \cdot \sum_{i=j}^{N} C_i^j (1 - \frac{m_{t-k}}{N})^{i-j} (\frac{m_{t-k}}{N})^j \cdot \frac{4}{k(k+2)} \cdot i(1 - \frac{2}{k+2})^i}{\sum_{i=1}^{N} [1 - (1 - \frac{m_{t-k}}{N})^i] \cdot \frac{4}{k(k+2)} \cdot i(1 - \frac{2}{k+2})^i}$$

$$= \frac{\sum_{i=1}^{N} \sum_{j=1}^{i} j \cdot C_i^j (1 - \frac{m_{t-k}}{N})^{i-j} (\frac{m_{t-k}}{N})^j \cdot \frac{4}{k(k+2)} \cdot i(1 - \frac{2}{k+2})^i}{\sum_{i=1}^{N} [1 - (1 - \frac{m_{t-k}}{N})^i] \cdot \frac{4}{k(k+2)} \cdot i(1 - \frac{2}{k+2})^i}$$

$$= \frac{\sum_{i=1}^{N} i \cdot \frac{m_{t-k}}{N} \cdot \frac{4}{k(k+2)} \cdot i(1 - \frac{2}{k+2})^i}{\sum_{i=1}^{N} [1 - (1 - \frac{m_{t-k}}{N})^i] \cdot \frac{4}{k(k+2)} \cdot i(1 - \frac{2}{k+2})^i}$$

$$\approx \frac{\frac{m_{t-k}}{N} \cdot t^3 \int_0^{\infty} x^2 e^{-\frac{2t}{k+2}x} dx}{t^2 \int_0^{\infty} x(1 - e^{-\frac{m_{t-k}t}{N}x}) \cdot e^{-\frac{2t}{k+2}x} dx}$$

$$\approx \frac{(\frac{m_{t-k} \cdot k}{N} + 2)^2}{\frac{m_{t-k} \cdot k}{N} + 4}.$$

Given a random $x \in RT_{t-k}$, the expected number of pre-images of x under F^{t-k} that belongs to RT_0 is $\frac{m_0}{m_{t-k}}$, then we have

$$\mathcal{C}(k,t) = \mathcal{C}(k,k) \cdot \frac{m_0}{m_{t-k}} = \frac{(\frac{m_{t-k} \cdot k}{N} + 2)^2}{\frac{m_{t-k} \cdot k}{N} + 4} \cdot \frac{m}{m_{t-k}}.$$

$\square$

Non-perfect Rainbow Tradeoff without Checkpoints. For a non-perfect table without checkpoints, at the k-th iteration during the online phase, the probability of an alarm is $Pr\{F^k(x) \in RT_t\} = \frac{1}{N}\{m_t(1+k)(1 - \frac{m_t k}{4N})\}$. The expected number of chains to be regenerated for every alarm is $\mathcal{C}(k,t)$. Then the expected number of chains to be regenerated at the k-th iteration is

$$\mathcal{C}(k,t) \cdot \frac{1}{N}\{m_t(1+k)(1 - \frac{m_t k}{4N})\} \approx \frac{m(1+k)}{N}. \tag{2}$$

Thus the expected number of chains to be regenerated due to false alarms at the k-th iteration is $\frac{1}{N}(m(1+k) - m)$. It is exactly what the authors claimed in [8].

Non-perfect Rainbow Tradeoff with n Checkpoints. Let $c_1, c_2, \cdots, c_n$ $(c_1 < c_2 < \cdots < c_n)$ be the positions of n 1-bit checkpoints. That is the n checkpoints are located at the $(t - c_j)$-th columns for $j = 1, \cdots, n$. Let $c_0 = 0$ and $c_{n+1} = t$.

We compute the expected number of chains to be regenerated at the k-th iteration such that $c_j < k \leq c_{j+1}$ $(j = 1, \cdots, n)$. Given a random $x \in \mathcal{N}$, we have

$$Pr\{F^{k-c_j}(x) \in RT_{t-c_j}\} = \frac{m_{t-c_j}(1 + k - c_j)}{N}[1 - \frac{m_{t-c_j}(k - c_j)}{4N}].$$

In such a case, an alarm always occurs and the expected number of chains to be regenerated is

$$Pr\{F^{k-c_j}(x) \in RT_{t-c_j}\} \cdot \mathcal{C}(k - c_j, t - c_j) = \frac{m(1 + k - c_j)}{N}.$$

For $0 \leq u \leq j - 1$,

$$Pr\{F^{k-c_u}(x) \in RT_{t-c_u}\} = \frac{m_{t-c_u}(1 + k - c_u)}{N}[1 - \frac{m_{t-c_u}(k - c_u)}{4N}].$$

Then the expected number of pre-computed chains that merge with an online chain before the $(t - c_u)$-th column is

$$Pr\{F^{k-c_u}(x) \in RT_{t-c_u}\} \cdot \mathcal{C}(k - c_u, t - c_u) = \frac{m(1 + k - c_u)}{N}.$$

Thus the expected number of pre-computed chains that merge with an online chain between the $(t - c_{u+1})$-th column and the $(t - c_u)$-th column is

$$\frac{m(1 + k - c_u)}{N} - \frac{m(1 + k - c_{u+1})}{N}.$$

In such a case, an alarm occurs with probability $1/2^{j-u}$. Therefore the expected number of chains to be regenerated at the k-th iteration such that $c_j < k \leq c_{j+1}$ $(j = 1, \cdots, n)$ is

$$\frac{m(1+k-c_j)}{N} + \sum_{u=0}^{j-1} \frac{1}{2^{j-u}} [\frac{m(1+k-c_u)}{N} - \frac{m(1+k-c_{u+1})}{N}].$$

Combined with Equation (2), we get the expected decreasing number of chains to be regenerated due to checkpoints. This simplifies to the same results as in [12].

Simulation Results. Our one-way function is built from a reduced version of MD5 hash function with $N = 2^{24}$. We built our pre-computed table from $m = 2^{16}$ different starting point and the chain length is $t = 300$. Table 1 shows that Proposition 2 agrees well with the experiment.

Table 1. Verification of Proposition 2

k	$\mathcal{C}(k,t)$	
	Theory	Experiment
50	1.6363	1.6333
100	1.6900	1.6916
150	1.7473	1.7230
200	1.8087	1.8199
250	1.8745	1.8661
300	1.9453	1.9507

4   Checkpoints for Perfect Rainbow Tradeoff

Perfect rainbow table is constructed by eliminating merged chains and thus reduces the cost of false alarms. Most rainbow tables available online are perfected before they are released to the public. It requires much more pre-computation for the generation of a perfect table, because chains with duplicate endpoints are removed.

We consider a perfect rainbow created with m_0 starting points and denote the chain length by t. Then we expect to collect $m = \frac{N}{N/m_0+t/2}$ non-merging chains. Let $r = \frac{m_0 t}{N}$ be the pre-computation coefficient. When a perfect table is created with $m_0 = N$ starting point, we have $m = \frac{N}{N/m_0+t/2} = \frac{2N}{t+2}$, and the table is referred to as a maximal perfect rainbow table. Let $\bar{r} = \frac{mt}{N}$, then $\bar{r} \leq \frac{2t}{t+2} \approx 2$. Table 2 shows that building a maximal perfect rainbow table (with $\bar{r}$ close to 2) is very costly and is seldom used in practice. An analysis of multiple checkpoints in maximal perfect tables was given in [4]. In this section, we give the first way

Table 2. Relations in a perfect rainbow table

r	$\bar{r}$	success rate	r	$\bar{r}$	success rate
1.0607	0.6931	50%	1.6911	0.9163	60%
3.0251	1.2040	70%	4.5178	1.3863	75%
8.2407	1.6094	80%	18.4363	1.8971	85%

to find optimal positions of multiple checkpoints even when the perfect table is not maximum.

Suppose n checkpoints are located at the $(t - c_j)$-th columns for $j = 1, \cdots, n$ ($c_1 < c_2 < \cdots < c_n$). Let $c_0 = 0$ and $c_{n+1} = t$. In a perfect table for every false alarm only one chain need to be regenerated, so we only need to compute the probability of false alarms at the k-th iteration, for $c_j < k \le c_{j+1}$ ($j = 1, \cdots, n$). Given a random $x \in \mathcal{N}$, we have

$$Pr\{F^{k-c_j}(x) \in RT_{t-c_j}\} = \frac{m(1 + k - c_j)}{N}[1 - \frac{m(k - c_j)}{4N}].$$

In such a case, an alarm always occurs. For $0 \le u \le j - 1$,

$$Pr\{F^{k-c_u}(x) \in RT_{t-c_u}\} = \frac{m(1 + k - c_u)}{N}[1 - \frac{m(k - c_u)}{4N}].$$

Thus the probability of a merge of the online chain with pre-computed chain between the $(t - c_{u+1})$-th column and the $(t - c_u)$-th column is

$$\frac{m(1 + k - c_u)}{N}[1 - \frac{m(k - c_u)}{4N}] - \frac{m(1 + k - c_{u+1})}{N}[1 - \frac{m(k - c_{u+1})}{4N}].$$

In such a case, an alarm occurs with probability $1/2^{j-u}$. Also the expected number of alarms at the k-th iteration without checkpoints is

$$Pr\{F^k(x) \in RT_t\} = \frac{m(1 + k)}{N}(1 - \frac{mk}{4N}).$$

Therefore the expected decreasing number of false alarms at the k-th iteration such that $c_j < k \le c_{j+1}$ ($j = 1, \cdots, n$) is

$$D(k,j) = \frac{m(1 + k)}{N}(1 - \frac{mk}{4N}) - \left\{ \frac{m(1 + k - c_j)}{N}[1 - \frac{m(k - c_j)}{4N}] \right.$$

$$+ \sum_{u=0}^{j-1} \frac{1}{2^{j-u}} \left(\frac{m(1 + k - c_u)}{N}[1 - \frac{m(k - c_u)}{4N}] - \frac{m(1 + k - c_{u+1})}{N}[1 - \frac{m(k - c_{u+1})}{4N}] \right) \right\}$$

$$= \frac{1}{N}\{(1 - \frac{1}{2^j}) \cdot m(1 + k)(1 - \frac{mk}{4N}) - \sum_{u=0}^{j-1} \frac{1}{2^{j-u}} m(1 + k - c_{u+1})(1 - \frac{m(k - c_{u+1})}{4N})\}.$$

The k-th iteration of the online phase is executed with probability $(1 - \frac{m}{N})^k$ and every verification of a false alarm requires $(t - k + 1)$ iterations of F. This leads us to the following theorem.

Theorem 3. *The decreasing number of invocations of F due to n checkpoints $(c_1 < c_2 < \cdots < c_n)$ is*

$$S = \sum_{j=1}^{n} \{ \sum_{c_j < k \le c_{j+1}} (t - k + 1) \cdot D(k,j) \cdot (1 - \frac{m}{N})^k \}. \qquad (3)$$

Simplification. We rewrite Equation (3) to the sum of 4 parts.

$$S.1 = \sum_{j=1}^{n} \{ \sum_{c_j < k \le c_{j+1}} (t - k + 1) \frac{1}{N} \{ (1 - \frac{1}{2^j}) \cdot m(1 + k)(1 - \frac{mk}{4N}) \cdot (1 - \frac{m}{N})^k \},$$

$$S.2 = -\sum_{j=1}^{n} \{ \sum_{c_j < k \le c_{j+1}} (t - k + 1) \frac{1}{N} \cdot \sum_{u=0}^{j-1} \frac{1}{2^{j-u}} m(1 + k)(1 - \frac{mk}{4N}) \cdot (1 - \frac{m}{N})^k \},$$

$$S.3 = -\sum_{j=1}^{n} \{ \sum_{c_j < k \le c_{j+1}} (t - k + 1) \frac{1}{N} \{ m \cdot (\frac{m(2k + 1)}{4N} - 1) \cdot \sum_{u=0}^{j-1} \frac{c_{u+1}}{2^{j-u}} \cdot (1 - \frac{m}{N})^k \} \},$$

$$S.4 = \sum_{j=1}^{n} \{ \sum_{c_j < k \le c_{j+1}} (t - k + 1) \frac{1}{N} \{ \frac{m^2}{4N} \cdot \sum_{u=0}^{j-1} \frac{c_{u+1}^2}{2^{j-u}} \cdot (1 - \frac{m}{N})^k \} \}.$$

Computation of S.2:

$$S.2 = -\sum_{j=1}^{n} \{ \sum_{c_j < k \le c_{j+1}} (t - k + 1) \frac{1}{N} \cdot \sum_{u=0}^{j-1} \frac{1}{2^{j-u}} m(1 + k)(1 - \frac{mk}{4N}) \cdot (1 - \frac{m}{N})^k \}$$

$$= -\sum_{j=1}^{n} \{ \sum_{c_j < k \le c_{j+1}} (t - k + 1) \frac{1}{N} \cdot (\sum_{u=0}^{j-1} \frac{1}{2^{j-u}}) \cdot m(1 + k)(1 - \frac{mk}{4N}) \cdot (1 - \frac{m}{N})^k \}$$

$$= -\sum_{j=1}^{n} \{ \sum_{c_j < k \le c_{j+1}} (t - k + 1) \frac{1}{N} \cdot (1 - \frac{1}{2^j}) \cdot m(1 + k)(1 - \frac{mk}{4N}) \cdot (1 - \frac{m}{N})^k \}$$

$$= -S.1.$$

Computation of S.3:

$$S.3 = -\sum_{j=1}^{n} \{ \sum_{c_j < k \le c_{j+1}} (t - k + 1) \frac{1}{N} \{ m \cdot (\frac{m(2k + 1)}{4N} - 1) \cdot \sum_{u=0}^{j-1} \frac{c_{u+1}}{2^{j-u}} \cdot (1 - \frac{m}{N})^k \} \}$$

$$\approx -\frac{mt^2}{N} \cdot \sum_{j=1}^{n} \{ [\sum_{c_j < k \le c_{j+1}} (1 - \frac{k}{t}) \cdot (\frac{mt}{2N} \cdot \frac{k}{t} - 1) e^{-\frac{mt}{N} \cdot \frac{k}{t}}] \cdot \frac{1}{t} \cdot \sum_{u=0}^{j-1} \frac{c_{u+1}}{2^{j-u}} \}$$

$$\approx -\frac{mt^2}{N} \sum_{j=1}^{n} \{ \int_{c_j/t}^{c_{j+1}/t} (1 - x) e^{-\frac{mtx}{N}} (\frac{mt}{2N} \cdot x - 1) \, dx \cdot \sum_{u=0}^{j-1} \frac{c_{u+1}}{2^{j-u}} \}.$$

Computation of S.4:

$$S.4 = \sum_{j=1}^{n} \{ \sum_{c_j < k \le c_{j+1}} (t - k + 1) \frac{1}{N} \{ \frac{m^2}{4N} \cdot \sum_{u=0}^{j-1} \frac{c_{u+1}^2}{2^{j-u}} \cdot (1 - \frac{m}{N})^k \} \}$$

$$= \frac{m^2 t^2}{4N^2} \cdot \sum_{j=1}^{n} \{ [\sum_{c_j < k \le c_{j+1}} (1 - \frac{k}{t}) e^{-\frac{mt}{N} \cdot \frac{k}{t}}] \cdot \frac{1}{t} \cdot \sum_{u=0}^{j-1} \frac{c_{u+1}^2}{2^{j-u}} \}$$

$$= \frac{m^2 t^2}{4N^2} \cdot \sum_{j=1}^{n} \{ \int_{c_j/t}^{c_{j+1}/t} (1 - x) e^{-\frac{mtx}{N}} \, dx \cdot \sum_{u=0}^{j-1} \frac{c_{u+1}^2}{2^{j-u}} \}.$$

Thus Equation (3) simplifies to

$$S = -\frac{mt^2}{N} \sum_{j=1}^{n} \{ \int_{c_j/t}^{c_{j+1}/t} (1 - x) e^{-\frac{mtx}{N}} (\frac{mt}{2N} \cdot x - 1) \, dx \cdot \sum_{u=0}^{j-1} \frac{c_{u+1}}{2^{j-u}} \}$$

$$+ \frac{m^2 t^2}{4N^2} \cdot \sum_{j=1}^{n} \{ \int_{c_j/t}^{c_{j+1}/t} (1 - x) e^{-\frac{mtx}{N}} \, dx \cdot \sum_{u=0}^{j-1} \frac{c_{u+1}^2}{2^{j-u}} \}.$$

Simulation Results. We experiment with $N = 2^{24}$, $m = 65536$, $t = 300$. Table 3 shows the experiment results with 3 checkpoints, located at the 177-th, 218-th and 251-th columns. We used Maple to obtain these optimal positions. The data are averaged over 10000 random inversion targets. The success probability (69.5%) is also close to the theoretical expectation (69.02%).

Table 3. Experiment for 3 checkpoints

	without checkpoint		with 3 checkpoints	
	Theory	Experiment	Theory	Experiment
#total operations	30255	30154	26687	26540
#operation for FA	8812	8833	5265	5219
#false alarms	69.4235	69.4529	42.8058	42.0807

5   Conclusion

Checkpoint is a useful technique to quickly rule out false alarms with a little additional memory. While the positions of checkpoints significantly affect the tradeoff efficiency, one of the key issue is to locate the optimal setting of multiple checkpoints. In this paper, we revisited the analysis of multiple checkpoints in rainbow tradeoff. For non-perfect table we gave a new sight to the computation of the expected decreasing number of false alarms at the k-th iteration. This helps to better understand the real nature of false alarms. For perfect rainbow table, we obtained the first full analysis applicable even if the perfect rainbow table is not maximum. Considering in practice the table available are mostly perfect and not maximum, this part of our work is of value to the ongoing research projects, e.g. the RainbowCrack Project. Through experiment we saw a drastic decrease of cost due to false alarms, with only little additional memory.

References

1. Rainbowcrack project, `http://project-rainbowcrack.com/`
2. Avoine, G., Bourgeois, A., Carpent, X.: Discarding the endpoints makes the cryptanalytic time-memory trade-offs even faster
3. Avoine, G., Junod, P., Oechslin, P.: Time-memory trade-offs: False alarm detection using checkpoints. In: Maitra, S., Veni Madhavan, C.E., Venkatesan, R. (eds.) INDOCRYPT 2005. LNCS, vol. 3797, pp. 183–196. Springer, Heidelberg (2005)
4. Avoine, G., Junod, P., Oechslin, P.: Characterization and improvement of time-memory trade-off based on perfect tables. ACM Transactions on Information and System Security (TISSEC) 11(4), 17 (2008)
5. Biryukov, A., Shamir, A., Wagner, D.: Real time cryptanalysis of A5/1 on a PC. In: Schneier, B. (ed.) FSE 2000. LNCS, vol. 1978, pp. 1–18. Springer, Heidelberg (2001)
6. Borst, J., Preneel, B., Vandewalle, J.: On the time-memory tradeoff between exhaustive key search and table precomputation. In: Symposium on Information Theory in the Benelux, pp. 111–118. Citeseer (1998)
7. Hellman, M.: A cryptanalytic time-memory trade-off. IEEE Transactions on Information Theory 26(4), 401–406 (1980)
8. Hong, J.: The cost of false alarms in hellman and rainbow tradeoffs. Designs, Codes and Cryptography 57(3), 293–327 (2010)
9. Hong, J., Lee, G.W., Ma, D.: Analysis of the parallel distinguished point tradeoff. In: Bernstein, D.J., Chatterjee, S. (eds.) INDOCRYPT 2011. LNCS, vol. 7107, pp. 161–180. Springer, Heidelberg (2011)
10. Hong, J., Moon, S.: A comparison of cryptanalytic tradeoff algorithms. Journal of Cryptology, 1–79 (2010)
11. Kim, B.-I., Hong, J.: Analysis of the non-perfect table fuzzy rainbow tradeoff. In: Boyd, C., Simpson, L. (eds.) ACISP. LNCS, vol. 7959, pp. 347–362. Springer, Heidelberg (2013)
12. Kim, J.W., Seo, J., Hong, J., Park, K., Kim, S.-R.: High-speed parallel implementations of the rainbow method in a heterogeneous system. In: Galbraith, S., Nandi, M. (eds.) INDOCRYPT 2012. LNCS, vol. 7668, pp. 303–316. Springer, Heidelberg (2012)
13. Lee, G.W., Hong, J.: A comparison of perfect table cryptanalytic tradeoff algorithms. Technical report, Cryptology ePrint Archive, Report 2012/540 (2012)
14. Nohl, K.: Attacking phone privacy. BlackHat 2010 Lecture Notes (2010)
15. Oechslin, P.: Making a faster cryptanalytic time-memory trade-off. In: Boneh, D. (ed.) CRYPTO 2003. LNCS, vol. 2729, pp. 617–630. Springer, Heidelberg (2003)
16. Saarinen, M.-J.O.: A time-memory tradeoff attack against LILI-128. In: Daemen, J., Rijmen, V. (eds.) FSE 2002. LNCS, vol. 2365, pp. 231–236. Springer, Heidelberg (2002)

A   When Multiple Tables Are Used

It is easy to translate the results to the case when l tables are processed in parallel. We just give the results and omit the proof.

Corollary 1. *For non-perfect rainbow tables with the parameters m, t, and l, where l is number of tables. Given n checkpoints $c_1 < c_2 < \cdots < c_n$, the expected number of f invocations that can be removed through checkpoints is*

$$l \sum_{j=1}^{n} \left\{ \sum_{c_j < k \le c_{j+1}} (t - k + 1) \cdot \frac{m}{N} \sum_{u=0}^{j-1} \left(\frac{c_{u+1}}{2^{j-u}} \right) \cdot \prod (1 - \frac{m_{t-i}}{N})^l \right\}.$$

Corollary 2. *For perfect rainbow tables with the parameters m, t, and l, where l is number of tables. Given n checkpoints $c_1 < c_2 < \cdots < c_n$, the expected number of f invocations that can be removed through checkpoints is*

$$-\frac{mt^2 l}{N} \sum_{j=1}^{n} \left\{ \int_{c_j/t}^{c_{j+1}/t} (1-x) e^{-\frac{mtlx}{N}} \left(\frac{mt}{2N} \cdot x - 1 \right) dx \cdot \sum_{u=0}^{j-1} \frac{c_{u+1}}{2^{j-u}} \right\}$$

$$+ \frac{m^2 t^2 l}{4N^2} \cdot \sum_{j=1}^{n} \left\{ \int_{c_j/t}^{c_{j+1}/t} (1-x) e^{-\frac{mtlx}{N}} dx \cdot \sum_{u=0}^{j-1} \frac{c_{u+1}^2}{2^{j-u}} \right\}.$$

B   Maple Code for Optimal Checkpoints in Perfect Rainbow Tradeoff

```
>   with(Optimization);
>   N  := 2^24;
>   m  := 65536;
>   t  := 300;
>   l  := 3;
>   n  := 4;
>   c  := array(1 .. n);
>   S  := {}:
>   for i from 1 to n-1 do
>   S  := S union {c[i] <= c[i+1]}
>   end do:
>   S  := S union {c[n] <= t}:
>   eval(
>   -m^2*l*t^3/N/N/2*sum(int((1-x)*x*exp(-m*t*l/N*x),
>   x=c[j]/t..c[j+1]/t)*sum(c[u+1]*2^(u-j),u=0..j-1),
>   j=1..n-1)+m*l*t^2/N*sum(int((1-x)*exp(-m*t*l/N*x),
>   x=c[j]/t..c[j+1]/t)*sum(c[u+1]*2^(u-j),u=0..j-1),
>   j=1..n-1)+m^2*t^2*l/4/N/N*sum(int((1-x)*exp(-m*t*l/N*x),
>   x=c[j]/t..c[j+1]/t)*sum((c[u+1])^2*2^(u-j),u=0..j-1),
>   j=1..n-1)):
>   Maximize(%,S, assume=nonnegative);
```

Efficient Implementation of NIST-Compliant Elliptic Curve Cryptography for Sensor Nodes

Zhe Liu[1], Hwajeong Seo[2], Johann Großschädl[1], and Howon Kim[2]

[1] University of Luxembourg,
Laboratory of Algorithmics, Cryptology and Security (LACS),
6, rue R. Coudenhove-Kalergi, 1359 Luxembourg-Kirchberg, Luxembourg
{zhe.liu,johann.groszschaedl}@uni.lu
[2] Pusan National University,
School of Computer Science and Engineering,
San-30, Jangjeon-Dong, Geumjeong-Gu, Busan 609–735, Republic of Korea
{hwajeong,howonkim}@pusan.ac.kr

Abstract. In this paper, we present a highly-optimized implementation of standards-compliant Elliptic Curve Cryptography (ECC) for wireless sensor nodes and similar devices featuring an 8-bit AVR processor. The field arithmetic is written in Assembly language and optimized for the 192-bit NIST-specified prime $p = 2^{192} - 2^{64} - 1$, while the group arithmetic (i.e. point addition and doubling) is programmed in ANSI C. One of our contributions is a novel *lazy doubling* method for multi-precision squaring which provides better performance than any of the previously-proposed squaring techniques. Based on our highly optimized arithmetic library for the 192-bit NIST prime, we achieve record-setting execution times for scalar multiplication (with both fixed and arbitrary points) as well as multiple scalar multiplication. Experimental results, obtained on an AVR ATmega128 processor, show that the two scalar multiplications of ephemeral Elliptic Curve Diffie-Hellman (ECDH) key exchange can be executed in 1.75 s altogether (at a clock frequency of 7.37 MHz) and consume an energy of some 42 mJ. The generation and verification of an ECDSA signature requires roughly 1.91 s and costs 46 mJ at the same clock frequency. Our results significantly improve the state-of-the-art in ECDH and ECDSA computation on the P-192 curve, outperforming the previous best implementations in the literature by a factor of 1.35 and 2.33, respectively. We also protected the field arithmetic and algorithms for scalar multiplication against side-channel attacks, especially Simple Power Analysis (SPA).

1 Introduction

Wireless Sensor Networks (WSNs) are a key technology of the 21st century, enabling new applications in such domains as infrastructure protection, industrial automation and health monitoring, to name a few [1]. A WSN can be defined as a network composed of autonomous, battery-powered computing devices (called nodes) with sensing and wireless networking capabilities. The sensor nodes are

S. Qing et al. (Eds.): ICICS 2013, LNCS 8233, pp. 302–317, 2013.

deployed in a certain environment or area of interest to monitor a phenomenon or condition such as temperature, humidity, luminosity, etc. They cooperatively collect and aggregate sensor readings and send them to a central unit (the base station) for further processing and decision making. Unfortunately, WSNs face all security threats inherent in any wireless network, plus additional ones that are hard to protect against [24]. Since WSNs are often deployed in unattended areas, an attacker may be able to access individual nodes and perform various kinds of physical attacks, e.g. side-channel cryptanalysis [10]. The integration of countermeasures against such attacks is a nontrivial task due to the resource constraints (in particular limited energy) of battery-powered sensor nodes like the MICAz mote [8]. These constraints make a good case for using lightweight cryptosystems that can be effectively protected against side-channel attacks. In the context of public-key cryptography, elliptic-curve based algorithms such as ECDH and ECDSA are known to meet these requirements [15].

Energy is the most precious resource of a wireless sensor node. The MICAz mote [8], for example, is powered by two 1.5 V AA batteries, which can not be easily recharged or replaced after deployment. In general, the energy consumption of cryptographic software depends primarily on the execution time of the algorithm and the average power dissipation of the processor it is executed on [11]. However, a cryptographic engineer can only influence the former since the choice of the processor is normally not under his control. The overall execution time of most elliptic curve cryptosystems is dominated by the time needed to perform a scalar multiplication, which, in turn, depends on a number of factors such as the order of the elliptic-curve group, the actual implementation of the point arithmetic, and the efficiency of certain operations (e.g. multiplication) in the underlying finite field [15]. Another important aspect is the concrete form of the elliptic curve; for example, Montgomery curves [25] or Twisted Edwards curves [16] allow for more efficient point addition/doubling than conventional Weierstraß curves. Unfortunately, these special curve shapes are not standardized, which prevents their use in commercial applications that need to undergo a certification process. On the other hand, curves specified by standards bodies like the NIST facilitate inter-operability and maximize access to resources and services. Therefore, we decided to adopt the NIST-recommended elliptic curve P-192 from [26] for our implementation.

Elliptic Curve Cryptography (ECC) has been exhaustively researched in the past 25 years and is nowadays considered an excellent option for the implementation of key exchange and digital signatures. Virtually all ECC cryptosystems of practical importance require to execute one (resp. two) of the following three variants of scalar multiplication: (i) $k \cdot P$ where the point P is fixed and known a priori (called *fixed-point scalar multiplication*), (ii) $k \cdot Q$ with Q being an arbitrary point not known in advance, and (iii) $k \cdot P + l \cdot Q$ where P is fixed and Q is an arbitrary point (called *double scalar multiplication*). For example, the classical ECDH key exchange protocol consists of two stages; in the first stage a key-pair is created, which comprises a fixed-point scalar multiplication by the generator of an elliptic-curve group of prime order. The second stage involves a scalar multiplication by a point that, unlike to the first stage, is neither fixed nor known in advance. Something similar holds for ECDSA since the signature-generation process entails a fixed-point scalar multiplication like the first stage of ECDH. However, the verification of an ECDSA signature requires to execute a double scalar multiplication of the form $k \cdot P + l \cdot Q$, whereby one of the two points is not known in advance.

1.1   Overview of Related Work and Motivation for Our Work

In the past ten years, a multitude of ECC implementations for 8-bit processors appeared in the literature. The first milestone belongs to Gura et al [14], who introduced highly-optimized ECC software for 8-bit AVR microcontrollers like the ATmega128 [4] and reported an execution time of roughly 0.81 s and 1.24 s for a 160-bit and 192-bit scalar multiplication, respectively (at a frequency of 8 MHz). They also found that the relative performance advantage of ECC versus RSA increases with larger key sizes (i.e. larger groups). TinyECC [22] was one of the first publicly available and, hence, widely used ECC libraries for wireless sensor nodes. Most parts of TinyECC are implemented in nesC, but it contains also numerous processor-specific optimizations (written in Assembly language) for common 8-bit and 16-bit sensor platforms. It has been tested successfully on MICA2/MICAz, TelosB/Tmote Sky, BSNV3, and the Imote2 node. TinyECC supports the SECG-specified 128-bit and 160-bit domain parameters as well as the NIST curve P-192 through dedicated field and curve arithmetic operations [22]. There exist many other efficient ECC implementations for 8-bit AVR processors, e.g. WM-ECC [33], Nano-ECC [31], MIRACL [6], NaCl [17] using prime fields and RELIC [2] for binary fields.

All currently-existing prime-field based ECC libraries use either the hybrid multiplication technique [14] (or a variant of it [6,22,33,31,20]) or employ the Karatsuba method (e.g. NaCl [17]) for the performance-critical multi-precision multiplication and squaring. Recently, the operand caching method [18] and its successor, the consecutive operand caching method [28], were proposed as new techniques to speed up multi-precision multiplication on embedded micro-controllers, while Lee et al [21] developed several optimizations for multi-precision squaring. However, these recent papers focussed exclusively on multi-precision arithmetic and did not evaluate the impact of the described techniques on the overall execution time of a scalar multiplication. It is, therefore, interesting to combine these sophisticated multiplication and squaring techniques in order to push the envelope of ECC on AVR micro-controllers. However, performance is not our only goal since, as pointed out before, protection against side-channel cryptanalysis (i.e. timing and SPA attacks) is similarly important. Most of the previous ECC libraries, however, do not contain countermeasures; the only two exceptions are the work from [20] and NaCl [17]. Lederer et al [20] implemented ECDH for WSNs and protected the scalar multiplication against SPA attacks by adopting highly "regular" variants of the comb and window method, respectively. Their ECDH software uses a 192-bit prime field specified by the NIST as underlying algebraic structure and needs $5.20 \cdot 10^6$ and $12.33 \cdot 10^6$ clock cycles an ATmega128 processor to to compute a fixed-point and random-point scalar multiplication, respectively. NaCl is a cryptographic library whose ECC part is based on Curve-25519 [5] and, therefore, provides a (symmetric) security level of about 128 bits. Unfortunately, a scalar multiplication on Curve-25519 needs at least $22.95 \cdot 10^6$ clock cycles when executed on an ATmega128 micro-controller (i.e. 3.11 s at a frequency of 7.37 MHz), which naturally raises the question of how well Curve25519 is suited for battery-powered sensors nodes.

1.2   Our Contributions

We introduce a number of optimizations to improve both the performance and security (i.e. resistance against timing and SPA attacks) of scalar multiplication on the NIST curve P-192 when executed on an 8-bit AVR micro-controller. The contribution of this paper is threefold.

- *New approach for the efficient implementation of multi-precision squaring on 8-bit AVR micro-controllers.* The novel "lazy doubling" method we describe in this paper has been specially devised for multi-precision squaring. When executed on the ATmega128, it needs merely 2,064 clock cycles to square a 192-bit integer, which sets a new speed record for multi-precision squaring on an 8-bit processor.
- *Highly optimized arithmetic library for the NIST P-192 field.* All operations of our library (except inversion) are implemented in a highly regular fashion independent of the value of the operands, which helps to thwart timing and SPA attacks. Yet, our implementation of arithmetic operations modulo the 192-bit NIST prime is more than twice as fast as the widely-used TinyECC library, the current de-facto standard for ECC in WSNs [22].
- *Record-setting execution times for ECDH and ECDSA over a 192-bit prime field.* We employ a regular variant of the fixed-base comb technique for the fixed-point scalar multiplication and a window method with a window size of 4 when the point is not known a priori, while the double scalar multiplication is executed in an interleaved fashion with joint doublings. Practical results, obtained on an ATmega128, demonstrate that our work exceeds the state-of-the-art in ECDH key agreement and ECDSA signature generation (resp. verification), outperforming the best implementations reported in the literature by a factor of 1.35 [20] and 2.33 [22], respectively.

The rest of the paper is organized as follows. In Section 2, we briefly discuss the mathematical foundations of ECC and describe the basic properties of the NIST curve P-192 we adopt in our implementation. Thereafter, we explain the algorithms for fixed-point and arbitrary-point scalar multiplication (for ECDH) as well as double-scalar multiplication (for ECDSA). In Section 3, we introduce our implementation of the field operations for the 192-bit prime, including the new "lazy doubling" method for multi-precision squaring. The implementation results (e.g. execution time, energy consumption, RAM footprint) we achieved are summarized in Section 4. Finally, we conclude the paper in Section 5.

2   Elliptic Curve Cryptography

In this section, we first discuss some implementation aspects of ECC and then present the domain parameters we used in our implementation. Thereafter, we describe algorithms for fixed-point and arbitrary-point scalar multiplication as well as double scalar multiplication.

2.1   NIST Curve P-192

Let $\mathbb{F}_p$ be a prime field. An elliptic curve E over $\mathbb{F}_p$ can be defined through a short Weierstraß equation of the form $y^2 = x^3 + ax + b$, whereby $a, b \in \mathbb{F}_p$ and $4a^3 + 27b^2 \neq 0$. In order to improve efficiency, it is common practice to fix the curve parameter a to -3 (i.e. $a = p - 3$) since this choice allows for optimizing the point arithmetic, as will be discussed in more detail below. All prime-field curves standardized by the NIST in [26] adopt this approach; consequently, the so-called "NIST curves" can be defined via a short Weierstraß equation of the following form

$$E : \; y^2 = x^3 - 3x + b \tag{1}$$

Before an elliptic curve cryptosystem can actually be carried out, the involved parties need to agree on a set of domain parameters, which specifies besides the curve and field to be used also a base point $G = (x_G, y_G)$ that generates a large cyclic subgroup of $E(\mathbb{F}_p)$, the order n of this subgroup (which is a prime), and the co-factor $h = \#E(\mathbb{F}_p)/n$ [15]. All five NIST curves over prime fields have a co-factor of $h = 1$; consequently, any point P whose x and y coordinates fulfill Equation 1 has prime order n. This property prevents small subgroup attacks and, therefore, simplifies the implementation of ECDH key agreement. On the other hand, Edwards curves and Montgomery curves require specific measures to thwart these attacks since they always have a co-factor of $h \geq 4$. Among the five prime-field curves specified in [26], the curve P-192 is the most suitable one for resource-constrained sensor nodes as it offers a reasonable balance between security and execution time (i.e. energy consumption). This curve uses the field $\mathbb{F}_p$ defined by the generalized-Mersenne (GM) prime

$$p = 2^{192} - 2^{64} - 1 \tag{2}$$

as underlying algebraic structure to facilitate the modular reduction. As shown in [15], the product of two 192-bit integers can be reduced via three additions modulo p by exploiting the relation $2^{192} \equiv 2^{64} + 1 \bmod p$. The parameter b, the base point G, and the order n of curve P-192 can be found in [26].

In order to avoid expensive inversions in $\mathbb{F}_p$, we represent the points on the curve using projective coordinates. According to [15, Table 3.3], Jacobian projective coordinates yield the most efficient formula for point doubling, whereas mixed Jacobian-affine coordinates allows for the fastest point addition on curve P-192. Based on [15, Algorithm 3.22], a mixed addition needs 8 multiplications (8M) and 3 squarings (3S) in the underlying field. The doubling of a point costs only 4 multiplications and the same number of squarings (i.e. 4M + 4S).

2.2 Algorithms for Scalar Multiplication

The Elliptic Curve Diffie-Hellman (ECDH) key exchange technique has much in common with the "classical" Diffie-Hellman scheme, but operates in an elliptic curve group $E(\mathbb{F}_p)$ instead of $\mathbb{Z}_p^*$ [15]. There exist two principal variants of the ECDH protocol, namely static ECDH and ephemeral ECDH. The latter is computationally more demanding, but provides the important advantage of forward secrecy. Ephemeral ECDH requires each of the two involved parties to perform two scalar multiplications; the first to generate an ephemeral key pair, and the second to obtain the shared secret. The first scalar multiplication takes a fixed and a-priori-known point as input, namely the generator G, whereas the second scalar multiplication has to be carried out with an arbitrary point not known in advance. Consequently, ephemeral ECDH key agreement requires each party to execute both a fixed-point and an arbitrary-point scalar multiplication.

A fixed-point scalar multiplication can be efficiently performed through the so-called *fixed-base comb method* as described in Section 3.3.2 of [15]. The idea is to pre-compute and store 2^w multiples of the base point P and then process w bits of the scalar k at once, thereby reducing the number of point doublings by a factor of w and the number of point additions by roughly $w/2$ compared to the straightforward double-and-add method. A window size of $w = 4$ represents a good trade-off between performance and storage requirements since only 16 points need to be pre-computed. In this case, a fixed-point scalar multiplication on curve P-192 requires 48 point doublings and up to 48 point additions. The multiples of the base point to be pre-computed are linear combinations of the form $d_3 \cdot (2^{144} P) + d_2 \cdot (2^{96} P) + d_1 \cdot (2^{48} P) + d_0 \cdot P$ with $d_i \in \{0, 1\}$. As indicated before, our comb method represents (and processes) a 192-bit scalar k in 4-bit digits $K_i = 8k_{144+i} + 4k_{96+i} + 2k_{48+1} + k_i$ for $0 \leq i < 48$ (see [15] for an in-depth description of the fixed-base comb method).

A straightforward implementation of the comb method described above has an irregular execution pattern (and, hence, succumbs to Simple Power Analysis (SPA) attacks [19,15]) since the point addition is only carried out for non-zero digits K_i. Consequently, an attacker able to distinguish point additions from point doublings in the power consumption profile can get the position of 0 bits in the scalar k. One possibility to prevent this SPA leakage is to represent the 4-bit digits using a digit set not containing 0, e.g. $D' = \{\pm 1, \pm 3, \ldots, \pm 15\}$, instead of the ordinary set $D = \{0, 1, \ldots, 15\}$ and adapting the pre-computation of multiples of P accordingly. When doing so, the comb technique executes the same number of point additions and point doublings, independent of the actual value of k, since all K_i are non-zero. Liu et al introduced in [23] a simple (and highly regular) algorithm for the conversion of radix-2^4 integers represented via the canonical digit set D into an equivalent representation based on the zero-free digit set D'. We apply their algorithm to obtain the $K_i \in \{\pm 1, \pm 3, \ldots, \pm 15\}$ in an SPA-resistant fashion. Using D' instead of D also allows one to reduce the storage requirements of the comb method by half since we need to pre-compute only the multiples of P corresponding to the eight positive elements of D'. The negative multiples can be generated "on the fly" via the regular point-negation

---

Algorithm 1. Regular window method for scalar multiplication ($w = 4$)

Input: n-bit scalar $k = (k_{n-1}, \ldots, k_1, k_0)_2$, point $P \in E(\mathbb{F}_p)$.
Output: Scalar product $R = k \cdot P$.

1: Convert k into radix-2^4 representation $k' = (K_{s-1}, \ldots, K_1, K_0)_{16}$ where $s = \lceil n/4 \rceil$
    and $K_i \in \{\pm 1, \pm 3, \ldots, \pm 15\}$ for $0 \leq i \leq s - 1$ as described in [23].
2: Generate look-up table T consisting of 8 points $T[i] = (2i + 1) \cdot P$ for $0 \leq i \leq 7$.
3: $R \leftarrow T[(K_{s-1} - 1)/2]$ $\{K_{s-1}$ is always positive$\}$
4: **for** i from $s - 2$ by 1 down to 0 **do**
5:    $R \leftarrow 16 \cdot R$ $\{$four point doublings$\}$
6:    $R \leftarrow R + \text{sign}(K_i) \cdot T[(|K_i| - 1)/2]$ $\{$one point addition$\}$
7: **end for**
8: **return** R

---

technique described in [23]. In this way, the 4-bit comb method requires a mere 384 bytes in read-only memory (i.e. ROM or Flash) as the pre-computed points are stored in affine coordinates so that we can use the efficient mixed-addition formula given in [15, Algorithm 3.22]

Besides a fixed-point scalar multiplication, each of the two parties involved in an ECDH key agreement also has to perform a scalar multiplication with an arbitrary base point not known in advance. Unfortunately, the comb method involves an expensive pre-computation phase and is, therefore, only useful when the base point is fixed. If this is not the case, it is generally more efficient to employ a *window method* [15] such as shown in Algorithm 1 for a window size of $w = 4$. First, we convert the scalar k into a radix-2^4 representation based on the signed digit set $D' = \{\pm 1, \pm 3, \ldots, \pm 15\}$. Similar to the comb method, we follow the approach introduced in [23] to ensure this conversion does not leak any SPA-relevant information. The next step is then the generation of a table containing eight multiples of P, namely $P, 3P, 5P, \ldots, 15P$. Since all of these points are needed in affine coordinates, it makes sense to do a simultaneous inversion [15, page 44] of the Z coordinates so as to reduce the cost of the table computation. The loop in Algorithm 1 is similar to that of the double-and-add method, but we process a 4-bit digit K_i of k in each iteration instead of just a single bit. At line 6, the pre-computed point from table T corresponding to the absolute value of K_i is loaded from RAM. Even though the index for this table access depends on the secret scalar, there is no information leakage since load operations always have the same latency on an ATmega128. Depending on the sign of K_i, the loaded point is added to R either directly or negated. We again refer to [23] for a description of how this can be performed in a regular fashion without the need to execute conditional statements. The window method with $w = 4$ performs 192 point doublings and 48 point additions, idenpendent of the actual value of k. It occupies 384 byte in RAM for table T.

The Elliptic Curve Digital Signature Algorithm (ECDSA) is a variant of the DSA signature scheme operating in an elliptic curve group [15]. From an arithmetic point of view, the major operation of an ECDSA signature generation is a scalar multiplication by a fixed and a-priori-known base point, similar to the

---

Algorithm 2. Double scalar multiplication with joint doublings

---

Input: Two n-bit scalars k and l, two points $P, Q \in E(\mathbb{F}_p)$.
Output: Scalar product $R = k \cdot P + l \cdot Q$.
1: $(k', l') \leftarrow \mathrm{JSF}(k, l)$ { calculate JSF of (k, l) using [15, Algorithm 3.50]}
2: $R \leftarrow \mathcal{O}$, $S \leftarrow P + Q$, $T \leftarrow P - Q$
3: **for** i from n by 1 down to 0 **do**
4:     $R \leftarrow 2R$
5:     **if** $(k'_i = 1)$ and $(l'_i = 1)$ **then** $R \leftarrow R + S$
6:     **else if** $(k'_i = 1)$ and $(l'_i = -1)$ **then** $R \leftarrow R + T$
7:     **else if** $(k'_i = -1)$ and $(l'_i = 1)$ **then** $R \leftarrow R - T$
8:     **else if** $(k'_i = -1)$ and $(l'_i = -1)$ **then** $R \leftarrow R - S$
9:     **else if** $(k'_i = 1)$ and $(l'_i = 0)$ **then** $R \leftarrow R + P$
10:    **else if** $(k'_i = 0)$ and $(l'_i = 1)$ **then** $R \leftarrow R + Q$
11:    **else if** $(k'_i = -1)$ and $(l'_i = 0)$ **then** $R \leftarrow R - P$
12:    **else if** $(k'_i = 0)$ and $(l'_i = -1)$ **then** $R \leftarrow R - Q$ **end if**
13: **end for**
14: **return** R

---

first stage of ECDH key exchange. The fixed-base comb method with $w = 4$ is the natural choice to perform this operation in an efficient and secure (i.e. SPA-resistant) fashion. On the other hand, the verification of an ECDSA signature requires a so-called double scalar multiplication of the form $k \cdot P + l \cdot Q$ where one of the points is fixed and the other not. To reduce execution time, the two scalar multiplications $k \cdot P$ and $l \cdot Q$ can be carried out simultaneously (i.e. in an "interleaved" fashion) so that n point doublings suffice to get the result. Algorithm 2 shows a possible realization of this approach, sometimes referred to as *Shamir's Trick* (see e.g. [15, p. 109]). We represent the n-bit scalars k and l in *Joint Sparse Form (JSF)* [30], which means roughly $n/2$ point additions have to be performed. In our case, i.e. 192-bit scalars, the cost of Algorithm 2 amounts to 192 point doublings and some 96 point additions, not taking into account the pre-computation of $P + Q$ and $P - Q$ in line 2. Note that the verification of an ECDSA signature is a public-key operation and, therefore, does not need to be protected against side-channel attacks.

3   Efficient Field Arithmetic for Curve P-192

In the following, we describe our implementation of basic arithmetic operations modulo the 192-bit generalized-Mersenne prime $p = 2^{192} - 2^{64} - 1$.

3.1   Addition and Subtraction

To add two elements $a, b \in \mathbb{F}_p$, we firstly perform a conventional multi-precision addition of the two byte-arrays A and B representing them. As result we get a sum-array S consisting of 24 bytes and a carry bit c, which is either 0 or 1. The carry bit c is then used to generate a mask M that, depending on c, is either an

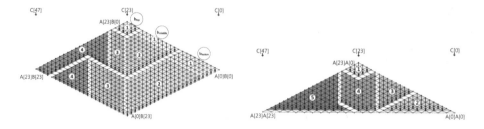

Fig. 1. COC multiplication (left) and "lazy doubling" squaring (right)

"all-1" byte (i.e. has the value 255) or an "all-0" byte. A mask of this form can be simply obtained via negation of the carry bit; we get the "all-1" byte if c is 1 and the "all-0" byte otherwise. Then, we perform two "masked" subtractions of the prime p, which means we do a logical "AND" of prime-byte $P[i]$ and the mask M before we actually subtract it from the corresponding byte of S. Two such subtractions are required to get a result of at most 192 bits, whereby the carry bit c must be updated after the first subtraction. In this way, always the same sequence of instructions is executed, independent of the value of the two operands a and b. Note, however, that the final result may not be fully reduced (even though it is always smaller than 2^{192}), but this is no problem because all functions of our arithmetic library can process incompletely reduced operands [34]. The modular subtraction is implemented in a very similar way.

3.2 Multiplication and Squaring

Multiplication and squaring are two extremely performance-critical arithmetic operations in ECC [2]. Our implementation employs an improved variant of the Consecutive Operand Caching (COC) method [28] for the former and a novel "lazy doubling" technique to speed up the latter. We use the following notation:

- n: operand size (192 bits in our case)
- w: word size of the processor (8 bits)
- m: number of elements in an operand-array, i.e. $m = n/w = 24$
- e: number of operand words (i.e. bytes) to be cached (10 in our case)
- r: number of row sections, $r = \lfloor m/e \rfloor$
- A, B: operands represented by byte arrays: $A = (A[m-1], \ldots, A[1], A[0])$ and $B = (B[m-1], \ldots, B[1], B[0])$
- C: $2n$-bit product $C = A \cdot B$ whereby $C = (C[2m-1], \ldots, C[1], C[0])$

As shown in Figure 1, we describe the execution flow using a rhombus and triangular forms. Each dot represents a byte-product of the form $A[i] \times B[j]$ or $A[i] \times A[j]$. The rightmost corner of the rhombus indicates the lowest indices (i.e. $i, j = 0$), whereas the highest indices (i.e. $i, j = m - 1$) can be found at the leftmost corner. All bytes $C[k]$ of the product C are located at the bottom edge of the rhombus, whereby $C[0]$ is at the right and $C[2m - 1]$ at the left.

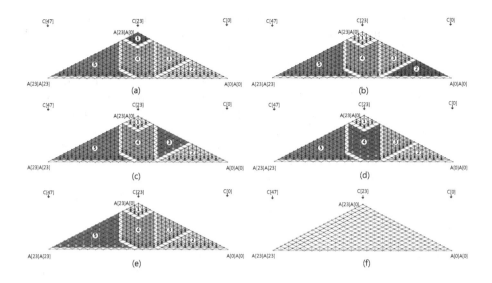

Fig. 2. Execution flow of the novel "lazy doubling" technique

To speed up the multiplication, we combine the COC method [28] with the so-called carry-once technique described in [29]. The COC method reduces the number of load instructions by re-scheduling the byte-multiplication sequences so that each byte is loaded only once (i.e. it fully prevents re-loadings). On the other hand, the carry-once technique minimizes the number of add instructions by first delaying and then updating intermediate results at once instead of doing it one-by-one. The execution flow is illustrated on the left of Figure 1. We have $r = \lfloor \frac{24}{10} \rfloor = 2$, which means there are two row sections, namely b_{bottom} and b_{middle}. First, we calculate the 16 byte-products in block b_{top} at the top of the rhombus; this requires to load the operand bytes $A[20-23]$ and $B[0-3]$. The latter four bytes are cached as they are used again in the next block, which is b_{bottom}. This block consists of four regions (labeled ① to ④ in Figure 1) and is processed from right (i.e. region ①) to left (i.e. region ④). The computations in the regions ① to ③ involve the loading of the bytes $A[0-9]$, $B[4-23]$, and $A[10-19]$. Following the carry-once strategy, we load in region ② and ③ the intermediate-result bytes $C[20-27]$ and update them pair-wise in the following order: $C[20, 21]$, $C[22, 23]$, $C[24, 25]$, and $C[26, 27]$. In this way, we save an add instruction in the processing of each of these pairs. Once b_{botton} is finished, we pass the bytes $A[10-19]$ to the block b_{middle}, which is processed similarly.

We describe now our novel "lazy doubling" approach for squaring. Unlike to multiplication, an optimized squaring algorithm does not need to calculate all m^2 byte products since there exist a large number of pairs that have the same value, e.g. $A[1] \cdot A[0]$ and $A[0] \cdot A[1]$. After elimination of these "duplicates," we get a squaring algorithm with a triangular execution flow as illustrated on the right of Figure 1. Figure 2 shows the main steps of the our squaring algorithm in more detail. At first, in step (a), all byte products on the top of the triangle are computed, which includes to load operand bytes $A[20-23]$ and to load and cache bytes $A[0-3]$. In step (b), all byte products of region ② are formed and the bytes $A[0-8]$ are cached. Thereafter, in step (c), we apply the carry-once technique, indicated by yellow dotted lines in Figure 2. This step uses operand bytes $A[9-17]$ and $A[0-8]$, but only the former ones are cached. The bytes $C[10-18]$ of the intermediate result are computed and updated in a pair-wise fashion, thereby saving one clock cycle per pair. In step (d), byte products are generated using bytes $A[10-23]$ and $A[0-13]$, and in step (e), computations are continued with $A[13-23]$ and $A[6-23]$, and the intermediate results are updated. Finally, in step (f), we double the whole intermediate result we got so far and then compute the remaining byte products. Our lazy doubling method requires only 2064 clock cycles to square a 192-bit integer, which improves the best previous result in the literature [21] by about 2%.

The result of a multiplication (or squaring) is a 384-bit integer, which must be reduced modulo $p = 2^{192} - 2^{64} - 1$ to get a 192-bit residue. As mentioned in Subsection 2.1 (and explained in more detail in [15, Section 2.2.6]), it is possible to perform this reduction via three 192-bit additions modulo p. However, in the worst case, three subtractions of p are necessary to get a reduced result, which can considerably slow down this operation, especially if one aims for resistance against SPA or timing attacks. Therefore, we use the "sum scanning" method for reduction modulo p proposed in [13, Algorithm 2] so that at most one final subtraction of p has to be carried out. We perform this final subtraction in an "unconditional way" using a byte-mask as described in Subsection 3.1.

3.3 Inversion

When using projective coordinates, it is generally necessary to invert the Z coordinate of the point obtained at the end of the scalar multiplication to have a final result in affine coordinates. The Extended Euclidean Algorithm (EEA) is commonly used for computing multiplicative inverses in $\mathbb{F}_p$. Unfortunately, the EEA has a very irregular execution profile and, therefore, may leak information about Z, which, in turn, could be used by an attacker to recover parts of the secret scalar. To thwart such attacks, we firstly multiply Z by a random value R, invert this product, and then multiply $(ZR)^{-1}$ again by R to get Z^{-1}.

4   Implementation Results

In this section, we firstly report the execution times of our implementation and compare them with the results of previous work. Then, we analyze the memory footprint and energy consumption of our ECC software.

4.1   Execution Time

We implemented all field operations (except of a few parts of the inversion) in AVR Assembly language and the rest (i.e. point addition, point doubling, and

Table 1. Execution time of 192-bit arithmetic operations (in clock cycles)

Implementation	mod-add	mod-sub	mod-mul	mod-sqr	mod-inv
Liu et al [22]	832	786	8,152	7,493	1,305,616
Chu et al [7]	632	632	4,845	4,052	476,055
This work	378	378	4,042	2,658	280,829

the scalar multiplication algorithms) in ANSI C. In order to achieve peak performance, we unrolled the loops of all field operations except inversion. Table 1 summarizes the execution times of the five basic arithmetic operations modulo the 192-bit NIST prime. The modular addition takes exactly the same time as the modular subtraction, namely 378 clock cycles on an 8-bit AVR ATmega128 processor. Our modular multiplication executes in about 4,000 cycles, whereas the modular squaring has an execution time of 2,658 clock cycles, which means the squaring requires merely two-third of the multiplication cycles. This result impressively demonstrates the efficiency of our "lazy doubling" technique since modular squaring is typically only about 20% faster than modular multiplication. A comparison with Liu et al's widely-used TinyECC software [22] shows that our implementation of modular addition, subtraction and multiplication is more than twice as fast as theirs, while the modular squaring gains a speed-up by a factor of roughly 2.8. Our implementation is also significantly faster than that of Chu et al [7], who used a 192-bit Optimal Prime Field (OPF) but did not unroll the loops. Our inversion modulo p has an (average) execution time of roughly 280k cycles, which means it is approximately 70 times slower than a modular multiplication. However, our inversion needs only 56% of the execution time reported in [7] and 21% of the time of the TinyECC inversion.

Table 2. Execution time (in cycles) of point addition and point doubling

Implementation	Point addition	Point doubling
Liu et al [22] (NIST P-192)	80,774	63,355
Chu et al [7] (Tw. Edwards)	54,158	41,630
This work (NIST P-192)	43,604	29,914

Table 2 shows the execution time of point addition and doubling. Compared to TinyECC, our addition achieves a speed-up of slightly below 2.0x, whereas the speed-up factor of point doubling is a bit above 2.0x. Interestingly, we are also faster than Chu et al [7], who used a twisted Edwards curve that features more efficient addition and doubling formulae than our NIST curve.

We also simulated the execution times of fixed-point and variable-point scalar multiplication as well as double scalar multiplication; they amount to some 3.67, 9.23, and 10.4 million cycles, respectively. Considering the MICAz mote's clock frequency of 7.37 MHz [8], these cycle counts translate to execution times of 0.5 s, 1.25 s, and 1.41 s. Each run of the (ephemeral) ECDH key agreement

Table 3. Comparison of fixed-point and arbitrary-point scalar multiplication, double scalar multiplication, ECDH, and ECDSA on an ATmega128 clocked at 7.37 MHz

Implementation	Field	$k \cdot P$	$l \cdot Q$	$k \cdot P + l \cdot Q$	ECDH	ECDSA
Gura et al [14]	160 b	0.88 s	0.88 s	n/a	1.76 s	n/a
Wang et al [33]	160 b	1.34 s	1.46 s	3.09 s	2.80 s	4.43 s
Szczechowiak et al [31]	160 b	1.27 s	1.27 s	n/a	2.54 s	n/a
Ugus et al [32]	160 b	0.57 s	1.03 s	n/a	1.60 s	n/a
Liu et al [22]	160 b	2.05 s	2.30 s	2.60 s	4.35 s	4.65 s
Großschädl et al [12]	160 b	0.74 s	0.74 s	n/a	1.48 s	n/a
Chu et al [7]	160 b	0.78 s	0.78 s	n/a	1.56 s	n/a
Liu et al [22]	192 b	2.99 s	2.99 s	n/a	5.98 s	n/a
Gura et al [14]	192 b	1.35 s	1.35 s	n/a	2.70 s	n/a
Lederer et al [20]	192 b	0.71 s	1.67 s	n/a	2.38 s	n/a
This work	192 b	0.50 s	1.25 s	1.41 s	1.75 s	1.91 s

protocol requires the two involved parties to execute both a fixed-point and an arbitrary-point scalar multiplication; adding them up gives an execution time of $12.9 \cdot 10^6$ clock cycles (1.75 s) altogether. On the other hand, the two main operations of ECDSA signature generation and verification, namely fixed-point scalar multiplication and double scalar multiplication, have an overall execution time of some $14 \cdot 10^6$ cycles (1.91 s). Table 3 compares our work with previous ECC implementations for 8-bit AVR-based processors. We are much faster than any other ECC software using a 192-bit prime field and outperform even some 160-bit implementations. For example, our ECDH key exchange improves the best result in the literature (which can be found in [20]) by a factor of 1.35. On the other hand, our ECDSA implementation is 2.33 times faster than the best ECDSA software reported in the literature, namely the one in [33].

4.2   Memory Footprint

Low memory footprint is another very important requirement on ECC software for sensor nodes, which becomes evident when considering that the ATmega128 on a MICAz mote has only 4 kB RAM and 128 kB flash ROM [3]. Our implementation occupies about 1.4 kB in RAM; this includes the two 384-bit tables of the comb and windows method for scalar multiplication. However, there are several options to reduce the RAM footprint. For example, when executing the comb method, it is not necessary to have the full table of pre-computed points in RAM since, at any time, only one entry of the table is required. Optimizing our implementation in this direction would reduce the RAM footprint by some 350 bytes at the expense of a slight performance degradation. The binary executable of our ECC software has a size of 28 kB, which leaves about 100 kB in flash memory for the operating system and applications.

4.3 Energy Consumption

According to [8], the ATmega128 processor of a MICAz mote draws an average current of about 8.0 mA (at a supply voltage of 3.0 V) when it is active. Since the clock frequency of the mote is known to be 7.37 MHz, we can evaluate the energy consumption of a scalar multiplication algorithm by simply forming the product of average power consumption, supply voltage, and execution time. In this way, the energy cost of a fixed-point scalar multiplication, arbitrary-point scalar multiplication, and double scalar multiplication amounts to roughly 12.0 mJ, 30.0 mJ, and 33.84 mJ, respectively. The energy consumption of the two scalar multiplications of ECDH key exchange is approximately 42.0 mJ, while the overall energy cost (for both nodes) is about 84.0 mJ. Normally, one also has to take into account the energy required for transmitting (i.e. sending and receiving) the public keys, but previous work in [9,20,27] shows that ECDH is clearly dominated by the computation energy cost. The energy required for the scalar multiplications to generate/verify an ECDSA signature is 45.84 mJ.

5 Conclusions

We introduced a carefully-optimized implementation of NIST-compliant ECC for sensor nodes equipped with an 8-bit AVR processor. Our software achieves record-setting execution times for fixed-point scalar multiplication, arbitrary-point scalar multiplication, and double scalar multiplication. For example, we outperform the best implementation of ephemeral ECDH key agreement in the literature by a factor of 1.35 and improve the state-of-the-art in ECDSA by a factor of 2.33. These speed-ups are mainly due to the performance of our field arithmetic, which is implemented in Assembly language and protected against SPA and timing attacks. We also conducted a simple energy evaluation for the ATmega128 and found that (ephemeral) ECDH key agreement consumes some 42.0 mJ per node. On the other hand, the two scalar multiplications needed to generate and verify an ECDSA signature have an energy cost of 45.84 mJ. The RAM footprint of our ECC software is 1.4 kB, which is just slightly more than one third of the total RAM of the MICAz mote. In summary, our results show that an efficient and secure (i.e. SPA-resistant) implementation of ECC on the NIST curve P-192 is possible.

References

1. Akyildiz, I.F., Su, W., Sankarasubramaniam, Y., Cayirci, E.: A survey on sensor networks. IEEE Communications Magazine 40(8), 102–114 (2002)
2. Aranha, D.F., Dahab, R., López, J.C., Oliveira, L.B.: Efficient implementation of elliptic curve cryptography in wireless sensors. Advances in Mathematics of Communications 4(2), 169–187 (2010)
3. Atmel Corporation. ATmega128(L) Datasheet (Rev. 2467O–AVR–10/06) (October 2006), http://www.atmel.com/dyn/resources/prod_documents/doc2467.pdf

4. Atmel Corporation. 8-bit ARV® Microcontroller with 128K Bytes In-System Programmable Flash: ATmega128, ATmega128L. Datasheet (June 2008), http://www.atmel.com/dyn/resources/prod_documents/doc2467.pdf

5. Bernstein, D.J.: Curve25519: New Diffie-Hellman speed records. In: Yung, M., Dodis, Y., Kiayias, A., Malkin, T. (eds.) PKC 2006. LNCS, vol. 3958, pp. 207–228. Springer, Heidelberg (2006)

6. CertiVox Corporation. CertiVox MIRACL SDK. Source code (June 2012), http://www.certivox.com

7. Chu, D., Großschädl, J., Liu, Z., Müller, V., Zhang, Y.: Twisted Edwards-form elliptic curve cryptography for 8-bit AVR-based sensor nodes. In: Xu, S., Zhao, Y. (eds.) Proceedings of the 1st ACM Workshop on Asia Public-Key Cryptography (AsiaPKC 2013), pp. 39–44. ACM Press (2013)

8. Crossbow Technology, Inc. MICAz Wireless Measurement System. Data sheet (January 2006), http://www.xbow.com/Products/Product_pdf_files/Wireless_pdf/MICAz_Datasheet.pdf

9. de Meulenaer, G., Gosset, F., Standaert, F.-X., Pereira, O.: On the energy cost of communication and cryptography in wireless sensor networks. In: Proceedings of the 4th IEEE International Conference on Wireless and Mobile Computing, Networking and Communications (WIMOB 2008), pp. 580–585. IEEE Computer Society Press (2008)

10. de Meulenaer, G., Standaert, F.-X.: Stealthy compromise of wireless sensor nodes with power analysis attacks. In: Chatzimisios, P., Verikoukis, C., Santamaría, I., Laddomada, M., Hoffmann, O. (eds.) MOBILIGHT 2010. LNICST, vol. 45, pp. 229–242. Springer, Heidelberg (2010)

11. Großschädl, J., Avanzi, R.M., Savaş, E., Tillich, S.: Energy-efficient software implementation of long integer modular arithmetic. In: Rao, J.R., Sunar, B. (eds.) CHES 2005. LNCS, vol. 3659, pp. 75–90. Springer, Heidelberg (2005)

12. Großschädl, J., Hudler, M., Koschuch, M., Krüger, M., Szekely, A.: Smart elliptic curve cryptography for smart dust. In: Zhang, X., Qiao, D. (eds.) QShine 2010. LNICST, vol. 74, pp. 623–634. Springer, Heidelberg (2012)

13. Großschädl, J., Savaş, E.: Instruction set extensions for fast arithmetic in finite fields gF(p) and gF(2^m). In: Joye, M., Quisquater, J.-J. (eds.) CHES 2004. LNCS, vol. 3156, pp. 133–147. Springer, Heidelberg (2004)

14. Gura, N., Patel, A., Wander, A., Eberle, H., Shantz, S.C.: Comparing elliptic curve cryptography and RSA on 8-bit cPUs. In: Joye, M., Quisquater, J.-J. (eds.) CHES 2004. LNCS, vol. 3156, pp. 119–132. Springer, Heidelberg (2004)

15. Hankerson, D.R., Menezes, A.J., Vanstone, S.A.: Guide to Elliptic Curve Cryptography. Springer (2004)

16. Hisil, H., Wong, K.K.-H., Carter, G., Dawson, E.: Twisted Edwards curves revisited. In: Pieprzyk, J. (ed.) ASIACRYPT 2008. LNCS, vol. 5350, pp. 326–343. Springer, Heidelberg (2008)

17. Hutter, M., Schwabe, P.: NaCl on 8-bit AVR microcontrollers. In: Youssef, A., Nitaj, A., Hassanien, A.E. (eds.) AFRICACRYPT 2013. LNCS, vol. 7918, pp. 156–172. Springer, Heidelberg (2013)

18. Hutter, M., Wenger, E.: Fast multi-precision multiplication for public-key cryptography on embedded microprocessors. In: Preneel, B., Takagi, T. (eds.) CHES 2011. LNCS, vol. 6917, pp. 459–474. Springer, Heidelberg (2011)

19. Kocher, P.C., Jaffe, J., Jun, B.: Differential power analysis. In: Wiener, M. (ed.) CRYPTO 1999. LNCS, vol. 1666, pp. 388–397. Springer, Heidelberg (1999)

20. Lederer, C., Mader, R., Koschuch, M., Großschädl, J., Szekely, A., Tillich, S.: Energy-efficient implementation of ECDH key exchange for wireless sensor networks. In: Markowitch, O., Bilas, A., Hoepman, J.-H., Mitchell, C.J., Quisquater, J.-J. (eds.) Information Security Theory and Practice. LNCS, vol. 5746, pp. 112–127. Springer, Heidelberg (2009)
21. Lee, Y., Kim, I.-H., Park, Y.: Improved multi-precision squaring for low-end RISC microcontrollers. Journal of Systems and Software 86(1), 60–71 (2013)
22. Liu, A., Ning, P.: TinyECC: A configurable library for elliptic curve cryptography in wireless sensor networks. In: Proceedings of the 7th International Conference on Information Processing in Sensor Networks (IPSN 2008), pp. 245–256. IEEE Computer Society Press (2008)
23. Liu, Z., Wenger, E., Großschädl, J.: MoTE-ECC: Energy-scalable elliptic curve cryptography for wireless sensor networks (submitted for publication, 2013)
24. Lopez, J., Zhou, J.: Wireless Sensor Network Security. Cryptology and Information Security Series, vol. 1. IOS Press (2008)
25. Montgomery, P.L.: Speeding the Pollard and elliptic curve methods of factorization. Mathematics of Computation 48(177), 243–264 (1987)
26. National Institute of Standards and Technology (NIST). Recommended Elliptic Curves for Federal Government Use. White paper (July 1999),
    http://csrc.nist.gov/encryption/dss/ecdsa/NISTReCur.pdf
27. Piotrowski, K., Langendörfer, P., Peter, S.: How public key cryptography influences wireless sensor node lifetime. In: Zhu, S., Liu, D. (eds.) Proceedings of the 4th ACM Workshop on Security of Ad Hoc and Sensor Networks (SASN 2006), pp. 169–176. ACM Press (2006)
28. Seo, H., Kim, H.: Multi-precision multiplication for public-key cryptography on embedded microprocessors. In: Lee, D.H., Yung, M. (eds.) WISA 2012. LNCS, vol. 7690, pp. 55–67. Springer, Heidelberg (2012)
29. Seo, H., Lee, Y., Kim, H., Park, T., Kim, H.: Binary and prime field multiplication for public key cryptography on embedded microprocessors. In: Security and Communication Networks (2013)
30. Solinas, J.A.: Low-weight binary representations for pairs of integers. Technical Report CORR 2001-41, Centre for Applied Cryptographic Research (CACR), University of Waterloo, Waterloo, Canada (2001)
31. Szczechowiak, P., Oliveira, L.B., Scott, M., Collier, M., Dahab, R.: NanoECC: Testing the limits of elliptic curve cryptography in sensor networks. In: Verdone, R. (ed.) EWSN 2008. LNCS, vol. 4913, pp. 305–320. Springer, Heidelberg (2008)
32. Ugus, O., Westhoff, D., Laue, R., Shoufan, A., Huss, S.A.: Optimized implementation of elliptic curve based additive homomorphic encryption for wireless sensor networks. In: Wolf, T., Parameswaran, S. (eds.) Proceedings of the 2nd Workshop on Embedded Systems Security (WESS 2007), pp. 11–16 (2007), http://arxiv.org/abs/0903.3900
33. Wang, H., Li, Q.: Efficient implementation of public key cryptosystems on mote sensors. In: Ning, P., Qing, S., Li, N. (eds.) ICICS 2006. LNCS, vol. 4307, pp. 519–528. Springer, Heidelberg (2006)
34. Yanık, T., Savaş, E., Koç, Ç.K.: Incomplete reduction in modular arithmetic. IEE Proceedings – Computers and Digital Techniques 149(2), 46–52 (2002)

Attacking and Fixing the CS Mode

Han Sui[1], Wenling Wu[1], Liting Zhang[1], and Peng Wang[2]

[1] Trusted Computing and Information Assurance Laboratory
Institute of Software, Chinese Academy of Sciences, Beijing 100190, P.R. China
{suihan,wwl,zhangliting}@tca.iscas.ac.cn
[2] Data Assurance and Communication Security
Institute of Information Engineering, Chinese Academy of Sciences,
Beijing 100093, P.R. China
wp@is.ac.cn

Abstract. The security of the Cipher-State (CS) mode was proposed to NIST as an authenticated encryption (AE) scheme in 2004. The usual SPRP blockcipher security for AE schemes may not guarantee its security. By constructing a special SPRP, one can easily make a key-recovery attack with a single block query. The distinguishing attacks and the forgery attacks can also be made with simpler SPRP constructions. The security flaw relies in the method for generating initial whitening values. To fix this shortcoming, we propose a modified version CS* which incorporates a new method for generating initial whitening values, while keeping the main structure of CS unchanged. As we show, CS* is secure when its underlying blockcipher is an SPRP and halves of which are unpredictable.

1 Introduction

Background. An authenticated encryption (AE) scheme is a shared-key encryption scheme whose goal is to provide both privacy and authenticity. There are usually two approaches to build AE schemes from blockciphers.

- A *two-pass* scheme combines essentially separate privacy and authenticity modes together, and has to process data twice; and
- a *one-pass* scheme tightly couples the parts of the mechanism responsible for both privacy and authenticity, and needs only one time to process data.

The latter schemes firstly emerged in 2001, with the work of Jutla [12] and developed by Katz et al. [13], Gilgor et al. [10] and Rogaway et al. [15]. Cipher-State mode is such a one-pass AE scheme.

The CS mode was firstly introduced by Anderson et al. in ACISP 2004 [3] and proposed to National Institute of Standards and Technology (NIST)[4] as submissions for modes development. Besides its advantage for processing data with only one time, it takes a special method for authentication with any round-based blockcipher. That is, it takes the internal states in the middle round of

S. Qing et al. (Eds.): ICICS 2013, LNCS 8233, pp. 318–330, 2013.
© Springer International Publishing Switzerland 2013

encryption for authentication information. This method provides a computationally low cost alternative to CBC mode. Furthermore, it can be fully parallelized, allowing fast execution.

It seems that little attention has been put to CS mode. It has been proposed and put on the NIST's web page for nearly a decade, however, seldom analysis can be found publicly. Švenda provided a brief analysis of CS mode in his comparison of AE modes [16]. Besides this, only an incomplete security analysis can be found in its designers' report [5] without any formal proof.

Our Contribution. Consider the wide requirements for secure AE schemes, especially with the recent motivation of CAESAR competition [1]. We find it necessary to give a formal analysis for such an interesting mode. We study CS mode from the provable-security point of view and discover that CS mode is totally insecure with a special SPRP as its underlying blockcipher. The problem is, $E_K(K \oplus \cdot)$ is used in generating initial whitening values and this may result in non-random internal values, and even the leakage of K. Such a way of XORing the key to a message block has been pointed out to be very dangerous by Furuya and Skurai [9]. By constructing a special permutation $F_K(\cdot)$, we show that one can build a key-recovery attack against CS mode with $F_K(\cdot)$ as its underlying blockcipher. Distinguishing attacks and forgery attacks can also be made using simpler SPRP constructions.

To fix CS mode, we build CS* which retains the main structure of CS and the update method of R_i unchanged, but replaces the method for generating initial whitening values R_0. To simplify the mode, we also take away the LFSR in T_i's updating and unnecessary pre-whiten and post-whiten process in generating a tag from T_m. However, we keep the convenient method that derives internal states from blockciphers to generate the tag. Therefore, CS* inherits the advantages of CS and becomes even simpler.

Due to its special method to compose the tag, we have to handle the detailed proof for CS* more carefully than usual. That is, we have to evaluate the properties of blockcipher internal states, and show how hard for adversaries to get a collision just before the last blockcipher encryption for authentication. To solve this, we introduce *unpredictability* into our proof. We argue that assuming the internal states in the middle of blockcipher encryption are unpredictable is quite suitable here. On the one hand, it is weaker than pseudorandomness, properly simulates the fact that the outputs of half-rounds blockcipher have less randomness than those of full-rounds. On the other hand, unpredictability of blockcipher internal states is sufficient to prevent collisions before the final encryption, allowing random tags for different messages. In the rest of this paper, we say "the internal states in the middle of blockcipher encryption" as "the internal states" for short.

Our fixing mode, CS*, is a secure AE scheme as we prove by assuming that the underlying block E is an SPRP and its internal states are unpredictable. For privacy, the success probability for an adversary to distinguish $CS^*[\mathrm{Perm}(n)]$ from a random function is upper bounded by

$$\frac{(\sigma + 2q + 1)^2}{2^n} + 1.5(\sigma + q + 1)^2 \mathbf{Adv}_{E_1}^{\mathrm{up}}(t, q, \sigma).$$

For authenticity, the success probability of making a forgery is upper bounded by

$$\frac{(\sigma + 2q + c + 5)^2}{2^n} + 1.5(\sigma + 2q + c + 2)^2 \mathbf{Adv}_{E_1, E_2}^{\mathrm{up}}(t, q, \sigma),$$

where E_1 and E_2 are two unpredictable permutations satisfying $E = E_2^{-1} \circ E_1$.

2 Preliminaries

2.1 Notation

A *string* is a finite sequence of symbols, each symbol being 0 or 1. The string of length 0 is called *empty string* and is denoted ϵ. Let $\{0,1\}^*$ denote the set of all strings. If $A, B \in \{0,1\}^*$ then AB, or $A\|B$, is their concatenation. 0^i and 1^i denote the strings of i-many 0s and 1s, respectively. Let $\{0,1\}^n$ denote the set of all strings of length n. If $A \in \{0,1\}^*$ then $|A|$ denotes the length of A in bits. If $A, B \in \{0,1\}^*$ are strings of same length then $A \oplus B$ is the bitwise xor of A and B. If A is a set, then $\#A$ denotes the size of set A, and $a \xleftarrow{\$} A$ denotes that a is chosen from set A uniformly at random.

If $M \in \{0,1\}^*$ then the padding rule used in this paper is $\mathrm{pad}(M) = M10^{n-1-(|M| \bmod n)}$. Furthermore, we assume that each message M used in this paper has already padded and $|M|$ is a multiple of n. In pseudocodes, "partition M into $M_1 \cdots M_m$" means "let m be the length of M in n-bit blocks and let $M_1 \cdots M_m$ be string such that $M_1 \cdots M_m = \mathrm{pad}(M)$ and $|M_i| = n$ for $1 \le i \le n$".

If π is a function on $\{0,1\}^n$, let $\mathrm{Dom}(\pi)$ and $\mathrm{Ran}(\pi)$ be the domain and range of π, respectively. Especially, if we defines the values of $\pi(x)$ point-by-point in game, $\mathrm{Dom}(\pi)$ is the set of values $x \in \{0,1\}^n$ such that $\pi(x) \notin$ undefined. Similarly, $\mathrm{Ran}(\pi)$ is the set of $y \in \{0,1\}^n$ such that there exists an $x \in \{0,1\}^n$ for which $\pi(x) = y$. If π is a fixed function, we use $\mathrm{Dom}(\pi)$ and $\mathrm{Ran}(\pi)$ to describe the sets of queried inputs and outputs, respectively.

2.2 Description of Cipher-State Mode

As illustrated in Fig.1, Cipher-State mode derives internal states from each round-based blockcipher invocations during data encryption for authentication information. It needs one blockcipher key K and one nonce N. An initial whitening value R_0 is created from K and N.

An LFSR is used as a pseudorandom number generator (PRNG) to pre-whiten the plaintext and post-whiten the ciphertext with the same parameter. The polynomial selected for the authentication combiner and the PRNG is the lexicographically least primitive polynomial, $p(x)$ of degree n.

The blockcipher E_K is split into two roughly equal pieces, $_{1:r/2}E_K$ and $_{(r/2+1):r}E_K$: $_{1:r/2}E_K$ returns the internal state after completing $r/2$ rounds of the blockcipher; while $_{(r/2+1):r}E_K$ takes the internal state as input and returns the final state after all rounds. If the blockcipher has odd rounds, it will be split into $_{1:\lceil r/2 \rceil}E_K$ and $_{(\lceil r/2 \rceil+1):r}E_K$.

Let M be a padded data and be split into m n-bit blocks M_i:

$$M = M_1\|M_2\| \cdots \|M_m.$$

The initial whitening value R_0 is computed with $R_0 = E_K(N \oplus K) \oplus K$. The plaintext block M_i is pre-whitened using R_i which updates after each step using LFSR with $p(x)$. A pre-authenticator value T_i is computed with internal states of the underlying blockcipher and updates in the same way.

$$R_i = R_{i-1} \times x \pmod{p(x)}, \quad i = 1, 2, \cdots, m.$$
$$T_m = \Sigma_{i=1}^{m} E_K(M_i \oplus R_{i-1}) \times x^{m-i}.$$

To prevent possible information leakages from using the internal cipher state, a final authenticator T is computed using an extra blockcipher invocation:

$$T = E_K(T_m \oplus R_m) \oplus T_m.$$

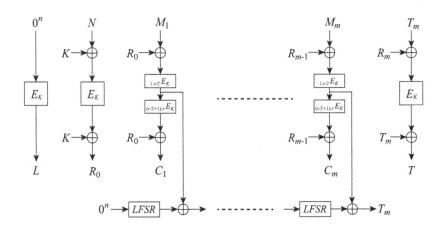

Fig. 1. Cipher-State Mode

2.3   Security Definitions

Adversaries. An *adversary* is a program with access to an oracle. Oracle queries are tuples of strings. An adversary is *nonce-respecting* if it never repeats the first component, N, to its oracle, regardless of oracle responses. In this paper, adversaries are always assumed to be nonce-respecting. We write an oracle as superscript to the adversary that uses it.

AE-schemes. We use the syntax of a nonce-using authenticated-encryption schemes and their security given by Bellare et al. [6] and extended by Rogaway et al. [15] [14]. An *authenticated-encryption scheme* (an AE-scheme) is a triple $\Pi = (\mathcal{K}, \mathcal{E}, \mathcal{D})$ and an associated number n (the blockcipher length). Here $\mathcal{K}$ is a finite set and $\mathcal{E}$ and $\mathcal{D}$ are deterministic algorithms. Encryption algorithm $\mathcal{E}$ takes $K \in \mathcal{K}$, $N \in \{0,1\}^n$, and $M \in \{0,1\}^*$, and returns a string $C \leftarrow \mathcal{E}_K(N, M)$. Decryption algorithm $\mathcal{D}$ takes $K \in \mathcal{K}$, $N \in \{0,1\}^n$, and $C \in \{0,1\}^*$, and returns $\mathcal{D}_K(N, M)$, which is either a string $M \in \{0,1\}^*$ or a distinguished symbol INVALID. If $C \leftarrow \mathcal{E}_K(N, M)$ then $\mathcal{D}_K(N, C) = M$.

Privacy. Consider an adversary $\mathcal{A}$ that has one of two types of oracles: a "real" encryption oracle or a "fake" encryption oracle. A real encryption oracle, $\mathcal{E}_K(\cdot, \cdot)$, takes as input N, M and returns $C \leftarrow \mathcal{E}_K(N, M)$. Assume that $|C| = l(|M|)$ depends only on $|M|$. A fake encryption oracle, $\$(\cdot, \cdot)$ takes as input N, M and returns a random string $C \xleftarrow{\$} \{0,1\}^{l(|M|)}$. Given adversary $\mathcal{A}$ and encryption scheme $\Pi = (\mathcal{K}, \mathcal{E}, \mathcal{D})$, define

$$\mathbf{Adv}_\Pi^{\mathrm{priv}} = |\Pr[K \xleftarrow{\$} \mathcal{K} : \mathcal{A}^{\mathcal{E}_K(\cdot,\cdot)} \Rightarrow 1] - \Pr[\$(\cdot,\cdot) \xleftarrow{\$} \mathrm{Rand}(*,*) : \mathcal{A}^{\$(\cdot,\cdot)} \Rightarrow 1]|.$$

Authenticity. Fix an encryption scheme $\Pi = (\mathcal{K}, \mathcal{E}, \mathcal{D})$ and run an adversary $\mathcal{A}$ with an oracle $\mathcal{E}_K(\cdot, \cdot)$ for some key K. Adversary $\mathcal{A}$ *forges* (in this run) if $\mathcal{A}$ is nonce respecting, $\mathcal{A}$ outputs (N, C), where $\mathcal{D}_K(N, C) \neq$ INVALID, and $\mathcal{A}$ made no earlier query (N, M) that resulted in a response C. Let $\mathbf{Adv}_\Pi^{\mathrm{auth}} = \Pr[K \xleftarrow{\$} \mathcal{K} : \mathcal{A}^{\mathcal{E}_K(\cdot,\cdot)} \text{ forges}]$. We stress that the nonce used in the forgery attempt may coincide with a nonce used in one of the adversary's queries.

Pseudorandom Functions. A *function family* from n-bit to n-bit is a map $E : \mathcal{K} \times \{0,1\}^n \to \{0,1\}^n$, where $\mathcal{K}$ is a finite set of strings. It is a *blockcipher* if each $E_K(\cdot) = E(K, \cdot)$ is a permutation. Let $\mathrm{Rand}(n)$ denote the set of all functions from $\{0,1\}^n$ to $\{0,1\}^n$. These sets can be regarded as function families by imagining that each member is specified by a string. For $\pi \in \mathrm{Perm}(n)$, let $\pi^{-1}(Y)$ be the unique string X such that $\pi(X) = Y$. Let

$$\mathbf{Adv}_E^{\mathrm{prf}}(\mathcal{A}) = |\Pr[K \xleftarrow{\$} \mathcal{K} : \mathcal{A}^{E_K(\cdot)} \Rightarrow 1] - \Pr[\rho \xleftarrow{\$} \mathrm{Rand}(n) : \mathcal{A}^{\rho(\cdot)} \Rightarrow 1]|$$

$$\mathbf{Adv}_E^{\mathrm{prp}}(\mathcal{A}) = |\Pr[K \xleftarrow{\$} \mathcal{K} : \mathcal{A}^{E_K(\cdot)} \Rightarrow 1] - \Pr[\pi \xleftarrow{\$} \mathrm{Perm}(n) : \mathcal{A}^{\pi(\cdot)} \Rightarrow 1]|$$

$$\mathbf{Adv}_E^{\mathrm{sprp}}(\mathcal{A}) = |\Pr[K \xleftarrow{\$} \mathcal{K} : \mathcal{A}^{E_K(\cdot), E_K^{-1}(\cdot)} \Rightarrow 1] - \Pr[\pi \xleftarrow{\$} \mathrm{Perm}(n) : \mathcal{A}^{\pi(\cdot), \pi^{-1}(\cdot)} \Rightarrow 1]|$$

be defined for the advantages of adversary $\mathcal{A}$ attacking blockcipher E. The security of E is defined as the maximum over all advantages of the adversaries with time complexity t, making at most q queries with at most σ blocks. If the advantage $\mathbf{Adv}_E^{\mathrm{prf}}(t, q, \sigma)$ is negligible, then E is said to be a *pseudorandom function* (PRF). The notions of *pseudorandom permutation* (PRP) and *strong pseudorandom permutation* (SPRP) are defined similarly.

Unpredictability. The notion of *"unpredictablilty"* is first proposed by Goldreich et al. in 1986 [11]. Let E be a blockcipher and $\mathcal{A}$ be an adversary with access to E for some key K. Consider this experiment.

$$\text{Experiment } \mathbf{Exp}_E^{\text{up}}(\mathcal{A})$$
$$K \xleftarrow{\$} \mathcal{K}$$
when $\mathcal{A}$ makes a query M to $E_K(\cdot)$, do
$$C \leftarrow E_K(M)$$
$\quad$ return C to $\mathcal{A}$
until $\mathcal{A}$ stops and outputs (M', C') such that
$\quad - E_K(M') = C'$, and
$\quad - M'$ was never queried to $E_K(\cdot)$
then return 1 else return 0

Let

$$\mathbf{Adv}_E^{\text{up}}(\mathcal{A}) = \Pr[\mathbf{Exp}_E^{\text{up}}(\mathcal{A}) = 1]$$
$$\mathbf{Adv}_E^{\text{up}}(t, q, \sigma) = \max_{\mathcal{A}}\{\mathbf{Adv}_E^{\text{up}}(\mathcal{A})\}$$

where t, q, σ stand for the total time, number of queries, and the total length of queries respectively. If $\mathbf{Adv}_E^{\text{up}}(t, q, \sigma)$ is sufficiently small, we say E is unpredictable. Unpredictable is a wekaer notion than pseudorandomness, examples can be found in [2].

3 Attacks against CS

In this section, we will show CS mode could not be secure with some special SPRPs $F : \{0,1\}^k \times \{0,1\}^n \to \{0,1\}^n$. By constructing three different SPRPs, we give a distinguishing attack, a forgery attack and a key-recovery attack against CS[F] respectively, with only one query of length no more than two blocks.

3.1 Distinguishing Attack against CS

Let $E : \{0,1\}^k \times \{0,1\}^n \to \{0,1\}^n$ be a randomly chosen SPRP, and $A \in \{0,1\}^n$ be a randomly chosen constant. The special permutation $F : \{0,1\}^k \times \{0,1\}^n \to \{0,1\}^n$ is built with E with a special property: $F_K(K \oplus A) = K$ for any key $K \in \{0,1\}^n$. This will help us building the distinguishing attack against CS mode.

$$F_K(M) = \begin{cases} K & \text{if } M = K \oplus A, \\ E_K(K \oplus A) & \text{if } M = E_K^{-1}(K), \\ E_K(M) & \text{else.} \end{cases}$$

A similar PRP (PRP-RK) has been constructed with $A = 0^{n-1}1$ by Peng Wang et al. to show that 2-Key XCBC using this PRP (PRP-RK) is totally insecure[17]. They proved that the special permutation F is a PRP as long as E is a PRP. And more specifically, F and E are indistinguishable. We can show that F is an SPRP as long as E is an SPRP.

Theorem 1. *If E is an SPRP, then F is an SPRP. More spexifically, for any adversary $\mathcal{A}$ with q queries trying to distinguish F and E, there exists an adversary $\mathcal{B}$ with no more than $(q+1)$ queries such that*

$$|\Pr[\mathcal{A}^{F,F^{-1}} \Rightarrow 1] - \Pr[\mathcal{A}^{E,E^{-1}} \Rightarrow 1]| \leq 2q\mathbf{Adv}_E^{\mathrm{sprp}}(\mathcal{B}) + \frac{2q}{2^n - q}.$$

Furthermore, $\mathcal{B}$ runs in approximately the same time as $\mathcal{A}$.

If CS takes F as its underlying blockcipher, it is distinguishable from CS with a random permutation. Let $\mathcal{O}$ be an oracle, with equal probability to be CS$[F]$ or CS$[\pi]$, where π is a random permutation. One query with nonce $N = A$ will lead to $R_0 = E_K(N \oplus K) \oplus K = 0^n$. Notice that if $R_0 = 0^n$, the algorithm will set $R_0 = K$. A distinguishing algorithm is built using this information:

> **Algorithm** $\mathcal{A}^{\mathcal{O}(\cdot,\cdot)}$:
>   query (A, A) to $\mathcal{O}(\cdot,\cdot)$ and get (C, T)
>   if $C = 0^n$ return 1
>   else return 0

We can see that $\Pr[\mathcal{A}^{\mathrm{CS}[F_K]} \Rightarrow 1] = 1$ and $\Pr[\mathcal{A}^{\mathrm{CS}[\pi]} \Rightarrow 1] = 1/2^n$, so the advantage is $1 - 1/2^n$.

3.2 Forgery Attack against CS

Let $E : \{0,1\}^k \times \{0,1\}^n \to \{0,1\}^n$ be a randomly chosen SPRP and $I : \{0,1\}^k \times \{0,1\}^n \to \{0,1\}^n$ be an identity function. The special permutation F is built by combining E and I: $_{1:r/2}F_K(\cdot) = E_K(\cdot)$, $_{(r/2+1):r}F_K(\cdot) = I(\cdot)$. Obviously, F is an SPRP as long as E is an SPRP. Taking F as the underlying blockcipher, there will be $C_j \oplus R_{j-1} = Z_{j-1}(j = 1, \ldots, c)$ in CS.

Noticing that the tag T is generated by underlying blockcipher $E_K(\cdot)$ with R_m and $T_m = \sum_{i=1}^m Z_i \cdot x^{m-i}$, and verified with R_c and $T_c = \sum_{j=1}^c Z_j \cdot x^{m-j}$, where $Z_i(i = 1, \ldots, m)$ in former situation is the internal state of $E_K(M_i \oplus R_{j-1})$ and $Z_j(j = 1, \ldots, c)$ in latter situation is the internal state of $E_K^{-1}(C_j \oplus R_{j-1})$. Suppose (N, C, T) is valid, if we can find $C_1^*, \ldots, C_c^*$ satisfying

$$\sum_{j=1}^c {}_{1:r/2}E^{-1}(C_j^* \oplus R_{j-1}) \cdot x^{m-j} = \sum_{j=1}^c {}_{1:r/2}E^{-1}(C_j \oplus R_{j-1}) \cdot x^{m-j},$$

then (N, C^*, T) will be valid. A forgery attack using only one query of two blocks to CS.Enc can be built as following.

> **Algorithm** $\mathcal{A}^{\mathrm{CS}[F](\cdot,\cdot)}$:
>   randomly choose $N, M_1, M_2 \in \{0,1\}^n$
>   query $(N, M_1 \| M_2)$ to $\mathcal{O}(\cdot,\cdot)$ and get $(C_1 \| C_2, T)$
>   randomly choose $C_1^* \in \{0,1\}^n$ satisfying $C_1^* \neq C_1$
>   let $C_2^* = C_2 \oplus (C_1 \oplus C_1^*) \cdot x$
>   forgery$(N, C_1^* \| C_2^*, T)$

We can see that

$$\begin{aligned}
T_2^* &= Z_1^* \cdot x \oplus Z_2^* \\
&= (C_1^* \oplus R_0) \cdot x \oplus (C_2^* \oplus R_1) \\
&= (C_1 \oplus R_0) \cdot x \oplus (C_2 \oplus R_1) \\
&= Z_1 \cdot x \oplus Z_2 \\
&= T_2
\end{aligned}$$

Therefore, $T^* = F_K(T_2^* \oplus R_2) \oplus T_2^* = F_K(T_2 \oplus R_2) \oplus T_2 = T$. The probability of the forgery success is 1.

This attack shows the CS security requires some randomness on the blockcipher internal states. We will show unpredictability is a proper choice in Section 4.

3.3 Key-Recovery Attack against CS

Let $E : \{0,1\}^k \times \{0,1\}^n \to \{0,1\}^n$ be a randomly chosen SPRP. Similar to the permutation we used in distinguishing attack, by modifying several ordered pairs in $E_K(\cdot)$ we can get:

$$F_K(M) = \begin{cases}
E_K(A_1) & \text{if } M = A_2 \oplus K, \\
A_3 \oplus E_K(A_1) & \text{if } M = A_3 \oplus K \oplus E_K(A_1), \\
E_K(A_2 \oplus K) & \text{if } M = A_1, \\
E_K(A_3 \oplus K \oplus E_K(A_1)) & \text{if } M = E_K^{-1}(A_3 \oplus E_K(A_1)), \\
E_K(M) & \text{else.}
\end{cases}$$

where A_1, A_2, A_3 are randomly chosen from $\{0,1\}^n$. What we do is exchanging the values of $E_K(A_1)$ and $E_K(A_2 \oplus K)$, and the values of $E_K(A_3 \oplus K \oplus E_K(A_1))$ and $E_K(E_K^{-1}(A_3 \oplus E_K(A_1)))$. Noting that, some chooses of (A_1, A_2, A_3) may lead to collisions happen in $\mathcal{X} = \{A_2 \oplus K, A_3 \oplus K \oplus E_K(A_1), A_1, E_K^{-1}(A_3 \oplus E_K(A_1))\}$, which may make this construction fail. The probability of no collision happens in $\mathcal{X}$ is more than at least $1 - 6/2^n$. We can proof that F is an SPRP as long as E is an SPRP.

If CS takes this permutation F as underlying blockcipher, then we can build a key-recovery attack as following.

> **Algorithm** $\mathcal{A}^{\mathrm{CS}[F](\cdot,\cdot)}$:
> query (A_2, A_3) to $\mathrm{CS}[F](\cdot, \cdot)$ and get (C, T)
> $K \leftarrow C \oplus A_3$
> **return** K

Noting that $R_0 = K \oplus E_K(A_1)$, and

$$\begin{aligned}
C \oplus A_3 &= (F_K(M \oplus R_0) \oplus R_0) \oplus A_3 \\
&= (F_K(A_3 \oplus (K \oplus E_K(A_1))) \oplus (K \oplus E_K(A_1))) \oplus A_3 \\
&= ((A_3 \oplus E_K(A_1)) \oplus (K \oplus E_K(A_1))) \oplus A_3 \\
&= (A_3 \oplus K) \oplus A_3 \\
&= K
\end{aligned}$$

Noting that, some choices of (A_1, A_2, A_3) may lead this attack to fail. For example, if $E_K(A_1) = 0^n$ and R_0 will be set to K not $E_K(A_1)$. The probability of choosing such (A_1, A_2, A_3) is less than $1/2^{n-1}$. Therefore, the success probability of this attack is at least $(1 - 6/2^n)(1 - 1/2^{n-1})$.

4   Fixing CS and Its Security Proof

The main problem of CS comes from the method for generating the initial whitening value R_0 with nonce and key. We naturally consider modifying only the generation method of R_0 and analyze the fixing mode CS*.

4.1   CS* Mode

CS* mode retains the updating way of R_i unchanged, but changes the method for generating the initial whitening value R_0.

$$R_0 = E_K(N \oplus L) \oplus L \quad \text{with } L = E_K(0^n).$$

To make the mode simpler, the LFSR in T_i's updating and the unnecessary pre-whiten and post-whiten process in generating a tag from T_m are taken away.

The algorithm given below illustrates the CS* construction for a m-block message, $M = M_1, \ldots, M_m$, initialization vector, IV, and encryption key, K. Let E_K be a r-round blockcipher.

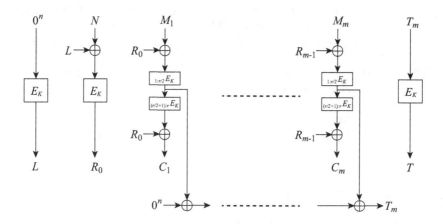

Fig. 2. CS* Mode

Algorithm CS.Enc$_K(N, M)$	Algorithm CS.Dec$_K(N, C, T)$
Partition M **into** $M_1 \cdots M_m$	**Partition** C **into** $C_1 \cdots C_c$
$L \leftarrow E_K(0^n)$	$L \leftarrow E_K(0^n)$
$T_0 = 0^n$	$T_0 = 0^n$
$R_0 \leftarrow E_K(N \oplus L)$	$R_0 \leftarrow E_K(N \oplus L)$
for $i \leftarrow 1$ **to** m **do** $R_i \leftarrow R_{i-1} \cdot x$	**for** $i \leftarrow 1$ **to** c **do** $R_i \leftarrow R_{i-1} \cdot x$
for $i \leftarrow 1$ **to** m **do**	**for** $i \leftarrow 1$ **to** c **do**
$\quad Z_i \leftarrow_{1:r/2} E_K(M_i \oplus R_{i-1})$	$\quad Z_i \leftarrow_{1:r/2} E_K^{-1} E_K(C_i \oplus R_i)$
$\quad C_i \leftarrow_{(r/2+1):r} E_K(Z_i) \oplus R_{i-1}$	$\quad M_i \leftarrow_{(r/2+1):r} E_K^{-1}(Z_i) \oplus R_{i-1}$
$\quad T_i \leftarrow T_{i-1} \oplus Z_i$	$\quad T_i \leftarrow T_{i-1} \oplus Z_i$
$T \leftarrow E_K(T_m)$	$T' \leftarrow E_K(T_m)$
return (C, T)	**if** $T = T'$ **then return** M
	else return $\perp$

Fig. 3. The specification of CS*

4.2 The Security of CS* Mode

We now proceed to show the security of CS*. For this we assume the underlying blockcipher of CS*, P, is an SPRP and it can be split into two unpredictable permutations P_1 and P_2 satisfying $P = P_2^{-1} \circ P_1$. Theorems as following show the information-theoretic bounds and the computational bounds on the privacy and authenticity of CS*.

Theorem 2. *Let $\mathcal{A}$ be a nonce-respecting adversary that asks q queries and then makes its forgery attempt. Suppose the q queries have aggregate length of σ blocks, and the adversary's forgery attempt has at most c blocks. Then*

$$\mathbf{Adv}_{CS^*[\mathrm{Perm}(n)]}^{\mathrm{priv}}(\mathcal{A}) \leq \frac{(\sigma + 2q + 1)^2}{2^n} + 1.5(\sigma + q + 1)^2 \mathbf{Adv}_{P_1}^{\mathrm{up}}(t, q, \sigma),$$

$$\mathbf{Adv}_{CS^*[\mathrm{Perm}(n)]}^{\mathrm{auth}}(\mathcal{A}) \leq \frac{(\sigma + 2q + c + 3)^2}{2^n} + 1.5(\sigma + 2q + c + 2)^2 \mathbf{Adv}_{P_1, P_2}^{\mathrm{up}}(t, q, \sigma).$$

This theorem can be easily translated to the computational complexity setting by adding a advantage of distinguishing blockcipher E and its inverse E^{-1} with a random permutation π and π^{-1}, where E can be split into two unpredictable permutation E_1 and E_2^{-1}.

Theorem 3. *Suppose $E : \{0,1\}^k \times \{0,1\}^n \to \{0,1\}^n$ is an SPRP-secure block-cipher. Let $E_1 =_{1:r/2} E$ and $E_2 =_{1:r/2} E^{-1}$. Let $\mathcal{A}$ be an nonce-respecting adversary that asks q queries and then makes its forgery attempt. Suppose the q queries have aggregate length of σ blocks, and the adversary's forgery attempt has at most c blocks. Then*

$$\mathbf{Adv}_{\mathrm{CS}^*[E]}^{\mathrm{priv}}(\mathcal{A}) \leq \frac{(\sigma + 2q + 1)^2}{2^n} + 1.5(\sigma + q + 1)^2 \mathbf{Adv}_{E_1}^{\mathrm{up}}(t, q, \sigma) + \mathbf{Adv}_E^{\mathrm{sprp}}(t', q', \sigma'),$$

$$\mathbf{Adv}_{\mathrm{CS}^*[E]}^{\mathrm{auth}}(\mathcal{A}) \leq \frac{(\sigma + 2q + c + 3)^2}{2^n} + 1.5(\sigma + 2q + c + 2)^2 \mathbf{Adv}_{E_1, E_2}^{\mathrm{up}}(t, q, \sigma)$$
$$+ \mathbf{Adv}_{E, E^{-1}}^{\mathrm{sprp}}(t', q', \sigma'),$$

where $t' = t$, $q' = q + 1$, and $\sigma' = \sigma + c + 2q + 3$.

For privacy, the initial whitening value R_0 is generated by $E_K(\cdot)$ with a new nonce N in each query and is kept secret from $\mathcal{A}$. Pre-whiten values are then generated from R_0 and they make the inputs to blockciphers pair-wise distinct, resulting in random ciphertexts because E is an SPRP. Furthermore, noticing E_1 is unpredictable, it is easy to find T_m is collision-resistant, and the final tag T is random after the final encryption. Therefore, both the ciphertexts and the tag are random bits. For authenticity, if the forgery is composed with a new nonce N, then it has a close-to-1 probability that the inputs to E_2 are pairwise distinct and also distinct from former blockcipher outputs. By the unpredictability of E_2, T_m would be new and the final tag is random. On the other side, if the forgery is composed with a used nonce N, then there still exists large probability that at least one of the inputs to E_2 is new, resulting in a new T_m by the unpredictability of E_2 and a random tag by the SPRP of E. In either case, the probability to make a valid forgery is negligible.

In CS* mode, the internal states of the underlying blockcipher are hidden from adversaries and their sum is again encrypted before being output, these features result in no information leakage, except the collision before the last blockcipher encryptions for authentication.

Noting that, in our proofs, we assume that the underlying blockcipher E is an SPRP and constructed by $E = E_2^{-1} \circ E_1$, where E_1, E_2 are two independently unpredictable permutations. However, this doesn't mean in theory that the concatenation of two unpredictable permutations can make up an SPRP.

Despite the above, our assumption on blockciphers for the security of CS* is no stronger than the usual and solo SPRP assumption. This can also be reflected by the security of practical blockciphers. That is, a full-round blockcipher behaves like an SPRP and its internal states are unpredictable for adversaries.

5 Conclusion

The CS mode was submitted to NIST in 2004, and is still in NIST's modes development list. However, only a few of papers involve this mode in and no formal proof has been proposed before. In this paper, we pointed out that there exist some security problems in its method for generating initial whiten values. By constructing a special SPRP F, a key-recovery attack against CS[F] with a single block query can be made.

A slight modification for generating initial whiten values leads to a new authenticated encryption mode, CS*, which uses the same way of generating initial whiten values as the OCB mode and retains most parts of CS. Assuming internal states of the underlying blockcipher behave as "unpredictable" while the blockcipher is super pseudorandom, it can be proved that CS* is a secure AE scheme.

Acknowledgments. The authors would like to thank the anonymous referees for their valuable comments. This work was supported by the National Grand Fundamental Research 973 Program of China (Grant No. 2013CB338002), and the National Natural Science Foundation of China (Grant No. 61272476,61232009,61272477 and 61202422).

References

1. CAESAR: Competition for Authenticated Encryption: Security, Applicability, and Robustness (2013), http://competitions.cr.yp.to/index.html
2. An, J.H., Bellare, M.: Constructing VIL-MACs from FIL-MACs: message authentication under weakened assumptions. In: Wiener, M. (ed.) CRYPTO 1999. LNCS, vol. 1666, pp. 252–269. Springer, Heidelberg (1999)
3. Anderson, E., Beaver, C., Draelos, T., Schroeppel, R., Torgerson, M.: ManTiCore: encryption with joint Cipher-State authentication. In: Wang, H., Pieprzyk, J., Varadharajan, V. (eds.) ACISP 2004. LNCS, vol. 3108, pp. 440–453. Springer, Heidelberg (2004)
4. Anderson, E., Beaver, C., Draelos, T., Schroeppel, R., Torgerson, M.: Submission to NIST: Cipher-State (CS) mode of operation for AES (2004), http://csrc.nist.gov/CryptoToolkit/modes/proposedmodes/cs/cs-spec.pdf
5. Anderson, E., Beaver, C., Draelos, T., Schroeppel, R., Torgerson, M.: Manticore and CS mode: parallelizable encryption with joint Cipher-State authentication (2004), http://dx.doi.org/10.2172/919631
6. Bellare, M., Desai, A., Jokipii, E., Rogaway, P.: A concrete security treatment of symmetric encryption: analysis of the DES modes of operation. In: Goldberg, A.V., Rao, S. (eds.) FOCS 1997, pp. 394–403. ACM Press, IEEE (1997)
7. Bellare, M., Namprempre, C.: Authenticated encryption: relations among notions and analysis of the generic composition paradigm. In: Okamoto, T. (ed.) ASIACRYPT 2000. LNCS, vol. 1976, pp. 531–545. Springer, Heidelberg (2000)
8. Bellare, M., Rogaway, P.: Encode-then-encipher encryption: How to exploit nonces or redundancy in plaintexts for efficient cryptography. In: Okamoto, T. (ed.) ASIACRYPT 2000. LNCS, vol. 1976, pp. 317–330. Springer, Heidelberg (2000)
9. Furuya, S., Sakurai, K.: Risks with raw-key maksing - the security evaluations of 2-key XCBC. In: Deng, R.H., Qing, S., Bao, F., Zhou, J. (eds.) ICICS 2002. LNCS, vol. 2513, pp. 327–341. Springer, Heidelberg (2002)
10. Gligor, V., Donescu, P.: Fast encryption and authentication: XCBC encryption and XECB authentication modes. In: Matsui, M. (ed.) FSE 2001. LNCS, vol. 2355, pp. 92–108. Springer, Heidelberg (2002)
11. Goldreich, O., Goldwasser, S., Micali, S.: How to construct random function. Journal of the ACM 33(4), 792–807 (1986)

12. Jutla, C.: Encryption modes with almost free message integrity. In: Pfitzmann, B. (ed.) EUROCRYPT 2001. LNCS, vol. 2045, pp. 529–544. Springer, Heidelberg (2001)

13. Katz, J., Yung, M.: Unforgeable encryption and chosen ciphertext secure modes of operation. In: Schneier, B. (ed.) FSE 2000. LNCS, vol. 1978, pp. 284–299. Springer, Heidelberg (2001)

14. Rogaway, P.: Authenticated-encryption with associated-data. In: Atluri, V. (ed.) CCS 2002, pp. 98–107. ACM, ACM press (2002)

15. Rogaway, P., Bellare, M., Black, J.: OCB: A block-cipher mode of operation for efficient authenticated encryption. ACM Trans. on Information and System Security 6(3), 365–403 (2003); Earlier version, with Krovetz, T. in CCS 2001

16. Švenda, P.: Basic comparison of modes for authenticated-encryption (IAPM, XCBC, OCB, CCM, EAX, CWC, GCM, PCFB, CS) (2004), http://www.fi.muni.cz/~xsvenda/docs/AE_comparison_ipics04.pdf

17. Wang, P., Feng, D., Wu, W., Zhang, L.: On the unprovable security of 2-key XCBC. In: Mu, Y., Susilo, W., Seberry, J. (eds.) ACISP 2008. LNCS, vol. 5107, pp. 230–238. Springer, Heidelberg (2008)

Integral Attacks on Reduced-Round PRESENT

Shengbao Wu[1,2] and Mingsheng Wang[3]

[1] Trusted Computing and Information Assurance Laboratory, Institute of Software,
Chinese Academy of Sciences, Beijing 100190, PO Box 8718, China
[2] Graduate School of Chinese Academy of Sciences, Beijing 100190, China
[3] State Key Laboratory of Information Security, Institute of Information Engineering,
Chinese Academy of Sciences, Beijing, China
wangmingsheng@iie.ac.cn

Abstract. Integral attack is a powerful technique to recover the secret
key of block ciphers by usually exploiting the fact that specific parts
of the output after several round encryptions has a zero-sum property
in a set of chosen plaintexts. In FSE 2008, bit-based integral attack
proposed by Z'aba et al. revealed that integral attacks may be not only
suitable for byte-based block ciphers but also still applied to bit-based
block ciphers. In this work, we show that integral attack against bit-
based block ciphers can be improved not only by the theorem of higher-
order differential attack but also by using specific algebraic properties of
Sboxes, and the order of plaintexts in a set, which is important in bit-
based integral attack, is not required here. We focus on the block cipher
PRESENT. Based on some algebraic properties of its Sbox, we propose
two integral distinguishers: a 5 round (4-th order) integral distinguisher
and a 7 round (16-th order) integral distinguishers, which can be used
to attack 10 (out of 31) round PRESENT. As far as we know, it is the
first time that a 7 round integral distinguisher of PRESENT is reported.
Algebraic techniques used in this paper may be also applied to other
block ciphers to improve their known integral attacks.

Keywords: Integral Attack, PRESENT, Higher Order Differential
Attack, Boolean Function.

1 Introduction

The integral attack is one of the most popular cryptanalytic tools for block
ciphers. It was first known as "Square attack" due to its efficiency in attacking
the Rijndael-predecessor Square [8]. Later, several variants of Square attack have
been proposed, including saturation attack [13] and multiset attack [5]. In FSE
2002, Knudsen and Wagner introduced the definition of integral and unified these
kinds of attacks as integral attack [11].

The basic idea of integral attack is to analyze the propagation of sums of
(many) values. Thus, it can be seen as a dual to the differential cryptanalysis.
When applying integral attack to a block cipher, an attacker first selects a d-th
order integral, that is, he/she chooses a set of 2^d plaintexts, where d bit positions

S. Qing et al. (Eds.): ICICS 2013, LNCS 8233, pp. 331–345, 2013.

take on all values through the set, and the other bits are chosen to be arbitrary constants. Then, he/she traces the evolvement of the sum of this set of plaintexts through the encryption algorithm and builds an integral distinguisher as long as possible. Finally, the integral distinguisher will be used to verify key guesses. In practice, a zero-sum property in specific parts of the ciphertext is often used as the integral distinguisher.

In quite a long time, integral attack has not been thought suitable for bit-based block ciphers, such as Noekeon [9], Serpent [1] and PRESENT [2]. Until 2008, Z'aba et al. proposed the bit-based integral attack [16], which was applied to Noekeon, Serpent and PRESENT reduced up to 5, 6 and 7 rounds, respectively. Although the bit-based integral attack does not pose a serious threat to known block ciphers, it reveals that integral attacks may be not only suitable for byte-based block ciphers but also still applied to bit-based block ciphers.

Many cryptanalysis methods may be not so powerful as nowadays in their first proposals. However, with the studies getting further, they became more and more powerful. On the one hand, new techniques may be introduced to improve known cryptanalysis methods. For example, the partial-sum techniques proposed by Ferguson et al. [10] enhance the ability of integral attack. On the other hand, a cryptanalysis method may be improved using the theorem of other cryptanalysis methods if they have some links. For example, the data complexity of a zero-correlation attack [4] may be improved using the theorem of integral attack [3].

Integral attack and higher-order differential attack also have some links in constructing distinguishers. To construct a d-th order integral distinguisher with a zero-sum property is equivalent to show that the algebraic degree of specific parts of the ciphertext is at most $d - 1$, if XOR difference is considered in the higher-order differential attack. This technique has been used, for instance, in [15].

In this paper, we show that integral attack against bit-based block ciphers can be improved not only by the theorem of higher-order differential attack but also by using specific algebraic properties of Sboxes. What is more, the order of plaintexts in a set, which is important in bit-based integral attack, is not required here.

We focus on the bit-based block cipher PRESENT. Firstly, we analyze the algebraic properties of PRESENT's Sbox. We observe that the rightmost co-ordinate of the Sbox is quadratic while other three coordinates has algebraic degree 3. Combined it with the properties of diffusion layer, we find that, for the rightmost bit of the output, the growth rate of its algebraic degree is slower than other bits. Than, we propose two integral distinguishers: the first one uses that the rightmost bit of the output after 5 rounds has a zero-sum property in the 4 rightmost bits of the input. Similarly, the second distinguisher is based on the fact that the rightmost bit of the output after 7 rounds has a zero-sum property in the 16 rightmost bits of the input. Our distinguishers improve the 3.5 round (4-th order) integral distinguisher proposed by Z'aba et al. and the 5 round (32-th order) integral distinguisher proposed by Zhang et al [17].

Finally, we applied our distinguishers to recover the keys up to 10 (out of 31) rounds of PRESENT. All known integral attacks on reduced-round PRESENT are summarized in Table 1.

Table 1. Summary of integral attacks on reduced-round PRESENT

Rounds	Key Size	Data	Time	Memory	Attacks & Source
5	all	$N \cdot 2^{32}$ CP†	-	-	(32-th order) integral distinguisher [17]
5	80	$2^{6.4}$ CP	$2^{25.7}$	-	Bit-Pattern Based Integral [16]
6	80	$2^{22.4}$ CP	$2^{41.7}$	-	Bit-Pattern Based Integral [16]
7	128	$2^{24.3}$ CP	$2^{100.1}$	2^{77}	Bit-Pattern Based Integral [16]
7	80	$2^{8.3}$ CP	2^{60}	2^{17}	Section 5
8	80	$2^{10.1}$ CP	$2^{72.6}$	2^{66}	Section 5
9	80	$2^{20.3}$ CP	2^{60}	2^{17}	Section 5
10	128	$2^{22.4}$ CP	$2^{99.3}$	2^{81}	Section 5

† N is the number of sets required in a key-recover attack.

Even though we only restrict our attention on PRESENT in this work, the algebraic techniques used in constructing longer integral distinguishers here may be also applied to other block ciphers to improve their known integral attacks.

Outline of This Paper. In Section 2, we introduce the encryption process of PRESENT, the definition of boolean functions and the basic idea of integral attack. In Section 3, we analyze the properties of PRESENT's S-box and present some observations on the degree of boolean functions. The integral distinguishers are constructed in Section 4 and attacks based on them are given in Section 5. Finally, we conclude this paper.

2 Preliminaries

In this section, we briefly describe the block cipher PRESENT, boolean functions and the integral attack.

2.1 Description of PRESENT

PRESENT [2], proposed by A. Bogdanov et.al in CHES 2007, is a 31-round ultra-lightweight block cipher with block length 64 bits. It has two versions supporting key length 80 bits and 128 bits, which will be denoted as PRESENT-80 and PRESENT-128, respectively. The underlying structure of PRESENT is a typical SP-network which has three layers in every round: AddRoundKey, SBoxLayer and PLayer. In the AddRoundKey layer, a round key with 64 bits is XORed to the current state. Then, one 4-bit Sbox is applied 16 times in parallel in the SBoxLayer. Finally, a fully wired permutation P on the 64-bit state is employed in the PLayer. The outline of one round PRESENT is shown in Fig. 1. Notice that there is an AddRoundKey layer after round 31. The Sbox

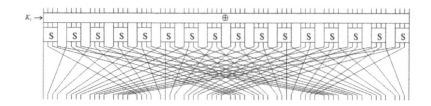

Fig. 1. One round PRESENT

Table 2. The Sbox of PRESENT

x	0	1	2	3	4	5	6	7	8	9	A	B	C	D	E	F
$S(x)$	C	5	6	B	9	0	A	D	3	E	F	8	4	7	1	2

and P permutation used in PRESENT are illustrated in Table 2 and Table 3, respectively.

The key schedule of PRESENT-80 is given below. Firstly, the 80-bit key is stored in a key register K and represented as $k_{79}k_{78} \ldots k_0$. In round i, the most significant 64-bit keys are extracted as the subkey $K^{(i)}$, that is, $K^{(i)} = k_{79}k_{78} \ldots k_{16}$. Then, key register $K = k_{79}k_{78} \ldots k_0$ is updated as follows:

$$[k_{79}k_{78} \ldots k_1 k_0] = [k_{18}k_{17} \ldots k_{20}k_{19}],$$
$$[k_{79}k_{78}k_{77}k_{76}] = S[k_{79}k_{78}k_{77}k_{76}],$$
$$[k_{19}k_{18}k_{17}k_{16}k_{15}] = [k_{19}k_{18}k_{17}k_{16}k_{15}] \oplus round\_counter.$$

We omit the key schedule of PRESENT-128 here since we do not use it in this paper.

Table 3. The PLayer of PRESENT. Bit i of state is moved to bit position $P(i)$.

i	0	1	2	3	4	5	6	7	8	9	10	11	12	13	14	15
$P(i)$	0	16	32	48	1	17	33	49	2	18	34	50	3	19	35	51
i	16	17	18	19	20	21	22	23	24	25	26	27	28	29	30	31
$P(i)$	4	20	36	52	5	21	37	53	6	22	38	54	7	23	39	55
i	32	33	34	35	36	37	38	39	40	41	42	43	44	45	46	47
$P(i)$	8	24	40	56	9	25	41	57	10	26	42	58	11	27	43	59
i	48	49	50	51	52	53	54	55	56	57	58	59	60	61	62	63
$P(i)$	12	28	44	60	13	29	45	61	14	30	46	62	15	31	47	63

2.2   Boolean Functions

A *boolean function f of n variables* is a map from $\mathbb{F}_2^n \to \mathbb{F}_2$. It can be expressed as a polynomial in $\mathbb{F}_2[x_1, \ldots, x_n]/(x_1^2 - x_1, \ldots, x_n^2 - x_n)$, called *algebraic normal form*. That is,

$$f(x_1, x_2, \ldots, x_n) = \bigoplus_{\Lambda \subseteq \{1,2,\ldots,n\}} a_\Lambda \prod_{k \in \Lambda} x_k. \tag{1}$$

In the subsequent discussions, we denote by $\mathcal{B}_2[x_1, x_2, \ldots, x_n]$ the set of all boolean functions with variables $x_1, x_2, \ldots, x_n$. The *algebraic degree* (or *degree*) of f, denoted by $deg(f)$, is the number of variables in the highest order term with nonzero coefficient. For a further step, the *degree* of a vectorial boolean function from $\mathbb{F}_2^n \rightarrow \mathbb{F}_2^m$ is defined as the highest degree of its coordinates.

2.3 Integral Attack

Let $E = E_1 \circ E_0$ be the encryption function of an r round block cipher, where E_0 is the first k rounds of E and E_1 is the last $r - k$ rounds. It can be written formally as

$$Y = E(X, K) = E_1(E_0(X, K_0), K_1),$$

or equivalently,

$$E_1^{-1}(Y, K_1) = E_0(X, K_0), \tag{2}$$

where E_1^{-1} is the inverse function of E_1, K is the master key, K_0 and K_1 are subkeys in the first k rounds and the last $r - k$ rounds, respectively.

In integral attacks, an attacker first selects a set of 2^d plaintext, where d bit positions of X take on all values through the set and the other bits of X are chosen to be arbitrary constants. Then, a zero-sum property of the set of plaintexts propagating through k round encryptions is proved, that is, an attacker demonstrates that

$$\bigoplus_{X \in \Lambda} E_0(X, K_0) = 0, \tag{3}$$

where Λ is the set of 2^d plaintexts. Finally, the subkey K_1 in the last $r - k$ rounds is guessed and equation

$$\bigoplus_{X \in \Lambda, Y = E(X, K)} E_1^{-1}(Y, K_1) = 0 \tag{4}$$

is used to verify the guess. The remaining key bits in the master key K will be obtained by exhausting method.

Notice that, the integral distinguisher (3) can be built upon a specific parts of the output of E_0, that is, the zero-sum property may be only valid in some specific bits. Based on the theorem of higher-order differential attack, (3) can be proved by showing that some specific bits of the output of E_0 have degree at most $d - 1$.

3 Degree of Boolean Functions and PRESENT's Sbox

In this section, we discuss some properties for evaluating the degree of boolean functions and then analyze the algebraic properties of PRESENT's Sbox.

Some trivial bounds for operations between (vectorial) boolean functions are summarized in Proposition 1.

Proposition 1. *Suppose $f, g \in \mathcal{B}_2[x_1, x_2, \ldots, x_n]$ are two boolean functions, h is a vectorial boolean function from $\mathbb{F}_2^n \to \mathbb{F}_2^n$, then the degree of composed function $f \circ h$, product $f \cdot g$ and sum $f \oplus g$ can be evaluated as*

$$deg(f \circ h) \leq deg(f)deg(h),$$
$$deg(f \cdot g) \leq deg(f) + deg(g),$$
$$deg(f \oplus g) \leq max\{deg(f), deg(g)\}.$$

Moreover, $deg(f), deg(g), deg(f \circ h), deg(f \cdot g)$ and $deg(f \oplus g)$ are less than or equal to n.

These bounds are so loose that they are unfitted in some cases. Here, we analyze the product of boolean functions and show a tighter degree bound in a specific situation. First, we introduce the definition of *m-partition*.

Definition 1. *Nonempty sets $U_1, \ldots, U_m$ is called an m-partition of $U = \{x_1, x_2, \ldots, x_n\}$, if $U = U_1 \cup \cdots \cup U_m$ and $U_i \cap U_j = \emptyset$ for $1 \leq i < j \leq m$.*

Let n_i be the number of variables in U_i, then $n = n_1 + \cdots + n_m$. Our observation is given below.

Proposition 2. *Suppose $U_1, \ldots, U_m$ is an m-partition of $U = \{x_1, x_2, \ldots, x_n\}$, $f_1, f_2, \ldots, f_k$ is a list of boolean functions satisfying:*

1. *For each f_i, there exists a $j \in \{1, 2, \ldots, m\}$ such that $f_i \in \mathcal{B}_2[U_j]$,*
2. *$deg(f_i) \leq n_j - 1$,*

then, for any $k \leq 2m - 1$, we have

$$deg(f_1 \cdot f_2 \cdots f_k) \leq n - 1.$$

Proof. This can be explained as an allocation problem. Now, we have k tokens $f_1, \ldots, f_k$ and m boxes $\mathcal{B}_2[U_1], \ldots, \mathcal{B}_2[U_m]$. When throwing $k \leq 2m - 1$ tokens to m boxes, there must exist a box with the condition that it contains no more than one token. Without loss of generality, suppose this box is $\mathcal{B}_2[U_1]$.

If it's empty, then all f_is do not involve variables in U_1, which implies

$$deg(f_1 \cdot f_2 \cdots f_k) \leq n - n_1 \leq n - 1.$$

If it contains a token f_i, then, from Proposition 1, we have

$$deg(f_1 \cdot f_2 \cdots f_k) \leq deg(f_i) + deg(f_1 \cdots f_{i-1} \cdot f_{i+1} \cdots f_k)$$
$$\leq (n_i - 1) + (n - n_i) \leq n - 1.$$

$\square$

This property will be used for constructing integral distinguishers of PRESENT, combining with the subsequent observations on PRESENT's Sbox.

Proposition 3. *The Sbox of PRESENT is a permutation $S : \mathbb{F}_2^4 \to \mathbb{F}_2^4$. It can be expressed as a vectorial boolean function with four coordinates. Suppose its input is a vector $x = (x_3, x_2, x_1, x_0)$ and output is a vector $y = (y_3, y_2, y_1, y_0)$, where $x_i, y_i \in \mathbb{F}_2$ and $0 \le i \le 3$. Then, the algebraic normal form of PRESENT's Sbox is:*

$$
\begin{cases}
y_3 = 1 \oplus x_0 \oplus x_1 \oplus x_3 \oplus x_1 x_2 \oplus x_0 x_1 x_2 \oplus x_0 x_1 x_3 \oplus x_0 x_2 x_3; \\
y_2 = 1 \oplus x_2 \oplus x_3 \oplus x_0 x_1 \oplus x_0 x_3 \oplus x_1 x_3 \oplus x_0 x_1 x_3 \oplus x_0 x_2 x_3; \\
y_1 = x_1 \oplus x_3 \oplus x_1 x_3 \oplus x_2 x_3 \oplus x_0 x_1 x_2 \oplus x_0 x_1 x_3 \oplus x_0 x_2 x_3; \\
y_0 = x_0 \oplus x_2 \oplus x_3 \oplus x_1 x_2;
\end{cases}
$$

The correctness of Proposition 3 can be easily checked. From Proposition 3, we immediately have

Corollary 1. *The degree of PRESENT's Sbox S is 3. However, its rightmost coordinate is only quadratic, that is, $\deg(y_0) = 2$.*

Corollary 2. *Let $f = c_f \oplus f_0 \oplus f_2 \oplus f_3 \oplus f_1 f_2$ and $g = c_g \oplus g_0 \oplus g_2 \oplus g_3 \oplus g_1 g_2$, where $f_i, g_i \in \mathcal{B}_2[x_i]$ for $0 \le i \le 3$ and $c_f, c_g \in \mathbb{F}_2$ are constants, then we have $\deg(f \cdot g) \le 3$.*

According to the PLayer of PRESENT (see Fig. 1), all 16 quadratic coordinates of Sboxes are translated to the rightmost 16 bits after one round encryption. Thus, we have

Observation. *The growth rate of algebraic degree for the bits in the right side of the output is slower than those in the left side.*

After several rounds of encryption, the effect is finally accumulated to the rightmost bit of the output. Therefore, in the subsequent discussions, we only consider the degree for the rightmost bit of the output.

4   Integral Distinguishers of PRESENT

In this section, we proposed two integral distinguishers of PRESENT. We denote by $X^{(i)}$ the state entering round i, $Y^{(i)}$ the state before the SBoxLayer, $Z^{(i)}$ the state after the SBoxLayer and $K^{(i)}$ the subkey of round i. Thus, $Y^{(i)} = X^{(i)} \oplus K^{(i)}$. Each state and subkey can be represented as a vector of 64 bits, for example, $X^{(i)} = (x_{63}^{(i)}, x_{62}^{(i)}, \ldots, x_0^{(i)})$, where $x_0^{(i)}$ is the least significant (rightmost) bit of $X^{(i)}$. Additionally, let $x_{[j-k]}^{(i)}$ be the consecutive $j - k + 1$ bits of $X^{(i)}$ from bit k to bit j, and $x_{[j,\ldots,k]}^{(i)}$ represents several separate bits $x_j^{(i)}, \ldots, x_k^{(i)}$ of $X^{(i)}$.

4.1   A 5 Round (4-th Order) Integral Distinguisher

In this subsection, we show a 4-th order integral distinguisher of PRESENT, which provides us a 5-round integral distinguisher.

Proposition 4. *Choose a set of 2^4 values in the input of round 2, where all values of bits $x^{(2)}_{[48,32,16,0]}$ of input $X^{(2)}$ are chosen and other bits are chosen to be arbitrary constants. Then, the rightmost bit of $X^{(6)}$, that is, the bit $x^{(6)}_0$, has a zero-sum property.*

Proof. Consider $x^{(6)}_0$ as a boolean function of $X^{(2)}$, then we only need to prove that $x^{(6)}_0 \in \mathcal{B}_2[x^{(2)}_{48}, x^{(2)}_{32}, x^{(2)}_{16}, x^{(2)}_0]$ has degree at most 3. The proof process is shown in the phase T1 of Fig. 2.

In round 2, since $x^{(2)}_{[3-1]}$ are fixed, then $z^{(2)}_{[3-0]}$ are affine functions with only one variable $x^{(2)}_0$, that is, $z^{(2)}_{[3-0]} \in \mathcal{B}_2[x^{(2)}_0]$. Similarly, we have $z^{(2)}_{[19-16]} \in \mathcal{B}_2[x^{(2)}_{16}]$, $z^{(2)}_{[35-32]} \in \mathcal{B}_2[x^{(2)}_{32}]$ and $z^{(2)}_{[51-48]} \in \mathcal{B}_2[x^{(2)}_{48}]$. Other bits of $Z^{(2)}$ are constants.

In round 3, we have $x^{(3)}_{[48,32,16,0]} \in \mathcal{B}_2[x^{(2)}_0]$, $x^{(3)}_{[52,36,20,4]} \in \mathcal{B}_2[x^{(2)}_{16}]$, $x^{(3)}_{[56,40,24,8]} \in \mathcal{B}_2[x^{(2)}_{32}]$ and $x^{(3)}_{[60,44,28,12]} \in \mathcal{B}_2[x^{(2)}_{48}]$.

In round 4, we have $x^{(4)}_{[12,8,4,0]} \in \mathcal{B}_2[x^{(2)}_0]$, $x^{(4)}_{[13,9,5,1]} \in \mathcal{B}_2[x^{(2)}_{16}]$, $x^{(4)}_{[14,10,6,2]} \in \mathcal{B}_2[x^{(2)}_{32}]$ and $x^{(4)}_{[15,11,7,3]} \in \mathcal{B}_2[x^{(2)}_{48}]$.

In summary, bits marked with red color (resp. green color, blue color and purple color) in Fig. 2 are affine functions with only one variable $x^{(2)}_0$ (resp. $x^{(2)}_{16}$, $x^{(2)}_{32}$ and $x^{(2)}_{48}$). Other bits are not considered here since they are independent of $x^{(6)}_0$.

In round 5, from the expression of Sbox, we have

$$y^{(5)}_i = k^{(5)}_i \oplus y^{(4)}_{4i} \oplus y^{(4)}_{4i+2} \oplus y^{(4)}_{4i+3} \oplus y^{(4)}_{4i+1} \cdot y^{(4)}_{4i+2},$$

where $y^{(4)}_{4i+j} \in \mathcal{B}_2[x^{(2)}_{16j}]$ for $0 \le j \le 3$ and $0 \le i \le 3$.

Finally,

$$\begin{aligned}
deg(x^{(6)}_0) &= deg(y^{(5)}_0 \oplus y^{(5)}_2 \oplus y^{(5)}_3 \oplus y^{(5)}_1 \cdot y^{(5)}_2) \\
&\le max\{deg(y^{(5)}_0), deg(y^{(5)}_2), deg(y^{(5)}_3), deg(y^{(5)}_1 \cdot y^{(5)}_2)\} \\
&\le max\{2, 2, 2, 3\} = 3,
\end{aligned}$$

where the final inequation comes from Corollary 2.   □

A 5-round integral distinguisher is obtained by adding one round to the upper side of the distinguisher given in Proposition 4.

Theorem 1. *Choose a set of 2^4 values in the plaintext, where all values of bits $x^{(1)}_{[3,2,1,0]}$ of input $X^{(1)}$ are chosen and other bits are chosen to be arbitrary constants. Then, the rightmost bit of $X^{(6)}$, that is, the bit $x^{(6)}_0$, has a zero-sum property.*

Proof. It's based on the fact that $x^{(1)}_{[3-0]} \rightarrow x^{(2)}_{[48,32,16,0]}$ is a permutation (see the phase T2 of Fig. 2 with bold line). We have

$$\bigoplus_{x^{(2)}_{[48,32,16,0]} \in \mathbb{F}_2^4} R_{K^{(5)}} \circ \cdots \circ R_{K^{(2)}} (x^{(2)}_{[48,32,16,0]}, c') = \bigoplus_{x^{(1)}_{[3-0]} \in \mathbb{F}_2^4} R_{K^{(5)}} \circ \cdots \circ R_{K^{(1)}} (x^{(1)}_{[3-0]}, c),$$

(5)

where $R_{K^{(i)}}$ is the round function with key $K^{(i)}$, c is the constant chosen in the plaintext and c' is the constant deduced from c by one round encryption. $\square$

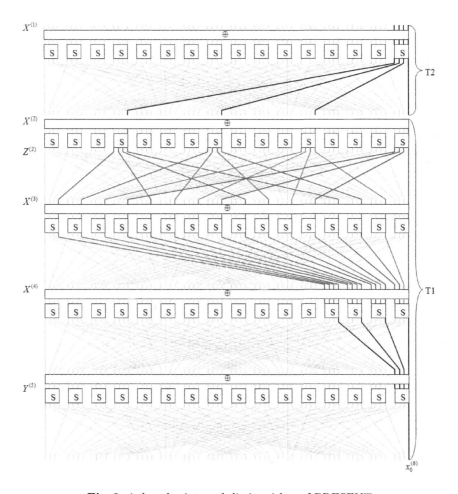

Fig. 2. 4-th order integral distinguisher of PRESENT

4.2   A 7 Round (16-th Order) Integral Distinguisher

In this subsection, we show a 16-th order integral distinguisher of PRESENT, which provides us a 7-round integral distinguisher.

Proposition 5. *Choose a set of 2^{16} values in the input of round 3, where all values of bits $x_{4j}^{(3)}$ ($0 \leq j \leq 15$) of input $X^{(3)}$ are chosen and other bits are chosen to be arbitrary constants. Then, the rightmost bit of $X^{(8)}$, that is, the bit $x_0^{(8)}$, has a zero-sum property.*

Proof. Consider $x_0^{(8)}$ as a boolean function of $X^{(3)}$, then we only need to prove that $x_0^{(8)} \in \mathcal{B}_2[x_{60}^{(3)}, x_{56}^{(3)}, \dots, x_4^{(3)}, x_0^{(3)}]$ has degree at most 15. The proof process is shown in the phase T1 of Fig. 3.

In round 3, we have $z_{[4j+3, 4j+2, 4j+1, 4j]}^{(3)} \in \mathcal{B}_2[x_{4j}^{(3)}]$ ($0 \leq j \leq 15$).

In round 4, we have $y_i^{(4)} \in \mathcal{B}_2[x_{4j}^{(3)}]$ ($0 \leq i \leq 63$), where $j = i \bmod 16$.

In round 5, from the expression of PRESENT's Sbox, we have $y_i^{(5)} \in \mathcal{B}_2[x_{16j+12}^{(3)}, x_{16j+8}^{(3)}, x_{16j+4}^{(3)}, x_{16j}^{(3)}]$ and $deg(y_i^{(5)}) \leq 3$, where $0 \leq i \leq 63$ and $j = i \bmod 4$.

In summary, bits marked with red color (resp. green color, blue color and purple color) in Fig. 3 are boolean functions in $\mathcal{B}_2[x_{12}^{(3)}, x_8^{(3)}, x_4^{(3)}, x_0^{(3)}]$ (resp. $\mathcal{B}_2[x_{28}^{(3)}, x_{24}^{(3)}, x_{20}^{(3)}, x_{16}^{(3)}]$, $\mathcal{B}_2[x_{44}^{(3)}, x_{40}^{(3)}, x_{36}^{(3)}, x_{32}^{(3)}]$ and $\mathcal{B}_2[x_{60}^{(3)}, x_{56}^{(3)}, x_{52}^{(3)}, x_{48}^{(3)}]$) and have degree at most 3.

Now, we consider $x_0^{(8)}$ as a boolean function of $Y^{(5)}$. Then, $x_0^{(8)} \in \mathcal{B}_2[y_{[63-0]}^{(5)}]$ has representation

$$x_0^{(8)} = \bigoplus_{\Lambda \subseteq \{0,1,2,\dots,63\}} a_\Lambda \prod_{k \in \Lambda} y_k^{(5)}. \tag{6}$$

Notice that $x_0^{(8)}$ is also a boolean function in $\mathcal{B}_2[x_{60}^{(3)}, \dots, x_4^{(3)}, x_0^{(3)}]$. Thus, in the following discussions, we have to show that each term $a_\Lambda \prod_{k \in \Lambda} y_k^{(5)} \in \mathcal{B}_2[x_{60}^{(3)}, \dots, x_4^{(3)}, x_0^{(3)}]$ with $a_\Lambda \neq 0$ has degree at most 15.

First, we show that $deg(\prod_{k \in \Lambda} y_k^{(5)}) \leq 15$ if $|\Lambda| \leq 7$. Here, $|\Lambda|$ is the number of elements in set Λ. Denote by $U = \{x_{4j}^{(3)} | 0 \leq j \leq 15\}$ and $U_k = \{x_{16k+12}^{(3)}, x_{16k+8}^{(3)}, x_{16k+4}^{(3)}, x_{16k}^{(3)}\}$ for $0 \leq k \leq 3$, then $U_0, \dots, U_3$ is a 4-partition of U. Notice that $y_i^{(5)}$ ($0 \leq i \leq 63$) satisfies the condition of Proposition 2, which implies that $deg(\prod_{k \in \Lambda} y_k^{(5)}) \leq 15$ if $|\Lambda| \leq 7$. Therefore, we only need to check the terms $a_\Lambda \prod_{k \in \Lambda} y_k^{(5)}$ with $a_\Lambda \neq 0$ and $|\Lambda| \geq 8$.

Secondly, we show that a_Λ is always zero in (6) if $|\Lambda| > 8$. According to Proposition 3 and Proposition 1, we have $deg(y_{[15-0]}^{(6)}) \leq 2$, $deg(y_{[3-0]}^{(7)}) \leq 4$ and $deg(x_0^{(8)}) \leq 8$ if $y_{[15-0]}^{(6)}, y_{[3-0]}^{(7)}$ and $x_0^{(8)}$ are viewed as boolean functions in $\mathcal{B}_2[y_{[63-0]}^{(5)}]$. Thus, in (6), all $a_\Lambda = 0$ if $|\Lambda| \geq 9$, which implies that we only need to consider the terms with $|\Lambda| = 8$.

Thirdly, we show that only one term in (6) may have $|\Lambda| = 8$. According to the algebraic normal form of PRESENT's Sbox, $x_0^{(8)} \in \mathcal{B}_2[y_{[63-0]}^{(5)}]$ can be expressed as follows.

$$
\begin{aligned}
x_0^{(8)} &= y_0^{(7)} \oplus y_2^{(7)} \oplus y_3^{(7)} \oplus y_1^{(7)} y_2^{(7)} \simeq y_1^{(7)} y_2^{(7)} \\
&= (k_1^{(7)} \oplus y_4^{(6)} \oplus y_6^{(6)} \oplus y_7^{(6)} \oplus y_5^{(6)} y_6^{(6)})(k_2^{(7)} \oplus y_8^{(6)} \oplus y_{10}^{(6)} \oplus y_{11}^{(6)} \oplus y_9^{(6)} y_{10}^{(6)}) \\
&\simeq y_5^{(6)} y_6^{(6)} y_9^{(6)} y_{10}^{(6)} \simeq y_{21}^{(5)} y_{22}^{(5)} y_{25}^{(5)} y_{26}^{(5)} y_{37}^{(5)} y_{38}^{(5)} y_{41}^{(5)} y_{42}^{(5)},
\end{aligned}
$$

where $\simeq$ means that the terms with degree 8 can only appear in these products. Thus, the remaining work is to prove that $y_{21}^{(5)} y_{22}^{(5)} y_{25}^{(5)} y_{26}^{(5)} y_{37}^{(5)} y_{38}^{(5)} y_{41}^{(5)} y_{42}^{(5)}$ is a boolean function with degree at most 15 in $\mathcal{B}_2[x_{60}^{(3)}, x_{56}^{(3)}, \ldots, x_4^{(3)}, x_0^{(3)}]$.

Finally, we show that $y_{21}^{(5)} y_{22}^{(5)} y_{25}^{(5)} y_{26}^{(5)} y_{37}^{(5)} y_{38}^{(5)} y_{41}^{(5)} y_{42}^{(5)} \in \mathcal{B}_2[x_{60}^{(3)}, \ldots, x_4^{(3)}, x_0^{(3)}]$ has degree less than 15. Since $y_{[41,37,25,21]}^{(5)} \in \mathcal{B}_2[x_{28}^{(3)}, x_{24}^{(3)}, x_{20}^{(3)}, x_{16}^{(3)}]$ and $y_{[42,38,26,22]}^{(5)} \in \mathcal{B}_2[x_{44}^{(3)}, x_{40}^{(3)}, x_{36}^{(3)}, x_{32}^{(3)}]$, we have

$$
deg(y_{21}^{(5)} y_{22}^{(5)} y_{25}^{(5)} y_{26}^{(5)} y_{37}^{(5)} y_{38}^{(5)} y_{41}^{(5)} y_{42}^{(5)}) \leq 8.
$$

In summary, $x_0^{(8)} \in \mathcal{B}_2[x_{60}^{(3)}, x_{56}^{(3)}, \ldots, x_4^{(3)}, x_0^{(3)}]$ has degree

$$
deg(x_0^{(8)}) = max\{deg(\prod_{k \in \Lambda, |\Lambda| \leq 7} y_k^{(5)}), deg(y_{21}^{(5)} y_{22}^{(5)} y_{25}^{(5)} y_{26}^{(5)} y_{37}^{(5)} y_{38}^{(5)} y_{41}^{(5)} y_{42}^{(5)})\} \leq 15.
$$

$\square$

A 7-round integral distinguisher is obtained by adding two rounds to the upper side of the distinguisher given in Proposition 5.

Theorem 2. *Choose a set of 2^{16} values in the plaintext, where all values of bits $x_{[15-0]}^{(1)}$ of input $X^{(1)}$ are chosen and other bits are chosen to be arbitrary constants. Then, the rightmost bit of $X^{(8)}$, that is, the bit $x_0^{(8)}$, has a zero-sum property.*

Proof. It's based on the fact that $x_{[15-0]}^{(1)} \to x_{[60,56,\ldots,4,0]}^{(3)}$ is a permutation. This permutation is shown in phase T2 of Fig. 3 with bold line. $\square$

5   Integral Attack on Reduced-Round PRESENT

In this section, we attack reduced-round PRESENT using the 4-th order integral distinguisher and 16-th order integral distinguisher.

The general attack procedure is given as follows.

1. Choose a set of 2^n ($n = 4$ or $n = 16$) plaintexts to construct a structure, where the rightmost n bits take all possible values of $\mathbb{F}_2^n$ while other bits are chosen to be arbitrary constants over $\mathbb{F}_2$. Obtain the corresponding ciphertexts after r-round encryption.

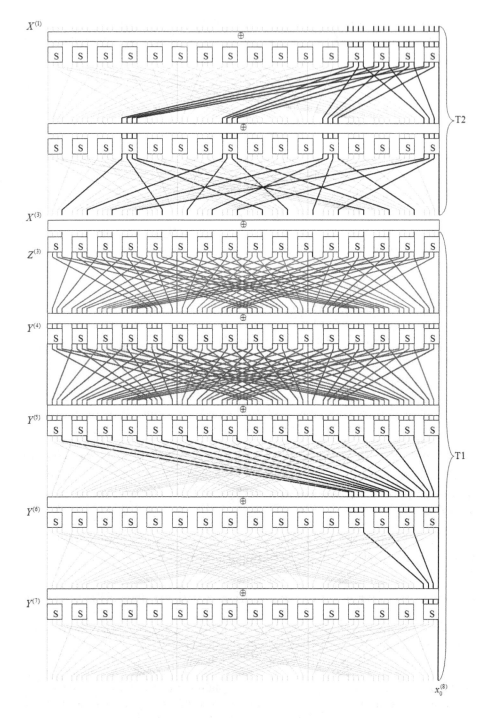

Fig. 3. 16-th order differential characteristics of PRESENT

2. For every guessing of the corresponding subkeys in the last $(r - m)$ rounds, decrypt the ciphertexts to obtain the one bit state $y_0^{(m+1)}$ after the m-th round, where m is the length of integral distinguishers.
3. Check whether $\bigoplus_\Lambda y_0^{(m+1)} (= \bigoplus_\Lambda x_0^{(m+1)})$ is zero, where Λ with $|\Lambda| = 2^n$ is the set of chosen plaintexts. If the equation is not satisfied, we know the guessed subkey is wrong. Then, we guess another subkey and repeat until the correct subkey is found.
4. Recover the remaining key bits in the master key by exhausting method.

Suppose we need to guess k bit subkey in the last $(r - m)$ rounds, the complexity of this attack can be estimated as follows. Step 1 needs about 2^n plaintexts which requires 2^n encryptions. In step 2 and step 3, a subkey needs about $\frac{r-m}{r} \times 2^n$ encryptions. For a wrong subkey guess, equation $\bigoplus_\Lambda y_0^{(m+1)} = 0$ holds with probability $\frac{1}{2}$. Therefore, to discard all the wrong k-bit subkey guesses, we need about k plaintext structures. Suppose the master key has $|K|$ bits, then the time complexity of step 4 is about $2^{|K|-k}$ r-round encryptions.

Thus, the data complexity is about $k \times 2^n$ chosen plaintexts. The time complexity in recovering these k key bits is about

$$\sum_{i=1}^{k} (2^n + 2^n \times \frac{r-m}{r} 2^k \times (\frac{1}{2})^{i-1}) \approx \frac{r-m}{r} \times 2^{n+k+1} \quad (7)$$

r-round encryptions. So, the final time complexity is $max\{\frac{r-m}{r} \times 2^{n+k+1}, 2^{|K|-k}\}$. A total of 2^k bits are required to keep track of possible values for the k key bits, so the memory complexity is 2^{k-3} bytes.

To attack $r = m + 2$ round PRESENT, we need to guess 4 key bits $k_{[48,32,16,0]}^{(m+2)}$ in $K^{(m+2)}$, 16 key bits $k_{4j}^{(m+3)}$ for $0 \le j \le 15$ in $K^{(m+3)}$ to obtain state $y_0^{(m+1)}$. Thus, when considering the 4-th order integral attack, we have $n = 4$, $m = 5$, $r = 7$ and $k = 20$. In this case, we can recover 20 bit keys of 7-round PRESENT with data complexity $20 \times 2^4 \approx 2^{8.3}$, time complexity $\frac{2}{7} \times 2^{4+20+1} \approx 2^{23.2}$ 7-round encryptions and memory 2^{17} bytes. To recover the master key of PRESENT-80, we have to exhaust the remaining 60 key bits. Thus, the final time complexity is 2^{60}. Similarly, when considering 16-th order differential attack, we can recover 20 bit keys of 9-round PRESENT with data complexity $2^{20.3}$, time complexity $2^{34.8}$ 9-round encryptions and memory 2^{17} bytes. To recover the master key of PRESENT-80, the final time complexity is 2^{60}.

To attack $r = m + 3$ round PRESENT, we need to guess all of 64 key bits in $K^{(m+4)}$ additionally, totally guessing 84 key bits. Utilizing the 16-th order integral, we can attack 10 rounds of PRESENT-128 with data complexity $2^{22.4}$, time complexity $2^{99.3}$ 10-round encryptions and memory 2^{81} bytes. The remaining 44 key bits can be obtained easily by exhausting method. To attack 8 rounds of PRESENT-80 using 4-th order integral, we need some properties of the key schedule. After examining the key schedule for 80-bit keys, we find that bits $k_{4j}^{(m+3)}$ for $j = 0$ or $5 \le j \le 15$ in $K^{(m+3)}$ and bits $k_{[48,16,0]}^{(m+2)}$ in $K^{(m+2)}$ are given from guessing all of $K^{(m+4)}$. Thus, in total we need to guess

$64 + (16 - 12) + (4 - 3) = 69$ bits of key, which leads to an attack of 8-round PRESENT-80 with data complexity $2^{10.1}$, time complexity $2^{72.6}$ 8-round encryptions and memory 2^{66} bytes. The remaining 11 key bits can be obtained easily by exhausting method.

6 Discussions and Conclusions

In this paper, we discuss the integral attack against bit-based block ciphers. We focus on the block cipher PRESENT and show that integral attack can be improved not only by the theorem of higher-order differential attack but also by using specific algebraic properties of Sboxes. What is more, the order of plaintexts in a set, which is important in bit-based integral attack, is not required here.

Combined with the algebraic properties of PRESENT's Sbox and its diffusion layer, we proposed two integral distinguishers: one 5 round (4-th order) integral distinguisher and one 7 round (16-th order) integral distinguisher, where the latter is the longest integral distinguisher of PRESENT as far as we know. Based on the integral distinguishers proposed in this paper, 10 (out of 31) rounds of PRESENT can be attacked.

Although the number of attack rounds in this paper are not so impressive as other statistical attacks [6,7,14], it is the first time that some new algebraic properties for constructing integral distinguishers of PRESENT are reported. For a further step, the algebraic techniques used in constructing longer integral distinguishers here may be also applied to other block ciphers to improve their known integral attacks.

Acknowledgements. We are grateful to the anonymous reviewers for their valuable comments on this paper. This work was supported by the National Basic Research Program of China (Grant No. 2013CB834203 and Grant No. 2013CB338002) and the National Natural Science Foundation of China (Grant No. 11171323).

References

1. Anderson, R., Biham, E., Knudsen, L.: Serpent: A Proposal for the Advanced Encryption Standard. NIST AES Proposal (1998),
   http://www.cl.cam.ac.uk/rja14/serpent.html
2. Bogdanov, A., Knudsen, L.R., Leander, G., Paar, C., Poschmann, A., Robshaw, M.J.B., Seurin, Y., Vikkelsoe, C.: PRESENT: An ultra-lightweight block cipher. In: Paillier, P., Verbauwhede, I. (eds.) CHES 2007. LNCS, vol. 4727, pp. 450–466. Springer, Heidelberg (2007)
3. Bogdanov, A., Leander, G., Nyberg, K., Wang, M.: Integral and Multidimensional Linear Distinguishers with Correlation Zero. In: Wang, X., Sako, K. (eds.) ASIACRYPT 2012. LNCS, vol. 7658, pp. 244–261. Springer, Heidelberg (2012)
4. Bogdanov, A., Rijmen, V.: Linear Hulls with Correlation Zero and Linear Cryptanalysis of Block Ciphers. Designs, Codes and Cryptography (2012)

5. Biryukov, A., Shamir, A.: Structural Cryptanalysis of SASAS. In: Pfitzmann, B. (ed.) EUROCRYPT 2001. LNCS, vol. 2045, pp. 394–405. Springer, Heidelberg (2001)
6. Cho, J.Y.: Linear Cryptanalysis of Reduced-Round PRESENT. In: Pieprzyk, J. (ed.) CT-RSA 2010. LNCS, vol. 5985, pp. 302–317. Springer, Heidelberg (2010)
7. Collard, B., Standaert, F.X.: A Statistical Saturation Attack against the Block Cipher PRESENT. In: Fischlin, M. (ed.) CT-RSA 2009. LNCS, vol. 5473, pp. 195–210. Springer, Heidelberg (2009)
8. Daemen, J., Knudsen, L., Rijmen, V.: The block cipher Square. In: Biham, E. (ed.) FSE 1997. LNCS, vol. 1267, pp. 149–165. Springer, Heidelberg (1997)
9. Daemen, J., Peeters, M., Van Assche, G., Rijmen, V.: Nessie Proposal: NOEKEON. In: First Open NESSIE Workshop (2000), http://gro.noekeon.org/
10. Ferguson, N., Kelsey, J., Lucks, S., Schneier, B., Stay, M., Wagner, D., Whiting, D.: Improved cryptanalysis of Rijndael. In: Schneier, B. (ed.) FSE 2000. LNCS, vol. 1978, pp. 213–230. Springer, Heidelberg (2001)
11. Knudsen, L., Wagner, D.: Integral Cryptanalysis. In: Daemen, J., Rijmen, V. (eds.) FSE 2002. LNCS, vol. 2365, pp. 112–127. Springer, Heidelberg (2002)
12. Lai, X.: Higher order derivatives and differential cryptanalysis. In: Proc. Symposium on Communication, Coding and Cryptography, in Honor of J. L. Massey on the Occasion of his 60th Birthday, Kluwer Academic Publishers, Dordrecht (1994)
13. Lucks, S.: Attacking seven rounds of Rijndael under 192-bit and 256-bit keys. In: Proc. 3rd AES Candidate Conf., pp. 215–229 (2000)
14. Wang, M.: Differential Cryptanalysis of reduced-round PRESENT. In: Vaudenay, S. (ed.) AFRICACRYPT 2008. LNCS, vol. 5023, pp. 40–49. Springer, Heidelberg (2008)
15. Yu, X., Wu, W., Li, Y., Zhang, L.: Cryptanalysis of Reduced-Round KLEIN Block Cipher. In: Wu, C.-K., Yung, M., Lin, D. (eds.) Inscrypt 2011. LNCS, vol. 7537, pp. 237–250. Springer, Heidelberg (2012)
16. Z'aba, M.R., Raddum, H., Henricksen, M., Dawson, E.: Bit-pattern based integral attack. In: Nyberg, K. (ed.) FSE 2008. LNCS, vol. 5086, pp. 363–381. Springer, Heidelberg (2008)
17. Zhang, W., Su, B., Wu, W., Feng, D., Wu, C.: Extending Higher-Order Integral: An Efficient Unified Algorithm of Constructing Integral Distinguishers for Block Ciphers. In: Bao, F., Samarati, P., Zhou, J. (eds.) ACNS 2012. LNCS, vol. 7341, pp. 117–134. Springer, Heidelberg (2012)

Computationally Efficient Expressive Key-Policy Attribute Based Encryption Schemes with Constant-Size Ciphertext

Y. Sreenivasa Rao and Ratna Dutta

Indian Institute of Technology Kharagpur
Kharagpur-721302, India
{ysrao,ratna}@maths.iitkgp.ernet.in

Abstract. In this paper, we present two attribute based encryption (ABE) schemes for monotone access structure (MAS) in the key-policy setting, where secret key is generated according to a MAS, ciphertext is associated with a set of attributes and decryption is possible only if the attribute set satisfies the MAS. The first scheme is secure against chosen plaintext attacks (i.e., CPA secure) while the second scheme is secure against chosen ciphertext attacks (i.e., CCA secure). The security proofs are free from the random oracle heuristic. The most interesting features of both schemes are *constant-size* ciphertext, *constant* number of bilinear pairing evaluations and *low* computation cost (in terms of exponentiations) compared with previous schemes. We further propose two non-monotone access structure (nonMAS) variants, one is CPA secure and another is CCA secure, by using the idea of transforming a non-MAS over attributes to a MAS over attributes and their negation. These key-policy ABE schemes for nonMAS preserve the same functionality as that of MAS primitives. While the secret key in all our constructions has quadratic size in the number of attributes, the number of pairing evaluations is constant. The (CPA and CCA) security of all our schemes are proved under the decisional n-Bilinear Diffie-Hellman Exponent assumption over prime order groups in the selective model.

Keywords: key-policy, attribute-based encryption, constant-size ciphertext, (non-)monotone access structure, chosen ciphertext security.

1 Introduction

Functional Encryption (FE) [4] is a new version of public key encryption that facilitates sophisticated and flexible relations between the "parameters" of secret keys and ciphertexts where either (i) secret key is generated according to a parameter $\mathbb{A}$ and ciphertext is associated with another parameter W, yielding *Key-Policy* FE (KP-FE) or (ii) ciphertext is created according to a parameter $\mathbb{A}$ and secret key is associated with another parameter L, yielding *Ciphertext-Policy* FE (CP-FE). Decryption is successful in key-policy (or ciphertext-policy) FE if and only if a relation $\mathcal{R}^{KP}(\mathbb{A}, W)$ (or $\mathcal{R}^{CP}(L, \mathbb{A})$) holds. A FE is an Attribute

S. Qing et al. (Eds.): ICICS 2013, LNCS 8233, pp. 346–362, 2013.

Based Encryption (ABE) [1,2,3] if one of the parameters for ciphertext and secret key is a tuple of attributes, and the other is an access structure or monotone span program over a set of attributes, wherein the relation $\mathcal{R}^{KP}$ (or $\mathcal{R}^{CP}$) is an "inclusion" relation, i.e., $\mathcal{R}^{KP}(\mathbb{A}, W)$ (or $\mathcal{R}^{CP}(L, \mathbb{A})$) holds if and only if $W \in \mathbb{A}$ (or $L \in \mathbb{A}$). In this case, KP-FE (or CP-FE) is called as Key-Policy ABE (KP-ABE) [2] (or Ciphertext-Policy ABE (CP-ABE) [3]).

The first ABE system introduced by Sahai and Waters [1] is considered as a KP-ABE with threshold access policy. Later, Goyal et al. [2] designed the first KP-ABE for Monotone Access Structure (MAS). There are quite a number of KP-ABE schemes [6,5,4] that allow Non-Monotone Access Structure (nonMAS). While all the schemes mentioned so far are proven to be *selectively* Chosen Plaintext Attacks (CPA) secure where the adversary commits to her target before the simulation is set up, the works presented in [7,4] achieve *full* CPA security. Attrapadung et al. [8] proposed the first constant-size ciphertext selectively CPA secure KP-ABE for MAS as well as nonMAS over prime order groups with constant number of bilinear pairings, but secret key size is quadratic in the number of attributes. Independent of this work, Wang and Luo [9] proposed another KP-ABE for MAS with the same functionality as that of [8]. However, their scheme is proven to be secure in the random oracle assumption, while [8] does not use any such random oracle heuristic.

Security against Chosen Ciphertext Attacks (CCA) for ABE is a challenging task and has received little attention so far. The KP/CP-ABE schemes [2,11,4] used CHK (Canetti-Halevi-Katz) technique [10] to achieve CCA security in the standard model (without random oracles). They associate one-time signature keys with each encryption operation in combination with the delegation mechanism that uses key of one access structure $\mathbb{A}$ to construct a key for another access structure $\mathbb{A}'$ which is more restricted than $\mathbb{A}$. Resulting CCA secure ABE schemes have linear-size ciphertexts. Generalizing this idea, Yamada et al. [12] proposed a generic construction of CCA secure ABE and proved that any CPA secure ABE scheme preserving either delegatability or verifiability generically yields a CCA secure ABE primitive in the standard model. Note that it is easy to extend CPA security to CCA security in the random oracle model by applying Fujisaki-Okamoto transformation [13]. To the best of our knowledge, there is no constant-size ciphertext KP-ABE for expressive access policies (MAS as well as nonMAS) that is CCA secure in the standard model.

Our Contribution. The main focus of this article is to construct computationally efficient constant-size ciphertext KP-ABE schemes for Linear Secret-Sharing Scheme (LSSS)-realizable MAS as in [8,9] as well as nonMAS providing both CPA and CCA security in the standard model. To this end, we propose four KP-ABE schemes having the following unique features: (i) constant-size ciphertext, (ii) constant number of bilinear pairing evaluations, (iii) constant computation cost during encryption, (iv) $\mathcal{O}(|I|)$ exponentiations in decryption, where $|I|$ is the number of rows of LSSS matrix used in the decryption, and (v) secret key size $\mathcal{O}(\ell \cdot n)$ group elements, where ℓ is the number of rows in the user LSSS matrix, n is the number of attributes in the attribute space.

Table 1. Comparison of constant-size ciphertext KP-ABE for MAS and nonMAS

	Scheme	SK Size $E_{\mathbb{G}}$	CT Size $E_{\mathbb{G}} + E_{\mathbb{G}_T} + E_{\mathbb{Z}}$	Enc. Cost $\mathsf{Ex}_{\mathbb{G}}$	$\mathsf{Ex}_{\mathbb{G}_T}$	Dec. Cost $\mathsf{Ex}_{\mathbb{G}}$	Pairings	Security
MAS	[8,9]	$\mathcal{O}(\ell \cdot \overline{n})$	$2+1+0$	$\mathcal{O}(\phi)$	1	$\mathcal{O}(|I| \cdot \phi)$	2	sCPA
	Scheme I	$\mathcal{O}(\ell \cdot n)$	$2+1+0$	2	1	$\mathcal{O}(|I|)$	2	sCPA
	Scheme II	$\mathcal{O}(\ell \cdot n)$	$3+1+1$	5	1	$\mathcal{O}(|I|)$	6	sCCA
nonMAS	[8]	$\mathcal{O}(\ell \cdot \overline{n})$	$3+1+0$	$\mathcal{O}(\phi)$	1	$\mathcal{O}(|I| \cdot \phi)$	3	sCPA
	Scheme III	$\mathcal{O}(\ell \cdot n)$	$3+1+0$	3	1	$\mathcal{O}(|I|)$	3	sCPA
	Scheme IV	$\mathcal{O}(\ell \cdot n)$	$4+1+1$	6	1	$\mathcal{O}(|I|)$	9	sCCA

$E_{\mathbb{G}}$ *(resp. $E_{\mathbb{G}_T}, E_{\mathbb{Z}}$) = number of elements in a group $\mathbb{G}$ (resp. $\mathbb{G}_T, \mathbb{Z}_p$), $\mathsf{Ex}_{\mathbb{G}}$ (resp.* $\mathsf{Ex}_{\mathbb{G}_T}$*) = number of exponentiations in a group $\mathbb{G}$ (resp. $\mathbb{G}_T$), ℓ = number of rows in the user LSSS access structure matrix, n = number of attributes used in the system, ϕ = number of attributes in a ciphertext, $\overline{n}$ = maximum number of attributes that can be associated with a ciphertext, $|I|$ = number of rows of LSSS matrix used in the decryption, sCPA (resp. sCCA) = selective CPA (resp. CCA) security, SK = Secret Key and CT = Ciphertext. Note that $\overline{n} = n$ in the small universe setting.*

We use the threshold public key encryption framework of [14] to design our basic construction, referred as Scheme I, which realizes monotone LSSS access structure. We further extend our monotone KP-ABE approach to non-monotone KP-ABE by using the technique of [6] for transforming a nonMAS over attributes to a MAS over attributes and their negation. The resulting nonMAS KP-ABE construction is referred as Scheme III. Both the Scheme I and Scheme III are proven to be selectively CPA secure (as [8,9]) in the standard model under the decisional n-Bilinear Diffie-Hellman Exponent (n-BDHE) assumption over prime order bilinear groups. Finally, to enhance the CPA security of our basic constructions for MAS and nonMAS to CCA security, we incorporate the technique of CCA secure public key encryption of [15]. The generic conversions proposed in [12] transform the existing constant-size ciphertext KP-ABE schemes [8,9] to CCA secure schemes which no longer exhibit constant ciphertext-size as the conversion appends additional (dummy) attributes to the ciphertext. This new attribute addition incurs additional overhead which is linear to the number of attached attributes. In sum, we believe that our Scheme II for MAS and Scheme IV for nonMAS are the *first* CCA secure KP-ABE schemes with all the properties listed above.

In Table 1, we provide a detailed comparison between our schemes and the previous KP-ABE schemes [8,9] with constant-size ciphertext proposed so far. As the number, n, of attributes in the attribute universe is a factor of the secret key size, our constructions deal only with small attribute universe, thereby the attributes are fixed at system setup phase as in [7,1,2,16,8]. The KP-ABE schemes [8,9] are large universe constructions with a bound, $\overline{n}$, on the number of attributes that can be annotated to a ciphertext. For a fair comparison, we consider the small universe variants of the schemes [8,9]. Under this assumption, $\overline{n} = n$, i.e., there is no bound on the number of ciphertext attributes. Our

Table 2. Comparison of our large universe KP-ABE for MAS with [8,9]

		Public Key Size	SK Size $E_{\mathbb{G}}$	CT Size $E_{\mathbb{G}} + E_{\mathbb{G}_T}$	Enc. Cost $\mathsf{Ex}_{\mathbb{G}}$	$\mathsf{Ex}_{\mathbb{G}_T}$	Dec. Cost $\mathsf{Ex}_{\mathbb{G}}$	Pairings	Security
MAS	[8,9]	$\mathcal{O}(\overline{n})$	$\mathcal{O}(\ell \cdot \overline{n})$	$2+1$	$\mathcal{O}(\overline{n})$	1	$\mathcal{O}(|I| \cdot \overline{n})$	2	sCPA
	Scheme V	$\mathcal{O}(1)$	$\mathcal{O}(\ell^2)$	$(\phi+1)+1$	$\mathcal{O}(\phi)$	1	$\mathcal{O}(|I|)$	2	sCPA

schemes need only $\mathcal{O}(|I|)$ exponentiations and 2 pairing computations to decrypt any ciphertext, $|I|$ being the number of rows of LSSS matrix used in the decryption. On the contrary, the existing constant-size ciphertext KP-ABE schemes [8,9] perform $\mathcal{O}(|I| \cdot \phi)$ exponentiations followed by 2 pairing computations to decrypt a ciphertext, where ϕ denotes the number of attributes associated with a ciphertext. This could be very expensive in terms of exponentiations in certain situations. For instance, if a decryptor receives a ciphertext with 1000 attributes, our schemes require 20 exponentiations (if $|I| = 10$) and 2 pairing operations to decrypt that ciphertext. On the other hand, the schemes [8,9] require 10,000 exponentiations and 2 pairing operations to decrypt the same ciphertext. The encryptor executes 1000 exponentiations to compute the above ciphertext in [8,9], while that for our Scheme I is only 2. Thus, the schemes [8,9] in the large universe setting cannot yield directly KP-ABE constructions for small attribute universe that are computationally efficient, supporting expressive access policies and achieving constant-size ciphertext. We believe that our new constructions are of independent interest in the small universe setting as they outperform the KP-ABE schemes of [8,9] in terms of exponentiations, thereby can efficiently be deployed in practice.

By using the similar ideas in [16,14], our basic construction, Scheme I, can be extended to large universe setting (referred as Scheme V, see Section 5) wherein the attribute parameters are dynamically computed after the system setup by using a hash function, while the ciphertext-size is proportional to the number of attributes in it. However, it still preserves the decryption efficiency analogous to our small universe construction. The large universe constructions of [8,9] place a bound, $\overline{n}$, on the maximum number of attributes to encrypt each message in the system. This makes the system infeasible and the size of public key is proportional to this bound $\overline{n}$. On the other hand, Scheme V is free from any such system-wide limitations and exhibits constant-size public parameters. But, as in [9], the scheme is secure in the random oracle model. The secret key size of [8,9] increases by a factor of $\overline{n}$, while that for our Scheme V *only* increases by a factor of the number of attributes in user secret key. In sum, while all the proposed schemes present faster decryption capabilities over previous proposals, we achieve a controllable trade-off between the ciphertext size and the attribute universe size. In Table 2, we compare our large universe construction with the previous schemes [8,9]. Even though we show some of the improvements over previous schemes [8,9], the work of Attrapadung et al. [8] is a major step forward in designing expressive KP-ABE schemes with constant-size ciphertexts.

2   Background

Notation. Let $x \in_R X$ denote the operation of picking an element x uniformly at random from the set X. We denote the set $\{1, 2, \ldots, n\}$ as $[n]$.

In this section, we recall necessary background from [16,7].

Definition 1 (Access Structure). *Let U be the universe of attributes and $\mathcal{P}(U)$ be the collection of all subsets of U. Every subset $\mathbb{A}$ of $\mathcal{P}(U) \setminus \{\emptyset\}$ is called an access structure. An access structure $\mathbb{A}$ is said to be monotone access structure (MAS) if for any $C \in \mathcal{P}(U)$, with $C \supseteq B$ where $B \in \mathbb{A}$ implies $C \in \mathbb{A}$.*

2.1   Linear Secret-Sharing Schemes (LSSS)

Let U be the universe of attributes. A secret-sharing scheme $\Pi_{\mathbb{A}}$ for the access structure $\mathbb{A}$ over U is called *linear* (in $\mathbb{Z}_p$) if $\Pi_{\mathbb{A}}$ consists of the following two polynomial-time algorithms, where $\mathbb{M}$ is a matrix of size $\ell \times k$, called the *share-generating matrix* for $\Pi_{\mathbb{A}}$ and $\rho : [\ell] \to I_U$ is a row labeling function that maps each row of the matrix $\mathbb{M}$ to an attribute in $\mathbb{A}$, I_U being the index set of U.

(i) Distribute$(\mathbb{M}, \rho, \alpha)$: This algorithm takes as input the share-generating matrix $\mathbb{M}$, row labeling function ρ and a secret $\alpha \in \mathbb{Z}_p$ which is to be shared. It randomly selects $z_2, z_3, \ldots, z_k \in_R \mathbb{Z}_p$ and sets $\boldsymbol{v} = (\alpha, z_2, z_3, \ldots, z_k) \in \mathbb{Z}_p^k$. It outputs a set $\{\boldsymbol{M_i} \cdot \boldsymbol{v} : i \in [\ell]\}$ of ℓ shares, where $\boldsymbol{M_i} \in \mathbb{Z}_p^k$ is the i-th row of matrix $\mathbb{M}$. The share $\lambda_{\rho(i)} = \boldsymbol{M_i} \cdot \boldsymbol{v}$ belongs to an attribute $\rho(i)$.

(ii) Reconstruct$(\mathbb{M}, \rho, W)$: This algorithm will accept as input $\mathbb{M}, \rho$ and a set of attributes $W \in \mathbb{A}$. Let $I = \{i \in [\ell] : \rho(i) \in I_W\}$, where I_W is index set of the attribute set W. It returns a set $\{\omega_i : i \in I\}$ of secret reconstruction constants such that $\sum_{i \in I} \omega_i \lambda_{\rho(i)} = \alpha$, if $\{\lambda_{\rho(i)} : i \in I\}$ is a valid set of shares of the secret α according to $\Pi_{\mathbb{A}}$.

Lemma 1. *Let $(\mathbb{M}, \rho)$ be a LSSS access structure realizing an access structure $\mathbb{A}$ over the universe U of attributes, where $\mathbb{M}$ is share-generating matrix of size $\ell \times k$, and $W \subset U$. If $W \notin \mathbb{A}$ (in other words, W does not satisfy $\mathbb{M}$), there exists a polynomial time algorithm that outputs a vector $\boldsymbol{w} = (-1, w_2, \ldots, w_k) \in \mathbb{Z}_p^k$ such that $\boldsymbol{M_i} \cdot \boldsymbol{w} = 0$, for each row i of $\mathbb{M}$ for which $\rho(i) \in I_W$.*

2.2   Bilinear Maps and Hardness Assumption

We use multiplicative cyclic groups $(\mathbb{G}, \mathbb{G}_T)$ of prime order p with an efficiently computable mapping $e : \mathbb{G} \times \mathbb{G} \to \mathbb{G}_T$ such that $e(u^a, v^b) = e(u, v)^{ab}, \forall\, u, v \in \mathbb{G}$, $a, b \in \mathbb{Z}_p$ and $e(g, g) \neq 1_T$, where 1_T is the unit element in $\mathbb{G}_T$.

Decisional n-BDHE Assumption. An algorithm (or distinguisher) $\mathfrak{D}$ for solving the decisional n-BDHE (Bilinear Diffie-Hellman Exponent) problem in $(\mathbb{G}, \mathbb{G}_T)$ takes as input a tuple $(\overrightarrow{y}_{a,s}, Z) \in \mathbb{G}^{2n+1} \times \mathbb{G}_T$, where $a, s \in_R \mathbb{Z}_p, g \in_R \mathbb{G}, g_i = g^{a^i}, \forall i \in [2n], \overrightarrow{y}_{a,s} = (g, g^s, g_1, \ldots, g_n, g_{n+2}, \ldots, g_{2n})$ and determines

whether $Z = e(g_{n+1}, g^s)$ or a random element in $\mathbb{G}_T$. The advantage of a 0/1-valued algorithm $\mathfrak{D}$ in solving the decisional n-BDHE problem in $(\mathbb{G}, \mathbb{G}_T)$ is defined to be $\mathsf{Adv}_{\mathfrak{D}}^{n\text{-dBDHE}} = |\Pr[\mathfrak{D}(\overrightarrow{y}_{a,s}, Z) = 1 | Z = e(g_{n+1}, g^s)]$
$$- \Pr[\mathfrak{D}(\overrightarrow{y}_{a,s}, Z) = 1 | Z \text{ is random}]|.$$

Definition 2. *The decisional n-BDHE problem in $(\mathbb{G}, \mathbb{G}_T)$ is said to be $(\mathcal{T}, \epsilon)$-hard if the advantage $\mathsf{Adv}_{\mathfrak{D}}^{n\text{-dBDHE}} \leq \epsilon$, for any probabilistic polynomial-time (PPT) distinguisher $\mathfrak{D}$ running in time at most $\mathcal{T}$.*

2.3   KP-ABE Template

Let U be the attribute universe. A single trusted central authority (CA) manages all the attributes and its keys, and is responsible for issuing secret keys to users according to access structure of user attributes. The KP-ABE scheme consists of the following four algorithms.

Setup(κ, U). This algorithm is run by the CA and takes as input a security parameter κ and the attribute universe U. It returns public key PK and master secret key MK. The secret key MK is kept secret by CA and the public key PK is made public.

KeyGen$(\mathsf{PK}, \mathsf{MK}, \mathbb{A})$. The CA runs this algorithm with the input PK, MK and an access structure $\mathbb{A}$. It outputs the secret key $\mathsf{SK}_{\mathbb{A}}$ associated with $\mathbb{A}$.

Encrypt(PK, M, W). An encryptor will execute this algorithm with the input PK, a message M to be encrypted under a set W of attributes. It then returns a ciphertext CT_W in such a way that only the user with access structure $\mathbb{A}$ satisfied by W can decrypt CT_W.

Decrypt$(\mathsf{PK}, \mathsf{SK}_{\mathbb{A}}, \mathsf{CT}_W)$. This algorithm is run by decryptor and takes as input $\mathsf{PK}, \mathsf{SK}_{\mathbb{A}}$ and CT_W. It outputs the message M encrypted under a set W of attributes if the access structure $\mathbb{A}$ embedded in decryptor's secret key $\mathsf{SK}_{\mathbb{A}}$ is satisfied by W, otherwise decryption will fail.

2.4   Selective-Set Security Model for KP-ABE

We describe IND-sCPA (ciphertext indistinguishability under selective-set chosen plaintext attacks) security model in terms of a game $\mathsf{Game}^{\mathsf{IND-sCPA}}$ carried out between a challenger and an adversary. The challenger executes the relevant KP-ABE algorithms in order to answer the queries from the adversary. The game is as follows:

Init. The adversary announces a set W^* of attributes that he wishes to be challenged upon.

Setup. The challenger executes the **Setup** algorithm and gives public key PK to the adversary.

Query Phase 1. The adversary is allowed to make secret key queries for an access structure $\mathbb{A}$ subject to the constraint that W^* must not satisfy the access structure $\mathbb{A}$. The challenger then runs **KeyGen** algorithm and returns the corresponding secret key $\mathsf{SK}_{\mathbb{A}}$ to the adversary. This process can be repeated polynomial number of times.

Challenge. The adversary submits two equal length messages M_0, M_1. The challenger flips a random coin $\mu \in \{0, 1\}$ and runs **Encrypt** algorithm in order to encrypt M_μ under W^*. The resulting challenge ciphertext CT_{W^*} is given to the adversary.

Query Phase 2. Query Phase 1 is repeated.

Guess. The adversary outputs a guess bit $\mu' \in \{0, 1\}$ for the challenger's secret coin μ and wins if $\mu' = \mu$.

The advantage of an adversary $\mathcal{A}$ in the IND-sCPA game is defined to be $\mathsf{Adv}_{\mathcal{A}}(\mathsf{Game}^{\mathsf{IND-sCPA}}) = |\Pr[\mu' = \mu] - \frac{1}{2}|$, where the probability is taken over all random coin tosses of both adversary and challenger.

We note that the foregoing security model can easily be extended to IND-sCCA (ciphertext indistinguishability under selective-set chosen ciphertext attacks) security model by allowing decryption queries in Query Phase 1, 2, with the restriction that no decryption query is allowed on challenge ciphertext CT_{W^*}.

Definition 3. *A KP-ABE scheme is said to be $(\mathcal{T}, q, \epsilon)$-IND-sCPA secure if the advantage $\mathsf{Adv}_{\mathcal{A}}(\mathsf{Game}^{\mathsf{IND-sCPA}}) \leq \epsilon$, for any PPT adversary $\mathcal{A}$ running in time at most $\mathcal{T}$ that makes at most q secret key queries in the foregoing selective-set CPA security game.*

Definition 4. *A KP-ABE scheme is said to be $(\mathcal{T}, q, q_D, \epsilon)$-IND-sCCA secure if the advantage $\mathsf{Adv}_{\mathcal{A}}(\mathsf{Game}^{\mathsf{IND-sCCA}}) \leq \epsilon$, for any PPT adversary $\mathcal{A}$ running in time at most $\mathcal{T}$ that makes at most q secret key queries and q_D decryption queries in the selective-set CCA security game.*

3   KP-ABE for Monotone Access Structures

In this section, we first present our efficient KP-ABE scheme with constant-size ciphertext that provides selective CPA (sCPA) security. We further enhance the sCPA security to selective CCA (sCCA) security by using the technique of CCA secure public key encryption of [15]. In these two constructions, every monotone access structure (MAS) is represented by LSSS access structure $(\mathbb{M}, \rho)$.

3.1   Scheme I: Basic sCPA Secure Scheme

Setup(κ, U). On receiving the implicit security parameter κ, this algorithm generates a prime number p, a bilinear group $\mathbb{G}$, a generator $g \in_R \mathbb{G}$ and a bilinear map $e : \mathbb{G} \times \mathbb{G} \to \mathbb{G}_T$, where $\mathbb{G}$ and $\mathbb{G}_T$ are multiplicative groups of order p. It then chooses a random $\alpha \in_R \mathbb{Z}_p$ and $h_0 \in_R \mathbb{G}$, and for each attribute $att_j \in U$, it randomly chooses $h_j \in_R \mathbb{G}$, for all $j \in [n]$. The public key is $\mathsf{PK} = \langle p, g, h_0, Y = e(g, g)^\alpha, h_1, h_2, \ldots, h_n \rangle$ and the master secret key is $\mathsf{MK} = \alpha$.

KeyGen$(\mathsf{PK}, \mathsf{MK}, (\mathbb{M}, \rho))$. Here $\mathbb{M}$ is a share-generating matrix of size $\ell \times k$ and ρ is a mapping from each row i of $\mathbb{M}$ to an attribute $att_{\rho(i)}$. The CA first executes $\mathsf{Distribute}(\mathbb{M}, \rho, \alpha)$ and obtains a set $\{\lambda_{\rho(i)} = \boldsymbol{M_i} \cdot \boldsymbol{v} : i \in [\ell]\}$ of ℓ shares, where $\boldsymbol{v} \in_R \mathbb{Z}_p^k$ such that $\boldsymbol{v} \cdot \boldsymbol{1} = \alpha$ (here, $\boldsymbol{1} = (1, 0, \ldots, 0)$ is a vector of length k). For each row $i \in [\ell]$, it chooses a random exponent $r_i \in_R \mathbb{Z}_p$ and computes

$D_i = g^{\lambda_{\rho(i)}}(h_0 h_{\rho(i)})^{r_i}, D_i' = g^{r_i}, D_i'' = \{D_{i,j}'' : D_{i,j}'' = h_j^{r_i}, \forall j \in [n] \setminus \{\rho(i)\}\}$.
The CA then returns the secret key $\mathsf{SK}_{(\mathbb{M},\rho)} = \langle (\mathbb{M}, \rho), \{D_i, D_i', D_i'' : i \in [\ell]\} \rangle$
associated with $(\mathbb{M}, \rho)$.

Encrypt(PK, M, W). To encrypt a message $M \in \mathbb{G}_T$ under a set W of attributes, the encryptor selects $s \in_R \mathbb{Z}_p$ and computes $C = MY^s, C_1 = g^s$
and $C_2 = (h_0 \prod_{att_j \in W} h_j)^s$. It outputs the ciphertext $\mathsf{CT}_W = \langle W, C, C_1, C_2 \rangle$.

Decrypt$(\mathsf{PK}, \mathsf{SK}_{(\mathbb{M},\rho)}, \mathsf{CT}_W)$. The decryptor first runs $\mathsf{Reconstruct}(\mathbb{M}, \rho, W)$ to
obtain a set $\{\omega_i : i \in I\}$ of reconstruction constants, where $I = \{i \in [\ell] :
att_{\rho(i)} \in W\}$. If W satisfies the access structure $(\mathbb{M}, \rho)$, then $\sum_{i \in I} \omega_i \lambda_{\rho(i)} = \alpha$. The decryptor computes E_1, E_2 as follows:

$$E_1 = \prod_{i \in I}\left(D_i \cdot \prod_{att_j \in W, j \neq \rho(i)} D_{i,j}'' \right)^{\omega_i}, \quad E_2 = \prod_{i \in I}(D_i')^{\omega_i}.$$

The message M can be obtained by computing $C \cdot e(C_2, E_2)/e(C_1, E_1)$.

Theorem 1 (Security Proof). *If the attribute universe U has n attributes
then our Scheme I is $(\mathcal{T}, q, \epsilon)$-IND-sCPA secure, assuming that the decisional
n-BDHE problem in $(\mathbb{G}, \mathbb{G}_T)$ is $(\mathcal{T}', \epsilon')$-hard, where $\mathcal{T}' = \mathcal{T} + \mathcal{O}(n^2) \cdot q \cdot \mathcal{T}_e$ and
$\epsilon' = \epsilon/2$. Here, $\mathcal{T}_e$ denotes the running time of one exponentiation in $\mathbb{G}$.*

Proof. Suppose that an adversary $\mathcal{A}$ can $(\mathcal{T}, q, \epsilon)$-break our Scheme I in the
IND-sCPA security model. We will show that the decisional n-BDHE problem
in $(\mathbb{G}, \mathbb{G}_T)$ is *not* $(\mathcal{T}', \epsilon')$-hard.

Suppose a distinguisher $\mathfrak{D}$ is given the decisional n-BDHE challenge $(\overrightarrow{y}_{a,s}, Z)$,
where $\overrightarrow{y}_{a,s} = (g, g^s, g_1, \ldots, g_n, g_{n+2}, \ldots, g_{2n})$, $g_i = g^{a^i}$, and $Z = e(g_{n+1}, g^s)$ or
Z is a random element of $\mathbb{G}_T$. Now, the distinguisher $\mathfrak{D}$ plays the role of a
challenger in $\mathsf{Game}^{\mathsf{IND-sCPA}}$ and interacts with $\mathcal{A}$ in order to solve the decisional
n-BDHE problem (i.e., $\mathfrak{D}$ attempts to output 1 if $Z = e(g_{n+1}, g^s)$ and 0 otherwise) as follows.

Init. The adversary $\mathcal{A}$ outputs the target attribute set W^*.

Setup. The distinguisher $\mathfrak{D}$ selects a random value $\alpha' \in_R \mathbb{Z}_p$ and implicitly sets
$\alpha = \alpha' + a^{n+1}$ by letting $Y = e(g, g)^\alpha = e(g, g)^{\alpha'} e(g^a, g^{a^n})$.

The distinguisher $\mathfrak{D}$ then programs the parameters $\{h_i : i \in [n]\}$ as follows.
For $i \in [n]$, $\mathfrak{D}$ chooses a random value $t_i \in_R \mathbb{Z}_p$ and computes $h_i = g^{t_i} g_{n+1-i}$.
Furthermore, to program h_0, the distinguisher selects a random $t_0 \in_R \mathbb{Z}_p$ and
computes $h_0 = g^{t_0} \prod_{att_j \in W^*} h_j^{-1}$. We note that the parameters h_i are distributed
randomly due to the g^{t_i} factor, for $i = 0, 1, \ldots, n$.

Finally, the public key $\mathsf{PK} = \langle p, g, h_0, Y, h_1, h_2, \ldots, h_n \rangle$ will be given to the
adversary $\mathcal{A}$.

Query Phase 1. In this phase, the adversary $\mathcal{A}$ requests for secret keys corresponding to the LSSS access structures $(\mathbb{M}, \rho)$ subject to the condition that W^*
does not satisfy $\mathbb{M}$ and then the distinguisher responds as follows.

Let the size of a share-generating matrix $\mathbb{M}$ be $\ell \times k$. Since W^* does not
satisfy $\mathbb{M}$, by Lemma 1, there exists a vector $\boldsymbol{w} = (-1, w_2, \ldots, w_k) \in \mathbb{Z}_p^k$ such
that $\boldsymbol{M_i} \cdot \boldsymbol{w} = 0$, for all rows i where $att_{\rho(i)} \in W^*$.

The distinguisher randomly selects $y'_2, y'_3, \ldots, y'_k \in_R \mathbb{Z}_p$ and implicitly sets

$$\boldsymbol{v} = (\alpha' + a^{n+1}, -(\alpha' + a^{n+1})w_2 + y'_2, \ldots, -(\alpha' + a^{n+1})w_k + y'_k) \in \mathbb{Z}_p^k$$

which will be used for generating shares of α as in the original scheme. Note that $\boldsymbol{v}$ can be written as $\boldsymbol{v} = -(\alpha' + a^{n+1})\boldsymbol{w} + \boldsymbol{v}'$, where $\boldsymbol{v}' = (0, y'_2, \ldots, y'_k) \in \mathbb{Z}_p^k$. Observe that $\lambda_{\rho(i)} = \boldsymbol{M_i} \cdot \boldsymbol{v}$ contains the term a^{n+1} and hence $g^{\lambda_{\rho(i)}}$ contains terms of the form $g^{a^{n+1}} = g_{n+1}$ which is unknown to $\mathfrak{D}$. Therefore, $\mathfrak{D}$ must make sure that there are no terms of the form g_{n+1} involved in secret key components. To this end, the distinguisher implicitly creates suitable r_i values in such a way that the unknown terms will be canceled out automatically. Now, the secret key corresponding to each row $\boldsymbol{M_i}, i \in [\ell]$, of M is computed as one of the following two cases:

Case 1: For i where $att_{\rho(i)} \in W^*$.

In this case, the distinguisher randomly chooses $r'_i \in_R \mathbb{Z}_p$ and implicitly sets $r_i = r'_i - a^{\rho(i)}$. Since $att_{\rho(i)} \in W^*$, $\boldsymbol{M_i} \cdot \boldsymbol{w} = 0$ and hence $\boldsymbol{M_i} \cdot \boldsymbol{v} = -(\alpha' + a^{n+1})\boldsymbol{M_i} \cdot \boldsymbol{w} + \boldsymbol{M_i} \cdot \boldsymbol{v}' = \boldsymbol{M_i} \cdot \boldsymbol{v}'$. Then the distinguisher computes

$$D_i = g^{\boldsymbol{M_i} \cdot \boldsymbol{v}'}(h_0 h_{\rho(i)})^{r'_i} g_{\rho(i)}^{-t_0} \prod_{att_j \in W^*,\ j \neq \rho(i)} \left(g_{\rho(i)}^{t_j} \cdot g_{n+1-j+\rho(i)}\right),$$

$$D'_i = g^{r'_i} g_{\rho(i)}^{-1}, \quad D''_i = \left\{D''_{i,j} : D''_{i,j} = h_j^{r'_i} g_{\rho(i)}^{-t_j} g_{n+1-j+\rho(i)}^{-1}, \forall j \in [n] \setminus \{\rho(i)\}\right\}.$$

Case 2: For i where $att_{\rho(i)} \notin W^*$, i.e., $\rho(i) \neq j$, for all $att_j \in W^*$.

Note that $\boldsymbol{M_i} \cdot \boldsymbol{v} = \boldsymbol{M_i} \cdot (\boldsymbol{v}' - \alpha'\boldsymbol{w}) - (\boldsymbol{M_i} \cdot \boldsymbol{w})a^{n+1}$. In this case, the distinguisher selects a random $r'_i \in_R \mathbb{Z}_p$ and implicitly sets $r_i = r'_i + (\boldsymbol{M_i} \cdot \boldsymbol{w})a^{\rho(i)}$. Then the secret key components are computed as

$$D_i = g^{\boldsymbol{M_i} \cdot (\boldsymbol{v}' - \alpha'\boldsymbol{w})}(h_0 h_{\rho(i)})^{r'_i} g_{\rho(i)}^{(\boldsymbol{M_i} \cdot \boldsymbol{w})(t_0 + t_{\rho(i)})} \cdot \prod_{att_j \in W^*} \left(g_{\rho(i)}^{-(\boldsymbol{M_i} \cdot \boldsymbol{w})t_j} g_{n+1-j+\rho(i)}^{-(\boldsymbol{M_i} \cdot \boldsymbol{w})}\right),$$

$$D'_i = g^{r'_i} g_{\rho(i)}^{(\boldsymbol{M_i} \cdot \boldsymbol{w})}, \quad D''_i = \left\{D''_{i,j} = h_j^{r'_i} g_{\rho(i)}^{(\boldsymbol{M_i} \cdot \boldsymbol{w})t_j} g_{n+1-j+\rho(i)}^{(\boldsymbol{M_i} \cdot \boldsymbol{w})}, \forall j \in [n] \setminus \{\rho(i)\}\right\}.$$

Since $1 \leq \rho(i) \leq n$ and $j \neq \rho(i)$, the secret key components D_i, D'_i and D''_i do not contain any term which implicitly contains g_{n+1} and hence the distinguisher can correctly distribute the secret key components. Therefore, the distribution of the secret key is identical to that of the original scheme. Finally, the distinguisher sends the secret key $\mathsf{SK}_{(\mathbb{M},\rho)} = \langle(\mathbb{M},\rho), \{D_i, D'_i, D''_i : i \in [\ell]\}\rangle$ associated with $(\mathbb{M}, \rho)$ to the adversary.

Challenge. The adversary $\mathcal{A}$ submits two equal length messages M_0 and M_1 to the distinguisher $\mathfrak{D}$. Now, the distinguisher flips a random coin $\mu \in \{0, 1\}$ and encrypts M_μ under the challenge attribute set W^*. The components of challenge ciphertext CT_{W^*} are computed as follows: $C = M_\mu Z \cdot e(g^s, g^{\alpha'}), C_1 = g^s, C_2 = (g^s)^{t_0}$. The challenge ciphertext $\mathsf{CT}_{W^*} = \langle W^*, C, C_1, C_2 \rangle$ is returned to $\mathcal{A}$.

If $Z = e(g_{n+1}, g^s)$, then the challenge ciphertext CT_{W^*} is a valid encryption of the message M_μ under the attribute set W^* as $C_1 = g^s, C_2 = (g^s)^{t_0} = (g^{t_0})^s =$

$(h_0 \prod_{att_j \in W^*} h_j)^s$ and $C = M_\mu Z \cdot e(g^s, g^{\alpha'}) = M_\mu \cdot e(g_{n+1}, g^s) \cdot e(g^s, g^{\alpha'}) = M_\mu \cdot e(g, g)^{(\alpha' + a^{n+1})s} = M_\mu \cdot e(g, g)^{\alpha s}$.

On the contrary, if Z is a random element in $\mathbb{G}_T$, then the challenge ciphertext CT_{W^*} is independent of μ in the adversary's view.

Query Phase 2. $\mathfrak{D}$ proceeds exactly as it did in Query Phase 1.

Guess. The adversary $\mathcal{A}$ outputs his guess $\mu' \in \{0, 1\}$ on μ. If $\mu' = \mu$, then $\mathfrak{D}$ outputs 1 in the decisional n-BDHE game to guess that $Z = e(g_{n+1}, g^s)$; otherwise it outputs 0 to indicate that Z is a random element in $\mathbb{G}_T$.

If $Z = e(g_{n+1}, g^s)$, then the adversary's view in the above game is identical to that in a real attack. In that case $|\Pr[\mu = \mu'] - 1/2| > \epsilon$. On the other hand, if Z is a random element in $\mathbb{G}_T$, then $\mathcal{A}$ cannot obtain any information about M_μ and hence $\Pr[\mu = \mu'] = 1/2$. Since the events $Z = e(g_{n+1}, g^s)$ and Z is random element in $\mathbb{G}_T$ are equiprobable, it is easy to see that $\mathsf{Adv}_{\mathfrak{D}}^{n\text{-dBDHE}} > \epsilon/2$. Thus, the decisional n-BDHE problem in $(\mathbb{G}, \mathbb{G}_T)$ is not $(\mathcal{T}', \epsilon')$-hard, where $\mathcal{T}' = \mathcal{T} + \mathcal{O}(n^2) \cdot q \cdot \mathcal{T}_e$ and $\epsilon' = \epsilon/2$. $\qquad\qquad\Box$

3.2 Scheme II: Extension to sCCA Security

Setup(κ, U). This algorithm generates a tuple $(p, \mathbb{G}, g, \mathbb{G}_T, e)$ according to the implicit security parameter κ. It then chooses a random $\alpha \in_R \mathbb{Z}_p$ and $h_0, h_1, \ldots, h_n, \delta_1, \delta_2, \delta_3 \in_R \mathbb{G}$. It also selects a collision-resistant hash function $\mathcal{H} : \{0, 1\}^* \to \mathbb{Z}_p$. Now, it outputs the public key and master secret key as $\mathsf{PK} = \langle p, g, h_0, Y = e(g, g)^\alpha, h_1, h_2, \ldots, h_n, \delta_1, \delta_2, \delta_3, \mathcal{H} \rangle$ and $\mathsf{MK} = \alpha$, respectively.

KeyGen$(\mathsf{PK}, \mathsf{MK}, (\mathbb{M}, \rho))$. This algorithm is similar to the KeyGen algorithm of sCPA secure construction given in Section 3.1.

Encrypt(PK, M, W). To encrypt a message $M \in \mathbb{G}_T$ under a set W of attributes, the encryptor selects at random $s, \gamma \in_R \mathbb{Z}_p$ and computes

$$C = MY^s, \quad C_1 = g^s, \quad C_2 = (h_0 \prod_{att_j \in W} h_j)^s, \quad C_3 = (\delta_1^\beta \delta_2^\gamma \delta_3)^s,$$

where $\beta = \mathcal{H}(W, C, C_1, C_2)$. The encryptor outputs the ciphertext CT_W as $\mathsf{CT}_W = \langle W, C, C_1, C_2, C_3, \gamma \rangle$.

Decrypt$(\mathsf{PK}, \mathsf{SK}_{(\mathbb{M}, \rho)}, \mathsf{CT}_W)$. The decryptor first checks the following two identities: $e(g, C_2) \stackrel{?}{=} e(C_1, h_0 \prod_{att_j \in W} h_j)$ and $e(g, C_3) \stackrel{?}{=} e(C_1, \delta_1^\beta \delta_2^\gamma \delta_3)$, where $\beta = \mathcal{H}(W, C, C_1, C_2)$. If one of the two identities does not hold, decryption will fail. Otherwise, it will proceed similar to the Decrypt algorithm of sCPA secure construction given in Section 3.1.

Theorem 2 (*Security Proof*). *Assume that the attribute universe U has n attributes and collision-resistant hash function exists. Then our Scheme II is $(\mathcal{T}, q, q_D, \epsilon)$-IND-sCCA secure, assuming that the decisional n-BDHE problem in $(\mathbb{G}, \mathbb{G}_T)$ is $(\mathcal{T}', \epsilon')$-hard, where $\mathcal{T}' = \mathcal{T} + \mathcal{O}(n^2) \cdot q \cdot \mathcal{T}_e + \mathcal{O}(1) \cdot q_D \cdot \mathcal{T}_p$ and $\epsilon' = (1 - q_D/p) \cdot \epsilon$. Here, $\mathcal{T}_e$ denotes the running time of one exponentiation in $\mathbb{G}$ and $\mathcal{T}_p$ denotes the running time of one pairing computation in $\mathbb{G}_T$.*

Proof. Suppose that there exists an adversary $\mathcal{A}$ which can $(\mathcal{T}, q, q_D, \epsilon)$-*break* our Scheme II in the IND-sCCA security model. We can then build a distinguisher $\mathfrak{D}$ which uses $\mathcal{A}$ to show that the decisional n-BDHE problem in $(\mathbb{G}, \mathbb{G}_T)$ is *not* $(\mathcal{T}', \epsilon')$-hard. On input the decisional n-BDHE challenge $(\overrightarrow{y}_{a,s}, Z)$, where $\overrightarrow{y}_{a,s} = (g, g^s, g_1, \ldots, g_n, g_{n+2}, \ldots, g_{2n})$, $g_i = g^{a^i}$, and $Z = e(g_{n+1}, g^s)$ or Z is a random element of $\mathbb{G}_T$, the distinguisher $\mathfrak{D}$ attempts to output 1 if $Z = e(g_{n+1}, g^s)$ and 0 otherwise. Now, $\mathfrak{D}$ plays the role of a challenger in $\mathsf{Game}^{\mathsf{IND-sCCA}}$ and interacts with $\mathcal{A}$ as follows.

Init. The adversary $\mathcal{A}$ outputs the target attribute set W^* that he wishes to be challenged upon.

Setup. This Setup phase is same as the Setup phase described in the proof of Theorem 1. In addition, the distinguisher $\mathfrak{D}$ randomly chooses $\tau_2, \tau_3, \theta_1, \theta_2, \theta_3 \in_R \mathbb{Z}_p$ and sets $\delta_1 = g_1 g^{\theta_1}, \delta_2 = g_1^{\tau_2} g^{\theta_2}, \delta_3 = g_1^{\tau_3} g^{\theta_3}$. Note here that $\delta_1, \delta_2, \delta_3$ are distributed randomly due to the g^{θ_i} factor. The public key $\mathsf{PK} = \langle p, g, h_0, Y, h_1, h_2, \ldots, h_n, \delta_1, \delta_2, \delta_3, \mathcal{H} \rangle$ will be given to the adversary $\mathcal{A}$, where $\mathcal{H} : \{0,1\}^* \to \mathbb{Z}_p$ is a collision-resistant hash function.

Query Phase 1. In this phase, the distinguisher $\mathfrak{D}$ answers secret key queries as well as decryption queries from the adversary.

Secret Key Query: On adversary's secret key query, the distinguisher proceeds exactly as it did in Query Phase 1 in the proof of Theorem 1.

Decryption Query: When $\mathfrak{D}$ is given a ciphertext $\mathsf{CT}_W = \langle W, C, C_1, C_2, C_3, \gamma \rangle$ as an input to decryption query, $\mathfrak{D}$ first computes $\beta = \mathcal{H}(W, C, C_1, C_2)$ and performs the following pairing test on ciphertext components

$$e(g, C_2) \stackrel{?}{=} e(C_1, h_0 \prod_{att_j \in W} h_j) \text{ and } e(g, C_3) \stackrel{?}{=} e(C_1, \delta_1^\beta \delta_2^\gamma \delta_3).$$

If one of the two pairing test identities does not hold, it returns $\perp$. Otherwise, it checks whether $\beta + \gamma\tau_2 + \tau_3 = 0$ (this happens with probability at most $1/p$). If so, the distinguisher $\mathfrak{D}$ aborts (we refer to this event as **abort**) and outputs a random bit, else it returns

$$C \cdot e\left(C_3/C_1^{\beta\theta_1 + \gamma\theta_2 + \theta_3}, g_n^{(\beta + \gamma\tau_2 + \tau_3)^{-1}}\right)^{-1} \cdot e\left(C_1, g^{\alpha'}\right)^{-1} = M.$$

Challenge. The adversary $\mathcal{A}$ submits two equal length messages M_0 and M_1 to the distinguisher $\mathfrak{D}$. Now, the distinguisher flips a random binary coin $\mu \in \{0,1\}$ and encrypts M_μ under the challenge attribute set W^*. The components of challenge ciphertext CT_{W^*} are computed as follows

$$C^* = M_\mu Z \cdot e(g^s, g^{\alpha'}), \ C_1^* = g^s, \ C_2^* = (g^s)^{t_0}, \ C_3^* = (g^s)^{\beta^*\theta_1 + \gamma^*\theta_2 + \theta_3},$$

where $\beta^* = \mathcal{H}(W^*, C^*, C_1^*, C_2^*)$ and $\gamma^* = -(\beta^* + \tau_3)/\tau_2$. The challenge ciphertext $\mathsf{CT}_{W^*} = \langle W^*, C^*, C_1^*, C_2^*, C_3^*, \gamma^* \rangle$ is returned to the adversary $\mathcal{A}$.

If $Z = e(g_{n+1}, g^s)$, then the challenge ciphertext CT_{W^*} is a valid encryption of the message M_μ under the attribute set W^* as explained below.

$C_1^* = g^s, \ C_2^* = (g^s)^{t_0} = (g^{t_0})^s = (h_0 \prod_{att_j \in W^*} h_j)^s.$
Since $\gamma^* = -(\beta^* + \tau_3)/\tau_2$, we have $\beta^* + \gamma^*\tau_2 + \tau_3 = 0$ and hence $C_3^* = (g^s)^{\beta^*\theta_1 + \gamma^*\theta_2 + \theta_3} = (g_1^s)^{\beta^* + \gamma^*\tau_2 + \tau_3} (g^s)^{\beta^*\theta_1 + \gamma^*\theta_2 + \theta_3} = (\delta_1^{\beta^*} \delta_2^{\gamma^*} \delta_3)^s.$ Finally, $C^* = M_\mu Z \cdot e(g^s, g^{\alpha'}) = M_\mu \cdot e(g_{n+1}, g^s) \cdot e(g^s, g^{\alpha'}) = M_\mu \cdot e(g, g)^{(a^{n+1} + \alpha')s} = M_\mu \cdot e(g, g)^{\alpha s}.$

If Z is a random element in $\mathbb{G}_T$, then the challenge ciphertext CT_{W^*} is independent of μ in the adversary's view.

Query Phase 2. The adversary $\mathcal{A}$ issues more secret key and decryption queries and the distinguisher $\mathfrak{D}$ responds as in **Query Phase 1.**

We point out here a couple of facts. First, the adversary is not allowed to make a decryption query on challenge ciphertext CT_{W^*}. If so, $\mathfrak{D}$ aborts. Second, if the adversary is able to create a ciphertext $\mathsf{CT}_W = \langle W^*, C, C_1, C_2, C_3, \gamma \rangle$ with $\beta^* = \mathcal{H}(W^*, C, C_1, C_2)$ such that $\mathsf{CT}_W \neq \mathsf{CT}_{W^*}$, this represents a collision in the hash function $\mathcal{H}$. However, the probability that this event happens is negligible since $\mathcal{H}$ is a collision-resistant hash function.

Guess. The adversary $\mathcal{A}$ outputs his guess $\mu' \in \{0, 1\}$ on μ. If any abort happens, the distinguisher $\mathfrak{D}$ outputs 0. Otherwise, $\mathfrak{D}$ outputs 1 in the n-dBDHE game to guess that $Z = e(g_{n+1}, g^s)$ if $\mu' = \mu$, and it outputs 0 to indicate that Z is a random element in $\mathbb{G}_T$ if $\mu' \neq \mu$. Therefore, as long as $\mathfrak{D}$ does not abort in the simulation, $\mathfrak{D}$ can use the $\mathcal{A}$'s advantage to show that the decisional n-BDHE problem is not $(\mathcal{T}', \epsilon')$-hard. This can be checked as follows.

If $Z = e(g_{n+1}, g^s)$, then the distinguisher $\mathfrak{D}$ provides a perfect simulation and hence

$$\epsilon < \mathsf{Adv}_{\mathcal{A}}(\mathsf{Game}^{\mathsf{IND-CPA}}) = \Pr\left[\mu' = \mu | [Z = e(g_{n+1}, g^s)] \wedge \overline{\mathsf{abort}}\right] - \tfrac{1}{2}$$
$$= \Pr\left[\mathfrak{D}(\overrightarrow{y}_{a,s}, Z) = 1 | [Z = e(g_{n+1}, g^s)] \wedge \overline{\mathsf{abort}}\right] - \tfrac{1}{2},$$

i.e., $\Pr\left[\mathfrak{D}(\overrightarrow{y}_{a,s}, Z) = 1 | [Z = e(g_{n+1}, g^s)] \wedge \overline{\mathsf{abort}}\right] > \epsilon + 1/2$.

If Z is a random element $X \in \mathbb{G}_T$, then $\mathcal{A}$ cannot obtain any information about M_μ and therefore, $\Pr\left[\mathfrak{D}(\overrightarrow{y}_{a,s}, Z) = 1 | [Z = X] \wedge \overline{\mathsf{abort}}\right] = \tfrac{1}{2}$.

Since the event abort is independent of whether $Z = e(g_{n+1}, g^s)$ or a random element $X \in \mathbb{G}_T$, we have that

$$\Pr\left[\mathfrak{D}(\overrightarrow{y}_{a,s}, Z) = 1 | [Z = e(g_{n+1}, g^s)] \wedge \mathsf{abort}\right] = \tfrac{1}{2} \text{ and}$$
$$\Pr\left[\mathfrak{D}(\overrightarrow{y}_{a,s}, Z) = 1 | [Z = X] \wedge \mathsf{abort}\right] = \tfrac{1}{2}.$$

The probability of the event abort in the simulation is $\Pr[\mathsf{abort}] = q_D/p$, where q_D is the maximum number of decryption queries the adversary can make during simulation. Now,

$$\mathsf{Adv}_{\mathfrak{D}}^{n\text{-dBDHE}} = \Pr[\mathfrak{D}(\overrightarrow{y}_{a,s}, Z) = 1 | Z = e(g_{n+1}, g^s)] - \Pr[\mathfrak{D}(\overrightarrow{y}_{a,s}, Z) = 1 | Z = X]$$
$$= \Pr[\mathsf{abort}] \cdot \Pr\left[\mathfrak{D}(\overrightarrow{y}_{a,s}, Z) = 1 | [Z = e(g_{n+1}, g^s)] \wedge \mathsf{abort}\right]$$
$$+ \Pr[\overline{\mathsf{abort}}] \cdot \Pr\left[\mathfrak{D}(\overrightarrow{y}_{a,s}, Z) = 1 | [Z = e(g_{n+1}, g^s)] \wedge \overline{\mathsf{abort}}\right]$$
$$- \Pr[\mathsf{abort}] \cdot \Pr\left[\mathfrak{D}(\overrightarrow{y}_{a,s}, Z) = 1 | [Z = X] \wedge \mathsf{abort}\right]$$
$$- \Pr[\overline{\mathsf{abort}}] \cdot \Pr\left[\mathfrak{D}(\overrightarrow{y}_{a,s}, Z) = 1 | [Z = X] \wedge \overline{\mathsf{abort}}\right]$$
$$> \frac{q_D}{p} \cdot \frac{1}{2} + (1 - \frac{q_D}{p}) \cdot (\epsilon + \frac{1}{2}) - \frac{q_D}{p} \cdot \frac{1}{2} - (1 - \frac{q_D}{p}) \cdot \frac{1}{2} = (1 - \frac{q_D}{p})\epsilon.$$

Thus, the decisional n-BDHE problem in $(\mathbb{G}, \mathbb{G}_T)$ is not $(\mathcal{T}', \epsilon')$-hard, where $\mathcal{T}' = \mathcal{T} + \mathcal{O}(n^2) \cdot q \cdot \mathcal{T}_e + \mathcal{O}(1) \cdot q_D \cdot \mathcal{T}_p$ and $\epsilon' = (1 - q_D/p) \cdot \epsilon$. $\square$

4   KP-ABE Variants for Non-monotone Access Structures

This section is dedicated to the presentation of our constant-size ciphertext KP-ABE schemes for Non-Monotone Access Structure (nonMAS) that provide both sCPA and sCCA security.

To build a KP-ABE for nonMAS with constant-size ciphertext, we employ the *moving from MAS to nonMAS* technique [6] that represents non-monotone access structures in terms of monotone access structures with *negative* attributes (NOTcrypto is a negative attribute of the attribute crypto). We discuss here the technique for completeness. For ease of reference, we call the attribute crypto, a *positive* attribute and we denote its negation NOTcrypto by ¬crypto. Let U be a positive attribute universe.

Given a family $\mathfrak{F} = \{\Pi_{\mathbb{A}} : \mathbb{A} \in \mathsf{MA}\}$ of linear secret-sharing schemes for a set of possible monotone access structures MA, and $\widetilde{U} = U \bigcup \{\neg att : att \in U\}$ is the underlying attribute universe for each monotone access structure $\mathbb{A} \in \mathsf{MA}$, a family NM of non-monotone access structures can be defined as follows. For each access structure $\mathbb{A} \in \mathsf{MA}$ over $\widetilde{U}$, one defines a possibly non-monotone access structure $N_{\mathbb{A}}$ over U in the following way.

- For every set $W \subset U$, form $N(W) = W \bigcup \{\neg att : att \in U \setminus W\} \subset \widetilde{U}$.
- Now, define $N_{\mathbb{A}}$ by saying that W is authorized in $N_{\mathbb{A}}$ if and only if $N(W)$ is authorized in $\mathbb{A}$, i.e., $W \in N_{\mathbb{A}}$ iff $N(W) \in \mathbb{A}$.

The family of non-monotone access structures is $\mathsf{NM} = \{N_{\mathbb{A}} : \Pi_{\mathbb{A}} \in \mathfrak{F}\}$. Note that the non-monotone access structure $N_{\mathbb{A}}$ will have only positive attributes in its access sets.

We combine the foregoing methodology with our KP-ABE schemes for MAS in order to construct desired KP-ABE schemes for nonMAS.

4.1   Scheme III: sCPA Secure Construction

Setup(κ, U). This algorithm first generates $p, \mathbb{G}, \mathbb{G}_T, e$ according to the implicit security parameter κ. It then picks a random generator $g \in_R \mathbb{G}$, random elements $h_0, k_0 \in_R \mathbb{G}$ and a random exponent $\alpha \in_R \mathbb{Z}_p$. For each attribute $att_j \in U$, it randomly chooses $h_j, k_j \in_R \mathbb{G}$, for all $j \in [n]$. Now, it outputs the public key and master secret key respectively as
$$\mathsf{PK} = \langle p, g, h_0, k_0, Y = e(g,g)^{\alpha}, \{h_j, k_j\}_{j \in [n]} \rangle \text{ and } \mathsf{MK} = \alpha.$$

KeyGen$(\mathsf{PK}, \mathsf{MK}, \widetilde{\mathbb{A}})$. Given a non-monotone access structure $\widetilde{\mathbb{A}}$ such that we have $\widetilde{\mathbb{A}} = N_{\mathbb{A}}$ for some monotone access structure $\mathbb{A}$ over $\widetilde{U} = U \bigcup \{\neg att : att \in U\}$ and associated with a linear secret sharing scheme $\Pi_{\mathbb{A}} = (\mathbb{M}_{\ell \times k}, \rho)$, this algorithm first runs Distribute$(\mathbb{M}, \rho, \alpha)$ and obtains a set $\{\lambda_{\rho(i)} = \boldsymbol{M}_i \cdot \boldsymbol{v} : i \in [\ell]\}$ of ℓ shares, where $\boldsymbol{v} \in_R \mathbb{Z}_p^k$ such that $\boldsymbol{v} \cdot \boldsymbol{1} = \alpha$ (here, $\boldsymbol{1} = (1, 0, \ldots, 0)$ is a vector of length k). Note that each row $i \in [\ell]$ of $\mathbb{M}$ is associated with an attribute $\widetilde{att}_{\rho(i)} \in \{att_{\rho(i)}, \neg att_{\rho(i)}\}$. For each row $i \in [\ell]$, it chooses a random exponent $r_i \in_R \mathbb{Z}_p$ and computes
$$D_i = g^{\lambda_{\rho(i)}} (\widetilde{h}_0 \widetilde{h}_{\rho(i)})^{r_i}, D_i' = g^{r_i}, D_i'' = \left\{ D_{i,j}'' : D_{i,j}'' = \widetilde{h}_j^{r_i}, \forall j \in [n] \setminus \{\rho(i)\} \right\},$$

where, for each $j = 0, 1, \ldots, n$, $\widetilde{h}_j = \begin{cases} h_j, & \text{if } \widetilde{att}_{\rho(i)} = att_{\rho(i)}, \\ k_j, & \text{if } \widetilde{att}_{\rho(i)} = \neg att_{\rho(i)}. \end{cases}$ It then re-

turns the secret key $\mathsf{SK}_{\widetilde{\mathbb{A}}} = \langle \widetilde{\mathbb{A}}, \{D_i, D'_i, D''_i : i \in [\ell]\} \rangle$ associated with the non-monotone access structure $\widetilde{\mathbb{A}}$.

Encrypt(PK, M, W). To encrypt a message $M \in \mathbb{G}_T$ under a set $W \subset U$ of attributes, this algorithm selects at random $s \in_R \mathbb{Z}_p$ and computes $C = MY^s, C_1 = g^s$, $C_2 = (h_0 \prod_{att_j \in W} h_j)^s$ and $C_3 = (k_0 \prod_{att_j \in W} k_j)^s$. It outputs the ciphertext $\mathsf{CT}_W = \langle W, C, C_1, C_2, C_3 \rangle$.

Decrypt(PK, $\mathsf{SK}_{\widetilde{\mathbb{A}}}, \mathsf{CT}_W$). This algorithm first checks whether $W \in \widetilde{\mathbb{A}}$. If not, it outputs $\bot$. Otherwise, since $\widetilde{\mathbb{A}} = N_{\mathbb{A}}$ for some monotone access structure $\mathbb{A}$ over $\widetilde{U}$ associated with a linear secret sharing scheme $\Pi_{\mathbb{A}} = (\mathbb{M}_{\ell \times k}, \rho)$, we have $N(W) \in \mathbb{A}$. It runs $\mathsf{Reconstruct}(\mathbb{M}, \rho, N(W))$ and obtains a set $\{\omega_i : i \in I\}$ of reconstruction constants such that $\sum_{i \in I} \omega_i \lambda_{\rho(i)} = \alpha$, where $I = \{i \in [\ell] : \widetilde{att}_{\rho(i)} \in N(W)\}$. Let $I^+ = \{i \in [\ell] : \widetilde{att}_{\rho(i)} = att_{\rho(i)} \in N(W)\}$ and $I^- = \{i \in [\ell] : \widetilde{att}_{\rho(i)} = \neg att_{\rho(i)} \in N(W)\}$. Then $I = I^+ \bigcup I^-$. It now computes E_1, E_2, E_3 as follows:

$$E_1 = \prod_{i \in I} \left(D_i \cdot \prod_{att_j \in W, j \neq \rho(i)} D''_{i,j} \right)^{\omega_i}, \quad E_2 = \prod_{i \in I^+} (D'_i)^{\omega_i}, \quad E_3 = \prod_{i \in I^-} (D'_i)^{\omega_i}.$$

The message M is obtained by computing $C \cdot e(C_2, E_2) \cdot e(C_3, E_3) / e(C_1, E_1)$.

Security Proof: The proof of the following theorem is straightforward from the proof of Theorem 1 with the modification that in the simulation, the secret key generation uses h_j elements for positive attributes and k_j elements for negative attributes. Due to page limitation, the detailed proof is omitted.

Theorem 3. *If the attribute universe U has n attributes then Scheme III is $(\mathcal{T}, q, \epsilon)$-IND-sCPA secure, assuming that the decisional n-BDHE problem in $(\mathbb{G}, \mathbb{G}_T)$ is $(\mathcal{T}', \epsilon')$-hard, where $\mathcal{T}' = \mathcal{T} + \mathcal{O}(n^2) \cdot q \cdot \mathcal{T}_e$ and $\epsilon' = \epsilon/2$. Here, $\mathcal{T}_e$ denotes the running time of one exponentiation in $\mathbb{G}$.*

4.2 Scheme IV: Extension to sCCA Security

Similar to KP-ABE schemes for MAS, we can extend our Scheme III to sCCA secure KP-ABE construction for non-monotone access structure by employing the same technique used in Scheme II. We describe the sCCA secure scheme as a set of the following four algorithms.

Setup(κ, U). This algorithm randomly selects $\delta_1, \delta_2, \delta_3 \in_R \mathbb{G}$ and a collision-resistant hash function $\mathcal{H} : \{0,1\}^* \to \mathbb{Z}_p$. The other public parameters and master secret are chosen analogous to the Setup algorithm of Scheme III. It finally outputs the public key and master secret key respectively as
$\mathsf{PK} = \langle p, g, h_0, k_0, Y = e(g,g)^\alpha, \{h_j, k_j\}_{j \in [n]}, \delta_1, \delta_2, \delta_3, \mathcal{H} \rangle$ and $\mathsf{MK} = \alpha$.

KeyGen(PK, MK, $\widetilde{\mathbb{A}}$). This algorithm acts as KeyGen algorithm of Scheme III.

Encrypt(PK, M, W). To generate the ciphertext, this algorithm selects at random $s, \gamma \in_R \mathbb{Z}_p$ and computes $C = MY^s, C_1 = g^s, C_2 = (h_0 \prod_{att_j \in W} h_j)^s,$
$C_3 = (k_0 \prod_{att_j \in W} k_j)^s$ and $C_4 = (\delta_1^\beta \delta_2^\gamma \delta_3)^s$, where $\beta = \mathcal{H}(W, C, C_1, C_2, C_3)$. It outputs the ciphertext $\mathsf{CT}_W = \langle W, C, C_1, C_2, C_3, C_4, \gamma \rangle$.

Decrypt$(\mathsf{PK}, \mathsf{SK}_{\widetilde{\mathbb{A}}}, \mathsf{CT}_W)$. This algorithm first checks the following identities:
$$e(g, C_2) \stackrel{?}{=} e(C_1, h_0 \prod_{att_j \in W} h_j), \quad e(g, C_3) \stackrel{?}{=} e(C_1, k_0 \prod_{att_j \in W} k_j) \text{ and}$$
$e(g, C_4) \stackrel{?}{=} e(C_1, \delta_1^\beta \delta_2^\gamma \delta_3)$, where $\beta = \mathcal{H}(W, C, C_1, C_2, C_3)$. If one of the three identities does not hold, decryption will fail. Otherwise, it will proceed similar to the Decrypt algorithm of Scheme III in order to recover the message M.

Theorem 4 (*Security Proof*). *Assume that the attribute universe U has n attributes and collision-resistant hash function exists. Then our Scheme IV is $(\mathcal{T}, q, q_D, \epsilon)$-IND-sCCA secure, assuming that the decisional n-BDHE problem in $(\mathbb{G}, \mathbb{G}_T)$ is $(\mathcal{T}', \epsilon')$-hard, where $\mathcal{T}' = \mathcal{T} + \mathcal{O}(n^2) \cdot q \cdot \mathcal{T}_e + \mathcal{O}(1) \cdot q_D \cdot \mathcal{T}_p$ and $\epsilon' = (1 - q_D/p) \cdot \epsilon$. Here, $\mathcal{T}_e$ denotes the running time of one exponentiation in $\mathbb{G}$ and $\mathcal{T}_p$ denotes the running time of one pairing computation in $\mathbb{G}_T$.*

5   Scheme V: Large Universe KP-ABE for MAS

In this section, we extend our basic construction Scheme I to the large attribute universe setting as the set of the following four algorithms.

Setup(κ). Let $(p, \mathbb{G}, \mathbb{G}_T, e)$ be as in Section 4.1 and $U = \{0, 1\}^*$ is assumed to be the attribute universe. Choose a hash function $H : \{0, 1\}^* \to \mathbb{G}$, which will be modeled as a random oracle, to compute attribute values dynamically. Pick $\alpha \in_R \mathbb{Z}_p$ and set $Y = e(g, g)^\alpha$. The public key and master secret key are $\mathsf{PK} = \langle p, g, Y, H \rangle$ and $\mathsf{MK} = \alpha$, respectively.

KeyGen$(\mathsf{PK}, \mathsf{MK}, (\mathbb{M}, \rho))$. Here $\mathbb{M}$ is a share-generating matrix of size $\ell \times k$ and ρ is a mapping from each row i of $\mathbb{M}$ to an attribute $\rho(i) \in \{0, 1\}^*$. Let L be the set of attributes appeared in LSSS access structure $(\mathbb{M}, \rho)$. The CA first executes Distribute$(\mathbb{M}, \rho, \alpha)$ and obtains a set $\{\lambda_{\rho(i)} = \boldsymbol{M_i} \cdot \boldsymbol{v} : i \in [\ell]\}$ of ℓ shares, where $\boldsymbol{v} \in_R \mathbb{Z}_p^k$ such that $\boldsymbol{v} \cdot \boldsymbol{1} = \alpha$. For each row $i \in [\ell]$, it chooses $r_i \in_R \mathbb{Z}_p$ and computes
$$D_i = g^{\lambda_{\rho(i)}} H(\rho(i))^{r_i}, D_i' = g^{r_i}, D_i'' = \{D_{i,y}'' : D_{i,y}'' = H(y)^{r_i}, \forall y \in L \setminus \{\rho(i)\}\}$$
The CA then returns the secret key $\mathsf{SK}_{(\mathbb{M}, \rho)} = \langle (\mathbb{M}, \rho), \{D_i, D_i', D_i'' : i \in [\ell]\} \rangle$.

Encrypt(PK, M, W). To encrypt a message $M \in \mathbb{G}_T$ under a set W of attributes, the encryptor selects $s \in_R \mathbb{Z}_p$ and computes
$$C = MY^s, C_1 = g^s, C_2 = \{C_{2,y} : C_{2,y} = H(y)^s, \forall y \in W\}.$$
It outputs the ciphertext $\mathsf{CT}_W = \langle W, C, C_1, C_2 \rangle$.

Decrypt$(\mathsf{PK}, \mathsf{SK}_{(\mathbb{M}, \rho)}, \mathsf{CT}_W)$. The decryptor first runs Reconstruct$(\mathbb{M}, \rho, W)$ to obtain a set $\{\omega_i : i \in I\}$ of reconstruction constants, where $I = \{i \in [\ell] : \rho(i) \in W\}$. If W satisfies the access structure $(\mathbb{M}, \rho)$, then $\sum_{i \in I} \omega_i \lambda_{\rho(i)} = \alpha$. The decryptor computes E_1, E_2, C_2' as follows:
$$E_1 = \prod_{i \in I} \left(D_i \cdot \prod_{y \in W', y \neq \rho(i)} D_{i,y}'' \right)^{\omega_i}, \quad E_2 = \prod_{i \in I} (D_i')^{\omega_i}, \quad C_2' = \prod_{y \in W'} C_{2,y},$$

where $W' = \{y \in W : \exists\ j \in I$ such that $\rho(j) = y\}$. The message M can be obtained by computing $C \cdot e(C_2', E_2)/e(C_1, E_1)$.

Note. Due to lack of space, the security proof will be given in the full version.

6 Conclusion

In this paper, we proposed efficient CPA as well as CCA secure KP-ABE schemes for both MAS and nonMAS with constant-size ciphertext and constant number of bilinear pairing computations. Security of all our schemes against selective adversary has been proven under the decisional n-BDHE assumption in the standard model. Our schemes outperform the existing schemes in terms of computation cost during encryption and decryption.

References

1. Sahai, A., Waters, B.: Fuzzy Identity-Based Encryption. In: Cramer, R. (ed.) EUROCRYPT 2005. LNCS, vol. 3494, pp. 457–473. Springer, Heidelberg (2005)
2. Goyal, V., Pandey, O., Sahai, A., Waters, B.: Attribute Based Encryption for Fine-Grained Access Control of Encrypted Data. In: ACM Conference on Computer and Communications Security, pp. 89–98 (2006)
3. Bethencourt, J., Sahai, A., Waters, B.: Ciphertext-Policy Attribute-Based Encryption. In: IEEE Symposium on Security and Privacy, pp. 321–334 (2007)
4. Okamoto, T., Takashima, K.: Fully Secure Functional Encryption with General Relations from the Decisional Linear Assumption. In: Rabin, T. (ed.) CRYPTO 2010. LNCS, vol. 6223, pp. 191–208. Springer, Heidelberg (2010)
5. Lewko, A., Sahai, A., Waters, B.: Revocation Systems with Very Small Private Keys. In: IEEE Symposium on Security and Privacy, pp. 273–285 (2010)
6. Ostrovksy, R., Sahai, A., Waters, B.: Attribute Based Encryption with Non-Monotonic Access Structures. In: ACM Conference on Computer and Communications Security, pp. 195–203 (2007)
7. Lewko, A., Okamoto, T., Sahai, A., Takashima, K., Waters, B.: Fully Secure Functional Encryption: Attribute-Based Encryption and (Hierarchical) Inner Product Encryption. Cryptology ePrint report 2010/110 (2010)
8. Attrapadung, N., Herranz, J., Laguillaumie, F., Libert, B., de Panafieu, E., Ràfols, C.: Attribute-Based Encryption Schemes with Constant-Size Ciphertexts. Theor. Comput. Sci. 422, 15–38 (2012)
9. Chang-Ji, W., Jian-Fa, L.: A Key-policy Attribute-based Encryption Scheme with Constant Size Ciphertext. In: CIS 2012, pp. 447–451. IEEE (2012)
10. Canetti, R., Halevi, S., Katz, J.: Chosen-Ciphertext Security from Identity-Based Encryption. In: Cachin, C., Camenisch, J.L. (eds.) EUROCRYPT 2004. LNCS, vol. 3027, pp. 207–222. Springer, Heidelberg (2004)
11. Cheung, L., Newport, C.: Provably Secure Ciphertext Policy ABE. In: ACM Conference on Computer and Communications Security, pp. 456–465 (2007)
12. Yamada, S., Attrapadung, N., Hanaoka, G., Kunihiro, N.: Generic Constructions for Chosen-Ciphertext Secure Attribute Based Encryption. In: Catalano, D., Fazio, N., Gennaro, R., Nicolosi, A. (eds.) PKC 2011. LNCS, vol. 6571, pp. 71–89. Springer, Heidelberg (2011)

13. Fujisaki, E., Okamoto, T.: How to Enhance the Security of Public-Key Encryption at Minimum Cost. In: Imai, H., Zheng, Y. (eds.) PKC 1999. LNCS, vol. 1560, pp. 53–68. Springer, Heidelberg (1999)
14. Qin, B., Wu, Q., Zhang, L., Domingo-Ferrer, J.: Threshold Public-Key Encryption with Adaptive Security and Short Ciphertexts. In: Soriano, M., Qing, S., López, J. (eds.) ICICS 2010. LNCS, vol. 6476, pp. 62–76. Springer, Heidelberg (2010)
15. Lai, J., Deng, R.H., Liu, S., Kou, W.: Efficient CCA-Secure PKE from Identity-Based Techniques. In: Pieprzyk, J. (ed.) CT-RSA 2010. LNCS, vol. 5985, pp. 132–147. Springer, Heidelberg (2010)
16. Waters, B.: Ciphertext-Policy Attribute-Based Encryption: An Expressive, Efficient, and Provably Secure Realization. Cryptology ePrint report 2008/290 (2008)

Privacy-Preserving Decentralized Ciphertext-Policy Attribute-Based Encryption with Fully Hidden Access Structure

Huiling Qian, Jiguo Li, and Yichen Zhang

College of Computer and Information Engineering
Hohai University, Nanjing, P.R. China, 210098
lijiguo@hhu.edu.cn

Abstract. To make multi-authority ABE schemes collusion-resistant, a user in the system must be tied with a globally verifiable identifier GID. The drawback of this approach is that it compromises the user's privacy. Malicious authorities can collect user's attributes by tracing the user GID, thus compromises the privacy of the user. The other privacy concern is access structures that sent along with ciphertext in traditional CP-ABE schemes may have sensitive information. In this paper, we propose a multi-authority ABE scheme with fully hidden access structure that authorities can get nothing about user GID when generating and issuing user private keys and access structures are hidden to receivers. We prove the security of our scheme under a standard complexity assumption of decisional bilinear Diffie-Hellman (DBDH) assumption. The access structure we used in our scheme is AND, OR gates on multi-valued attributes.

1 Introduction

In distributed file systems, it allows users to access files from different hosts via network. Thus multiple users can share files and store data. To protect the sensitive data, a complicated access control policy is needed to specify who can access those data. However, traditional access control policies may have some drawbacks, especially in distributed systems. The first drawback is management of user identities. In traditional access control policies, a user identity must be validated by the authority when accessing files or data. So, it can be very hard to manage numerous identities in large distributed file systems. Another drawback is privacy concerns. To overcome these problems and drawbacks, Sahai and Waters [1] introduced the concept of ABE. In this scheme, user's secret key and ciphertext are labeled with a set of attributes, when there is a match between the secret keys and ciphertext, the user can decrypt the message. To share his data, the user can specify an access structure on who can access the data. Therefore, ABE schemes make it possible for users to be validated by descriptive attributes rather than a unique identity. Furthermore, ABE schemes enable one-to-many encryption; one can specify an access structure on who can

S. Qing et al. (Eds.): ICICS 2013, LNCS 8233, pp. 363–372, 2013.

decrypt the data without knowing specific identity. Users whose attributes satisfy the access structure can decrypt the data and access the file.

There are two forms of ABE schemes, key-policy attribute based encryption (KP-ABE) and ciphertext-policy attribute based encryption (CP-ABE). In a KP-ABE scheme [2], secret keys are associated with an access structure and ciphertext is labeled by a set of attributes. If and only if the set of attributes in the ciphertext satisfy the access structure in the secret keys, the user can access the encrypted data. Conversely, in a CP-ABE scheme [3], ciphertext is associated with an encryptor specified access structure and secret keys are labeled by a set of attributes.

1.1   Related Work

The scheme proposed by Sahai and Waters [1] in 2005 can only express simple (t, n) threshold access structure. The limited expressive power is a restriction to the applicability of ABE schemes. Some efforts have been made to enhance the expressibility of ABE schemes. Goyal et al. [2] greatly improved the expressibility of ABE schemes by proposing an ABE scheme with fine-grained access control. Ostrovsky et al. [4] gave the first KP-ABE scheme supporting non-monotonic access structure.

The first CP-ABE scheme is proposed by Bethencourt et al.[3]. In this scheme, it allows the encryptor to specify an access structure in terms of any monotonic access formula. Cheung and Newport [5] constructed a CP-ABE scheme, its complexity assumption is bilinear Diffie-Hellman assumption. However, the scheme only supports positive and negative attributes and wildcards in the access structure. To enhance the expressibility of the access structure, Balu et al. [6] proposed a new CP-ABE scheme, the access structure in this scheme can be expressed by AND, OR gates on multi-valued attributes. In traditional CP-ABE schemes [3,5], access structures are sent to receivers along with ciphertexts. However, access structures may contain some sensitive information. To address this issue, Boneh and Waters [7] proposed a predicate encryption scheme based on hidden vector encryption. Nishide et al. [8] proposed CP-ABE schemes with hidden access structure. In [9], the authors proposed a fully secure CP-ABE with partially hidden access structures.

In all the schemes we discussed above, there is only one authority monitoring and issuing user secret keys. However, there will often be more than one party that acts as authority in reality. Chase [10] proposed the first multi-authority ABE scheme in 2007. In this scheme, there are multiple authorities responsible for monitoring attributes and issuing secret keys. There also exists a central authority generating public and secret keys for other authorities. Users get their secret keys from multiple authorities. Different approaches have been provided to remove the trusted central authority. In [11], a technique named distributed PRF is used to remove the central authority. Moreover, the authors first give the concern that malicious authorities might collect user's attributes and combine their own information to build a full profile, thus compromises the privacy of the user. In [12], the scheme removes the need of cooperation with authorities in the setup stage. They also remove the need of central authority, thus making the system more scalable.

Multi-authority ABE scheme is more in line with reality, different authorities monitor different sets of attributes. However, being different from single authority ABE scheme, to resist collusion attacks in multi-authority ABE schemes is difficult. Chase [10] solved this problem by introducing global identifier GID. However, this solution compromises user's privacy. Malicious authorities can collaborate and collect user's attributes by tracing user's GID, thus compromises the privacy of the user. Han et al. [13] addressed this issue by involving a 2-party secure computation protocol based on the ideas in [11].

1.2 Our Contributions

In this paper, we propose a decentralized multi-authority CP-ABE scheme. Multiple authorities monitor different kinds of attributes. Moreover, we remove the need of trusted central authority. Even parts of the authorities are not honest, our scheme remains secure. Authorities in our scheme do not need to collaborate in the setup stage. Authorities can join and leave the system freely. In our scheme, the access structure is fully hidden, and authorities in our scheme can get nothing about user GID. Thus we protect user privacy from both malicious users and malicious authorities.

2 Preliminaries

Definition 1. (Bilinear Maps).*Let $\mathbb{G}$, $\mathbb{G}_T$ be two multiplicative cyclic groups of prime order p. Let g be a generator of $\mathbb{G}$ and e be a bilinear map, $e : \mathbb{G} \times \mathbb{G} \rightarrow \mathbb{G}_T$. The bilinear map e has the following properties:*

- *Bilinearity: for all $g, h \in \mathbb{G}$, and $a, b \in \mathbb{Z}_p$, we have $e(g^a, h^b) = e(g, h)^{ab}$.*
- *Non-degeneracy: $e(g, g) \neq 1$.*
- *Computability: Group operation $e(g, h)$ is efficiently computable, where $g, h \in \mathbb{G}$.*

Definition 2. (Decisional   Bilinear   Diffie-Hellman   (DBDH) Assumption)[14]. *Let $a, b, c, z \in \mathbb{Z}_p$ be chosen at random and g be a generator of group $\mathbb{G}$. The DBDH assumption holds when no polynomial-time algorithm $\mathcal{B}$ can distinguish the tuple $(A, B, C, Z) = (g^a, g^b, g^c, g^{abc})$ from the tuple $(A, B, C, Z) = (g^a, g^b, g^c, g^z)$ with non-negligible advantage. The advantage of algorithm $\mathcal{B}$ is*

$$\text{Adv}_{\mathcal{B}}^{DBDH} = |Pr[\mathcal{B}(A, B, C, g^{abc}) = 1] - Pr[\mathcal{B}(A, B, C, g^z) = 1]|.$$

Definition 3. (Access Structure)[15]. *Let $P = \{P_1, P_2, ..., P_n\}$ be a set of parties. A collection $\mathbb{A} \subseteq 2^P$ is considered to be monotone if $\forall B, C$ satisfies that if $B \in \mathbb{A}$ and $B \subseteq C$, then $C \in \mathbb{A}$. An access structure (resp., monotonic access structure) is a collection (resp., monotone collection) $\mathbb{A}$ that $\mathbb{A} \subseteq 2^P \{\emptyset\}$. The sets in $\mathbb{A}$ are called the authorized sets, and the sets not in $\mathbb{A}$ are called the unauthorized sets.*

Commitment. A commitment scheme allows someone to commit a chosen value without leaking the value for a period of time and reveal the committed value later when it is needed. The commitment scheme used in our scheme is a perfectly hiding commitment scheme named as Pedersen commitment scheme [16].

Zero-Knowledge Proof. A zero-knowledge proof is an interactive proof for a prover to prove some knowledge without revealing the knowledge. The zero-knowledge proof scheme involved in our construction is introduced by Camenisch and Stadler [17].

3   Formal Definition and Security Model

3.1   Outline of Decentralized CP-ABE Encryption

A decentralized CP-ABE scheme consists of the following five algorithms.

Global Setup: This algorithm takes an implicit security parameter l as input and returns the system parameters params for the system.

Authority Setup: This algorithm is run by authorities in the system. Each authority A_k generates his secret keys SK_k and public keys PK_k, where $k = 1, 2, ..., N$.

KeyGen: This algorithm takes authority's secret keys SK_k, a set of attributes L^k and a global identifier GID as input, returns the secret keys SK_U^k for user U. Here $L^k = \hat{A}_k \cap L$, $\hat{A}_k$ denotes the attributes monitored by the authority A_k, L denotes the list of attributes corresponding to the GID.

Encryption: The encryption algorithm takes the system parameters params, a message M, authority's public keys PK_k and an access structure W as input, returns the ciphertext C_T.

Decryption: This algorithm takes the global identifier GID, a collection of secret keys corresponding to user attributes and the ciphertext C_T as input, and outputs the message M when user attributes satisfy the encryptor specified access structure.

3.2   Security Model

The security game is played between adversary and challenger as follows:

Initialization: Adversary $\mathcal{A}$ submits the challenge access structure W_0^*, W_1^* and a list of corrupted authorities $C_\mathcal{A}$ to algorithm $\mathcal{B}$, where $|C_\mathcal{A}| < N$.

Global Setup: The challenger runs the algorithm **Setup** and outputs the system parameters params to adversary $\mathcal{A}$.

Authorities Setup: For the corrupted authorities, the challenger sends his public and secret keys (PK_k, SK_k) to the adversary $\mathcal{A}$. For the honest authorities, the challenger sends his public keys PK_k to the adversary $\mathcal{A}$. For the third kind of authorities, the challenger sends his public keys PK_k and parts of secret keys SK_k to the adversary $\mathcal{A}$.

Phase 1: The adversary $\mathcal{A}$ sends an attribute list L to the challenger for secret keys queries, where $(L \not\models W_0^*$ or $L \not\models W_1*)$ and $(L \not\models W_0^*$ and $L \not\models W_1*)$. The challenger returns secret keys for these attributes.

Challenge: The adversary $\mathcal{A}$ submits two equal length messages M_0 and M_1. The challenger chooses a random bit $\xi \in_R \{0,1\}$ and runs the algorithm **Encryption**. The challenger gives the ciphertext $C^*_{T,\xi}$ to the adversary $\mathcal{A}$. Note that if $L \not\models W_0^*$ and $L \not\models W_1^*$, then $M_0 = M_1$.

Phase 2: Phase 1 is repeated.

Guess: Finally adversary $\mathcal{A}$ outputs his guess ξ' on ξ.

Definition 4. *A decentralized CP-ABE scheme is (t, q, ϵ) secure in the selective-set model if all t-time adversary makes at most q secret key queries and succeeds in the above game with negligible advantage ϵ.*

3.3 Outline of Privacy-Preserving Decentralized CP-ABE Encryption

To protect user privacy from malicious authorities, we replace the algorithm **KeyGen** in the decentralized CP-ABE encryption scheme with **BlindKeyGen**. Other algorithms remain the same. The algorithm **BlindKeyGen** is described as follows.

BlindKeyGen: User U runs the algorithm Commit and returns *com* to the authority A_k. Authority A_k uses *com* to verify whether the user U has GID u or not in zero-knowledge. If the proof is correct, authority A_k computes partial secret keys for the user. The user verifies whether the authority A_k has the correct secret keys in zero-knowledge through partial secret keys. If the proof is correct and Decommit returns 1, the user U can compute his secret keys successfully and authority A_k gets empty. Otherwise, algorithm aborts and outputs $(\perp, \perp)$ for the authority and user.

To be secure against both malicious users and malicious authorities, algorithm **BlindKeyGen** should satisfy two properties: leak freeness and selective-failure blindness [18,13]. Leak freeness requires that a malicious user can get nothing by executing algorithm **BlindKeyGen** with an honest authority. Selective-failure blindness requires that a malicious authority cannot get anything about user's GID u and cannot fail the algorithm according to user's GID u through running algorithm **BlindKeyGen**.

4 Our Construction

In this section, we propose a decentralized CP-ABE scheme which can fully hide access structure specified by the encryptor.

4.1 Decentralized CP-ABE Encryption Scheme with Fully Hidden Access Structure

Our scheme is constructed as follows.

Global Setup: Given the security parameter l, the algorithm returns a bilinear group $(e, p, \mathbb{G}, \mathbb{G}_T)$ with prime order p. Let g, h and h_1 be the generators of group $\mathbb{G}$. Suppose there are N authorities in the system, namely $A_1, A_2, ..., A_N$.

Authority Setup: Each authority A_k chooses $\alpha_k \in_R \mathbb{Z}_p, \beta_k \in_R \mathbb{Z}_p$ and $t_{i,j}^k \in_R \mathbb{Z}_p (i \in [1,n], j \in [1, n_i])$, and computes $Y_k = e(g,g)^{\alpha_k}, Z_k = g^{\beta_k}$, and $T_{i,j}^k = g^{t_{i,j}^k}$. The secret keys and public keys of authority A_k are $SK_k = (\alpha_k, \beta_k, \{t_{i,j}^k\}_{i \in [1,n], j \in [1,n_i]})$ and $PK_k = (Y_k, Z_k, \{T_{i,j}^k\}_{i \in [1,n], j \in [1,n_i]})$.

KeyGen: Denote the user's global identifier GID by u, where $u \in \mathbb{Z}_p$. Let L be the attribute list of the user U. To generate a key for the user U, authority A_k selects $r_k, \tau_k \in_R \mathbb{Z}_p, \omega_i \in_R \mathbb{Z}_p^*$ for $1 \le i \le n$ and computes

$$D_{i,1}^k = g^{\alpha_k} h^{r_k} h_1^{\frac{1}{u+\beta_k}}, D_{i,2}^k = h^{\omega_i t_{i,j}^k}, D_{i,3}^k = h^{\omega_i}, D_0^k = h^{r_k} h_1^{-\tau_k}, D_1^k = h_1^{\tau_k + \frac{1}{u+\beta_k}}$$

for $t_{i,j}^k \in L^k$, where $L^k = \hat{A}_k \cap L$, for $k = 1, 2, ..., N$, $\hat{A}_k$ denotes the attributes monitored by the authority A_k.

Encryption: An encryptor chooses a random number $s \in_R \mathbb{Z}_p$, and computes

$$C_1 = M \cdot \prod_{k \in I_c} Y_k^s, C_2 = g^s,$$

where I_c is an index set of authorities A_k.

The encryptor sets the value of root node to be s, marks the root node as assigned and all the child nodes as un-assigned.

For each non leaf node that is un-assigned, the encryptor proceeds as follows.

1. If the symbol in the access structure is $\wedge$ and its child nodes are un-assigned, the encryptor selects a random number $s_i \in_R \mathbb{Z}_p, 1 \le s_i \le p - 1$. For the last child node, set $s_j = s - \sum_{i=1}^{j-1} s_i \mod p$. Mark this node assigned.
2. If the symbol in the access structure is $\vee$, the encryptor sets the value of this node to be s and mark this node assigned.
3. The encryptor computes $C_{i,j,1} = \prod_{k \in I_c} (T_{i,j}^k)^{s_i}, C_{i,j,2} = g^{s_i}$.

The encryptor outputs the ciphertext $C_T = (C_1, C_2, \{C_{i,j,1}, C_{i,j,2}\}_{i \in [1,n], j \in [1,n_i]})$.

Decryption: To decrypt the ciphertext C_T, the user computes $E = \prod_{k \in I_c} e(D_1^k, C_2), F = \prod_{k \in I_c} e(D_0^k, C_2), P = e(D_{i,3}^k, C_{i,j,1}), Q = \prod_{k \in I_c} e(D_{i,1}^k, C_2), H = \prod_{k \in I_c} e(D_{i,2}^k, C_{i,j,2})$ and $M = C_1 \cdot \frac{PEF}{QH}$.

Now we prove the correctness of our scheme.

$$E = \prod_{k \in I_c} e(D_1^k, C_2) = \prod_{k \in I_c} e(h_1^{\tau_k + \frac{1}{u+\beta_k}}, g^s) = \prod_{k \in I_c} e(g, h_1)^{s(\tau_k + \frac{1}{u+\beta_k})},$$

$$F = \prod_{k \in I_c} e(D_0^k, C_2) = \prod_{k \in I_c} e(h^{r_k} h_1^{-\tau_k}, g^s) = \prod_{k \in I_c} e(g, h)^{sr_k} e(g, h_1)^{-s\tau_k},$$

$$P = e(D_{i,3}^k, C_{i,j,1}) = e(h^{\omega_i}, \prod_{k \in I_c} g^{s_i t_{i,j}^k}) = e(g, h)^{\sum_{k \in I_c} s_i \omega_i t_{i,j}^k},$$

$$H = \prod_{k \in I_c} e(D_{i,2}^k, C_{i,j,2}) = \prod_{k \in I_c} e(g, h)^{\sum_{k \in I_c} s_i \omega_i t_{i,j}^k},$$

$$Q = \prod_{k \in I_c} e(D_{i,1}^k, C_2) = \prod_{k \in I_c} e(g^{\alpha_k} h^{r_k} h_1^{\frac{1}{u+\beta_k}}, g^s)$$
$$= \prod_{k \in I_c} e(g, g)^{s\alpha_k} e(g, h)^{sr_k} \prod_{k \in I_c} e(g, h_1)^{\frac{s}{u+\beta_k}},$$

$$C_1 \cdot \frac{PEF}{QH} = M \cdot \frac{e(g,h)^{\sum_{k \in I_c} s_i \omega_i t_{i,j}^k} \prod_{k \in I_c} e(g,h_1)^{\frac{s}{u+\beta_k}} e(g,h)^{sr_k} e(g,g)^{s\alpha_k}}{e(g,h)^{\sum_{k \in I_c} s_i \omega_i t_{i,j}^k} \prod_{k \in I_c} e(g,g)^{s\alpha_k} e(g,h)^{sr_k} e(g,h_1)^{\frac{s}{u+\beta_k}}} = M.$$

Theorem 1. *Our decentralized CP-ABE scheme is (Γ, q, ϵ) semantically secure in the selective-set model, if the (Γ', ϵ') DBDH assumption holds in $(e, p, \mathbb{G}, \mathbb{G}_T)$, where*

$$\Gamma' = \Gamma + \mathcal{O}(\Gamma) \quad and \quad \epsilon' = \frac{1}{2}\epsilon.$$

4.2   BlindKeyGen Protocol

The first part of secret keys in the scheme we proposed in section 4.1 is $D_{i,1}^k = g^{\alpha_k} h^{r_k} h_1^{\frac{1}{u+\beta_k}}$. In order to obtain secret keys blindly from authority A_k, the user has to prove his possess of GID u in zero-knowledge. However, if the random number r_k is chosen by authority A_k as the same as we described in section 4.1, then he can compute $h_1^{\frac{1}{u+\beta_k}} = \frac{D_{i,1}^k}{g^{\alpha_k} h^{r_k}}$ or $h_1^{\frac{1}{u+\beta_k}} = \frac{D_1^k}{h_1^r}$. Since h_1 and u are public, β_k is the part of secret key of authority A_k, authority A_k can identify user GID u by computing $h_1^{\frac{1}{u+\beta_k}}$, which is not allowed according to the property selective-failure blindness of protocol **BlindKeyGen**. Therefore, we use the technique 2-party secure computing to generate the random number r_k and τ_k. The protocol **BlindKeyGen** is described as follows.

1. The user U and authority A_k first use the technique 2-party secure computing to generate $\rho_1(u + \beta_k)$, where ρ_1 is a random number selected by user U. They can operate as follows. Firstly, the user U selects $\rho_1 \in_R \mathbb{Z}_p$, computes $x = u\rho_1$, and returns x to the authority A_k. Secondly, authority A_k selects $\rho_3 \in_R \mathbb{Z}_p$, computes $y = \beta_k\rho_3, x' = \rho_3 x$, and returns (x', y) to the user U. Then, user U computes $y' = \rho_1 y$ and returns y' to authority A_k. Authority A_k computes $X = \frac{x'+y'}{\rho_3}$, and then authority A_k selects $\theta, p_1, x_1, x_2, x_3, x_4 \in_R \mathbb{Z}_p$, computes $T = h_1^{\frac{\theta}{X}}, T_1 = g^{\alpha_k\theta}, P_1 = h^{p_1}, Q_1 = h_1^{p_1}, T' = h_1^{x_1}, T_1' = g^{x_2}, P_1' = h^{x_3}$ and $Q_1' = h_1^{x_4}$ and returns $(T, T_1, P_1, Q_1, T', T_1', P_1', Q_1')$ to the user U.
2. User U selects $c \in_R \mathbb{Z}_p$ and returns c to the authority A_k. Authority A_k computes $a_1 = x_1 - c\frac{\theta}{X}, a_2 = x_2 - c\alpha_k\theta, a_3 = x_3 - cp_1, a_4 = x_4 - cp_1$. Authority A_k returns (a_1, a_2, a_3, a_4) to the user U.
3. User U checks whether $T' = h_1^{a_1}T^c, T_1' = g^{a_2}T_1^c, P_1' = h^{a_3}P_1^c$ and $Q_1' = h^{a_4}Q_1^c$. If the equations hold, user U selects $\rho_2, p_2, y_1, y_2, y_3, y_4, y_5, y_6, y_7 \in_R \mathbb{Z}_p$ and computes $T_2 = (T^{\rho_1}T_1)^{\rho_2}, P_2 = h^{p_2}, Q_2 = h_1^{p_2}, T_3 = T^{\rho_1\rho_2}, P = (P_1P_2)^{\rho_2}, Q = (Q_1Q_2)^{\rho_2}, T_2' = T^{y_1}T_1^{y_2}, P_2' = h^{y_3}, Q_2 = h_1^{y_4}, T_3' = T^{y_5}, P' = (P_1P_2)^{y_6}$ and $Q' = (Q_1Q_2)^{y_7}$. The user U returns $(T_2, P_2, Q_2, T_3, P, Q, T_2', P_2', Q_2', T_3', P', Q')$ to the authority A_k. The user U should prove his possess of (ρ_2, p_2) to authority A_k in zero-knowledge.
4. Authority A_k selects $c' \in_R \mathbb{Z}_p$ and returns c' to the user U. User U computes $b_1 = y_1 - c'\rho_1\rho_2, b_2 = y_2 - c'\rho_2, b_3 = y_3 - c'p_2, b_4 = y_4 - c'p_2, b_5 = y_5 - c'\rho_1\rho_2, b_6 = y_6 - c'\rho_2, b_7 = y_7 - c'\rho_2$. User U returns $(b_1, b_2, b_3, b_4, b_5, b_6, b_7)$ to the authority A_k.
5. Authority A_k checks whether $T_2' = T^{b_1}T_1^{b_2}T_2^{c'}, P_2' = h^{b_3}P_2^{c'}, Q_2' = h_1^{b_4}Q_2^{c'}, T_3' = T^{b_5}T_3^{c'}, P' = (P_1P_2)^{b_6}P^{c'}$ and $Q' = (Q_1Q_2)^{b_7}Q^{c'}$. If the equations hold,

then authority A_k selects $r_k, \tau_k, z_1, z_2, z_3, z_4, z_5, z_6 \in_R \mathbb{Z}_p$, $\omega_i, t_i, \eta_i \in_R \mathbb{Z}_p^*$ for $1 \leq i \leq n$ and computes $\tilde{D}_{i,1}^k = T_2^{\frac{1}{\theta}} P^{r_k}, D_{i,2}^k = h^{\omega_i t_{i,j}^k}, D_{i,3}^k = h^{\omega_i}, \tilde{D}_0^k = P^{r_k} Q^{-\tau_k}, \tilde{D}_1^k = T_3^{\frac{1}{\theta}} Q^{\tau_k}, (\tilde{D}_{i,1}^k)' = T_2^{z_1} P^{z_2}, (D_{i,2}^k)' = (D_{i,3}^k)^{\eta_i}, (\tilde{D}_{i,3}^k)' = h^{t_i}, (\tilde{D}_0^k)' = P^{z_3} Q^{-z_4}, (\tilde{D}_1^k)' = T_3^{z_5} Q^{z_6}$ and returns $(\tilde{D}_{i,1}^k, D_{i,2}^k, D_{i,3}^k, \tilde{D}_0^k, \tilde{D}_1^k, (\tilde{D}_{i,1}^k)', (D_{i,2}^k)', (\tilde{D}_{i,3}^k)', (\tilde{D}_0^k)', (\tilde{D}_1^k)')$ to the user U. Here, we replace the random number r_k and τ_k in the original scheme with $(p_1 + p_2) r_k$ and $(p_1 + p_2) \tau_k$, where p_1 is only known to authority A_k and p_2 is only known to user U. Thus malicious authority cannot compute $h_1^{\frac{1}{u+\beta_k}}$ and selectively fail the algorithm.

6. User U selects $c'' \in_R \mathbb{Z}_p$ and returns c'' to the authority A_k. Authority A_k computes $c_1 = z_1 - \frac{c''}{\theta}, c_2 = z_2 - c'' r_k, c_3 = z_3 - c'' r_k, c_4 = z_4 - c'' \tau_k, c_5 = z_5 - \frac{c''}{\theta}, c_6 = z_6 - c'' \tau_k, d_i = \eta_i - c' t_{i,j}^k$ and $e_i = t_i - c' \omega_i$ and returns $(c_1, c_2, c_3, c_4, c_5, c_6, d_i, e_i)$ to user U.

7. User U checks whether $(\tilde{D}_{i,1}^k)' = T_2^{c_1} P^{c_2} (\tilde{D}_{i,1}^k)^{c''}, (D_{i,2}^k)' = (D_{i,3}^k)^{d_i} (D_{i,2}^k)^{c''}, (D_{i,3}^k)' = h^{e_i} (D_{i,3}^k)^{c''}, (\tilde{D}_0^k)' = P^{c_3} Q^{-c_4} (\tilde{D}_0^k)^{c''}$ and $(\tilde{D}_1^k)' = T_3^{c_5} Q^{c_6} (\tilde{D}_1^k)^{c''}$ or not. If the equations hold, user U computes $D_{i,1}^k = (\tilde{D}_{i,1}^k)^{\frac{1}{p_2}}, D_0^k = (\tilde{D}_0^k)^{\frac{1}{p_2}}$ and $D_1^k = (\tilde{D}_1^k)^{\frac{1}{p_2}}$. Otherwise, the algorithm aborts.

Theorem 2. *Our **BlindKeyGen** protocol is leak-free and selective-failure blind.*

4.3   Security and Performance Comparison

We compared our scheme to other schemes [6,19,20] with hidden access structure in Table 1.

Table 1. Security and Performance Comparison

Scheme	Multi-Authority	Anonymity of Access Structure	Access Structure	Security Model	Ciphertext Size
LRZW's scheme [19]	No	Partially hidden	AND-gates on multi-valued attributes with wildcards	Selective-set	Linear
LOSTW's scheme [20]	No	Fully hidden	Inner product predicates	Fully secure	Linear
BK's scheme [6]	No	Fully hidden	AND, OR gates on multi-valued attributes	Selective-set	Linear
Our scheme	Yes	Fully hidden	AND, OR gates on multi-valued attributes	Selective-set	Linear

5   Conclusions

In this paper, we proposed a decentralized CP-ABE with fully hidden access structure. The access structure in our scheme is AND, OR gates on multi-valued attributes. Moreover, we considered user privacy from two aspects. On one hand, the access structure in our scheme is fully hidden, so intermediate user can get nothing about user attributes and policy from the access structure. On the other hand, malicious authorities cannot collaborate to collect user attributes by tracing user GID. The security of our scheme is proved under a standard DBDH complexity assumption.

Acknowledgement. This work is supported by the National Natural Science Foundation of China (60842002, 61272542, 61103183, 61103184), the Fundamental Research Funds for the Central Universities(2013B07014, 2010B07114), the Six Talent Peaks Program of Jiangsu Province of China (2009182) and Program for New Century Excellent Talents in Hohai University.

References

1. Sahai, A., Waters, B.: Fuzzy Identity-Based Encryption. In: Cramer, R. (ed.) EUROCRYPT 2005. LNCS, vol. 3494, pp. 457–473. Springer, Heidelberg (2005)
2. Goyal, V., Pandey, O., Sahai, A., Waters, B.: Attribute-Based Encryption for Fine-Grained Access Control of Encrypted Data. In: Juels, A., Wright, R.N., di Vimercati, S.D.C. (eds.) CCS 2006. Proc. ACM Conf. Computer and Communications Security, pp. 89–98 (2006)
3. Bethencourt, J., Sahai, A., Waters, B.: Ciphertext-Policy Attribute-Based Encryption. In: SP 2007. IEEE Symposium on Security and Privacy, pp. 321–334 (2007)
4. Ostrovsky, R., Sahai, A., Waters, B.: Attribute-Based Encryption with Non-Monotonic Access Structures. In: Ning, P., di Vimercati, S.D.C., Syverson, P.F. (eds.) CCS 2007. Proc. ACM Conf. Computer and Communications Security, pp. 195–203 (2007)
5. Cheung, L., Newport, C.: Provably Secure Ciphertext Policy ABE. In: Ning, P., di Vimercati, S.D.C., Syverson, P.F. (eds.) CCS 2007. Proc. ACM Conf. Computer and Comm. Security, pp. 456–465 (2007)
6. Balu, A., Kuppusamy, K.: Privacy Preserving Ciphertext Policy Attribute Based Encryption. In: Meghanathan, N., Boumerdassi, S., Chaki, N., Nagamalai, D. (eds.) CNSA 2010. CCIS, vol. 89, pp. 402–409. Springer, Heidelberg (2010)
7. Boneh, D., Waters, B.: Conjunctive, Subset, and Range Queries on Encrypted Data. In: Vadhan, S.P. (ed.) TCC 2007. LNCS, vol. 4392, pp. 535–554. Springer, Heidelberg (2007)
8. Nishide, T., Yoneyama, K., Ohta, K.: Attribute-Based Encryption with Partially Hidden Encryptor-Specified Access Structures. In: Bellovin, S.M., Gennaro, R., Keromytis, A.D., Yung, M. (eds.) ACNS 2008. LNCS, vol. 5037, pp. 111–129. Springer, Heidelberg (2008)
9. Lai, J., Deng, R.H., Li, Y.: Expressive CP-ABE with Partially Hidden Access Structures. In: Youm, H.Y., Won, Y. (eds.) ASIACCS 2012. Proc. ACM Conf. Computer and Communications Security, pp. 18–19 (2012)

10. Chase, M.: Multi-Authority Attribute Based Encryption. In: Vadhan, S.P. (ed.) TCC 2007. LNCS, vol. 4392, pp. 515–534. Springer, Heidelberg (2007)
11. Chase, M., Chow, S.S.M.: Improving Privacy and Security in Multi-Authority Attribute-Based Encryption. In: Al-Shaer, E., Jha, S., Keromytis, A.D. (eds.) CCS 2909. Proc. ACM Conf. Computer and Comm. Security, pp. 121–130 (2009)
12. Lewko, A., Waters, B.: Decentralizing Attribute-Based Encryption. In: Paterson, K.G. (ed.) EUROCRYPT 2011. LNCS, vol. 6632, pp. 568–588. Springer, Heidelberg (2011)
13. Han, J., Susilo, W., Mu, Y., Yan, J.: Privacy-Preserving Decentralized Key-Policy Attribute-Based Encryption. IEEE Transantions on Parallel and Distributed System 23(11), 2150–2162 (2012), Nayak, A. (ed.)
14. Boneh, D., Boyen, X.: Efficient Selective-ID Secure Identity-Based Encryption Without Random Oracles. In: Cachin, C., Camenisch, J.L. (eds.) EUROCRYPT 2004. LNCS, vol. 3027, pp. 223–238. Springer, Heidelberg (2004)
15. Beimel, A.: Secure Schemes for Secret Sharing and Key Distribution. PHD thesis, Israel Inst. of Technology, Technion, Haifa, Israel (1996)
16. Pedersen, T.P.: Non-Interactive and Information-Theoretic Secure Verifiable Secret Sharing. In: Feigenbaum, J. (ed.) CRYPTO 1991. LNCS, vol. 576, pp. 129–140. Springer, Heidelberg (1992)
17. Camenisch, J., Stadler, M.: Efficient Group Signature Schemes for Large Groups. In: Kaliski Jr., B.S. (ed.) CRYPTO 1997. LNCS, vol. 1294, pp. 410–424. Springer, Heidelberg (1997)
18. Green, M., Hohenberger, S.: Blind Identity-Based Encryption and Simulatable Oblivious Transfer. In: Kurosawa, K. (ed.) ASIACRYPT 2007. LNCS, vol. 4833, pp. 265–282. Springer, Heidelberg (2007)
19. Li, J., Ren, K., Zhu, B., Wan, Z.: Privacy-Aware Attribute-Based Encryption with User Accountability. In: Samarati, P., Yung, M., Martinelli, F., Ardagna, C.A. (eds.) ISC 2009. LNCS, vol. 5735, pp. 347–362. Springer, Heidelberg (2009)
20. Lewko, A.B., Okamoto, T., Sahai, A., Takashima, K., Waters, B.: Fully Secure Functional Encryption: Attribute-Based Encryption and (Hierarchical) Inner Product Encryption. In: Gilbert, H. (ed.) EUROCRYPT 2010. LNCS, vol. 6110, pp. 62–91. Springer, Heidelberg (2010)

Toward Generic Method
for Server-Aided Cryptography

Sébastien Canard[1], Iwen Coisel[2], Julien Devigne[1,3], Cécilia Gallais[4],
Thomas Peters[5], and Olivier Sanders[1,6]

[1] Orange Labs - Applied Crypto Group
42 rue des coutures - 14000 CAEN - France
[2] European Commission - Joint Research Centre (JRC)
Institute for the Protection and the Security of the Citizen - Digital Citizen Security
21027 ISPRA (VA) - Italy
[3] Université de Caen Basse-Normandie - Laboratoire GREYC
Esplanade de la Paix - 14000 Caen - France
[4] Tevalis
80 av. des Buttes de Cosmes - 35700 Rennes - France
[5] Université catholique de Louvain - ICTEAM/Crypto Group
1348 Louvain-la-Neuve - Belgium
[6] Ecole Normale Supérieure - Département d'Informatique
45 rue dUlm - 75230 Paris Cedex 05 - France

Abstract. Portable devices are very useful to access services from anywhere at any time. However, when the security underlying the service
requires complex cryptography, implying the execution of several costly
mathematical operations, these devices may become inadequate because
of their limited capabilities. In this case, it is desirable to adapt the way
to use cryptography. One possibility, which has been widely studied in
many particular cases, is to propose a server-aided version of the executed
cryptographic algorithm, where some well-chosen parts of the algorithm
are delegated to a more powerful entity. As far as we know, nothing
has been done to generically change a given well-known secure instance
of a cryptographic primitive in its initial form to a secure server-aided
version where the server (called the intermediary) may be corrupted by
the adversary. In this paper, we propose an almost generic method to
simplify the work of the operator who wants to construct this secure
server-aided instance. In particular, we take into account the efficiency
of the resulting server-aided instance by giving the best possible way to
separate the different tasks of the instance so that the resulting time
efficiency is optimal. Our methodology can be applied to most of public
key cryptographic schemes.

1 Introduction

Constrained devices (*e.g.* mobile phones, smart cards or RFIDs) are more and
more used in our daily life. Practical applications may require them to execute
cryptographic algorithms. However, in return for their low-cost, these devices are

S. Qing et al. (Eds.): ICICS 2013, LNCS 8233, pp. 373–392, 2013.

generally resource constrained and/or do not implement all the necessary mathematical/cryptographic tools to perform such executions. This is not a major drawback in protocols requiring a low user's workload, but it can become appalling for some modern and complex protocols allying contradictory properties (such as anonymity and accountability, or confidentiality and sharing). Then, some applications may not be developed if the time taken by a device to execute required operations is too long. Thus, cryptographic protocols sometimes need to be further studied when executed in such environments. One solution is to use preprocessing (see *e.g.* [30]) which permits some data to be computed in advance so that the whole algorithm does not require heavy computation to be efficiently executed. This has the drawback of consuming a lot of space memory and may not be applicable all the time. Another possibility is to modify the cryptographic mechanism to fit the device restrictions. This has already been done in the RFID case [18,26] or when considering the integration of *e.g.* group and ring signatures in a smart card [10,32]. This approach sometimes necessitates important modifications of the initial algorithm, and may imply some stronger (and questionable!) assumptions such as *e.g.* the tamper-resistance one.

This paper focus on the approach which consists in speeding up the cryptographic operation by delegating a substantial part of computations to a more powerful entity, generally called a server or an *intermediary*.

RELATED WORK. Many papers in the literature propose a way to outsource cryptographic operations to servers. Regarding efficiency, the result should be more efficient than the non-server-aided execution. Regarding security, the possibility to corrupt the intermediary should be taken into account in the server-aided version. This work has been done *e.g.* in the case of RSA [25,5], where the aim is to help the restricted device to perform a modular exponentiation with an RSA modulus[1], or in the case of the signature/authentication verification [23,19], for several existing schemes. Multi-party computation techniques (see *e.g.* [33]) permit several entities to jointly compute a function over their inputs, while each entity keeps its own input secret.

When dealing with more complicated protocols, especially those dealing with anonymity, a lot of research has also been carried out. For group signature schemes [12], Maitland and Boyd [24] and then Canard *et al.* [9] proposed variants of existing schemes where the group member is helped by some semi-trusted entity to produce a group signature. This trick is also part of the Direct Anonymous Attestation framework (see *e.g.* [8,13]).

Another approach, called *wallet with observers*, has been taken in the CAFE project [11,16]. Here, a powerful prover interacts with a non-trusted smart card to perform some computations, such that the prover is unlinkable *w.r.t.* the smart card.

Hohenberger and Lysyanskaya [20] have proposed a new security model where the server is necessarily split into two different components. For signature/authentication schemes, Girault and Lefranc [19] have given the theory for

---

[1] Even if most of them have later been broken [29,28,27].

server-aided verification. However, nothing has been done to generically transform a given secure instance of a cryptographic primitive in its initial form into a secure server-aided version where the server may be corrupted by the adversary. Such a transformation permits creating automatically the previous systems, with a potentially more efficient outcome.

OUR CONTRIBUTION. In this paper, we provide an almost generic method to simplify the work of an operator for the above problem. More precisely, we focus on an entity $\mathcal{E}_0$ and its execution of a cryptographic algorithm ALG_0 underlying a secure instance of a cryptographic primitive. We first divide $\mathcal{E}_0$ into two roles: a trusted entity $\mathcal{T}$ which manages the inputs of ALG_0 but is not necessarily powerful (typically a smart card or a PC) and an intermediary $\mathcal{I}$ which is not necessarily trusted but is considered as more powerful (typically a mobile phone or a cloud server). Our aim is then to produce a secure server-aided variant which is as efficient as possible.

We first focus on the data manipulated inside ALG_0. All the inputs and outputs of the algorithm are known by $\mathcal{E}_0$ and, as we trust it, by $\mathcal{T}$ too. Regarding $\mathcal{I}$, this may be different since it depends on the possibility of corruption of $\mathcal{I}$ by the adversary (who can passively listen to the interactions between $\mathcal{T}$ and $\mathcal{I}$, can obtain the data given to $\mathcal{I}$ or can corrupt $\mathcal{I}$). Our method allows the operator to choose the power of the adversary on each expected security property, and automatically outputs, for most of manipulated data, whether this data can be *known* or *unknown* (called the status of the data) to $\mathcal{I}$.

We then consider the studied algorithm ALG_0 as a set of tasks. Then, depending on the status of the inputs and outputs, we decide whether each task can be performed by $\mathcal{T}$ alone, $\mathcal{I}$ alone or by both (using some well-known server-aided computations).

We finally provide an algorithm which outputs the best possible secure variant, depending on the time performances of both $\mathcal{T}$ and $\mathcal{I}$. All along the paper, we use as a running example the case of group signatures (to make a comparison with the work in [9]) but our method can also be applied to most existing cryptographic primitives.

ORGANIZATION OF THE PAPER. The next section describes our framework and introduces the notion of intermediary. Section 3 describes how one can fill in the data status table according to the chosen security. Section 4 defines task statuses and explains how one can determine them. Section 5 is devoted to the description of the way to efficiently distribute the computations.

2 Background and Definitions

All along the paper, any entity is denoted using calligraphic typography (e.g. $\mathcal{E}$), an object or a data using sans font typography (e.g. d), algorithm using small capital letters (e.g. ALG), list using true type typography (e.g. `list`), and sets using greek letters (e.g. Ω). A task is always denoted t.

When a single entity is required to perform a procedure, it is generally called an algorithm, whereas it is called a protocol when interactions between several entities are required. However, protocols can be split into as many parts (algorithms) executed by a single entity as needed. We thus only focus on the notion of algorithm in the following.

2.1 Definitions

NOTION OF PRIMITIVE. A *cryptographic primitive* Π describes the main guidelines of a cryptographic application. Informally, a primitive Π is defined by a set Ξ of entities, a set Ω of objects, a set $\Lambda = \{\text{ALG}_1, \ldots, \text{ALG}_v\}$ of algorithms and a set Σ of security properties. An instance of a given primitive Π is a precise description of all the algorithms and the associated objects which ensure the security properties of Π. We consider in the following that each algorithm is realized thanks to a sequence of *tasks*, defined below.

CONSIDERED TASKS. The instance of an algorithm ALG_i is a set of tasks, denoted Θ_i, related to cryptographic or mathematical operations, that formally describes how to reach the output of the focused algorithm, denoted out, from its input, denoted inp. In this paper, we group these tasks by types which are assigned an identifier: (1) pseudo-random generation (*e.g.* $r \in_R \mathbb{Z}_p^*$), (2) multilinear combination evaluation (*e.g.* $s = a \cdot b + c$), (3) exponentiation evaluation (*e.g.* $T = g^x$), (4) group operation (*e.g.* $z = g \cdot h$), (5) pairing evaluation (*e.g.* $h = e(P, Q)$), (6) hash function evaluation (*e.g.* $\text{hash}(m)$) and (7) communication. This list is totally arbitrary and our generic transformation still works if other types of tasks are introduced. As an example, exponentiations in a *regular* finite field and in an elliptic curve group might be considered as two different tasks while leading to the same result.

THE DATA. In an instance π of a primitive Π, data can come from two different ways. Some of them represent the objects of the primitive, and so inputs and outputs of the algorithms. But there are also data used as "intermediate values" within a sequence of tasks of a given algorithm. The former data are called *intrinsic*, while the latter data are called *ephemeral*.

DEFINITION OF AN INSTANCE. To sum up, an instance π of a primitive Π is defined by a set $\Theta = \bigcup_i^v \Theta_i$ of tasks, a set $\Phi = \bigcup_i^v \Phi_i$ of *intrinsic data* and a set $\Psi = \bigcup_i^v \Psi_i$ of *ephemeral data*, where each subset is related to one specific algorithm ALG_i. In the following, $\text{ALG}_i(\mathcal{E}, \text{inp}) = \text{out}$ denotes that the (intrinsic) data contained in out $\in \Phi$ have been obtained by the execution of the algorithm ALG_i by the entity $\mathcal{E}$ using the data contained in inp $\in \Phi$ as inputs.

2.2 Our Running Example: Group Signatures

In the group signature primitive [12], the set of entities is composed of one group manager (sometimes called the issuer), several group members, one opener and several verifiers. In this primitive, any member of a group can sign messages on behalf of the group. Such signatures remain anonymous and unlinkable for anyone except a designated authority, the opener, who has the ability to identify the signer. Anyone, called in this case a verifier, can check the validity of a group signature. The objects related to this primitive are the issuer, members, and opener keys as well as all the possible messages (generally defined by a message space). Following [6], such primitive is composed of 7 procedures called SETUP (to compute secret keys and public parameters), USERKG (for users), JOIN (a protocol for users to become group members), GSIGN (for the production of a group signature), GVERIFY (for the verification step), OPEN (for anoymity revocation) and JUDGE (for the public verification of an anonymity revocation). An interested reader may refer to *e.g.* [6] for details.

2.3 Our Method in a Nutshell

Let π_0 be a particular instance (*e.g.* XSGS [17]) of a given primitive Π_0 (*e.g.* group signature scheme). Let Θ_i be an instance of one particular algorithm ALG$_0$ (*e.g.* the GSIGN algorithm) which is executed by the entity $\mathcal{E}_0$ (*e.g.* a group member). This task description is called the *initial version* of the algorithm. Our aim is to improve its time complexity without compromising the security of π_0, or in a controlled way.

In the literature, the notion of server-aided cryptography is most of the time related to the split of an entity $\mathcal{E}_0$ into two components, namely a trusted entity, denoted[2] $\mathcal{T}$, which manages all inputs of the algorithm, and an intermediary[3], denoted $\mathcal{I}$ with which $\mathcal{T}$ can interact and delegate some of his workload. We will speak in this case of a *server-aided version* of the algorithm. From one initial version of the instance π_0, it is possible to design several secure server-aided versions $\overline{\pi}_0^{(1)}, \overline{\pi}_0^{(2)}, \ldots$.

To decide which one is the most efficient, we first need to decide which data (intrinsic or ephemeral) can be given to the intermediary. This is done in accordance with the security properties of the studied primitive Π_0 (see Section 3). Then, depending on this result, we focus (in Section 4) on each task of ALG$_0$ and try to say whether it can be executed by $\mathcal{T}$ alone, $\mathcal{I}$ alone, and/or cooperatively (both $\mathcal{T}$ and $\mathcal{I}$ participate in its execution). This leads to a bunch of different secure repartitions. Our method finally outputs the most efficient one according to the performances of $\mathcal{T}$ and $\mathcal{I}$ (see Section 5).

3   Status of the Data

Our methodology is in particular based on the definition of a status for each manipulated data. In this section, we define the status of a data *w.r.t.* an entity of an instance. Then, we adapt the adversary against the server-aided instance in the security properties.

---

[2] We should have used the notation $\mathcal{T}_{\mathcal{E}_0}$ but, as it is not ambiguous, we simplify it.
[3] $\mathcal{I}$ is not necessarily a new entity in the system but can be in fact seen as a new role played by one existing entity.

3.1 Data Status and Intermediary

Traditionally in cryptography, some data are said *secret*, and some others are said *public*. This can be formalized by the notion of *known* data *w.r.t.* a specific entity, and we argue that this is enough to handle all possible cases. On the one hand, the status of a data is secret if an entity is the only one to *know* it. On the other hand, its status is public if all involved entities know such data. It also permits to formalize intermediate cases where a data is known by several entities, but not all. By the way, the only relevant status in our case is that of *known* data.

Let $\Pi = (\Xi, \Omega, \Lambda, \Sigma)$ be a primitive and let $\pi = (\Theta, \Phi, \Psi)$ be an instance of Π. The security properties verified by π determine the status of each intrinsic data *w.r.t.* the different entities. The status of an ephemeral data $\mathsf{ed} \in \Psi$ is known by an entity $\mathcal{E}$, denoted $\mathsf{st}_{\mathcal{E}}[\mathsf{ed}] = \mathsf{kn}$, if ed is an output of an elementary task t run by $\mathcal{E}$ for which the inputs are all known by $\mathcal{E}$. Otherwise the status of the data is unknown (noted ukn).

Now let us consider an algorithm ALG_0, executed by an entity $\mathcal{E}_0$, the status of intrinsic (Φ_0) and ephemeral (Ψ_0) data are thus known *w.r.t.* this entity. Now, if $\mathcal{E}_0$ is divided into the two entities $\mathcal{T}$ and $\mathcal{I}$, we should focus on the status of intrinsic data *w.r.t.* $\mathcal{I}$ since it follows from our above choices that the status of these data *w.r.t.* $\mathcal{T}$ is necessarily *known*.

SECURITY EXPERIMENT AND ADVERSARIES. Let us consider a security property, denoted secu, expected by the primitive Π. We assume that the studied instance π verifies this security property. We thus need to clearly describe the server-aided security property $\overline{\mathsf{secu}}$ expected by a server-aided execution of the primitive Π. We recall that $\mathcal{I}$ is only implicated in the execution of the ALG_0 procedure.

Since $\mathcal{T}$ and $\mathcal{I}$ are two distinct entities, possible corruption of $\mathcal{I}$ by an adversary must be taken into account, while we assume all along this paper that $\mathcal{T}$ is never corrupted (if $\mathcal{E}_0$ is not). We should then modify the related security experiments accordingly. First, we give the following definition which states the possible strategies given to the adversary against a server-aided version of π.

Definition 1 (server-aided adversary). *Let* $\overline{\mathsf{secu}}$ *be a security property related to a server-aided instance* $\overline{\pi}$. *Let* $\mathcal{A}$ *be an adversary against* $\overline{\mathsf{secu}}$ *in the server-aided setting. For the related experiment, an adversary is said to have the power of a*

- listener-receiver *if* $\mathcal{A}$ *can obtain all the communication between* $\mathcal{T}$ *and* $\mathcal{I}$ *and is given access to all the data known by* $\mathcal{I}$.
- controller *if* $\mathcal{A}$ *totally controls* $\mathcal{I}$.

It is obvious that a *controller* is necessarily *listener-receiver*. Then, there are three different types of adversary to study: *standard* (with no extra power), *listener-receiver* and *controller*.

DEALING WITH SEVERAL SECURITY PROPERTIES. In most of the complex cryptographic primitives, several security properties are required at the same time (see the example of group signatures in Section 2.2). In order to build a server-aided instance with an improved efficiency it can make sense to relax some of them in regards of the intermediary, while the others are preserved[4].

Several server-aided instances of the initial instance π can thus be generated depending of the combinations of desired properties. For example: the adversary may *e.g.* be standard for the server-aided security property $\overline{\text{secu}}_1$ but controller for $\overline{\text{secu}}_2$.

3.2   Filling the Data Status Table

We should now make the link between the security properties and the status of all the data manipulated in ALG_0.

GENERIC OR NOT GENERIC. Again, our aim is to design a generic autonomous (as possible) method to obtain the best secure server-aided variant of a secure instance. In fact, from the security point of view, it seems hard to completely automate our work.

One solution is to make use of some formal analysis dedicated to cryptographic protocols, such as the (non exhaustive) work given in [7,1,3,4]. For this purpose, we first need to precisely formalize the operations available to the adversary. We then make use of the description of the experiment, depending on the power of the adversary (see above) and execute formal methods to find a way for the adversary to break the security, using its available operations as defined above. This execution is done several times by having the status of all the data vary. Finally, each set of data status which leads to "no attack" by formal analysis can be given to the next step of the procedure (with the deletion of some redundant choices). Such work requires a complete and deep study and it is not our aim in this paper to study this independent research topic.

Another possibility is to ask an operator to perform such choice(s). We give him the new experiment and ask him on output the status of all data. We then assume that such output is good regarding security.

In the following, we have chosen a compromise between the two. We have succeeded, using some results given below, in simplifying the work of this operator by automatically treating some cases. The way we assign a status to each task depends on their nature (intrinsic or ephemeral) and their type.

STATUS OF INTRINSIC DATA. Informally, we do not want that a non-standard adversary uses his extra power to get access to more data than the adversary in the original security experiment. We then use the following result.

Definition 2. *Let* $\Sigma = \{\text{secu}[1], ..., \text{secu}[t]\}$ *be the security properties ensured by* π. *For all* $i \in I = [1, t]$, Δ_i *is the set of all intrinsic data known by* $\mathcal{A}_i$, *the*

---

[4] In [9], the authors argue that the anonymity property may be relaxed *w.r.t.* the intermediary as this latter may already know the identity of $\mathcal{T}$, while it should not be able to produce a group signature without the help of $\mathcal{T}$, and thus break the traceability property.

adversary of the security experiment defining secu[i]. *Let* $\overline{\mathcal{A}_i}$ *be the adversary against* $\overline{secu}[i]$ *in the server-aided setting. We define* $\Delta = \bigcap_{i \in I} \Delta_i$ *where* $i \in I$ *if* $\overline{\mathcal{A}_i}$ *has extra power (i.e. has the power of a listener-receiver or a controller).*

We then consider that an intrinsic data d is stated as known to $\mathcal{I}$ iff $d \in \Delta$. We illustrate this method in Section 3.3 using the XSGS group signature scheme given in [17].

STATUS OF EPHEMERAL DATA. A server-aided version should not compromise the security of the instance π. One way is to make use of a strong notion, related to the zero-knowledge property used for proofs of knowledge.

Definition 3. : *A server-aided version* $\overline{\pi}$ *of an instance* π *is said to be*

- listener-receiver secure iff *there exists a simulator* $\mathcal{S}$, *whose inputs are known intrinsic data, such that the output of* $\mathcal{S}$ *is computationally indistinguishable from the view of the real communications between* $\mathcal{T}$ *and (a non-controller)* $\mathcal{I}$.
- controller secure iff, *for any intermediary* $\mathcal{I}^*$, *there exists a simulator* $\mathcal{S}_{\mathcal{I}^*}$, *whose inputs are known intrinsic data, such that the output of* $\mathcal{S}_{\mathcal{I}^*}$ *is computationally indistinguishable from the view of the real communications between* $\mathcal{T}$ *and* $\mathcal{I}^*$.

Definition 4. *Let* Π *be a primitive and* π *an initial instance of* Π *ensuring* $\Sigma = \{secu[1], ..., secu[t]\}$. *Let* secuvec *be a vector of length* t, *defining the class of each adversary* $\mathcal{A}_i$, *such that for all* $i \in [1, t]$, secuvec[i] $\in \{standard, listener-receiver, controller\}$. *Let* $\overline{\pi}$ *be a server-aided version of the instance* π. *The server-aided instance* $\overline{\pi}$ *is a* secuvec *secure server-aided version of* π *if for all* $i \in [1, t]$ *such that* secuvec[i] $\neq$ standard, $\overline{\pi}$ *is* secuvec[i] *secure.*

The next result helps for a partial automation of the filling of the data status table.

Lemma 1. *Let* Π *be a primitive and* π *an initial instance of* Π *ensuring* $\Sigma = \{secu[1], ..., secu[t]\}$. *If* $\overline{\pi}$ *is a* secuvec *secure server-aided version of the instance* π *then* $\overline{\pi}$ *ensures* $\overline{\Sigma} = \{\overline{secu}[1], ..., \overline{secu}[t]\}$.

Proof. First, let $\overline{\mathcal{A}_i}$ be a standard adversary against $\overline{secu}[i]$. Since it does not have access to the data given to $\mathcal{I}$ and cannot listen to the communication between $\mathcal{T}$ and $\mathcal{I}$, it is equivalent to an adversary against the initial security property secu[i]. Thus the security of the initial instance implies the security of the server-aided instance $\overline{\pi}$.

Now we consider $\overline{\mathcal{A}_i}$, a non-standard adversary against $\overline{secu}[i]$. We recall that the status of intrinsic data are known to $\mathcal{I}$ iff they are known by any adversary $\mathcal{A}$ of the security properties verified by π. Since we assume the existence of $\mathcal{S}$ which is able, using these known intrinsic data, to simulate the communications between $\mathcal{T}$ and $\mathcal{I}$, we do not give more information to the adversary than in the original experiment. Thus, the security of the initial instance implies the one of the server-aided version. □

One can argue that we could reach the security property $\overline{\text{secu}}$ without this strong "zero-knowledge" requirement. Indeed, in some experiments, if we allow the adversary to get access to some additional information, we can get a more efficient repartition of the tasks without endangering the security of π. Yet it then seems hard to guarantee the security of π without asking the operator which ephemeral data can be stated as known.

In practice, the way our algorithm assigns status to each ephemeral data depends on the type of task in which it is involved. For example, if a secret data is involved in a multi-linear combination then another data involved in the same task has to be set as *unknown w.r.t.* $\mathcal{I}$. Now, if we consider a hash function evaluation we could consider the output as *known*, regardless of the status of the inputs. We still refer to Section 3.3 for a more explicit example.

CONCLUSIONS. The filling of the data status table by the operator is done by first choosing the security vector **secuvec**, enabling him to determine Δ, the set of intrinsic data known by $\mathcal{I}$. Then he runs our algorithm that will automatically assign a status to most of the ephemeral data. Finally, the operator just has to indicate the status of the non treated ephemeral data, using the security notions given in Definition 3.

3.3   Example of Group Signatures

Let us consider the XSGS group signature scheme given in [17,9] and we focus on the data. The whole GSIGN algorithm is given in Figure 1.

Group signature scheme [17] - $\text{GSIGN}(\mathsf{m}, \mathsf{gsk}[i] = (A, x, y))$					
$t_1.$	$\alpha_1 \in_R \mathbb{Z}_p^*$	$t_{15}.$	$r_1 \in_R \mathbb{Z}_p^*$	$t_{29}.$	$t_5'' = y_2^{-r_8}$
$t_2.$	$\beta_1 \in_R \mathbb{Z}_p^*$	$t_{16}.$	$r_2 \in_R \mathbb{Z}_p^*$	$t_{30}.$	$t_5 = t_5' \cdot t_5''$
$t_3.$	$\alpha_2 \in_R \mathbb{Z}_p^*$	$t_{17}.$	$r_3 \in_R \mathbb{Z}_p^*$	$t_{31}.$	$t_6 = T_3^{r_5}$
$t_4.$	$\beta_2 \in_R \mathbb{Z}_p^*$	$t_{18}.$	$r_4 \in_R \mathbb{Z}_p^*$	$t_{32}.$	$e_1 = e(t_6, g_2)$
$t_5.$	$\gamma_1 = \alpha_1 + \beta_1$	$t_{19}.$	$r_5 \in_R \mathbb{Z}_p^*$	$t_{33}.$	$t_7 = e(y_1, \Gamma)^{-r_7}$
$t_6.$	$\gamma_2 = \alpha_2 + \beta_2$	$t_{20}.$	$r_6 \in_R \mathbb{Z}_p^*$	$t_{34}.$	$t_7' = e(y_1, g_2)^{-r_6}$
$t_7.$	$T_1 = g^{\alpha_1}$	$t_{21}.$	$z = \gamma_1 \cdot x + y$	$t_{35}.$	$t_8 = e_1 \cdot t_7 \cdot t_7'$
$t_8.$	$T_2 = g'^{\beta_1}$	$t_{22}.$	$r_7 = r_1 + r_2$	$t_{36}.$	$c = \mathcal{H}(\mathsf{m}\|T_1\| \dots \|T_6\|t_1\| \dots \|t_8)$
$t_9.$	$T_3' = y_1^{\gamma_1}$	$t_{23}.$	$r_8 = r_3 + r_4$	$t_{37}.$	$s_1 = r_1 + c \cdot \alpha_1 \pmod p$
$t_{10}.$	$T_3 = A \cdot T_3'$	$t_{24}.$	$t_1 = g^{r_1}$	$t_{38}.$	$s_2 = r_2 + c \cdot \beta_1 \pmod p$
$t_{11}.$	$T_4 = g^{\alpha_2}$	$t_{25}.$	$t_2 = g'^{r_2}$	$t_{39}.$	$s_3 = r_3 + c \cdot \alpha_2 \pmod p$
$t_{12}.$	$T_5 = g'^{\beta_2}$	$t_{26}.$	$t_3 = g^{r_3}$	$t_{40}.$	$s_4 = r_4 + c \cdot \beta_2 \pmod p$
$t_{13}.$	$T_6' = y_2^{\gamma_2}$	$t_{27}.$	$t_4 = g'^{r_4}$	$t_{41}.$	$s_5 = r_5 + c \cdot x \pmod p$
$t_{14}.$	$T_6 = A \cdot T_6'$	$t_{28}.$	$t_5' = y_1^{r_7}$	$t_{42}.$	$s_6 = r_6 + c \cdot z \pmod p$
Output: $\sigma = (T_1, T_2, T_3, T_4, T_5, T_6, c, s_1, s_2, s_3, s_4, s_5, s_6)$					

Fig. 1. The XSGS GSIGN algorithm [17,9]

DEALING WITH SECURITY PROPERTIES. The security properties required from a group signature scheme [6] are: correctness, traceability, anonymity and non-frameability. We consider a standard adversary against the correctness and listener-receiver against traceability and non-frameability. We use, as in [9], the relaxed anonymity property $w.r.t.$ the intermediary since it has other ways to identify the signature issued by $\mathcal{E}_0$, and then consider a standard adversary against the anonymity. Using the above order for security properties we then set the corresponding security vector to secuvec $=$ [standard, listener-receiver, standard, listener-receiver].

STATUS OF INTRINSIC DATA. We now have to determine Δ using Definition 2. The status of most of the intrinsic data is obvious since the adversaries of the different security experiments have access to the public parameters $(g, g', ...)$, the message (m) and the group signature. We thus have:

$$\{g, g', y_1, y_2, \Gamma, g_2, e(y_1, \Gamma), e(y_1, g_2), m, T_1, T_2, T_3, T_4, T_5, T_6, c, s_1, s_2, s_3, s_4, s_5, s_6\} \subset \Delta.$$

Now let consider the user's key: $\mathcal{A}, x, y$. We have chosen non-standard adversaries for the traceability and non-frameability, the status of the user's key only depends on the knowledge of the adversaries of these experiments. Since the issuer is adversary-controlled in both experiments, the adversaries know A and x and thus we have: $\{A, x\} \subset \Delta$. The only intrinsic data that has to remain unknown to $\mathcal{I}$ is then y.

STATUS OF EPHEMERAL DATA. Once the status of each intrinsic data is set, the operator runs the algorithm SETSTATUSDATA, described in Section 5, which outputs $st_{\mathcal{I}}[\{r_6, z\}] = ukn$ and $st_{\mathcal{I}}[\Psi_0 \setminus \{r_6, z\}] = kn$.

4   Status of a Task

We will now focus on each task of the studied algorithm ALG_0 and decide which entity(ies) can execute it. For this purpose, each task of the algorithm is characterized by a status. More precisely, let us consider independently each task $t_i \in \Theta$ of the procedure ALG_0. We focus on the inputs and outputs of t_i and make use of the data status which has been stated as explained in the previous section.

4.1   Execution of a Task by the Intermediary

Based on the data status table, there are initially two cases that can be seen as trivial.

1. All input and output data of t_i are known to $\mathcal{I}$: for obvious reasons, this task may be executed by either $\mathcal{T}$ or the intermediary $\mathcal{I}$. We denote such case $st(t_i) = 1$.

2. At least one output data of t_i is not known to $\mathcal{I}$: we first consider that t_i is executed by $\mathcal{T}$ and we say that the status of t_i is 0, which is denoted $\text{st}(t_i) = 0$. However, depending on the existence of a cooperative version of this task, this status could be changed (see Section 4.2).

MULTIPLICITY OF THE CHOICES. One important thing is that a task with status 1 will not necessarily be executed by $\mathcal{I}$. Indeed, we consider that it can be either executed by $\mathcal{T}$ or by $\mathcal{I}$. Our main objective is to determine the best possible server-aided instance, which may include a task that can be executed by $\mathcal{I}$ will possibly be executed by $\mathcal{T}$ (if the latter has nothing more to do during enough time for example). This will be taken into account in our main method below.

We now try to do better by searching in the literature some tasks where $\mathcal{I}$ can help $\mathcal{T}$ even if some of the manipulated data are secret.

4.2 Server-Aided Execution of a Task

There are numerous papers about outsourcing some specific cryptographic tasks (for example [25,5,20,31,2]). We here talk about a "cooperative" execution of a task.

COOPERATIVE EXECUTION OF A TASK. We have previously made some choices regarding the set Θ of tasks. Then, for each type of task in Θ, we can say whether it exists in the literature a way to execute such task cooperatively or not, depending on the status of the different inputs and outputs. For example, the authors of [15,14] provide a method to compute $e(A, B)$ when A and B are secret. Appendix A lists some existing cooperative methods for the tasks in Θ. In the following, the database `CoopMeth` contains the status of each task depending on the status of the inputted and outputted data.

4.3 Status of a Task

Using the above results, we can now formally define the status of a task.

Definition 5 (status of a task). *Let $\Pi = (\Xi, \Omega, \Lambda, \Sigma)$ be a primitive and let $\pi = (\Theta, \Phi, \Psi)$ be an instance of Π. The status of a task $t \in \Theta$ is defined as $\text{st}[t] = 0$ if t has to be executed by $\mathcal{T}$; $\text{st}[t] = 1$ if t can be executed by either $\mathcal{T}$ or $\mathcal{I}$; $\text{st}[t] = \star$ if t can be executed cooperatively, or by $\mathcal{T}$ alone; $\text{st}[t] = 1\star$ if t can be executed cooperatively, or by $\mathcal{I}$ or $\mathcal{T}$ alone; $\text{st}[t] = 2$ if t should be entirely executed by $\mathcal{I}$.*

The last item ($\text{st}[t] = 2$) corresponds to the case where the trusted entity $\mathcal{T}$ is not able to perform a task. For example, most of today's smart cards do not implement a bilinear pairing (even cooperatively), which makes all the other statuses impossible. However, depending on the chosen security vector, the introduction of such status may imply that no possible secure server-aided version of a given instance can be designed (the result is that all the tasks should be performed by $\mathcal{T}$ sole). As it may occur in practice, we prefer to keep it.

TABLE OF STATUS TASK. Each task t_i of ALG$_0$ (in Θ_0) has to be associated to one of these status in order to design the server-aided version, which is done by the SETSTATUSTASK algorithm. In order to ease the execution of this algorithm, we list in a database the existing possibilities of execution for all elementary tasks depending on the status of their inputs and outputs.

- If a task cannot be executed by $\mathcal{T}$, then the status is necessarily stated to 2.
- If all the inputs and outputs of t_i are known to $\mathcal{I}$ (except when the adversary is a controller $w.r.t.$ the correctness), then it can be totally executed by $\mathcal{I}$ and the status includes a 1.
- We then focus on existing server-aided executions of the task. Regarding the status of all inputs and outputs, we are able to say whether such cooperative method exists or not (see Appendix A for some examples). If one exists, then we can introduce the $\star$ in the task status (which implies the possibility to obtain a status $1\star$ with the previous case). In addition, the cooperative method is inserted in the database.
- Otherwise, the status of t_i is set to 0.

Now the task status table is filled, we can explain how we determine the best variant, which will be done in the next section. We first illustrate our purpose on task status with our example of group signatures.

4.4   Example of Group Signatures

When considering the elementary tasks of the XSGS group signature we find two types of them which can be executed cooperatively, namely the pairing and the exponentiation. However, cooperative executions of the these tasks remain inefficient (for example the delegation of pairing provided by [15] and [14] requires respectively 10 and 7 exponentiations in $\mathbb{G}_T$ which is costlier than computing the pairing) or insecure [5,28]. We then do not consider in our example the status "$\star$" and get the following repartition:

$$\mathtt{st}[\{t_{20}, t_{21}, t_{42}\}] = 0 \text{ and } \mathtt{st}[\Theta_0 \setminus \{t_{20}, t_{21}, t_{42}\}] = 1.$$

5   Producing the Most Efficient Server-Aided Variant

Before formally describing the algorithms that construct the most efficient server-aided version, we introduce some useful notations for this section. The best server-aided version of an algorithm mainly depends on the efficiency of both actors, namely the trusted entity $\mathcal{T}$ and the intermediary $\mathcal{I}$. Consequently, a database denoted $\mathtt{Perf}$ containing the performances of both entities for all types of tasks must be set. $\mathtt{Perf}[\mathcal{X}][t]$ returns the time taken by the entity $\mathcal{X}$ (either $\mathcal{T}$ or $\mathcal{I}$) to perform the task t. If it is not able to perform this task, the associated time is arbitrarily fixed to ∞.

Each task is defined by its identifier, its type (exponentiation, pairing,...), its inputs and its outputs.

5.1 Description of the Global Method

We here make a high level description of our algorithms by taking again our running example of the XSGS group signature phase. The more formal description of the main algorithms is further given by Algorithms 1, 2 and 3.

We first run the algorithm SETSTATUSDATA to determine the status of each epheme-ral data depending on the status of the intrinsic data and on rules defined by the operator. For example, if a secret data is involved in a multi-linear combination over $\mathbb{Z}_p$, then another data involved in the same task has to be kept secret from $\mathcal{I}$. Considering the task $t_{21} : z = \gamma_1 x + y$, this means that the algorithm will have to set γ_1 or z as *unknown* because y is secret and $st_{\mathcal{I}}[x] = kn$. Using the same methodology for each task, the algorithm will finally output the status of each data. The resulting status of ephemeral data will be *known*, except for r_6 and z. We are then able to determine the status of each task. As already explained, we will consider that a task can be executed by $\mathcal{I}$ if the status of all inputs and outputs are known to $\mathcal{I}$ because of the lack of efficient cooperative protocol for the considered tasks.

Before allocating each task to $\mathcal{T}$ or $\mathcal{I}$ we first have to ensure that their order is respected. Indeed, some tasks take as inputs the output of other ones and thus have to be computed after. For example tasks $t_{37}, t_{38}, t_{39}, t_{40}, t_{41}, t_{42}$ require the data c and thus have to be computed after the task t_{36}. We then assign to each task, using the algorithm REPROUND described below, a *round* number such that every task of a same round only takes as input intrinsic data or ephemeral data produced during previous rounds. We may thus look for the best repartition of the tasks in the round without caring for their order of execution.

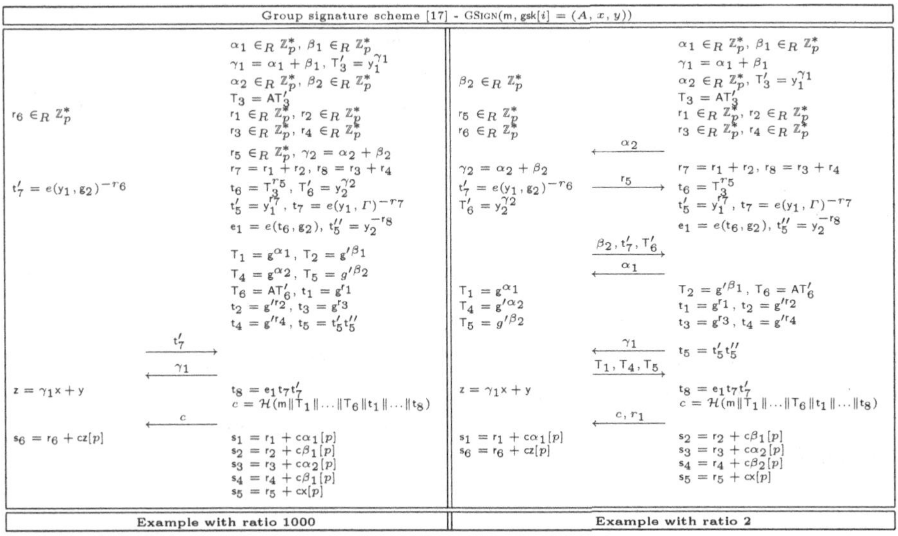

Fig. 2. The XSGS GSIGN algorithm [17,9]

We get this best repartition using the algorithm REP which focus on the different types of tasks of the round rather than on the tasks themselves. This algorithm will determine how many tasks of each type have to be executed by $\mathcal{T}$ and by $\mathcal{I}$. For example, the round 7 is composed of the tasks $t_7, t_8, t_{11}, t_{12}, t_{14}, t_{24}, t_{25}, t_{26}, t_{27}, t_{30}$ and t_{35}, *i.e.* 8 exponentiations and 3 group operations. The algorithm REP will then decide how many exponentiations and group operations have to be computed by $\mathcal{T}$ in order to minimize the execution time of this round. For a ratio of 2 between $\mathcal{T}$ and $\mathcal{I}$ we get the following repartitions: 3 exponentiations for $\mathcal{T}$ and the rest for $\mathcal{I}$. Now we must choose the 3 exponentiations among the 8 that will require the less communication time. This is done by the ATTRIBUTETASK algorithm which is described in appendix B. In a nutshell, it mainly depends on the number of successors of each task. Indeed, since $\mathcal{T}$ handles less tasks than $\mathcal{I}$, the goal is to assign the tasks with the fewest successors to $\mathcal{T}$ since the probability that their output will be required by $\mathcal{I}$ is smaller.

Using the same methodology for each round finally gives us the repartitions described in Figure 2 for 2 different ratios (1000 and 2).

Considering the intermediary $\mathcal{I}$ as far more powerful than $\mathcal{T}$ is a typical approach in cryptography [9,15,22], the resulting protocols trying to delegate as many tasks as possible to the delegatee. The left side of figure 2 describes the result of our algorithm in such case, the only tasks handled by $\mathcal{T}$ being those who require knowledge of secret data (y, r_6, z) and thus cannot be delegate to $\mathcal{I}$. One may note that we exactly find the same repartition as the one from [9]. Yet, the gap between $\mathcal{T}$ and $\mathcal{I}$ may not be so important, the right side of the figure describes a different repartition for a smaller ratio.

5.2   Round Attribution

The REPROUND algorithm takes as inputs the number of tasks, *taskNumber*, an array *RepRound* and a matrix *SuccNumber* such that $SuccNumber[i, j] = 1$ if t_j takes as input the output of t_j. It assigns the current round to every tasks t with no successor and then removes t from the successor lists of all the other tasks.

5.3   Rep Algorithm

The REP algorithm takes as inputs five arrays $TaskRoundT$, $TaskRoundI$, $TaskT$, $TaskI$, and $Index$ and an integer $typeNumber$ that is the number of different types of tasks. $TaskRoundT$ stores, for each type, the number of tasks that have to be executed by $\mathcal{T}$ while $TaskRoundI$ stores, for each type, the number of tasks that can be executed by $\mathcal{I}$. $Index$ ensures that the while loop tests all possible combinations. Finally, the best repartition is stored in $TaskT$ and $TaskI$.

Algorithm 1. REPROUND($RepRound, taskNumber, SuccNumber$)

$round = 1; count = 0;$
while $count \: != \: taskNumber$ **do**
$\quad$ **for** $i \in [0; taskNumber[$ **do**
$\quad\quad$ **if** $RepRound[i] == 0$ **then**
$\quad\quad\quad$ /*If no round has been assigned to t_i */
$\quad\quad\quad$ $succNumber = 0;$
$\quad\quad\quad$ **for** $j \in [0; taskNumber[$ **do**
$\quad\quad\quad\quad$ $succNumber+ = Succ[i * taskNumber + j];$
$\quad\quad\quad$ **if** $succNumber == 0$ **then**
$\quad\quad\quad\quad$ $RepRound[i] = round; count + +;$

$\quad$ /* We remove each task assigned in this round from the successor list */
$\quad$ **for** $i \in [0; taskNumber[$ **do**
$\quad\quad$ **if** $RepRound[i] == round$ **then**
$\quad\quad\quad$ **for** $j \in [0; taskNumber[$ **do**
$\quad\quad\quad\quad$ $Succ[i * taskNumber + j] = 0;$

$\quad$ $round + +;$

Algorithm 2. REP($TaskRoundT, TaskRoundI, TaskT, TaskI, typeNumber, Index$)

$bestTime = +\infty; constTimeT = 0;$
for $i \in [0; typeNumber[$ **do**
$\quad$ /*We first compute the computation time of the tasks that have to be executed by T*/
$\quad$ $constTimeT+ = TaskRoundT[i] * Perf[T][i];$
$i = 0$
while $i! = typeNumber$ **do**
$\quad$ $timeT = constTimeT; timeI = 0;$
$\quad$ **for** $j \in [0; typeNumber[$ **do**
$\quad\quad$ $timeT+ = Index[j] * Perf[T][j];$
$\quad\quad$ $timeI+ = (TaskRoundI[j] - Index[j]) * Perf[I][j];$
$\quad$ **if** $timeT > timeI$ **then**
$\quad\quad$ $timeMax = timeT$
$\quad$ **else**
$\quad\quad$ $timeMax = timeI$
$\quad$ **if** $timeMax < bestTime$ **then**
$\quad\quad$ $bestTime = timeMax$
$\quad\quad$ **for** $j \in [0; typeNumber[$ **do**
$\quad\quad\quad$ $TaskT[round * typeNumber + j] = TaskRoundT[j] + Index[j];$
$\quad\quad\quad$ $TaskI[round * typeNumber + j] = TaskRoundI[j] - Index[j];$
$\quad$ $Index[0] + +; i = 0;$
$\quad$ **while** $Index[i] > TaskRoundI[i]$ **and** $i < typeNumber$ **do**
$\quad\quad$ $Index[i] = 0; Index[i + 1] + +;$
$\quad\quad$ $i + +;$

---

6   Conclusion

In this paper, we have proposed an almost generic method to simplify and precise the work of an operator wanting to construct the most possible efficient secure server-aided instance of a cryptographic primitive. Our work can easily be applied or adapted to any instance of any primitive.

This is obviously a first step and it remains a lot of work to do to improve the final result. For example, regarding cooperative execution of elementary tasks such as modular exponentiations or pairings, the related work clearly lacks of efficient and secure dedicated solutions. Regarding our main methodology, we also need to work on a true operator-free solution, especially regarding the security part. As said before, one option seems to work with formal methods, but it needs to be confirmed by additional work.

Acknowledgments. The work of the first, third and sixth author has been partially supported by the French ANR-11-INS-0013 LYRICS Project. The fifth author was supported by the Camus Walloon Region project. We are grateful to Nicolas Desmoulins for helpful discussions on the implementation aspects, and to anonymous referees for their valuable comments.

References

1. Abadi, M., Blanchet, B., Comon-Lundh, H.: Models and proofs of protocol security: A progress report. In: Bouajjani, A., Maler, O. (eds.) CAV 2009. LNCS, vol. 5643, pp. 35–49. Springer, Heidelberg (2009)
2. Atallah, M.J., Frikken, K.B.: Securely outsourcing linear algebra computations. In: ASIACCS, pp. 48–59 (2010)
3. Barthe, G., Daubignard, M., Kapron, B., Lakhnech, Y.: Computational indistinguishability logic. In: Proceedings of the 17th ACM Conference on Computer and Communications Security, CCS 2010, pp. 375–386. ACM (2010)
4. Barthe, G., Grégoire, B., Heraud, S., Béguelin, S.Z.: Computer-aided security proofs for the working cryptographer. In: Rogaway, P. (ed.) CRYPTO 2011. LNCS, vol. 6841, pp. 71–90. Springer, Heidelberg (2011)
5. Béguin, P., Quisquater, J.-J.: Fast server-aided RSA signatures secure against active attacks. In: Coppersmith, D. (ed.) CRYPTO 1995. LNCS, vol. 963, pp. 57–69. Springer, Heidelberg (1995)
6. Bellare, M., Shi, H., Zhang, C.: Foundations of group signatures: the case of dynamic groups. In: Menezes, A. (ed.) CT-RSA 2005. LNCS, vol. 3376, pp. 136–153. Springer, Heidelberg (2005)
7. Blanchet, B., Pointcheval, D.: Automated security proofs with sequences of games. In: Dwork, C. (ed.) CRYPTO 2006. LNCS, vol. 4117, pp. 537–554. Springer, Heidelberg (2006)
8. Brickell, E.F., Camenisch, J., Chen, L.: Direct anonymous attestation. In: ACM Conference on Computer and Communications Security 2004, pp. 132–145. ACM (2004)
9. Canard, S., Coisel, I., De Meulenaer, G., Pereira, O.: Group signatures are suitable for constrained devices. In: Rhee, K.-H., Nyang, D. (eds.) ICISC 2010. LNCS, vol. 6829, pp. 133–150. Springer, Heidelberg (2011)

10. Canard, S., Girault, M.: Implementing group signature schemes with smart cards. In: CARDIS 2002, pp. 1–10. USENIX (2002)
11. Chaum, D., Pedersen, T.P.: Wallet databases with observers. In: Brickell, E.F. (ed.) CRYPTO 1992. LNCS, vol. 740, pp. 89–105. Springer, Heidelberg (1993)
12. Chaum, D., van Heyst, E.: Group signatures. In: Davies, D.W. (ed.) EUROCRYPT 1991. LNCS, vol. 547, pp. 257–265. Springer, Heidelberg (1991)
13. Chen, L.: A daa scheme requiring less tpm resources. In: Bao, F., Yung, M., Lin, D., Jing, J. (eds.) Inscrypt 2009. LNCS, vol. 6151, pp. 350–365. Springer, Heidelberg (2010)
14. Chevallier-Mames, B., Coron, J.-S., McCullagh, N., Naccache, D., Scott, M.: Secure delegation of elliptic-curve pairing. Cryptology ePrint Archive, Report 2005/150 (2005), http://eprint.iacr.org/
15. Chevallier-Mames, B., Coron, J.-S., McCullagh, N., Naccache, D., Scott, M.: Secure delegation of elliptic-curve pairing. In: Gollmann, D., Lanet, J.-L., Iguchi-Cartigny, J. (eds.) CARDIS 2010. LNCS, vol. 6035, pp. 24–35. Springer, Heidelberg (2010)
16. Cramer, R., Pedersen, T.P.: Improved privacy in wallets with observers (extended abstract). In: Helleseth, T. (ed.) EUROCRYPT 1993. LNCS, vol. 765, pp. 329–343. Springer, Heidelberg (1994)
17. Delerablée, C., Pointcheval, D.: Dynamic fully anonymous short group signatures. In: Nguyên, P.Q. (ed.) VIETCRYPT 2006. LNCS, vol. 4341, pp. 193–210. Springer, Heidelberg (2006)
18. Girault, M., Lefranc, D.: Public key authentication with one (online) single addition. In: Joye, M., Quisquater, J.-J. (eds.) CHES 2004. LNCS, vol. 3156, pp. 413–427. Springer, Heidelberg (2004)
19. Girault, M., Lefranc, D.: Server-aided verification: theory and practice. In: Roy, B. (ed.) ASIACRYPT 2005. LNCS, vol. 3788, pp. 605–623. Springer, Heidelberg (2005)
20. Hohenberger, S., Lysyanskaya, A.: How to securely outsource cryptographic computations. In: Kilian, J. (ed.) TCC 2005. LNCS, vol. 3378, pp. 264–282. Springer, Heidelberg (2005)
21. Kawamura, S.I., Shimbo, A.: Fast server-aided secret computation protocols for modular exponentiation. IEEE Journal on Selected Areas in Communications 11(5), 778–784 (1993)
22. Kang, B.G., Lee, M.S., Park, J.H.: Efficient delegation of pairing computation. IACR Cryptology ePrint Archive, 2005:259 (2005)
23. Lim, C.H., Lee, P.J.: Server (prover/signer)-aided verification of identity proofs and signatures. In: Guillou, L.C., Quisquater, J.-J. (eds.) EUROCRYPT 1995. LNCS, vol. 921, pp. 64–78. Springer, Heidelberg (1995)
24. Maitland, G., Boyd, C.: Co-operatively formed group signatures. In: Preneel, B. (ed.) CT-RSA 2002. LNCS, vol. 2271, pp. 218–235. Springer, Heidelberg (2002)
25. Matsumoto, T., Kato, K., Imai, H.: Speeding up secret computations with insecure auxiliary devices. In: Goldwasser, S. (ed.) CRYPTO 1988. LNCS, vol. 403, pp. 497–506. Springer, Heidelberg (1990)
26. Moradi, A., Poschmann, A., Ling, S., Paar, C., Wang, H.: Pushing the limits: A very compact and a threshold implementation of aes. In: Paterson, K.G. (ed.) EUROCRYPT 2011. LNCS, vol. 6632, pp. 69–88. Springer, Heidelberg (2011)
27. Nguyên, P.Q., Shparlinski, I.E.: On the insecurity of a server-aided RSA protocol. In: Boyd, C. (ed.) ASIACRYPT 2001. LNCS, vol. 2248, pp. 21–35. Springer, Heidelberg (2001)

28. Nguyên, P.Q., Stern, J.: The béguin-quisquater server-aided RSA protocol from crypto '95 is not secure. In: Ohta, K., Pei, D. (eds.) ASIACRYPT 1998. LNCS, vol. 1514, pp. 372–379. Springer, Heidelberg (1998)

29. Pfitzmann, B., Waidner, M.: Attacks on protocols for server-aided RSA computation. In: Rueppel, R.A. (ed.) EUROCRYPT 1992. LNCS, vol. 658, pp. 153–162. Springer, Heidelberg (1993)

30. Schnorr, C.-P.: Efficient identification and signatures for smart cards. In: Brassard, G. (ed.) CRYPTO 1989. LNCS, vol. 435, pp. 239–252. Springer, Heidelberg (1990)

31. van Dijk, M., Clarke, D.E., Gassend, B., Edward Suh, G., Devadas, S.: Speeding up exponentiation using an untrusted computational resource. Des. Codes Cryptography 39(2), 253–273 (2006)

32. Xu, S., Yung, M.: Accountable ring signatures: a smart card approach. In: CARDIS 2004, pp. 271–286. Kluwer (2004)

33. Yao, A.C.-C.: Protocols for secure computations (extended abstract). In: FOCS, pp. 160–164. IEEE Computer Society (1982)

A   Cooperative Execution of Elementary Tasks

We here provide some cooperative protocols one can find in the literature. Our goal is not to be exhaustive but to show that they are relevant to our methodology. To the best of our knowledge there is no general method to cooperatively perform a pseudo random generation or a hash computation. We focus on the costliest types of tasks introduced in section 2.1.

A.1   Exponentiation

Let g be an element of a group $\mathbb{G}$ and $a \in \mathbb{Z}_p$. The cooperative execution of g^a depends on the status of g and a. Since our method only considers one intermediary $\mathcal{I}$, we do not use the method proposed by [20], secure under the strong assumption that $\mathcal{T}$ has access to two intermediaries that cannot communicate with each other.

The method of [31] describes the way to outsource the computation of an exponentiation with verifiability of the result (*i.e.* the intermediary cannot convince $\mathcal{T}$ to accept a false value for g^a). Nevertheless, this method requires that g and a are both public.

Several papers [25,21,5] provide protocols for secret data, however, they were later proven insecure [29,5]. We then do not consider cooperative execution of exponentiation when secret data are involved.

A.2   Bilinear Map

In [19], Girault and Lefranc have proposed a way to compute $e(A, B)$ for secret A or B. Their solution works as follows. First, $\mathcal{T}$ chooses at random u and v in $\mathbb{Z}_p$, computes $X = A^u$ and $Y = B^v$ and sends theses values to $\mathcal{I}$. Then, $\mathcal{I}$ computes $z = e(X, Y)$, sends it to $\mathcal{T}$ which recovers $e(A, B)$ by computing $z^{(uv)^{-1}}$. Since X and Y are random elements of $\mathbb{G}_1$ and $\mathbb{G}_2$ we are able to simulate the communication between $\mathcal{T}$ and $\mathcal{I}$ without knowledge of A and B. The above cooperative execution of a pairing is then listener-receiver secure.

However, this protocol does not ensure verifiability of the result. Indeed, if $\mathcal{I}$ returns a random value from $\mathbb{G}_T$ instead of $e(X, Y)$, then $\mathcal{T}$ is unable to detect it. In [15] and [22], the authors provide verifiability but their protocol remain inefficient since they require respectively 10 and 7 exponentiations in $\mathbb{G}_T$ to check the validity of the result.

B   AttributeTask Algorithm

The algorithm ATTRIBUTETASK takes as input $TaskT$, the output of the REP algorithm, $AssignedTaskT$, an array storing for each round and each type the number of tasks with status 0, $StatusTask$, $TypeTask$ and $RepRound$, arrays indicating the status, the type and the round of each task and three integers $typeNumber$, $roundNumber$ and $taskNumber$. Recall that the REP algorithm has chosen, for each type of tasks, how many of them $\mathcal{T}$ must compute to get the best repartition. However, it remains to choose which ones will be computed by this entity to minimize communication time. Since some tasks, involving secret data, are already assigned to $\mathcal{T}$, the algorithm only has to find n (see algorithm 3) other ones. It proceeds as follows. It counts, for each task of this type, the number of successors $succNumber$ and stores the n of them with the fewest number in $BestRep$. Once this is done, we get the best repartition and it only remains to add the communication time.

Algorithm 3. ATTRIBUTETASK($TaskT$, $AssignedTaskT$, $StatusTask$, $TypeTask$, $RepRound$, $typeNumber$, $roundNumber$, $taskNumber$)

---

for $i \in [1, roundNumber]$ **do**

  for $j \in [0, typeNumber[$ **do**

    /* n is the number of tasks with status 1 that T has to compute */

    $n = TaskT[(i-1) * typeNumber + j] - AssignedTaskT[(i-1) * typeNumber + j]$;

    if $n \mathrel{!=} 0$ **then**

      $repNumber = 0$;

      $minIndex = 0$;

      for $k \in [0, taskNumber[$ **do**

        $succNumber = 0$;

        if $RepRound[k] == i$ and $StatusTask[k] == 1$ and $TypeTask[k] == j$ **then**

          for $l \in [0, taskNumber[$ **do**

            $succNumber\mathrel{+}= Succ[k * taskNumber + j]$;

          if $taskNumber < n$ **then**

            /*$BestRep$ stores the best repartition at this stage */

            $BestRep[repNumber] = k$;

            $BestSucc[repNumber] = succNumber$;

            $repNumber + +$;

            if $BestSucc[minIndex] < succNumber$ **then**

              $minIndex = repNumber$;

          else

            if $BestSucc[minIndex] > succNumber$ **then**

              $BestRep[minIndex] = k$;

              $BestSucc[minIndex] = succNumber$;

              for $l \in [0; n[$ **do**

                if $Bestsucc[l] > succNumber$ **then**

                  $minIndex = l$;

Generation and Tate Pairing Computation of Ordinary Elliptic Curves with Embedding Degree One

Zhi Hu[1,2], Lin Wang[3], Maozhi Xu[2], and Guoliang Zhang[2]

[1] Beijing International Center for Mathematical Research, Peking University,
Beijing, 100871, P.R. China
[2] LMAM, School of Mathematical Sciences, Peking University,
Beijing, 100871, P.R. China
[3] Science and Technology on Communication Security Laboratory,
Chengdu, 610041, P.R. China
{huzhi,linwang,mzxu}@math.pku.edu.cn,
{guoliang_tj}@126.com

Abstract. We generalize Boneh-Rubin-Silverberg method [3] to construct ordinary elliptic curves with embedding degree one, which provides composite order groups for cryptographic protocols based on such bilinear groups. Our construction is more efficient and almost optimal for parameter setting. In addition, we analyze the non-degeneracy of symmetric pairing derived from the reduced Tate pairing on such curves, and prove that its non-degeneracy only relies on the existence of distortion maps. Based on this observation, we propose a new method for computing the reduced Tate pairing on ordinary curves with embedding degree one. Compared with previous methods, our formulae provide faster computation of the reduced Tate pairing on such curves, which also implies that the reduced Tate pairing may be preferred to use as symmetric pairing instead of the modified Weil pairing in certain cases.

Keywords: Elliptic Curve, Complex Multiplication, Symmetric Pairing.

1 Introduction

The idea of using composite order groups in pairing-based cryptography comes from Boneh, Goh, and Nissim [2] for partial homomorphic public key encryption, and now it has been used in a number of other important applications including group signatures [5], ring signatures [23], non-interactive zero-knowledge proofs [10], traitor tracing [4] and so on. Though there exist generic techniques to translate protocols from composite-order to prime-order groups [17], some properties cannot be achieved in the prime-order setting [22]. Thus composite-order pairing-friendly elliptic curves remain interesting.

The construction [2] of composite pairing-friendly groups is based on supersingular elliptic curves. Boneh, Rubin and Silverberg showed that it is possible

S. Qing et al. (Eds.): ICICS 2013, LNCS 8233, pp. 393–403, 2013.

to obtain composite groups from ordinary elliptic curves [3]. So elliptic curve $E/\mathbb{F}_q$ which has small embedding degree k with respect to a composite number N (e.g. an RSA modulus) is considered for such cryptographic applications. Freeman et al. [8] deduced that pairing-friendly curves of composite order should have ρ-values ($\rho = \log q / \log N$) and embedding degrees k chosen to minimize $\rho \cdot k$. They also concluded that both $k = 1$ ordinary curves and $k = 2$ supersingular curves provided the minimum possible value for $\rho \cdot k$ and are thus optimal for such cryptographic setting. Koblitz [16] described a security weakness for such cryptographic setting when $k > 2$.

Since the cryptographic applications mentioned above need symmetric pairings on such curves, faster pairing computation is required. The computation of symmetric pairing on desired curves has been considered in several papers. Koblitz and Menezes [15] examined the efficiency of the modified Weil pairing as opposed to the modified Tate pairing. Zhang and Lin [30] gave an optimal Omega pairing based on the Weil pairing which would halve the length of Miller loop. Zhao et al. [31] and Wu et al. [29] proposed faster computation of self pairing (some kind of symmetric pairing) based on the Weil pairing. Their work concentrated on ordinary elliptic curves with embedding degree $k = 1$ and complex multiplication discriminant $D = -3$ or $D = -4$.

This work concentrates on ordinary elliptic curves with embedding degree one. We generalize Boneh-Rubin-Silverberg method to construct composite order ordinary elliptic curves with embedding degree one. Our construction is very efficient and reaches almost optimal parameter setting. Since the cryptographic applications mentioned above need symmetric pairings on such curves, we consider the use of the reduced Tate pairing, whose non-degeneracy only relies on the existence of distortion maps. We give formulae under Jacobian coordinate for the computation of the reduced Tate pairing on desired curves, with $8M + 10S$ for each doubling step and $12M + 5S$ for each addition step. It is shown that our method achieves better performance than the previous methods for the reduced Tate pairing computation.

Our manuscript is organized as follows. Section 2 gives some basic knowledge of ordinary elliptic curves. In Section 3 we review Boneh-Rubin- Silverberg method for constructing composite order ordinary elliptic curves with $k = 1$, and propose our generalized method. In Section 4 we analyze the non-degeneracy of symmetric pairing derived from the reduced Tate pairing on the desired curves, and propose faster computation formulae for such pairing. At last in Section 5 we conclude this work.

2   Preliminaries

2.1   Ordinary Elliptic Curve with CM

Let E be an elliptic curve defined over $\mathbb{F}_p$ with $p \geq 5$, and $End(E)$ be its endomorphism ring. E is said to be *ordinary* if it satisfies any of the following equivalent conditions [24, Theorem V.3.1]:

1. $E[p^m] \cong \mathbb{Z}/p^m\mathbb{Z}$ for all positive integers m;
2. $End(E)$ is an order in a quadratic imaginary extension of $\mathbb{Q}$;
3. The dual of the p-th power Frobenius endomorphism π is separable;
4. The trace of π (denoted by t) is co-prime to p.

If E is not *ordinary*, then E is said to be *supersingular*.

The complex multiplication (CM) method [1] is very important for constructing elliptic curve. Let D be a negative integer, and p be a prime such that $4p = t^2 - Ds^2$, where $t, s \in \mathbb{Z}$. Then the CM method generates an elliptic curve $E/\mathbb{F}_p$ with $\#E(\mathbb{F}_p) = p + 1 - t$, and the Frobenius map $\pi = \frac{t+s\sqrt{D}}{2}$. Let $K = End(E) \otimes \mathbb{Q}$ and $\mathcal{O}_K$ be its integral closure, then $D = m^2 Disc(K)$ for some $m \in \mathbb{Z}$, where $Disc(K)$ denotes the discriminant of K.

2.2   Pairings on Elliptic Curve

Let r be a prime integer dividing $\#E(\mathbb{F}_p) = p + 1 - t$, and k be the embedding degree with respect to r, that is, the smallest positive integer such that $r|p^k - 1$. Let $P \in E(\mathbb{F}_p)[r]$, $Q \in E(\mathbb{F}_{p^k})$ and $\mathcal{O}_\infty$ be the identity element of $E(\mathbb{F}_p)$. For any $m \in \mathbb{N}$, let $f_{m,P}$ be the rational function on E such that $div(f_{m,P}) = m(P) - ([m]P) - (m-1)(\mathcal{O}_\infty)$. Assume that D_Q is a divisor which is equivalent to $(Q) - (\mathcal{O}_\infty)$ with its support disjoint from $div(f_{r,P})$. Let μ_r denote the group of the r-th roots of unity in $\mathbb{F}_{p^k}$. The reduced Tate pairing [7] is a bilinear map

$$t : E(\mathbb{F}_p)[r] \times E(\mathbb{F}_{p^k})/rE(\mathbb{F}_{p^k}) \to \mu_r, \quad t(P,Q) = f_{r,P}(D_Q)^{(p^k-1)/r}.$$

Let $P, Q \in E[r]$, $P \neq Q$, D_P, D_Q be two divisors which are respectively equivalent to $(P) - (\mathcal{O}_\infty)$ and $(Q) - (\mathcal{O}_\infty)$. Assume that $f_{r,P}, f_{r,Q}$ are two rational functions satisfying $div(f_{r,P}) = rD_P$ and $div(f_{r,Q}) = rD_Q$. The Weil pairing [18] is a bilinear map

$$e : E[r] \times E[r] \to \mu_r, \quad e(P,Q) = f_{r,P}(D_Q)/f_{r,Q}(D_P).$$

Both pairings can be efficiently computed via Miller's Algorithm [19]. Let $l_{[m]P,[n]P}$ and $v_{[m+n]P}$ be the rational function with $div(l_{[m]P,[n]P}) = ([m]P) + ([n]P) + (-[m+n]P) - 3(\mathcal{O}_\infty)$ and $div(v_{[m+n]P}) = ([m+n]P) + (-[m+n]P) - 2(\mathcal{O}_\infty)$ respectively, then for any $m, n \in \mathbb{N}$, the Miller iteration is

$$f_{m+n,P} = f_{m,P} \cdot f_{n,P} \cdot l_{[m]P,[n]P}/v_{[m+n]P}.$$

There are some variants derived from the above two basic pairings. These pairings usually are not symmetric, but under certain conditions they can be modified to be symmetric with the help of *distortion* map . The *distortion* map ψ is an endomorphism which maps a point $P \in E(\mathbb{F}_p)$ to $\psi(P) \in E(\mathbb{F}_{p^k}), \psi(P) \notin \langle P \rangle$ [28]. Distortion map always exists on supersingular elliptic curves, but only exists on ordinary curves with $k = 1$ [28].

3   Constructing Ordinary Elliptic Curves with $k = 1$

3.1   Boneh-Rubin-Silverberg Method

Let N be a positive integer (e.g., an RSA modulus) or a large prime. Below is the method given by Boneh, Rubin and Silverberg [3] for constructing ordinary composite order elliptic curves with embedding degree 1.

1. Choose a negative integer D suitable for the CM method and

$$p = \begin{cases} 1 - DN^2 & \text{if } D \equiv 0, 2 \bmod 6, \\ 1 - 4DN^2 & \text{if } D \equiv 3, 5 \bmod 6, \\ (1 - N)^2 - DN^2 & \text{if } D \equiv 1 \bmod 6, \\ (1 - 2N)^2 - DN^2 & \text{if } D \equiv 4 \bmod 6. \end{cases}$$

such that p is prime.

2. Use the CM method to construct an elliptic curve E over $\mathbb{F}_p$ with

$$\#E(\mathbb{F}_p) = \begin{cases} -DN^2 & \text{if } D \equiv 0, 2 \bmod 6, \\ -4DN^2 & \text{if } D \equiv 3, 5 \bmod 6, \\ (1 - D)N^2 & \text{if } D \equiv 1 \bmod 6, \\ (4 - D)N^2 & \text{if } D \equiv 4 \bmod 6. \end{cases}$$

3.2   Our Construction

Let N be a positive integer (e.g., an RSA modulus or a large prime), D be a negative integer and $\gcd(N, [\mathcal{O}_K : End(E)] \cdot D) = 1$.

Lemma 1. *Let p be an odd prime where $4p = t^2 - Ds^2$ for some $t, s \in \mathbb{Z}$, and $E/\mathbb{F}_p$ be the elliptic curve with $\#E(\mathbb{F}_p) = p + 1 - t$. Then the embedding degree of $E/\mathbb{F}_p$ with respect to N is 1 if and only if $t \equiv 2 \bmod N, s \equiv 0 \bmod N$.*

Proof. Since Verheul's condition [28] for E of embedding degree 1 with respect to N can be given by

$$t \equiv 2 \bmod N,$$
$$\#E(\mathbb{F}_p) = \frac{(t - 2)^2 - Ds^2}{4} \equiv 0 \bmod N,$$

thus it must have $t \equiv 2 \bmod N$ and $s \equiv 0 \bmod N$.   □

If we let $t = 2 + 2uN, s = 2vN$ (usually we choose u, v very small compared with N), the parameters for the desired curves are set by

$$p = (1 + uN)^2 - D(vN)^2,$$
$$\#E(\mathbb{F}_p) = (u^2 - Dv^2)N^2. \tag{1}$$

Theorem 1. *Let the parameters of elliptic curves be set as Eqn.1. If* $\gcd(N, [\mathcal{O}_K : End(E)]Disc(K)) = 1$, *then* $E[N] \subseteq Ker(\pi - 1) = E(\mathbb{F}_p)$, *i.e., the embedding degree of* $E/\mathbb{F}_p$ *with respect to* N *is* 1.

Proof. Since $\pi - 1 = N(u + v\sqrt{D}) \in N \cdot End(E)$, then $[\pi - 1](E[N]) = \{\mathcal{O}_\infty\}$, and thus $E[N] \subseteq Ker(\pi - 1) = E(\mathbb{F}_p)$. $\square$

To generate ordinary composite order elliptic curves with embedding degree 1, we describe our method as the following algorithm.

Algorithm 1. Generating Elliptic Curve

Input: CM discriminant D and positive integer N.

Output: Elliptic curve $E/\mathbb{F}_p$.

1. Choose proper integers u, v such that $p = (1 + uN)^2 - D(vN)^2$ is prime;

2. For two special cases:

(1) If $D = -3$, choose a proper $b \in \mathbb{F}_p^\times$ such that the elliptic curve $E/\mathbb{F}_p : y^2 = x^3 + b$ satisfying $\#E(\mathbb{F}_p) = (u^2 + 3v^2)N^2$;

(2) If $D = -4$, choose a proper $a \in \mathbb{F}_p^\times$ such that the elliptic curve $E/\mathbb{F}_p : y^2 = x^3 + ax$ satisfying $\#E(\mathbb{F}_p) = (u^2 + 4v^2)N^2$;

3. For the other cases:

(1). Compute the Hilbert class polynomial H_D of $\mathbb{Q}(\sqrt{D})$;

(2). Compute a root $j \in \mathbb{F}_p$ of $H_D \mod p$;

(3). Let $m = j/(1728 - j)$, choose a proper $c \in \mathbb{F}_p^\times$ such that the elliptic curve $E/\mathbb{F}_p : y^2 = x^3 + 3mc^2x + 2mc^3$ satisfying $\#E(\mathbb{F}_p) = (u^2 - Dv^2)N^2$.

The main expenditure step in Algorithm 1 is the computation of Hilbert class polynomial H_D. Current computational power admits the above algorithm when $|D| < 10^{13}$ and the class number $h(D) < 10^6$ [26]. Under the assumption of Generalized Riemann Hypothesis, Algorithm 1 has an expected running time of $O(|D|^{1+\epsilon})$.

Remark 1. Algorithm 1 provides parameters with $\log p \approx 2 \log N$ which is almost optimal for embedding degree 1 ordinary curves as mentioned in [8]. The curve given by Koblitz and Menezes ($D = -4$) [15] and the curve given by Hu et al. ($D = -3$) [11] can be viewed as special cases in our construction. Moreover, the Verheul's theorem [28] (usually considered as an evidence for the difficulty of pairing inversion) could be generalized to such curves with embedding degree $k = 1$, answering an open problem given by Moody [20].

Example 1. We choose a 1024-bit RSA modulus $N = p_1 p_2$ used in [14] as

$p_1 = 10255011809224889372719081312267071525523427198331787650924765783668946195914019904657448967015565448927912751782149864907464901841782492454031263306824711,$

$$p_2 = 10871883181590817218945857405537842626311518852786946779992871285229819789842666582176885062701923174345579393609134702776143459315515232095349365641880549.$$

For $D = -3$, $u = 7$ and $v = 5$, $p = (1 + 7N)^2 + 3(5N)^2$ is a prime number. The elliptic curve is $E/\mathbb{F}_p : y^2 = x^3 + 3$, with $\#E(\mathbb{F}_p) = 124N^2$. For $D = -4$, $u = 16$ and $v = 2$, $p = (1 + 16N)^2 + 4(2N)^2$ is a prime number. The elliptic curve is $E/\mathbb{F}_p : y^2 = x^3 + 4x$, with $\#E(\mathbb{F}_p) = 272N^2$.

Example 2. Let N be the RSA challenge number RSA-2048 (bit) [21], for $D = -7$, $u = 5$ and $v = 17$, $p = (1 + 5N)^2 + 7 \cdot (17N)^2$ is a prime number. The elliptic curve is $E/\mathbb{F}_p : y^2 = x^3 - 35x + 98$, with $\#E(\mathbb{F}_p) = 2048N^2$. When we run the Boneh-Rubin-Silverberg method, the output D with the smallest absolute value is $D = -1893$. For randomly selected RSA modulus N in our experiments, we can usually find much smaller $|D|$ by our method to meet the desired setting than that given by Boneh et al. [3], and thus reduce the computation of Hilbert class polynomial. Therefore, our method is more efficient.

4   Symmetric Pairing Based on the Reduced Tate Pairing

4.1   Non-degeneracy of the Reduced Tate Pairing

Previous non-degeneracy symmetric pairing on desired curves are usually derived from the Weil pairing e and a distortion map $[\tau]$. Let $E/\mathbb{F}_p$ be an ordinary elliptic curve with embedding degree $k = 1$ as generated by Algorithm 1, r be a prime factor of N and $P \in E(\mathbb{F}_p)$ of order r, then $\{P, [\tau]P\}$ generates $E(\mathbb{F}_p)[r]$ and thus the modified Weil pairing $\hat{e} : \langle P \rangle \times \langle P \rangle \to \mu_r \subset \mathbb{F}_p^\times, \hat{e}([a]P, [b]P) = e([a]P, [b][\tau]P)$ is non-degenerate.

In this section, we analyze the non-degeneracy of symmetric pairing based on the reduced Tate pairing t and distortion map τ. Obviously, at least one of $t : \langle P \rangle \times \langle P \rangle \to \mu_r$ and $t : \langle P \rangle \times \langle [\tau]P \rangle \to \mu_r$ must be non-degenerate ($t(P, P)$ can be alternatively computed by $t(P, P+R)/t(P, R)$ for some $R \in E(\mathbb{F}_p)$). Note that the first pairing is degenerate for any elliptic curve with embedding degree $k > 1$ [9, Lem. IX.13]. However, we have the following result:

Theorem 2. *Let $E/\mathbb{F}_p$ be the curve generated by Algorithm 1. Let $t : \langle P \rangle \times \langle P \rangle \to \mu_r$ be the reduced Tate pairing, where $P \in E(\mathbb{F}_p)$ has order r. Denote $(\frac{\cdot}{\cdot})$ as the Legendre symbol.*

1. *If $(\frac{D}{r}) = -1$, then t is non-degenerate for any non-trivial $P \in E(\mathbb{F}_p)[r]$;*
2. *If $(\frac{D}{r}) = 1$, then t is non-degenerate for non-trivial P belonging to all but two subgroups of $E(\mathbb{F}_p)[r]$ having distortion maps.*

Proof. Let $\bar{\mathbb{F}}_p$ be the algebraic closure of $\mathbb{F}_p$. Since $E[r] \subset E(\mathbb{F}_p)$, by [24, VIII. §1, §2] we can define two isomorphisms

$$\delta_E : E(\mathbb{F}_p)/rE(\mathbb{F}_p) \to Hom(G_{\bar{\mathbb{F}}_p/\mathbb{F}_p}, E[r]), \ \delta_E(P)(\sigma) = \sigma(Q) - Q,$$

where $Q \in E(\bar{\mathbb{F}}_p)$ is chosen so that $[r]Q = P$, and

$$\delta_{\mathbb{F}_p} : \mathbb{F}_p^\times / \mathbb{F}_p^{\times^r} \to Hom(G_{\bar{\mathbb{F}}_p/\mathbb{F}_p}, \mu_r), \ \delta_{\mathbb{F}_p}(b)(\sigma) = \beta^\sigma / \beta,$$

where $\beta \in \bar{\mathbb{F}}_p^\times$ is chosen so that $\beta^r = b$. By [24, Thm. X.1.1], we have $e(\delta_E(P), P) = \delta_{\mathbb{F}_p}(t(P, P))$.

Let $End(E) = \mathbb{Z}[\tau]$ and π be the Frobenius map, π can be represented as $\pi = 1 + r(m + n\tau)$ for some $m, n \in \mathbb{Z}$ and $n \not\equiv 0 \bmod r$. In the above let $\sigma = \pi$, then by Hilbert's Theorem 90, we have

$$t(P, P) \neq 1 \Leftrightarrow e(\delta_E(P), P) \neq 1 \Leftrightarrow \delta_E(P) = \pi(Q) - Q \notin \langle P \rangle.$$
$$\Leftrightarrow \forall s \in \mathbb{Z}/r\mathbb{Z}, [m - s + n\tau](P) \neq \mathcal{O}_\infty.$$

Therefore, by the above result and [6, Thm. 2] we deduce that

1. If $(\frac{D}{r}) = -1$, then $[\tau]$ acts on $E(\mathbb{F}_p)[r]$ as a distortion map, and hence $[m - s + n\tau]P \neq \mathcal{O}_\infty$ for any non-trivial $P \in E(\mathbb{F}_p)[r]$;
2. If $(\frac{D}{r}) = 1$, then $[\tau]$ acts on all but two subgroups of $E(\mathbb{F}_p)[r]$ as a distortion map, and hence $t(P, P) \neq 1$ for all non-trivial $P \in E(\mathbb{F}_p)[r]$ except these two subgroups.

□

Remark 2. Interestingly, Ionica also gave a similar result in [13] for the non-degeneracy of self pairing but used a different proof. By Theorem 2 we can use $t : \langle P \rangle \times \langle P \rangle \to \mu_r$ as symmetric pairing if there exists a distortion map $[\tau]$ for P, even we do not know the explicit form of $[\tau]$. To avoid attack for Subgroup Decision Problem [2], we usually require $(\frac{D}{r}) = -1$ for any prime factor r of N, which implies that distortion maps always exist. From Algorithm 1 and Theorem 2 if we choose $\eta = (u + v\sqrt{D})/\gcd(u, v) \in End(E) \backslash \mathbb{Z}$, then $\pi = 1 + N \gcd(u, v)\eta$ and $\pi(Q) - Q \in \langle [\eta]P \rangle$, therefore $t(P, [\eta]P) = 1$ for any $P \in E(\mathbb{F}_p)[r]$. Represent $\eta = u_1 + v_1\tau$ for some $u_1, v_1 \in \mathbb{Z}$. If chosen D very small, $[\tau]$ can be efficiently computed by Vélu formula [27] or Stark algorithm [25]. Thus $[\eta]P$ can also be efficiently computed if D, u, v are very small.

Example 3. Let $E/\mathbb{F}_p$ be the curve defined in Example 1 with $D = -3, u = 7, v = 5$. Define $[\zeta](x, y) = (\zeta x, y)$, where $\zeta \in \mathbb{F}_p$ and $\zeta^2 + \zeta + 1 = 0$. Set $\eta = 12 + 10\zeta$, then for any $P \in E(\mathbb{F}_p)[p_j], j = 1, 2$, the reduced Tate pairing $t(P, [\eta]P) = 1$; Also, let $E/\mathbb{F}_p$ be the curve defined in Example 1 with $D = -4, u = 16, v = 2$. Define $[i](x, y) = (-x, iy)$, where $i \in \mathbb{F}_p$ and $i^2 + 1 = 0$. Set $\eta = 8 + 2i$, then for any $P \in E(\mathbb{F}_p)[p_j], j = 1, 2, t(P, [\eta]P) = 1$.

4.2 The Computation of the Reduced Tate Pairing

For $D = -3, -4$, Zhao et al. [31] and Wu et al. [29] defined some self pairing on ordinary elliptic curve with embedding degree $k = 1$ based on the Weil pairing, where they accelerated the pairing computation by using the technique of *denominator* elimination or *numerator* elimination respectively. Moreover, if

$(\frac{D}{r}) = 1$, we could use the technique given by Zhang and Lin [30] to halve the Miller loop length of the Omega pairing based on the Weil pairing. But for $D < -4$, the computation of the reduced Tate pairing is usually faster than that of the Weil pairing, since the latter usually needs two Miller loops.

For $P, Q \in \langle P \rangle$ ($P = Q$ also known as self pairing) we usually can not compute $t(P,Q)$ directly but use an alternative method as $t(P,Q) = t(P, Q + R)/t(P, R)$ for some $R \in E(\mathbb{F}_p)$. Koblitz and Menezes [15] chose $R = (0,0)$ for the case $D = -4$. By Remark 2, suppose $t(P, [\eta]P) = 1$ for some distortion map $[\eta]$, we can choose $R = [\eta]P$ which can be pre-computed, and then $t(P,Q) = t(P, Q + R) = f_{N,P}(Q + R)^{(p-1)/N}$. Let I, M and S denote the cost of inversion, multiplication and squaring in $\mathbb{F}_p$ respectively. Based on the work of Zhao et al. [31], we analyze the cost of the doubling and addition steps for computing $t(P,Q)$ in Miller's algorithm [19].

Doubling Step: Suppose E has short Weierstrass form $E : y^2 = x^3 + ax + b, a, b \in \mathbb{F}_p$, usually we choose a very small. Let $Q + R = (x_{Q+R}, y_{Q+R})$, $T = (x_T, y_T)$ and $2T = (x_{2T}, y_{2T})$ in affine coordinate systems. The function $l_{T,T}$ and v_{2T} correspond to the tangent line at the point T and the vertical line through $2T$, respectively. For each bit of N we do

$$\lambda = \frac{3x_T^2 + a}{2y_T}, \quad x_{2T} = \lambda^2 - 2x_T, \quad y_{2T} = \lambda \cdot (x_T - x_{2T}) - y_T,$$

$$l_{T,T}(Q + R) = y_{Q+R} + y_{2T} - \lambda \cdot (x_{Q+R} - x_{2T}), \quad v_{2T}(Q + R) = x_{Q+R} - x_{2T},$$

$$f_1 \leftarrow f_1^2 \cdot l_{T,T}(Q + R), \quad f_2 \leftarrow f_2^2 \cdot v_{2T}(Q + R).$$

It needs $1I + 5M + 4S$ to compute the doubling step in affine coordinates. We also consider the operation count for the doubling step in Jacobian coordinates. A point $(X, Y, Z, W = Z^2)$ in the modified Jacobian coordinates corresponds to the point (x, y) in affine coordinates with $x = X/Z^2, y = Y/Z^3$. Let $T = (X_T, Y_T, Z_T, W_T = Z_T^2)$ and $2T = (X_{2T}, Y_{2T}, Z_{2T}, W_{2T} = Z_{2T}^2)$, the following formulae compute a doubling in $8M + 10S$.

$$B = X_T^2, \quad C = Y_T^2, \quad E = C^2, \quad F = W_T^2, \quad S = 2((X_T + C)^2 - B - E),$$

$$M = 3B + aF, \quad X_{2T} = M^2 - 2S, \quad Y_{2T} = M \cdot (S - X_{2T}) - 8E,$$

$$Z_{2T} = (Y_T + Z_T)^2 - C - W_T, \quad W_{2T} = Z_{2T}^2, \quad G = W_{2T} \cdot x_{Q+R} - X_{2T},$$

$$l_{T,T}(P + R) = Z_{2T} \cdot W_{2T} \cdot y_{Q+R} + Y_{2T} - M \cdot G,$$

$$v_{2T}(P + R) = Z_{2T} \cdot G, \quad f_1 \leftarrow f_1^2 \cdot l_{T,T}(Q + R), \quad f_2 \leftarrow f_2^2 \cdot v_{2T}(Q + R).$$

Addition Step: Let $P = (x_P, y_P)$, $Q + R = (x_{Q+R}, y_{Q+R})$, $T = (x_T, y_T)$, and $T + P = (x_{T+P}, y_{T+P})$. The function $l_{T,P}$ and v_{T+P} correspond to the line through the points T, P and the vertical line through $T + P$, respectively. The formulae for the addition step can be given by

$$\lambda = \frac{y_T - y_P}{x_T - x_P}, \quad x_{T+P} = \lambda^2 - x_T - x_P, \quad y_{T+P} = \lambda \cdot (x_P - x_{T+P}) - y_P,$$

$$l_{T,P}(Q + R) = y_{Q+R} - y_P - \lambda \cdot (x_{Q+R} - x_P), \quad v_{T+P}(Q + R) = x_{Q+R} - x_{T+P},$$

$$f_1 \leftarrow f_1 \cdot l_{T,P}(Q + R), \quad f_2 \leftarrow f_2 \cdot v_{T+P}(Q + R).$$

The total cost of the operation for the addition in affine coordinates will be $1I + 5M + 1S$. Consider the operation count for the addition step in Jacobian coordinates. Let $T = (X_T, Y_T, Z_T, W_T = Z_T^2)$, and $T+P = (X_{T+P}, Y_{T+P}, Z_{T+P}, W_{T+P} = Z_{T+P}^2)$, the following formulae compute an addition in $12M + 5S$.

$$U = x_p \cdot W_T, \ S = y_p \cdot Z_T \cdot W_T, \ H = U - X_T, \ H_2 = H^2, \ I = 4H_2, \ J = H \cdot I,$$
$$L = S - Y_T, \ M = 2L, \ L_2 = L^2, \ M_2 = 4L_2, \ V = X_T \cdot I, \ X_{T+P} = M_2 - J - 2V,$$
$$Y_{T+P} = M \cdot (V - X_{T+P}) - 2Y_T \cdot J, \ Z_{T+P} = (Z_T + H)^2 - W_T - H_2,$$
$$W_{T+P} = Z_{T+P}^2, \ M_3 = (L + Z_{T+P})^2 - L_2 - W_{T+P},$$
$$l_{T,P}(Q + R) = W_{T+P} \cdot (y_{Q+R} - y_P) - M_3 \cdot (x_{Q+R} - x_P),$$
$$v_{T+P}(Q + R) = W_{T+P} \cdot x_{Q+R} - X_{T+P},$$
$$f_1 \leftarrow f_1 \cdot l_{T,P}(Q + R), \ f_2 \leftarrow f_2 \cdot v_{T+P}(Q + R).$$

We summarize the computational costs of basic doubling and addition steps for the reduced Tate pairings on desired curves into the following table.

Table 1. Comparison of Computation for the reduced Tate pairings on Desired Curves

Coordinate System	Method	Doubling Step	Addition Step
Affine coordinate	[31]	1I+8M+4S	1I+8M+1S
	This work	1I+5M+4S	1I+5M+1S
Jacobian coordinate	[15]	13M+ 9S	−
	[12,31]	10M+10S	18M+3S
	This work	8M+10S	12M+5S

Remark 3. Note that in Table 1, the cost estimations for [15,12] are only applicable for $D = -4$, while our result is applicable for various D. Moreover, for $D = -3$ and $P = Q$ (self pairing), we could choose proper R such that $y_P = y_{P+R}$, then the cost of addition step would be reduced to $11M + 5S$.

5   Conclusion

We propose a very efficient method to construct composite order ordinary elliptic curves with embedding degree one, and analyze the non-degeneracy of symmetric pairing based on the reduced Tate pairing, which provides the cryptographic bilinear pairing for protocols mentioned in [2,4,5,10,23]. We also give faster computation for the reduced Tate pairing on desired curves, and see that the reduced Tate pairing may be preferred to use as symmetric pairing instead of the modified Weil pairing in case with $D < -4$.

Acknowledgments. The authors would like to thank the anonymous reviewers for their insightful comments and helpful suggestions. This work was supported by the Natural Science Foundation of China (Grants No. 61272499 and No. 10990011) and the Science and Technology on Information Assurance Laboratory (Grant No. KJ-11-02).

References

1. Atkin, A.O.L., Morain, F.: Elliptic Curves and Primality Proving. Math. Comput. 61, 29–68 (1993)
2. Boneh, D., Goh, E.J., Nissim, K.: Evaluating 2-DNF Formulas on Ciphertexts. In: Kilian, J. (ed.) TCC 2005. LNCS, vol. 3378, pp. 325–341. Springer, Heidelberg (2005)
3. Boneh, D., Rubin, K., Silverberg, A.: Finding Composite Order Ordinary Elliptic Curves Using the Cocks-Pinch Method. J. Number Theor. 131(5), 832–841 (2011)
4. Boneh, D., Sahai, A., Waters, B.: Fully Collusion Resistant Traitor Tracing with Short Ciphertexts and Private Keys. In: Vaudenay, S. (ed.) EUROCRYPT 2006. LNCS, vol. 4004, pp. 573–592. Springer, Heidelberg (2006)
5. Boyen, X., Waters, B.: Compact Group Signatures without Random Oracles. In: Vaudenay, S. (ed.) EUROCRYPT 2006. LNCS, vol. 4004, pp. 427–444. Springer, Heidelberg (2006)
6. Charles, D.: On the Existence of Distortion Maps on Ordinary Elliptic Curves. Cryptology ePrint Archive Report 2006/128, http://eprint.iacr.org/2006/128/
7. Frey, G., Rück, H.: A Remark Concerning m-divisibility and The Discrete Logarithm in The Divisor Class Group of Curves. Math. Comp. 62, 865–874 (1994)
8. Freeman, D., Scott, M., Teske, E.: A Taxonomy of Pairing-friendly Elliptic Curves. J. Cryptol. 23, 224–280 (2010)
9. Galbraith, S.D.: Pairings-Advanced in Elliptic Curve Cryptography. In: Blake, I.F., Seroussi, G., Smart, N.P. (eds.) Cambridge Univ. Press, Cambridge (2005)
10. Groth, J., Sahai, A.: Efficient Non-interactive Proof Systems for Bilinear Groups. In: Smart, N.P. (ed.) EUROCRYPT 2008. LNCS, vol. 4965, pp. 415–432. Springer, Heidelberg (2008)
11. Hu, Z., Xu, M., Zhou, Z.H.: A Generalization of Verheul's Theorem for Some Ordinary Curves. In: Lai, X., Yung, M., Lin, D. (eds.) Inscrypt 2010. LNCS, vol. 6584, pp. 105–114. Springer, Heidelberg (2011)
12. Ionica, S., Joux, A.: Another Approach to Pairing Computation in Edwards Coordinates. In: Chowdhury, D.R., Rijmen, V., Das, A. (eds.) INDOCRYPT 2008. LNCS, vol. 5365, pp. 400–413. Springer, Heidelberg (2008)
13. Ionica, S.: Algorithmique des couplages et cryptographie. PhD thesis of the Versailles Saint-Quentin-en-Yvelines University (2010)
14. Keller, S.: The RSA Validation System (November 9, 2004)
15. Koblitz, N., Menezes, A.J.: Pairing-based Cryptography at High Security Levels. In: Smart, N.P. (ed.) Cryptography and Coding 2005. LNCS, vol. 3796, pp. 13–36. Springer, Heidelberg (2005)
16. Koblitz N.: A Security Weakness in Composite Order Pairing Based Protocols with Embedding Degree $k > 2$. Cryptology ePrint Archive Report 2010/227, http://eprint.iacr.org/2010/227/
17. Lewko, A.: Tools for Simulating Features of Composite Order Bilinear Groups in the Prime Order Setting. In: Pointcheval, D., Johansson, T. (eds.) EUROCRYPT 2012. LNCS, vol. 7237, pp. 318–335. Springer, Heidelberg (2012)

18. Menezes, A.J., Okamoto, T., Vanstone, S.A.: Reducing Elliptic Curve Logarithms to Logarithms in a Finite Field. IEEE Trans. Inf. Theory. 39(5), 1639–1646 (1993)
19. Miller, V.S.: The Weil Pairing, and Its Efficient Calculation. J. Cryptol. 17, 235–261 (2004)
20. Moody, D.: The Diffie-Hellman Problem and Generalization of Verheuls Theorem. Des. Codes Cryptogr. 52, 381–390 (2009)
21. The RSA Challenge Numbers, http://www.rsa.com/rsalabs/node.asp?id=2093
22. Seo, J.H.: On the (Im)possibility of Projecting Property in Prime-Order Setting. In: Wang, X., Sako, K. (eds.) ASIACRYPT 2012. LNCS, vol. 7658, pp. 61–79. Springer, Heidelberg (2012)
23. Shacham, H., Waters, B.: Efficient Ring Signatures without Random Oracles. In: Okamoto, T., Wang, X. (eds.) PKC 2007. LNCS, vol. 4450, pp. 166–180. Springer, Heidelberg (2007)
24. Silverman, J.: The Arithmetic of Elliptic Curves. Springer, New York (1986)
25. Stark, H.M.: Class Numbers of Complex Quadratic Fields. In: Kuyk, W. (ed.) Modular Functions of One Variable I. Lecture Notes in Math., vol. 320, pp. 153–174. Springer, New York (1973)
26. Sutherland, A.: Computing Hilbert class polynomials with the Chinese Remainder Theorem. Math. Comput. 80(273), 501–538 (2011)
27. Vélu, J.: Isogénies entre courbes elliptiques. C.R. Acad. Sc. Paris, Série A 273, 238–241 (1971)
28. Verheul, R.: Evidence that XTR Is More Secure than Supersingular Elliptic Curve Cryptosystems. J. Cryptol. 17, 277–296 (2004)
29. Wu, H., Feng, R.: Efficient Self-pairing on Ordinary Elliptic Curves. In: Chan, T.-H.H., Lau, L.C., Trevisan, L. (eds.) TAMC 2013. LNCS, vol. 7876, pp. 282–293. Springer, Heidelberg (2013)
30. Zhang, X.S., Lin, D.D.: Efficient Pairing Computation on Ordinary Elliptic Curves of Embedding Degree 1 and 2. In: Chen, L. (ed.) IMACC 2011. LNCS, vol. 7089, pp. 309–326. Springer, Heidelberg (2011)
31. Zhao, C.A., Zhang, F.G., Xie, D.Q.: Fast Computation of Self-pairings. IEEE Trans. Inf. Theory 58(5), 3266–3272 (2012)

Threshold Secret Image Sharing

Teng Guo[1,2], Feng Liu[1], ChuanKun Wu[1], ChingNung Yang[3], Wen Wang[1,2], and YaWei Ren[1,2,4]

[1] State Key Laboratory of Information Security, Institute of Information Engineering, Chinese Academy of Sciences, Beijing 100093, China
[2] University of Chinese Academy of Sciences, Beijing 100190, China
[3] Department of Computer Science and Information Engineering, National Dong Hwa University, Hualien 974, Taiwan
[4] School of Information Management, Beijing Information Science and Technology University, Beijing 100192, China
{guoteng,liufeng,ckwu,wangwen}@iie.ac.cn,cnyang@mail.ndhu.edu.tw

Abstract. A (k, n) threshold *secret image sharing scheme*, abbreviated as (k, n)-TSISS, splits a secret image into n shadow images in such a way that any k shadow images can be used to reconstruct the secret image exactly. In 2002, for (k, n)-TSISS, Thien and Lin reduced the size of each shadow image to $\frac{1}{k}$ of the original secret image. Their main technique is by adopting *all coefficients* of a $(k - 1)$-degree polynomial to embed the secret pixels. This benefit of small shadow size has drawn many researcher's attention and their technique has been extensively used in the following studies. In this paper, we first show that this technique is neither information theoretic secure nor computational secure. Furthermore, we point out the security defect of previous (k, n)-TSISSs for sharing textual images, and then fix up this security defect by adding an AES encryption process. At last, we prove that this new (k, n)-TSISS is computational secure.

Keywords: Secret image sharing, Security defect, Computational secure.

1 Introduction

Secret image sharing has drawn considerable attention in recent years [2, 5, 12, 14, 18–21, 25–27]. A (k, n) threshold *secret image sharing scheme*, abbreviated as (k, n)-TSISS, encrypts a secret image into n shadow images (also referred to be shadows) in such a way that any k shadows can be used to reconstruct the secret image exactly, but any less than k shadows should provide no information about the secret image. The secret pixel can be hidden in the *constant term* of a $(k-1)$-degree polynomial using Shamir's (k, n) secret sharing scheme, abbreviated as Shamir's (k, n)-SSS [17], and the secret image can be perfectly reconstructed from any k shadows by Lagrange's interpolation. In such a case, each shadow is the same size as the secret image. For example, to encrypt a $10GB$ satellite image by a $(5, 10)$-TSISS, we get 10 shadows, each with size $10GB$; and to

S. Qing et al. (Eds.): ICICS 2013, LNCS 8233, pp. 404–412, 2013.

reconstruct the $10GB$ satellite image, we have to collect 5 shadows, which sum up to $50GB$. The larger the amount of information grows, the severer the above problem suffers from. To solve this large shadow size problem in secret image sharing, Thien and Lin [18] embed the secret pixels in *all coefficients* of a $(k-1)$-degree polynomial and reduce the shadow size to $\frac{1}{k}$ of the secret image. This *variant* use of Shamir's (k, n)-SSS is denoted as (k, n)-VSSS in this paper. Since the smaller shadow size makes the transmission and storage more convenient, the (k, n)-VSSS has drawn many attentions in the following studies [2, 3, 5, 12, 14, 18–22, 24–28] of TSISS ever since. Initially, Thien and Lin [18] adopt $GF(251)$ as the coefficient field, and the pixel's gray-level degrees has to be modified to less than 251. Therefore, Thien and Lin's scheme is in fact a lossy secret image sharing scheme, in which the reconstructed secret image may be distorted slightly in gray-level. In 2007, Yang et al. [23] adopt $GF(2^8)$ as the coefficient field, avoiding the losses in gray-level. Recently, (k, n)-TSISS has been combined with steganography and authentication [2, 3, 5, 24, 27], which divides a secret image into several shadows and embeds the produced shadows in the cover images to form the stego images, which can be transmitted to authorized recipients without causing suspicion. In addition, these schemes also have some authentication mechanisms to verify the integrity of the stego images, so that the secret image can be reconstructed correctly. (k, n)-TSISS has also been combined with visual cryptography [1, 8–11, 15, 16], which provides a two-in-one (k, n)-TSISS [14, 25] with two decoding options: the first option is stacking shadows to see a vague reconstructed image like visual cryptography; and the second option is to perfectly reconstruct the original gray-level secret image by Lagrange's interpolation.

However, there is no free lunch. The (k, n)-VSSS is no longer information theoretic secure, and to the best of our knowledge, no research has conjectured that the inverting of a $k - 1$ degree polynomial $f(x)$ from less than or equal to $k - 1$ shadows is computational infeasible. From this viewpoint, all of the above mentioned studies of (k, n)-TSISS provide neither of the two currently well-known security guarantees: 1, *information theoretic security* (also known as perfect secrecy), which is based on Shannon's information theory, e.g. the one-time pad, Shamir's secret sharing scheme, visual cryptography; 2, *computational security*, which is based on computational hardness assumptions, e.g. RSA, AES, DES. Motivated by the above observation, we in fact find the security defect of previous (k, n)-TSISSs for sharing textual images, in which the secret can be perceived from any single shadow. Please refer to Section 3.

To avoid the above security defect, we suggest to add an AES encryption process before the sharing process to form a computational secure (k, n)-TSISS, which is denoted by (k, n)-CSTSISS. Then we prove it is computational secure by giving a construction that transforms any efficient attack of the (k, n)-CSTSISS to an efficient attack of AES. In addition to theoretic analysis, experimental results are given to show feasibility of the proposed scheme. Compared to previous (k, n)-TSISSs, the proposed (k, n)-CSTSISS needs $256n$ bits more storage space in overall, and more time for the AES encryption and decryption processes.

This paper is organized as follows. In Section 2, we give some preliminaries of TSISS. In Section 3, we point out the security defect of the previous (k, n)-TSISSs. In Section 4, we propose a computational secure (k, n)-TSISS. The paper is concluded in Section 5.

2   Preliminaries

In this section, we first give some basic knowledge of Shamir's secret sharing and its variant version that is commonly used in studies of TSISS, and then analyze their security properties sequentially.

Suppose the secret we are going to share is in some finite field, e.g. prime fields $GF(p)$ or prime power fields $GF(2^n)$. For simplicity, we will take $GF(p)$ for example to illustrate the sharing process in the following. This will not cause any limitations, for the underlying principle is the same except that the operations in $GF(2^n)$ are modular of some irreducible polynomial of degree n, while those of $GF(p)$ are modular of prime number p.

In *Shamir's* (k, n)-*SSS*, to divide the secret $S \in GF(p)$ into n shadows $S_i \in GF(p)$ $(1 \leq i \leq n)$, we first pick up $k - 1$ random numbers $a_1, a_2, \ldots, a_{k-1}$ from $GF(p)$ and form a $k - 1$ degree polynomial $f(x) = a_0 + a_1x + a_2x^2 + a_3x^3 + \ldots + a_{k-1}x^{k-1}$ with $a_0 = S$. Then we evaluate each shadow by $S_i = f(i)$ $(1 \leq i \leq n)$. From any k-subset of these S_i values, we can reconstruct $f(x)$ by Lagrange's interpolation and compute the secret by $S = f(0)$. However, from any $(k - 1)$-subset of these S_i values, we get no information about S. Detailed analysis can be found in [17].

In *the* (k, n)-*VSSS*, which is widely used in the studies of (k, n)-TSISS, to divide the secret $D = (D_0, D_1, \ldots, D_{k-1})$ with $D_0, D_1, \ldots, D_{k-1} \in GF(p)$ into n shadows $S_i \in GF(p)$ $(1 \leq i \leq n)$, we first form a $k - 1$ degree polynomial $f(x) = D_0 + D_1x + D_2x^2 + D_3x^3 + \ldots + D_{k-1}x^{k-1}$. Then we evaluate each shadow by $S_i = f(i)$ $(1 \leq i \leq n)$. From any k-subset of these S_i values, we can reconstruct $f(x)$ by Lagrange's interpolation and obtain all the coefficients $(D_0, D_1, \ldots, D_{k-1}) = D$. Detailed analysis of the information leakage can be found in the proof of Theorem 2.

To analyze the information leakage of the (k, n)-VSSS from less than k shadows, we have to assume a probability distribution on the secret. For the simplicity of analysis and consistency with our proposed scheme, we assume that the secret is uniformly distributed in its space. For some knowledge of information theory, one can refer to [4]. Here we only give some necessary backgrounds. *Entropy* is a measure of the uncertainty associated with a random variable. Suppose X is a random variable, its entropy is defined by $H(X) = \sum_{x \in X} p(x) \log \frac{1}{p(x)}$[1]. The amount of randomness in random variable X given that you know the value of random variable Y is defined by $H(X|Y) = \sum_{x \in X, y \in Y} p(x, y) \log \frac{p(y)}{p(x, y)}$, which is

---

[1] In this paper, the base of logarithm is 2.

also known as the conditional entropy of X and Y. Briefly speaking, a (k,n)-SSS is information theoretic secure if any $k-1$ shadows provide no information about the secret. Formally, this notion is given as follows.

Definition 1 (Information theoretic secure). *In a (k,n)-SSS, suppose the secret is distributed according to random variable S and the n shadows are distributed according to random variables $S_1, S_2, \ldots, S_n$. The (k,n)-SSS is information theoretic secure if $H(S) = H(S|S_{i_1}, \ldots, S_{i_{k-1}})$ holds for any $k-1$ shadows $S_{i_1}, \ldots, S_{i_{k-1}}$.*

Theorem 1 ([17]). *Shamir's (k,n)-SSS is information theoretic secure.*

Theorem 2. *In the (k,n)-VSSS, there is only $\frac{1}{k}$ fraction of the uncertainty of the secret left, given the knowledge of any $k-1$ shadows.*

Due to page limit, the proof of Theorem 2 is omitted in this version. If you are interested in details of the proof, you can refer to the full version on eprint.

In the following, we present the common subprogram that all the above studies of (k,n)-TSISS share formally as Construction 1.

Construction 1.

Input: *A secret image S.*
Output: *n shadows $S_1, S_2, \ldots, S_n$.*
Step 1. *Adopt all coefficients of a $k-1$ degree polynomial $f(x)$ to embed the secret pixels of S. Each time we share k successive pixels, say $p_1, p_2, \ldots, p_k$. Then fix $f(x) = p_1 + p_2 x + p_3 x^2 + \ldots + p_k x^{k-1}$. The pixel value for each shadow is calculated as $q_i = f(i)$ for $i = 1, 2, \ldots, n$. Repeat the above process until all pixels of S have been shared. The shadows are denoted as $S_1, S_2, \cdots, S_n$.*
Step 2. *Participant i is distributed S_i for $i = 1, 2, \ldots, n$.*

Remark: In Step 1., we use the (k,n)-VSSS, whose security is not guaranteed. This may cause hidden security risk to Construction 1. Indeed we have found its security defect for sharing textual images, please refer to Section 3.

3   The Security Defect of Construction 1

In this section, we present some experimental results to illustrate the security defect of Construction 1, while concrete theoretical analysis of the experiment is given in Appendix of the full version on eprint.

Here we only give a general idea of the cause of the security defect. Since the sharing process (Step 1.) of Construction 1 is deterministic, the same combination of k secret pixels will always contribute to the same combination of n share values. In such a case, if the secret image is of little variation in gray-level, e.g. textual images, its content might be leaked from a single shadow.

For Construction 1 of $(2, 3)$ threshold access structure, the experimental results on coefficient fields $GF(251)$ and $GF(2^8)$ can be found in Figures 1 and 2 respectively, in which any single shadow reveals the content of the secret image.

LOIS LOIS LOIS LOIS

(a)   (b)   (c)   (d)

Fig. 1. Experimental results of Construction 1 on $GF(251)$, (a) the original secret image with image size 300×300, (b) shadow 1 with image size 150×300, (c) shadow 2 with image size 150×300, (d) shadow 3 with image size 150×300

(a)   (b)   (c)   (d)

Fig. 2. Experimental results of Construction 1 on $GF(2^8)$, (a) the original secret image with image size 300×300, (b) shadow 1 with image size 150×300, (c) shadow 2 with image size 150×300, (d) shadow 3 with image size 150×300

Remark: The above security defect seems to be obvious, so why it is not discovered in previous studies? One of the reasons may be that in previous experiments, they only use Construction 1 to encode natural dithered images and never use Construction 1 to encode textual images. But we think a good secret image sharing scheme should be able to deal with all kinds of images, and shouldn't make any restriction on the content of the image.

4   The Proposed Computational Secure (k, n)-TSISS

In this section, we first propose a new (k, n)-TSISS. Then we will prove that this (k, n)-TSISS is computational secure.

Definition 2 (Computational secure). *Let the secret s be drawn from $GF(2^m)$. A (k, n)-SSS is computational secure if for any probability polynomial-time (PPT) algorithm A, $Pr[A(s_{i_1}, \ldots, s_{i_{k-1}}) = s]$ is negligible in m, which is the success probability of getting the secret s from any $k-1$ shadows $s_{i_1}, \ldots, s_{i_{k-1}}$.*

Remark: In other words, it is computational infeasible to invert the (k, n) secret sharing scheme from any $k - 1$ shadows $s_{i_1}, \ldots, s_{i_{k-1}}$.

To achieve computational security, we need to have a computational hardness assumption. For some knowledge of computational security and AES in CBC mode, one can refer to [7, 13]. In this paper, we will use the following assumption:

Assumption 1. *It is computational infeasible to invert AES in CBC mode without the key.*

The proposed computational secure (k,n)-TSISS, also abbreviated as (k,n)-CSTSISS, contains two parts: *Construction 2*, which is the sharing program run by the dealer in the encoding phase; *Construction 3*, which is the revealing program run by the shadow holders in the decoding phase.

Construction 2.

Input: *A secret image S.*
Output: *n shadows $(S_1, K_1, IV), (S_2, K_2, IV), \ldots, (S_n, K_n, IV)$.*
Step 1. *Pick up a random 128 bit key K and a random 128 bit initialization vector IV.*
Step 2. *Encrypt the secret image S by AES with key K and initialization vector IV in CBC mode. Each time we encrypt a 128 bit block, which contains 16 pixels for gray level image. The encrypted secret image is denoted as D.*
Step 3. *Fix $f(x) = p_1 + p_2 x + p_3 x^2 + \ldots + p_k x^{k-1}$, where $p_1, p_2, \ldots, p_k$ are k successive pixels. Then the pixel value for each shadow is calculated as $q_i = f(i)$ for $i = 1, \ldots, n$. Repeat the above process until all pixels of D have been shared. The shadows are denoted as $S_1, S_2, \cdots, S_n$.*
Step 4. *Pick up a random $k-1$ degree polynomial $g(x) = a_1 + a_2 x + a_3 x^2 + a_4 x^3 + \ldots + a_k x^{k-1}$ with $a_1 = K$ and $a_2, \ldots, a_k \overset{r}{\in} GF(2^{128})$. Then the shadows are calculated by $K_i = g(i)$ for $i = 1, \ldots, n$.*
Step 5. *Participant i is distributed (S_i, K_i, IV) as his shadow, where $i = 1, 2, \ldots, n$.*

Remark: In Step 3., we use the (k,n)-VSSS, whose security is not guaranteed, and in Step 4., we use Shamir's (k,n)-SSS, which is information theoretic secure. The coefficient field that we use in Step 3. is $GF(2^8)$.

Construction 3.

Input: *Any k shadows: $(S_{i_1}, K_{i_1}, IV), \ldots, (S_{i_k}, K_{i_k}, IV)$.*
Output: *A image S.*
Step 1. *Use $K_{i_1}, \ldots, K_{i_k}$ and Lagrange's interpolation to recover the constant term K of $g(x)$.*
Step 2. *Use $S_{i_1}, \ldots, S_{i_k}$ and Lagrange's interpolation to recover all coefficients $p_1, p_2, \ldots, p_k$ of $f(x)$. Repeat the above process until all pixels of D have been recovered.*
Step 3. *Decrypt D by AES in CBC mode with key K and initialization vector IV. The output is S.*

Theorem 3. *If Assumption 1 holds, then the proposed (k,n)-CSTSISS is computational secure.*

Due to page limit, the proof of Theorem 3 is omitted in this version. If you are interested in details of the proof, you can refer to the full version on eprint.

Compared to previous (k, n)-TSISSs, the price we have payed out is $2 \times 128 \times n$ bits more storage space in overall, and more time for the AES encryption and decryption processes.

The experimental results of the proposed $(2, 3)$-CSTSISS can be found in Figure 3, in which shadow images (b,c,d) are noise-like and provide no information about the content of the secret image (a). Compared to previous (k, n)-TSISSs, the proposed (k, n)-CSTSISS indeed does not have security defect for sharing textual images.

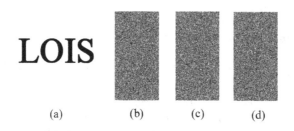

(a)   (b)   (c)   (d)

Fig. 3. Experimental results of the proposed $(2, 3)$-CSTSISS: (a) the original secret image with image size 300×300, (b) shadow 1 with image size 150×300, (c) shadow 2 with image size 150×300, (d) shadow 3 with image size 150×300

5   Conclusions

In this paper, we have shown that the (k, n)-VSSS, being extensively used in the studies of (k, n)-TSISS, does not have security guarantees. Furthermore, we have found those studies' security defect for sharing textual images and then patched up this security defect by adding an AES encryption process before the sharing process, which combines the beauty of small shadow size with computational security guarantee.

Acknowledgments. This work was supported by NSFC grant No. 60903210, the "Strategic Priority Research Program" of the Chinese Academy of Sciences No. XDA06010701 and the IIE's Projects No. Y1Z0011102, No. Y3Z001B102, No. Y2Z0011102 and No. Y3Z0071C02.

References

1. Ateniese, G., Blundo, C., Santis, A.D., Stinson, D.: Visual cryptography for general access structures. Information and Computation 129, 86–106 (1996)
2. Chan, C., Sung, P.: Secret image sharing with steganography and authentication using dynamic programming strategy. In: PCSPA, pp. 382–395 (2010)
3. Chang, C., Hsieh, Y., Lin, C.: Sharing secrets in stego images with authentication. Pattern Recognition 41, 3130–3137 (2008)

4. Cover, T., Thomas, J.: Elements of information theory, 2nd edn. Wiley Interscience, New York (2006)
5. Elsheh, E., Hamza, A.B.: Robust approaches to 3D object secret sharing. In: Campilho, A., Kamel, M. (eds.) ICIAR 2010. LNCS, vol. 6111, pp. 326–335. Springer, Heidelberg (2010)
6. Goldreich, O.: Randomized methods in computation (2001), http://www.wisdom.weizmann.ac.il/~oded/rnd.html
7. Goldwasser, S., Bellare, M.: Lecture notes on cryptography (2008), http://cseweb.ucsd.edu/~mihir/papers/gb.pdf
8. Guo, T., Liu, F., Wu, C.: Multi-pixel encryption visual cryptography. In: Wu, C.-K., Yung, M., Lin, D. (eds.) Inscrypt 2011. LNCS, vol. 7537, pp. 86–92. Springer, Heidelberg (2012)
9. Guo, T., Liu, F., Wu, C.: On the equivalence of two definitions of visual cryptography scheme. In: Ryan, M.D., Smyth, B., Wang, G. (eds.) ISPEC 2012. LNCS, vol. 7232, pp. 217–227. Springer, Heidelberg (2012)
10. Guo, T., Liu, F., Wu, C.: Threshold visual secret sharing by random grids with improved contrast. The Journal of Systems and Software 86, 2094–2109 (2013)
11. Guo, T., Liu, F., Wu, C.: k out of k extended visual cryptography scheme by random grids. Signal Processing 94, 90–101 (2014)
12. Huang, C., Hsieh, C., Huang, P.: Progressive sharing for a secret image. The Journal of Systems and Software 83, 517–527 (2010)
13. Katz, J., Lindell, Y.: Introduction to modern cryptography. CRC Press (2007)
14. Li, P., Ma, P., Su, X., Yang, C.: Improvements of a two-in-one image secret sharing scheme based on gray mixing model. Journal of Visual Communication and Image Representation 23, 441–453 (2012)
15. Liu, F., Guo, T., Wu, C., Qian, L.: Improving the visual quality of size invariant visual cryptography scheme. Journal of Visual Communication and Image Representation 23, 331–342 (2012)
16. Naor, M., Shamir, A.: Visual cryptography. In: De Santis, A. (ed.) EUROCRYPT 1994. LNCS, vol. 950, pp. 1–12. Springer, Heidelberg (1995)
17. Shamir, A.: How to share a secret. Communications of the ACM 22(11), 612–613 (1979)
18. Thien, C., Lin, J.: Secret image sharing. Computers and Graphics 26, 765–770 (2002)
19. Thien, C., Lin, J.: An image-sharing method with user-friendly shadow images. IEEE Transactions on Circuits and Systems for Video Technology 13, 1161–1169 (2003)
20. Ulutas, M., Ulutas, G., Nabiyev, V.: Medical image security and epr hiding using shamir's secret sharing scheme. The Journal of Systems and Software 84, 341–353 (2011)
21. Wang, R., Chien, Y., Lin, Y.: Scalable user-friendly image sharing. Journal of Visual Communication and Image Representation 21, 751–761 (2010)
22. Wang, R., Shyu, S.: Scalable secret image sharing. Signal Processing: Image Communication 22, 363–373 (2007)
23. Yang, C., Chen, T., Yu, K., Wang, C.: Improvements of image sharing with steganography and authentication. The Journal of Systems and Software 80, 1070–1076 (2007)

24. Yang, C., Ciou, C.: A comment on "sharing secrets in stegoimages with authentication". Pattern Recognition 42, 1615–1619 (2009)
25. Yang, C., Ciou, C.: Image secret sharing method with two-decoding-options: Lossless recovery and previewing capability. Image and Vision Computing 28, 1600–1610 (2010)
26. Yang, C., Huang, Y., Syue, J.: Reversible secret image sharing based on shamir's scheme with discrete haar wavelet transform. In: ICECE, vol. 16-18, pp. 1250–1253 (2011)
27. Yang, C., Ouyang, J., Harn, L.: Steganography and authentication in image sharing without parity bits. Optics Communications 285, 1725–1735 (2012)
28. Zhao, R., Zhao, J., Dai, F., Zhao, F.: A new image secret sharing scheme to identify cheaters. Computer Standards and Interfaces 31, 252–257 (2009)

Author Index